ALSO BY TOM WICKER

ONE OF US

★

Richard Nixon
and the
American Dream

For Steve —
with many Thanks
for a great day
at The Intimate —

Tom Wicker

ONE OF US

★

Richard Nixon
and the
American Dream

★

TOM WICKER

RANDOM HOUSE
NEW YORK

Grateful acknowledgment is made to the following for permission to reprint previously published material:

DOUBLEDAY, A DIVISION OF BANTAM, DOUBLEDAY, DELL PUBLISHING GROUP, INC.: Excerpts from *Six Crises* by Richard M. Nixon. Published by Doubleday, 1962. Reprinted by permission.

FOREIGN AFFAIRS: Excerpt from "Asia After Viet Nam" by Richard M. Nixon, *Foreign Affairs;* October 1967, Volume 46, Number 1; excerpts from an article by Clark M. Clifford, *Foreign Affairs,* July 1969, Volume 47, Number 4. Copyright © 1967, 1969 by the Council on Foreign Relations, Inc. Reprinted by permission of *Foreign Affairs.*

LITTLE, BROWN AND COMPANY: Excerpts from *The White House Years* by Henry Kissinger. Copyright © 1979 by Henry A. Kissinger. Reprinted by permission of Little, Brown and Company.

THE NEW YORK TIMES: Excerpts from Tom Wicker article of August 28, 1968, and "Recapturing Bobby" by William Manchester from the August 7, 1988, *New York Times Book Review.* Copyright © 1968, 1988 by The New York Times Company. Reprinted by permission.

SIMON AND SCHUSTER, INC.: Excerpts from *Witness to Power* by John D. Ehrlichman. Copyright © 1982 by John D. Ehrlichman. Reprinted by permission of Simon and Schuster, Inc.

UNIVERSITY PRESS OF AMERICA: Excerpts from *The Nixon Presidency: Twenty-two Intimate Portraits of Richard M. Nixon* (Vol 6. of *Portraits of American Presidents*). Published by University Press of America. Reprinted by permission.

WARNER BOOKS, INC.: Excerpts from *RN: The Memoirs of Richard Nixon* by Richard Nixon. Copyright © 1978 by Richard Nixon. Reprinted by permission of Warner Books/New York.

Library of Congress Cataloging-in-Publication Data

Wicker, Tom.
One of us : Richard Nixon and the American dream/Tom Wicker.
p.   cm.
Includes bibliographical references.
ISBN 0-394-55066-8
1. Nixon, Richard M. (Richard Milhous), 1913–   .   2. Presidents—
United States—Biography.   3. United States—Politics and
government—1945– I. Title.
E856.W52   1991
973.924′092—dc20   89-42779

Manufactured in the United States of America
24689753
First Edition

Designed by Oksana Kushnir

To the memory of
RICHARD HARRIS,
who would have hated this book

. . . I can safely assure my readers that he is not the product of oddly perverted thinking. . . . I saw his form pass by—appealing—significant—under a cloud—perfectly silent. . . . It was for me, with all the sympathy of which I was capable, to seek fit words for his meaning. He was "one of us."

—Joseph Conrad, Introduction to
Lord Jim

Preface

★

The genesis of this book was a quick and perplexing encounter in a corridor of the national Capitol more than thirty years ago.

In 1957, I was reporting from Washington for the *Winston-Salem Journal,* mostly on the congressional delegation from North Carolina, and on matters of particular interest to that state—such as the medical consensus, just then forming, that cigarettes cause lung cancer. I was also getting my first experience in covering national politics.

The first of the modern civil rights bills was being debated and its eventual passage gave me a lasting admiration for the legislative mastery of Lyndon B. Johnson of Texas, the Democratic leader. Johnson, John F. Kennedy, W. Stuart Symington of Missouri, and Richard Nixon—as vice president of the United States, the presiding officer—were all active in the Senate that year, and beginning to maneuver for their parties' 1960 presidential nominations.

One night, after the Senate session had ended and most congressional reporters had left the Capitol, I worked late in the Senate press gallery—the only office I had. When I had filed my story with Western Union, I went down to the "principal floor," on which the Senate chamber is located, intending to walk across to the "House side" and out to Independence Avenue for a streetcar downtown.

As I came down the ornate staircase from the gallery floor, Jack Sherwood, Vice President Nixon's Secret Service agent, passed below me in the silent Senate lobby. Not far behind was the vice president himself. I had until then seen him only distantly from the press gallery, but he was and remains an eminently recognizable man.

I was surprised, first, at seeing Nixon at all, because as a rookie in Washington I had supposed high officials to be cloistered, and afforded general immunity to prying eyes; and second, because as far as I could see Nixon was alone except for Sherwood preceding him. I had observed that even junior members of the House usually paraded the congressional halls with at least one aide in tow, as if to appear without the semblance of a retinue was to acknowledge lowly status.

But the greatest surprise, as Nixon and I approached each other, was to see the vice president walking along rather slowly, shoulders slumped, hands jammed in his trousers pockets, head down and his eyes apparently fixed—though perhaps on nothing—on the ornate Capitol floor. What I could see of his face seemed darker than could be accounted for by the trademark five o'clock shadow; it was preoccupied, brooding, gloomy, whether angry or merely disconsolate I was unable to tell.

Altogether, as Nixon walked toward me in the empty corridor with no sign that he realized anyone was nearby, although my footsteps as well as his were clacking on the tiled floor, his was an unappealing presence. (My friend Hugh Sidey of *Time* magazine had a similar experience at about the same time; years later, he recalled Nixon as "secretive even then. . . . Of course he had to sit up in front of the Senate, but when he was off duty you would see that hunched figure trying to skulk off down the back ways.")

I had expected Nixon to be taller, and of better posture, and would have thought he'd have a politician's ready greeting for a voter unexpectedly encountered. But as he went his way without the slightest recognition that someone else was in that shadowy hall, I realized that I was seeing a man bound up in his inner being, unaware that he was meeting another person, unaware of the impression he was making, unaware even that he was making an impression, too absorbed in himself to present the facade with which—I know now but did not know then—most of us guard the truth of that inner self, that secret life, we rarely share with anyone.

What, in Richard Nixon's case, was that truth? What, in that dark face, had I seen? The small mystery of his presence in the Capitol was solved later: he had an inner-sanctum hideaway somewhere in its bowels; no doubt he was returning from it to his primary office in what now is called the Russell Office Building. But I concluded then only that I had glimpsed a profoundly unhappy man, for once unsheltered behind practical defenses; I was young and found it hard to fathom why a vice president, who could even become president, should appear so desolate, and so alone.

I believe now that I had glimpsed more of the authentic man than most Americans had seen of "the real Nixon," who was even then something of a conundrum. And it seems plain that the peculiar reserve and ambivalence in the public's attitude toward this man, ostensibly so well known for so long to so many, lies in the fact that his public self always has seemed palpably to be concealing a private self we do not know.

Just as I could not be sure what I had seen that night in the echoing Capitol corridor, Americans seldom have been sure of what lies beneath the facade Richard Nixon constantly presents. From behind his appearance of pious responsibility and somewhat strained good-fellowship, someone else has looked out at us over the years, with a gaze shrewd, sharp, measuring, menacing to some, enigmatic even to those who believe in him.

From that evening in the Capitol, I was convinced that Nixon was a highly interesting, if not an attractive, man. Three decades later, after the lengthy national drama of his defeats, revival and resignation from the presidency, followed by still another unlikely recovery to the position of thoughtful elder statesman, and after my own struggles, disappointments and survival in the same decades, I consider him one of the two most interesting public men I have known. The other was Lyndon Johnson, who was not particularly likable either.

As a journalist active through most of the Nixon saga, I was more often his critic—in retrospect, not always knowledgeably—than his admirer. As the decades passed, however, and Nixon remained somehow central to American life—a fixture sometimes in the foreground, sometimes in the background, nearly always in the picture—it seemed to me that no American of my time more nearly deserved study and reflection; and perhaps none might so reward them. So it has proved, at least for me.

Save for the famous "last press conference," I have passed over the Nixon campaign for governor of California in 1962. I concede its political importance at the time, but in the context of his long career it seems mostly a misadventure.

Nor have I retold the Watergate saga. Events leading to it are detailed and I have made suggestions as to why Nixon "stonewalled" instead of cleaning house and clearing himself if he could have. But what followed that fateful decision seems to me familiar enough to need no retelling that does not solve some of the remaining Watergate mysteries. Besides, Richard Nixon had a fully formed personality and lengthy experience—my primary concerns—when he began the cover-up.

As I worked on this book, I realized also that few people remembered much about the Nixon presidency, or about Richard Nixon himself, *except* Watergate; to many, Watergate seemed to be the only episode of his career that signified. I thought it more useful to focus on what people had forgotten, or never knew, than on the one thing with which Nixon's name is inevitably associated. And it seemed to me, anyway, that the man Nixon had become by 1972, as well as the general atmosphere of his administration, were the most important elements of Watergate.

The resulting book is not a biography, nor is it a comprehensive account of Nixon's career, or even of his presidency. It is not a condemnation and certainly not a celebration. It is too factual to be a speculation and too speculative to be the last word. Nixon was not interviewed for it, though interviews were sought. I do not pretend that I have come fully to understand the man—"You will never do that," Arthur Burns told me—or what has driven him to his extraordinary career.

For all these reasons, I told friends—many of them appalled at the idea—only that I was writing "a book about Richard Nixon." But it is also a book about American politics, American lives, American dreams, American reality.

I made no attempt to use footnotes in the comprehensive manner of the formal historian. For each chapter, however, a general note on my sources has been provided, together with such specific citations as seemed required or useful. Material on the public record—say, a quotation from a presidential news conference, or a broadcast speech, or a well-reported event of a political campaign or an international conference—has not been cited unless some special reason seemed to warrant it. Usually, such material has been identified in the text.

This also has been the procedure, wherever possible, with material taken from published works and from my personal interviews. A few references by persons who wished not to be publicly identified can be verified from my files.

Special thanks are due to Abby Wasserman and Joy Hackel, who at separate times served ably as research assistants. Rosemary Breslin, Justine Kaplan and Jim McKinley, who followed each other in drudgery for me at the New York Times, each took much spare time to assist me. Sam Vaughan of Random House was a splendid and understanding editor. As always, my indispensable secretary, Inell Willis, helped hold my life together during what must have seemed to her, as they did to me, the interminable years devoted to this book.

I am also heavily indebted, as will be obvious from the notes, to the White Burkett Miller Center for the Study of Public Affairs at the University of Virginia, and its director, Dr. Kenneth Thompson; to the Richard Nixon Oral History Project at California State University, Fullerton, California, directed by Professor Harry P. Jeffrey of the CSU history department; and to the many associates, acquaintances and critics of Richard Nixon who shared their experiences with me.

Except where specifically attributed to someone else, however, the interpretations and analyses of Nixon's life and work, especially in the first and last chapters, are mine alone.

A final word: I grew up in a small railroad town in the South and I too, as Richard Nixon did in the California of his youth, heard lonely whistles in the long-ago nights; and I too, as he did in his far different young world, dreamed of great things to be done, and believed that I would do them. Poles apart though we may otherwise be, that seems to me not an insignificant bond.

—TOM WICKER
Rochester, Vermont
October 12, 1990

Contents

★

BOOK I

★

THE MAN
IN THE
ARENA

★

There's no question but that a person in politics is always hurt when he loses, because
people like to play a winner. But the one sure
thing about politics is that what goes up
comes down, and what goes down often
comes up.

—Richard Nixon

1

★

Cardboard Man

★

I knew that what was most important was
that I must be myself.

—Richard Nixon, *Six Crises*

In the spring of 1963, Elmer Bobst may have been the only prominent man
in America who firmly believed in the political future of Richard Milhous
Nixon—not excluding Nixon himself. What Bobst did about it led ultimately to Nixon's return from political oblivion and to his place in history
as one of the most important presidents of the United States—if far from
the most respected.

Although vice president during Dwight D. Eisenhower's eight years in
the White House (1953–1961), Richard Nixon had suffered two disastrous
political defeats—one for president in 1960, one for governor of California
in 1962. He had seemed to fall apart emotionally after the latter loss,
tossing dumbfounded reporters one of the most famous exit lines in American political history: "You won't have Nixon to kick around anymore,
because, gentlemen, this is my last press conference. . . ."

But Elmer Bobst, the wealthy chairman of the Warner-Lambert Company, felt a "kind of brotherhood" with Nixon that had overtones instead
of a father-son relationship. Bobst thought Nixon's outburst at "the last
press conference" was justified because "he had been more unfairly, even
destructively, treated by the press than any modern political leader"—
which may have been true. Bobst also comforted himself that this was the
"first and only time" Nixon ever had "lost his public composure"—thus
demonstrating the convenient memory of a partisan.

The votes sending Nixon to his second major defeat had hardly been counted in California before Bobst, a man of large affairs and bold action, began pressing Nixon, as he had after the presidential loss, to move to New York. In the East, Bobst had thought two years earlier, Nixon would have "a respectable vantage point from which to rebuild his political strength." If he returned to California, Bobst had foreseen in 1960, the former vice president would be under heavy pressure to run for governor in 1962—a race in which Bobst believed Nixon would have everything to lose and nothing to gain. His prediction having come disastrously true, Bobst renewed his pleas for Nixon to come East and start over.

So Bobst was not particularly surprised, one morning in the spring of 1963, to be summoned off the course at Spring Lake Golf and Country Club in New Jersey, to take a call from California. Nor could Nixon, who was on the line, have been surprised to locate Elmer Bobst at Spring Lake. For it had been there, ten years earlier, when Bobst was club president, that he and Richard Nixon had begun what Bobst considered "perhaps the strongest, certainly the most propitious friendship of my life." For Nixon, the relationship always had been personally rewarding; and it was becoming professionally indispensable.

In 1953, Bobst had been chairman of the U.S. Savings Bond drive in New Jersey, and in that capacity had invited two hundred of the state's leading businessmen to a dinner at his Spring Lake club. Eisenhower's secretary of the treasury, George Humphrey, was to speak; but at the last minute, Humphrey had begged off and recommended Richard Nixon to take his place. Bobst, a Republican stalwart, readily agreed; he had met but did not really know the vice president—although Nixon's "Checkers" speech, which saved his career during the 1952 presidential campaign, had brought tears to Bobst's eyes.

In fact, with all due respect to Humphrey, Bobst suspected he was trading up. And when he and Nixon were seated side by side at the head table for the Spring Lake dinner, they hit it off beautifully. At the end, Bobst later recalled, Nixon told him: "My name is Dick and yours is Elmer. Let's cut out the Mr. Vice President."

Later that summer, the Nixon family took a vacation house near Spring Lake; every day, Nixon and his new friend played golf at the club or met for a talk. Each deeply impressed the other. The vice president's young daughters began calling the older man "Uncle Elmer." Bobst's wife had died a few months before the savings bond dinner, and the lonely widower no doubt was cheered by the friendship of the Nixon family—then held together by warm and conventional relationships not yet strained by later political stress. As the years passed, Bobst was invited to spend family occasions and holidays with the Nixons, and at an official reception for Queen Elizabeth during her visit to the U.S. in 1957, the vice president presented Bobst to her with the words: "Your Highness, Elmer Bobst is family to us."

There's no reason to doubt the genuine affection and admiration that developed between Elmer Bobst and Richard Nixon. To some extent the kindly, generous and highly successful Bobst may have compensated for Nixon's relatively hard experience with his own father—an overbearing, exacting and verbose man of little accomplishment, who had settled for the operation of a moderately prosperous neighborhood grocery and service station in Whittier, California. And Bobst's affection and loyalty call into question—as do several other close relationships—the common view of Nixon as an opportunistic and calculating man without much human warmth.

So when Bobst picked up the phone that morning in the Spring Lake clubhouse, it was as part of a friendship that he considered "serious, illuminating and private," one in which Bobst could and did tell the former presidential candidate "exactly what was on my mind, without pulling punches." For his part, Nixon could and did use Bobst "as a backboard" for his ideas without fear that the older man "would react as a sycophant."

And Nixon need have had no hesitancy that morning in telling Bobst that he had come around to the older man's view: he wanted a job in New York. But it had to be the right kind of a job. Though formally taking the position that his political career was finished, Nixon agreed with Bobst that there was no reason he should not remain available for political opportunity—that in a new private-sector career an experienced public man should stay alert and in touch, in case lightning should strike.

There was also the question of money; Nixon, who had little material gain to show for fourteen years in government service, needed a lot of it. Adams, Duque and Hazeltine, the Los Angeles law firm he had joined in 1961, was paying him $100,000 a year—even in 1963 not a huge income for a national figure. He had made about $250,000 from *Six Crises,* his best-selling memoir. But he was asking his family to give up a well-loved Beverly Hills house with seven baths and a swimming pool, and he wanted them to be able to live well in New York—a city, then as now, where living well is perhaps more expensive than anywhere else in the U.S.

But Bobst advised against offers from industry, no matter how lucrative; they would mostly be from companies hoping to exploit Nixon's well-known name, he said, in ways that would not be helpful politically. Nor did Bobst think his own company, Warner-Lambert, the right place for a man he regarded as a surrogate son whom Bobst still wanted to become president.

Some law firms, moreover, would not want to take in a new partner whose prime activity, they would fear, would be political rather than legal. Others, of the "Eastern Establishment" sort, might not consider Richard

Nixon, the nemesis of Alger Hiss, the beard-shadowed butt of hundreds of acerbic Herblock cartoons in the *Washington Post,* a name they wanted on the letterhead. In fact, after Nixon's move to New York, Irving Mitchell Felt, then the head of the Madison Square Garden Corporation, tried to arrange a dinner party for about five couples in honor of the newcomer.

"It took two or three weeks to get the others," a Nixon associate recalled. "They just didn't want to go to dinner with Nixon."[1]

There was a political problem, too, despite Nixon's avowals that he was through with politics. New York in 1963 was the home turf of Governor Nelson A. Rockefeller, favorite of liberal Republicans, briefly Nixon's rival for the nomination in 1960 and sure to be a presidential candidate again in 1964. Rockefeller could hardly help seeing a latent political challenge in Nixon's move to New York.

As it turned out, Nixon never dabbled much in New York City or State politics. But after Rockefeller had lost the nomination, and Barry Goldwater the presidency, at a news conference on the day after the 1964 election Nixon did call Rockefeller a "party divider" and "spoilsport" who had not worked hard enough for the Goldwater ticket—a longheaded first step on the road to Nixon's 1968 presidential bid.

Not long after that news conference, I arrived in Spain on a trip with Arthur O. Sulzberger, the publisher of the *New York Times.* As we checked into the Ritz Hotel in Madrid, we encountered Rockefeller checking out. Grinning his famous grin, the governor spoke what may have been his true feelings about Nixon: "Got to get back to New York to take care of that political gypsy!"

But Elmer Bobst, pondering Richard Nixon's future in 1963, was little concerned about possible future conflict with Rockefeller. An immediate place for his friend was needed, and Bobst had a good idea where to find it. Warner-Lambert was a major client of the Wall Street law firm Mudge, Stern, Baldwin and Todd; and one of its three senior partners, Milton Rose, handled Bobst's personal legal affairs.

Quickly, once he had Nixon's go-ahead, Bobst seized the opportunity of a conference with Rose. Bobst's pitch was direct: "Milton, you have a very good law firm and we have received excellent service," he said. "But it seems to me that you're pretty badly in need of new blood."

Bobst made it clear he meant

> new blood at the top. Somebody who can serve to bring the firm into the eyes of Wall Street and to the attention of industry throughout the country. Now, for instance, supposing you could get Richard Nixon to join the firm and head it. What would you think of that?

Bobst's account of what followed seems too specific to be doubted; and it's impossible to suppose that his and his company's heavy involvement in Mudge, Stern, Baldwin and Todd, together with the closeness of his well-known friendship with Nixon, had nothing to do with Milton Rose's response. Rose said he would "say 'yes' right away" and thought he could persuade his partners "to say 'yes' by tomorrow."

That was on a Tuesday. By Wednesday the partners had agreed. Nixon flew East on Friday; and on Saturday, Nixon, Bobst and the other two senior partners made up a foursome—unfortunately for historical symmetry, not at Spring Lake but at Baltusrol Golf Club in New Jersey.

"After a conversation at the nineteenth hole, I felt the negotiations were completely and perfectly satisfactory to all concerned," Bobst recalled with deserved satisfaction.

Former Vice President Richard Milhous Nixon was to become a senior partner of the renamed firm of Nixon, Mudge, Rose, Guthrie and Alexander as soon as he could be admitted to the New York bar; until then, he would be "of counsel" to the firm. And he would be paid $250,000 a year.[2]

Nixon insisted to Bobst that he looked on this immense change in his life as a professional commitment rather than a political opportunity. But the elderly engineer of the new arrangement had other ideas; he was sure that the new Wall Street lawyer—then only fifty years old—at last would be in the right place to stage a political comeback, perhaps all the way to the top. And he believed that sooner or later the country would demand his still-young friend's return to what Richard Nixon liked to call "the arena."

Nixon actually may have believed that his move to New York was primarily personal and professional—that in fact his political career had been terminated by "the last press conference," if not by his defeat in California. At about the time of the move, the Nixons were joined for dinner one evening by their old friends, former attorney general and Mrs. William P. Rogers of Washington; Rogers carried away the belief that Nixon was convinced he had no political future.[3]

Leonard Garment, who headed the litigation department at Nixon's new law firm, had a quite different impression. He believed almost from the beginning that whatever his new senior partner thought or said, he probably had not given up, in his deepest self, all hope of winning the presidency. It is an ambition, or a disease, not easily shed.

Garment was a Democrat with, at first, a conventional early-sixties view of Nixon as an illiberal opportunist; but Garment was observant, too. He saw Nixon's skills as a leader within the law firm and he watched the effect Nixon's presence and fame had on others—including some New York political operators. Surely, he thought, the presidency still was a possibility for such a man.

A gregarious and generous person, Garment held the former vice president and presidential candidate in some awe; but he befriended the new man from the day of Nixon's arrival, a stranger and alone at 20 Broad Street. Soon a strong friendship formed. As a result, Leonard Garment could see that, no matter his political fame, Nixon was uneasy with the manner and jargon of what he saw as the smooth, experienced Wall Street lawyers now surrounding him.[4]

Nixon's practical legal experience, after all, consisted of four years of small-town practice in Whittier, California, a quarter century earlier (before World War II), and about a year full-time with Adams, Duque and Hazeltine in Los Angeles, before he had embarked on his gubernatorial campaign. Now he was expected to lead a firm of impressive New York lawyers to a new eminence, in the very heart of the Eastern Establishment.

More than Nixon's comparative legal inexperience was troubling the new partner. After his graduation—third in a class of twenty-five—from the Duke University School of Law in 1937, he had sought and failed to get a job with just the kind of prestigious New York law firm that Mudge et al. must have seemed to him in 1963. The Federal Bureau of Investigation also had turned down his application (for lack of an opening, although Nixon thought for many years that he had simply been rejected), and he had been forced to go back to Whittier to a hometown legal practice.

This apparently depressed him. His cousin, Lucille Parsons, recalled in an oral history that when Nixon first returned from the East, "he didn't want to go into a law office here in Whittier—he wanted something better. . . . [H]e was a little bit uppity when he came home from Duke." After "a couple of weeks," she had to force him to return a call from Tom Bewley, a local attorney who offered him the place that Nixon finally accepted.[5]

This dampening if not humiliating experience had helped to confirm in the adult Nixon the conviction, evident in his adolescence, that he was an outsider—not "sophisticated," not privileged, perhaps not even brilliant enough for the traditional Establishment, one who could make his mark in the world only by hard work, determination and persistence.

Upon entering Whittier College, for example (the Nixon family was too poor to permit him to accept a possible tuition scholarship at Yale), he had not sought membership in the Franklins, the campus club for men, which had high social standing. Instead, Nixon was one of the founding members and—though only a freshman—the first president of the Orthogonian Society.

The name meant "Square Shooters," he wrote in his memoirs, *RN,* and the members were "mostly athletes and men who were working their way through school." The Franklins had their pictures taken for the college annual in tuxedos; the Orthogonians wore open-necked shirts. The Franklins "were the haves, and we were the have-nots, see?" Nixon told the journalist Stewart Alsop many years later. In one way or another, whether socially, financially, intellectually, or all three, this distinction was to remain important in his life and career, in both of which, despite considerable achievements, he seemed always to regard himself as a kind of have-not; and he never appears to have felt himself part of an Establishment—save possibly that of Republican party professionals.[6]

"I won my share of scholarships, and of speaking and debating prizes in school," he writes of his Whittier College career (1930–1934) in *Six Crises,* "not because I was smarter but because I worked longer and harder than some of my gifted colleagues."

This theme is a constant in Nixon's life: success belongs to the hard worker, the person who sticks to the job and masters it by unremitting effort, and *not* necessarily to those more talented or more fortunate. It is an American faith—the tortoise can overtake the hare—and Nixon never seems to have questioned it, or its relevance to his own abilities and achievements. He proudly recounts in *Six Crises,* for instance, the comment of a Duke law school classmate "who had noted the long hours" Nixon spent studying in the library: that he had "what it takes to learn the law. . . . An iron butt."

Nixon not only had an iron butt; he had faith in what it represented. But inevitably, in him as in many another ambitious and hardworking American, that faith had generated a degree of bitterness toward, sometimes contempt for, those "gifted colleagues" in their tuxedos, to whom good things came more easily, who therefore somehow deserved them less.

"What starts the process," Nixon told a friend many years after he moved to New York in 1963,

> really are laughs and slights and snubs when you are a kid. Sometimes it's because you're poor or Irish or Jewish or Catholic or ugly or simply that you are skinny. But if you are reasonably intelligent and *if your anger is deep enough and strong enough,* you learn that you can change those attitudes by excellence, personal gut performance, while *those who have everything are sitting on their fat butts.*[7] [Emphasis added.]

It's not exactly clear whose "laughs and slights and snubs" Richard Nixon suffered in his boyhood. Mostly, he's remembered by contemporaries as intelligent, hardworking, serious, what would be called today "an achiever." Schoolmates rewarded him with success in school politics and his grades were always near the top. He was a poor athlete but his dogged determination to make the football team at Whittier College inspired more admiration than derision from those who remembered his scrawny form sitting on the bench or being bowled over in practice.

Lucille Parsons did remember in her oral history that he was sensitive about the work he did in his father's store—particularly his assigned task of bringing fresh produce from the Los Angeles market.

> We worked in the store many, many hours together. Dick would get up early and go get his vegetables. He didn't want anybody to see him go get vegetables, so he got up real early and then got back real quick. And he didn't like to wait on people in the store.

Numerous contemporaries noted, in other oral histories, that Richard Nixon was not a favorite with young women. Mrs. Dean (Jill) Triggs, who had been a schoolmate, observed, for example:

> He wasn't the type that was queening all the girls or all the girls were crazy about him because he was a student leader. . . . He didn't have the glamor about him that interests the opposite sex. He wasn't sexy.

Nothing can hurt a sensitive young man more than that attitude among the girls he knows, since he will inevitably become aware of it. Still, the young Nixon "liked to be at places where people were," Jill Triggs recalled:

> "He would ask a date and he would be there, but that wouldn't mean that he was crazy about the girl . . . but he liked to be where people were."

Nixon was not much of a dancer, either, although he campaigned successfully for student body president at Whittier College primarily on his demand that dancing be permitted on what was then a staid Quaker campus. His election does not seem to have improved his standing with the girls he knew; thus, his youthful relations with women—or lack of such relations—may well have been a source of inner anger later in life. That would not be unusual among American men.

In any case, and quite aside from his legal qualifications, Richard Nixon, the small-town California lawyer moved east, the Orthogonian from Whittier who'd made good only in the suspect world of politics and who even then had missed the ultimate prize, who even as vice president never had been invited by Dwight and Mamie Eisenhower to the private living quarters in the White House—Richard Nixon, for the deepest of reasons, looked at his sleek new partners, Wall Street lawyers all, *the Establishment,* with trepidation and envy, perhaps seeing them as among *those who have everything . . . sitting on their fat butts.*

Leonard Garment, sensing Nixon's unease if not entirely comprehending its sources, told him to relax; the other lawyers in the firm, he assured the new partner, were far more in awe of a former vice president and presidential candidate than he was of them. Besides, Garment said, what Nixon took as the knowledge and sophistication of his partners was to some extent a show aimed at impressing *him.*

Nixon maintained to Garment, too, that he had no further political expectations. But after Garment told him frankly that he thought the presidency was still a possibility, even if a long shot, the two worked together tacitly, then explicitly, toward that goal.

In early 1966, Garment was getting ready to argue the *Hill* case, an invasion-of-privacy suit against *Life* magazine. James J. Hill had won a thirty-thousand-dollar judgment against *Life* in 1963, on grounds that his family's privacy had been invaded by the magazine's story about a play called *The Desperate Hours.* The play concerns escaped convicts who take over a family's house and hold them captive. This had happened to the Hill family; but many incidents in the play had not been part of the Hills' experience. They had since moved from the Philadelphia suburbs to Connecticut. When the play tried out in Philadelphia, *Life* photographed the cast in the Hills' old house; Hill argued that this defeated his attempts to maintain his family's privacy, and a New York court agreed.

As Garment prepared to argue against *Life*'s appeal to the U.S. Supreme Court, he decided the case was tailor-made for Richard Nixon—a good one to build his legal reputation, and one centered on an individual-rights issue. The case, Garment reasoned, might help overcome the lingering resentments of liberals and others at Nixon's earlier anti-Communist zeal, which supposedly had led him to run over just such individual rights.

In 1965, that reputation had been revived when Nixon unwisely intervened in a New Jersey gubernatorial election. He had supported Wayne Dumont, the Republican nominee, routinely; later, he backed Dumont's insistence that Eugene D. Genovese, a professor at Rutgers, New Jersey's state university, should be fired for having said he would welcome a Communist victory in Vietnam.

In a statement that sounded not unlike "the old Nixon," the supposed new one said Genovese therefore had given "aid and comfort to the enemy." Eventually, Nixon and Dumont lost the argument, Dumont lost the election, and Nixon lost much of whatever ideological redemption his move to the East might have afforded him.

When Garment urged him to argue the *Hill* case in the Supreme Court, Nixon protested that he knew little of the applicable law and precedents.

He also feared that the high court's well-known liberals—Hugo Black, William O. Douglas, William Brennan—would react against him and, therefore, against the case he would be pleading. And Chief Justice Earl Warren, the former governor of California, had cause dating to 1952—or thought he had—to mistrust Nixon.

Warren had hoped to be a compromise presidential nominee if, as seemed possible, Eisenhower and Robert A. Taft deadlocked the Republican convention that year. Nixon, like the other California delegates, was pledged to Governor Warren until Warren released the whole delegation from his support. In fact, however, Nixon was for Eisenhower, though keeping publicly neutral; and some of Eisenhower's major sponsors— Governor Dewey of New York in particular—had given Nixon reason to believe he had a chance to be Eisenhower's running mate.

When Nixon polled his California precinct workers before the convention to determine their views on the strongest Republican nominee—a poll Eisenhower was almost sure to win—Warren and his aides thought Nixon was undercutting them, despite his pledge. They persuaded him not to publish the poll results.

Nevertheless, aboard the California delegation's train to Chicago, Nixon was reported, at the time and later, to have moved busily among the delegates seeking second-ballot support for Eisenhower. That is consistent with his attitude at the time, although he always has denied the reports.

At the convention itself, Nixon persuaded the California delegation to support the so-called fair-play resolution on the seating of contested delegates—another move bound to help Eisenhower. Warren then became convinced of Nixon's perfidy and banned him, a U.S. senator at the time, from the Warren convention headquarters.*

After Eisenhower won the nomination and chose Nixon for his vice presidential candidate, the Warren organization was reinforced in its mistrust. On the other hand, the notably independent Warren had given Nixon no significant help in any of Nixon's California campaigns and had little standing to demand loyalty from him; and while Nixon undoubtedly maneuvered for the vice presidential nomination in 1952, he also believed that Eisenhower was the strongest possible Republican candidate.

The breach with Warren, never healed, had serious political repercussions in the 1952 campaign and in Nixon's run for governor of California in 1962. In 1966, it provided another good reason for Nixon to resist

*Paul W. Walter of Cleveland, who had charge of Senator Taft's delegate organization at the 1952 convention, asserted in a letter to the author (dated August 12, 1988) that Nixon had agreed with Governor Warren that California would abstain from voting on the fair-play resolution. Nixon later persuaded the California delegation to support the resolution, Mr. Walter wrote, on grounds that Nixon would "benefit" from that support—presumably by receiving the vice presidential nomination.

arguing the *Hill* case before the Warren court. But Garment persisted and Nixon finally agreed.

The result was predictable: the man who believed in hard work and persistence, who was proud of his "iron butt," and whose formidable intellectual capacity considerably exceeded his public—perhaps even his private—appraisal of it, soon mastered a sufficient amount of First Amendment law, the issues involved, and the precedents relevant to the case.[8]

While Garment was helping Nixon prepare their arguments for the high court, Nixon had to keep a Florida business engagement—a meeting with the board of directors of Investors' Diversified Services. He invited Garment to make the trip with him, so that they could continue their preparations.

The IDS meeting was scheduled for a country club near Miami; but Nixon and Garment flew to West Palm Beach on the day before, to have dinner with Elmer Bobst. By then, Bobst had been remarried, to a Lebanese woman he called "Dodo." Nixon had sponsored her for American citizenship. The four had a pleasant dinner, then the two visiting lawyers were driven by limousine to the house outside Miami where they were to be put up for the night.

When they arrived, however, they realized the house was new and unoccupied, in a neighborhood just being developed. Nixon, the experienced politician, immediately sensed that the developers wanted to exploit his name and fame; he feared they'd have photographers on hand in the morning to take publicity pictures of him leaving their new house in their new development. In the middle of the Florida night, he ordered himself and Garment driven back to Elmer Bobst's house in Palm Beach, perhaps forty miles distant.

The hour, Nixon thought, was too late to check into a suitable hotel. But when they reached the Bobst house, near the Palm Beach compound of the Kennedy family, all was dark and the gate was locked. A wall surrounded Bobst's grounds.

"Come on, Garment," the former vice president commanded, on impulse confounding his reputation as both a formal and a calculating man. "Let's climb the wall."

And so they did, two well-dressed New York lawyers with briefcases and luggage clambering into Elmer Bobst's compound in the dark of night. Nixon, who had often visited the place, remembered there was a poolhouse with twin beds; they managed to gain entrance and settled down for the night. But not to sleep.

"Like kids in a summer camp," Leonard Garment recalled years later, the two talked far into the early morning hours. Nixon, who was no longer protesting—at least to Garment—that he was finished with politics, confided that his greatest interest was in foreign affairs, which he had studied closely, in his thoroughgoing fashion. He intended, he confessed, to dedicate a large part of his life to the "great purposes" he had set himself in the field of international relations.

In fact, Garment remembers, the recurrent theme of this rambling nocturnal talk was "the life of 'great purposes.' " Nixon told him—the sort of thing even a more outgoing man would be unlikely to confide except in circumstances as unconventional as those of that night in the poolhouse— that

> he would give anything, make any sacrifice, to be able to utilize his talents and experience. Making money, belonging to exclusive clubs, playing golf, was not his idea of a worthwhile life. His life up to then had been "in the arena," and that's where he wanted to be—even if it meant "a much shorter life."

Nixon also spoke that night of the necessity for personal tenacity; if a man wanted to lead a life of "great purposes," he must never give up, always keep trying.

This, too, is a recurrent theme in Nixon's life; in fact, that life is almost a symbol of indomitability, a quality that, even in 1966, Nixon's worst enemy hardly would have denied him: the young lawyer who could not make it in the world of the big Eastern firms but who had succeeded extravagantly in politics; the young politician who survived a supposed secret-fund scandal in 1952 and the "dump Nixon" movement President Eisenhower secretly pushed in 1956, only to become his party's presidential candidate in 1960; the old pro who already was on his way back from the defeats of 1960 and 1962 and was moving toward another presidential candidacy.

Nixon's old Whittier College football coach, "Chief" Wallace Newman (a Native American), had been a persuasive teacher of tenacity. He "not only taught his players how to win," Nixon was to recall; he "also taught them that when you lose you don't quit, that when you lose you fight harder the next time."

Fighting was what life was about. That was the reason Richard "tried and tried and tried" to make Chief Newman's team, despite his lack of size and football skill: "To get the discipline for myself and to show the others that here was a guy who could dish it out and take it. Mostly, I took it."[9]

Tenacity ran in the family. Nixon's mother, Hannah, a Quaker—some who knew her thought her a "saint"—also instilled in him this respect for tenacity. At about the time of his trip to Florida with Garment, Nixon visited his mother in the hospital, at a time when she was believed to be dying. But she was not too ill to hear his urgent, characteristic exhortation: "Mother, don't give up!"

As he remembered in *RN*, she rose a little in the bed, "and with sudden strength in her voice" replied: "Richard, don't *you* give up. Don't let anybody tell you you are through." Years later, Nixon observed that "if my mother hadn't said that, I might have given up. She didn't live to see what her advice did."[10]

It was not just from a sickbed that Hannah Nixon taught her son; especially in her marriage, she exemplified tenacity.

"I think that they would have called him a sort of a little man, common man," Richard Nixon said of his father, Frank Nixon, in his farewell speech to the White House staff in 1974. "He was a streetcar motorman first, and then he was a farmer, and then he had a lemon ranch. It was the poorest lemon ranch in California, I can assure you." Frank Nixon during most of Richard's youth also was a grocer and a butcher, not very successful in any of his enterprises, a loud and argumentative man, a "punishing and often brutal" father.[11]

At the service station across from the Nixon store, as he recalled in an oral history, Merle West often could hear Frank Nixon "holler" at his sons.

> He was a lot of mouth, the little rascal. . . . Honest as the day is long. But he would argue with you and let you pick which side you wanted to argue on. You would make him happy if you argued on either side. He was just a big old Irish loud type.

But West, a descendant of the Milhous family and a brother of the novelist Jessamyn West, thought Richard Nixon "out-maneuvered Frank" rather than "out-shouting" him.

Frank "didn't mind screaming his head off at you," Lucille Parsons remembered, only partially in amusement.

> He was a gruff character, nobody got the best of him . . . he'd do anything for you. But he sure could scream and yell. . . . He didn't like a lot of the customers that came in. It was the same with them. They didn't like him either. . . . He didn't mince any words about people that got in his way or bothered him . . . if you got in his way, woe be unto you. And you wouldn't want to do it again.

Frank Nixon was not only difficult, he was a tough disciplinarian who used the strap or the rod on his sons. Richard's younger brother, Edward, once referred to "my mother as the judge and my father as the executioner," a choice of words that may or may not have been significant. But Richard appears to have escaped physical punishment. In trying to "out-maneuver" Frank, he learned early "to abide by the rules [his father] laid down. Otherwise, I would probably have felt the touch of a ruler or the strap as my brothers did." His mother said later that she did not remember that her husband ever "spanked Richard."[12]

Richard's first cousin, Floyd Wildermuth, who lived with the Nixon family for a while after his own father died, had a high regard for his uncle, Frank Nixon, as "the biggest-hearted man I think I've ever known." But in his oral history, he too recalled Frank as "a shouter, very vociferous. . . . He sure was loud. He'd blow you out of the place when he got upset."

It would not be surprising if Richard suffered embarrassment, even shame, at such a "grouchy and impatient" father, a man of "volatile nature and explosive temper." That, too, could have contributed to the later internal anger Nixon spoke of in remembering "slights and snubs" in his youth.[13]

The marriage of the gentle Quaker Hannah Nixon to Frank can only have been frequently a trial to her; yet she never disclosed—certainly not to her children—bitterness or disappointment or anger at her and their plight, tied as they were to an unpleasant bully they could not acknowledge as such. In that sense, visible every day to an observant youth like Richard, Hannah Nixon "never gave up" on the life she had had to make for herself or the future she tried to make for her children.

However unconsciously, Richard Nixon's youth and family were a living presence in Elmer Bobst's poolhouse, as Nixon talked on and on about "great purposes" and indomitable will. His father, lacerated by ulcers and failure, may have been a hard man to please and quick to punish, but he was knowledgeable and passionate about politics; and Richard had been deeply influenced by him as well as by Hannah. Frank Nixon and his lack of achievement were at the root of his son's conscious identification of himself as an Orthogonian, and of his determination.

"Because of illness in the family," Nixon recalled in *Six Crises,* Frank Nixon "had to leave school after only six years of formal education. Never a day went by when he did not tell me and my four brothers how fortunate we were to be able to go to school. *I was determined not to let him down.*"

In such youthful resolution, "great purposes" often begin. If so, Nixon's were not mocked by his Grandmother Milhous, whose idol was Abraham Lincoln. On Richard's thirteenth birthday, she gave him a picture of Lincoln, inscribed in her own hand with the well-known lines from Longfellow:

> Lives of great men oft remind us
> We can make our lives sublime.
> And, departing, leave behind us
> Footprints on the sands of time.

The picture and inscription had hung over Richard Nixon's bed all through his high school and college years.[14]

But to Leonard Garment, listening from the other poolhouse bed, Nixon's midnight confidences seemed to form a beacon into the future rather than a shadow of the past. Garment fell asleep more certain than ever that great achievements still lay before his impressive colleague.

Nixon had instructed their driver to return for him at 7:30 A.M. and, when Garment woke to the Florida sun, Nixon had already departed to keep his appointment near Miami. Before leaving, Nixon had alerted Elmer Bobst to their night in the poolhouse, and the older man welcomed Garment cordially with a sumptuous breakfast. Afterward, they sat by the pool, soaking up sun and talking away most of the five or six hours of Nixon's absence.

Then eighty-one years old, Bobst was a thoughtful and kindly gentleman—though Garment remembers him, too, as formal to the point of pomposity: "When he said good morning, it was almost like a speech to his stockholders."

But if Leonard Garment, a Democrat, had become a convert to the political future of Richard Nixon, he found Elmer Bobst evangelical on the subject. Bobst had no doubt, two years before the election of 1968, that Nixon would yet be president. He and Nixon, he confided that morning in the Florida sun, often had talked about what Nixon would do when he reached the White House.

Bobst had the typically conservative attitudes of a wealthy businessman, but on two important subjects Garment was surprised by the man's heretical views. Bobst had been the son of an American missionary to China, had spent his childhood in that country and was still fascinated by it. Though nearly twenty years had passed without free exchange of travel and commerce between China and the U.S., Bobst treated Garment to a long and knowledgeable disquisition, not only on his early life in China, but on the history, future, power, beauty and importance of that immense and mysterious nation—which was far more enigmatic in 1966 than now.

China, Bobst continued, was one of the subjects he and Nixon had most frequently discussed. And, he went on, they agreed that "the most important thing" to be done in world affairs was "bringing China into the world"—whether Communist or not.

Garment was surprised to hear that Richard Nixon, of all people, agreed with this. He was well aware of the long Nixon history of opposition to what Americans called "Red China" and his frequent castigations of those—mostly Democrats and State Department bureaucrats—he had accused of having "lost China" to the Communists.

After his first foreign trip as vice president, for instance, Nixon had returned from the Far East to inform the American people on radio and television that "China is the basic cause of all our troubles in Asia. If China had not gone Communist, we would not have had a war in Korea. If China were not Communist, there would be no war in Indochina, there would be no war in Malaya."

In more than a decade of campaigning across the nation, Nixon had given few people reason to believe that his long-held views on China had changed; far from it. Debating John Kennedy during the 1960 presidential campaign, he had answered one of his own rhetorical questions roundly: "Now, what do the Chinese Communists want? . . . They want the world."

In a postelection meeting with Kennedy at Key Biscayne, Nixon also had advised the president-elect not to recognize Communist China or admit it to the United Nations. That "would give respectability to the Communist regime which would immensely increase its power and prestige in Asia."

Nevertheless, Garment was left in no doubt that Bobst, who seemed sure in his knowledge of Nixon's views, believed that when he became president—there was no if about it, in Bobst's view—Nixon would bring China into the world. That plan was all the more surprising as the war in Vietnam, then widely assumed to be the handiwork of what Secretary of State Dean Rusk called "Asian communism with its headquarters in Peiping," was becoming a major issue of American politics.*

It was on the question of Vietnam that Elmer Bobst surprised Garment a second time. Bobst was, remarkably, a strong opponent of the war, considering it a disaster from which the U.S. needed to extricate itself as quickly as possible. In 1966, this was a highly unusual view, particularly among conservatives. Nixon disagreed, Bobst told Garment—who was familiar, anyway, with Nixon's hawkish support for the war.

More than merely supporting it, in fact, Nixon then publicly contended that the Johnson administration should escalate and widen the war with naval and air interdiction of North Vietnamese supply routes into South Vietnam and destruction of Communist facilities in North Vietnam and Laos. Negotiating with the Vietcong or "neutralizing" South Vietnam, Nixon was then arguing, would be "surrendering on the installment plan."

A few months *after* the Nixon-Garment trip, Nixon was campaigning for congressional candidates in Pennsylvania; I was traveling with him, as was Joseph Stern of the *Baltimore Sun.* As we sat in a private plane parked off the runway at the Philadelphia airport, Nixon said that if the Republican party wanted to nominate a "peace candidate" in 1968, "I could not be that candidate."

I had left a briefcase at an earlier stop; at considerable expense and with the courtesy his close acquaintances say he often shows, Nixon had arranged for it to be flown to us at Philadelphia.* While we waited, Stern

---

*Owing to his State Department experience in the fifties, Rusk always referred to the Chinese capital with the old usage "Peiping."
*Or perhaps he was only showing a politician's deference to the press, as suggested by

and I asked him about the war in Vietnam. He was convinced it had to be fought and won, Nixon said, to maintain the American position in Asia and the world—which was why he insisted he would not and could not be a "peace candidate," even if that stand should cost him the nomination.

But as Bobst talked on, that morning at poolside, Garment saw that there was not as much disagreement between the older man and Nixon about Vietnam as the latter's public pronouncements would suggest. Bobst said Nixon thought the American position in Vietnam was that of "a cork in the bottle"; pulling it out could have disastrous consequences (which is consistent with what Nixon later said to Stern and me). But Bobst pictured Nixon as little more optimistic than Bobst himself that the war could be won, or brought to some fruitful conclusion.

To his consternation, Garment realized that the primary difference—at least in Bobst's telling—between Nixon the hawk and Bobst the dove was whether the U.S. should "get out quickly or slowly." Bobst thought immediately; Nixon believed the cork could not be extracted so abruptly without serious dislocations of American influence and power elsewhere.

Thus, the testimony of two of those who then knew him best is that in early 1966 Nixon was already clear about what would in less than three years become his presidential policies on China and the war in Vietnam. Not uncharacteristically, he was saying something quite different to the American people—many of whom would have expected little but indirection from Richard Nixon anyway.

He was a long-familiar figure to every American by then, though few knew or perceived him as fully as most thought they did. He had been in the arena for a long time—since 1946, and for twenty of his fifty-three years, although out of public office for the last five. In the House, the Senate, the second-highest office of the government, as candidate for president and for governor of the most populous state, he had become a presence in the land.

Throughout that long, portentous post–World War II period in which the legacy of Franklin Roosevelt and the policies of Truman, Stalin, Churchill, Attlee, Adenauer, Mao Tse-tung, Eisenhower, and Khrushchev had shaped the modern world—through the entire era, that is, of his country's evolution into one of the two superpowers—Richard Nixon (to borrow Dean Acheson's phrase) had been "present at the creation."

---

a similar occurrence earlier that year. On a trip to Birmingham, Nixon had been accompanied by a single reporter, Jules Witcover. Misunderstanding the departure time, Witcover had to take a taxi to the airport, expecting to be left behind; but Nixon waited a half hour for him and graciously waved away his apologies. Witcover wrote of this experience: "I was grateful and genuinely impressed by his courtesy and act of generosity (even when I later learned he had told those aboard who wanted to leave me behind: 'He's the only reporter we've got')."[15]

In 1960, moreover, he had contested with John Kennedy—who by 1966 was virtually deified—not merely for the presidency; both had knowingly sought the leadership of that new world built in the years of Truman, Stalin and Eisenhower—the leadership, too, of those Kennedy was to call in his inaugural address "a new generation of Americans, born in this century, tempered by war, disciplined by a hard and bitter peace. . . ."

Nixon lost that epic contest, though by only a handful of votes out of the sixty million cast. Quite possibly, he had not really lost at all but had been the victim of stolen votes in Illinois and Texas. Millions of his countrymen thought so, with ample if not conclusive evidence to back them up.

Present at the creation in more ways than one: Richard Nixon, among other things, had been a pioneer in television, a newfangled and mistrusted political medium in his early years in the arena, but one that not least by his use of it was to become the fundamental instrument of today's politics—not an altogether felicitous development. His 1952 Checkers speech (famous or infamous, in 1966, to virtually every American) had been one of the first major events of presidential politics to reach a national audience of home viewers—the largest, in fact, up to then assembled, about sixty million people.

Not without pride, Nixon pointed out in *Six Crises* that this record had lasted for eight years, until he and John Kennedy broke it in their first debate, on September 26, 1960. In 1958, Nixon also became the first American to address the people of the Soviet Union on Soviet television.

He was an innovator in national campaigning, too—a man to whom Lyndon Johnson later referred derisively as a "chronic campaigner," although Nixon once told one of the few reporters with whom he was close, Earl Mazo of the *New York Herald Tribune,* that he "shudder[ed] at the thought" of any more campaigning.[16]

As a vice presidential candidate, Nixon had stumped the nation in 1952 in classic whistle-stop fashion, from the rear platform of a campaign train. In 1954 and 1958 he led the Republican congressional campaigns, from which Eisenhower shrank; in 1956 he even took the leading part in the Eisenhower reelection campaign. Then, in 1960, as he and Kennedy abandoned the rails for jet flight, Nixon became the first presidential candidate to visit every one of the fifty states, including Alaska and Hawaii.

Nixon's performance as vice president also had been ground-breaking. He had carried an unprecedented share of the Eisenhower administration's domestic political burdens, not only as lead campaigner but as high-level lobbyist in Congress, as liaison to the Republican party, and as counselor on the political ramifications of administration policy decisions.

He was also the first vice president to attend cabinet and National Security Council meetings as a matter of routine, and to be given extensive—if not highly substantive—foreign assignments, a responsibility that arose from an expanded American presence in the world, combined with the rapid postwar development of international flight. And the task Eisenhower delegated to him as chairman of a cabinet committee on government contracts made Nixon one of the few vice presidents to have been given an actual executive function.

Nixon also had been given high marks for his performance as vice president during the periods following Eisenhower's heart attack in 1955 and two other major illnesses. In those trying times, he had skillfully walked a fine line, continuing necessary executive activity without appearing to reach for presidential powers that were not his. In this delicately balanced political act, together with his other vice presidential achievements, Nixon had constantly transcended the classic description of the office by one of his predecessors, John Nance Garner: "not worth a pitcher of warm spit."

Thus, in the sense that an actor creates a role on the stage, Richard Nixon essentially had created the modern vice presidency. The office he had helped expand, in turn, had helped greatly in making him a candidate for the presidency in his own right (despite Eisenhower's ill-concealed doubts), as it has made every vice president since (save Spiro T. Agnew, who was forced to resign the office, and Nelson Rockefeller, Gerald Ford's appointee).

Since Thomas Jefferson in 1800, only one vice president, Martin Van Buren (who, rather like Nixon, was said to "row to his object with muffled oars"), had been elected president (in 1836) without first having succeeded a president who died in office. Nixon had come closest, in 1960.*

And yet, for all his imposing record and his prominence, Nixon's return to the presidential arena, if Elmer Bobst's expectations were met, would bring no easy triumph. For there was something elusive, unknown, perhaps unknowable, about the man. True, a great many Americans admired and respected—some loved—him. Perhaps as many feared and disliked—some despised—him. Few of those with even minimal public concern were neutral or uncaring.

Adlai Stevenson had spoken for Nixon's critics when he envisioned a place called "Nixonland—a land of slander and scare, of sly innuendo, of a poison pen, the anonymous phone call, and hustling, pushing, shoving—the land of smash and grab and anything to win." And some wag had said: "If Dick Nixon ever wrestled with his conscience, the match was fixed."

But Herbert Hoover had spoken as surely for Nixon's admirers when he credited him with exposing "the stream of treason that has existed in our country." They did not doubt that Richard Nixon was a patriotic scourge

*In 1988, George Bush became the first vice president since Van Buren to win the White House in an election.

of Communists in government and a stand-up battler for America, able and willing to take on the powerful forces of greed, corruption and subversion.

The "evidence" on which such polar beliefs rested, as is frequently the case with the reputations of public men, was often distorted, misunderstood or insufficient. But these claims were primarily underpinned, anyway, less by evidence than by strong reactions to Nixon's *manner*—by powerful impressions that stirred the public to faith and admiration or to dislike and mistrust, but seldom to indifference.

This is not unusual in American politics. "I just can't stand him" or "He's my kind of guy" is, as often as not, the reason we vote for or against a political candidate. The stuffy image of "the little man on the wedding cake" had nothing to do with political issues but it helped ruin Thomas E. Dewey. "I Like Ike," perhaps the most inspired political slogan in American history, was not merely a catchy rhyme; it was a resounding truth for millions who could have cited little besides General Eisenhower's smile to account for their sentiment.

But Richard Nixon had none of the grace and charm, the easy touch, that distinguished Eisenhower and later Ronald Reagan, nor did he appear smug and self-satisfied, as had been widely supposed about Dewey and punishingly symbolized by the wedding-cake image. More important, the general impression of these politicians was that they were very much what they seemed to be—good guys or insufferable. Nixon's problem was the opposite: *the instinct of many Americans that he was not what he seemed.*

Taken at face value—and his heavy beard shadow, immortalized in so many cartoons, caused many a "Nixon hater" to take him all too literally at "face" value—Nixon had appealed throughout his career to patriotism and the love of family; he had expressed devotion to hard work and free enterprise, constantly exalted "the people," professed religious faith and— perhaps more important—faith in religion. He had extolled the virtues of military might and peace, suggesting that the former was necessary to guarantee the latter; and he had left no doubt of his confidence in the manifest destiny of an American nation favored by God (the one of your choice).

The 34,108,000 people who had voted for Richard Nixon for president in 1960 (only 113,000 more had voted for John Kennedy, as far as can be determined) attested to the apparent success of this political Nixon with roughly half the voting public of the time. The journalist Richard Rovere sought valiantly to explain his appeal:

> As a person and as a personality, he embodies much that is held to be precious by a large and growing number of Americans— especially in that segment of the middle class to which he belongs. . . . He is young, he is enterprising, he is successful. . . . He lacks humor, but exudes earnestness and frankness. . . .

His sales-executive manner and his account-executive rhetoric are the very stuff of the good life to his constituency. The fact that his ideas are obscure and his positive achievements few detracts not in the slightest from the charm of the public image. . . . His general appearance, his dress, his whole style of living and being, commend him to the multitudes who share his aspirations for a clear title to a ranch-house, furs for the wife, and pets for the children.[17]

In describing his own voting attitudes, Merle West—though naturally a supporter because of childhood acquaintance—may have described a lot of other Nixon voters:

> Kennedy wanted to give, give, give—Roosevelt did, Rockefeller did. I'm a stingy man. . . . I work hard and I don't want to give it to everybody. I'm willing to share a little but I don't want to throw it around. It seems like these people that had it so easy feel guilty because they inherited all that . . . because they never had to work for it. I think maybe somebody that has to work hard for it isn't as inclined to be as generous about it. . . . I don't think Dick has promised blue sky, pie in the sky, so much as these other guys do.

But even to many such admirers, Nixon appeared stiff, calculating, calculated. With practiced professionalism, rarely referring to a text, he could deliver speeches precisely attuned to his audience and the moment; but the very shrewdness of these supposedly spontaneous performances called their validity into question, particularly to a political press that conveyed to the American electorate most of what it knew about public persons.

Even Nixon's stump-speaking gestures, of which he had an extensive repertoire—many appearing a little too stagy—could betray him, for sometimes the sweep of his arms or the twists of his body or the counting of points on his long fingers seemed ill-timed with his words, as if speech and gesture had gotten out of sync, like a film running a few frames ahead or behind its sound track. Could either speech or gesture, therefore, proceed from genuine emotion or impulse?

With his shadowed face, his eyes set protectively deep beneath lowering brows, his rather sour mouth turning down at the corners, Nixon could present a forbidding appearance. Must that not, some critics wondered, reflect a profound inner discontent rather than the upbeat spirit of American confidence his constituency valued and his political speeches so often extolled? Even the ski-jump nose, though a more amiable trademark than his five o'clock shadow and as much a butt of jokes as Bob Hope's, could not make Richard Nixon seem, like the comedian, a "regular guy" whose human flaws made him the more ordinary and likable.

Nixon did project the kind of barbershop joviality that among American men often passes for wit. He was well informed and a prolific talker about sports; he sometimes appeared to have researched the subject. Even these labored efforts at Rotary Club and locker-room good fellowship seemed to reinforce the impression of a man distant, uncomfortable, engaged in unnatural acts—the public arts of politics.

Despite his defeats, Nixon was mostly a successful politician; but he lacked the gregariousness that usually marks the vote-getter. The late Bryce Harlow (who worked with him in both the Eisenhower and the Nixon administrations) recalled that Nixon had no small talk and "had to force himself to be out there pressing the flesh. He had to be something he didn't want to be." Nixon was "stiff," Harlow observed, even with friends.[18]

That had been true of Nixon as far back as Whittier College days. The Orthogonians had a ritual they called "knock and boost," a primitive kind of encounter group, in which they sat in a circle and each member could "stand and give his colleague a knock or a boost." Perhaps "the member gave constructive criticism that he thought might be helpful," Byron Netzley remembered in an oral history. "One time . . . one of the men told [Nixon] that he needed more of the common touch—that he should make an effort to be friendly."

The seriousness with which the ambitious and introspective young Nixon took this can be imagined; but the result, in all probability, was more of the rather heavy-handed efforts he made, all of his life, to *appear* outgoing and friendly—which belied his nature and usually emphasized his inability to be casual and easy.

Once, during a layover in the middle of his 1956 campaign for the Eisenhower-Nixon ticket, the Nixon staff and the accompanying reporters were cavorting in a hotel swimming pool. Vice President Nixon suddenly appeared in his bathing suit, dived in, swam several lengths, climbed out and walked off—without having exchanged a word or a smile or even a look with anyone.[19]

William Rogers, a close friend who became Nixon's secretary of state, believes Nixon had felt since boyhood that people didn't like him, and that as a consequence he tried too hard to be "one of the boys"—for instance, in his almost suicidal determination to play college football, for which he had no talent, and his obvious later efforts to talk sports. Nixon was too often "trying to fit a mold that wasn't his," Rogers told me.

"I'm fundamentally relatively shy," Nixon himself conceded to Stewart Alsop. "It doesn't come natural to me to be a buddy-buddy boy. When I meet a lot of people, I tend to seek out the shy ones. . . . I can't really let my hair down with anyone . . . not even with my family."[20]

A passage in *Six Crises* suggests the problem Nixon presented to the public. One crisis was the presidential election of 1960, and in giving his account of it, written while memory was still fresh, Nixon went into considerable detail about his debates with Kennedy.

In the view of the huge television audience and most political professionals, Nixon decisively lost the first of these, although a quarter century later the text of the exchange seems to yield no particular advantage to Kennedy. Ralph McGill, the editor of the *Atlanta Constitution,* checked with people who *heard* the debate on radio rather than watching on television, and reported that "they unanimously thought Mr. Nixon had the better of it." So it was not the substance of what Nixon said that damaged his candidacy—although he may have taken the occasion too lightly and failed to do his homework as extensively as was usual with him.

The radio audience that McGill checked was small compared to the eighty million who watched on the home screen. Thus, in the first of the televised presidential debates that have now become standard, their essential flaw appeared: these contrived confrontations tend to subordinate the substance of the issues to the appearance and manner of the debaters.

In Nixon's case in 1960, the impression he made was sabotaged by powder that failed to conceal his five o'clock shadow, by a too loose shirt collar (he had lost weight from a brief illness) and by his lack of ease and charm as compared with his cool young millionaire opponent (who was, in Whittier terms, an obvious "Franklin").

None of that has much to do with substantive qualifications. But that Kennedy appeared with Nixon on the same platform and discussed the same issues without obvious disadvantage shook the public's belief that eight years in the vice presidency as the revered Eisenhower's heir presumptive must have better qualified Nixon to be president. His gaunt appearance and relatively uneasy manner further undermined confidence in him, and the television broadcast of the first debate thus struck a severe, perhaps fatal, blow to Nixon's candidacy.

Well aware that much of the public had judged him the loser, Nixon—who prided himself on the realism of his political judgments—resolved to recoup. In *Six Crises* he portrays himself and his state of mind in some detail as he prepared for the second debate. This time, he did his usual iron-butt stint, studying and cramming, reading as widely as possible and listening to as many briefings as time permitted. But, he wrote,

> In the final analysis, I knew that what was most important was that *I must be myself.* . . . I went into the second debate determined to do my best to convey three basic impressions to the television audience—knowledge in depth of the subjects discussed, *sincerity,* and confidence. [Emphasis added.]

Nixon was, indeed, the consensus winner of the second debate—though, significantly, the television audience dropped by twenty million viewers from the first, probably decisive, confrontation. But that passage from *Six Crises* makes an essential point about its author: Richard Nixon, in his public presentations of himself, seemed constantly to be *trying to be sincere.*

But sincerity that can be resolved upon is not really sincerity. An *effort* to be sincere ("sincerity as a cram course," as James R. Schlesinger, once Nixon's secretary of defense, described this quality to me) belies the very meaning of sincerity, which comes naturally if at all; even the subjective question in a person's mind whether he or she is or should be sincere, let alone concern about *appearing* to be sincere, presupposes a basic *in*sincerity.[21]

It was a central fact of Richard Nixon's political life that even some of his most ardent supporters, as well as others who disliked and mistrusted him, so often saw him as a performer, a man not only trying to make an impression but constantly calculating precisely *what* impression he wanted to make—whether of sincerity, candor, boldness or some other desirable quality.

His critics saw a fraud and a demagogue, a gut-fighter who pretended to be a preacher. Nixon's backers, like Bobst and Herbert Hoover, saw a preacher often pretending, for reasons not of his own making, to be a politician.

They believed him an honorable, dedicated man forced by the self-interested attitudes of the public to assume sometimes the slashing and deceitful ways of a hard campaigner. They believed that beneath the palpably vote-seeking exterior, a less politically motivated man had to conceal himself if he was to win the power to assert and defend traditional American values against the relentless forces of greed and corruption, joined in postwar America by those of subversion.

How else explain the mixture of virtue bordering on piety with alley-fighting tactics, both of which marked Nixon as a campaigner? If this patriotic, public-spirited man was to win elections and exercise power in the jungle of American politics, did he have any choice but to fight with any weapon at hand? Was that not, in fact, the manly and responsible thing to do? Or so his admirers reasoned.

There were better explanations, had the public known them, for Nixon's calculated presentations of himself. This painfully inward and introverted man, who had forced himself to adopt the hearty, one-of-the-boys manner of an extraverted calling, was an intellectual in a decidedly unintellectual business. Dr. Arthur Burns, who had known him well in the Eisenhower administration, concluded "early in that period that Mr. Nixon could have held down a chair in political science or law in any of our major universities and would have served with great distinction."[22]

Good teachers are not necessarily intellectuals; nor are persons of high intelligence. Nixon probably would not label himself—perhaps has never thought of himself—as an intellectual. Certainly, he never trusted in disinterested rationality, if that can be considered the usual mark of an intellectual, over and above the passions, moods and interests of the American public.

Nixon's intellect, however, was more often and more intricately engaged in his work than is usual for a politician; those who know him well speak again and again of his special skill at the *tour d'horizon*—pulling together known but disparate facts into a single, compelling picture, perhaps of "American interests" worldwide at any given moment, or of the essential elements of a presidential campaign. Maurice Stans, an unstinting admirer who served in Nixon's cabinet, recalled him as "a keen student in evaluating the pros and cons of a problem," a man who tried "to innovate in major national and international events rather than merely respond to them."[23]

Elliot Richardson, who filled many offices in both the Eisenhower and Nixon administrations, termed Nixon "a man of great powers of intellect, as well as quickness of mind" with—in many ways as important—"a long memory." In different circumstances it seems likely that Richard Nixon might well have made a mark as a man devoted to learning and intellect, rather than as a politician.[24]

Still, just as satire loses on Saturday night, intellect tends to lose at the polls. Nixon thought so, anyway. Raymond Price—a skilled and widely admired aide from 1966 until well after Nixon left the White House—conceded to me that his boss often was not the man he tried, usually transparently, to appear to be. Price insisted, however, that Nixon the politician was not pretending to be *better* than he really was, but *worse*—or less than he was, in the sense of concealing his introverted and cerebral self in order to become more appealing to voters.[25]

Nixon's political success appears to have been built on the calculated (however necessary) presentation of a public persona that brutally distorted the essential Nixon within—an introverted intellectual—though at what price to his self-esteem can only be imagined.

No wonder, then, as the years wore along, that much of the public suspected that Richard Nixon was not what he tried to appear in his public performances; he wasn't. No wonder that so many in the press with which his career was so inextricably involved came to regard him as a "cardboard man" (as one described him to Bryce Harlow). Reporters are not much inclined or encouraged to look past what meets the eye, and in Nixon they tended only to see the performer—to their experienced eyes, the faker.

No wonder that for so many years this man, strangely persisting in the national consciousness, so fascinated a public, much of which constantly sought "the real Nixon"—seldom understanding that he was only to be found as "one of us," shaped as much by circumstance and inheritance as by choice, a victim of chance as often as the master of his fate, as driven by private demons and dreams as by the gross ambitions of American life.

Before anything else, he was the son of Hannah and Frank Nixon, the Quaker "saint" and the brooding, bullying, politically minded Irishman, both of whom, as noted, had a profound impact upon him in his impressionable youth, and thus upon his adult personality.

To Hannah his frequent assertions of morality and idealism surely can be traced; and to Frank his hard-hitting, sometimes unscrupulous campaign style. The one was no less a heritage than the other; both enabled, or perhaps forced, him to adopt his strange coupling of idealism expressed in terms of moral *values* with the value-free language and tactics of a politics that emphasized *interests* and power. In Merle West's opinion:

> If Dick just had Milhous in him, nice as we think they are, he wouldn't have had the go-power to go and put up with what he has through the years and come back as strong as he has. He wouldn't be the scrapper he is. . . . It's some of that Nixon blood that did him a lot of good, too. He needed both.

Beyond an obvious inheritance, something more elusive, glimpsed only tantalizingly in his childhood and later recollections but perhaps more powerful than any other influence, may have arisen from his mother's quiet dominance of the Nixon family. Hannah Nixon clearly *was* dominant, despite the contrast of her Quaker ways with the "volatile nature and explosive temper" of Frank.

"At nights she'd go to the meetings, and Frank would stay home with the children," Ollie Burdg remembered in an oral history; he worked for the Nixons and lived in their house in Richard's early childhood. Hannah Nixon also "arranged diplomatically," the Reverend Harold Walker of the First Friends Church of Whittier suggested, that:

> instead of waiting on customers—for whom Hannah had the patience of an angel—Frank did the buying by driving into the Los Angeles wholesale markets early in the morning, doing maintenance work, and helping with the meat cutting and the heavier stock work.[26]

In all the wealth of recollections of Hannah Nixon by her contemporaries, whether in books about her famous second son or in oral histories, not an unkind word about her can be found. Reverend Walker's "angel" reference above is typical—she was "an angel on earth," Merle West said.

"I never heard her not willing to help and not do what she could do, whatever your problem was, she would do her best to help you out."

Hannah is always remembered as extraordinarily patient with her difficult husband and a houseful of boys—a quiet woman who never showed anger, deeply religious, hardworking, obviously of powerful character and self-discipline in the Quaker tradition.

"The only dominance she had," as Lucille Parsons saw it,

> was telling [Richard] what was right and what was wrong . . . she saw to it that the boys always went to church and Sunday school. On Sunday they went to Christian Endeavor in the evening.

Religion was at the center of Hannah Nixon's concern—"she put it first in the family life." But Mrs. Parsons also pictured a woman too busy keeping her household together, in difficult circumstances, to have much time for personal relationships.

> Gosh, she worked so darned hard all her life she didn't have time to do anything. . . . As for their home life they didn't have too much because they were so busy working. . . . She just didn't have too much time to even visit Grandmother.

Or, as Merle West put it: "Never anything but work, work as hard as she could."

In no recollection, to my knowledge, is Hannah Nixon described, however, as given to *physical* expressions of warmth toward her sons. The emphasis is invariably on her near "saintliness," a quality that for young children may be less important than a close embrace, a kiss, a rollicking bounce on a mother's lap. Remembering his mother with near adulation in *RN,* Nixon nevertheless added that "she was intensely private in her feelings and emotions."

At times, moreover, Hannah Nixon was literally distant from Richard. When his older brother Harold was ill with tuberculosis, she lived for two years with Harold in Arizona—characteristically washing and scrubbing for other patients to help defray expenses. For a time, also, Richard lived with his aunt, Carrie Wildermuth, while he attended high school in Fullerton; earlier, in 1925, when he was only twelve years old, he had been sent to study music and live with his aunt, Jane Beeson, whose home was more than a hundred miles away in Lindsay.

Richard later wrote in a college essay about the death of his younger brother Arthur, that when the Nixon family came to get him after the year in Lindsay "finally" ended:

As soon as [Arthur] saw me alone, he solemnly kissed me on the cheek. I learned later that he had dutifully asked my mother *if it would be proper for him to kiss me,* since I had been away for such a long time.[27] [Emphasis added.]

Repeating this story in *RN,* Nixon added: "Even at that early age [Arthur] had acquired our family's reticence about open displays of affection." Indeed, a child "dutifully" asking his mother if it would be "proper" to kiss a long-absent brother does not suggest a family in which displays of warm physical affection were commonplace. The descriptions are of a household centered on keeping up the store, and later the restaurant, that provided the Nixon family's living.

Even the death of two sons—Harold the eldest, Arthur the youngest; a double loss that might have caused a less controlled person to shake her fist at heaven—seems not to have shattered the religious equanimity of Hannah Nixon. "We mustn't question God's decision," she told Richard's friendly biographer, Bela Kornitzer, when speaking of Harold's illness and death. "He let me learn understanding and compassion through the suffering of my son."

But to an unformed boy like Richard Nixon, twice exiled—as it might have seemed—from his mother's concern, the care and attention she necessarily devoted to Harold and Arthur, in contrast, might have been unsettling. Even before that, is there not an implicit cry for attention and affection in the letter he wrote Hannah ("My Dear Master") at age ten, which he concluded with the words "I wish you would come home right now" and signed "Your good dog Richard"?[28]

Such a remarkable woman unquestionably was an imposing figure in the development of Richard Nixon's character and personality. But in the formative years, emotions are more powerful than intellect or moral example, however admirable; the emotional signals, the physical demonstrations, the tangible evidence of love and caring and protection, have continuing influence throughout life; so does their absence. In the saintly detachment, the emotional quiescence faintly discernible in Hannah Nixon's blameless character may perhaps be glimpsed an unadmitted— perhaps unrecognized—but real fact of Richard's restrained childhood and youth: an essential coldness at the center of a relationship from which he needed warmth and affection more than moral guidance.

If so, his own remoteness, his self-control and self-discipline, even his apparently unemotional calculation of political tactics and advantage can be seen to have the kind of ineradicable roots in early experience that so profoundly affect most of our lives. If reassuring, physically demonstrated affection was not provided at a time when Richard Nixon most sorely needed it, by the one from whom he most desired it, he might himself have been unable later to offer others affection, or even consciously to consider it valuable.

"As a young person," Bryce Harlow speculated, speaking with the surety of a man who had given the matter long thought, Nixon "was hurt very deeply by somebody . . . a sweetheart, a parent, a dear friend, someone he deeply trusted. Hurt so badly he never got over it and never trusted anybody again. But in life we get back what we plow into it." If a man trusts no one—and Harlow believed Nixon did not—it will not be easy for anyone to trust him.[29]

A sense of emotional deprivation deep in Nixon's innermost personality might go far to explain his fear, perceived by friends like William Rogers, that people didn't like him, perhaps subconsciously that he was not worthy of their liking—a fear causing him in his political career to try too hard and too obviously, sometimes too clumsily, to appear to be an ordinary, patriotic, hardworking, God-fearing, sports-loving, public-spirited American humbled by prominence and responsibility.

Whether or not a lack of motherly warmth in his childhood affected Richard Nixon in that way, Hannah Nixon's calmness and quiet, her ability to soothe the angers and resentments Frank's belligerence sometimes caused, her diplomatic interventions with her husband on her sons' behalf, her strongly held Quaker beliefs—all of which, as Richard approached manhood, would have become more visible to him—provided a formidable, even daunting example for a son who longed to achieve "great purposes." In his 1968 acceptance speech to the Republican National Convention, for example, he spoke of Hannah's "passionate concern for peace," and her Quaker voice can almost be heard in a later passage:

> We extend the hand of friendship to all people. To the Russian people. To the Chinese people. To all people in the world. And we work toward the goal of an open world, open sky, open cities, open hearts, open minds.

Most men and women, of course, long for peace, at least as an abstraction, and everyone who runs for high office pays lip service to the idea. But it does not seem fanciful to suggest that the idealized and challenging example of Hannah Nixon was at the heart of the high hopes, intellectual effort and political risk her son was to invest in the search for a literal, negotiated peace among nations—the "structure of peace" that became virtually an obsession with him, the obvious monument he hoped to erect to the Nixon name.

Nixon has confided his inmost feelings to few people. But the young member of Congress and the later vice president chose to talk intimately with one man* who concluded that the supposedly ruthless and calculating politician suffered "guilt feelings" for having followed so often in politics the example of his rancorous, partisan father rather than that of his "saintly" mother. Nixon's strongest wish, this confidant deduced from their conversations, was finally to be able to go in spirit to Hannah Nixon— despite all the tumult, the shouting, the un-Quakerish grapplings and betrayals of his political life—and say: "Mother, I have made peace. Now I am worthy of you."

That goal, in time, was to come as nearly within Richard Nixon's reach as it has to any president. In the long and often bitter years from Whittier to the White House, it could only have been a punishing personal burden, to be borne at any cost, in hope of absolution.

*Who chose not to be identified. Notes of my interview with him are in my files.

2

★

Tricky Dick

★

**Nice guys and sissies don't win
many elections.**

—Roy Day

Shortly after he defeated Helen Gahagan Douglas in the California Senate
campaign of 1950, Richard Nixon and his wife Pat attended a Sunday-
night supper at the Washington house of the newspaper columnist Joseph
Alsop. After they had arrived, Averell Harriman came in and spotted
Nixon sitting quietly in a deep wing chair.

Harriman, then a White House assistant to President Truman, was
slightly deaf and spoke loudly, his voice carrying through the room: "I will
not break bread with that man!"

Then Harriman switched off his hearing aid and stalked out of the
party.[1]

Nixon has not referred to the Harriman incident in any of his writings,
although it was just the sort of thing that might have aroused his none too
deeply buried Orthogonian hostility toward the rich and fortunate, which
Averell Harriman certainly was. But Harriman's distaste for Nixon had
nothing to do with their different backgrounds. Its immediate cause was
Nixon's "rocking, socking" campaign in California against Helen Douglas,
to whom Harriman at the request of President Truman had lent his presence, assistance, and no doubt a lot of money.

Harriman, who had been Franklin Roosevelt's wartime ambassador to
the Soviet Union and was anything but soft on communism, no doubt

thought also, as most other Democrats then did, that well before the 1950 Senate campaign Nixon and the House Un-American Activities Committee had used unfair smear tactics in their investigations into Communist activities within the Roosevelt and Truman administrations. Truman himself had insisted that Nixon's and the committee's activities, particularly in the celebrated case of Alger Hiss, had been a "red herring . . . to keep the Congress's attention from the things they ought to be doing about inflation." That view was widely shared, particularly among Democrats.

Harriman's animus might have gone even further back—all the way to Nixon's election to the House in 1946, when as a political newcomer he had unseated Jerry Voorhis, a respected Democrat, in the Twelfth District of California. Less vituperative than that against Mrs. Douglas, the Voorhis campaign nevertheless gave Nixon from the start of his career a reputation as a tough—some thought unscrupulous—campaigner.

These early episodes, especially the Hiss case, had carried Nixon in only four years to political prominence and high favor in the Republican party. But, as Averell Harriman's refusal to dine with him suggested, Nixon had paid a steep price for those four years of rapid ascent; and none of his later activities ever erased from the sensibilities of a large segment of the American public—that same public before which he had still to play out the greater part of his career—the impression that Richard Nixon was a gutfighter to be feared, a politician not to be trusted.

On the night of September 13, 1946, not much more than a year after the end of World War II and the beginning of both the atomic era and the American ascent to superpower status, about five hundred Californians gathered in the auditorium of South Pasadena High School to hear a political debate between Representative Jerry Voorhis and his thirty-three-year-old challenger.

"Gathered" suggests casual arrivals and seatings; in fact, though, the hall had been carefully "diamonded" by the Nixon campaign. Known Nixon supporters had arrived early in four separate groups; each sat together, one down front in the middle, one at center left, one at center right, one in the middle rear. All raucously applauded Nixon and jeered Voorhis, and their distribution left Voorhis backers either surrounded by the Nixonites or isolated in the four corners of the hall.

Even so, the experienced Voorhis, a Democrat who had represented the Twelfth District for five terms, might have been expected to demolish his Republican opponent, who never before had campaigned for public office and was less than a year out of the U.S. Navy. But Richard Nixon—already displaying methodical preparation—repeatedly threw the congressman off stride.

In the question period, for example, an obviously prepared Nixon supporter read, then demanded an explanation of, an out-of-context quotation from a book Voorhis had written about monetary reform—a subject on which he held idiosyncratic views that were anathema to banking interests. Voorhis's rambling answer on such an esoteric subject was unconvincing and appeared to lose the attention of the audience.

Perhaps trying to strike back, a Voorhis backer then ran right into a trap: why, he asked, did Nixon claim that Voorhis had been endorsed by the CIO-PAC—the Political Action Committee of the Congress of Industrial Organizations—when there had been no such endorsement?

Some analysts think that question cost Voorhis the election. It certainly marked the beginning of Richard Nixon's reputation for falsely accusing opponents of being "soft" or naive or dangerously uninformed about communism—and perhaps, by implication, of lacking patriotism or proper devotion to American values.

The CIO-PAC had been established in 1943 to mobilize organized labor's political potential. Formally nonpartisan, it nevertheless, in the nature of things, more often supported Democrats than Republicans. Both the organization and its president, Sidney Hillman of the Amalgamated Clothing Workers, had gained national fame in 1944 when President Roosevelt advised Democrats proposing the vice presidential nomination for Harry S Truman to "clear it with Sidney."

The *Los Angeles Times*—so partisanly Republican in 1946 that the factual accuracy of its political reporting often was questionable—said on March 16, 1946, that the CIO-PAC, with a goal of affecting one hundred congressional races that year, had authorized a drive for six million dollars. But its support could be a mixed blessing because Communists were widely believed to have considerable influence in the CIO—though Hillman and the other PAC officers were not Communists. Apparently with this problem in mind, Jerry Voorhis—who had been endorsed by the CIO-PAC in 1944—had informed its leaders that he did not want their endorsement for 1946.

That September night in Pasadena, Nixon had anticipated the question. He pulled a paper from his pocket and read Voorhis's name from a list purporting to be endorsements by the Los Angeles chapter of the National Citizens Political Action Committee—a group Voorhis remembered Nixon calling "Communist-dominated."

Nixon showed Voorhis the paper—a copy of the Los Angeles organization's mimeographed bulletin—then read the names of board members of both PACs to show that the two organizations were closely linked. Voorhis protested that the CIO-PAC and the National Citizens PAC were two different groups, but Nixon recalled in *RN,* "I could tell from the audience reaction that I had made my point."

Which was, of course, that the two PACs were so nearly one that an endorsement by either bore out Nixon's charge—in a newspaper ad—that "a vote for Nixon is a vote against the Communist-dominated PAC with its gigantic slush fund," and supported the implication that a vote for Voorhis was a vote *for* "the PAC" and its supposedly Communist leanings.

Thirty years later, in *RN,* Nixon insisted that "the question of which PAC had endorsed [Voorhis] was a distinction without a difference." In fact, Sidney Hillman headed both PACs. The National Citizens PAC, too, had close ties to the CIO, though it had been formed to project the political power of liberals—literary, religious, academic and entertainment figures—who had few if any formal ties to organized labor. The *Daily People's World,* a West Coast Communist newspaper, had listed the National Citizens PAC as a member of the " 'Big Five' labor and progressive coalition," along with the CIO-PAC, the railroad brotherhoods, the Progressive AFL, and the Hollywood Independent Citizens' Committee of the Arts, Sciences and Professions.

Voorhis, moreover, played into Nixon's hands a few days later when he telegraphed the National Citizens PAC to request that "whatever qualified endorsement the Citizens PAC may have given me be withdrawn." That could only foster the impression Nixon had sought to create, that one PAC was as bad, or as Red, as another.

Nevertheless, the two organizations were *not* the same; the reputation of the CIO-PAC, if transferred to Voorhis, was more damaging. And even if Nixon's later defense of his use of the National Citizens PAC is accepted at face value, he still took deliberate advantage of confusion about the two PACs in an attempt to hang the most damaging of them around Voorhis's neck. If he did not literally misstate the facts, he stated them in such a way as to create confusion damaging to Voorhis. Nixon's high school and college debating experience was at work; in formal debates, it's considered fair to score points on an opponent, if they aren't refuted, whether or not the points are literally justified.

Here was the first step along a slippery political slope—for Richard Nixon more than for Jerry Voorhis. The object, of course, was to link Voorhis loosely to Communist influence. Actually, that *object,* in the context of Republican politics in 1946, may have been marginally more understandable than the deceptive *maneuver* Nixon used to accomplish it.

For one thing, Nixon then had no real political experience; he was young, ambitious, up against a favored incumbent who already had carried the Twelfth District five times. Kyle Palmer, the veteran political editor of the *Los Angeles Times* and a partisan Republican, at first thought Nixon had embarked on "a sort of giant-killer operation. The man he proposed to unseat was a very popular and well-entrenched Democrat. The Republicans—including myself—generally felt that it was a forlorn effort."[2]

On June 4, seeming to bear out Palmer's early judgment, Voorhis had taken 53.5 percent of the total Democratic and Republican primary vote, under the California cross-filing system then in effect. That Nixon was an underdog who felt he had to reach for any available issue if he was to have a chance cannot, of course, excuse demagoguery; but it is at least a mitigating factor in Nixon's turn to what must have seemed, in 1946, a promising new Republican tactic—the imputation of quasi-Communist positions to an opponent.

The atmosphere was ripe for such suggestions. In that year of reconversion to a peacetime economy—the World War II armed forces already had been cut back from eleven million to about one million men—the Soviet Union was no longer seen by most Americans as a stout wartime ally but was coming to be considered an international menace; aggressive communism abroad, subversive communism at home, soon would be national obsessions.

Labor, moreover, was a powerful and controversial force, threatening to many Americans. Union membership, encouraged by official wartime policy, had grown by 50 percent, to about fifteen million during the war; in the immediate postwar years strikes were hamstringing the economy. Nearly two million workers, at one point, had been on strike.

In May 1946, President Truman—supposedly a friend of labor—had proposed, with widespread public approval, to break a crippling railroad strike by drafting the strikers into the armed forces. The proposal was outrageous but Truman had reason to be exasperated.

> In one year, he had seized the coal mines twice; he had seized the railroads; he had seized 134 meat-packing plants; he had seized ninety-one tugboats; he had seized the facilities of twenty-six oil-producing and refining companies; he had seized the Great Lakes Towing Company. And all he had on his hands now was disaster. He had grappled with huge strikes against General Motors and United States Steel. He had proposed labor legislation only to see Congress ignore it. He had felt double-crossed . . . that there should have been any strikes at all after he had agreed to relax [wartime] wage controls.[3]

A Gallup poll found Americans favoring by 54 to 36 a law to forbid strikes and lockouts for one year; the public was exasperated too. Another poll found voters ranking "strikes and labor trouble" the most important issue of the 1946 elections.

In this situation, some Republican party leaders—out of power since 1933 and hungry for a return to the trough—theorized that since Americans feared communism and were wary of organized labor's power, the linkage of labor to communism would be plausible and helpful to Republicans. Some labor leaders, like some other Americans, did have personal ties to, or had displayed sympathy for, communism; and since organized labor already was loosely associated in the public mind with the Democratic party, the supposed flow of influence from Communists to labor to Democrats could be used as a political blackjack with which to beat Democratic candidates over the head.

The Soviet Union's aggressive international conduct tended to reinforce the Communist threat. On March 5, 1946, Winston Churchill gave his famous Iron Curtain speech at Fulton, Missouri, warning against Soviet domination of Europe. Campaigning in California, young Richard Nixon—as he recalled in *RN*—found his attitude toward communism and the Soviet Union "profoundly affected" by this landmark speech. He was not alone; that month a Gallup poll showed 71 percent of Americans alarmed by Soviet foreign policy.

On June 14 the so-called Baruch Plan for ultimate international control of atomic energy—which would have left the U.S. with an atomic monopoly for many years—was submitted to the U.N. It was spurned by the suspicious Soviets after they learned that they had to accept or reject in its entirety a plan they thought designed to preserve American advantages. Most Americans, however, believed the Baruch Plan a generous international gesture (see chapter 4).

The Soviet rejection helped to convince Americans of Moscow's aggressive intent. By September, Gallup found that relations with Russia had replaced labor troubles as the voters' first concern. And with an eye to just such public attitudes, a Western Republican Conference at Salt Lake City condemned the "alien philosophy" of the Truman administration and urged Americans to turn to the Republican party for "tried and true Americanism."

This was not idle talk; during the war, anticommunism had been strong medicine in American politics at least since the "Red scare" of the twenties. As early as the 1944 presidential election, when the Soviets still were allied to the West, Senator John W. Bricker of Ohio, the Republican candidate for vice president, declared that "first the New Deal took over the Democratic Party and destroyed its very foundation; now these Communist forces have taken over the New Deal and will destroy the very foundations of the Republic." With the war over and no need existing to "rally round" the president or the government, and with the Soviets beginning to provoke trouble in Eastern Europe and elsewhere, Americans in 1946 were ripe for shedding wartime tolerance and setting out on another anti-Communist crusade.[4]

B. Carroll Reece of Tennessee, the Republican national chairman, made the labor-Communist connection in a radio speech denouncing the CIO-

PAC as "the spearhead of Red reactionism." In other speeches, he extended the supposed connection to the Democrats, declaring the 1946 elections a "fight basically between Communism and Republicanism" because the Democrats had been taken over "by a radical group devoted to Sovietizing the United States." Their goal, in Reece's apocalyptic (and demagogic) vision, was "a one-party system and a police state."

Even Senator Robert Taft of Ohio, "Mr. Republican" and "Mr. Integrity," charged that the Democratic party was "divided between Communism and Americanism." Governor Earl Warren of California, who was considered a liberal Republican, reacted strongly against a campaign tour of California by Henry Wallace, whose call for a less militant attitude toward the Soviet Union had triggered his expulsion from the Truman administration. Warren said Wallace was leading the attack of "leftist organizations that are attuned to the Communist movement." J. Edgar Hoover, the FBI director and an unchallenged icon of American life in 1946, told the American Legion that "at least 100,000 Communists" were at large in the nation.[5]

Thus, Nixon's attempt to paint Jerry Voorhis with the Red brush was consistent with the approach of conservative Republicans in 1946. Though the belief persists that he virtually invented the tactic, in reality he adopted it, following the general lead of many national and state Republican leaders. And his use of it was relatively tame stuff compared to others' inflammatory rhetoric. California's Young Republicans declared with straight faces, for instance, that the Democratic party had been "taken over by a combination of leftists, Communists and political bosses"—as if Sidney Hillman, Earl Browder and Frank Hague had joined hands!

In such an atmosphere, and with Soviet actions abroad exacerbating the fear of communism at home, many voters of the time could agree with Nixon's view, as he somewhat disingenuously described it in *RN,* that "Communist infiltration of labor and political organizations was a serious threat . . . and a candidate's attitude toward endorsements by heavily infiltrated organizations was a barometer of his attitude toward that threat."

Voorhis's CIO-PAC endorsement in 1944 and his tardy disavowal of National Citizens PAC support in 1946 lent verisimilitude to the campaign against him. So, probably, did the unsought endorsement Henry Wallace gave him. And Nixon assiduously pointed out that Voorhis had resigned from the Communist-hunting House Un-American Activities Committee—to which he had been assigned against his will—and spoke and voted against the committee's continued existence.

Voorhis had been a registered Socialist in the twenties, another fact Nixon emphasized, since most Americans then and later made little dis-

tinction between Socialists and Communists. But Voorhis had fought hard
against Communist infiltration of the Socialist party.

As the campaign wore on, Nixon resorted to more trickery to underline
his Red charges. Beginning October 17, the Nixon campaign ran a series
of newspaper ads charging that Voorhis had voted in the House with the
"Communist-dominated PAC" on forty-three out of forty-six votes. So
even if he didn't want the PAC endorsement, the ads claimed, Voorhis had
earned it. But the ads mentioned neither the substance of the votes nor the
sources of the information.

By the time Voorhis got Nixon to identify those sources six days later,
it was almost too late to answer the charge; and the pamphlet Voorhis
finally got out in response was confusing and ill-prepared. It nevertheless
demonstrated that the Nixon ads, based on several different surveys of
House voting, had counted *separately* a number of the same votes that
appeared in all the surveys. Overall, a total of only twenty-seven votes, not
forty-six, was covered by these studies.

Most of the twenty-seven were unexceptionable, whether or not Voorhis
and the CIO-PAC went the same way—for example, a postwar loan to
Great Britain, a bill to provide school lunches, and one to abolish poll
taxes. But in one significant case, Voorhis had *supported* and the PAC
opposed a bill to make antiracketeering statutes apply to organized labor.
Voorhis's pamphlet made the essential point, but not powerfully or prominently:

> How foolish it would be for a member of Congress to follow Mr.
> Nixon's formula of voting the opposite on every issue from the
> position taken by the PAC or any other organization. Just because
> the PAC [votes a certain way] certainly should not cause a member
> who wants to serve the best interests of his country to vote against
> its interests just to be on the opposite side from the PAC. . . . What
> Mr. Nixon needs to do instead of talking about 46 mysterious votes
> is to discuss the specific issues involved and point out where he
> believes Mr. Voorhis was wrong in the votes he cast.[6]

But as every journalist and politician knows—even one so new at the
game as Richard Nixon in 1946—a rebuttal rarely catches up to a charge,
and almost never demolishes it. Jerry Voorhis later calculated sadly that
perhaps 5 percent of the Twelfth District voters who read the Nixon ads
ever saw his answering pamphlet.[7]

The common assumption of Nixon watchers who mistrust his every
word and deed is that these tactics gave him a victory he could not
otherwise have won, over a veteran congressman who had been chosen by

his colleagues in a *Pageant* magazine survey as the hardest-working member of the House. That heightens the drama. Yet, though it can never be proved, the likelihood is that Nixon would have defeated Jerry Voorhis with no reference at all to the so-called Red issue. Even Kyle Palmer had been deceived; in 1946, not a "giant-killer operation" but just a shove was needed to topple Jerry Voorhis.

Voorhis *was* a good congressman; he also was an inept campaigner who was at least to some extent out of touch and out of step with a changing district, and who suffered from both local and national issues having little to do with communism. Nixon *was* a beginner; he also proved to be an aggressive and resourceful campaigner—more nearly a professional than Voorhis. He was backed by a united party and had those local and national issues going his way.

Voorhis, moreover, never before had faced a tough campaign—and, as has happened to many another member of Congress, his first strong opponent found him not up to the challenge. He had been elected in the Great Depression year of 1936, when it was helpful to be a friend of labor, a practicing liberal, a former Socialist and prominent supporter of Upton Sinclair's End Poverty in California (EPIC) campaign. And that year, there had been no incumbent congressman in the general election. Even so, the major factor in Voorhis's first victory was the long coattail of Franklin Roosevelt, who swept forty-six of forty-eight states, including California, to win his second presidential term.

Voorhis, who by 1946 was forty-five, had been reelected four times—all in depression or war years—even though a Republican legislature had tried to gerrymander him in 1942, remapping his stronghold, East Los Angeles, out of the Twelfth District. He survived in part through communications that were good for that time—a weekly column he sent to district newspapers and a weekly radio speech for a local station. But Roy O. Day, chairman of the district's Republicans, believed the main reason for Voorhis's five victories was "the poor caliber of candidates the Old Guard Republicans" put up against him.[8]

For ten years, moreover, Voorhis had been building up opposition because of his liberal voting record, which became more and more dissonant in his basically Republican district. He antagonized the banks with his "funny-money" views. He opposed a bill backed by insurance companies to exempt them from antitrust laws. He angered oil companies by working for federal control of offshore oil and by exposing a wartime Standard Oil contract to develop the Elk Hills navy reserve at a huge profit, with little benefit to the navy.

He offended other corporations by trying to limit their tax deductions for advertising and their control of patents. He advocated higher inheritance taxes. Farmers were upset with him for supporting agricultural

unions; and by 1946, even without CIO-PAC support, his general record
of support for labor was a liability.

All these positions had been arrived at with admirable independence and
no doubt justified Voorhis's reputation as an idealist. Nixon himself later
told Stewart Alsop: "I don't suppose there was scarcely ever a man with
higher ideals than Jerry Voorhis, or better motivated than Jerry Voorhis."

But what was to happen in November 1946 is perhaps suggested by
Voorhis's estrangement: he had not set foot in the Twelfth District since
late 1945, did not return even to campaign in the June primary, and only
arrived to take up the fight against a vigorous opponent after the Seventy-
ninth Congress adjourned on August 2, 1946. The Twelfth District also
was changing. Like others across America, it would vote for the first time
in nearly two decades without an overhanging shadow of depression or
war. In the new postwar spirit of enterprise and technological advance,
"Socialist" views like Jerry Voorhis's tax and monetary ideas had little of
the political value they might have had in the thirties.

The postwar immigration that was to make California the most populous state had started; between the 1944 and 1946 elections, the once-sleepy
Twelfth District—swiftly falling into the environs of Los Angeles—had
gained 9,212 new voters, and 5,594 had registered as Republicans against
only 2,831 Democrats.

Under the California cross-filing system then in effect, candidates sought
the nominations of both parties and ran in both Republican and Democratic primaries. In the June 1946 primaries, Republicans voting for Nixon,
Voorhis and a minor candidate totaled 37,054; Democrats cast only 31,315
votes for the three.

From the primaries came another warning, and Voorhis's late start
suggests he failed to heed it: the 53.5 percent of the total Republican and
Democratic votes that he received was drastically down from the 60 percent he had taken in 1944.

It was therefore a district ripe for a new young Republican candidate,
a war veteran in tune with the postwar era: in short, Richard Nixon—a
native of the district, from Whittier, who had compiled a splendid college
record and practiced law there, and who had come home from the navy
in January 1946 with ten full months of campaign time ahead of him.

It's a pleasant myth that Nixon became the Republican nominee by
answering a want ad. Actually, Roy Day had put together a committee of
104 Republicans from the principal cities and towns of the Twelfth District; this committee's appeal for would-be congressional candidates was
not an ad but a front-page story in most district newspapers.

Nixon, still in the navy and renegotiating contracts all the way across
the continent in Baltimore, did not respond; the committee had to ask him,
by letter, to come to California for an interview that was more nearly a

tryout. A local Republican pulled strings to get him a scarce reservation on American Airlines; the committee sent him a three-hundred-dollar expense check, and he flew to California for his "interview." On November 28, 1945, the committee voted 63 to 12 for Nixon, then made his nomination unanimous.[9]

There were glitches. Nixon's first campaign photos showed him in officer's uniform; that didn't sit well with most ex-enlisted men, and he turned to civilian clothes for good. One Republican woman, looking over Pat Nixon, complained to Roy Day that the candidate's wife didn't "even know what color finger-nail polish to wear." Day himself had to reprove the new candidate—though it seems hard to believe in view of the later sobersided Nixon—for wearing neckties the chairman considered too flashy. Aside from such minor matters, the committee and Nixon were soon launched on a campaign that left Jerry Voorhis in the dust.[10]

When he returned to California in August, Voorhis brought heavy baggage with him—not just his own record but the peacetime reconversion policies of the Truman administration, and the unpopularity of the president himself. In addition to the labor unrest Truman seemed unable to handle, the problems of shortages, prices and inflation plagued the Democrats, who controlled the White House and Congress.

In the summer of 1946, wrangling with Capitol Hill over the continuation of the Office of Price Administration, Truman let price and rent controls lapse. Weaker new controls went into effect after July 25, but in the short period of no controls, prices took off for the skies; and when meat price controls went into effect in August, farmers held beef off the market and caused severe shortages.

In May, a Gallup poll had found more than two thirds of Americans in favor of controls; by October, less than half the public wanted controls on anything except rents. Nixon remembered in *RN* that some Twelfth District butcher shops had signs in their windows: NO MEAT TODAY? ASK YOUR CONGRESSMAN! The meat shortage in southern California was acute in September and October, doing Jerry Voorhis no good. It was so bad nationally that on October 14, Truman ordered the OPA to remove meat price controls.

On this major issue of wage and price regulation, Richard Nixon was ideally situated. He had been an OPA bureaucrat early in the war and could claim to know from experience that the agency was inefficient, ineffective and leftist in its aims. In *RN* he said the impression had stayed with him that some government workers "became obsessed with their own power and seemed to delight in kicking people around, particularly those in the private sector."

Such views found a sympathetic audience in the atmosphere of 1946 (and would still today). One of Nixon's campaign slogans foreshadowed another that was to be a feature of a presidential campaign nearly forty years later. "Where's the Meat?" Nixon's slogan asked, long before Clara Peller and Walter Mondale immortalized "Where's the Beef?" in 1984.

Not the least of Voorhis's problems was Truman himself. Virtually unknown until April 13, 1945, Franklin Roosevelt's successor fared ill by comparison. Labor was disenchanted with him. Worse, he seemed unable to control his own political house, causing Harold L. Ickes to resign as secretary of the interior because of the appointment of Edwin Pauley to be undersecretary of the navy; then Pauley's nomination had to be withdrawn under pressure.

One day before the Voorhis-Nixon debate of September 13, 1946, Secretary of Commerce Henry A. Wallace vehemently attacked the Truman foreign policy in a speech at Madison Square Garden; he called for greater cooperation with the Soviet Union and for open recognition of Soviet and American spheres of influence. Truman, forced to stand by either Wallace, then still a New Deal hero, or Secretary of State James F. Byrnes, a South Carolina conservative, fired Wallace—a move triggering Wallace's third-party presidential candidacy two years later.

The furthest left wing of the Democratic party was outraged (though Voorhis, like Nixon, strongly endorsed the tough Truman-Byrnes approach to American-Soviet relations). In 1946, Americans generally were questioning Truman's ability to govern, and whether his party had been in power too long. As in Britain, where Winston Churchill had been ousted the year before, postwar pressures for a new government were great. Truman was no Churchill, and Republican slogans like "Had Enough?" were right to the point. On the eve of the 1946 elections, Gallup predicted that 58 percent of the national vote would go Republican.

Voorhis was no better off on strictly local matters. A particularly damaging aspect of Republican unity behind Nixon was the treatment Voorhis received from the district's thirty-five newspapers, most of them Republican owned. They shut Voorhis out while giving Nixon a tremendous ride. On election day, the *Alhambra Post-Advocate,* for example, ran Nixon's picture but not the incumbent congressman's. Only one paper supported Voorhis—and it went out of business right after the election. Stephen Zetterberg, a Voorhis activist (who was to lose both Republican and Democratic primaries as a candidate against Nixon in 1948), claims that an editor of the *San Gabriel Sun* was fired for saying he would give the two candidates equal treatment. Voorhis himself recalled that merchants were warned not to sign newspaper statements supporting him, or their bank credit would be cut off.[11]

Not only district newspapers supported Nixon. So did the *Los Angeles Times* and its powerful political editor, Kyle Palmer, who soon saw that in the newcomer he had thought couldn't win, "we had an extraordinary man on our hands." Palmer introduced Nixon to the *Times*'s publisher,

Norman Chandler, who then told Palmer, "He has a lot of fight and fire. Let's support him." Support from the *Los Angeles Times* in those days meant all-out, favorable coverage as well as editorial endorsement.[12]

Nixon's campaign employed a Los Angeles advertising agency, Lockwood and Shakelford. The result was hard-hitting, well-conceived newspaper ads, billboards and slogans. Voorhis had no advertising assistance, and the resulting differences in the two candidates' public messages were apparent. Even in campaign gimmickry, Nixon's efforts outdid his supposedly more experienced opponent's; he distributed, for example, thousands of thimbles printed with the slogan ELECT NIXON: PUT A NEEDLE IN THE PAC.

In virtually every way, the Nixon campaign was skilled and effective, while Voorhis bumbled along ineffectually, without much organization or planning—or money. Nixon and his Twelfth District backers are reliably estimated to have spent about thirty-two thousand dollars on the general election campaign, a sizable figure for 1946, as against less than ten thousand for Voorhis.

One sum well spent went to the professional campaign manager Murray Chotiner, whose alliance with Nixon was to be famous and fateful. Chotiner was running William Knowland's campaign for the Senate in 1946, but for a five-hundred-dollar fee also provided part-time counsel to Nixon. This brought into the Twelfth District a skilled and shrewd operator, a pioneer among the political "consultants," who have since proliferated.[13]

Chotiner agreed with Roy Day's political credo (or it may be more likely that Day took his view from Chotiner): "I like to win and I play hard to win. You have to carry the fight all the way; never get on the defensive. Nice guys and sissies don't win many elections." That was to be the political attitude Richard Nixon, too, carried forward from 1946; though bluntly stated, it would not be refuted by many political professionals today.[14]

As the election approached, all political signs pointed so convincingly to a national Republican victory that Nixon's ads dared to argue that one of the Democrat Voorhis's greatest assets—his ten years of seniority— would count for little in a Republican-controlled House. Still, Voorhis allowed himself to be maneuvered into a series of five face-to-face debates, providing an opportunity that no strongly challenged incumbent should ever give his opponent.

These confrontations showcased the personal contrasts between Nixon—a tough debater, fast on his feet, quick with a word or slogan, amply in command of "facts," superbly prepared—and Voorhis—a nervous, almost jittery man, rambling and discursive, pedantically pushing his irrelevant (to the campaign) monetary views, almost invariably ill-prepared for Nixon's sharp attacks.

After the first debate and the raising of the PAC issue, Voorhis asked his campaign manager, Chet Holifield—later to be a Democratic member of Congress from California—for his verdict.

"Jerry," Holifield said, "he cut you to pieces. He had you on the defensive all the way. He picked the battleground and you let him fight on his own terms."[15]

For the Voorhis campaign, that seems an appropriate epitaph.

In the end, Nixon won with ease, 65,586 to 49,994—better than 57 percent of the vote, or about what the Republican party was polling nationally in House races. Gallup had called it on the nose.

Nixon's was scarcely a margin to validate the idea that a "Red smear" could enable an underdog to pull off an upset. In fact, Jerry Voorhis failed to carry even his hometown, San Dimas, while Whittier went for its native son by two to one.

Nationally, the Republicans won the Senate and gained fifty-five House seats, to take control of Congress for the first time since 1933. Seven of the new Republican House seats were from California—Nixon's prominent among them. So he was not going to Congress as a junior member of the minority but as part of the new postwar majority; he had come to politics at just the right time.

From beginning to end, as his opportunity had unfolded, Nixon had rarely put a foot wrong, despite those neckties and such egregious overstatements as: "I see no difference whatever between the dictatorial practices of labor and those of Hitler and Mussolini." To contemporary ears, he may also sound extreme in charging that "the [Truman] Administration is guilty of criminal negligence in allowing the people to go hungry and homeless merely to further aims of socializing basic industries and free American institutions."[16]

But in 1946, to Americans hungry for meat and for the consumer goods they had been denied so long by depression and war, such accusations against the administration hit the mark. Nixon's attacks on the OPA's "lopsided regulation," on labor, on Truman's reconversion policies and on Truman himself were far more nearly the essential stuff of his winning campaign than the more celebrated Red smear.

"Had all the lying then been necessary?" the historian Fawn Brodie asked, reasonably enough. "Could [Nixon] have won the campaign with a conventional campaign and without all the deception?" The answer seems clearly yes, but Brodie's implication as clearly is that "all" the lying and deception are the more to be condemned for having been unnecessary—as if they had been mere whims of a sociopathic candidate.[17]

Jerry Voorhis was the first opponent in what, by strange fortune, was to become a chain of Nixon opponents who were much like the Franklins—those tuxedo-clad college mates he had considered "the haves" and in rivalry with whom he had helped to organize those he saw as "have-nots" like himself into the Orthogonians. If so, an old, mostly buried but still-virulent class hostility might have sharpened the edge of his attacks on Voorhis—the millionaire banker's son about whom Nixon remarked rather contemptuously to Stewart Alsop: "Then there are the Don Quixotes, who never accomplish anything, the idealistic men—like Jerry Voorhis."

For the most part, however, Nixon's use of "the PAC" and the "forty-six votes" to suggest that Voorhis was a Communist sympathizer or dupe seems more nearly to have been motivated by the temper of the times, by the national example of many Republican leaders, above all by the general assumption—seemingly confirmed by the June primary results—that Nixon was an underdog up against an entrenched incumbent.

No polls of the Twelfth District were taken. According to Nixon's claim in *RN,* even after he flaunted the PAC issue in the first debate, on September 13, Murray Chotiner the professional thought he was running behind. Commenting after Nixon's victory, *Time* said his campaign had been "dubbed 'hopeless' by wheelhorse Republicans." Nixon and Chotiner no doubt *thought* Nixon would win, particularly in the final days; but they could not *know* he would win—certainly not on September 13 and maybe not as late as October 17—and they could take no chances. Politicians seldom do; they campaign as hard as they can for as big a victory as they can achieve.

The Communist implications were nevertheless deplorable; so were "all the lying" and "all the deception." But a certain amount of lying and deception, sadly enough, are staples in democratic, not least American, politics—exaggerations, dark and uncheckable implications, ambiguities, sophistical statements and the like, almost always aimed at the selfish interests of voters or at arousing their fears and prejudices.

Save perhaps for the PAC charges, what went on in the Twelfth District of California in 1946—the distortion of Voorhis's voting record, for example—was not untypical of what goes on in elections all across the nation, every year, in every state and locality. Campaign tactics, in fact, may be even more deplorable since the advent of television with its emphasis on images, its almost subliminal flashes of "information" that can never really be challenged.

Those who are outraged at politicians for "lying" and "deception" are not always themselves free from devious tactics, in business, the professions, in personal relations. The politician's purpose is of course to win votes, not just to deceive for deception's sake; and perhaps few would use devious campaign methods if such methods did not succeed, in some cases even seem necessary—as businessmen must occasionally convince themselves that it's necessary to employ deceptive advertising or pricing policies, or lawyers that a jury must be bamboozled, or a college president that his athletes be exempt from tough academic standards.

Besides, which came first, people or politicians? If we the people governed ourselves always by reason and the public interest, and were not instead so often creatures of our fears, prejudices and interests, politicians would have less reason to appeal to them, and little success in doing so.

So if Nixon's conduct in 1946 can't be excused, neither should it be considered entirely unworthy of those who were to choose between him and Voorhis, nor singled out as indefensibly darker and more threatening than most American political behavior. In a game the ethic of which is to win, it should not be surprising that players will go to great lengths to win. Jerry Voorhis appears to have been a rare exception; Nixon certainly was not.

It was the national trend to the Republicans, together with Voorhis's campaign ineptitude and liberal record in a district where he was less and less in step with the voters, that gave the ambitious, quick-learning and well-counseled young newcomer his opportunity. Nixon did not fail to seize it, if with more enthusiasm and less scruple than some Americans want their politicians to display.

Roy Day had not been wrong in his estimate that Nixon was "saleable merchandise"—which may say something we do not like to concede about the prospective buyers. But even Day probably did not foresee what, across more than forty chaotic years, now seems undeniable: that in 1946 Richard Nixon found not just his chance but his métier, his calling, his life—in politics, in campaigning, above all in battle.[18]

Nixon's autobiographical writings are peppered with them: references to "battle," sometimes called "crisis"—to the need for coolness and resolve in the midst of it, and how to handle the inevitable letdown in its aftermath. "I knew these were simply the evidences of preparing for battle," he wrote in *Six Crises,* for instance, of his fatigue and ill temper at a tense stage of the Hiss case, and added: "One must always be keyed up for battle." Not long after he came to Congress, Nixon told a reporter that he was there to "smash the labor bosses."[19]

Fawn Brodie quoted Nixon's remark to Donald Jackson of *Life* on his war experience: "I didn't get hit, or hit any one, all I got was a case of fungus," and there may be, as she suggested (though Brodie invariably put the worst interpretation on Nixon's words and deeds, and sometimes tortured the record to do so), a note of regret in the words.[20]

More significantly, Nixon told the journalist Earl Mazo that after the battle with Jerry Voorhis, he entered Congress with "the same lost feeling that I had when I first went into the military service." Campaigning—the battle, the crisis—was more exhilarating than the mundane duties of a junior officer behind the lines, or of a junior member of the House.

There was little battle and no real crisis in the latter role until near the end of Nixon's first term, though he had become a member of the notorious

House Un-American Activities Committee—whose old Democratic chairman, Martin Dies of Texas, had been an unconscionable Red-baiter and whose new Republican chairman, J. Parnell Thomas of New Jersey, was soon to be jailed for accepting kickbacks from his staff. William Costello, a knowledgeable journalist and commentator of the time, nevertheless speculated that the freshman Nixon must have maneuvered for, and been the beneficiary of, "powerful influence" in landing "such a plum."

It was *not* such a plum to everyone. In 1947, the committee was widely despised for its irresponsibility and bigotry, had never produced any legislation, had achieved the conviction of no one it had investigated, and could only give Nixon more of what the Voorhis campaign already had given him too much of—a reputation as a smear artist. It "was such a harebrained committee," Nixon's friend William Rogers suggested to me, that having been a member of it hurt him "forever."

Nixon asserted in *RN* that the new Speaker of the House, Joseph W. Martin of Massachusetts, knowing that the Republicans who had taken over Congress now would have to bear the responsibility for the committee's activities, asked him as a "personal favor" to go on the committee to "smarten it up." Robert Stripling, who was then chief investigator for HUAC, recalled to me that Speaker Martin had called Nixon a "comer." Martin told Stripling, "I want you to push him."

That seems a more plausible explanation than the idea of Nixon scheming and pulling wires to join what, as a quick learner, he surely would have realized was a virtually discredited committee; and it hardly took a quick learner to grasp the truth of former Speaker Sam Rayburn's adage about getting ahead in the House of Representatives: "To get along, go along"— especially with a new Speaker and doubly so for a freshman.

Nixon, moreover, stayed clear of the committee's famous "communism in Hollywood" hearings, which he'd hardly have done if, as Costello suspected, he merely wanted to reap publicity benefits from a Red hunt. In 1949, he was to suggest in another way that he was not necessarily the kind of wild-eyed Red-hunter usually associated with the committee.

On June 7 of that year, in a closed-door session with great publicity potential, the committee interviewed J. Robert Oppenheimer, the renowned physicist who had led in the development of the atomic bomb at Los Alamos—but whose leftish leaning and connections had caught the interest of the FBI and other security agencies. The committee wanted his testimony in an investigation of a supposed Communist cell in the Berkeley Radiation Laboratory at the University of California, where Oppenheimer had taught before World War II.

Oppenheimer, as later became clear, was not entirely candid with the committee at the 1949 hearing. But Joseph Volpe, who as the general counsel of the Atomic Energy Commission sat with the physicist at the witness table, recalled that "Robert seemed to have made up his mind to charm those Congressmen out of their seats." He was so successful that all six committee members who were present shook his hand at the conclusion of his testimony; and Representative Nixon took it upon himself to say: "Before we adjourn . . . and I am sure this is the sense of all who are here—I have noted for some time the work done by Dr. Oppenheimer, and I think we all have been tremendously impressed with him and are mighty happy we have him in the position that he has in our program."[21]

That would not be the last time Richard Nixon defended Robert Oppenheimer; as will be seen, he even did so later at some risk to his own political career.

During his committee tenure, Nixon and Karl Mundt of South Dakota put together and shepherded through the House the so-called Mundt-Nixon bill—the committee's first legislative product. It died in the Senate, which was just as well; the measure required the registration of Communist party members and would have established a Subversive Activities Control Board two years before the McCarran Act did it in 1950.

In the early stages of the Mundt-Nixon effort, Nixon had toyed with the idea of outlawing the Communist party altogether; he debated the point in a committee hearing with Arthur Garfield Hays of the American Civil Liberties Union, who eloquently opposed it. By the time Nixon wrote *Six Crises,* however, he claimed that he had believed outlawing the party would be "inefficient and counterproductive," driving the "hard core of true believers underground." Perhaps Hays convinced him.

During the well-publicized House consideration of Mundt-Nixon, Thomas E. Dewey and Harold Stassen, campaigning in the Oregon primary for the 1948 Republican presidential nomination, met in a radio debate in which Stassen supported the bill but Dewey scornfully termed it "nothing but the method of Hitler and Stalin . . . an attempt to beat down ideas with a club."

Dewey was generally thought to have won the debate and went on to take the nomination, Stassen's career took a probably decisive downward turn, and their debate helped sink both the Mundt-Nixon bill and Nixon's early leaning toward Stassen. (Stassen had endorsed him during his campaign against Voorhis but was later to keep turning up as a sort of thorn in Nixon's side).

Nixon also played a minor, freshman's role in passage of the anti-labor Taft-Hartley Act, and in fending off Truman's veto; but in his two House terms he proved not much more effective in getting bills passed than he had accused Voorhis of being.

"When I got to Washington," Nixon acknowledged to Stewart Alsop just before his first presidential campaign fourteen years later, "I realized soon it wasn't easy to get through legislation with your name on it. . . .

[Y]ou get here and you've got to learn how to operate—the boring and frustrating committee system and so on." That system did not usually provide enough "battle" for one who craved it.

Nixon did have two important experiences in his four years in the House, the first of which was his service in 1947 on the select Herter committee. It was assigned to study postwar conditions in Europe and report on the need for the so-called Marshall Plan for European recovery that the secretary of state, George C. Marshall, had proposed. This time, Nixon accepted appointment to a committee *against* the advice of Speaker Martin. "If you go on that committee," Martin warned him, "you'll lose your Republican credentials, being for all those giveaways."[22]

Nixon joined the Herter committee anyway and his appointment to such an important mission suggests that he was considered a standout in a standout class of freshman Republicans—including Kenneth Keating of New York, Thruston Morton of Kentucky, Charles Potter of Michigan and Norris Cotton of New Hampshire, all of whom, like Nixon, ultimately went to the Senate; J. Caleb Boggs, who was later governor of Delaware; Melvin Laird of Wisconsin, whom Nixon appointed secretary of defense in 1969; John Lodge of Connecticut, who became ambassador to Spain; and John Byrnes of Michigan, who rose to be House Republican leader.

"Stars fell on that class," the late Bryce Harlow told me forty years later: "the best I've seen."

Harlow had seen a lot of them by the time I interviewed him about a year before he died. A former congressional aide, speech writer for Presidents Eisenhower and Nixon, senior adviser to both, congressional liaison for Nixon, and a retired Washington public-relations official for Proctor and Gamble, the diminutive but voluble Harlow seemed to have lost none of his asperity or animation when confined, in his last years, to a motorized wheelchair. He was a "wise old head" within the Republican party, widely respected also among Democrats and journalists.

Harlow first met Richard Nixon when the latter was a freshman in the House; he quickly saw that Nixon was "unusually gifted, a smart sonovagun," a "workaholic" who had "tunnel vision" about any job at hand. Peers in the House, Harlow recalled, "thought highly of him," in contrast to another newcomer of 1946, Democrat John Kennedy of Massachusetts—"a dope" and "a totally amoral playboy, a ubiquitous stud." Kennedy served with Nixon on the Education and Labor Committee.

The Herter committee appointment was a *real* plum and Nixon owed it to Joe Martin, despite Martin's reluctance to name him to a "giveaway" committee. A decade later, when some Republican congressmen were trying to oust Martin as Speaker, he found out that Nixon—by then vice president—was part of the movement. Martin was not amused: "I expected that Nixon would come out in my favor," he remarked. "After all, I gave him his first break in Congress." Nixon was getting ready to run for president in 1960 and was supporting efforts to "modernize" his party—which certainly required turning Martin out to pasture.[23]

The experience in Europe with the Herter committee—thanks to Joe Martin—made Nixon permanently an internationalist and marked his baptism in what would become his consuming interest and greatest strength: foreign affairs.

Robert Finch, one of Nixon's closest friends, who was to serve in his cabinet, considers the Herter committee experience the source of Nixon's "abiding interest, his fundamental interest," the subject that really got him excited. Herbert Klein, Nixon's press secretary in many campaigns, calls the Herter committee appointment the "keystone" of Nixon's political career.[24]

Travel to Europe in those immediate postwar years could hardly help but be enlightening to a raw young congressman. And what the committee found on the Continent, as Richard Nixon remembered in *RN*, seemed clear to him: "Without our food and aid, Europe would be plunged into anarchy, revolution and, ultimately, Communism."

That was not the kind of thing most Twelfth District Republicans wanted to hear, but Nixon stuck to his guns, at considerable political risk; in a series of public appearances in the district, and in columns in its Republican newspapers, he urged the case for extending economic aid. In December 1947, the House approved the Marshall Plan, owing not least to the Herter committee's findings; and Nixon's arguments must have been persuasive to his constituency, because in June 1948 he won both the Republican *and* Democratic primaries in the Twelfth District. This double nomination, in effect, meant that he had been reelected and would not even have to wage a fall campaign.

Nixon thus had plenty of time for the second major experience of his House tenure. On August 3, 1948, before startled members of the Un-American Activities Committee, a self-confessed former courier in the Communist underground, Whittaker Chambers, who had become an editor of *Time* magazine, identified Alger Hiss as having been part of that underground. Chambers said Hiss, in 1948 the president of the Carnegie Endowment for International Peace and a well-known former State Department official, had been part of a Communist group that in the thirties had infiltrated important levels of the Roosevelt administration.

It was less than three years since Lieutenant Commander Nixon, slogging through navy contract renegotiations in Baltimore, had received that exploratory letter from Roy Day's Republican search committee. Thus quickly had fate tapped him on the shoulder a second time. Not only was he given again an opportunity to follow his deepest instincts into "crisis"; this time the "battle" would make him famous and lead ultimately to his nomination for vice president.

Nixon was one member of the Un-American Activities Committee, probably the only one, who was *not* startled to hear Alger Hiss's name on Whittaker Chambers's lips.

In 1947, the young congressman had met several times in Baltimore with Father John Cronin, a priest involved in the labor movement; that activity had led Father Cronin to investigate Communist penetration of dockside unions, and these inquiries had put him in touch with the FBI. Its files had been opened to him, enabling Father Cronin to write a lengthy report on Communist infiltration and activities to be distributed among American Catholic bishops. Nixon read the report, which specifically named Alger Hiss, and heard more about him in a number of long conversations with Father Cronin.[25]

In view of what is now known, Alger Hiss seems to have been lucky, before Chambers's testimony, to have escaped public accusation as a Communist or fellow traveler. At the time, Nixon and Father Cronin probably thought something more sinister than luck had been at work.

After his own break with the Communist party ten years earlier in 1938, Whittaker Chambers had told his story—including his charge against Hiss—to Adolf Berle, then an assistant secretary of state with certain responsibilities for internal security. Historians Fawn Brodie and Allen Weinstein quote the journalist Isaac Don Levine as saying that Berle actually took the story to President Roosevelt, who dismissed it.

But Berle didn't mention such a meeting with the president either in his diary or in his later testimony to the Un-American Activities Committee; and he did nothing with his written notes of Chambers's story until the FBI, to whom Chambers had repeated it in 1942, asked for the notes in 1943.

Truman's first secretary of state, James F. Byrnes, and other officials became suspicious of Hiss from other sources—Canadian and French intelligence; Premier Édouard Daladier of France, who spoke about Hiss to American Ambassador William C. Bullitt; and Igor Gouzenko, the Soviet code clerk who defected in Canada in 1945 and told a story that pointed to Hiss. The FBI had questioned Hiss in 1942 and again in 1946.

For a year after November 1945, in fact, Hiss was under FBI surveillance, including a telephone tap, owing to Gouzenko's story and new testimony to the FBI by a former Communist, Elizabeth Bentley—both tending to confirm Whittaker Chambers's previous declaration. Early in 1946, J. Edgar Hoover, the FBI director, sent Byrnes, Attorney General Tom Clark and President Truman a report making the charge—still unproven by hard evidence, as Hoover had to concede—that Alger Hiss was a security risk.

Hiss strongly and repeatedly denied communist sympathies or ties to the Communist party; he denied these allegations to his friend Dean Acheson, then the undersecretary of state, to Secretary Byrnes, to the FBI and later to John Foster Dulles—who was the chairman of the board of the Carnegie Endowment at the time Hiss was made its president. Nevertheless, the State Department, after its own investigation, put a hold on any possible promotion for Hiss and restricted his assignments and his access to classified information. Acheson personally encouraged him, in late 1946, to leave the department for the nonsensitive job at the endowment; the cloud over Hiss, Acheson advised, was unlikely ever to be dispelled.

No one from the State Department or elsewhere in the administration, however, said an accusing word to Chairman Dulles, at least not in time to stop or delay Hiss's appointment to the endowment job. Nevertheless, Dulles soon learned of the charges against his new president. Letters to Dulles from Alfred Kohlberg, financier of the right-wing monthly *Plain Truth,* and Representative Walter Judd of Minnesota, a zealous Red-hunter, repeated but could not document the charges against Hiss, who continued to deny them.[26]

Nixon may not have known all of this long history of the gathering case against Alger Hiss, but he knew what the FBI knew in 1948—which was a lot, and no doubt enough to convince him in advance that Hiss was being protected, or at least that the Roosevelt and Truman administrations had little zeal for rooting out high-level security risks.

Nixon also knew from Father Cronin enough about Hiss to predispose him to believe Whittaker Chambers's testimony, that sultry morning of August 3 in the House Ways and Means Committee room, where Chambers told his story. But Nixon took only a minor part in the questioning and did not disclose to anyone on the committee or its staff that he was well informed about Hiss's background.

Why, then, did Nixon state in *Six Crises,* published in 1962, that he had never heard of Alger Hiss before Chambers testified on August 3, 1948? And why, in writing his memoirs in the late seventies did he still make no mention of his prior knowledge about Hiss's background—although he no longer made the explicit claim put forward in *Six Crises*?

The fact of his prior knowledge had been made public in books about Nixon, by Earl Mazo in 1959 and by Bela Kornitzer in 1960, though neither attributed the information directly to Nixon. Either could have gotten it from Father Cronin, who was well known as a Nixon confidant and speech writer in the fifties; but Kornitzer in particular seems to imply that Nixon himself may have been the source of the story.

One reason for Nixon's failure to tell other committee members what he knew, before, during or after the Hiss hearings, could have been that he was plotting to manage personally an investigation of Hiss, and to take the political credit for disclosing what he knew was already in the government's files. If so, his prior knowledge enabled him to press for a continued investigation, reasonably sure of results, when the rest of the committee wanted to drop the matter. This motivation also would explain Nixon's later silence in his two books (although not his telling Mazo and Kornitzer, if he did, about Father Cronin's briefings).

But those who have advanced this explanation have had to assume a lot—that, for instance, Nixon foresaw that Chambers would be such an unimpressive witness before the committee, and that Hiss would so dazzle its members with his manner and appearance on August 5, his career record, his plausibility in denying any knowledge of Chambers or Communist activities, that every one of them except Nixon would want to drop the case.

This theory also assumes that Nixon knew or guessed that on the very day of Hiss's convincing first testimony President Truman would attack the committee, making his famous "red herring" response at his news conference. Truman also reaffirmed that morning an earlier executive order directing that no federal agency release to committees of Congress information relating to the loyalty of any government employee. This presidential counterattack was a major factor in the desire of most committee members to drop the Hiss matter and get on to what they thought would be firmer ground.

By the time the committee met in executive session on August 5, after Hiss's testimony and Truman's statement, Karl Mundt, the acting chairman, warned that members had to develop another issue that would "deflect public attention from the Hiss case." Only Nixon argued for continuing the investigation, making the point that while the committee might not be able to prove Hiss a Communist, it ought to be able to prove whether or not Chambers had known Hiss—hence whether Hiss was lying when, after examining pictures of Chambers, he told the committee under oath that he had never known the man.

Mundt finally named Nixon chairman of a special subcommittee to question Chambers further. Had Nixon calculated it that way? Hardly. He couldn't have been sure in advance that Chambers would be unprepossessing, Hiss would persuade the committee and the press of his innocence, Truman would speak out at just the right moment, or even, if all that happened, that the rest of the committee members would panic. He couldn't even be sure their panic, if he had counted on it, would not carry the day and shut off the investigation he supposedly was scheming to head.

The idea, in fact, seems to be one of those conclusions about Nixon that critics often have seemed eager to reach—that his methods, unless proven otherwise, must have been devious and his motives probably bad. In this case, had he been determined from the start to pursue Hiss, surely he would have been better off informing the committee that the government had a lot of damaging material on Hiss already in its files; that would have assured an investigation and given Richard Nixon just as much if not more chance to head it.

There can be no doubt that once the committee appeared ready to opt out of the investigation, Nixon's prior knowledge reinforced him in his argument for continuing it; but he was more likely taking advantage of an unexpected opening than reaping the rewards of devious calculation. That he told committee members neither then nor later of his early knowledge of the Hiss case can be explained without conspiratorial undertones: it gave him an advantage over them, as secret knowledge always does, and Richard Nixon was not a man to pass up an advantage.

This one didn't last long. That very night, August 5, 1948, John Peurifoy, the assistant secretary of state with responsibility for security affairs (Adolf Berle's old job), defied the spirit if not the letter of Truman's just-repeated executive order. Peurifoy secretly spread the State Department file on Hiss in front of Karl Mundt. The file convinced the acting chairman of Hiss's complicity in Communist penetration, and from then on Mundt took an active part in the investigation.[27]

Then, too, Truman's executive order may have influenced Nixon to insist on further investigation. As Mundt was to learn from Peurifoy, a lot of damaging information about Alger Hiss was in administration files. But much of that information had been there since 1942, with little having been done about it; now HUAC or any other congressional committee had been denied any hope of *legitimate* access to those files. A zealous anti-Communist investigator naturally would suspect a cover-up, perhaps even destruction of those files; an ambitious young Republican politician would be eager to expose the information, embarrass the administration and get the credit. Richard Nixon was both.

He had been given, moreover, leaked information from FBI files, through Father Cronin and perhaps by then through other associations. During the Hiss case, Cronin boasted later, an FBI agent named Ed Hummer supplied him with much information on what the bureau was turning up on Hiss. The priest said he passed these useful leaks on to Nixon, who then "knew just where to look for things, and what he would find." Another good reason for Nixon's silence at the time may well have been to avoid the risk of disclosing his sources of FBI information, or that he had such sources.[28]

That may also be a reason why in his later books Nixon maintained the pretense that he had never heard of Alger Hiss before Chambers testified on August 3, 1948. Probably, too, he did not want to admit that he had not been honest with his colleagues. And the tone of both books, on the matter of Nixon's insistence on pursuing the investigation, suggests that he was proceeding only on hunch and instinct and a shrewd reading of a few off notes in Hiss's first testimony. That's a much more attractive picture to paint of one's self than that of a man who had been tipped off in advance.

Besides, Nixon had another reason for wanting to pursue Hiss, one that he may not have fully realized and would not have wished to talk about if he did: Hiss was a classic Franklin to Nixon's eternal Orthogonian.

A graduate of Johns Hopkins University and Harvard Law School, a former clerk for Justice Oliver Wendell Holmes, a student and protégé of Justice Felix Frankfurter, with a distinguished record as a government official and diplomat, the man who had sat behind Secretary of State Edward Stettinius at Yalta and presided over the founding meetings of the United Nations—besides all those things, Alger Hiss was tall, handsome, elegantly mannered and impeccably dressed. He was everything the "have-not" and proudly "self-made" Richard Nixon could not or would not claim for himself—everything he tended to envy and disdain.

In testifying to the committee on the morning of August 5, moreover, Hiss had been "coldly courteous and, at times, almost condescending"—so Nixon put it in *Six Crises,* written in 1961 and 1962. A year or so before that, in a memorandum on the Hiss case that he prepared for Earl Mazo, Nixon was even more explicit: Hiss "was rather insolent toward me . . . and from that time my suspicion concerning him continued to grow." *And,* it seems likely, his antipathy. Even after thirty years' reflection, Nixon recorded in *RN* that Hiss was "too suave, too smooth, and too self-confident to be an entirely trustworthy witness."

That conclusion was reached after only one relatively calm encounter with Hiss. Recalling in his memorandum for Mazo the later committee session in New York on August 17, at which the first confrontation between Hiss and Chambers took place, Nixon noted almost gleefully that "of course [Hiss's] manner and tone were insulting in the extreme . . . he was visibly shaken and had lost [his] air of smoothness."

Robert Stripling, the committee's chief investigator in 1948, had spotted Nixon's personal animosity after the first encounter with Hiss on August 3. From then on, he told the historian Allen Weinstein, "Nixon had his hat set for Hiss. . . . It was a personal thing. He was no more concerned about whether or not Hiss was [a Communist] than a billygoat." Stripling later cited to me a remark by Hiss to Nixon: "I graduated from Harvard. I heard your school was Whittier."

Nixon "got his finger out for Hiss right there," Stripling recalled.

Stripling may not have seen the matter whole. As the case wore on, Nixon's instinctive hostility—born partially of his class sense of a world divided into "haves" and "have-nots"—seems clearly to have been amplified by his growing certainty, to which his briefings from Father Cronin had predisposed him, that Hiss was lying when he denied having known Chambers and having taken part in the Communist activities Chambers described.

Whittaker Chambers kept in his mind "a vivid picture of [Nixon] in the blackest hours of the Hiss case . . . saying in his quietly savage way: 'If the American people understood the real character of Alger Hiss, they would boil him in oil.' " Stripling remembers Nixon pounding his desk and declaring of Hiss: "That son of a bitch is lying!"[29]

And something of Nixon's intensity in pursuit is captured in his response to Hannah Nixon, when she urged him at a low point in the investigation to drop it: "Mother, I think Hiss is lying. Until I know the truth, I've got to stick it out."[30]

But as the committee member most interested in and responsible for the investigation, Nixon moved against Hiss—whatever myth may hold—with circumspection and caution. One reason surely was his target's prominence and the long list of powerful public men Hiss could count as friends and colleagues.

Though it was not publicly known until many years later, on the morning of his first day of testimony, August 5, Hiss had conferred, for example, with Dean Acheson, soon to be Truman's secretary of state. That afternoon Hiss wrote a long letter of explanation and thinly veiled pleading for support to "Dear Foster"—John Foster Dulles, the Carnegie Endowment chairman and the foreign affairs adviser to Tom Dewey, who was by then the 1948 presidential candidate of Richard Nixon's party. That Hiss was advantageously connected and highly regarded was well known to Nixon, and was bound to have been cautionary to such an ambitious politician.

Dulles's position in the Dewey campaign gave Nixon an additional reason for being careful. If Alger Hiss was exposed as a Communist or fellow traveler, it would do Dewey little good if not some harm that his future secretary of state (as Dulles was assumed to be) had either hired a Communist sympathizer to head the endowment, or been duped by him. Thus, if substantial doubt about Chambers's story developed, it would be the better part of political policy for Richard Nixon to back away. But if Chambers was confirmed, Nixon could be blamed for damaging Dulles and, through him, Dewey.

Nixon was absorbing from Whittaker Chambers still another reason to make sure of his ground. He paid several long visits to Chambers's old, barely furnished Maryland farmhouse—which, Stripling thought, "smelled of another generation. A stuffed raven stared at us from the wall. An old German Bible lay opened on a table."[31]

In these surroundings, Nixon and Stripling talked intently with the older man, probing him for details that would prove his knowledge of Hiss, and learning from him what Chambers thought about communism, Soviet espionage and the American response. Chambers had come to believe that the Roosevelt and Truman administrations, in order to maintain power and credibility, were covering up Communist activities and protecting

Communists and fellow travelers—such as Alger Hiss—who had held office under their auspices.

Nixon accepted that view (Chambers "played Nixon like a monkey on a string," Stripling remembers) or at least expressed it politically, as later demonstrated in his campaign attacks on Truman and particularly on Acheson (an arch-Franklin). In 1948, it might well have caused him to be careful not to overstep himself, lest his own reputation be damaged in attacks by the powerful and unscrupulous opposition he and Chambers envisioned.

And why should the possibility be excluded (as Nixon critics tend to do) that he did not want to ruin an innocent man, even one he disliked? Chambers was an unattractive witness. ("Never in the stormy history of the Committee," Nixon wrote in *Six Crises,* "was a more sensational investigation started by a less impressive witness.") From FBI reports, Nixon probably knew (though he never mentioned it publicly or in his books) that Chambers had confessed to homosexual cruising in New York some years earlier.

Also, at that stage of the investigation, and for whatever reasons, Chambers was lying to Nixon and the committee on two important, related points: that the Communist group to which he said Hiss had belonged had not been engaged in espionage, and that he had no documentary evidence to support his charges. From his FBI sources, Nixon should have been aware that Chambers was holding back on the first point, if not the second.

Nixon was, moreover, a lawyer who presumably knew the rules of evidence; and he had shown—as in his absence from the Hollywood hearings—his reluctance to join in the committee's usual scattershot approach. People's motives, after all, are usually mixed, the idealistic or the dishonorable, and sometimes both, mingling with the practical. Except for those incapable of ascribing other than evil or cynical motives to Richard Nixon, readers of the Hiss case record will find little reason to believe that Nixon was eager to destroy Hiss—despite his visceral dislike—by hook or crook, fair means or foul.

Instead, Nixon and Stripling moved astutely but not unethically to get Chambers's considerable knowledge of Hiss and his family on the record, then used the information to lead Hiss—at a committee hearing on August 16—into admissions that left them in little doubt that he had known Chambers well and intimately. Then, at Nixon's direction, the committee staff quickly arranged the famous confrontation of August 17, in which Hiss "lost [his] air of smoothness" and finally had to admit his knowledge of Chambers (under another name).

The August 17 meeting was arranged, in Nixon's telling, before Hiss could have time "to make his story fit the facts." In *Six Crises* Nixon portrays this confrontation as a masterpiece of timing; Hiss suspected it had been ordered so quickly to smother the news of the death, a day earlier, of Harry Dexter White, another Roosevelt-Truman administration official who had recently denied Communist activity in committee testimony. The unexpected (by Hiss) staging of the August 17 hearing may also have been a product of Nixon's fondness, dating to Whittier College days, for theatricality and melodrama.

It hardly matters. Nixon, Stripling and the committee had established that Hiss and Chambers had known each other—not that Hiss was a Communist or a traitor. Their work made it impossible for the matter to be covered up, if anyone had so intended, more or less vindicated the committee (at least in the Hiss case), and made it all but inevitable that either Hiss or Chambers would be indicted.

By then Hiss had so enmeshed himself in a web of lies and deception that he never since has been able convincingly to extricate himself. No one but his wife, for example, has ever corroborated his story that he had known Chambers only as "George Crosley," a free-lance journalist to whom he said he had given harmless assistance in the thirties.

The further details of the Hiss-Chambers affair, though fascinating—the confrontation on August 17 in the old Commodore Hotel in New York, with Hiss peering into Chambers's teeth; the prothonotary warbler, the old Ford car, the Woodstock typewriter, the "pumpkin papers," and the two trials—are too complex for brief retelling and too familiar to many Americans to require it. Only two points about the case seem important to an inquiry into Richard Nixon's life and works.

The first is that during Nixon's major role in the case—establishing that Alger Hiss indeed had known Whittaker Chambers, even if by another name—he showed himself an able and resourceful investigator but did not use unprincipled smear techniques or hurl reckless false charges or concoct or acquiesce in schemes to frame Hiss.

On the contrary, he took the information Chambers had given him on Hiss to William Rogers, the chief counsel for the Senate Internal Security Subcommittee, which was considered to have conducted a fair and effective investigation into an earlier case, that of William Remington. Nixon and Rogers, who had not previously known each other, hit it off at once—perhaps, Rogers believes, because they both had been "poor guys from small towns who went to school on scholarships and got good marks."

Rogers, who became attorney general under Dwight Eisenhower and secretary of state under Nixon, found his new acquaintance "a very thoughtful fellow, quite intellectual." As for the Hiss case, Nixon told him that if the committee had made a mistake, "we should admit it and clear Hiss." But Rogers felt sure that because Chambers had provided so many details that could be checked, it could be established whether Chambers really had known Hiss.

Nixon also took Chambers's testimony to Representative Christian Herter of Massachusetts, renowned for probity, who also was to become a secretary of state; to Representative Charles Kersten of Ohio, who had introduced him to Father Cronin; to Bert Andrews, the *New York Herald Tribune*'s Washington Bureau chief, a Pulitzer Prize winner; and to Foster and Allen Dulles. All agreed Nixon had ample grounds to proceed—that Chambers's testimony could only have come from someone who had known Alger Hiss, and that Hiss probably had lied to the committee.

Foster Dulles in particular is a solid witness for Nixon's concern, because Dulles would have had good reason to want to discredit charges against a man he had chosen as president of the Carnegie Endowment. But Dulles would not dismiss the evidence.

Nixon "wanted to be careful about hurting reputations and sought the opinions of people who knew Hiss as to the weight of the evidence," Dulles recalled. "I formed a very high judgment of the sense of responsibility under which [Nixon] operated." Allen Weinstein, the most meticulous chronicler of the Hiss-Chambers affair, and by no means an admirer of Richard Nixon, found "no evidence that a demonic Dick Nixon participated in an effort to frame Alger Hiss."[32]

Thus, the common notion that Richard Nixon cynically "destroyed" Alger Hiss is insupportable. Hiss destroyed himself; and even less than in the campaign against Jerry Voorhis did Nixon win his "battle" only by the use of foul and lying tactics.

In *Six Crises* Nixon relates that during his 1952 campaign for the vice presidency, William Rogers overheard a lady say she didn't like Nixon. When asked why not, she replied: "He was mixed up with that awful Alger Hiss."

There may be more meaning to this story than the obvious—that the lady knew little about the Hiss case and less about why she disliked the vice presidential candidate. It suggests the second important point about Nixon's participation in the Un-American Activities Committee's most famous investigation: he not only has been blamed for things he never did; he also sought and got credit for more than he deserved.

The result is that Nixon's real and rather limited role has been so confused—distorted by critics and exaggerated by himself and his admirers—that few, perhaps not even Nixon himself, any longer know or remember what he did and didn't do. Thus, he can be, and is, blamed or praised for almost any aspect of the case, whether or not he bears responsibility.

From the start, Nixon certainly recognized the potential in proving Chambers's charges of Communist penetration in two Democratic administrations. In *RN* he conceded that the case had given him publicity "on a scale most congressmen only dream of achieving."

In *Six Crises* he recorded all his ostensible reasons, in every case admirable, for plunging ahead—the search for truth, the need to alert Americans to the Communist threat, the need to vindicate what he saw as the committee's educational efforts and what he thought was the just cause of proving Chambers truthful. He pointed out, too, what he pictured as the fearful dangers of going ahead—the unwillingness of the public and press to believe in the guilt of a man like Alger Hiss, the opposition of Truman and the administration, possible Communist retaliation, the disdain in which the committee would be held if the investigation proved fruitless.

Even if all this were taken at face value, the very seriousness of these dangers would have been magnetic to so publicity conscious a politician as Richard Nixon. (Another committee member, F. Edward Hebert of Louisiana, had chided Nixon and Mundt about "hysteria for headlines.") If these dangers could be overcome, he would score a double political triumph: much personal attention to advance his career, and an issue with which he and other Republicans could belabor Truman and the Democrats (assuming Dulles's connection to Hiss could be sufficiently played down).

Thus, after the series of committee hearings that established the Hiss-Chambers link, at the time and later, Nixon sought as much publicity as possible. He held news conferences, gave interviews and confided privately in interested reporters like Bert Andrews, spoke in the House, traveled widely to make partisan speeches on the subject, and later used his participation in the case as his springboard into a successful campaign for the Senate in 1950. On page one of *Six Crises* he quotes a "friend"—one of those ubiquitous but anonymous sources of pithy remarks with which his speeches and writings are filled: "If it hadn't been for the Hiss case, you never would have been Vice President of the United States or a candidate for President."

That's undoubtedly true; the Communists-in-government issue was a major Republican weapon by 1952, and Richard Nixon not only had done much to substantiate it; second only to Joe McCarthy, if more responsibly, he personified the scourge. Dwight Eisenhower—who as president of Columbia University had been elected to the board of the Carnegie Endowment the same day Alger Hiss was elected its president—later presented Nixon to the Republican National Convention that had nominated him for vice president as a man who "has a special talent and an ability to ferret out any kind of subversive influence wherever it may be found, and the strength and persistence to get rid of it."

By then, and owing greatly to his own publicity seeking, Nixon's role in the Hiss case had been exaggerated out of all recognition. His efforts had not, for example, despite the claim of one of his 1950 campaign leaflets, "broke[n] the Hiss-Chambers espionage case." His work had had little to do with espionage, and nothing important, until *after* the pumpkin papers had been turned over to HUAC investigators. If anything, in sharp contrast to his able earlier performance, Nixon displayed in the later stages of the case a nervous irascibility and strange lack of interest that almost shut himself and the committee out of *any* role in exposing Hiss's espionage activities.

On November 17, 1948, while being deposed by Hiss's attorneys in a libel suit Hiss had filed, Whittaker Chambers dumbfounded his interrogators by handing over to them sixty-five pages of retyped State Department documents from the thirties; he said Alger Hiss had given them to him years before. Chambers also surrendered four notes he said were written in Hiss's own hand. Abandoning the pretense that he had no documentary evidence, he finally offered such evidence, to link Hiss to espionage.

Nixon had long since considered the case over and done with; as far as he was concerned, it had effectively ended after he engineered the climactic Hiss-Chambers confrontations. In *Six Crises* he recalled that, after this drama, "the committee would be vindicated and I personally would receive credit for the part I had played." Any further committee investigation—here is the special Nixon touch of piety—"might interfere with judicial proceedings."

After the confrontations, Nixon pretty clearly had what he'd most wanted from the case—personal fame, a Republican issue, and perhaps the humbling of Alger Hiss. Throughout the 1948 fall campaign, as Dewey magnanimously squandered what he and almost everyone else thought was his sure victory over Truman—reinforcing Nixon's belief in Chotiner's thesis that elections are won on the attack—the now-renowned young congressman roamed the nation and his California district, speaking repeatedly on the Hiss case, his role in it, and the cover-up he alleged to the Democrats.

But on December 1, 1948, with the campaign over and Nixon back in Washington, he saw two conflicting stories in the Washington press. One, in the *Post,* reported new and "startling information" in the Hiss-Chambers case; the other, a United Press report in the *Daily News* (now defunct), stated that for lack of information the Justice Department was about to drop its investigation of Alger Hiss.

That same morning, Nicholas Vazzana, an attorney employed by *Time* to assist Chambers—one of *Time*'s editors—told Nixon and Stripling about the documents Chambers had produced on November 17.* No information about these had been made public or available to the committee, and the documents themselves had been turned over to the Justice Department (the "startling information" mentioned in the *Post*).

*Henry Luce, the publisher of *Time,* paid for Chambers's legal defense, according to Robert Stripling.

Vazzana had been told by the Justice Department that he could not discuss the contents of the documents. But the contradictory *Daily News* piece caused him to alert Stripling and Nixon anyway. All three feared that, again, with a Democratic administration reelected, nothing was going to be done about Alger Hiss.[33]

Nixon was scheduled to leave the next day, December 2, on a vacation cruise to Panama with Mrs. Nixon and other congressional couples. Stripling tried repeatedly to persuade him to drive to the Maryland farm and confront Chambers on the turn of the case toward espionage. Nixon, first irritably, then angrily, refused: "I'm so goddamned sick and tired of this case, I don't want to hear any more about it and I'm going to Panama. And the hell with it and you and the whole damned business!"

Now it was Stripling who persisted, amazed that Nixon apparently did not see the opportunity for the committee to reenter the case, disclose the existence of Chambers's documents and force the Justice Department to continue the investigation. It was even possible that the committee could get sensational documents of its own from whatever cache Chambers had maintained.

Nixon was adamant that he was no longer interested; but as Stripling was about to drive to Maryland alone, Nixon capitulated almost childishly: "Goddammit! If it'll shut your mouth, I'll go!" It is not difficult to discern that he knew he *should* confront Chambers, whether he wanted to or not.*

At the Maryland farm, Chambers conceded that he had turned over to the Hiss defense a "bombshell" of documents, of which the Justice Department had taken possession. But he had retained "another bombshell in case they try to suppress this one." Nixon urged him to give the second bombshell only to the committee, but did not demand that Chambers hand over anything then and there.

In fact, on the drive back to Washington, the once-zealous investigator who was to portray himself as having instinctively believed Chambers on first hearing his charges against Hiss, told Stripling: "I don't think he's got a damned thing." He still planned to go to Panama.

Talking with Bert Andrews that night, Nixon told the reporter about the two bombshells. Andrews advised him to have Stripling serve "a blanket subpoena on Chambers to produce anything and everything he still has in his possession." Nixon said he would think it over.[34]

The next morning, Nixon tried to meet Stripling at the committee offices before leaving for New York and the cruise ship on an 8:00 A.M. train. They missed connection and Nixon called, either from the station or on

---

*Stripling, who makes no secret of his dislike for Nixon today, theorizes that Nixon had been "brown-nosing" Chambers for information with which he intended to write a book. Because Chambers had not told Nixon about the documents he had handed to the FBI, Stripling believes, Nixon was angered and "terribly disillusioned."

the train's radio phone, to tell Stripling to serve a subpoena. Stripling already had had one signed by Speaker Joe Martin. That evening, in response, Chambers dug five rolls of microfilm out of a pumpkin on his farm, where he had hidden them earlier in the day, and surrendered them to committee investigators.

Nixon's curious reluctance to get into the matter was not publicly known at the time, when he was regarded as the hero of the Hiss case. And his own later account of these events in *Six Crises* differs startlingly in several important instances, all self-serving. He wrote, for one thing, that when he saw the report that the Justice Department might drop the Hiss case, "playing a long hunch, I suggested to Stripling that we drive to [Chambers's farm] at once." Vazzana's information, the long argument with Stripling, and Nixon's skepticism do not appear.

Nixon claimed, further, that he considered postponing his vacation trip that day, "but I didn't have the heart to tell Pat the bad news. . . . [T]aking no chances, however, I stopped off at the committee office [on December 1] and signed a subpoena *duces tecum* on Chambers for any and all documents" relevant to the case. In *RN* Nixon drops the spurious signed-subpoena claim: "I spent much of the night trying to decide whether to issue a subpoena." Finally, in the later version, he asks "Stripling to have subpoenas served." Neither book mentions the conversation with Bert Andrews, the missed morning meeting with Stripling or Joe Martin's signature on the crucial subpoena.

Nixon's strange, almost irresponsible behavior was kept from the press at the time and he continued publicly to play a hero's role. Stripling did tell some of the story in a series of articles written by Bob Considine of the Hearst press in 1949, and republished as the book *Red Plot against America*. But his carefully limited story had little effect on the tide of favorable publicity Nixon was receiving from the belief that he had "broken" the Hiss case. If anything, the finding of the pumpkin papers—which owed little if anything to Nixon—increased the flow of congratulatory coverage.

The discovery of the microfilm caused Stripling and Andrews to wire the cruise ship for Nixon to return to Washington. He did, by seaplane and train, and as Weinstein observed, "rarely did his name leave the headlines or his picture the front pages until a New York grand jury indicted Hiss for perjury on December 15," 1948.

Nixon also was less than decisive and self-possessed—the images he appears to prefer above all others—in one more dramatic episode of the Hiss case. But again he escaped damaging leaks about his behavior.

A routine check with the Eastman Kodak Company had disclosed that the film from the pumpkin had not been manufactured until 1945—years after Chambers said Alger Hiss had stolen the State Department documents photographed on the film. This seemed to mean that Chambers had manufactured the pumpkin papers.

"Oh my God, this is the end of my political career!" Nixon wailed. To Nicholas Vazzana he became "abusive," shouting: "You got us into this. . . . [W]hat are you going to do about it?"

Vazzana protested, but Nixon angrily declared: "You'd better get hold of Chambers!" And Stripling had to insist that Nixon not call off a scheduled news conference, telling the congressman: "No, damn it, we won't. We'll go down and face the music. We'll tell them that we were sold a bill of goods . . . that we were all wet."

Again, Nixon's *Six Crises* account is wholly different: he pictures himself calmly calling Chambers in New York and asking him to explain the discrepancy in the film's manufacture date. In his orotund style, Chambers replies: "I can't understand it. God must be against me."

Only then, to hear Nixon tell it, in tones of a man goaded beyond endurance: "I took out on him all the fury and frustration that had built up within me. 'You'd better have a better answer than that!' " for the committee's scheduled hearing that night in New York, he shouted. Then he "slammed the receiver down without giving [Chambers] a chance to reply."

But when Stripling asked him, "What'll we do now?" the Nixon of *Six Crises* is again in full control of his emotions and clearheaded about procedure: "There's only one thing we can do. I want you to have the staff call the reporters . . . and ask them to come to my office." He was ready, he wrote, for "the biggest crow-eating performance in the history of Capitol Hill." And again the whiff of piety: he "reminded Stripling that it was the committee's responsibility not to prove Hiss guilty but to find out who was telling the truth."[35]

As it turned out, in Nixon's as well as the Vazzana-Stripling account, no one had to eat crow. Eastman Kodak called back to correct its earlier statement: the type of film in question *had* been manufactured until 1938 and then it was discontinued, but production resumed in 1945. Once again, Whittaker Chambers's veracity had been confirmed.

There was almost a tragic aftermath to this incident, important otherwise only for what it may reveal about Richard Nixon in "battle." That night Whittaker Chambers, not knowing about Eastman Kodak's second call, despondent at God's apparent desertion, bungled a suicide attempt. (Nixon had tried and failed to reach him with the good news.)

For Nixon's account of his participation in the later stages of the Hiss case, Robert Stripling, not surprisingly, offered a succinct judgment many years later: *"Six Crises,"* Stripling told Allen Weinstein, "is pure bull-shit!"*

---

*Stripling claimed to me that when he later encountered Richard and Pat Nixon in an elevator of the Longworth House Office Building, Mrs. Nixon said: "Strip, we know you broke the Hiss case." But Nixon was going to run for the Senate in 1950, she

The result of all the publicity, the speeches, the exaggerations and the deceptions, which began long before *Six Crises,* was that Nixon's name came to be inextricably linked with all aspects of the Hiss case. However people felt about the *case,* so they tended to feel about Richard Nixon; and a great many Americans in those years and for many to come were convinced of Hiss's innocence, or at least that his transgressions were no greater than those of other well-meaning liberal and antifascist Americans in the twenties and the depression thirties. So powerful were the emotions raised that even after the emerging facts made it hard to believe in Hiss's *innocence,* many Americans still found it difficult to accept his *guilt.*

Hiss himself never has admitted it, neither during his prison term for perjury nor in his years of relative obscurity since. I interviewed him in the seventies, when Nixon's later career was at a low point following the Vietnam War, Watergate and his resignation from the presidency. Hiss, ironically, had become a minor celebrity again, because he was widely if erroneously thought to have been one of the first victims of Nixon's villainy.

I found Hiss a mild and affable man who wanted mostly to discuss his application for readmission to the Massachusetts bar (later successful) rather than the great case of a quarter century earlier. It was hard to believe he was a man who could have betrayed his country (or who had been in prison). Like many Americans, I *wanted* to believe Hiss innocent, a victim of witch-hunting and frame-up, even though I considered most of his claims—such as Chambers's supposed "forgery by typewriter"—improbable in the extreme.

Not until 1978, when Allen Weinstein published *Perjury,* the definitive account of the case, were my instinctive doubts finally overcome. I suspect that may have been true for many Americans, particularly those old enough, as I was, to remember the case itself and the passions it aroused, with Alger Hiss and Richard Nixon their focus. For many, the Hiss-Chambers-Nixon imbroglio was all of a piece with "McCarthyism," though McCarthyism's progenitor did not emerge as such until 1950.

After all, if such a man as Hiss—wellborn, Harvard trained, one of the "best and brightest" of his time—could succumb to foreign ideology and betray his country, *anyone* could. In that sense—the idea that the Communists had penetrated everywhere, threatened the U.S. from within as well as without, were diabolically clever and insidiously present—the Hiss case did plow fertile ground for the later outrages of Joseph R. McCarthy and other Red-baiters of the fifties, and for the large followings they achieved.

But in another sense—the idea that if Alger Hiss could be smeared and

---

continued, so "Do you mind if Dick claims credit for it?" Stripling didn't then, but decidedly does today.

ruined, anyone could be—the case powerfully evoked, for the first time on a national scale, the kind of anger and resentment McCarthyism was also to evoke. Either way, as hero or villain, Richard Nixon was a visible symbol.

American liberalism, moreover, was pushed on the defensive, first by the Hiss case, and later by McCarthyism. After Hiss was exposed, it became routine for liberals to assert their anticommunism, on the assumption that to be effective, maybe even tolerated, liberalism had to be free of any taint of Communist influence. To be anti-Communist became more important for some than to be liberal; and there were those who turned against and denounced old colleagues in liberal and antifascist activities, for reasons ranging from cowardice to conviction.

Thus, animosity and fear obviously stunted the growth of an American Left that never had been too vigorous anyway. Even three decades later, the powerful antiliberalism of the Reagan years, tinged as it was with the belief that liberals were somehow un-American, perhaps even un-Christian, had visible roots in the passions first widely aroused by the Hiss case. The actor Ronald Reagan's personal views probably were influenced by the Hiss case, as he was turning in those years toward politics and cooperation with HUAC.

Many Americans, like Hiss and Chambers, had had strong antifascist or pro-Communist or even Communist views in the depression years, or before; but few had engaged in espionage and treason. Few, however, had had the opportunity; what would they have done if they had had the chance? Had Alger Hiss, given that chance, simply followed their shared outlook to its logical end?

In this way of thinking, the way of Whittaker Chambers after his break with the party, lay guilt and renunciation, and not a few took that path. But others hated the fact that political and social ideas in which as Americans they profoundly believed had been falsely tainted with treason by Alger Hiss's activities—and by his assumed nemesis, Richard Nixon.

Politically, it was the Democratic administrations of Roosevelt and Truman that had been penetrated, as the Hiss case demonstrated—though to what extent was open to question. In 1951, to the Young Republicans' Convention in Boston, Nixon—only five years after he had entered politics—laid out a 1952 campaign line that became a model for Republican candidates that year:

> Communists infiltrated the very highest councils of this Administration. . . . [Yet] our top Administration officials have refused time and time again to recognize the existence of the fifth column in this country and to take executive action to clean subversives out of the administrative branch of government. . . . But one thing

can be said to [Republicans'] credit which cannot be said for the party in power, that is, that we have never had the support of the Communists in the past. . . . And for that reason a Republican Administration, we can be sure, will conduct a thoroughgoing housecleaning of Communists and fellow-travelers . . . because we have no fear of finding any Communist skeletons in our political closets.

So the Hiss case—for the first time providing seeming evidence that a fifth column existed—became a partisan issue, too, and no one made it so more effectively than Richard Nixon, who never hesitated to link Truman, Acheson and later Adlai Stevenson to Alger Hiss, if not quite to communism itself. Not unnaturally, they and Democrats generally saw this tactic as making a distinction without much difference, and resented it deeply— resenting Nixon most of all.

Worse, the linkage of the Democratic party to Communist subversion had the effect of bringing into question the Roosevelt-Truman postwar foreign policy, beginning with Yalta—where Hiss had been so prominent. Had it all been influenced or even brought about by high-level subversives? From Whittaker Chambers to Jesse Helms, that question persists in a certain kind of conspiratorial mind—of which there are many.

Such doubts, together with McCarthyism and the real events of the Cold War, poisoned the minds of generations of Americans on the subject of better relations with the Soviet Union or a less militant American policy in a world that, after the Hiss case, was constantly pictured as divided between "us and them," good and evil. For that, too, despite his internationalist voting record and later presidential policies, many Americans blamed and have never forgiven Richard Nixon; even before McCarthy, he had helped force the "Communist threat" into the nation's nightmares.

But Nixon's early triumph *was* to a great extent his fate: he had made his name synonymous with the case. In 1986, in a reflective article, Nixon recalled that Dwight Eisenhower had told him in 1952 that "one of the reasons I picked you [for running mate] was that you got Hiss and got him fairly." What millions of Americans believed was simply that "Nixon got Hiss."[36]

So if the case was a frame-up or if at worst Hiss had acted from "higher" notions of patriotism and antifascism shared by many Americans, and if exposing him had had adverse consequences for liberals, for the Democratic party, for Soviet-American relations, for the worldview of fearful Americans, in some cases for one's friends and heroes, all the anger, fear and resentment centered on Nixon.

Or if, on the other hand, Hiss's pursuer had brilliantly and courageously exposed, even against the powerful efforts of presidents, what Herbert

Hoover called "the stream of treason that has existed in our government" and aroused the nation to the mortal threat of communism—then, all the admiration and gratitude also went to Nixon. Animosity and approbation shared the same easy target: the rising young politician who had so zealously pushed and capitalized upon the case.

In making sure he got the credit, Richard Nixon had made it equally sure he would get the blame. It may be the irony—even the poetic justice—of his life that he fully deserved neither.

Nineteen-fifty, to any American who lived through it, was a year of trauma, perhaps not to be equaled until 1968. Here is a partial chronology of memorable events of that year of the half century:

> *January 21:* Alger Hiss is convicted of two counts of perjury.
> *January 31:* President Truman announces that he had ordered work to start on the hydrogen bomb.
> *February 2:* The physicist Klaus Fuchs confesses in London to having spied for the Soviet Union while he worked on Anglo-American atomic research.
> *February 9:* Senator Joseph R. McCarthy of Wisconsin tells the Women's Republican Club of Wheeling, West Virginia, that 205 Communists are employed in the State Department.
> *May 2:* Representative George Smathers defeats Senator Claude Pepper in the Florida Democratic primary, after an anti-Communist campaign in which Smathers labeled his opponent "Red Pepper." In other famous campaigns involving one degree or another of Red-baiting, three incumbent Democratic senators were defeated in 1950: Millard Tydings (by John Marshall Butler) in Maryland; Elbert Thomas (by Wallace Bennett) in Utah; and Frank P. Graham (by Willis Smith) in North Carolina.
> *June 28:* North Korea invades South Korea across the 38th parallel.
> *June 30:* President Truman sends American troops to fight in defense of South Korea.
> *August 17:* Julius and Ethel Rosenberg are charged with atomic espionage.
> *September 20:* The Senate, by 70 to 7, completes passage of the McCarran Act on internal security, which embodies much of the old Mundt-Nixon bill. Truman's veto will be overridden and the bill will become law on September 23.
> *November 3:* Republicans gain five Senate seats and twenty-eight in the House.

In California, one of the bitterest of 1950's nasty Senate campaigns had opened early, in October 1949, when Representative Helen Douglas, a former Broadway actress who had served three House terms and was a close friend of Eleanor Roosevelt, announced that she would compete in the Democratic primary against the incumbent senator, Sheridan Downey. Other than Downey, the most interested recipient of this news was Mrs. Douglas's Republican colleague in the House, Richard Nixon.

Nixon had been set back when the Republican party lost control of Congress (and Dewey's supposedly sure victory) in 1948. Other than for the Hiss case, he had not found life in the House sufficiently battle oriented to be satisfying even for a member of the majority. Being relegated to the minority was too much.

Against the advice of his Twelfth District supporters—having found a congressman, they wanted to keep him—he began thinking about challenging Senator Downey, mostly on "the worth of the nationwide publicity the Hiss Case had given me." Nixon's correspondence for the period discloses that he had decided that he did not want to be "a 'comer' with no place to go." He had been about ready to announce his candidacy when Mrs. Douglas leaped into the race.

The Douglas announcement clinched Nixon's decision, because she—a controversial figure with a liberal record—insured a divisive Democratic primary that was bound to benefit any Republican candidate. But Nixon moved with his customary attention to prepare his ground; he did not want a primary race himself. So with the assistance of Kyle Palmer, he made sure of the support of the *Los Angeles Times* (published by Chandler), the *San Francisco Chronicle* (Hearst) and the *Oakland Tribune* (Knowland). Herbert Hoover backed him privately. Harold Stassen, still a presidential hopeful, caused his California organization to lend its endorsement. Governor Earl Warren, always the independent, was preoccupied with his own reelection campaign.

All that meant no other serious Republican need apply. On November 3, one year before the 1950 election, with the Republican nomination his for the asking, Richard Nixon announced his candidacy for the Senate. His opening speech telegraphed what was to be his major theme.

California faced, he declared, a choice between "freedom and state socialism" because "the Democratic party today nationally and in our own state . . . has been captured and is completely controlled by a group of ruthless, cynical seekers-after-power who have committed that party to policies and principles which are completely foreign to those of its founders."

This theme was all the more powerful in the foreign and domestic contexts of the time. In late 1949, a victorious Mao Tse-tung had proclaimed the People's Republic of China and Chiang Kai-shek had fled ignominiously to the island of Formosa. The Soviet Union, moreover, had put an end to the American atomic monopoly by exploding its own atomic bomb. The second perjury trial of Alger Hiss in New York was making daily headlines; the first had ended in a hung jury. It was not hard for Americans to link the "loss of China" and the sooner-than-expected Soviet bomb to tales of espionage like that of which Hiss was a symbol. The arrests of Fuchs in February 1950 and of the Rosenbergs in August 1950 seemed to confirm this public impression and to emphasize Nixon's foresight and pioneer role in exposing Hiss.

Given these conditions and his own taste for "battle," Nixon promised "a fighting, rocking, socking campaign." But the rocking and socking, at first, was mostly on the Democratic side. Mrs. Douglas, the wife of the movie star Melvyn Douglas, aggressively charged Sheridan Downey with being subservient to big business and power interests. He replied that she was linked to extremists.

So it went for several months. But whether because Downey feared defeat or because he was physically unable to wage a tough campaign, he withdrew from the race in April 1950, saying he was not up to "a personal and militant campaign against the vicious and unethical propaganda" of his opponent, Helen Douglas.

The publisher of the *Los Angeles Daily News,* Manchester Boddy, then announced his own candidacy for the Democratic nomination. "The same old plot with a new leading man," the sharp-tongued Mrs. Douglas remarked. But Downey endorsed Boddy in a move that may have sunk the Douglas candidacy—not in the primary, but in the fall election.

Downey's statewide radio speech included one point that Boddy later repeated endlessly, and which Nixon and Murray Chotiner, who was managing Nixon's campaign, carefully noted for future reference: Mrs. Douglas, Downey said, had "joined Representative Vito Marcantonio, an admitted friend of the Communist party," in voting against an appropriation for the House Un-American Activities Committee.

Downey also tried to link Mrs. Douglas to Henry Wallace, whom she had supported for vice president in 1944, but whose third-party presidential candidacy she had opposed in her congressional district in 1948. Then, in an era when women in politics, or anywhere out of the kitchen and bedroom, were suspect anyway, Downey may have damaged Mrs. Douglas the most when he said she did not "have the fundamental ability and qualifications for a U.S. senator. She has shown no inclination, in fact no ability, to dig in and do the hard and tedious work required to propose legislation and push it through Congress." He might as well have said she was "just a woman."

This attack further split California Democrats, improving Nixon's chances for November. Also, since Downey had been a favorite of California oil interests, which he had faithfully served, his withdrawal had opened the way for Nixon to seek the oilmen's backing. (A Senate committee investigation later absolved Nixon of charges that he had accepted fifty-two thousand dollars from the Union Oil Company; letters making this allegation turned out to be forgeries.)

While the Democrats tore each other up, Nixon, characteristically, had been working hard. Systematically touring the state in a sound-equipped station wagon, with Mrs. Nixon, a driver and an aide, he made as many as fourteen curbside speeches a day, sometimes more than one an hour, over a thousand in sixteen weeks, anywhere the recorded popular music from his station wagon attracted a half dozen or so Californians. At each stop he answered questions from the audience, a technique that was to become familiar in his national campaigns. His favorite subject was Alger Hiss.[37]

But in May, he stepped sharply out of his established campaign character. Not long before primary day, the California Committee on Un-American Activities took testimony in Oakland from a woman named Sylvia Crouch, the wife of Paul Crouch, a former Communist who had become a paid consultant to the Department of Justice. Mrs. Crouch described a meeting she had attended in July 1941 in Berkeley, a "session of a top-drawer Communist group known as a special section, a group so important that its makeup was kept secret from ordinary Communists."

The host for the meeting, held in his home, Mrs. Crouch said, had been J. Robert Oppenheimer. The scientist was, by 1950, a target of numerous security agencies owing to his supposedly leftist views and his opposition (then unknown to the public) to development of the hydrogen bomb.

Oppenheimer promptly issued a statement denying that he had been host for or attended any such meeting, or had any knowledge of the Crouches. But in the Red-charged atmosphere of California in 1950, with Downey and Boddy imputing Communist sympathies to Helen Douglas and with Nixon exploiting and exaggerating his part in the exposure of Alger Hiss, the charge against Oppenheimer looked like another chance for Nixon to brandish his anti-Communist experience.

Instead, and without being asked to do so by Oppenheimer or the press, on May 10 the Republican candidate inserted into a speech he was making in the small town of Oakdale a statement of "complete confidence in Dr. Oppenheimer's loyalty." Citing HUAC's meetings with the physicist, Nixon added that he was "convinced that Dr. Oppenheimer has been and is a completely loyal American, and further, one to whom the people of the United States owe a great debt of gratitude for his tireless and magnificent job in atomic research."[38]

Boddy, meanwhile, citing Mrs. Douglas and Marcantonio in the same breath as often as he could, was charging that there was a "statewide conspiracy on the part of a small subversive clique of red-hots to capture, through stealth and cunning, the nerve center of our Democratic party." Nixon's unexpected defense of Oppenheimer notwithstanding, he couldn't have stated his own theme more concisely, and no one doubted what Boddy meant by "red-hots."

Mrs. Douglas—who was "a bitch," Marcantonio actually thought, and whom even Harry Truman privately regarded as a nuisance—was not too busy responding to Boddy to pay acerbic respects to Nixon: "I have utter scorn for such pipsqueaks as Nixon and McCarthy," she declared. But Nixon reluctantly held his fire for the general election, accepting Chotiner's thesis that "we wanted her to be the Democratic nominee on the basis that it would be easier to defeat her than a conservative Democrat."

On primary day, June 6, 1950, Nixon polled a total of about a million votes, Mrs. Douglas 890,000, Boddy only 535,000 (all three running in both party primaries). But many Boddy votes—no doubt including Boddy's own—clearly would be Nixon's in November. Nixon had, moreover, a united Republican party behind him. Victory seemed certain.

The Korean War, erupting on June 25, might have hurt a lesser competitor, because Truman's immediate dispatch of American troops to fight the North Korean Communist invaders hardly bore out the idea of a Democratic party and president controlled by left-wing extremists (a political consideration that actually had influenced Truman's decision to fight). Some of Nixon's advisers cautioned him to soft-pedal the Communist issue; but after four years in politics, he knew well enough how to turn developments to his advantage.

As a strong anti-Communist, he enthusiastically supported Truman's resistance—probably recognizing, too, that at least in the first stages of combat involving American forces, the instinct of Americans, as usual, would be to "support our boys" and "rally round the president." At the same time, to underline the "Communist threat," he emphasized the iniquity of the North Korean invasion. He also called for Dean Acheson's resignation as secretary of state because Acheson supposedly was responsible for excluding Korea from the announced area the U.S. had determined to defend in Asia.

Actually (although Nixon could not have known it), the Truman administration's attitude toward the Soviet Union and the Cold War had been significantly transformed by the Soviet bomb and developments in China. Not only had Truman secretly ordered a crash program to develop the "super" (hydrogen) bomb; an administration review of the world scene, formally stated in National Security Council document number 68, had abandoned the view that Soviet communism presented primarily a political and economic threat, to be "contained" by political and economic means.

NSC-68 predicted the possibility of a surprise Soviet atomic attack on the U.S. by 1954, and Russian "piecemeal" aggression "anywhere in the world," based on Moscow's supposed assumption that the U.S. would not resist for fear that confrontation would lead to atomic war. If the threat was thus military, and if indeed atomic war was to be avoided as the consequence, then the U.S. had to build up its conventional forces and be ready to meet Soviet challenges anywhere in the world. The North Korean invasion across the 38th parallel seemed to confirm this thesis; even had it not been launched, the Truman administration would have embarked on a conventional arms buildup in 1950 or soon thereafter.

Nevertheless, Nixon campaigned confidently—charging, for example, that Helen Douglas had "consistently supported the State Department's policy of appeasing communism in Asia, which finally resulted in the Korean War."

In reality, Mrs. Douglas had supported the Marshall Plan, reciprocal trade, Truman's mutual aid program, and aid to Korea; but she had laid herself open to political trouble by voting against Truman's showcase policy, openly anti-Communist and anti-Soviet, of aid to Greece and Turkey. That lent some underpinning to the otherwise farfetched idea that she had not sufficiently opposed Soviet adventurism.

The campaign reached its undoubted low point—one few other campaigns, before or since, have witnessed—when Senator Joseph McCarthy in all his Communist-hunting glory came to Los Angeles on October 10 to denounce "the blunders and traitorous acts of the crowd whom the Democratic candidates are pledged to protect" and to declare: "The chips are down . . . between the American people and the administration Commiecrat party of betrayal!"

Fawn Brodie called the occasion a "Nixon rally" and wrote that Nixon "applauded the speech, saying of McCarthy, 'God give him the courage to carry on.'"

Murray Chotiner, however, told Earl Mazo that McCarthy had been invited to California by "some arch-conservative group" and that he personally had told McCarthy that Nixon "didn't want outside help." And Brodie's own footnotes dispute her text. She cites the Nixon remark to a *Los Angeles Times* report of March 23, 1950, nearly *seven months* before the ugly McCarthy speech.

She also wrote that in Los Angeles McCarthy was making his response to Dean Acheson's statement that he would not "turn [his] back on Alger Hiss." McCarthy did declare in the October speech that Acheson "must go," but Acheson's remarks about Hiss had been made on January 25, 1950, nine months before McCarthy's Los Angeles diatribe.[39]

Nixon's primary instrument for driving home the "party-line" charges against Mrs. Douglas was the so-called pink sheet—a further refinement, if that is the word, of the tactic he had first used when he compared Jerry Voorhis's voting record to that of "the PAC." In 1950, taking up where Manchester Boddy had left off, Nixon compared Mrs. Douglas's votes to those of Vito Marcantonio.

Marcantonio had become a favorite conservative target, although he had originally run for office as a Republican. He was, by 1950, a member of the American Labor party but voted and held seniority in the House as a member of the Democratic majority, compiling a record that more or less justified the usual description of him as "the notorious Communist party-line congressman from New York."

Marcantonio took good care of his mostly slum-dwelling constituents in New York, and they usually responded with a "bullet vote" for him—that is, they voted for Marcantonio and no one else or, after voting for him on the ALP line, switched to candidates for other offices on the Democratic or Republican line.[40]

As the fall campaign was beginning, Nixon's Southern California campaign manager referred to Mrs. Douglas as "the pink lady"—some analysts think an appellation inspired by George Smathers's "Red Pepper" coinage. Nixon himself later said she was "pink right down to her underwear"—a reference that seems out of step with the priggishness he usually displayed.

Since "pink" was well understood then and now to mean at least slightly Red, or too close to it for innocence, it was not surprising that Nixon's linkage of the Douglas-Marcantonio voting records was printed on pink paper and promptly became known as the pink sheet. Chotiner ordered fifty thousand copies, one of his rare errors on the side of restraint; within a week, he went back to the printer for a half million more.[41]

High in the pink-sheet message came Nixonian notes of piety: "Many persons have requested a comparison of the voting records" of Mrs. Douglas and "the notorious Communist party-liner," etc. (This no doubt could be reprinted in the *New Yorker* under the heading "Requests we doubt ever got requested.")

Also: "While it should not be expected that a member of the House of Representatives should always vote in opposition to Marcantonio. . . ." Of course not. But then the pink sheet got down to business.

Mrs. Douglas, it related, had voted with "the notorious Communist party-liner" 354 times since January 1, 1945. Twenty-four of these votes were discussed briefly, and the pink sheet then asserted that Richard Nixon had voted "exactly opposite to the Douglas-Marcantonio Axis." That last word, not exactly a popular reference that soon after World War II, of course implied a formal alliance between the pink lady and the notorious Communist party-liner.

In 1960, William Costello provided devastating—if not exactly dispassionate—factual analysis of the pink sheet. Many of the 354 votes, to begin with, were of minor importance, including some on Democratic majority procedural matters. Richard Nixon, moreover, though in the House two fewer years than Mrs. Douglas, and a Republican at that, also had voted with Marcantonio no less than 111 times! That proved no more about him than the pink sheet proved about Helen Douglas—but the fact was not so widely distributed.

An *Editorial Research Reports* study found only 76 "outstanding"—or truly important—roll-call votes during the five years covered by the pink sheet. On 66 of these, Marcantonio and Mrs. Douglas *had* voted alike—but in 53 instances both were with a majority of the House or a majority of the Democratic party. The 13 others dealt with such matters as rent and price controls, except for two issues of internal security: the Mundt-Nixon bill of 1948 and the McCarran Act of 1950. Both Mrs. Douglas and Marcantonio voted *against* these two measures—of which the Senate had rejected the former and Truman had vetoed the latter (only to be overridden, though Helen Douglas had voted to sustain).

Of the 10 "outstanding" roll calls on which Mrs. Douglas and Marcantonio *differed*—the "Axis" splintering!—8 dealt in some way with the Communist threat, and on all 8 the pink lady had voted in a manner that would support an American policy *against* some real or feared Communist threat overseas.

Thus, the only tangible support for the ostensible meaning of the pink sheet came, first, from Mrs. Douglas's several votes against the majority, and with Marcantonio, to oppose contempt citations for witnesses who had invoked Fifth Amendment protection on questions about communism; and, second, her vote against the Greek-Turkish aid program—and even in the latter case, she was voting not just with Marcantonio but also with ninety-four Republicans!

The pink sheet took the Voorhis-PAC tactic a long step further into outright deception. In *RN* Nixon emphasized Mrs. Douglas's personal deficiencies, which were numerous, and cited a thousand-dollar contribution he received from Democratic Representative John Kennedy ("It isn't going to break my heart if you turn the Senate's loss into Hollywood's gain," Kennedy told him). Nixon also felt it necessary to insist: "I never questioned her patriotism."

This is classic "deniability." No doubt Nixon never did "question her patriotism" in so many words. With the pink sheet in hand, he didn't have to.

He also told Stewart Alsop a decade later: "I never said *or implied* that Helen Douglas was a Communist. I specifically said she was not" (emphasis added). He hardly had to say it; the pink sheet implied it for him, right down to the color of the paper, if not of Mrs. Douglas's underwear.

As if in mitigation, Nixon also urged Alsop "to put that campaign in the context of the times—1950 and the Korean War."

It's true that his direct attacks on Mrs. Douglas did not begin until after the North Korean invasion of June 25, 1950; but that was primarily because his campaign strategy called for refraining from such attacks until after the primary on June 6. The campaign's general direction was apparent from Nixon's announcement of his candidacy in November 1949, and those hundreds of street-corner speeches from his station wagon.

Helen Douglas, unfortunately, perhaps in desperation, also waged an unappetizing campaign; but by comparison to the skilled tactics of Nixon and Chotiner, and even with assistance from Averell Harriman and other Democrats, hers was inept. As with Voorhis, Nixon did not have competition worthy of his skills, as Mrs. Douglas's own wild charges soon made clear. She characterized Nixon and his aides as "a backwash of young men in dark shirts," about as clear an imputation of fascism to him as the pink sheet was of communism to her. She issued a leaflet headed THE BIG LIE: HITLER INVENTED IT—STALIN PERFECTED IT—NIXON USES IT. She hated "Mundt-Nixon totalitarianism," she said, as much as Communist or fascist totalitarianism.

In a statewide broadcast she called her opponent a reactionary "beside whom Bob Taft is a flaming liberal"—mild rhetoric for that campaign but a charge not borne out by Nixon's votes in Congress. And she further distorted his voting record on aid to Korea and Europe.

Worse, Mrs. Douglas herself turned to Red-baiting, in a patently unbelievable attempt to picture *Nixon* as pink. "On every key vote," she declared in what seems, in retrospect, a pathetic ad, "Nixon stood with party liner Marcantonio against America in its fight to defeat Communism." The victim, *in extremis,* had resorted to the victimizer's tactics.[42]

This bizarre development—the useless business of trying to outattack as expert an attacker as Nixon—may have diverted Mrs. Douglas from whatever issues could have given her a chance. "She made the fatal mistake of attacking our strength," Chotiner observed, "instead of sticking to attacking our weaknesses."[43]

In the last week of the campaign, the Chinese Communist Army—six divisions of which had flooded secretly across the Yalu River—made its devastating combat appearance in Korea. That led to one of the worst defeats the U.S. Army ever suffered and plunged the Douglas campaign—already sinking under the weight of its own ineptitude, a disastrous Democratic party split and Nixon's relentless attacks—to the bottom.

The "Communist threat," of which Richard Nixon had been a relentless prophet, had been dramatically validated—at least as it seemed to many Americans. Like their president, they incorrectly assumed that the Soviet Union was behind the Chinese intervention in Korea. (For further discussion of this point, see chapter 4).

On election day, Nixon ran seven percentage points ahead of the Republican congressional slate in California, winning by almost 2.2 million to 1.5 million. Nationally, the Republican party gained substantially in House and Senate, foreshadowing the narrow Republican congressional victory of 1952. One who lost his reelection campaign in 1950 was Representative Vito Marcantonio of New York.

Nixon's Republican victory was a rare one of which the Democratic Speaker, Sam Rayburn of Texas, did not wholly disapprove. It rid him and his beloved House of both the unpopular Helen Douglas *and* Richard Nixon—who, Rayburn recklessly predicted, would be "buried" in the Senate.

That election night, the exuberant senator-elect from California hopped from party to party, playing "Happy Days Are Here Again" on any piano he could find. But the exuberance probably was short-lived, as the Harriman incident at Joseph Alsop's house suggests. Nixon was never quite to live down his 1950 campaign—in which there was far less excuse than in the 1946 campaign against Jerry Voorhis for a seasoned campaigner and member of Congress to smear his opponent with overblown charges of Communist sympathies.

In 1957, David Astor, the British publisher, interviewed Vice President Nixon at length. The *New Republic* in its May 5, 1958, issue reported that Astor had asked the vice president about the 1950 campaign, and that Nixon had replied: "I'm sorry about that episode. I was a very young man."

He had been thirty-seven, had served four years in the House and had fought the "battle" of Alger Hiss. What might have been a barely acceptable excuse after 1946 hardly seems an adequate explanation of his campaign in 1950.

As for Helen Douglas, whose political life was finished, she made at least one enduring contribution to American politics and to Richard Nixon's continuing career; it might be called her revenge. She had picked up from an editorial in the *Independent Review* a phrase that she thereafter used repeatedly and effectively, affixing it indelibly—and it does not seem too much to say "fairly"—to her aggressive opponent: Tricky Dick.

3

★

Honor, if Possible

★

> There has just been a meeting of all Eisen-
> hower's top advisers, and they have asked me
> to tell you that it is their opinion that at the
> conclusion of the broadcast tonight you
> should submit your resignation to Eisen-
> hower.
>
> —Thomas E. Dewey to Richard Nixon,
> September 23, 1952

On Thursday, September 18, 1952, the *New York Post* broke a story with a sensational headline: SECRET RICH MAN'S TRUST FUND KEEPS NIXON IN STYLE BEYOND HIS SALARY.

No evidence ever justified any part of that headline, because the $18,000 fund (scarcely a vast sum even in 1952) was public, audited, reserved for legitimate campaign expenses not chargeable to the taxpayers, and had been raised from donors of no more than $500 each. The Nixons, more-over, lived modestly on a senator's $15,000 salary and on lecture fees that he reported for 1951 income tax purposes as $6,611.45.

The political fund had been raised and disbursements were made by a trustee. The fund was not illegal or even unethical—although the latter word has little meaning, anyway, in the jungle world of political money.

The *Post* story itself did not claim, as the headline did, that the fund was "secret." But the implications of that glaring headline over a story written, appropriately enough, by the *Post*'s Hollywood reporter—at a time when Republicans were charging the Truman administration with numerous improprieties—were stunning.

In retrospect, Dwight Eisenhower's vast popularity in the presidency makes his election to it seem to have been inevitable; but it did not necessar-ily seem so to everyone in September 1952. Only a few weeks before, the sympathetic Scripps-Howard newspapers had commented editorially (and scathingly) that the general, a newcomer to electoral politics, was "running like a dry creek."

Enthusiasm for Adlai Stevenson, the former Illinois governor who was the Democratic candidate, had risen as the nation became acquainted with his eloquence and wit. Early that September, Stevenson trailed in the Gallup poll with 40 to Eisenhower's 55, with 5 percent undecided; but that was not as big a margin as had been expected and the Democrat was thought to be gaining. No one had forgotten, either, Harry Truman's upset victory only four years earlier, or the unreliability of that year's polls. Eisenhower's party still was bitterly divided between the "Eastern Establishment" that had engineered his nomination and the "Old Guard" emotionally committed to Robert Taft of Ohio.

The supposed "mess in Washington"—concerning "five-percenters" and other accused or convicted officials of the Truman administration—was one of General Eisenhower's two major issues, aside from his own presumed qualities of magisterial leadership. The campaign plan was for him, as a war hero of unchallenged integrity, to hammer away at "the mess" while his running mate, the scourge of Alger Hiss, was to concentrate on the second big Republican issue—Communists in government.

Thus, if the fund story discredited Richard Nixon, both of Eisenhower's prime issues would be blunted, perhaps irreparably. Not only would the general have his own corruption scandal to explain, but his anti-Communist spokesman would be effectively silenced.

Many Republicans—including most of those on the Eisenhower campaign train, then moving through Iowa and Nebraska—immediately assumed that the surest way to avoid such consequences was to get Richard Nixon off the ticket. Advice to that effect poured in from Republicans who believed Eisenhower was their guarantee of a return to power after twenty years in the wilderness.

Former governor Sherman Adams of New Hampshire—later to be forced by his own ethical entanglement to resign as Eisenhower's chief of staff—and former attorney general Herbert Brownell, two of the general's most important advisers, went so far as to telephone William Knowland, California's other senator, to fly from Hawaii to board the Eisenhower train. They did not tell Knowland they had him in mind as a replacement for Nixon.

There were, however, severe problems with this "drop Nixon" scenario. Though the fact was not given much consideration on the panicked Eisenhower train or in the press, nothing had been proven that warranted such a drastic remedy. A major midcampaign change in the ticket, moreover, would be in itself a political setback, suggesting carelessness and incompetence by the supposedly peerless Eisenhower and his advisers in making one of his most important choices.

Eisenhower himself told Sherman Adams on first hearing of the fund

charges: "There is one thing I believe. If Nixon has to go, we cannot win."
Thirty-eight years later, that may seem hard to believe; but it probably was
sound political thinking in 1952.[1]

George McGovern—ironically enough while running against President
Richard Nixon in 1972—suffered disastrous consequences when he decided to drop his running mate, Senator Thomas Eagleton of Missouri,
after charges that the senator had suffered mental health problems. Whatever chance to win McGovern might have had—somewhere between slim
and none—went glimmering with the Eagleton problem.

Walter Mondale, too, was hurt badly in 1984 by mounting evidence that
in his historic choice of Geraldine Ferraro to run for vice president, he had
not investigated adequately her background and her husband's business
record. Vice presidents may be relatively obscure, and vice presidential
candidates more so, but Americans, if forced to think about it, do not want
their vice president, who has only one important reason for being, to have
been picked lightly or for obviously cynical reasons.

Like most vice presidential candidates before and since, unfortunately,
Richard Nixon *had* been picked both lightly and cynically—which was the
major problem with forcing him off the ticket.

The possibility of the vice presidential nomination had become real for
Nixon in the spring of 1952. He had rejected, by then, a request for support
from Taft, Eisenhower's principal rival for the presidential nomination,
"Mr. Republican" himself and the leader of the Old Guard that had hoped
to regain party dominance through Taft's candidacy. But Nixon was not
a free agent who could deal straightforwardly with the Eisenhower forces.

Paul Hoffman, the head of Citizens for Eisenhower, first raised with
Nixon the question of whether the California delegation, after ritual first-
ballot support for Governor Earl Warren, might swing to Eisenhower on
the second ballot. The seventy-seat California delegation, with its strategic
early position in the alphabetical roll call, obviously would be a major
convention factor. But Nixon could make no commitment, since the delegation was pledged to Governor Warren until he released it; the conversation with Hoffman nevertheless made it clear that Nixon could expect to
be rewarded if he could somehow influence California to help Eisenhower.

At the Gridiron Club's annual Washington dinner in that same spring
of 1952, Herbert Brownell, a close political associate of Governor Thomas
E. Dewey of New York, went further; to Nixon, he hinted at the vice
presidential nomination if something could be done for Eisenhower in
California. On the Senate floor, Henry Cabot Lodge of Massachusetts, who
was to be Eisenhower's floor manager at the convention, whispered the
same suggestion in his California colleague's attentive ear.

After Nixon, at Dewey's invitation, had made on May 8, 1952, a well-received speech to a New York Republican dinner, Dewey turned to him and said: "Make me a promise. Don't get fat, don't lose your zeal, and you can be President some day." Later that night, at a small gathering in Dewey's hotel suite, he asked if he could suggest Nixon's name for the vice presidency. Nixon's answer, though not recorded in *RN,* is not hard to imagine. But by then, more was on Dewey's highly political mind than second-ballot California votes.

The Taft-Eisenhower contest, fiercely waged, was sharpening the inherent conflict between the Eastern Establishment led by Dewey, and the Old Guard that Taft championed; particularly on foreign policy, the factional differences were profound. Not only was the race close—Nixon publicly predicted in June that each of the two leading candidates, needing 604 delegates to win, would go to the convention in Chicago with more than 500 committed to him—but the victor would have a hard time pulling the party together after such a bruising fight.

Though Nixon the internationalist was on many issues more moderate than the Old Guard, he was in generally good standing with them as a westerner, because of his strong anti-Communist record and his tireless travels to speak and work for Republican candidates. He was not part of the Eastern Establishment; above all, he was not, as many Old Guardsmen then considered Eisenhower, an outsider and a political interloper; they thought the general was, as Richard Rovere later put it, "a parvenu, an amateur, a boob, and a heretic of sorts."

Dewey and other Eisenhower strategists thus saw Nixon not only as a mole within the California delegation but as a possible vice presidential sop to a disappointed Old Guard, a ticket balancer who might assure the Taft wing's support for Eisenhower if the general could be nominated. That Nixon was a tough campaigner who could speak to the "Communist issue" only added to his appeal.

No one is on record as having wondered what kind of president he might make should he have to take over the office—although Nixon recalled in *RN* that he had spent an afternoon at the Mayflower Hotel in Washington in "a wide-ranging discussion of foreign and domestic policy" with Brownell and others of Eisenhower's inner circle.

Before and during the Chicago convention, as we have seen (see chapter 1), Nixon did what he could for Eisenhower within the California delegation—particularly in persuading it against Governor Warren's wishes to vote for the so-called fair-play resolution, the adoption of which assured Eisenhower's nomination. But after the general's narrow, rather strong-armed victory, more than a reward for Nixon preoccupied Dewey and the inner circle. They needed someone to bring the disgruntled Old Guard into line and to more than reluctant support of Eisenhower in what might prove to be a close election.

To a small meeting of these men—Dewey, Lodge, Brownell, Arthur Summerfield of Michigan, and Senator Frank Carlson of Kansas—a reluctant Eisenhower was persuaded to give a list of those he would accept for his running mate. He had had so little to do with his own nomination that he had not even realized the vice presidential choice was his to make.

Eisenhower's list included Governors Thornton of Colorado, Langlie of Washington and Driscoll of New Jersey, Lodge, Knowland and Stassen. None of them could act as a bridge to Taft and still retain the enthusiasm of the Eastern Establishment. The seventh name—actually first on the list—was that of Richard Nixon, who presumably could do both.

A much larger group of Eisenhower leaders made the final choice, in a proverbial smoke-filled room at the Conrad Hilton Hotel. Taft himself was suggested, but Dewey's representative, J. Russell Sprague, vetoed him. Senator Everett McKinley Dirksen of Illinois was as quickly ruled out. Nixon's name then was put forward; everyone knew he was in good standing with the Old Guard, and Paul Hoffman said the Californian had the right foreign policy views to go with Eisenhower's. He also, probably decisively, hinted that Dewey was ready to fight for Nixon's nomination.

With no more discussion, certainly not of presidential qualifications, the choice was made and Dwight Eisenhower was told who his running mate would be. Later, in the so-called Surrender at Morningside Heights, Eisenhower approved a statement of principles by Taft that resembled Taft's own preconvention platform; Taft then urged the Old Guard to support Eisenhower. That episode, and Nixon's nomination, were parts of a concerted effort by Eisenhower's managers to pull the party together for a united campaign.*

The danger of Republican disunity was real because the emotions involved were profound. In the convention's decisive struggle over delegate seating, Everett Dirksen, perhaps second only to Taft in the hearts of Old Guardsmen, had pointed down from the podium at Tom Dewey, the loser of 1944 and 1948, the leader of the Eastern Establishment, the Svengali of the Eisenhower nomination—and the smiling "little man on the wedding cake."

"We followed you before," Dirksen thundered, voicing all the fury and frustration of the Old Guard, "and you took us down the path to defeat. Don't do it to us again!"

After Nixon had been chosen, he recalled in *RN,* he asked Senator John Bricker of Ohio, a pillar of the Old Guard, to make a seconding speech for

*Paul Waltler, Taft's delegate manager, in his letter of August 12, 1988, to the author, said that after a poorly received speech by Eisenhower at his birthplace, Abilene, Kansas, Nixon approached *Taft* to "make a deal" for the vice presidency. Taft rebuffed him, Mr. Waltler wrote. He rejected the idea of Nixon as a "sop" to the Taft conservatives.

him on the convention floor. "Tears filled [Bricker's] eyes. 'Dick,' he said, 'there isn't anybody in the world I would rather make a speech for but after what they have said and done to Bob Taft over the last few months, I just cannot bring myself to do it.' "

Such attitudes ran the other way, too. In his acceptance speech to the convention, Nixon made the obligatory tribute to Taft, setting off an ovation for the defeated candidate that some thought more enthusiastic than the one for Eisenhower had been. Nixon wrote in *RN* that some of the general's "liberal advisers" thought he had deliberately contrived this somewhat embarrassing display, and may have held it against him in the crisis over the supposedly secret fund.

When Eisenhower and Nixon went to the podium for their acceptance speeches, the highly charged atmosphere of the convention barely could be concealed from television viewers—of whom there were not yet all that many—and the radio audience. To a cheering throng of delegates who seemed more enthusiastic than about half of them actually were, Eisenhower proclaimed his crusade—one, in part, to "get out of the governmental offices . . . people who have been weak enough to embrace communism." Nixon already had declared that the most important issue of the campaign would be "destroying the forces of communism at home and abroad."

Following the September *New York Post* story about Nixon's political fund, one of the first big-name Republicans to come out in full support of the vice presidential candidate was Robert Taft—which suggests how sound, if cynical, the Nixon nomination had been. So to throw Nixon overboard—particularly with no illegality or even indiscretion proven—was to risk the renewed alienation of Bob Taft and the Old Guard, not to mention Republican and independent voters, perhaps some Democrats too, to whom Richard Nixon was an anti-Communist hero aptly suited to Eisenhower's "crusade."

Despite the unofficial tapping of Knowland by Adams and Brownell, moreover, a furious intraparty battle might have had to be waged over the choice of a successor. It was not even clear whether that choice legally would be Eisenhower's or that of the Republican National Committee—a Nixon stronghold whose chairman, Arthur Summerfield, was Nixon's most important (almost his only) backer on the Eisenhower train.

Eisenhower chose to remain publicly silent as his train rolled through the midwest. That only fueled press and Republican speculation that he was getting ready to drop Nixon, and allowed both Democratic attacks and press sensationalism to blow the story out of proportion. Steven Mitchell, the Democratic national chairman, for example, was demanding stridently that Nixon be thrown off the ticket to prove that Eisenhower meant what he was saying about morality and ethics in politics.

Those who disliked Nixon anyway, for his pursuit of Alger Hiss, or for his participation in what was widely believed to be the "smear tactics" of HUAC, or for his aggressive campaigns for House and Senate, or for all of the above, saw in the fund charges the opportunity to bring him down. It was an opportunity that seemed especially sweet because he and other Republicans had been so noisily, often unfairly, attacking the "mess in Washington." So there was a receptive audience for the charges against Nixon, and his supporters' detailed explanations of the fund's legality and openness were lost in the uproar; quickly, that uproar caused the political good sense of the men around Eisenhower to succumb to panic.

Nixon himself, as he campaigned with his own entourage in Northern California, at first did not take the matter seriously. He knew there were no irregularities in the fund's administration and that it was neither illegal nor particularly unusual in politics. A few days before the *Post*'s exaggerated headline, he had been asked about the fund by Peter Edson, a respected syndicated columnist. Undisturbed, Nixon readily told Edson to get all the details he wanted from Dana Smith, an attorney in Pasadena, who was the fund trustee; Nixon even gave Smith's phone number to Edson.

On the first day of Nixon's official campaign, as his train moved up the West Coast from a kickoff in Pomona, California, at which even Earl Warren had appeared, word was received that a story about the fund was to appear in the *Los Angeles Mirror.* Assuming this to be Edson's column, Nixon still was unworried but called his traveling party together to review the matter.

Among the group was William Rogers, the affable and levelheaded lawyer who had become Nixon's close friend during and after the Hiss case. Rogers knew nothing about the fund until the session on the train, but after hearing the details he told Nixon that he didn't "see anything to worry about." Murray Chotiner, Nixon's campaign manager and political mentor, thought the matter "ridiculous, a tempest in a teapot." Herbert Klein, in later years a Nixon press secretary, left the train and returned to California headquarters convinced that there was no problem.

Even the appearance on September 18 of the *Post* story, first disclosing the existence of the fund, and definitely not Peter Edson's column, did not trouble Nixon seriously. He thought the *Post* such a partisan Democratic paper—as it then was—that no one would take its charges seriously. But that day, as he whistle-stopped through California's Central Valley, numerous reporters boarded the train to demand a response to the fund story—which was being amplified nationally by the Democrats, by repetition elsewhere in the press and by Eisenhower's failure to make a quick statement of support for his running mate.

A brief press release from the Nixon train, detailing the facts about the fund, went almost unnoticed. "An attack," Chotiner had taught Nixon in his first campaign, "always makes more news than defense." Nixon himself had acted on that precept in all his campaigns. Now he was to see its full implications.

By Friday, September 19, public outcry forced the vice presidential nominee to defend himself publicly. He did so characteristically, by trying to go on the offensive with a familiar and usually effective argument. At one whistle-stop, when heckled about the fund by a group of Young Democrats sent out by Stevenson's Northern California headquarters, Nixon blamed "the Communists and the left-wingers." He'd been warned, he declared, that if he "continued to attack the Communists and crooks *in this government* they would continue to smear me." (Emphasis added.)

No Communist in or out of "this government" (the Truman administration) had had anything to do with the story, which came from California Republicans. In the overheated party politics of 1952, they thought that Nixon had betrayed Governor Earl Warren's presidential candidacy, before and during the national convention, in return for the vice presidential spot on the Eisenhower ticket. They knew about the fund because some had been solicited for contributions; and to receptive reporters, some of them pictured it in the worst light.

The Communist-smear story was persuasive enough to vanquish the hecklers, and Nixon repeated it at other stops that day. But it didn't silence the press and the Democrats, nor satisfy the Eastern Establishment Republicans who had chosen young Senator Nixon—then thirty-nine and just six years a member of Congress—to share the ticket with General Eisenhower. The fund story suddenly made Nixon seem damaged goods and a liability to the great man, possibly threatening his defeat and the demolition of the hopes of his promoters.

A none too strong statement from the general in Kansas City—"the facts will show that Nixon would not compromise with what is right"—and the release by Dana Smith of the list of donors also failed to choke off the story. The attack was now too strong for a merely factual defense or for hopeful statements to blunt. But in the hermetic world of a campaign train, neither Nixon nor Chotiner, the old pro, yet grasped the intensity of the national controversy.

When the train was sidetracked for the night in southern Oregon, however, the full dimensions of the crisis came brutally clear. Word was received that an editorial in the *New York Herald Tribune* (the late, lamented voice of Eastern Establishment Republicans) called for Nixon's resignation from the ticket—just two days after the *Post* story had appeared, *before* he had been allowed to make his case directly to Eisenhower (who had not yet even called his running mate) and without a shred of proof of wrongdoing.

Nixon recognized the editorial as an ultimatum, "a real blockbuster," and took it as perhaps "the view of Eisenhower himself"—at least as representing "the thinking of the people around" the general.

Aroused at last to the political body blow that had been struck him from out of the blue, Nixon spent most of that night debating his course with Chotiner and Rogers. Both were as shaken by the editorial as Nixon himself, but they could not get through to anyone in authority on the Eisenhower train, nor get any direct word about the origins of the *Herald Tribune*'s demand.

With the piety that many Americans came to distrust, Nixon later described himself in *Six Crises* as most concerned, throughout the fund crisis, not to damage Eisenhower's election prospects. No doubt this was calculated hindsight; the loyal and experienced Chotiner probably expressed more nearly the real tenor of the deliberations that night on the train: "If those damned amateurs around Eisenhower just had the sense they were born with, they would recognize that this is a purely political attack."

After the inconclusive conference, Nixon told his wife about the blockbuster *Herald Tribune* editorial and wondered out loud if he should resign. "Much of the fight had gone out of me," he later recalled; but he was bucked up when Mrs. Nixon, "with fire in her eyes," told him that if he withdrew, Eisenhower would lose and "you will destroy yourself."

The vice presidential candidate, distraught but concealing it beneath the iron self-control he usually forced himself to maintain, put in a full campaign day through Oregon on Saturday, September 20, while the hecklers pursued him at every stop and the mob outcry for his scalp rose across the nation—although the *Los Angeles Times*, in its friendly political reporting, did not run the fund story for three days, and then headlined Nixon's defense rather than the charge itself.

Nixon had no such protection elsewhere. On the Eisenhower train, reporters polled themselves and opted, 40 to 2, for a Nixon resignation. (By today's presidential campaign standards this is twice surprising—that there were so few of them, and that they would so unprofessionally involve themselves in a political question.)

Conversing later with the press party, but not allowing direct quotation, Eisenhower insisted that there would be no whitewash. "Of what avail," he asked pointedly, "is it for us to carry on this crusade against this business of what has been going on in Washington if we aren't ourselves as clean as a hound's tooth?"

Attribution of this remark only to "highest authorities" could fool few people and none on the Nixon train—from which at Eugene, Oregon, the candidate had angrily replied to a heckler holding a sign that proclaimed NO MINK COAT FOR NIXON, JUST COLD CASH. "That's absolutely right,"

Nixon shouted, pointing at the sign, "my wife Pat wears a good old Republican cloth coat!"

That night, as they entered the Benson Hotel in Portland, the Nixons were jeered and jostled by a hostile crowd; candidates had no Secret Service protection in those days long before the assassination of Robert Kennedy in 1968. A message to call Sherman Adams awaited. But by then, coming out of his earlier funk, Nixon had made the first of several bold decisions— he would not talk to anyone on the Eisenhower train but the general himself. To deal with anyone at a lower level, he reasoned, would be to lower himself to that level. Chotiner gave the message to Adams.

That done, Nixon again thrashed things out with his advisers—although in view of the way things were going, Rogers recalls, "quite a few of his associates [had] left the train."

The advisory group was joined by James Bassett, Nixon's press secretary, and Representative Pat Hillings, who held Nixon's old House seat. Still they could reach no conclusion and still they had no authoritative word from the presidential candidate. Told for the first time of the "hound's tooth" remark and that reporters were interpreting it as a call for Nixon to prove himself innocent, he felt uncomfortably "like the little boy caught with jam on his face."

Most other reports were discouraging, too. Those on the Eisenhower train were known to be overwhelmingly in favor of a Nixon resignation. Television and radio commentators and newspaper columnists—who often tend to follow each other like sheep—were predicting it. But Hillings could report that many senators and congressmen—more sensibly than the "amateurs around Eisenhower"—wanted Nixon to stay and fight.

Belying his many protestations over the years about his coolness in crisis, Nixon apparently was in bad shape—as anyone might have been. Chotiner recalled that he "was more worried about Dick's state of mind than about the party. He was edgy and irritable." Hillings, opening a door in the hotel suite, saw that "Dick was sitting in a huge leather chair, his arms stretched out, his hands dangling in that characteristic way of his. His brooding face and his posture reminded me of the statue in the Lincoln Memorial in Washington. I knew I was in the presence of total despair. This scene is so deeply etched in my memory that I will never forget it."[2]

Nixon was so hard hit emotionally because he never before had been attacked severely in print. He and some of his admirers have insisted over the years that Nixon's legendary hostility to the press was a reaction against newspaper opposition to his part in the Hiss case. But that is unsupportable; most of the press gave it heavy and ultimately supportive play, painting Nixon in attractive colors. Many reporters covering the affair and HUAC regarded Nixon as their best and most credible source;

and such criticism as he suffered was mostly from predictably "liberal" editorial pages.

In the Voorhis and Douglas campaigns, Nixon had been the beneficiary of a California press almost uniformly in his corner; his opponents had been all but shut out of equal or even adequate coverage. Given Kyle Palmer's attitude and that of the *Los Angeles Times,* Nixon had been *sheltered* from criticism and from reporters' searching inquiry into his affairs. In the fund crisis, despite Palmer's protectionism, Nixon felt for the first time the full force of a questioning press; in the glare of the sensational headlines that resulted, he began to wilt and perspire, as had many a lesser man, and even some better ones who had had to take similar heat.

Nixon believed that some of those who wanted him off the ticket probably wanted to be on it themselves—a thought no doubt stimulated by a sanctimonious telegram from Harold Stassen, urging Nixon's withdrawal. But the Nixon group surely recognized, and the outspoken Chotiner probably said, that the "indecision and delay" Nixon complained of resulted mostly from Eisenhower's unwillingness to squash the story by declaring his faith in Nixon—putting himself on the line for his running mate.

But there seemed no way to force the general's hand; and the Benson Hotel deliberations—interrupted by a speech to a Portland audience that cheered Nixon—went on fruitlessly until 3:00 A.M. The only decision was to explore the possibility of a speech on television to put Nixon's defense directly before the public.

Then Nixon went into seclusion for two more hours. He took with him the advice of Rogers and Hillings to fight for his place on the ticket, and these blunt remarks from the hardheaded Chotiner:

> This is politics. The prize is the White House. The Democrats have attacked you and will continue to attack you because they are afraid to take on Eisenhower. You are the lightning rod. If they weren't taking you on this way, they would be taking you on on something else because they don't know how to get at Eisenhower and they are afraid he is too popular for a frontal assault. If you get off this ticket because Eisenhower forces you off, or if you do so on your own volition, Eisenhower won't have the chance of a snowball in hell to win in November. Your friends and those who supported Taft will never forgive him, and the Democrats will beat him over the head for his lack of judgment in selecting you in the first place.

Armed with such views, Nixon came—in a pattern that was to become familiar—to a second vital decision, taken in solitude. "I did what I always do," he told the journalist Stewart Alsop several years after the episode.

"I considered all the worst alternatives, as cold-bloodedly as I could, and I made an analytical decision—that if I withdrew, Ike would probably lose. So I decided to make the effort to stay on, *if possible with honor.*" (Emphasis added.)[3]

Just what "if possible with honor" means is not clear. Did Nixon intend to stay on the ticket if it could be done without losing his honor? Or did he aim to stay on the ticket in any case and keep his honor if he could? In *Six Crises,* written a year or two after the Alsop interview, Nixon described this decision in significantly different words:

> If I were to resign from the ticket it would be an admission of guilt, Eisenhower might well lose the election, and I would forever afterward be blamed for it. I decided that I had to do everything in my power to stay on the ticket—with honor.

When Nixon wrote later memoirs in the seventies, however, he said only that he had decided "I would stay and fight."

For whatever reasons, Nixon had made a hard decision—the courage of which was not mitigated by the fact that he had set himself on the only course that offered a chance to clear his name and save his career. He could have been in little doubt that Eisenhower was willing to have him resign, perhaps wanted him to—but did not wish to take the heat for *ordering* him off the ticket. So Nixon was taking a decision that defied those who had engineered his nomination and might threaten—if his political judgment proved to be wrong—Eisenhower's election.

Sunday, September 21, had finally brought high-level contact with the East—and it must have shaken any newfound Nixon resolve. Thomas E. Dewey, the two-time loser who had been the major force behind both Eisenhower's and Nixon's nominations in 1952, called first, to say that "all the fellows in New York"—in 1952, a lot of Republican clout—wanted the vice presidential candidate to state his case on television, weigh the response and let that decide his course. If the public registered no more than 60–40 in his favor, he should resign; but if 90–10, he could stay on the ticket.

Putting it that way, Dewey seemed to want Nixon forced off. Ninety percent victories in American politics are not to be expected, and 60 percent exceeds most presidential majorities. Moreover, the whole proposition implied that Nixon *was,* in effect, guilty of wrongdoing—that Eisenhower and "all the fellows in New York" would *believe* he was guilty—unless he could prove himself innocent in the unreliable court of public opinion. Dewey did not help matters either when he reported that seven of the nine people at his dinner table believed Nixon should resign immediately.

After delivering another speech in Portland that Sunday night—canceling would only have increased speculation that he was off the ticket—Nixon received at last the long-awaited call from Eisenhower himself, *three days* after the *Post* story had appeared. But the general was not calling to state his readiness to support his running mate; instead, he repeated Dewey's proposal and added on his own: "Tell them everything there is to tell, everything you can remember since the day you entered public life. Tell them about any money you have ever received."

This was not the finest hour of the hero who had ordered the cross-Channel invasion in 1944—especially considering the dubious record of accepting gifts and preferment that he himself was to compile during his presidency.* Eisenhower knew that a Price Waterhouse audit of the Nixon fund would be in his hands within hours, together with a report from a major law firm on all legal aspects of the matter. No public judgment was needed because Eisenhower soon would have the evidence on which to render his own verdict.

But as Nixon quickly perceived, Eisenhower did not want either to stand behind his ticket mate or to take the onus for demanding his resignation. "You are the one who has to decide what to do," the general blandly decreed—when in fact it was his own indecision, or unwillingness to act, that had allowed the controversy to mushroom into crisis. But Nixon may already have decided that he would stay on the ticket unless Eisenhower specifically called for his resignation. The proposed television speech looked like the inevitable next step.

Would Ike, Nixon asked, support him if such a broadcast satisfied his doubts? With little of the superior political instinct that he was so often to display as president, Eisenhower said he hoped he wouldn't have to make any announcement at all, and in any case would still want to gauge public reaction, which might take three or four days.

At this further evasion, knowing that three or four more days would be an impossible time to let a major political crisis fester in the middle of a campaign, the young and beleaguered vice presidential candidate, his probity in question and his career at stake, sensing himself abandoned by those who had chosen him and to whom he had been impeccably loyal, delivered to the revered five-star general on the other end of the line a stinging political lecture that gradually rose into an eruption of anger.

Eisenhower, Nixon said, should not listen to "some of those people around you who don't know a damn thing about it" (Chotiner's "amateurs" thesis). Then he turned the responsibility squarely back where it belonged:

*Including some of the cattle and equipment on his Gettysburg farm, "Mamie's Cottage" at the Augusta National Golf Club, and other gifts from the wealthy friends with whom he played bridge and golf.

I will get off the ticket if you think my staying on it would be harmful. You let me know and I will get off and I will take the heat, but this thing has got to be decided at the earliest possible time. After the television program, if you think I should stay on or get off, I think you should say so either way.

Then, in language that surely had not been addressed to the majestic Eisenhower since his days in the barracks room, Nixon drove home the point: "There comes a time in matters like these when you have to shit or get off the pot!"

Immediately, as if to soften this lèse-majesté, Nixon added: "The great trouble here is the indecision."[4]

It seems to me impossible not to think better of Richard Nixon, as he was then, than at almost any of the innumerable moments the American public, in one way or another, has had to share with him over the more than forty years of his public life.

It took courage to speak so sharply to an American hero, more particularly to one who held Nixon's fate in his hands; it took a loner's tough fiber to challenge Eisenhower at all. Nixon's understanding of the political realities, moreover, was clear and levelheaded, unlike Ike's. And it was spontaneous, *natural,* that the hardworking young candidate should feel outraged and betrayed. He had a right to feel that way. He had every reason to express his anger. Few incidents in Nixon's career suggest so strongly that he is not—contrary to what is so widely believed—always guarded, calculating, posturing, never acting or reacting genuinely.

On the other hand, the outburst suggests again an angry sense of persecution and alienation seething not far beneath his surface conventionality. The opposition of the privileged Eastern Establishment probably touched Nixon's deep resentment of more fortunate, more "sophisticated" persons that Nixon believed scorned those like himself—those "Franklins," who, in his self-decrying view, disdained others who had had to scratch for everything they had. With his back to the wall, he was showing a gutfighter's instinct to strike back, as well as a readily available (if apt) vulgarity that belied his practiced public piety.

For years, however—as long as he was an active candidate, or might have been—Nixon tried to sugarcoat this conversation, finding excuses for Eisenhower in the general's "inexperience," emphasizing his concern for the general's election and the good of the country, and denying his own profane language. Nixon, his intimates knew, could "swear like a sailor but does it only among friends, mostly when it becomes necessary to open a safety valve on pent-up frustrations and anger"—as it certainly was in his response to Eisenhower that Sunday night in Portland.[5]

Years later, Nixon's cousin Floyd Wildermuth visited in the vice president's office in Washington:

[Dick] closed the door so no one could get in. He just let himself go. All those foul words that I taught him when he was young . . . I think he let them all out. "This is the first chance I've had to relax for a long time" [Nixon said]. I think he was doing it because he . . . needed to unwind.[6]

Stewart Alsop finally asked Vice President Nixon, just before his 1960 presidential campaign, if he had said to the general, that night in 1952, what had not then been publicly reported: "The time comes when you've got to pee or get off the pot." No doubt mindful of his forthcoming campaign and the need for Eisenhower's support, Nixon weaseled; the words, he told Alsop, "may be part of the mythology. . . . I don't remember."[7]

In *Six Crises,* published in 1962 when Nixon was running for governor of California, he records that in the telephone conversation he had told Eisenhower "you've got to fish or cut bait." But by the time he was out of elective office and the general was long dead, Nixon was willing in *RN* to be even more blunt than Alsop had been told. He had told the great man, Nixon wrote in this final version, "There comes a time in matters like this when you've got to shit or get off the pot."

Whatever the exact words, the picture of a defiant Nixon profanely lecturing General Dwight D. Eisenhower on political strategy and necessity seems far more attractive—it's certainly more plausible—than the more unctuous image of selfless propriety he had tried to foster. Ironically enough, in depicting himself as having maintained a proper deference, Nixon had obscured one of his most appealing moments of authority and audacity, and contributed instead to the popular view that he was a devious and calculating political poseur.

Dwight Eisenhower had not commanded the invasion of Europe by chance. He was tough too; and he held to his policy of leaving it to Nixon and the public. That left Nixon no alternative but to go ahead with the television broadcast. Hard telephone bargaining as well as the presidential candidate's endorsement of the idea forced reluctant Republican officials to provide the necessary seventy-five thousand dollars for airtime; and at 1:00 A.M. on Monday, September 22, Nixon announced in Portland that he'd make a national television appearance Tuesday night.

To announce his withdrawal? Reporters were left to guess, and to help build suspense and the audience.

On Monday afternoon, the Nixon party abandoned the campaign train upon which they had embarked so hopefully and flew to Los Angeles, where the national broadcast had to originate—an indication of the primitive television technology of the time. Ever disciplined and hardworking, and putting aside the angry reflection that he "had been deserted by so many I had thought were friends but who had panicked in battle when the first shots were fired," Nixon passed his time on the flight by making notes and plans for what he knew by then would be "the most important speech" of his life.

He noted his "Republican cloth coat" put-down of the heckler at Eugene. Remembering Franklin Roosevelt's devastating use of his "little dog Fala" to torment Republicans in 1944, Nixon decided with a certain malicious humor to turn the tables and refer to his own dog—Checkers. He reluctantly decided also to "lay out for everyone to see my entire personal financial history from the time I entered public life."

This would not be unusual in today's politics; in 1952 it was a sensational thing to do—and politically difficult for Nixon, product as he was of Hannah Nixon's Quaker insistence on maintaining strict privacy in personal matters. He felt strongly that "what we owned and what we owed was our own business and nobody else's," but in another of what he called his "cold-blooded" assessments he concluded that there was no other way to silence the fund charges completely or with such dramatic impact. He may have been right, but this was a decision that was to haunt the rest of his public life.

Nixon reached another conclusion, of equal importance, on that United Airlines flight. Chotiner's teachings and Nixon's instinct required him not just to defend himself but to counterattack. He knew he would have one of the largest audiences of the campaign, and he determined to take advantage of it for more than explaining the fund.

Once in Los Angeles and ensconced in the Ambassador Hotel—a Republican haven owned by G. David Schine—Nixon learned that the instrument for counterattack was at hand; almost providentially, it had been disclosed that Adlai Stevenson had a fund, too.

Stevenson had conceded in response to charges that as governor of Illinois he had administered a cash fund "left over from [his] 1948 campaign for governor, together with subsequent general contributions," to pay supplemental salaries to officials he had appointed to state office. But Stevenson gave few details and declined to answer questions; unlike Nixon's fund, moreover, Stevenson's had not been public or audited.

Nixon spent the rest of Monday and all day Tuesday preparing, in his methodical way, a speech he intended to give without notes. He took several long walks with William Rogers, whose advice was primarily, "Don't be defensive." Nixon's confidence was growing anyway. "If I can't convince people that I'm honest," he told Rogers, "I shouldn't be on the ticket."[8]

But Eisenhower, campaigning in Ohio, found his mail and messages running three to one against Nixon. Hundreds of letters and telegrams, wishing Nixon well or ill, also arrived at the Ambassador. Big-name reporters, who normally wanted no part of a vice presidential campaign, were streaming in from the East—seeking "front-row seats for the hanging," Nixon's press secretary, Jim Bassett, quipped.

That Tuesday, September 23, 1952, Sherman Adams called Chotiner and abruptly demanded to know what Nixon would say that night. But to keep the audience as large and the impact of his speech as great as possible, Nixon had imposed strict secrecy; even his closest associates were not sure of his intent. Adams at first refused to believe that there was no script or that Chotiner did not know the contents of the speech.

"Sherm," Chotiner said, "if you want to know what's going to be said, you do what I'm going to do. You sit in front of the television set and listen." It was, in effect, another defiant Nixon response to Dwight Eisenhower, who also would have to sit and listen.[9]

Telegrams of encouragement arrived that afternoon from many Republicans—most notably from Representative Gerald Ford of Michigan, a former colleague of Nixon's in the House, and Warren Burger, a party leader in Minnesota. In *RN* Nixon specifically recalls their loyalty, which suggests that it may well have influenced his later appointments (Ford became vice president, Burger chief justice.)

But by far the most important message of the day came from "Mr. Chapman"—a pseudonym Thomas E. Dewey, perhaps as a hangover from his days as a criminal investigator, sometimes used on the telephone. "Mr. Chapman" came on the line only an hour before the Nixons were to leave for the NBC studio at the El Capitan Theater; and it is hard not to believe that such timing must have been calculated to throw off Nixon psychologically (although he has never made that charge against Dewey).

"There has just been a meeting of all of Eisenhower's top advisers," Dewey said, "and they have asked me to tell you that it is their opinion that at the conclusion of the broadcast tonight you should submit your resignation to Eisenhower. As you know, I have not shared this point of view, but it is my responsibility to pass this recommendation on to you."

Stunned, Nixon could only ask if that was Eisenhower's opinion. Of course, Dewey said, the advisers wouldn't have asked him to make such a call unless they represented the view of Eisenhower himself—to whom, however, he personally had not spoken.

Nixon, alone in the room where he took the call—and by then about as alone psychologically as a high-level politician could be—once again managed not to buckle; once again he summoned the sheer nerve to stand alone against the Eisenhower entourage and the Eastern Establishment—knowing that *he* was innocent and that *they* cared little about that. And when Dewey asked if he'd do as he was told, Richard Nixon again responded spontaneously and angrily: "Just tell them . . . if they want to find out they'd better listen to the broadcast . . . and tell them I know something about politics too!"

But again, as with his sharp response to Eisenhower, Nixon since has tried to take the edge off this moment. In *Six Crises,* which appeared while Dewey was still a force, if a diminished one, in Republican politics, he contends that the tone of Dewey's voice disclosed that he "did not have his heart in what he had to tell me." This apologia disappears from *RN,* which came long after Dewey's death.

In that later book, moreover, Nixon adds what is not even mentioned in *Six Crises,* that Dewey had offered his own "mind-boggling" idea of how Nixon could "come out of all of it the hero rather than the goat." Nixon should resign from the ticket *and* from the Senate, Dewey suggested, then run in a special election to regain the seat "and vindicate yourself by winning the biggest plurality in history."

"The conversation," Nixon charitably remarks of this scheme, "was becoming unreal." But Dewey's outlandish proposal does not sustain Nixon's earlier plea that "Dewey did not have his heart" in the demand for Nixon's resignation. And it was *after* Dewey's remarkable suggestion that Nixon "exploded" in anger.

The call from "Mr. Chapman" understandably shook Nixon to his roots, however, and robbed him of the final uninterrupted time he needed to get the whole outline of his speech in his head. He reluctantly decided he would have to use his five pages of handwritten notes.

The call left *un*shaken his determination not to withdraw voluntarily, considering the disastrous consequences he foresaw for himself and the ticket if he did. And it settled in his mind—perhaps from sheer resentment at the treatment he was receiving from the Eisenhower camp—what he should ask for in conclusion.

As he had shouted to Dewey, moreover, Richard Nixon really did "know something about politics"—more, at that moment at least, than anyone who was trying to be rid of him.

The show he put on less than an hour later—without a text or cue cards, in an empty theater-studio, with reporters and staff watching monitors in an adjacent room and only Pat Nixon at his side—was, as charged, maudlin and mawkish, and its revelations of ordinarily private personal financial details embarrassed some viewers, who never forgot what they considered a debasing performance. Nixon's voice was hoarse and emotional; he appeared on the verge of breaking down, as he may have been. But it was not only Elmer Bobst, watching in New Jersey, who was moved; so were millions of Americans—some, like Bobst, to tears—including Mamie Eisenhower, watching with the general in Cleveland.

The most famous passage of this speech suggests the tone of most of it—that tone that evoked so much derision from critics but that profoundly

moved so many other Americans—and why it had an impact not unlike
that of a soap-opera deathbed scene, or a Norman Rockwell magazine
cover:

> One other thing I probably should tell you because if I don't they'll
> probably be saying this about me too, we did get something—a
> gift—after the election. A man down in Texas heard Pat on the
> radio mention the fact that our two youngsters would like to have
> a dog. And believe it or not, the day before we left on this cam-
> paign trip we got a message from Union Station in Baltimore
> saying that they had a package for us. We went down to get it. You
> know what it was? It was a little cocker spaniel dog in a crate that
> he sent all the way from Texas. Black and white spotted. And our
> little girl—Tricia, the six-year-old—named it Checkers. And you
> know the kids love that dog and I just want to say this right now,
> that regardless of what they say about it, we're going to keep it.

Such lachrymose appeals to an easily swayed public were not all that
infuriated many in the huge audience—mostly those opposed to Nixon
anyway. So did a certain holier-than-thou tone ("Now what I am going to
do—and incidentally this is unprecedented in the history of American
politics—I am going at this time to give to this television and radio audience a complete financial history . . .") that became a frequent presence
in Nixon speeches.

No doubt that tone owes much to the high moral content of Nixon's
Quaker background and upbringing; and in the case of the quoted comment his disclosures *were* unprecedented. Still, to some, pious rhetoric
from a politician known to be a no-quarter campaigner was bound to be
both infuriating and suspect.

But if in poor-mouthing again about Pat Nixon's "good old Republican
cloth coat" Nixon was hammily emphasizing his lack of affluence, his
impulse had genuine roots in republicanism with a small *r* and dramatized
Nixon's lifelong assertion of his bond to the commonality of the people.
Had not the Franklins, that prestigious men's club at Whittier College,
dressed in black tie for club occasions, while Nixon's Orthogonians wore
suits with open collars?

And when he quoted Lincoln ("The Lord must have loved the common
people because he made so many of them"), the epigram may have been
from the Emancipator at his most glib (and Nixon got it wrong*); but it

*Lincoln actually said, after being told that he was "common-looking": "Common-
looking people are the best in the world; that is the reason the Lord makes so many
of them."

stated an idea that millions of Americans cling to as an article of faith. Nixon always seems to have understood that, perhaps because he was one of them; and his powerfully effective "silent majority" speech on Vietnam nearly twenty years later was in that way clearly foreshadowed by the Checkers speech.

If, moreover, in detailing his finances—backed by the Price Waterhouse audit that cleared him of exploiting the fund for personal use—Nixon was indeed guilty of what critics called "indecent exposure," it was Eisenhower who had instructed him to tell "everything you can remember since the day you entered public life."

Besides, the details did prove more dramatically than anything else could have done that the Nixons did not, as charged in the fatal *New York Post* headline, live in a "style beyond his salary." Nixon had a 1950 Oldsmobile, a $20,000 equity in his Washington residence, a $3,000 equity in a California house where his parents lived, and $4,000 in life insurance. He owed $38,500 on the houses and in other debts. The worst that could be said was that Nixon was better off personally because the financial "burden of staying in politics had been lifted from [his] shoulders by the fund."[10]

But lifting that burden was precisely what the fund was designed to do; that was what he and Dana Smith, the fund's trustee, had said was its purpose; and that was what the audit showed it had been used for. No one has shown that contributors received any special favors, beyond those any constituent might expect. The American political system made it legitimate for a senator's supporters to finance the "burden of staying in politics" for him, so long as it was not done secretly or illegally; to argue otherwise is to say that only wealthy persons should be in public office, or that all political expenses ought to be borne by the public—a proposition the American people have yet to endorse, and certainly had not in 1952.

Nor was Nixon's speech a miscalculation of the American appetite for sentimentality, Horatio Alger stories and self-revelation. Public confession may or may not be good for the soul but, as many a celebrity has demonstrated since, it runs up the ratings.

Nixon's career, perhaps his livelihood, was at risk. More than that, he believed—probably rightly—that if he were forced off the ticket there would be a second risk: "that the ticket would lose, and that I would carry that responsibility for the balance of my life." Not inconsiderable stakes![11]

So if he also was guilty of playing to the public's vulgar tastes, he had correctly divined those tastes, was not responsible for them and had powerful reason to use any weapon at hand. A sentimental appeal, after all, is a weapon from which politicians from Lincoln to Ronald Reagan seldom have shrunk.

At the end of the performance and before the telegrams began to arrive,

Nixon himself was sure that he had failed. In fact, though, he had risen from political death. He had overcome odds no Alger hero could have imagined. But in what should have been his moment of triumph, he could not credit his own achievement. In the essence of his accepted philosophy—that hard work, courage and determination could overcome any obstacle—he could not at that moment really believe.

He threw his note pages to the studio floor and insisted to Pat Nixon and an elated Chotiner—who had watched a monitor and knew a triumph when he saw one—"I was an utter flop."[12]

Soon enough, he knew better. William Rogers pointed out camera crewmen—not a sentimental lot—with tears in their eyes. Word came that the switchboard was lit up "like a Christmas tree." A makeup man told Nixon there had "never been a broadcast like it." Crowds outside the theater waved and cheered.

As Nixon rode back to the Ambassador with Rogers, an Irish setter ran barking beside the car. "At least," Nixon said, conscious now of his victory, "I won the dog vote tonight."

He had won—and lost—far more than he could know. From that time on, he confessed in *RN,* his wife "would hate politics"—his calling, his life—and "dream of the day I would leave it behind." Nor was he himself ever to forget "my surprise and disappointment about those who turned against me overnight when it looked as if I would have to leave the ticket."

Nixon noted in *Six Crises* that a political scientist studying the 1960 election had concluded that he had been defeated by Kennedy because of continuing reaction *against* the Checkers speech. He could only point "cold-bloodedly" to the "hard reality of the alternative. If it hadn't been for that broadcast, I would never have been around to run for the Presidency."

That was the professional speaking, still hoping for office. But Nixon's true feeling was more accurately expressed in *RN,* his memoir. He recalled "how much the agony of the fund crisis had stripped the fun and excitement from campaigning for me." It was to be a long, hard penalty.

But by far the most extraordinary, if not the most remarked, aspect of the Checkers speech was Nixon's deft turning back of his ordeal, squarely onto his tormentors—not just the Democrats but General Eisenhower himself. His means to that end were Stevenson's just-disclosed fund, and the fact that Stevenson's running mate, John Sparkman of Alabama— unlike Richard Nixon—maintained his wife on his Senate payroll.

Fulsomely declaring that he would "condemn" neither "until the facts are in"—classic Nixonian piety but more charity than most of his attackers had extended to him—Nixon shrewdly capitalized on his own predicament and linked them to it:

I would suggest that under the circumstances both Mr. Sparkman and Mr. Stevenson should come before the American people *as I have,* and make a complete statement as to their financial history. If they don't it will be an admission that they have something to hide. . . . Because, remember, *a man who's to be President* and a man who's to be vice president must have the confidence of all the people. [Emphasis added.]

Robert Humphreys, an assistant to Chairman Summerfield of the Republican National Committee, was with the small Eisenhower party watching on television from a private room in a Cleveland auditorium, where a crowd waited for the general to speak. When Nixon called on "a man who's to be President" to make full financial disclosure, Humphreys saw the general jab a pencil point into a yellow legal pad on which he was taking notes; his face flushed with anger. Eisenhower had recognized, if the public didn't, that this exquisitely crafted passage—the more remarkable because Nixon was speaking only from notes—was aimed not just at Stevenson and Sparkman but at *him.* *

Eisenhower did have, if not "something to hide," something he had no wish to discuss—the special tax decision that declared the $635,000 he had been paid for his book, *Crusade in Europe,* to be subject to capital gains rather than ordinary income tax. He had paid only a $158,750 tax, and had become a wealthy man (by 1952 standards) as a consequence.[13] Eisenhower had not been generous, moreover, in his charitable contributions, which full disclosure would reveal.[14]

Knowing about the tax case, Nixon had forced the man who had forced *him* into his ordeal of "indecent exposure" to undergo it himself, at least partially. Eisenhower resisted mightily and angrily, but ultimately he, Stevenson and Sparkman had to make at least rudimentary disclosure— Eisenhower's tax returns for the past ten years were released—though none so fully or dramatically as had been forced upon Richard Nixon by his own political sponsors.

But the direct challenge to Eisenhower, from a man for whom the general had been willing to issue a ticket for oblivion, was the real measure of Nixon's response. And before the Checkers speech was over, he did it again. He said he was submitting the decision about his future to the public and the Republican National Committee—*not,* as Dewey had directed, a resignation to Eisenhower. Wire and write the national committee, Nixon

*William Rogers, for one, disagrees with this interpretation of Nixon's remarks. In a personal interview with the author on September 13, 1986, he recalled that Nixon was angrier at those around Eisenhower—he specified Dewey, Adams, Brownell and Lucius Clay—than at the general himself.

told the vast television audience, and he'd abide by its decision—not necessarily, it was implicit, by Eisenhower's.

Again, at this, Ike jabbed his pencil into the tablet, understanding this second challenge, too. Nixon was trying to take the decision on his fate out of the hands of the presidential candidate and "the fellows in New York" and give it to the party regulars, always more sympathetic to another regular like Dick Nixon than to an outsider like the general—and, in fact, mostly on record in public statements for retaining Nixon on the ticket.

So Eisenhower knew that his running mate was not giving up without a fight. Neither, of course, was a five-star general going to yield to that kind of pressure. Eisenhower at once wired Nixon (though news reports of the telegram's substance reached Nixon before the message itself):

> WHILE TECHNICALLY NO DECISION RESTS WITH ME, YOU AND I KNOW THE REALITIES OF THE SITUATION REQUIRE A PRONOUNCEMENT WHICH THE PUBLIC CONSIDERS DECISIVE. MY PERSONAL DECISION IS GOING TO BE BASED ON PERSONAL CONCLUSIONS. I WOULD MOST APPRECIATE IT IF YOU CAN FLY TO SEE ME AT ONCE. TOMORROW EVENING I WILL BE AT WHEELING, W. VA.

Something obviously had happened to the general's hope that he might not have to make any statement on Nixon's future. Nixon, as adept at reading between the lines as Eisenhower had been at hearing between them, realized that the general was asserting his authority at last and summoning Nixon to judgment—as Chotiner put it—"like a little boy to be taken to the woodshed."

That was too much for an exhausted and distraught Nixon: "I really blew my stack." To Chotiner, he cried in despair: "What more can he possibly want of me?" Then he dictated a telegram of resignation—to the Republican National Committee, *not* to Eisenhower.

Chotiner stopped the telegram and Nixon said later he "never had any serious intention of withdrawing." By then, anyway, a tidal wave of public approval of the Checkers speech had begun—eventually upward of two million telegrams, rolling down on the Eisenhower and Nixon camps and the national committee.[15]

Chotiner also persuaded Nixon to go to Missoula, Montana, to resume campaigning, rather than respond tamely to Eisenhower's summons—unless, Chotiner boldly told Chairman Summerfield, Nixon faced no further inquiry and could be sure of support from the top of the ticket when and if he reached Wheeling.

Soon Eisenhower, contemplating that flood of messages, and remembering the Cleveland audience he had addressed while it was still hoarse and weeping from the emotional impact of the Checkers speech, had little choice but to give the demanded assurances—leaving Nixon, who had continued his scheduled campaign, no choice but to go tamely to Wheeling to accept the general's gracious endorsement.

There, Eisenhower—perhaps in a subtle effort to reestablish himself as commander in chief—made his famous proclamation: "You're my boy!"

But Nixon was not, nor after the Checkers speech ever really would be. No matter how he tried to cover it over with labored excuses for Eisenhower's failure to support him in the fund crisis, Nixon never forgot that failure. In the depths of the Watergate crisis twenty years later, Nixon was to remark bitterly to John Mitchell (an important clue to the sources of his fatal decision to engage in cover-up and stonewalling): "That's what Eisenhower—that's all he cared about. He only cared about—Christ, 'be sure he was clean.' Both in the Fund thing and the Adams thing. But I don't look at it that way. . . . We're going to protect our people, if we can."[16]

An Eisenhower biographer, Stephen Ambrose, calls the general's behavior in the fund crisis "patient, calculated, clear-headed." And in the end, says Ambrose, Eisenhower "turned apparent disaster into stunning triumph."[17]

The only real credit the general deserves—which is substantial—is for not condemning Nixon out of hand. Even Eisenhower's trusted brother Milton, close advisers like Adams and Harold Stassen, and his personal friends—such as William Robinson, who had written the *Herald Tribune* editorial, and the banker Clifford Roberts—had urged Nixon's quick dismissal from the ticket. But Eisenhower was not to be stampeded; and Sherman Adams stated in *Firsthand Report* that the general was deeply impressed with the Checkers speech.

There was no reason, on the other hand, for him to have let the crisis drag on from Thursday until Sunday night before talking personally to Nixon—much less to let it continue two days more. Nixon's early denials of wrongdoing had not satisfied the public, predictably enough, but the general could have satisfied himself about the fund by a direct talk with Dana Smith, the trustee; and *Eisenhower's* word, plus an accounting from Smith, to be backed up by the Price Waterhouse audit, would have squelched the story far more quickly.

Nor was there need for Eisenhower, in the Sunday-night phone call, to foist the responsibility for decision on Nixon, while himself maintaining the right to act later on if he chose; or for the general to force Nixon to plead for his political life in what became the Checkers speech—the performance that, if anything did, ultimately produced "stunning triumph."

Similarly, Eisenhower later was to hold back from condemning Senator Joseph McCarthy directly—a tactic Nixon understood (the president was maintaining, he wrote, "the unique personal goodwill that enabled Eisenhower to lead his party even while representing only its minority wing") but did not particularly admire. In *RN* he pictures Eisenhower several times as "away on a golfing vacation" or practicing "chip shots on the South Lawn" when important decisions concerning McCarthy had to be made; and he states specifically that "Eisenhower himself had purposely avoided . . . determining the Administration's policy on McCarthy."

Eisenhower also shrank from forcing the resignation of Sherman Adams when the chief of staff became a political liability. Instead, he passed to Nixon and others the dirty work of telling Adams that he had to resign.

In none of these cases does Eisenhower's behavior seem personally admirable; but much of his great public stature—hence his power as president—was built on his instinctive avoidance of personal involvement in divisive political battles. Such involvements would have alienated one side or another, or both, and tarred him with the struggle and muck of combat. Such involvements could have pulled him off the above-the-battle pinnacle from which Americans like to think their presidents should preside nonpolitically over the public interest.

As in the case of Eisenhower and McCarthy, Nixon had mixed feelings—understanding yet criticizing—about this approach. He nowhere expresses explicit disapproval but quotes in *RN* the bitter remark of Eisenhower's wartime chief of staff, Walter Bedell Smith:

> I was just Ike's prat boy. Ike always had to have a prat boy, someone who'd do the dirty work for him. He always had to have someone else who could do the firing, or the reprimanding, or give any orders which he knew people would find unpleasant to carry out. Ike always has to be the nice guy. That's the way it is in the White House, and the way it will always be in any kind of an organization that Ike runs.

Two decades later, Ronald Reagan's "Teflon presidency" yielded him much the same lofty public standing that Eisenhower enjoyed, for less reason. Despite Nixon's evidently mixed feelings, he too sometimes tried as president to keep an above-the-battle stance—without much success, as will be seen.

In sharp contrast, President Jimmy Carter, incautiously mixing personally but too seldom successfully or decisively into every aspect and controversy of his administration, never while in office acquired the prestige and respect that are at the root of presidential power. What may be decent and honorable personal behavior is not necessarily sound politics for a president or a candidate—or necessarily in the underlying national interest. That's one good reason why the most decent of men might not be the best of presidents.

In the Nixon fund crisis, Eisenhower let his running mate take the heat, pay the price—and probably save the ticket. In return, the general certainly seethed over the "pot" remark, since lesser mortals are not supposed to speak that way to five-star generals. More important, Nixon's twin challenges, so buried in the Checkers speech that the public scarcely noticed them, angered Eisenhower at the time, and more so when he was forced to make public his tax returns; it's doubtful if as proud and commanding a man as the conqueror of Europe could ever forgive them. It probably never will be known to what extent the episode may have contributed to the "dump Nixon" movement that Eisenhower briefly countenanced in 1956, or to his seeming reluctance to give Nixon wholehearted support in 1960 (see chapters 5 and 6).

For his part, Nixon was to remain for nearly two more decades politically dependent on the great general he had so brashly defied. Eisenhower could have dumped him in 1956, ruined him in 1960 and badly hurt him in 1968, when Nixon pressed him hard for an endorsement.[18]

Why, therefore, did Nixon do what he did? The "pot" challenge may have been made only in the heat of the moment; but the words that twice caused Eisenhower to stab that pencil into his notepad were as calculated as Nixon's decision to cling to his place on the ticket "if possible with honor."

One reason surely was Murray Chotiner's political teaching that attack was always preferable to defense, and that an attack from someone else demanded counterattack. In the highly charged atmosphere of the fund crisis, Nixon and his aides came to see the Eisenhower camp as an opponent nearly as hostile as the Democrats, and far more dangerous.[19]

Nixon's political sense was backed strongly by personal instinct. He had been reared by a cantankerous and argumentative father, an Irishman by birth, a Quaker only by conversion; he had found his greatest youthful pleasures and triumphs in the cut-and-thrust of the college debate team he captained; and as he later remarked, he believed in "hitting back. . . . When somebody launches an attack, your instinct is to strike back. . . . [I]f you're always on the defensive, you always lose in the end." It was instinctive for Dick Nixon to strike back—even at Eisenhower himself.[20]

Later, carrying the Eisenhower-Nixon reelection campaign in 1956, for example, Nixon at first restrained himself, under the president's instructions, to "serious, low-keyed speeches without any of the tough campaign rhetoric [the press and Republican audiences] looked forward to hearing" from him. But Nixon was restive under Adlai Stevenon's "shrill and irresponsible" attacks, and at 5:30 A.M. in Eugene, Oregon—where four years earlier he had first mentioned Pat Nixon's "good old Republican cloth coat"—he got out of bed to work up some tough Nixonesque responses to Stevenson.

"Suddenly," he remembered in *RN,* "I felt as if a great weight had been lifted from me. I had not realized how frustrating it had been to suppress the normal partisan instincts and campaign with one arm tied behind my back. . . . I went over to the grand piano in one corner of the suite and began playing Brahms's Rhapsody in G."

If just the thought of counterattacking Stevenson could make Nixon feel so much better, his actual challenge to Eisenhower—coming at the lowest point of his career, when his self-esteem had been battered and his future was at stake—must have produced a positive elation. It was, at the least, necessary to his sense of himself.

Very likely the old Orthogonian in Nixon was subliminally at work. Men like Robinson, Roberts, Tom Dewey, Lucius Clay, perhaps even Eisenhower himself—not the Kansas or the army Eisenhower but the postwar Eisenhower—would have seemed, to Nixon, all too much like Franklins: the Establishment. Nixon's sense of himself as a self-made man, and some hidden form of the class sense that had led him into the Orthogonians might well have influenced his decision to force Eisenhower, and by extension Eisenhower's Establishment friends, to prove themselves, too, as clean as a hound's tooth. And although he was speaking of another time and place, he might have been describing the Eisenhower and Nixon trains when he told Alsop: "They were the haves, and we were the have-nots, see?"

Nixon's challenges to a man who had so much control over his destiny nevertheless may seem quixotic; and Nixon paid a high price over the years for his temerity. If so, however, the view that Nixon is a calculating trickster who acts only in his own self-interest seems to me badly undercut; if in some of the most crucial moments of the fund crisis, his actions were more instinctive than devised, and if at others he was "cold-blooded" and analytical, as advertised, the contradictions within him seem only the more evident.

People who watched the Checkers speech on television—and not a few who didn't—still argue about it, more than thirty-five years later. But one thing seems unarguable: considered, as it should be, entirely as a political exercise, Richard Nixon's performance that night was an American masterpiece—American in conception and American in its understanding of those to whom it was addressed. It saved Nixon's place on the ticket, perhaps saved that ticket itself, perhaps rescued two of the most remarkable American political careers—Eisenhower's as well as Nixon's—and thus echoed far into the future of the nation, beyond the lifetime of either principal.

The Scripps-Howard columnist Robert Ruark evaluated the speech at the time more shrewdly than many did:

> Dick Nixon stripped himself naked for all the world to see, and
> he brought the missus and the kids and the dog and his war record

into the act. . . . The sophisticates . . . sneer [but] this came closer to humanizing the Republican party than anything that has happened in my memory. . . . Tuesday night the nation saw a little man, squirming his way out of a dilemma, and laying bare his most-private hopes, fears and liabilities. This time the common man was a Republican for a change. . . . Dick Nixon . . . has suddenly placed the burden of old-style Republican aloofness on the Democrats.

The episode in one major respect was seminal for Nixon. He was, he wrote in *RN,* "bitterly disillusioned by the performance of the press. I regarded what had been done to me as character assassination, and the experience permanently and powerfully affected my attitude toward the press in particular and the news media in general." Nor did Nixon ever forget what he regarded as the double standard followed by reporters in their severe treatment of his political fund, but their lax coverage of Stevenson's.

Years after the Checkers speech, again battling for his political life in the ruins of Watergate, Nixon was to complain again and again about what he saw as the double standard of the press in its view of him and of earlier presidents—particularly Kennedy, that most obvious of Franklins. Nixon repeatedly suggested that he was the victim of "character assassination" by the press. The bitter memory of the fund crisis may have given all this a certain validity; but Nixon seemed to have no understanding that his own use of the press for what *others* saw as character assassination in the Voorhis and Douglas campaigns, and in 1952 and 1954, might have come back to haunt him. Richard Nixon's career is proof enough that he who lives by the press can die by the press.

The Checkers speech made Nixon a formidable national figure; if after that remarkable performance Eisenhower had little choice but to keep him on the ticket, the general also had to remember from then on, and he was to be forcibly reminded in 1956, that Richard Nixon had his own following, his own place in the political world.

It's strange and ironic, perhaps even sad, therefore—but typical of Richard Nixon's contradictory place in American life—that the Checkers speech has not passed into public memory as the political masterstroke it was, or at least as a moment of courageous personal achievement, when a young senator—abandoned, distraught, but shrewdly fighting back—won something more than a moral victory over the most imposing American of the day, not to mention the Eastern Establishment.

Instead, the speech has become legendary as a sort of comic and demeaning public striptease that cast Nixon forever as a vulgar political trickster who would disclose the most intimate private details and stoop even to exploiting his wife and his children's dog to grub votes. After watching the speech in his Washington living room, Walter Lippmann told a guest, John Miller of *The Times* of London, "That must be the most demeaning experience my country has ever had to bear."[21]

With almost equal disdain for the more complex story, Nixon's ardent admirers recall an American classic—the deeply moving recitation of a poor boy's rise to fame through hard work and high ideals (where but America could it happen?), his triumph over a vicious attack, his love of family and dog and his sacrificial devotion to a worthy cause: "And re-member, folks," he had concluded on a seemingly selfless note, "Eisen-hower is a great man. Folks, he is a great man, and a vote for Eisenhower is a vote for what is good for America."

On the morning after the Checkers speech, in the hotel coffee shop at Missoula, the waitresses "damn near fainted" when they saw Nixon come in—not because he was the vice presidential candidate but because they'd seen him on television the night before. The new medium already was creating the kind of instant celebrity that was to transform journalism and politics in America. And already, just six years into his political career, television had tagged and filed Richard Nixon in the public mind in ways good and bad that he was never quite to escape.[22]

With only one day's rest following the Wheeling meeting, Nixon re-turned to campaigning at Ogden, Utah—leaving his train for a chartered airliner, a move that symbolized the upturns in his own career and in the Eisenhower-Nixon campaign, as well as the coming abandonment of whis-tle-stopping. From then until election day, Nixon was constantly on the move, constantly on the attack.

The new celebrity television had created began to draw crowds unprece-dented for a vice presidential candidate, some as big as 20,000. Nixon was making as many as a dozen speeches a day. In *RN* he summed it all up statistically: 46,000 miles of travel by train and plane, 214 cities visited, 92 speeches, 143 whistle-stops. Another national television appearance on October 13, this one regularly scheduled, compounded his fame; in it he recounted in detail the Hiss-Chambers episode, exaggerating his own part and causing the *Washington Post*—a severe Nixon critic—to accuse him of trying to "make the nation's flesh creep."[23]

The campaign featured Eisenhower mostly on the high road and Nixon relentlessly pursuing what in reporters' shorthand was called "K-1, C-3"— Korea, communism, corruption and controls. He continued to assert that all Communists had not yet been rooted out of the Truman administration, that only Republicans could cleanse the government of the infestation. As if forgetting his concern about "character assassination," he tuned his attacks on Adlai Stevenson to a piercing pitch, terming Stevenson, for example, in a speech at Amarillo on September 26, "Sidesaddle Adlai"—

perhaps a hint at suspicions the Democratic candidate's bachelor status had aroused—"and like all sidesaddle riders his feet hang well out to the left."

Stevenson's deposition as a character witness for Hiss—whom, by then, Nixon had elevated into "the arch-traitor of our generation"—disqualified the Democratic candidate, Nixon contended, for public trust. In fact, though, Stevenson had said only the truth, that when he knew Hiss in various government posts Hiss's reputation had been good.

But Nixon went on to call Stevenson "a weakling, a waster and a small-caliber Truman . . . Adlai the appeaser" with a "Ph.D. from Dean Acheson's College of Cowardly Communist Containment." He did not omit the characteristic touch of sanctimony: "There is no question in my mind as to the loyalty of Mr. Stevenson." Whether Nixon left the question in the minds of his listeners may well be asked.

Acheson, as Truman's secretary of state, came to be another frequent Nixon target—although Acheson was the major architect of the Truman Doctrine and the Marshall Plan, the defense of which was a major reason Eisenhower had consented to run, and in support of which Nixon had risked his House seat in a conservative district in the 1948 election.

Now Nixon credited Acheson as the architect of "striped-pants confusion." Not only had Acheson's policies "lost" China and "invited" the war in Korea, Nixon proclaimed; but "Mr. Truman, Dean Acheson and other Administration officials for political reasons covered up Communist conspiracy and attempted to halt its exposure." Thus, Nixon trumpeted, "The word of Truman, Acheson, as well as that of Acheson's former assistant, Adlai Stevenson, gives the American people no hope for safety at home from the sinister threat of Communism."

In *RN,* Nixon conceded that Acheson's "clipped moustache, his British tweeds, and his haughty manner made him the perfect foil for my attacks on the snobbish kind of foreign service personality and mentality," a type that Nixon in the late seventies still was claiming "had been taken in hook, line and sinker by the Communists."

But Nixon also confessed that when *he* became president, Acheson served as "one of my most valued and trusted unofficial advisers. . . . [T]oday I regret the intensity of those attacks." In fact, neither the Hiss case nor Acheson's moustache made him less anti-Communist than Richard Nixon, then or later. Nixon might have been, he wrote, "unconsciously overreacting to the attacks made against me during and after the fund crisis."

Nixon stopped short, even in the heat of the "battle," of the depths to which Joe McCarthy by then was descending. But he came close on October 27 when, in a speech at Texarkana, he charged that Truman and Stevenson were "traitors to the high principles" of the Democratic party.

Truman, Stevenson and numerous press commentators heard the word "traitors" loud and clear and were not disposed to believe that Nixon had meant for the public to hear anything else—even if he had not literally called the two Democrats traitors to their country.

Still, Nixon's newfound celebrity did not provide the high point of the campaign nor did his attacks mark the low. Eisenhower gets credit for both. His failure to defend his great benefactor, General George C. Marshall, from McCarthy's charges of disloyalty—particularly his deletion of a defense of Marshall from a speech in Wisconsin, on McCarthy's turf and in his presence—was the least admirable moment of the campaign and perhaps of Eisenhower's career (see chapter 5).

On the other hand, the general's pledge on October 24 that he would go personally to Korea if he was elected provided the indisputable high— perhaps turning—point of the campaign. American voters clearly wanted to be out of a war few still believed in or understood, and what seemed to be the personal assurances of the great World War II commander broke open what until then had appeared to be a reasonably close election. Eisenhower had done little more than promise to take a look for himself, but that was enough to remind the nation of his recent triumph and to hold out the promise of another.

On November 4, the Eisenhower-Nixon ticket carried thirty-nine states, 55.1 percent of the popular vote, and 442 electoral votes—a little bit less than a landslide, perhaps, but an entirely conclusive result for a party returning to power after twenty years of Democratic presidents. Nixon was not responsible for the victory; that honor could not be denied the war hero at the head of the ticket. But Nixon had played his assigned part vigorously.

Four months earlier, as the general's inner circle at the convention had debated the vice presidential choice and Nixon argued with himself and his wife whether to accept it if it should be offered to him, Murray Chotiner had given him the advice of a hardened political professional: "Dick, there comes a time when you have to go up or go out."

Nixon had listened well. Now, in the national arena, at age thirty-nine a hardened professional himself, Richard Nixon would have to confront the larger truth of Chotiner's dictum.

4

★

Master and Student

★

If in order to avoid further communistic expansion in Asia and particularly in Indochina
. . . we must take the risk now by putting
American boys in . . . I personally would
support such a decision.

—Vice President Nixon, 1954

On Friday, February 21, 1947, Undersecretary of State Acheson received
from the British embassy notice that an important message was to be
delivered. The right-wing Greek government that Britain had been supporting was in dire straits; its repressive actions had caused a number of
resistance groups, the most powerful of which was the Communist-led
Popular Army of Liberation, to take to guerrilla warfare, threatening the
government's existence.

Arms for the guerrillas were coming in from Yugoslavia, Bulgaria and
Albania. On February 3, Britain—its economy still lagging from wartime
destruction and dislocations and newly disrupted by the terrible European
winter of 1946–1947—had had to announce the withdrawal of half its
forces from Greece, although those forces were the main prop of the Greek
government.

That same Friday, February 21, when Acheson awaited the British note,
Prime Minister Attlee's government had published a gloomy 1947 economic survey and forecast, disclosing a 1946 balance of payments deficit
of £450 million—"the most disturbing statement," said *The Times* of
London apocalyptically, "ever made by a British government."

Acheson, moreover, had received earlier that day a warning from American representatives in Greece that without additional assistance the Greek

government soon would be overthrown "and a totalitarian regime of the extreme left will come into power." This might result eventually in "the loss of the whole Near and Middle East and Northern Africa," Acheson was told, in what might well have been a model for the numerous dire warnings that were to pour into Washington in years to come.

So when the British embassy delivered that afternoon not one but two notes to Loy Henderson, then the director of the State Department's Office of Near Eastern and African Affairs (with responsibility for Greece), neither he nor Acheson could have been much surprised at their content. In one they found that the Attlee government considered it "impossible to grant further financial assistance to Greece"; in the other, they learned that it could not even "contemplate . . . making any further credits available to Turkey." Not surprising, but profoundly dismaying; an Acheson memo then told Secretary of State George Marshall in an uncharacteristically clumsy sentence: "This puts up the most major decision with which we have been faced since the war."

The British had proposed, in short, that the U.S. assume the burden of assistance—estimated at an immediate $240 to $280 million—for Greece, plus funds to help Turkey, the stronger of the two governments, modernize and maintain the armed forces needed to withstand Soviet pressures.

The new Republican majorities of the Eightieth Congress—tightfisted, near-isolationist and somewhat vengeful after fourteen years of Democratic ascendancy—were in no mood, however, to assist faraway countries with huge sums of taxpayers' dollars. Already the House, of which Richard Nixon had been a member for just over a month, had passed a resolution favoring a $6 billion *reduction,* including a cut in foreign assistance funds, in the Truman administration's budget.

Even if something for Greece and Turkey could be wheedled out of Capitol Hill, Acheson's memo to Marshall reflected the belief in the State Department that Britain's default posed a threat to American interests of far greater extent than the plight of two middle-rank Mediterranean governments. After a week of study, consultation and planning, Truman summoned congressional leaders to the White House—not to ask their advice but, in what was to become the postwar presidential pattern, to tell them what he already had decided: to aid Greece and Turkey. *Then* he asked their help with the necessary legislation and the $400 million he would request.

The prestigious but low-keyed Marshall made the administration's case: a Communist Greece under Soviet control, he said, would leave Turkey surrounded and possibly extend Soviet domination to the borders of India. That could lead to a series of crises, which ultimately might bring Europe and Asia also under Soviet sway.

This was strong medicine. But whatever was believed in the State Department in 1947, the Soviet Union did *not* intervene in Greece nor actively support the Communist insurgency there; as late as 1948, in fact, Stalin advised the Yugoslav government to put an end to the Greek uprising, lest it provoke an open confrontation with the West. In 1956, Winston Churchill wrote to President Eisenhower:

> Stalin always kept his word with me. I remember particularly saying to him . . . "You keep Rumania and Bulgaria in your sphere of influence, but let me have Greece." To this bargain he scrupulously adhered during months of fighting with the Greek Communists.[1]

When the Truman administration decided to intervene in Greece, however, it was the "Soviet threat" that was emphasized. Even so, stone-faced Republican congressional leaders appeared unimpressed with Marshall's dry analysis. Why, they wanted to know, should the U.S. "pull British chestnuts out of the fire"? Listening to the usually persuasive Marshall, Dean Acheson also was unimpressed—and alarmed.

"In desperation," he wrote in his memoir, *Present at the Creation*, "I whispered to [Marshall] a request to speak." Acheson's close personal friend, Wallace Carroll, later said that the undersecretary actually whispered: "Is this a private fight or can anyone get into it?"[2]

Marshall acquiesced, Acheson took the floor and passionately declared what was to be the enduring American attitude toward the Cold War, a doomsday view familiar now but stunning then: Soviet communism was seeking dominance of three continents, the encirclement of Western Europe—in effect, *world* domination.

"Not since Rome and Carthage has there been such a polarization of power on this earth," Acheson insisted. The Soviet Union and the U.S. stood at opposite poles of power and intent. Their struggle would be difficult, the outcome a long time off. But the U.S. alone had the power to thwart the Soviet drive for Communist dominion over two thirds of the globe, three quarters of the world's population. The place to begin to fight back was in Greece and Turkey.

Senator Arthur Vandenberg of Michigan, the chairman of the Foreign Relations Committee, quickly responded for the Republican leaders, who no longer looked bored: "Mister President, if you will say that to the Congress and the country, I will support you and I believe that most of the members will do the same."

This was a moment the importance of which was far greater than merely finding the key to Republican and congressional support for one aid program. Acheson had struck a note that for most of the rest of the twentieth century would ring through the American consciousness: the necessity for the U.S. to stop communism and the Soviet Union—whether either or both has not always been clear—from taking over the world. That idea was to become so nearly an article of American faith that in the following four decades few political leaders dared to dispute it; most politicians *proclaimed* it, often and loudly, reinforcing an idea that became an orthodoxy. Richard Nixon, for one, built his political career on it.

Acheson sounded a note tuned not only to the circumstances of the time but exactly to the American psyche. Whatever its other deficiencies, the U.S. is a nation not easily moved, in international affairs, by arguments of narrow self-interest or advantage. Americans, from John Winthrop to Ronald Reagan, have seen their country as "a city on a hill," a beacon to mankind, "the land of the free and the home of the brave," especially favored by God as both example to other peoples and as refuge from less exceptional societies. So seeing themselves, and endlessly encouraged by their leaders to do so, Americans have not wanted to fight wars merely to obtain commercial advantage, new territory or dominance over others— purposes beneath their view of themselves.

To get public support, American leaders have had to portray most American wars as idealistic, in keeping with American self-regard. The land-grabbing wars with Mexico and Spain had to be promoted as extensions of democracy to oppressed peoples; Woodrow Wilson declared the almost pointless American part in World War I a struggle to make the world "safe for democracy"; and FDR had to maneuver carefully to make Americans face up even to World War II, until the Japanese attack on Pearl Harbor erased the problem of motivation.

In 1947, Americans—a people who could rationalize the extermination of the Indians and the expropriation of their lands as necessary, if "civilization" was to be brought to areas once ruled by "savages"—were not being asked to enter a shooting war. But if meeting the Soviet threat was to be pictured as the cold equivalent of a hot war, Americans needed again to be given reasons beyond raw self-interest or softheaded charity. Acheson's impassioned speech to the Republican leaders provided the necessary messianic call, as Vandenberg quickly realized.

Acheson was not being cynical; a few days earlier he had told the journalist Louis Fisher that "the British are pulling out everywhere and if we don't go in the Russians will." And George Kennan's "long telegram" from Moscow (which was to be expanded and published in July 1947 by *Foreign Affairs* as "The Sources of Soviet Conduct," by "X") already had inspired the theme and tone of the overall American response: "containment" of Soviet military and political expansionism.

It remained only for Truman, under Acheson's skillful bureaucratic prodding, to propagate the message to the public—its real target. On

March 12, before a joint session of Congress, the president proposed the Greek-Turkish aid program, but went well beyond that specific response to the larger point:

> We shall not realize our objectives unless we are willing to help free peoples to maintain their free institutions and their national integrity against aggressive movements that seek to impose upon them totalitarian regimes. This is no more than a frank recognition that totalitarian regimes imposed upon free peoples, by direct or indirect aggression, undermine the foundations of international peace and hence the security of the United States.

Truman made it plain that he meant *Communist* totalitarianism. Then he drove home the message: "I believe it *must be the policy* of the United States to support free peoples who are resisting attempted subjugation by armed minorities or by outside pressures." (Emphasis added.)

This Truman Doctrine recognized the deficiencies of the rightist Greek government. But that government was anti-Communist, which in the context of the Truman Doctrine meant that it represented a "free people"—whatever the reality. More than forty years later, the U.S. remains willing to aid almost any professed anti-Communist government (South Korea, El Salvador) or movement (Jonas Savimbi's rebels in Angola) without much regard to its political practices.

Wise George Marshall, who was on his way to conferences in Moscow while the president's speech was being crafted by an interdepartmental group (chaired, of course, by Acheson), was sent a draft and replied that he thought it too broadly anti-Communist. George Kennan offered the same objection. So did George Elsey, Truman's preferred speech writer.

As Marshall was informed, however, the president was persuaded that Congress would not approve the Greek-Turkish aid program without a powerful emphasis on the worldwide Communist threat. And as Clark Clifford, Truman's astute White House aide, put it to Elsey, "we wanted to send a signal to Stalin."

When Truman spoke from the rostrum of the House of Representatives that March 12, three future presidents—Representatives John F. Kennedy and Lyndon B. Johnson, Democrats, and Richard M. Nixon, Republican—were in his audience. Truman's speech, Vandenberg said afterward, was "almost like a presidential declaration of war." And so the American people, Nixon among them, heard it—as a summons to arms against Communist totalitarianism and conquest.

The call had been sounded, the note of high American idealism properly struck. Freedom had been challenged to oppose Tyranny, and not for decades—not even after fifty thousand Americans died in Vietnam in futile pursuit of the Truman Doctrine as restated by those three young congress-men who went on to the White House—would the message be effectively questioned as fundamental American policy, much less laid aside.

As late as 1986, President Reagan could still wring from a reluctant and only half-persuaded Congress $100 million for a band of Nicaraguan "con-tras" organized by the CIA, on grounds that they were "freedom fighters" who not only sought to deliver their country from a Communist dictator-ship but were the U.S.'s first line of defense against a threatened Soviet military base in Central America.

By then, Reagan had even broadened the doctrine; he proclaimed Amer-ican support not just for anti-Communist governments resisting takeovers, but for anti-Communist political movements (like those of the contras and of Savimbi in Angola) that were seeking to *overthrow* established Commu-nist governments.

Looking back from the seventies, George Kennan testified that "the image of a Stalinist Russia, poised and yearning to attack the West . . . was largely a product of the Western imagination." But the Soviet threat did not seem exaggerated in 1947, either to the Truman administration or to the American people.

That threat seemed manifest when in late 1946 the Soviets rejected what most Americans took to be the idealistic Baruch Plan, an administration proposal for the international control of atomic energy—including the most destructive weapons yet devised by destructive men. Unfortunately, the Baruch Plan would have prevented the Soviet Union from developing its own atomic program; it permitted the U.S., however, to maintain its *existing* atomic stockpile (and thus its monopoly on the weapon) for a number of years. Even when international control came fully into effect, the U.S. probably could have dominated the envisioned international Atomic Development Agency.

The Baruch Plan also demanded considerable international penetration of the secretive society Lenin's heirs had built in the Soviet Union, and it would have barred a Soviet veto of such intrusions. Thus, the Soviets rejected the proposal as a devious means of spying on them and of prevent-ing development of their own atomic devices.

When the Soviets also turned down a Western plan for the reunification of Germany, and the U.S. responded by refusing to cooperate in further movement of war reparations from West to East, the formal division of Germany between East and West was all but assured. That coincided, anyway, with Truman's decision to build up West Germany's economy and to prevent, at all costs, a Soviet absorption of all Germany into the Com-munist sphere.

These and other events leading up to declaration of the Truman Doctrine had predisposed the American people to accept the president's Achesonian view of a polarized world. Truman then followed his joint-session speech of March 12, 1947, with an order—issued just over a week later—for loyalty investigations of all federal employees. The specter of Communist subversion at home thus was added officially to the menace of Soviet might abroad.

No one seems to have thought sufficiently about the irony of fighting to sustain democracy abroad, while undermining it at home with a loyalty scare that was necessarily a boon to orthodoxy and a threat to dissent. And to whatever extent Truman may have thought his loyalty order would negate the Republicans' "soft on communism" line of political attack, he was proven to be badly wrong.

Wartime destruction, ruined economies and hungry people, meanwhile were believed to be making the Western European nations vulnerable targets of communism; it was vital to save them for the West. American prosperity, moreover, depended greatly upon European markets, which had been all but destroyed by the war. The recovery of Europe therefore was essential to American political *and* economic interests, as well as a decent objective in itself.

On May 23, 1947, George Kennan and a small State Department planning staff produced the outlines of a program of economic assistance, with the initiative to come from the recipient nations acting in coordination with each other. As Kennan formulated it, and as Marshall announced it in a commencement address at Harvard on June 5, 1947, the plan was described as a recovery program rather than an anti-Communist instrument: "Our policy," the secretary declared, "is directed not against any country or doctrine but against hunger, poverty, desperation and chaos."

The Soviet Union and its satellites were technically eligible to take part in the Marshall Plan—although, as with the Baruch Plan, the conditions made their participation unlikely. Ultimately, the Soviets not only refused to participate but forced the Eastern European nations to stay out too—including Czechoslovakia, not then completely under Moscow's yoke.

"Here was the crucial event of the Cold War," Wallace Carroll wrote later. "The leaders of opinion in Europe . . . could see that the United States wanted Europe to become strong again; the Soviets wanted Europe divided and weak."[3]

Shortly afterward, the Soviets announced their own Molotov Plan to link the Eastern European economies more closely. Thus, the Marshall Plan, successful though it proved to be in reaching its goal of Western European recovery and restoring American markets, further polarized East and West, Communist and non-Communist blocs in Europe. The division was fast becoming irreparable.

Another result of the Marshall Plan, of no great importance at the time, had long consequences: for the first time it brought Representative Richard Nixon of California, then thirty-three years old, to the vast stage of world affairs, on which for the next forty years he would play every role from walk-on to star to character actor, from hero to heavy, from young leading man to elderly supporting player. It is as if that first experience had left him stagestruck, so that nothing but the arena of international affairs ever again quite satisfied his thirst for battle.

As sketched in chapter 2, while still a first-termer in what was then a Republican House, Nixon was appointed to the prestigious Herter committee, which was to travel in Europe in order to study conditions there and inquire into the need for the Marshall Plan. The committee saw firsthand the devastation war had wrought—for instance, Nixon recalled, "block after block, mile after mile of charred desolation" in Berlin. He also met leaders like Attlee and satisfied his yen for combat by debating such real Communists—in contrast to the hapless Jerry Voorhis—as Giuseppe Di-Vittorio, the secretary general of the Italian Labor Federation.

The latter's performance persuaded the young congressman, as he recalled in *RN*, that "Communists throughout the world owe their loyalties not to the countries they live in but to Russia." Nixon also witnessed Communist-inspired street violence in Trieste and showed an early tendency to what later became a dangerous obsession—getting off the beaten path, like an American politician campaigning for votes, in foreign countries.

Three decades later, in *RN*, Nixon remembered that the Herter committee trip had taught him respect for Communist leaders as tough, intelligent men, and given him an appreciation for their shrewd use of nationalist passions and Soviet money to advance their ideological and political goals. As he recalled:

> From just this brief exposure, I could see that the only thing the Communists would respect—and deal with seriously—was power at least equal to theirs and backed up by willingness to use it. I made a penciled note in Trieste that is as true today as it was thirty years ago: "One basic rule with Russians—never bluff unless you are prepared to carry through, because they will test you every time."

If this is taken at face value rather than as hindsight, the Herter committee tour of Europe remained a strong influence on Nixon even during his presidency. It also discloses what may have been a continuing—perhaps significant, surely very American—confusion of Communists with Russians. Not all Communists, of course, are Russians and few Communists that Nixon encountered in Western Europe in 1947 could have been, since the committee did not visit the Soviet Union.

What inspired the penciled note of 1947 is therefore obscure; but it raises the question whether the confusion it expressed conditioned Nixon's later conduct toward such non-Russian Communists as the North Vietnamese, or the Marxist Salvador Allende Gossens in Chile. That note also heightens the irony that Richard Nixon, masterminding his "opening to China" in 1970, was the first among American leaders to act importantly on the recognition that *not* all Communists are Russians, or even alike, and some may be useful to American purposes.

But Nixon's presidency was far in the future when he returned from Europe to campaign for the Marshall Plan in the Twelfth District of California—against the political advice of his sponsors and despite a district poll Nixon ordered that found 75 percent of respondents opposed to foreign aid. The Herter committee's favorable report to Congress was one reason—though only one—that the Republican House approved the Democratic president's proposal overwhelmingly, 313 to 82, on December 15, 1947, with Representative Nixon in the majority.

By then, Moscow had brought Hungary and Czechoslovakia—the most independent of Eastern European nations—firmly into Soviet control and had organized the Communist Information Bureau (COMINFORM), by which it sought to exert influence over Western European Communist parties. Three months later, in March 1948, Stalin fiercely denounced American, British and French plans for a separate West German government to participate in the Marshall Plan.

That March of 1948 was a landmark of the Cold War. On the 17th, Truman addressed another joint session of Congress and asked for Universal Military Training, the resumption of the military draft and swift action on the Marshall Plan. Ultimately, Congress gave him the draft and $4 billion for the Marshall Plan, but not UMT.

In Brussels, on the day Truman spoke, Britain, France, Belgium, the Netherlands and Luxembourg signed a fifty-year collective defense treaty—the forerunner of the North Atlantic Treaty Organization. In China, the situation had so deteriorated that Marshall warned Congress of "the possibility that the present Chinese [Nationalist] government may not be successful in maintaining itself against the Communist forces."

In that same ominous March, the Soviets walked out of the Allied Control Council for Germany, protesting the meetings of the Western representatives in London. The council never met again. On April 1, 1948, as if to commemorate the hard month just past, the Soviets blocked American trains bound for Berlin—the first step in what became the Berlin blockade.

It is not surprising, therefore, that a National Security Council policy paper, NSC-9, declared that the Marshall Plan needed to be supplemented by "concrete evidence of determination to resist" further Soviet aggression.

The so-called Vandenberg Resolution, vaguely suggesting an unprecedented alliance of Atlantic nations, passed the Senate by 68 to 4; a year or so earlier, that would have been unthinkable.

When in June 1948 the Western powers introduced a much-needed currency reform in their German occupation zones, the furious Soviets declared that the division of Germany was complete; on June 24, they cut off all rail, highway and water traffic to Berlin, deep in the Soviet zone. On June 28, Truman—not too busy with his underdog reelection campaign to react with his usual firmness—approved what was to be known as the Berlin airlift, and shifted two squadrons of B-29s to West Germany (keeping secret that the planes were not equipped to carry atomic bombs).

Most of these European troubles were well publicized by comparison to the problems caused by another divided nation on the rim of Asia. After V-J Day in 1945, both the U.S. and the Soviet Union had moved occupation troops into Korea, mutually agreeing upon a "temporary" dividing line at the 38th parallel—the Soviets halting north of it, the U.S. to the south. American pressures then led the U.N. General Assembly—still dominated by Washington—to call for election of a national assembly for all Korea.

The voting took place on May 10, 1948, while in Europe the Berlin crisis mounted; but only Koreans below the 38th parallel went to the polls, those in the Soviet sector refusing to take part, or having been prevented from doing so. This set Korea on the road to long-term partition; on August 15, 1948, Washington recognized a new Republic of South Korea, a rightist regime under President Syngman Rhee, an elderly but fierce anti-Communist who had spent decades in the U.S.

On September 9, the Democratic People's Republic of Korea was proclaimed in the northern zone; it was to be headed by Kim Il Sung, a Communist and a nationalist who—unlike Rhee—had fought with guerrillas against the Japanese during World War II. In late 1948, however, the General Assembly declared over Soviet protests and in defiance of reality that Rhee's republic was the lawful government of all Korea.

In Europe, the Berlin blockade and the responding American airlift began in June 1948 and were to last into May 1949. Allied planes soon were ferrying to West Berlin more than three thousand tons of supplies per day; 733 incidents between them and Soviet pilots were to be recorded. Thirty-nine British, thirty-one American and five German airmen were killed. Understandably, the blockade heightened Americans' view of themselves as being on the side of good, against Soviet and Communist evil.

By November 1948, when Harry Truman won his great upset victory over Thomas E. Dewey of New York, and Richard Nixon was elected—unopposed—to his second term in the House, the Cold War was a hard and dangerous reality, in Asia and in Europe. As a result of the Hiss case and the Herter committee's findings, Nixon's career was interwoven with the struggle, and the two were never to be separated.

Early in 1949, Dean Acheson returned to the Truman administration as secretary of state, succeeding Marshall. One of his first acts was to urge the Senate Foreign Relations Committee to approve an unprecedented treaty declaring the parties' agreement that "an armed attack against one or more of them in Europe or North America shall be considered an attack against all." For the first time in its history, if Acheson's advice was followed, the U.S. would enter into a formal peacetime alliance outside the Western Hemisphere.

The treaty did not commit the U.S. to go to war automatically in defense of European allies; Congress could decide in accordance with its constitutional powers if an armed attack had occurred, and how to respond if it had. But as Arthur Vandenberg put it: "Now we are not just the free agents that we were before we signed it."

Twelve nations signed the North Atlantic Treaty on April 4, 1949; eight days later, Truman submitted it to the Senate. Ratification, on July 21, was overwhelming—82 to 13—and passage of the North Atlantic Treaty may fairly be termed the official acceptance by the U.S. of great responsibility in world affairs—the formal step by which George Washington's policy of "no entangling alliances" finally had been put to rest.

Richard Nixon, after 1948, was a junior Republican in a Democratic House; he had nothing specifically to do with the treaty since the House was not required to approve it. He had nevertheless played a substantial role in ratification: the Hiss case, reinforcing public and congressional fears of communism, was a substantial factor in the Senate's willingness to make such a radical break with tradition.

Nixon did not mention the treaty debate in his memoirs, but his backing could hardly be questioned after his support for the Truman Doctrine and the Marshall Plan. From the start, he had been an "internationalist" in what had been traditionally an isolationist party—and he was certainly an anti-Communist.

During these same months of 1949, as Marshall had warned in March 1948, the situation in China was steadily moving from bad to very bad. The Truman administration was under heavy pressure from the "China lobby," from "China-firsters" like Henry Luce and from die-hard senators such as Knowland of California, Styles Bridges of New Hampshire and Kenneth Wherry of Nebraska, to send more aid to the anti-Communist forces of Chiang Kai-shek. Early in 1949, for example, fifty-one Republican congressmen—including the newly prominent Richard Nixon—wrote Truman demanding greater support for Chiang.

Truman and Acheson, generally backed by the military chiefs of staff, insisted that Nationalist China could not be saved by further American military or economic assistance. Despite $2 billion of such aid since 1945, Chiang's regime had become defeatist and corrupt; its support among the Chinese people was draining steadily away.

On October 1, 1949, Mao Tse-tung proclaimed the People's Republic of China. Two months later, Chiang fled to the island of Formosa (Taiwan), where he had thoughtfully sent three hundred thousand troops and his gold supply. The U.S., as Republicans began endlessly to declare, had "lost China." When early in January 1950 Mao's regime seized a building in the American compound in Peking, the State Department started withdrawing its personnel from mainland China. Twenty years of silence between two of the great nations of the world had begun.

One of the dominant political issues of the 1950 and 1952 political campaigns in the U.S. also had been opened: Who "lost" China and why? Never mind that China had not been the U.S.'s to lose—who lost it? Wasn't it those who protected the Communist subversives in the State Department and elsewhere in government? Richard Nixon was to be among the loudest and most frequent of those demanding answers they already had suggested.

Events in China were all the more shattering because on September 23, 1949, Truman had announced to shocked Americans that "we have evidence that within recent weeks an atomic explosion occurred in the Soviet Union." This dread news came at least a year or two earlier than was generally expected; it put an end to the American atomic monopoly after just four years and one month, and it demolished the old American sense of security that protective oceans had nourished.

The Truman administration's response was a forgone conclusion: power would meet power. The president ordered an enlargement of the atomic energy program, and just six days later the Atomic Energy Commission discussed the possibility of building what was then called "the super"—a fusion or hydrogen bomb, far more powerful and destructive than the Hiroshima weapon. On October 6, 1949, Admiral Lewis L. Strauss proposed to the other members of the AEC that they make "an intensive effort to get ahead with the super."

The "loss" of China and the explosion of the Soviet bomb were the more damaging to the Truman administration because that same winter, on January 22, 1950, Alger Hiss was found guilty of perjury by a federal jury in New York. In effect, the jury decided, Hiss had committed espionage for the Soviet Union, then lied about it. The statute of limitations prevented prosecution for the espionage, but not for the perjury.

Republicans immediately began suggesting that Hiss's spying and that of the other agents widely presumed to have penetrated the administrations of Roosevelt and Truman might have hurried along the victory of Mao and/or the Soviet development of atomic weapons. Richard Nixon, basking in the reflection of Hiss's conviction, declared on radio that the Roosevelt and Truman administrations had engaged in a "deliberate" effort to cover up the Hiss "conspiracy."

Neither he nor any other Republican ever explained how the idea of a Roosevelt-Truman cover-up of a Communist conspiracy squared with the anti-Communist Truman Doctrine, Marshall Plan and North Atlantic Treaty. But such charges appeared to receive dramatic backing on January 25, when Dean Acheson boldly but perhaps unwisely proclaimed that "I do not intend to turn my back on Alger Hiss." To reporters, Acheson cited Matthew 25:34–46, thus basing his remarkable statement on Christian charity. That hardly lessened the fury of the public reaction.*

Not so much attention had been paid or criticism leveled when Acheson, in an address to the National Press Club two weeks earlier, had described the American defense perimeter in Asia as a semicircle running from the Philippines through Okinawa and Japan to the Aleutian island chain off Alaska. Few noticed at the time that Korea apparently had been excluded; and even if anyone had, Acheson was saying nothing that the National Security Council, after due deliberation, had not approved (on December 30, 1949, in NSC-48/2). In 1949, even the revered General Douglas MacArthur, the Far East commander, had said as much.

In fact, however, South Korea was *not* excluded from American defense considerations; the White House and the Pentagon assumed that South Korea would be defended against Communist attack first by Syngman Rhee's American-supplied and -trained army, then if necessary by a U.N. force to which Washington would contribute troops.

Nor was Acheson's speech carelessly worded; it was a calculated reflection of the deliberate ambiguity of American policy toward Korea. On the one hand, the U.S. had created South Korea, opposed it to a similar Soviet creation north of the 38th parallel and committed not only its own prestige but that of the U.N. to South Korea's survival. On the other hand, the Joint Chiefs of Staff did not regard Korea as of major strategic importance and resisted either guaranteeing its security or providing high levels of military assistance.

Thus, the peninsula had low military but high political value, which dictated the ambiguity: Acheson and Truman wanted to prevent the bellig-

*One American did understand. Knowing that his statement had damaged the president politically, Acheson offered his resignation. Truman refused to accept it and Acheson later wrote his daughter: "He . . . said that one who had gone to the funeral of a friendless old man just out of the penitentiary had no trouble in knowing what I meant and in approving of it." In 1945, as vice president, Truman had attended the funeral of the former Kansas City political boss, Tom Pendergast, who had aided Truman's early career.

erent Rhee from moving north by refusing him a security guarantee and limiting military assistance; but they also wanted to deter Kim Il Sung from moving south by leaving him in doubt as to whether the U.S. and perhaps the U.N. would intervene to help Rhee.

Acheson's statement nevertheless *may* have made Kim more confident that he could attack across the 38th parallel without a significant American response. The speech *certainly* gave Republicans, for the not too distant future, cause to charge Acheson and Truman (but not MacArthur) with "inviting" a North Korean attack on the South.

But Korea, in January 1950, seemed far away and unimportant. So, no doubt, did Indochina, which most Americans then could not have found on a four-color map. On February 3, 1950, nevertheless, the Truman administration granted diplomatic recognition to a French-colonialist, anti-Communist Indochinese regime under a virtual puppet of the French, the ineffective Emperor Bao Dai, who would much have preferred to be on the Riviera.

The recognition of Bao Dai was forced by the administration's desire— primarily for reasons of European policy—to support the French, who were losing the battle for postwar control of their old Indochinese colonies to the revolutionary nationalist armies of Ho Chi Minh. Another reason was the triumph of the Chinese Communists a few months earlier, which caused Truman to want to be seen taking a strong stand somewhere in Asia. Moreover, Ho's government had been recognized in January 1950 by both Moscow and Peking; thereafter, Washington in the power-versus-power style of the Cold War felt compelled to oppose its enemies' friend.

A rare opportunity had been missed. In the crucial early postwar years, Stalin could *not* recognize Ho because to do so would have damaged the then-powerful French Communist party. If that party were to have any hope of taking power in Paris, it could hardly be seen as willing to abandon French control of Indochina. Neither, therefore, could Stalin.[4]

So if Truman, immediately after World War II, had recognized Ho and opposed a French return to Indochina, while Stalin was unwilling to do so, Ho might have become an Asian Tito. More important, the long ordeal of the U.S. in Vietnam might have been avoided. Truman's perhaps necessary focus on good relations with Paris prevented him from taking these steps, however; his formal support for Bao Dai marked an irrevocable turn away from Ho Chi Minh, putting the U.S. on the road to the first losing war in its history.

That grim winter of 1949–1950 also brought a significant though low-keyed announcement from the White House on January 31: the president had ordered the Atomic Energy Commission to continue working on "all forms of atomic weapons," including determining the feasibility of "the so-called hydrogen or superbomb." There was to be no crash program to develop the super, as many had hoped for, and for which much behind-scenes pressure had been exerted. Another irrevocable step had been taken, nonetheless, because no important scientific figure doubted feasibility, though some debated the super's military utility. The major opposition was moral and ethical—therefore weak, in the context of a Soviet-American arms race.

The Joint Chiefs of Staff, always eager for new and bigger weapons, of course were for proceeding. In the cabinet, Acheson and the new secretary of defense, Louis Johnson, were powerful proponents. The super also was pushed hard by Strauss, by Senator Brian McMahon of Connecticut, the chairman of the Joint Committee on Atomic Energy, and by many of the major figures of science: Ernest Lawrence, Edward Teller, Karl Compton.

Even Harold Urey, who had warned against an atomic arms race, advocated the hydrogen bomb. "I do not think we should intentionally lose the armaments race," he said. "To do this will be to lose our liberties."

This was the argument, however stated, that carried the day: the Soviets might get the super first and use it to coerce or destroy the U.S. Against that proposition, even Robert Oppenheimer, Enrico Fermi and Isidor Rabi, prestigious though they were, made little headway by arguing that a hydrogen bomb would be so destructive that it presented "extreme dangers to mankind [that] outweigh any military advantage" and was thus a weapon that "in practical effect is almost one of genocide."

Forty years later, that view is widely accepted. Even President Ronald Reagan, in the most succinct statement of the same attitude, has said: "A nuclear war cannot be won and must never be fought." But in 1950, Dean Acheson was scornful of the scientists' argument that if the U.S. refrained from developing the super, it might "by example" persuade the Soviets to observe the same "limitations on the totality of war." The secretary of state wanted to know: "How can you persuade a paranoid adversary to disarm 'by example'?"

Not for many years did Americans know that the AEC's general advisory committee of distinguished scientists—of which Oppenheimer, Fermi, Rabi and James B. Conant were members—had recommended *against* developing the hydrogen bomb. The opposition statements quoted above were classified, and were not published until long after Truman decided in January 1950 to proceed.

That decision was taken under great scientific and military pressures, to which Richard Nixon did not publicly contribute. Again, however, he was influential through the Hiss case; Hiss's conviction came only nine days before the White House announcement, no doubt reinforcing Truman's conclusion that "we have no choice." Only two days after Truman's public statement, moreover, on February 2, 1950, Dr. Klaus Fuchs, chief of theoretical physics for the British atomic research program, who formerly had worked on development of the American atomic bomb, was arrested in London and charged with spying for Moscow.

Fuchs actually provided the Soviets with little useful information, but in 1950, on top of the Hiss conviction, the sensational Fuchs arrest further forced Truman's hand. On March 10, 1950, he approved the crash program he had rejected in January. Thereafter, the American effort to build a hydrogen bomb, like that of the Soviets (who also began work on a superbomb in January 1950) went full speed ahead—each nation mistrustful and afraid of the other, neither making any effort to negotiate an agreement *not* to build the most destructive weapon in history.

Three times, moreover, in his remaining years in office, Harry Truman approved significant increases in American nuclear weapons production capacity; in none of the three instances was either public or congressional approval sought or given. The result was that by the end of the fifties, in ten short years and without any form of democratic deliberation or consent, the American arsenal included *eighteen thousand* nuclear weapons.[5]

On June 25, 1950, just under three weeks after Richard Nixon had won the Republican nomination for the U.S. Senate in California, the North Korean People's Army plunged south, across the 38th parallel, surprising the U.S. Far East Command, Syngman Rhee's South Korean government and the Truman administration.

In the U.S., certainly at Nixon campaign headquarters in California, the North Korean attack was believed to be a Soviet aggression carried out by a Soviet puppet. Kim Il Sung *had* gone to Moscow in late 1949, but not for instructions; he sought approval, instead, of his own scheme for unifying the Korean peninsula. Kim feared the possibility that Rhee would move north, and suspected that Washington was rebuilding Japan as the cornerstone of its Asian policy. In his press club speech, Acheson had appeared to confirm such a role for the Japanese, long hated by the Koreans—which may have been the speech's true significance for Kim.

Stalin approved Kim's plan and promised supplies—provided Korean troops took all the risk. Nikita Khrushchev, in his purported memoirs, said the Soviet dictator thought the plan would produce the appearance of "an internal matter which the Koreas would be settling among themselves," while unifying the peninsula before the U.S. could stop the invasion. The Communist Chinese apparently had no greater hand in planning Kim's invasion.

Candidate Nixon and most other politicians of both parties nevertheless proclaimed the invasion a confirmation of the worldwide Communist threat; and Nixon quickly turned the attack to his political advantage. He enthusiastically supported Truman's quick decision to resist and the dispatch of American ground forces from Japan to Korea on June 30; at the same time he cited the Korean war as evidence of his main theme against Helen Douglas—that the Democratic party had been so "captured" and was so "controlled" by Communist sympathizers that it had become committed to "policies and principles" which were making the nation vulnerable to the Communist onslaught.

This doubletalk required a shift of fire from Truman to Acheson; the secretary of state, Nixon declared repeatedly, should resign because in the press club speech he had "invited" the North Korean attack, and because what Republicans called "State Department Communists" were responsible for the "loss of China." The administration's refusal either to give greater assistance to Chiang Kai-shek or to guarantee his security on Formosa (which Americans were to learn to call Taiwan) also drew Nixon's scorn.

He was not, of course, the only American who believed the North Korean attack had originated in Moscow as part of a scheme for Soviet-Communist domination of the world. So did the Truman administration and its allies; so did even the American embassy in Moscow. Its counselor, Walworth Barbour, cabled within hours of the invasion the opinion that it represented "a clear-cut *Soviet challenge* which [the] U.S. should answer firmly and swiftly as it constitutes direct threat our leadership of free world against *Soviet Communist imperialism.*" (Emphasis added.)

The administration already had at hand an analysis that made such a conclusion all but inevitable. A National Security Council review (NSC-68) of the new situation brought about by the Soviet atomic bomb and a Communist-ruled China had concluded just two months earlier, in April 1950, that the Soviet Communist threat was primarily *military.* In the awful light of the Soviet bomb, it seemed clear to NSC-68's authors—principal among whom was Paul Nitze, then in the early stages of a long career in the national security establishment—that Moscow soon would have the capacity either to launch a surprise atomic attack on the U.S. or, more likely, to achieve an atomic stalemate in which Moscow's supposed advantages in conventional weapons and its vast manpower would give it a decisive edge in the Cold War.

An aggressive Soviet Union and/or its satellites, the document suggested, could engage in "piecemeal aggression" virtually anywhere, believing that the U.S. would not respond for fear of provoking a American-Soviet atomic war, to the devastation of both nations. The resulting Soviet gains would cause American allies to retreat into neutrality, if not the Soviet orbit; and the U.S. would have lost that grand confrontation of the superpowers that in 1947 Acheson had outlined so apocalyptically to dazzled congressional leaders.

Might not the U.S. have played the same game of "piecemeal aggression," particularly since it would take the Soviets some time to build an equal atomic arsenal? It is a measure of American exceptionalism, and the extent to which the Cold War was regarded as a contest between good and evil, that the authors of NSC-68 *knew* the U.S. would not so conduct itself but *assumed* the Soviets certainly would.

Acheson, as Truman's most trusted adviser, was at the peak of his influence; so NSC-68 fundamentally reflected his views—among them his belief that Truman's military budgets had been far too low to finance the worldwide commitments the administration already had made. NSC-68 demanded what Acheson had long wanted—rearmament. If accepted, that would require abandonment of those tight military budgets—and the departure of Louis Johnson, Acheson's cabinet rival, who had enforced the budget cuts against the pleas of Chairman Dwight D. Eisenhower of the Joint Chiefs of Staff.

NSC-68's authors thought military spending should be increased perhaps to the level of $40 billion—*three times* the administration's request for 1951. They wanted the U.S. to be able to counter the Soviets and/or their satellites at any level of war—atomic, conventional, guerrilla, limited—and anywhere. But with congressional elections coming in November, Truman had not been ready in the spring of 1950 for such a huge expansion in the military budget. Ironically, in June, Kim Il Sung and the Korean War created instant public support for the increased military spending Truman already had decided to propose.

Thus, it was a further irony—though unrecognized by Richard Nixon and the voters of California—that the tough young Republican Senate candidate of 1950, one of the clearest anti-Communist voices in the country, was demanding the scalp of the secretary of state, who had been largely responsible for the decision to rearm; the war Acheson supposedly had "invited," moreover, had made rearmament not only possible but popular.

Truman, of course, had ample other reasons for coming to Syngman Rhee's assistance. South Korea was the creation of the U.S. and a U.N. then largely influenced by Washington; the new republic could not be abandoned without damaging loss of credibility for both. The European allies (so the administration assumed) could not be expected to credit American guarantees if Washington proved unable or unwilling to defend South Korea—though that country was on the edge of a landmass dominated by the two great Communist powers.

These assumptions may have been reasonable in the case of South Korea; but in years to come, a high price would have to be paid for what became in Washington the ritual beliefs that every challenge had to be met, every position had to be defended, lest Moscow be emboldened and the allies disheartened by perception of an American loss of nerve and will. The disastrous war in Vietnam was continued far past any rational necessity on just such speculative geopolitical grounds, rather than on hardheaded analysis of tangible costs and benefits.

In June 1950, Truman also had a domestic problem—Senator Joseph McCarthy, in full cry since February, when at Wheeling, West Virginia, he had first raised his charges of Communists in the State Department. As a result, anti-Communists, Republican and Democrat alike, already fuming at the "loss of China," might have torn the administration apart had it backed away from the confrontation in Korea and allowed another Asian nation to fall to communism—this one following a brazen cross-border invasion.

Besides, Truman personally was outraged by the attack, convinced as he was that it had been masterminded from the Kremlin. "By God, I'm going to let them have it," he told aides.

He was favored by a stroke of luck, or a miscalculation by Kim Il Sung, which should have cast doubt on the idea that Moscow had instigated the invasion. On June 25 and immediately after, the Soviets were boycotting the U.N. Security Council because it had refused, under American pressures, to seat Mao's Communist regime as the legitimate representative of China.

So on the 25th, without a Soviet presence or veto, the security council resolved that North Korea should withdraw; and on the 27th that U.N. member nations should help South Korea resist aggression—both resolutions sponsored by Washington. Their passage gave the U.S. plausible opportunity to begin rearming and to use its military forces in Korea under a U.N. flag, in what could be billed legitimately as an international peacekeeping effort. If Stalin was the instigator of the invasion, he had been either stupid or careless to stage it while his representatives were absent from the security council.

The sudden outbreak of war in Korea confirmed the long-festering fear of Americans that they confronted a malevolent, diabolical enemy dedicated to their destruction and to conquest of the world. Could there be any doubt that such an enemy could be dealt with only by superior force and determination?

"I think it is a mistake," Acheson had told the Senate Foreign Relations Committee as early as 1947, "to believe that you can, at any time, sit down with the Russians and solve questions. . . . [Y]ou cannot sit down with them."

After June 25, 1950, if not before, that was the general conviction of Americans, passionately held by most, constantly reinforced by the politicians who wanted their votes. "Real war" in Korea meant that thenceforth the Cold War would be conducted more as confrontation than as competition, less as a contest between systems than as a clash of strengths. There would be no fundamental softening of the policies resulting from that attitude until the young senatorial candidate who endlessly charged that the Truman administration had been "captured" and "controlled" came himself to the White House, nearly twenty years later.

In Richard Nixon's two scant years in the Senate, he was only one of many Republican critics of Truman, particularly of the president's Asian policies. Nixon's early support for the war disappeared as the stalemate developed and General MacArthur was sacked, but he was busier on other matters, Republican politics not least: "I was caught up in this activity from my first days in the Senate," Nixon recalled in *RN*. Korea was distinctly a secondary interest.

As the Republican vice presidential candidate in 1952, Nixon belabored Truman and particularly Acheson on war issues, and pictured the Democratic presidential nominee, Adlai Stevenson, as perhaps worse—not only the anointed heir of Truman and Acheson, but a collaborator with Alger Hiss. Nixon and other Republican gladiators quickly became aware, too, that many who at first had supported Truman's strong response in Korea had by 1952 tired of its consequences—particularly after the Chinese intervened across the Yalu River in late 1950 and transformed a seeming American victory into one of the worst defeats the American military had ever suffered.

After that, what the American public saw was primarily a stalemate costly in lives, money and economic disruption. For the first time, and with memories of World War II still painfully fresh, Americans had to endure the frustrations of a limited war for limited objectives in a faraway country of little apparent significance, with victory only a hazy objective in the future. They did not like such a war; they wanted triumph, as over Germany and Japan, and the sooner the better.

That was what led Dwight Eisenhower, the hero of the well-remembered *good* war, to the decisive act of the 1952 campaign—his pledge that he would go personally to Korea in order to see what could be done about ending the stalemate. Truman might denounce Eisenhower's promise as a gimmick, and so it mostly was; but to the American people it seemed a promise to end the war.

Korea was the great preoccupation of the time; but perhaps the most important issue to come before the Senate in Nixon's brief tenure—though, curiously, he does not mention it in his memoirs—was the "great debate" about the sending of American troops to Europe in peacetime.

Truman had announced in September 1950 that he planned to assign ground forces to strengthen NATO positions in Europe. In December, he had appointed the immensely popular Eisenhower—then president of Columbia University—as supreme commander of NATO forces. (Some in the White House made the mistake of thinking that the appointment would keep the general out of the 1952 presidential campaign.)

When Congress had convened in January 1951, Nixon moving from the House to the Senate, Republicans introduced numerous resolutions putting

Congress on record *against* the assignment of American troops abroad without congressional approval. Truman promptly told a news conference that as commander in chief of the armed forces, he did not need congressional approval to send troops to Europe. In the Senate, Robert Taft flatly contradicted him: "The President has no power to agree to send American troops to fight in Europe a war between members of the Atlantic Pact and the Soviet Union."

Thus, the issue was constitutional as well as political, and in Taft the Republicans had a formidable intellectual leader. Nevertheless, Truman ignored an apparent compromise offer Taft held out in a National Press Club speech, and repeated that he had the constitutional authority to send troops anywhere in the world. As for Congress, "I don't ask their permission. I just consult them."

Senate debate on the key Republican resolution lasted for weeks, and was echoed in the press and in the universities and meeting places of the nation. The prestigious Eisenhower was a strong witness for the administration. George Marshall, who in the exigencies of the Korean War and rearmament had come out of retirement to replace Louis Johnson as secretary of defense, was allowed by Truman to specify that six American divisions—180,000 men, including two divisions still on postwar occupation duty—would be deployed in Europe.

Senator Nixon was not prominent in the great debate, despite his demonstrated internationalism ("I will oppose and fight any attempt to return to an isolationist or obstructionist attitude on foreign affairs," he had told Californians after his election to the Senate). His relative silence probably was dictated by his junior status and by politics. He was an internationalist with national political prospects that could have been endangered by support of the isolationist Republican position; but he was also a dutiful Republican who could hardly have served those same prospects by outspoken opposition to a party position and to a strong leader like Taft. Discretion and silence were for him the better part of valor.

In the end, Nixon did not have to choose; an innocuous substitute resolution prevailed, 89 to 21—Nixon in the majority—expressing the nonbinding sense of the Senate that no ground troops other than the four new divisions should be sent to Europe without further congressional approval. Even Truman could hail that as "further evidence that the country stands firm in its support of the North Atlantic Treaty."

Shortly after this vote, in May 1951, Nixon visited Geneva as a Senate observer of the World Health Organization—his second official trip to Europe. This time, he asserted in *RN,* "Senator Frank Carlson of Kansas, one of Eisenhower's early supporters, arranged for me to meet Eisenhower at NATO headquarters in Paris." More likely, Nixon arranged to have Carlson arrange the meeting; he knew the great general only slightly from a meeting the year before at Herbert Hoover's dinner table at the Bohemian Grove near San Francisco, but was already leaning toward Eisenhower for president.

When they talked in Paris, Eisenhower "carefully steered away" from politics but praised Nixon's work in the Hiss case ("You got him fairly") and the emphasis he had placed in some speeches "on the need to take into account economic and ideological as well as military factors in fashioning foreign policy." If so, it's probable that the painstaking Nixon sent Eisenhower these speeches in advance, since the NATO commander was unlikely to be keeping up with the utterances of junior senators.

Less than a year later, Nixon rejected Taft's request for support, telling him that he would back Eisenhower for president in 1952 as "the best qualified" in international affairs. Eisenhower clearly was more congenial than Taft to Nixon's internationalist views but these incidents reinforce Earl Warren's and his aides' later conclusion that Nixon was working for Eisenhower—thus against Warren—almost from the start. And however sincerely Nixon believed in Eisenhower's qualifications, it seems clear that his own vice presidential hopes also were at work.

His restless ambition, driving determination and shrewd calculations quickly rewarded, Nixon rode into high office and onto the international stage with Dwight D. Eisenhower. It was still the world of Truman and Acheson and Stalin that they looked out upon at noon on Inauguration Day 1953—but it was to be a world in new and untried hands, and not only theirs.

On March 8, 1953, less than two months after the inauguration, five days after a servant found Marshal Josef Stalin sprawled on the dining room floor in his fortresslike dacha, the Soviet dictator died of a brain hemorrhage. The world faced by Eisenhower and Nixon would be uncertain indeed.

After his wartime and NATO experiences, President Eisenhower took office with little wish to travel abroad; so he turned to his secretary of state, John Foster Dulles, and to Nixon to take that burden. Nixon was eager to oblige, because in the first months of the administration he had found himself something of a pariah. This probably did not surprise a moody and introspective man who, as William Rogers had observed, thought people generally didn't like him.

In early 1953, the problem was more specific. Many of Eisenhower's men in the cabinet and on the White House staff—a group among which Nixon never really was to count himself, nor was to be counted—thought he had almost cost them the election in the fund crisis of 1952. Some may have believed the fund was culpable, or held Nixon's Checkers dramatics against him.

The opportunity for diplomatic missions, however minor, helped Nixon over this unhappy beginning. And as his overseas experience mounted, he began to receive what his close friend, Robert Finch, later to be in Nixon's cabinet, called "an enormous education" in global affairs. During his vice presidency, Nixon came to know "more than a thousand foreign statesmen outside the Communist bloc." Among other adventures, he was "trapped in a Mexico City elevator, picketed in Burma, called 'son of a dog' in Casablanca, and plagued by dysentery and other maladies in Ethiopia, Afghanistan, Indonesia. . . ."[6]

Nixon's "enormous education" literally began on his first tour—mostly in Asia—when he delivered a letter from the president to Syngman Rhee. The tough old South Korean president was unreconciled to the Korean armistice Eisenhower had agreed to on July 27, 1953—a speedy accomplishment that gave rise to the persistent belief that, to achieve it, he had *threatened* China and North Korea with the use of atomic weapons. The atomic bomb story seems plausible primarily because an armistice had eluded Harry Truman throughout the last year and a half of his administration.

In fact, on May 7, 1953, two weeks *before* Dulles is supposed to have made the atomic bomb threat through Jawaharlal Nehru of India on May 22, the Chinese Communists offered important concessions on the deadlocked issue of repatriating prisoners of war.* Essentially, they turned about-face and accepted the terms of a U.N. resolution of December 1952, which the Truman administration had supported but China and North Korea then had rejected. After first refusing, Eisenhower too returned, by and large, to the U.N. formula of December 1952.

On June 4, 1953, the Communist powers agreed in principle to Eisenhower's second response, bringing an armistice close enough to grasp. That it was not finally signed until July 27 was due primarily to the fanatical resistance of Rhee, who wanted not an end to the war but the unification of Korea under *his* "republic." His resistance was so powerful that the Eisenhower administration considered—but finally rejected—ousting the old man and installing a compliant military government in South Korea.

Rhee's ROK—Republic of Korea—troops manned about two thirds of the U.N. military lines, giving him the acknowledged power to shatter the armistice—most disastrously by moving north in an attack on Chinese and North Korean forces. He was perfectly capable of such a move. To forestall it, the U.S. kept ROK troops on short supplies of gasoline and ammunition.

But the danger still was considered real that the headstrong Rhee might

*After the Chinese Communist intervention in late 1950, the primary problem was to make peace with them, though presumably they represented North Korean interests as well as their own.

gamble on right-wing Republicans forcing Eisenhower to support him if
he moved north against the Communists. The letter from Eisenhower that
Nixon delivered informed Rhee forcefully that if he reopened the war, the
president would give him no support at all.

Eisenhower's letter demanded Rhee's assurances that he would not
break the armistice. But even with that letter literally in hand, Rhee—"a
thin small man," Nixon recalled in *RN,* whose "firm handshake and spry
walk belied his seventy-eight years"—insisted that "a peace which leaves
Korea divided would inevitably lead to a war which would destroy both
Korea and the United States, and I cannot agree to such a peace." Since
a peace dividing Korea was exactly what had been arranged, the best
"assurance" Nixon could get from Rhee was hardly sufficient: "Before I
take any unilateral action at any time I shall inform President Eisenhower."

Rhee already had broken even such inadequate pledges, and he did not
ease Nixon's concern when he told the Korean press: "I hope I will be able
to convince President Eisenhower, through Vice President Nixon, that it
is the right policy to finish this thing in Korea." Nixon had been sent to
Seoul to convince Rhee—not the other way around.

During a second private meeting, Rhee took the opportunity to lecture
his young visitor:

> The moment the Communists are certain that the United States
> controls Rhee, you will have lost one of your most effective bar-
> gaining points. . . . The fear that I may start some action is a
> constant check on the Communists [who] think that America
> wants peace so badly that you will do anything to get it. At times,
> I am afraid they are right. But they do not think that is true as
> far as I am concerned, and I believe that you would be wrong to
> dispel their doubts in that respect.

Nixon never did get the kind of assurances from Rhee that Eisenhower's
letter had demanded. The vice president nevertheless left Korea not so
much offended by the old man's willfulness, intransigence and occasional
perfidy as "impressed . . . by the strength and intelligence of Syngman
Rhee." And "the more I travelled and the more I learned in the years that
followed, the more I appreciated," he recorded in *RN,* the tough old
Korean's "insight about the importance of being unpredictable in dealing
with the Communists."

Here was the seed of the so-called madman theory that Nixon later
brought to the presidency—the belief that an adversary would be more
willing to reach an agreement or back away from a position or moderate
a threat if he were not sure how his opponent might react.

Rhee had given his visitor a graphic lesson in the kind of stubborn willfulness President Nixon later was to encounter in Nguyen Van Thieu of South Vietnam, when Thieu did not like peace terms that were worked out, over his head, between North Vietnam and the Nixon administration.

But the primary lesson the vice president took with him from Seoul, as his extensive account of the meeting in *RN* suggests, was Rhee's "uncertainty principle."

After his election in 1968 but before his inauguration, Nixon described it this way to H. R. Haldeman:

> I want the North Vietnamese to believe I've reached the point where I might do *anything* to stop the war. We'll just slip the word to them that, "for God's sake, you know Nixon is obsessed about Communism. We can't restrain him when he's angry—and he has his hand on the nuclear button"—and Ho Chi Minh himself will be in Paris in two days begging for peace.[7]

The three nations—Vietnam, Cambodia, Laos—of French Indochina were, of course, important stops on Nixon's Asian itinerary. Since February 1950, when Truman had recognized the French puppet regime of Bao Dai, turning the American back on Ho Chi Minh's nationalist-Communist Vietminh, the war in Indochina had been greatly escalated; and Ho's forces had gained the advantage over a French army by then heavily dependent on supplies from the U.S.

Washington's commitment to the French effort, both in materiel and in political conviction, had grown steadily. Eisenhower himself was dubious about the French land war in Asia; but the French officials were seen by his administration, even more strongly than in the Truman-Acheson years, to be making a "free world" stand against Moscow and/or Peking, with their assumed master plans for global domination. One reason why Dulles had been unenthusiastic about a Korean armistice was his fear that peace on the peninsula would free Peking's forces to move to Ho's aid in Indochina—which Dulles and the Joint Chiefs regarded as strategically more consequential than Korea. They understood little, typically, of the ancient and portentous enmity between China and the Indochinese peoples.[8]

Naturally, Nixon's themes during his Indochina visit echoed the administration's attitude. "The threat to this nation," he said in Hanoi, in a toast to the French-appointed governor of Vietnam, "although it has taken the form of a civil war, still derives its strength from an alien source. This source, to call it by its name, is totalitarian Communism. . . . The struggle against the Vietminh in this country, therefore, is important far beyond the boundaries of Vietnam."

Visiting the troops, Nixon in battle fatigues preached the same sermon to Vietnamese who were fighting for the French; they were, he said, defending the outposts of freedom. He thought he "could see the inspiration" this message gave these men, forerunners of the ill-fated ARVN (Army of the Republic of Vietnam), on which President Nixon was to place so much hope and responsibility nearly two decades later.

But the sharp-eyed Nixon also saw something else about the Vietnamese soldiers: "The French had forfeited their loyalty by not talking to them" in the way *he* had, and by treating them with colonialist disdain and condescension, which prevented the development of a "working partnership."

Nixon already had come to believe, on a visit to Malaya, that the British were winning there a war against Communist guerrillas—not "by trying to fight a guerrilla war with conventional tactics and conventional strategy" but because they "had trained the natives and enlisted their wholehearted support."

A major reason the British could do this was that they had promised Malaya its independence once the insurgency was ended. Thus the British identified their fight against communism with Malayan nationalism. The French, on the other hand, were fighting to hang on to their colonial dominance in Indochina and were the *enemies* of Vietnamese nationalism; to the end, they resisted even the promise of independence. As a result, even those Vietnamese ostensibly on the French side were either lukewarm or mercenary.

If Nixon grasped this crucial distinction between the two situations, he does not mention it in *RN*—perhaps because he persisted in thinking the causes of the Indochina war lay in Moscow and Peking rather than in Indochina itself. He left Indochina

> convinced that the French had failed primarily because they had not sufficiently trained, much less inspired, the Indochinese people to be able to defend themselves. They had failed to build a cause— or a cadre—that could resist the nationalist and anti-colonialist appeals of the Communists.

He gives no hint, even, of understanding that the mere presence of the colonialist French in Indochina meant that they *could not* build such a resistance to Ho Chi Minh.

The success of the British in Malaya and the failure of the French in Indochina underpinned Nixon's later faith in his "Vietnamization" program—training and supplying the ARVN to fight for itself, rather than as a mere appendage of American forces. But neither in 1953 nor during his presidency nor in the later memoir did he ever suggest that he understood *nationalism* rather than international communism to be the most powerful force at work in those countries, or that in Indochina first the French and then the U.S. let themselves be regarded as *opposing* nationalism.

Instead, he concluded in 1953 that the Eisenhower administration had "to do everything possible to find a way *to keep the French in Vietnam* until the Communists were defeated." (Emphasis added.) These were irreconcilable goals, since the Communists also were nationalists; but those goals symbolized Nixon's and Washington's fixation on "totalitarian communism" as the evil at the root of every problem. When Nixon came to power fifteen years later, his actions showed that he *still* believed the root of the Indochinese problem to be in Moscow.

Nixon's foreign tour lasted more than two months—jet travel was still in the future and so was the big official and press party that's commonplace for traveling vice presidents today. The Nixons flew in an Air Force Constellation with a party of less than a dozen, including only two Secret Service agents and three wire service reporters. Covering more than forty-five thousand miles, they visited twenty-one countries in Asia, the Near East and Africa.

Characteristically, Nixon recalled his stop in Burma as the most "exciting," not because that country was particularly important or that he had any real diplomatic business to transact but because there he found the sort of "battle" he relished—a confrontation.

A crowd of Communist demonstrators were in view near the famous reclining Buddha at Pegu, fifty miles from Rangoon. Nixon insisted on walking into the crowd *ahead* of his escort, while debating with a demonstrator and—as he tells it in *RN*—backing him down and causing the crowd to disperse. This head-on approach became his future pattern—not always as successful—whenever he encountered such demonstrations.

Most of the industrious, exhausting trip was a learning experience. Nixon discreetly refrained from telling Chiang Kai-shek what he claims to have seen immediately—"that his chances of reuniting China under his rule were virtually non-existent"—and dutifully delivered Eisenhower's message that Chiang, like Syngman Rhee, could expect no American help if he launched a unilateral military effort—in Chiang's case, a return to the mainland.

In Japan, Nixon picked up valuable experience in diplomatic indirection by launching, on instruction, a "trial balloon" about possible Japanese rearmament; Dulles believed rearmament necessary to resist Communist domination of the Pacific.

The vice president liked Mohammed Ayub Khan of Pakistan, who was pro-American and "more anti-Communist than anti-Indian"; that perhaps foretold President Nixon's famous "tilt" later in the Indo-Pakistan War. He hinted even in 1953 that he might support arms aid for Pakistan, infuriating the Indians; and though he disliked Nehru for his "self-appointed role as spokesman for the underdeveloped nations," he picked up from the Indian leader and years later made famous the phrase "a generation of peace." Nehru, however, thought Nixon "an unprincipled cad."[9]

The extensive itinerary provided for meetings with many other prominent leaders—Sukarno of Indonesia ("his palaces were filled with some of the most exquisite women I have ever seen"), Prince Norodom Sihanouk of Cambodia ("totally unrealistic . . . prouder of his musical talents than his political leadership"), Ramón Magsaysay ("his death . . . was a tragedy for the Philippines and for all of free Asia") and Robert Menzies of Australia ("extraordinary intelligence and profound understanding").

The leader of India's Madras province, Rajagopalachani ("infinitely wise"), particularly impressed Nixon, though "Rajaji" confounded the conventional wisdom of the era by insisting that it had been disastrous to develop the atomic bomb. "It was wrong," he told his American visitor, "to seek the secret of the creation of matter. It isn't needed for civilian purposes. It is an evil thing and will destroy those who discovered it."

Nixon apparently did not interpret this as anti-American, and in *RN* reported no argument with Rajaji's ominous prophesy.

On one of his last stops, Nixon conferred with and was impressed by the shah of Iran, Mohammed Riza Pahlevi. In late 1953, the shah had been only briefly in actual—as opposed to titular—power; not long before Nixon's visit, as he later recalled it in *RN,* the military in a violent coup had overthrown the "pro-Communist" regime of Prime Minister Mohammed Mossadegh. Then "a government supporting the Shah . . . was installed under Prime Minister Fazollah Zahedi."

Even in 1953, Nixon probably knew, as the shah surely did, that it was not the Iranian military that had overthrown Mossadegh and handed power to Pahlevi and Zahedi, a Nazi collaborator during World War II. Britain and the Eisenhower administration had done it, acting through the British Secret Intelligence Service and the CIA, with the Iranian military merely taking advantage of conditions created by Western "covert" operations. Nor was it communism that had been at issue, whatever Washington's ideological fantasies; oil and nationalism had been at the root of the struggle, with the Iranian people the real losers.[10]

For years, Iranian oil had been pumped, refined and marketed by the Anglo-Iranian Oil Company. The firm paid Iran only about a tenth of company earnings while transferring out of the country about $2.4 billion of $3 billion in gross revenues from 1913 to 1951. No wonder, therefore, that Prime Minister Mossadegh—an elderly nationalist—and the Iranian parliament had nationalized Anglo-Iranian in May 1951.

That was enough to raise the fear of communism in Truman's Washington and later in Eisenhower's, although Mossadegh earlier had stopped a proposed Iranian oil concession to the Soviet Union. But the Truman administration was wary of a British proposal to "bring about a change" in the Mossadegh government, and it was not until Eisenhower took office that the CIA and the British SIS began actively to plot the "change."

Mossadegh, who was believed to be over eighty years old, a frail and weepy man who conducted most of his business from a sickbed, tried to be conciliatory. But Eisenhower publicly rebuffed his request for continuance of the foreign aid Truman had authorized. Privately, the new president approved Operation Ajax, the covert CIA-SIS scheme.

Mossadegh unwittingly played into the plotters' hands by moving to supplant the shah as commander in chief of the Iranian armed forces and opening trade talks with the Soviet Union. As a result, Eisenhower ordered Ajax into immediate effect. By prearrangement, the shah issued a decree dismissing Mossadegh and naming General Zahedi to replace him— though the monarch and Queen Soraya prudently departed for the Caspian seacoast and Italy before this drastic action became public.

Mossadegh's supporters poured into the streets in the kind of emotional demonstrations that were to become familiar on American television during the hostage crisis of 1979–1980. So did Communists of the Tudeh party. The American-British plotters had counted on such disorder and turned loose an estimated six thousand counter-rioters organized by the CIA and SIS. On August 18 and 19, 1953, chaos briefly ruled Teheran; Mossadegh—clinging to his office—called out the police to restore order.

The move backfired as the Iranian military then seized power, suppressed the demonstrations and arrested Mossadegh. The shah came home to begin twenty-six years of virtually unchecked power that frequently amounted to despotism. Eisenhower not only restored Truman's $23.4 million foreign aid program; he increased it to $85 million—and before his administration ended in 1961, he had poured nearly a billion dollars into the shah's Iran.

Iranian oil production resumed in August 1954; the Anglo-Iranian monopoly was ended, but British Petroleum was awarded 40 percent of output; five American oil companies and nine independents shared another 40 percent; and 20 percent went to Royal Dutch Shell and Compagnie Française des Pétroles. Iran was to be paid 50 percent of the revenues—an improvement on the former concession but scarcely what the Iranian people had a right to expect from their own oil.

Richard Nixon arrived in Teheran only a few months after Operation Ajax had given the shah vast personal power, though not the real support of Iranians. The vice president found Zahedi "intelligent and wise, with enormous strength of character"; in Pahlevi, he sensed the makings of "a strong leader"—for whom the vice president began to develop an admiration that was to have long consequences for American foreign policy.

Visiting Washington in December 1954, the shah offered a toast to

Eisenhower: "But for the grace of God and the help of your country I would not be here today." God had had mighty little to do with it. Instead a determined president had shown that when the U.S. decided to move in its own interest, it had the will and the means and the lack of scruple to do so.

Vice President Nixon did not fail to absorb the lesson; and the next year, in the fate of another "pro-Communist" government halfway around the world from Iran, he was to observe the same approach even more ruthlessly applied.

As Anglo-Iranian had dominated Iran, the United Fruit Company had dominated Guatemala. El Pulpo ("the Octopus"), as the company was known locally, ran the railways and the power company and owned 42 percent of Guatemalan land. United Fruit paid no taxes or import duties and managed Puerto Barrios, Guatemala's only port, and all its other transportation. Not least as a result, in midcentury Guatemala remained an outpost of poverty, feudalism and repression.

Just as the nationalization of Anglo-Iranian had hardly been surprising, neither was the Guatemalan revolution of 1944 that led to the freely elected governments of Juan José Arevalo and his successor in 1951, Jacobo Arbenz Guzmán. In 1947, Arevalo affirmed the right of workers to strike, and both El Pulpo and the Truman administration decided he was a "Communist dictator." Arbenz's land reform of 1951 brought him similar condemnation.

He persevered in the program—which took 178,000 acres of land from El Pulpo—and began a new electric plant and a network of roads, both threatening United Fruit's dominance. With the help of company protestations, Adolf A. Berle, the assistant secretary of state, had decided by 1952 that Arbenz's Guatemala was a "Russian-controlled dictatorship."[11]

In 1953, the Eisenhower administration took office, admirably reflecting United Fruit's interests. The Dulles brothers—Foster at the State Department, Allen as director of the CIA—had been partners in the Sullivan and Cromwell law firm, which worked for the company. John Moors Cabot, the assistant secretary of state for inter-American affairs, was a brother of a former company president. Walter Bedell ("Beetle") Smith, the undersecretary of state, later became a company director. John J. McCloy, president of the World Bank—which was heavily influenced by the administration and had refused loans to Arbenz—afterward became a United Fruit director.

In December 1953, when Vice President Nixon returned from his two-month world tour, including his meeting with the shah, he found Operation Success (a secret plan for another "change," this one in Guatemala) well advanced. Carlos Castillo Armas, a Guatemalan colonel who had led a failed revolt against Arevalo in 1949, had been found in Honduras and recruited by the CIA as a figurehead leader. Training soon was under way for Castillo's "rebel" army and air force. Some of the latter were from Taiwan.

In May 1954, Foster Dulles acknowledged to Latin ambassadors that it was "impossible to produce evidence clearly tying the Guatemalan government to Moscow"; but he insisted that "such a tie must exist"—apparently because he *believed* it did—and "therefore the Soviet Union could not be allowed to establish a puppet state in this hemisphere."[12]

In the McCarthyite atmosphere of Washington in the early fifties, "Red penetration" of a neighbor country was an idea that carried its own political imperative. As Eisenhower put it at a meeting of Republican legislative leaders on April 26, 1954: "The Reds are in control and they are trying to spread their influence . . . as a first step of the breaking out in Guatemala to other South American countries." Later in the meeting, he asked, not in reference to Guatemala but none too rhetorically: "Where in the hell can you let the Communists chip away anymore? We just can't stand it."[13]

In that spring of 1954, one development did seem to confirm the American view of Guatemala: Arbenz bought two thousand tons of arms from Communist Czechoslovakia. That meant, Eisenhower said, that Guatemala had become an "outpost" of "Communist dictatorship" in the Western Hemisphere; he did not note that Guatemala for years had been trying to buy arms from the U.S., without success.

Arbenz, in fact, had been conned by his supposed comrades. The weapons he received* were mostly large cannon, of little use in internal fighting and designed to be mounted on railway flatcars, of which Guatemala had only a few. There were also some antitank weapons, but there were then no tanks in Central America.

By then, anyway, Operation Success was in high gear. Colonel Castillo's "army"—never more than about 140 men—was being supplied by CIA airlift from Opa-Locka in Florida, and trained in Honduras. There, too, an "air force" of about a dozen planes—P-47s, P-51s and three old bombers—had been thrown together. The U.S. Information Agency was flooding the Latin press with CIA-prepared disinformation.

The stage was set; and on June 18, Castillo in an old station wagon and his tiny army in trucks advanced six miles into Guatemala. His ancient air force took off for action, too. REVOLT LAUNCHED IN GUATEMALA, proclaimed the front page of the *New York Times* that morning; LAND-AIR-SEA INVASION REPORTED: RISINGS UNDER WAY IN KEY CITIES.

There was only one problem. Despite the CIA and the *Times,* little was

*The weapons shipment reached Puerto Barrios aboard the Swedish freighter *Alfhem* on May 15. CIA teams tried but failed to block delivery by blowing up the railroad tracks leaving the port.

happening in Guatemala. The popular revolt Castillo was supposed to ignite never took place. The invading army invaded no farther. A seaborne strike at Puerto Barrios fizzled. The air force dropped leaflets, a few real bombs and a hand grenade and a stick of dynamite on the port. Two planes were knocked out by ground fire; another crash-landed in Mexico, where its American pilot's arrest had to be covered up by the CIA. By Sunday June 20, Operation Success was more nearly Operation Failure.

At this crucial moment, Anastasio "Tacho" Somoza, the American-backed dictator of Nicaragua, offered two P-51 fighter-bombers to support Castillo, provided the U.S. sent him two replacements. Eisenhower recalled in his memoirs that at a White House meeting to discuss this deal on June 22, he asked Allen Dulles: "What do you think Castillo's chances would be without the aircraft?"

"About zero."

"Suppose we supply the aircraft. What would be the chances then?"

"About twenty percent."

Somoza's planes went into action on June 23 and their attacks became the main effort on Castillo's behalf—and finally carried the day, psychologically, if not militarily. The "rebel" radio had jammed Guatemalan airwaves and constantly reported "major battles," with Castillo advancing; Arbenz could not tell for sure what was happening in his own country.

On June 27, the Guatemalan army gave Arbenz an ultimatum: resign or be ousted. Not surprisingly, he resigned and took asylum in the Mexican embassy. On July 3, Castillo flew into Guatemala City in the American embassy plane; American Ambassador John Peurifoy flew with him, wearing a pistol in a holster, John Wayne–style. In one of the most mendacious statements ever made by a deceitful man, John Foster Dulles then proclaimed: "Now the future of Guatemala lies at the disposal of the Guatemalan people themselves."[14]

Arbenz's agrarian reform law was canceled and 1.5 million acres were returned to their original owners. Unions were outlawed. Unknown numbers of *campesinos* were murdered under the new government, hundreds of political and labor leaders were exiled, over nine thousand people were arrested, all political parties were suspended and three quarters of the population was disenfranchised for being illiterate. From then until relatively free elections were finally held in 1986, Guatemala scarcely knew a day of tranquility, much less progress, as guerrilla warfare, coups and countercoups wracked the country; nor were things much better as late as 1990. Colonel Castillo Armas himself was assassinated in 1957.*

*Between 1970 and 1973 alone, Amnesty International reported, "deaths and disappearances" in Guatemala exceeded twenty thousand. After Guatemala's liberation from "Communist dictatorship" by the Eisenhower administration, it became the staging area for President Kennedy's abortive attempt in 1961 similarly to "liberate" Cuba, via the Bay of Pigs.

Vice President Nixon had little or no actual part in Operation Success—one of the most closely held secrets of the Eisenhower administration. But it probably afforded such an astute observer the opportunity to learn from the master what Eisenhower later told his aide, Andrew Goodpaster:

> If you at any time take the route of violence or support of violence . . . then you commit yourself to carry it through, and it's too late to have second thoughts, not having faced up to the possible consequences, when you're midway in an operation.[15]

Years later, in Indochina, Nixon acted as if following such impressive counsel. The vice president probably noticed also during Operation Success that despite his chief's frequent preachments about allies and collective security, when perceived American interests were at stake, Eisenhower acted alone and with ruthless disregard for allies.

Arbenz, for instance, wanted the U.N. Security Council to take up the "uprising" in Guatemala, and France and Britain at first announced that they would support his request. Eisenhower exploded, telling aides he'd show the British "they have no right to stick their noses into matters which concern this hemisphere entirely." Henry Cabot Lodge, Eisenhower's U.N. ambassador, was instructed to tell British and French representatives that if they followed an independent line on Guatemala, the U.S. would take an "equally independent" view on Egypt and North Africa. On the crucial vote, Britain and France abstained.[16]

When he became president, Nixon could be equally abrupt—consulting none of the allies, for instance, when he took the U.S. off the gold standard in 1971, or in leaving Japan to be confounded by his opening to China.

Watching the Guatemalan operation from the sidelines, Nixon could hardly have failed to see also that when Eisenhower thought it necessary, he did not hesitate to take illegal action—a naval blockade of Guatemala, for instance. "There is no general power of search on the high seas in peacetime," Foreign Minister Anthony Eden of Britain declared, correctly; and Jim Hagerty, the White House press secretary, recalled in his diary that the U.S. once had fought a war *against* Britain to make the same point.

But necessity may have appeared to Nixon, as to Eisenhower, to have legalized a president's illegality. "Well, when the president does it, that means it is not illegal," he later told David Frost (in a television interview on May 19, 1977):

> If the president approves . . . an action because of the national security, or . . . because of a threat to internal peace and order of, of significant magnitude, then the president's decision in that instance is one that enables those who carry it out to carry it out without violating the law.

Dwight Eisenhower never would have expressed such an expansive and unpalatable view of presidential powers; he had too strong an instinct to keep the mud off his shoes. But the example he set in Iran and Guatemala—the idea that the Communists could be beaten at the game of subversion, deception, infiltration and takeover—was to echo through American foreign policy for a generation. It could not have been irrelevant to Richard Nixon's developing view of presidential power.

An apt student, he was learning at the knee. But sometimes—for instance, in the Indochinese crisis that overlapped Operation Success in 1954—the pupil seemed more willing than the master to take "the route of violence" with the full power of the U.S.

Eisenhower was never willing to commit the U.S. fully in support of the French war to retain Indochina. Early in 1954, with that war on the verge of failure, the president did agree to provide ten B-26 bombers, with two hundred airmen to service (not to fly) them—less than half what the desperate French had requested.

The president was wary of being dragged too far into a war that he feared would be bloody and endless and would identify the U.S. with colonialism; such a war, moreover, would replace one he had ended only the year before in Korea. As a military man, he had doubts about the prospects for a French victory—particularly after Paris deployed its best units in a single fortress surrounded by high ground held by the Vietminh: Dienbienphu. Against that stronghold, General Vo Nguyen Giap had concentrated sixty thousand Vietminh and overwelming Chinese-supplied artillery.

Besides, Eisenhower's defense budget would not support American forces for Indochina. On the other hand, Indochina was considered critical to the West. "If Indochina goes, and Southeast Asia goes, it is extremely hard to insulate ourselves against the consequences of that," Dulles had argued to Eisenhower even before the inauguration.[17]

A continued drain on French resources would mean that France could not meet its NATO commitment or ratify the European Defense Community. But a French pullout from Indochina would leave Communists in power, and another Asian nation "lost." For these reasons, the U.S.—even before Eisenhower sent the B-26s—was paying about 75 percent of the costs of the French war.

On January 8, 1954, however, Eisenhower told the NSC "with vehemence" (and with great prescience) that he "simply could not imagine the United States putting ground forces anywhere in Southeast Asia . . . [H]ow bitterly opposed I am to such a course of action. This war in Indo-China would absorb our troops by divisions!"

Still, as French defeat at Dienbienphu neared certainty that spring, Eisenhower—with his taste for covert action—was doing more to help than he publicly disclosed. Besides the B-26s, the two hundred airmen and the substantial war costs Washington was bearing, he had ordered the so-called Civil Air Transport—an airline secretly owned by the CIA and later renamed Air America—to help supply Dienbienphu.

In all, CAT pilots flew 684 sorties to the surrounded base during an operation the CIA called "Squaw II"; one C-119 pilot, James B. McGovern, was shot down on May 6, 1954, and died on May 7, the day the fortress was surrendered.[18]

This covert support may have encouraged the French to believe that eventually the U.S. would come overtly to their aid. But Eisenhower had set conditions for American intervention that he was sure could not be met—a French grant of independence for the nations of Indochina, British participation in any rescue effort, and full congressional backing.

The last two points were connected. The British were resisting all persuasion to join in preserving a French position in Indochina. Bothered by American Cold War zeal, and fearing that an American-led intervention might turn into an attack on China, or bring Chinese retaliation, London fretted about the chilling possibility of a world war that would draw in the Soviet Union.

Prime Minister Churchill was not too infirm to realize Britain's vulnerability in a nuclear war; and the struggle in Indochina, he told Admiral Arthur Radford, the chairman of the Joint Chiefs of Staff, could only be won by using "that horrible thing." Besides, why should a people who had given up India fight to hold Indochina for France?

When the elderly Churchill visited Washington in the heat of the crisis, Vice President Nixon met him at National Airport. On the ride across the Potomac and into the city, the prime minister again mentioned his "concern" about the possible use of this "terrible weapon" in Indochina.[19]

Eisenhower knew, however, that if there were no British participation, Congress would not support a "go-it-alone" American intervention, despite Republican campaign bombast about "rolling back" communism. The president, at least, had learned from his predecessor's experience in Korea. To a news conference on March 10, he declared:

> There is going to be no involvement of America in a war unless
> it is a result of the constitutional process that is placed upon
> Congress to declare it. Now let us have that clear.

By April, however, Eisenhower had become reconciled to the loss of at least part of Indochina, and was moving in his own mind to the idea of partition, the unappetizing but effective solution already in effect in Germany and Korea. Not to undercut the French or his own schemes, he insisted that there could be no negotiated settlement. But his eye was on

Geneva, where an international conference on Korea was scheduled for late April. The Soviets had insisted on adding Indochina to the agenda.

Meanwhile, the French army chief of staff, Paul Ely, had concocted with Admiral Radford something called "Operation Vulture"—an American air strike against Giap's siege force at Dienbienphu. It's not clear whether the plan included use of atomic bombs; Nixon thought three would be dropped, but Foster Dulles believed Vulture called only for conventional air power. The French general and the American admiral apparently thought Eisenhower would yield to increasing French pressure.

Such an unlikely reversal by the president was definitively ruled out after a special meeting of eight Republican and Democratic congressional leaders in the White House on Saturday morning, April 3. Eisenhower asked only for a general resolution giving him brief discretionary authority to use American air and sea power to prevent "extension and expansion" of Communist aggression in Asia. Even that proved too much for the congressional leaders—among them Lyndon Johnson, the Senate Democratic leader.

Perhaps Democrats remembered Republican campaign attacks on Truman and Acheson, and Republican promises to seek victory over communism. "As ye sow, so shall ye reap," Senator Hubert Humphrey had warned Dulles, "and believe me, you have so sown and so you reap."

All the leaders may have been misled by a Radford briefing into thinking that immediate intervention in Indochina was planned. In any case, they agreed to seek the resolution *only* if Britain and other allies gave satisfactory commitments to support the effort, and if France granted independence to Indochina. Any possibility of unilateral intervention vanished with that congressional reaction.

On April 5, therefore, Eisenhower rejected the Ely-Radford plan, although Dulles tentatively favored it, and the report of a special study committee headed by "Beetle" Smith had recommended American intervention to seek "military victory" in Indochina. Without congressional approval, the president told Dulles, Vulture or any other operation would be "completely unconstitutional and indefensible."

When Nixon and others then argued in an NSC meeting on April 9 for a conventional air strike, Eisenhower rejected that idea too. As for atomic weapons, when Robert Cutler brought him on April 30 the draft of an NSC paper exploring the possibility of their use, Eisenhower recoiled: "You boys must be crazy," he said, if his memory in an interview with his biographer, Stephen Ambrose, is to be trusted. "We can't use those awful things against Asians for the second time in less than ten years. My God."[20]

Nixon was present at this meeting and gives a different account in *RN*—one that makes Eisenhower seem less appalled by the notion of using atomic weapons:

Eisenhower asked me what I thought about this idea; I said that
whatever was decided about using the bomb, I did not think it was
necessary to mention it to our allies before we got them to agree
on united action. . . . Eisenhower turned to Cutler and said, "First,
I certainly do not think that the atom bomb can be used by the
United States unilaterally, and second, I agree with Dick that we
do not have to mention it to anybody before we get some agreement on united action."

Nixon's account suggests again the relative ignorance, in that early stage
of the atomic era, of even informed officials about the catastrophic destruc-
tiveness of the new weapons. How could an atomic bomb be used against
the Vietminh in the hills around Dienbienphu without destroying the
French forces the explosion was intended to rescue? How could Nixon and
Eisenhower think that they need not forewarn allies of such a cataclysmic
step—one raising the specter of world war and terrible destruction?

Nixon's account of his meeting with Eisenhower and Cutler also suggests that he did not offer strenuous objection to the use of atomic bombs,
and perhaps even favored it. He certainly favored American intervention
in Indochina, as he had stated publicly. Even amid crisis, Eisenhower not
untypically had gone golfing in Augusta, Georgia; he asked Nixon to
substitute for him in a scheduled presidential appearance before the American Society of Newspaper editors. Nixon's speech was supposed to be off
the record; but in the question and answer session he was remarkably
candid. As he later recalled in *RN,* an editor asked if he thought "we would
send American troops to Indochina if the French decided to withdraw and
it was the only way to save Indochina from being taken over by the
Communists?" Nixon replied:

I recognize that he has put a hypothetical question. . . . However,
answering the question directly and facing up to it . . . if in order
to avoid further communistic expansion in Asia and particularly
in Indochina, if in order to avoid it we must take the risk now by
putting American boys in, I believe that the Executive Branch of
the government has to take the politically unpopular position of
facing up to it and doing it, and *I personally would support such
a decision.* [Emphasis added.]

Experienced as he was by then with the press, Nixon could hardly have
believed that such words from the vice president would be kept off the
record by an editors' group—and they weren't. As his remarks began to
circulate, they raised the question at home and abroad whether Nixon had

floated a "trial balloon" for Eisenhower. Inquiries poured in to the White House. Jim Hagerty noted in his diary for April 16, 1954:

> Checked with Nixon to see if this were right, and he said it was but that he was answering hypothetical questions. Played dumb in this in answer to all queries. Think it was foolish for Dick to answer as he did but will make the best of it.

This leaves little doubt that Nixon had spoken for himself; the question is why. The British were alarmed by his apparent belligerence, which made it all the less likely that they could be persuaded to join in any form of united action. Nixon knew Eisenhower and his views on Indochina, as well as his own place in the administration, too well to think he could pressure the president into an action he did not want to take.

Politically, Nixon was too knowledgeable to think he was helping the administration or the Republican party—in the middle of the 1954 elections—by raising the possibility of American involvement in another Asian war. At a White House meeting of the Republican congressional leaders a week later, in fact, House Majority Leader Charles Halleck reported that Nixon's words "had really hurt."

Nixon's remarks, therefore, usually have been regarded as a blunder; but since he was not long returned from his Asian tour, during which he had been convinced that the U.S. had "to do everything possible to find a way to keep the French in Vietnam until the Communists [are] defeated," he was more likely saying what he actually believed. He had dissociated himself from what he thought was a weak policy that might end in the loss of Indochina; if that happened, he could claim to have said "I told you so" in the ASNE speech.

Eisenhower put out the word that Nixon had enunciated American policy "hypothetically" but that an American intervention was "unlikely." On April 20, Nixon spoke in Cincinnati and prudently balanced his ticket; the administration's main goal, he said, was to "keep us from having to send American boys to fight in Indochina or anywhere else"—by no means a retraction of his remarks on April 16 but a far different emphasis.

Eisenhower, of course, had his own plans and moved ahead step by step. At his news conference on April 7, he had offered one of his most famous concepts, "the 'falling domino' principle": "You have a row of dominoes set up, you knock over the first one, and what will happen to the last one is the certainty that it will go very quickly."

That suggested the necessity for resistance to a Communist victory in Indochina to prevent further losses. On April 29, however, at another news conference, the president made his real purpose public. Conceding that the

Vietminh were winning, he argued that "the most you can work out is a practical way of getting along." Divided Germany and Berlin were examples of what he meant, he said: "If you could get that, that would be the most you could ask." To prevent a Communist triumph that would set the dominoes tumbling, he was willing to divide Indochina, limiting the Vietminh to incomplete victory.

On May 7, Walter Lippmann wrote in his influential syndicated column, *Today and Tomorrow,* that, without allied support in Asia,

> American military power which is on the sea and in the air can hold islands, can deny the use by an enemy of strategic points near the coast of the great continent. But it cannot occupy, it cannot pacify, it cannot control the mainland even in the coastal areas, much less the hinterland.[21]

The point was well taken, but by then intervention would have been futile. The French—having been reduced by lack of ammunition, in the last stages of the battle, to throwing grenades from behind barricades of the dead—surrendered Dienbienphu the next day. The Vietminh had defeated one of Europe's great armies, mostly because they had enlisted thousands of Vietnamese (whom the French once had disdained) to drag Chinese field pieces up hills that Western military experts believed too steep for artillery positions. Dienbienphu, General Giap observed thirty years later, "was like the toll of a bell heralding the decline, the twilight, of colonialism."[22]

Dienbienphu held a military lesson that anyone else who considered taking up arms against Vietnamese nationalism would ignore at his peril. The respected U.S. Army chief of staff, Matthew L. Ridgway, stated it clearly: "With reference to the Far East as a whole, Indochina is devoid of decisive military objectives and the allocation of more than token U.S. armed forces [there] would be a serious diversion of limited U.S. capabilities."[23]

On June 18, Pierre Mendès-France took over as French premier; he pledged to make peace in Indochina by July 20, and was ready to meet and deal with Chou En-lai at Geneva. But Eisenhower had no intention of allowing Communists the falling dominoes he thought would be the full fruits of their victory. Foster Dulles quickly demonstrated the intransigent American attitude; when by accident he encountered Chou at Geneva, Chou held out his hand and Dulles refused to shake it—quickly walking out of the room.

Chou was profoundly embarrassed—not just politically, but also as a Chinese whose sense of courtesy had been disdained. At the time, Richard Nixon might have done just as Dulles did (with better reason, since Dulles did not have to run for office). But much later, in 1971, circumstances had changed, and President Nixon had been well briefed on Chou's long memory of the Geneva incident.

"Therefore," Nixon recalled in *Leaders,* "when I reached the bottom step of the airplane ramp on my first arrival in Peking, I made a point of extending my hand as I walked toward him." On the drive to Peking, Chou told Nixon: "Your handshake came over the vastest ocean in the world—twenty-five years of no communication."

At their first plenary meeting, Chou again brought up the sore subject. "We shook hands," he said, "but John Foster Dulles didn't want to do that. . . . Dulles's assistant [at Geneva], Mr. Walter Bedell Smith, wanted to do differently, but he did not break the discipline of John Foster Dulles, so he had to hold a cup of coffee in his right hand. Since one doesn't shake hands with the left hand, he used it to shake my arm."

Nixon replied that, in his administration, the U.S. would look at "each country in terms of its own conduct rather than lumping them all together and saying that because they have this kind of philosophy they are all in utter darkness."

But in 1954, the "vastest ocean" and the "utter darkness" governed American attitudes, at Geneva as elsewhere. Though Eisenhower, like Mendès-France, wanted peace and partition as preferable to war and defeat, he was profoundly anti-Communist; he had his Republican right wing to contend with, his belligerent military and an American public that, if it did not want war, did not want Indochina "lost" to the Communists.

As the Vietminh continued to drive the French from Indochina after Dienbienphu, both French and American fears about Chinese military intervention were renewed—so much so that the NSC recommended that the U.S. strike directly at China, using atomic weapons. The Joint Chiefs concurred. From Korea, Syngman Rhee flew to Washington to persuade Eisenhower that the time had come to hit the Chinese.

With calm good sense, Eisenhower scotched this hysteria by reminding Dulles and others that an attack on China could bring retaliation by China's giant ally, the Soviet Union—an atomic power itself. If the U.S. were to attack China, Eisenhower pointed out, it would have to attack the Soviet Union too. Did anyone really want that?

Mendès-France and Chou quickly agreed at Geneva on the temporary partition of Vietnam, independence for Laos and Cambodia, and the withdrawal of all foreign troops—major Communist concessions to the West, since the Vietminh were capable of winning the war outright. Elections for the reunification of Vietnam were to be held in two years.

Eisenhower's virulent anticommunism and his plans for Indochina predictably—and fatally—intervened. He refused to allow the U.S. to sign the Geneva accords, though he announced that he would not use force to upset them. With his eye on Old Guard senators like Knowland of California, he emphasized that the U.S. was not "a party to or bound by the decisions taken."

In September, again fatefully, he acted on that defiant premise, extending to Laos, Cambodia and a new government in "South Vietnam" the protection of the Southeast Asia Treaty Organization concocted by Foster Dulles in the aftermath of the French defeat. The Geneva accords had specified that neither part of divided Vietnam could join an alliance. Eisenhower's true intention had begun to show.

In October, he pledged American aid in a letter to Ngo Dinh Diem—the mandarin Vietnamese the CIA had chosen to head a new South Vietnamese government—in order "to assist . . . in developing and maintaining a strong, viable state capable of resisting attempted subversion or aggression through military means."

The accords had promised reunification of Vietnam—not a separate, permanent state in the South. But accords or no accords, Eisenhower intended to back Diem when he refused to hold the elections that were supposed to bring reunification. (The CIA believed Ho Chi Minh would get 80 percent of the vote if the election were held.)

More than a decade later, President Lyndon Johnson was to argue repeatedly that Eisenhower's letter to Diem in October 1954 represented a "commitment" to South Vietnamese independence that required the U.S. to honor it. Johnson maintained this insistence even at the cost of a half-million troops sent to Southeast Asia, fifty thousand of them killed, and political dissension at home that nearly tore the nation apart.

The text of Eisenhower's letter, however, does not sustain Johnson's extravagant claim. But Eisenhower's decision to set up and aid an "independent" South Vietnam was a perhaps irreversible step down the shadowy road to the second Indochinese war—a mostly American war that Dwight Eisenhower had refused to countenance in his own time—a war that Richard Nixon, who was ready to fight in 1954, ultimately would expand and contract, and the American part of which he would have to liquidate.

Nixon hinted in *The Real War* that he continued to believe Eisenhower should have supported the French militarily in 1954:

> It has been estimated that a limited commitment of conventional American air power might have turned the tide of battle. [But] even if the strike had taken place, it is probable that the French would have lost in Indochina eventually because of their stubborn refusal to provide adequate guarantees of eventual independence.

Indeed. But if the Indochinese crisis of 1954 first caused Nixon to doubt Eisenhower's willingness to use American power, more explosive events

two years later were to have much the same effect—but also to give the
vice president a firsthand view of American *economic* power in action.

In the summer of 1956, Gamal Abdel Nasser of Egypt signed an arms
agreement with Czechoslovakia. For this and other "unacceptable" acts,
the Eisenhower administration canceled its agreement to help finance
Nasser's fondest dream, the Aswan High Dam on the Nile. Nasser responded by nationalizing the Suez Canal, through which moved half of the
90 percent of Britain's oil obtained from the Middle East.

Consequently, Anthony Eden—who finally had replaced Churchill as
prime minister—cabled Eisenhower that his government had firmly decided to fight for the canal and be rid of Nasser. Eden knew that if the oil
flow to Britain was curtailed, the pound would be weakened with troubling
consequences—including an end to Britain's pretensions to be a third
superpower. But Eisenhower was horrified at what he thought an unwarranted and impractical scheme.[24]

He made it clear to Eden that the U.S. would not join nor support an
attack on Nasser—who had every right, Eisenhower thought, to take over
a waterway running through Egypt's national territory. Throughout that
summer and fall, as the Eisenhower-Nixon reelection campaign heated up,
the president and Dulles worked to stall the British and possibly to bring
the Arab nations into the Western camp. They succeeded only in delaying
but not averting a showdown, though Nasser's pilots and bureaucrats had
proved that they could operate the canal.

On October 15, Eisenhower received ominous news. U-2 reconnaissance
flights had spotted sixty French Mystère jets *in Israel*—an apparent violation of an American-British-French agreement, in force since 1950, to
maintain the status quo in arms in the Middle East. Something was in the
wind that Washington neither was a part of nor knew about—possibly an
Israeli attempt, American analysts hypothesized, to wrest the West Bank
away from Jordan. Under cover of such an attack, Eisenhower feared,
Britain and France might try to retake the canal.

Secret U-2 flights also disclosed British and French troop buildups on
Cyprus. On October 28, Israel called up her reserves. The next afternoon,
as Eisenhower flew from Florida to Richmond, Virginia, for a campaign
appearance, the Israelis launched a massive attack—not against Jordan but
across the Sinai desert toward Egypt and the canal. By the early afternoon
of October 30, the aims of a British-French-Israeli cabal were made clear
in a British ultimatum—ostensibly to protect the canal, but redolent of
Victoria's imperial reign.

Egypt and Israel were both to withdraw their forces ten miles from the
canal within twelve hours, so that Britain and France could occupy important points along its length. If the Middle Eastern governments did not

heed this decree, the two European powers would take the canal by force, separating Israeli and Egyptian forces to stop their war.

This crude power play was all too easily seen through: posing as peacemakers between Israel and Egypt, Britain and France would regain control of the canal, Israel would keep its ill-gotten gains in the Sinai, and the brash Nasser probably could not survive politically. Israel promptly accepted the ultimatum. Nasser, of course, defied it.

Eisenhower brought powerful pressures for a cease-fire and British-French-Israeli withdrawals. On October 31, nevertheless, British aircraft bombed Cairo, Port Said and other Egyptian targets. Nasser retaliated as might have been expected, blocking the canal by sinking more than thirty ships loaded with cement and rocks. What Britain and France ostensibly had sought to prevent, they had brought about.

The U.S. pushed a cease-fire resolution through the U.N., but Eden ignored both it and all Eisenhower's protests. On November 5, British and French paratroopers landed in Egypt; amphibious landings followed. These operations "truly incensed the Eisenhower administration." Both were delayed, owing to botched military preparations, which only added to Eisenhower's anger and disgust at the mess he thought his allies had made of things in the sensitive Middle East.[25]

The Soviets, despite their simultaneous trouble in Hungary, threatened sanctimoniously to use force to restore Middle Eastern peace and brazenly proposed that the U.S. and the Soviet Union join forces against Washington's foremost allies in order to stop the burgeoning war. Eisenhower responded with a warning that if Moscow put troops into the region, the U.S. would resist them forcefully; the NATO alliance, he was resolved, would not be shattered by British-French foolishness and Soviet opportunism.

On November 6, Election Day in the U.S., Eden—stymied by Eisenhower's opposition, staggered by the huge costs of what had turned out to be an ineffective operation against Egypt, but minimally able to claim that Britain and France controlled the blocked canal—finally agreed to a cease-fire. A U.N. military team began moving in but Eisenhower had to withhold American oil and financial assistance to force the British out.

The president had the weapons. British currency reserves were to be published on December 3; if they were less than $2 billion—as they would be if the conflict dragged on—the pound sterling and the nations basing their currencies on it would be badly damaged. But the U.S. controlled Britain's possible sources of aid: a waiver of interest payments on the Anglo-American loan of 1945, a new loan from the U.S. Export-Import Bank, or a draw on the American-dominated International Monetary Fund. Eisenhower refused to permit any of them, as long as Britain remained in Egypt.

The outcome was foregone. By the key date of December 3, Eden had announced withdrawal plans. Eisenhower quickly turned loose the necessary aid. By Christmas, the invading force was gone.

The cabal had not succeeded in toppling Nasser; instead, his resistance to the tripartite attack by two European nations and Israel made him more than ever a hero in Egypt and the Third World. Eden, a sick man anyway, was ruined politically and soon resigned his office. To Eisenhower, this was one of the most distressing periods of his presidency.

He had at least two consolations. In the midst of the dual crisis—the Middle East and Hungary—he and Richard Nixon were reelected by a margin of nearly ten million votes, double that of their victory in 1952. And the American stand in defense of a Third World country, however distressing the necessity for it, was hailed around the globe.

In contrast to the simultaneous Soviet suppression of the Hungarian uprising, the U.S. had stood against force of arms, for law, for the rights of small nations and for peaceful settlement of disputes. In contrast to Eisenhower's own recent power plays in Iran and Guatemala—though these were little known or understood at the time—his opposition to war and big-power dominance in the Middle East amply demonstrated what the world wanted to believe of the free and democratic U.S.

In 1956, bearing as usual the brunt of the Republican political campaign, Nixon seems to have played little part in this drama—during the October-November crisis, Eisenhower scheduled few meetings of the formal NSC, which would have included the vice president. Even such a zealous student of foreign affairs as Nixon could have spared little time, anyway, from necessary speech-making, traveling and rally-going.

Nixon has been strangely critical of Eisenhower's conduct in the Suez crisis. In *RN,* for example, he suggested that "our actions [in 1956] were a serious mistake." In *Leaders* he observed further that Eisenhower's opposition to the invasion "in retrospect, I think was wrong." In *The Real War* Nixon was even more explicit, calling Eisenhower himself to witness:

> [Their] humiliating defeat in Suez had a devastating effect on the willingness of Britain and France to play a major role not only in the Mideast but in other areas of the world. . . . Years later, Eisenhower was to reflect that the U.S. restraint of Britain, France, and Israel when they were trying to protect their interests in Suez was a tragic mistake.

Nixon the elder statesman belabored the theme in an article in *The Times* of London for January 28, 1987, lamenting the death of Harold Macmillan. This was doubly infelicitous because in 1956, as a member of the Eden cabinet, Macmillan had *opposed* the Suez invasion; and because that operation caused Anthony Eden's downfall and brought Harold Macmillan to Number 10 Downing Street in his stead.

Nevertheless, Nixon wrote:

> If I may resort to British understatement, the role of the United States in handling that crisis was not admirable. The serious mistakes the US has made in dealing with Iran pale into insignificance compared with those made during the Suez crisis.

Understatement seems hardly the right word for this claim, which Nixon bolstered by stating that "as Eisenhower's vice president I followed events at first hand." Considering his political preoccupation at the time, "at first hand" also seems the opposite of British understatement. Nixon also insisted again on Eisenhower's change of heart:

> Years later, after he had left office, I talked with Eisenhower about Suez; he told me it was his major foreign policy mistake. . . . We agreed that the worst fallout from Suez was that it weakened the will of our best allies, Britain and France, to play a major role in the Middle East or in other areas outside Europe.

Eisenhower gave no hint in his memoirs of any such reconsideration. William Ewald, who helped write them, does not in any way suggest in his own book such a monumental change of view. Nor do Eisenhower's biographers. His well-recorded anger at the time of the crisis, moreover, seems incompatible with a later mea culpa. And long after his presidency, the old general proudly claimed that

> the United States never lost a soldier or a foot of ground in my Administration. We kept the peace. People asked how it happened—by God, it didn't just happen, I'll tell you that.[26]

He could hardly have made such a claim had he gone to war in aid of the British and French at Suez. So what can be said for Nixon's claims, made long after the fact?

It's true that Suez marked the decline of British "will" to play a major role in the Middle East and elsewhere; but in her straitened economic conditions, Britain could not have played a major role much longer. By 1956, too, the U.S. still wanted allies but was not overeager to have coequal partners in the actual leadership of the West. "Eisenhower [was] happy to aid the British and to work with them as long as they knew their place, which was not ahead of the Americans."[27]

It's true, too, that Nasser turned to the Soviet bloc, but he already had started to do so when the U.S. spurned the Aswan dam. American intervention on the side of the British, French and Israelis—or even American tolerance of their invasion—would hardly have stopped him from moving toward Moscow; quite the opposite. After Nasser's death on September 28, 1970, Egypt became a cooperative friend of the U.S. and reached a peace treaty with Israel. Neither might have happened had Eisenhower joined or abetted, rather than thwarted, the Suez cabal in 1956.

If Eisenhower was wrong, then Eden and his partners must have been mostly right. But it was more nearly *their* actions than Eisenhower's that caused the results Nixon deplores; invasion and retreat dramatized and heightened—they did not create—British and French weaknesses and Nasser's leanings. The Soviets might have been compelled to move forcefully into the Middle East on the side of Nasser, had the U.S. been complicitous with the cabal, bringing the unacceptable risk of superpower war that was never far from Eisenhower's mind in 1956.

Nothing sustains Nixon's repeated claims that in retirement the old general thought his Suez policy "his major foreign policy mistake." Are these, then, less Eisenhower's judgments than *Nixon's,* predicated perhaps on Eisenhower's mere agreement that Suez had precipitated British decline and advanced Nasser's turn to Moscow?

All these claims were published well after Eisenhower's death in 1969, so—to put the best face on it—Nixon might have reserved his criticism during the general's life. On the other hand, he may have been avenging himself for indignities he felt he had suffered during his vice presidency; or perhaps he was asserting, when Eisenhower could no longer contradict or damage him, that his own judgment had been better than that of the revered president—who, by implication, had come to agree with the Richard Nixon he at times had ignored.*

That's speculation. What seems clear from these writings is that Nixon, as he had in the Indochinese debate of 1954, thought in 1956 that American power ought to be used, this time for the assertion of Western interests in the Middle East, even at the risk of war with the Soviet Union. That was a judgment an uninvolved vice president or an elder, retired president could make more easily than the man who at the time carried actual responsibility for war and peace.

As vice president for eight years, Richard Nixon had numerous other occasions to observe foreign leaders and to watch, even advise, Dwight

*For this book, the author addressed to former president Nixon a written inquiry seeking details about Eisenhower's supposedly revised view and their conversation on this subject. No reply or acknowledgment was received.

Eisenhower in important episodes—whether or not his advice was taken. At the end of 1956, for example, after his and the president's reelection, Nixon paid a quick visit to a refugee camp at Andau in Austria, to which thousands of Hungarians were fleeing in the aftermath of the uprising the Soviets had just crushed.

Nixon's presence provided a symbol of American concern (and many of what later would be known as "photo opportunities"). More important to his education in world affairs, he listened to numerous refugees tell him that the Voice of America and Radio Free Europe (CIA-sponsored) had encouraged their abortive revolution.

Despite his anticommunism, the vice president concluded that it was "irresponsible" to raise the hopes of peoples to whom the U.S. could give no real help. In *RN,* many years later but long before the collapse of the Communist empire at the end of 1989, he confessed that he still felt "an utter hopelessness about what we can do to help the Communist countries of Central and Eastern Europe." He did not foresee, as indeed few did, that ultimately these countries would free themselves, or that an internally weakened Soviet Union would urge them on.

Upon his return from Austria, Nixon did recommend to Eisenhower that the McCarran-Walter Immigration Act—which strictly limited entrance to the U.S.—be amended to permit a "flexible response" to the Hungarian refugees. It was a little-noticed irony that the McCarran-Walter Act had become law only because President Truman's veto had been overridden by two votes—with Senator Richard Nixon among those voting to override.

Still, as the Alsop brothers observed in their syndicated column, "an adroit and intelligent man wishing to build himself up to the stature of a future Presidential candidate could hardly ask for a better chance" than Nixon's Christmas trip to the border of the free world.

When Eisenhower refused, in one of his less prescient moments, to see Fidel Castro during the young Cuban leader's visit to Washington in 1959, Nixon got another firsthand experience. He talked with Castro for three hours in the vice president's rococo formal office off the Senate floor. Immediately afterward, Nixon told his press secretary, Herbert Klein, that Castro was "an outright Communist, and he's going to be a real danger."[28]

More circumspectly, he reported to the president:

> Whatever we may think of [Castro], he is going to be a great factor in the development of Cuba and very possibly in Latin affairs generally. He seems to be sincere. He is either incredibly naive about Communism or under Communist discipline—my guess is the former. . . . [B]ecause he has the power to lead . . . we have no choice but at least to try to orient him in the right direction.

That was more, at the time, than most high officials perceived about Castro, but Eisenhower and, later, President Kennedy were too anti-Communist—or wanted to appear to be—to accept such sound advice.

As vice president, Richard Nixon seldom had more effect in foreign affairs than he did in the case of Castro, his later campaign puffery to the contrary. Nixon was primarily an astute and observant onlooker of world events during the eight important years when the Eisenhower administration was in power—and he forgot little of what he saw of those events or of what he learned from Eisenhower's reactions.

5

★

Prat Boy

★

Ike, what in hell does a man have to do to get
your support?

—Charles Jones, President Eisenhower's
friend, in 1956

In the summer of 1958, Dwight Eisenhower's popularity rating slipped
below 50 percent for the first time in his presidency. The American economy was in recession and the Democrats expected to score a big victory
in the November congressional elections. As if all that were not enough to
irritate the proud general, on July 14 the Middle East exploded once again.

King Faisal of Iraq was murdered in a military takeover by pro-Nasser
forces. King Hussein of Jordan was under Nasserite pressures, too. King
Saud of Saudi Arabia was demanding American intervention, and President Chamoun of Lebanon, fearing that Nasser's ally, Syria, might move
across their joint border, asked for American help. On July 14, Eisenhower ordered the marines into Lebanon, citing Chamoun's invitation to
distinguish this move from the British-French intervention at Suez in
1956.

That morning, Eisenhower also summoned Vice President Richard
Nixon to the White House. Nixon recalled in *RN* that he found the
president pacing the floor in frustration—but not just about Lebanon.
"Here on a day that I'm making a decision that could involve the United
States in war," he blurted, "I have to be worried about this damned
Goldfine-Adams business."

. . .

Not for the first time, Dick Nixon was about to be designated as "Ike's prat boy"—Walter Bedell Smith's phrase for a role to which, in war and peace, Smith himself had become unhappily accustomed.

As a constitutionally elected official, of course, Nixon did not literally have to take orders from Eisenhower; but before the 1956 election, he was well aware of the possibility that at the president's whim he could be left off the ticket that year—and after 1956, he knew Eisenhower had the power to kill or deeply depress Nixon's own presidential hopes for 1960. In fact, he had little choice but to become on occasion Ike's prat boy; the Adams affair was one of those times.

Sherman Adams, a cold and unemotional New Englander—as far as he ever showed anyone in Washington—was the keeper of the gates in the Eisenhower White House. Contrary to capital folklore, he had little influence on great decisions, but he ran the White House efficiently, an administrative skill the president highly valued.

Among other contributions, Adams saw to it that no one got into Eisenhower's office without his approval (save Foster Dulles, who had his own "back entrance" arrangement with Ann Whitman, the president's secretary). Adams kept the front door firmly closed, often with minimal courtesy. From that fact, it was easy to conclude that *any* White House rebuff stemmed from Adams. Many came to dislike this "abominable no-man," as wags called him, and few were his friends.

Adams had wanted to drop Nixon and substitute Senator Knowland on the 1952 ticket, and Nixon never forgave—or at least never forgot—those whom he felt had abandoned him in the fund crisis. Adams also was among those who had wanted to "dump Nixon" from the ticket in 1956, another offense that weighed heavily with the vice president. Besides, the two men had been tacit rivals for power within the administration, particularly when Eisenhower's illnesses had left a vacuum to be filled—Adams as staff chief and the champion of liberal Republicans, Nixon as the supposed heir apparent and ambassador from the Old Guard.

So Nixon had been dismayed only slightly, if at all, when in June 1958 a House investigating committee—controlled, of course, by the Democrats—stumbled on an Adams "indiscretion." The White House no-man had said yes and allowed some hotel bills he had incurred to be paid by one Bernard Goldfine, a none-too-reputable but wealthy investor in New England textiles and real estate, and a dabbler in politics.

Adams denied any wrongdoing, and Jim Hagerty, speaking for Eisenhower, characterized Democratic allegations of influence-peddling as "completely false." Nixon manfully swallowed whatever personal satisfaction he might have derived from Adams's plight and advised a group of Republican state chairmen not to act like "cannibals" when a fellow Republican was in trouble. Remembering his own disappointments during the fund crisis, Nixon added pointedly: "It doesn't take much guts to kick a guy when he's down."[1]

But Adams's numberless ill-wishers—all those he had offended with his frosty way of refusing requests, the Old Guardsmen who thought he had been instrumental in destroying their hopes for a conservative administration ("Most of the uproar against me," he grumbled in his memoirs, "came from the conservative Republicans"), the Democrats who saw in the case a needed weapon against Republicans seeking election to Congress in 1958—all these and more were delighted.[2]

So it often is with those who rely upon power alone, rather than decent human relations. And the press, of course, after so much Republican denunciation of the supposedly corrupt Truman administration, was delighted to keep Adams and Goldfine on the front page.

By the time Eisenhower called in Nixon on July 14, the day of the Lebanese intervention, the matter was out of hand; Republicans across the country were all but unanimous that Sherman Adams had to go. The *New York Post*—which had broken the Nixon fund story six years earlier—had dropped the kind of item into the Adams story that gave it color: Goldfine also had given Adams a vicuña overcoat. To this day, people who cannot recall Goldfine's name and who remember Adams only vaguely have heard that there was a "vicuña coat" scandal in the Eisenhower administration, just as they may know something about a "deep freeze" scandal under Harry Truman.

Appearing voluntarily and with the president's consent, Adams went before the House committee and admitted that he had been imprudent in his relations with Goldfine. But he denied any impropriety or influence-peddling; he had made only one phone call on Goldfine's behalf, he said—to the Securities and Exchange Commission, asking it to expedite hearings in a case involving his benefactor.

Eisenhower defended Adams's integrity and at a news conference confessed, to much Democratic derision: "I need him." That seemed to confirm the many stories that the president left a lot of his work to subordinates, including Adams. At any rate, Eisenhower's remark helped to keep the story going. Republicans like Knowland of California and Barry Goldwater of Arizona, both of whom were running for office in 1958, ignored Nixon's "cannibals" plea and demanded Adams's head. Republican state chairmen joined the hue and cry. The Democrats chortled.

Still, the story might have blown over, had the House committee not discovered that the innocuous-sounding hotel bills paid for Adams had totaled more than three thousand dollars—a lot of money in 1958—some of which Goldfine had deducted, as a business expense, from his income tax.

The president was in an embarrassing position. His party was insistent that if Adams stayed, Republican disaster would ensue in November. But Eisenhower had never liked to fire anyone who had worked loyally for him, and Adams had. He really did need Adams (or thought he did), believed in Adams's integrity and resented the political and personal motives in many of the attacks on his staff chief.

"How dreadful it is that cheap politicians can so pillory an honest man," he told Ann Whitman, who recorded the remark in her diary.

The president was in a weak position to punish anyone for accepting gifts, because Eisenhower himself was a similar offender. No one made an issue of expensive gifts from wealthy friends to a popular president, and none of the friends are known to have sought special favors; no doubt Eisenhower would have refused such requests, had any been made—*and* the gifts.

But that was essentially the same defense Adams had tried in vain to offer: *I took the gifts but did nothing in return.* Such a defense ignored the fact that in politics the *appearance* of conflict of interest—as Richard Nixon had learned in 1952—can be as important as an actual conflict. Dwight Eisenhower himself had set the standard—"clean as a hound's tooth"—and only the immense respect in which the nation held the World War II hero prevented gifts to Eisenhower from becoming the political issue they should have been.

By July 14, with the Middle East most prominently on his mind, the reluctant president had little choice but to remove Adams. Still, that morning in the White House, he could bring himself only to tell Nixon to keep him advised; but at least he had brought his most experienced political hand into the matter. In August, when the two talked about Adams again, Eisenhower, no doubt hopefully, said he'd heard "the issue has quieted down considerably."

Nixon knew better. "I felt I had to be completely frank," he recalled in *RN,* so he told the president that the Democrats would push the issue so hard that Republican candidates would have to take sides—and most would be *against* keeping Adams in the White House. Nixon thought the case could cost the party two dozen or more seats in Congress.

Eisenhower, his earlier loyalty to Adams disappearing under pressure, thought that such a prospect might give Adams a reason for resigning—to avoid being "an embarrassment to the Republican party or to me." This time, he asked Nixon to talk to "Sherm" after Congress had adjourned.

Nixon took his family on vacation instead, but they had no sooner arrived at The Greenbrier in West Virginia than the president called him back to Washington. The Republican National Committee was to meet in a few days; Eisenhower wanted the Adams matter resolved before then but still was unwilling for Adams to be told outright that the president wanted his resignation—although it was clear to Nixon that Eisenhower *did* want it.

Nixon could only tell Adams that most Republican leaders and candidates wanted him to quit. Adams, a tough player too, demanded to know what "the boss" thought. Nixon gave his "personal view" that Eisenhower "thinks you are a liability and that you should resign." But he saw that Adams did not plan to take even such a strong hint. In *Firsthand Report,* Adams's memoir, he did not even mention this meeting with Nixon.

The chief of staff saw Eisenhower the same day. That afternoon, the president and Nixon played golf at Burning Tree—Eisenhower's bad mood showing itself, Nixon recalled in *RN,* in a worse than usual game. On the drive home, with unconscious irony, Eisenhower unburdened himself: "Sherm won't take any of the responsibility. He leaves it all to me."

Nixon must have wondered why Adams *should* take a responsibility Eisenhower so resolutely shunned, and to whom the matter *should* be left, if not to the president. And he must have heard echoes of the general's lofty attitude in the fund crisis of 1952, as Eisenhower said: "Still, I can't fire a man who is sincere, just for political reasons. He must resign in a way I can't refuse." Of Adams personally, the president added: "With all these things that have been coming out one by one in the press, Sherm sees no wrong whatever in anything he has done."

But neither did Eisenhower himself see anything wrong in accepting gifts—not enough, at any rate, to give back the cattle or Mamie's Cottage, or to demand Adams's resignation. He told Nixon to ask Meade Alcorn, the Republican party chairman—thus twice removing himself from the ugly necessity—to "lay it on the line" with Adams.

That was August 26; but by September 15 nothing had been done, the Adams story had clung like a leech to the White House and the Republicans, and Eisenhower had been hearing even from wealthy friends and contributors that Adams had to go. Animosity toward Adams, Alcorn reported, was hampering Republican fund-raising. Eisenhower said he *knew* what to do but "the difficulty is to find a good way to do it." Then he told Alcorn that he and Nixon had to talk again to Adams, so that the case "isn't hanging around during the campaign."

Nixon and Alcorn did plot a strategy together, but to avoid alerting the press—as Nixon tells it in *RN*—only Alcorn went to Adams's office. William Ewald, recounting the same events, says that Alcorn was "miffed" at Nixon for backing out of the meeting. For whatever reason, Nixon clearly was as reluctant as the president to give Adams the bad news directly.

Alcorn did the job. After what must have been a difficult session, with Adams as flinty and resistant as New England granite, the party chairman phoned Nixon to say that Adams finally had been convinced that he had no choice, and that Alcorn, like Nixon before him, was acting at Eisenhower's request.[3]

In the end, despite all his evasions, Eisenhower could not avoid confrontation with Adams—who demanded not unreasonably to hear the bad news from the president himself. They met on September 17, Eisenhower still insisting that "you will have to take the initiative yourself"—as if he had left Adams any choice.

Adams said he would resign, but he wanted—incredibly, with the elections only six weeks off—to wait a month to wind up some White House business. Just as incredibly, Eisenhower agreed—but changed his mind as soon as Adams was out of the Oval Office. Then the president phoned him, finally to say what he should have said by mid-July—that he needed Adams out right away.

Even then, it was September 22 before the hard-shelled Adams flew to Eisenhower's vacation house at Newport, Rhode Island, and after another talk with the president announced his resignation. The "deepest regret" with which Eisenhower said he received it probably did not much impress the former chief of staff.

Even the sensational Adams affair was brief and unimportant compared to the years in which Eisenhower played the nice guy while using his vice president and others as his prat boys in dealing with the redoubtable Senator Joseph R. McCarthy of Wisconsin. In those years, "Tail-Gunner Joe," the maverick Red-baiter, carried Nixon's old campaign against "Communists in government" to depths Richard Nixon himself had never approached—attacking finally the Eisenhower administration itself.

The tone of Eisenhower's dealings with McCarthy had been set in the general's presidential campaign: as long as possible, he temporized, tacitly recognizing not only McCarthy's popularity (as late as January 1954, the Wisconsin senator had the favorable opinion of 50 percent of the respondents to a national poll) but also that Eisenhower himself represented only a moderately progressive minority in the conservative Republican party.

The general's dilemma, as Nixon described it in *RN,* was that he

> disliked McCarthy personally . . . because of his coarse familiarity, which Eisenhower found distasteful. But he was . . . aware that if he repudiated McCarthy or tried to discipline him, the Republican party would split right down the middle in Congress and in the country.

Nixon did not mention any distaste on Eisenhower's part for McCarthy's freewheeling, often slanderous tactics, other than for his attacks on General George Marshall. And in Milwaukee on October 3, 1952, Eisenhower had made it clear that he would not go to war with Joe McCarthy, whatever he thought of the rambunctious senator.

There was no doubt *what* Eisenhower thought, at least as far as

McCarthy's attacks on Marshall were concerned. At a news conference in Denver on August 22, 1952, his face flushed with anger, he had strongly defended General Marshall, his wartime chief and benefactor: "If he is not a perfect example of patriotism and loyal servant of the United States, I never saw one!" Obviously of McCarthy, who had called Marshall a traitor, Eisenhower had added cuttingly: "I have no patience with anyone who can find in [Marshall's] record of service for this country anything to criticize. . . . I am not going to support anything that smacks to me of un-Americanism."

Thus, the candidate sought to turn McCarthy's own stock in trade—communism and/or "un-Americanism"—against its proprietor.

At their only private meeting, Eisenhower may even have chewed out—in army terms—Tail-Gunner Joe. That was on October 2, 1952, in Peoria, where McCarthy had flown with Governor Walter Kohler of Wisconsin, a devout Eisenhower backer, to board the general's campaign train. Late that afternoon, the day before Eisenhower was to speak in Milwaukee, the presidential candidate demanded to see McCarthy in the Eisenhower suite at the Pere Marquette Hotel.

McCarthy later told reporters the half hour the two spent together was taken up with "a very, very pleasant conversation." Kevin McCann, an Eisenhower speech writer and loyalist, had a different story. He had been in the hallway outside the room, he remembered years later, and heard Eisenhower when he "just took McCarthy apart. I never heard the general so cold-bloodedly skin a man. The air turned blue—so blue in fact that I couldn't sit there listening. McCarthy said damned little. He just grunted and groaned."

A grain of salt is in order for this long-after-the-fact recollection; no reporter got wind of McCann's story at the time, which seems improbable, and in any case, a man so admiring of Eisenhower as Kevin McCann might well have exaggerated the McCarthy "skinning," to Eisenhower's benefit.*

By the day of the Milwaukee speech, October 3, as the Eisenhower train rolled into Wisconsin, at Green Bay, Appleton and Fond du Lac, the presidential candidate mildly criticized McCarthy's tactics. But in Sherman Adams's compartment, Governor Kohler and Senator Knowland of California had discovered a bombshell in Eisenhower's planned text for his major speech that night in Milwaukee. There was a paragraph in praise of George Marshall.

The Marshall statement had been proposed by Arthur Hays Sulzberger,

---

*I got to know McCann in 1962 when he, General Eisenhower, Earl Mazo of the old *New York Herald Tribune,* and I, then a *New York Times* political reporter, traveled in a small plane together for about a week. Eisenhower was appearing on behalf of Republican congressional candidates, and the amiable McCann showed himself clearly a profound if not slavish follower of the great man.

the publisher of the *New York Times,* long an Eisenhower supporter. The candidate had written Sulzberger to assure him he would use it at Milwaukee. Kohler and Knowland, both McCarthyites, saw immediately that on McCarthy's home turf the statement would be heard more as a criticism of him than as a defense of Marshall—who, they perhaps knew in their hearts, really needed no defense. The statement was "gratuitous," Kohler told Adams, and Knowland agreed. "Everybody knows," Kohler went on, "how Eisenhower feels about Marshall. This line is just out of place in this speech."

Knowland agreed again, vehemently. Gabriel Hauge, another speech writer, strongly resisted these arguments; but Adams finally capitulated, went to Eisenhower's compartment and recommended deletion of the Marshall defense.

"Are you telling me that paragraph is out of place?" Eisenhower demanded.

"Yes, sir."

"Then take it out."[4]

That may have been the worst mistake of Eisenhower's political career. Ordinarily, he could have deleted a paragraph from a speech in preparation, with no one the wiser; though Hagerty was preparing the text for release, he had not yet given it to the press. But William H. Lawrence, the *New York Times*'s veteran political correspondent, knew from Fred Seaton, then Adams's assistant (later secretary of the interior), that the Marshall defense was to be in the speech. Seaton repeatedly assured Lawrence that Eisenhower would make the statement, although McCarthy himself insisted to Lawrence that the defense of Marshall had been deleted.

"Wait and see," McCarthy urged.

Lawrence, a seasoned reporter, waited and saw that the promised statement was not in the mimeographed text Hagerty distributed; he demanded to know why. Hagerty and Seaton conceded that the Marshall paragraph had been taken out of the speech; Lawrence featured the deletion in his page one story for the *Times,* and the deletion quickly became a cause célèbre, the low point of the Eisenhower campaign.[5]

McCarthy triumphantly shook the general's hand after the truncated speech, which—rather as the straw that broke the camel's back—caused the long-suffering liberal Senator Wayne Morse of Oregon to quit the Republican party. So great was the outcry that it was an anticlimax when Richard Nixon, campaigning in Wisconsin three weeks later, endorsed "my good friend, Joe McCarthy," for reelection.

Once in office, Eisenhower showed no more inclination to "get down in the gutter with McCarthy" than he had on his campaign train. "I just won't get into a pissing contest with that skunk," he insisted.[6]

Vice President Nixon, however, volunteered at the second meeting of the cabinet, in January 1953, to broker differences between the White House and congressional Republicans—the most threatening of which arose from the Red-baiting of Senator McCarthy. The latter had been reelected rather easily, with 54 percent of the vote in Wisconsin—but even in his home state he ran well behind the Eisenhower-Nixon ticket, which took 61 percent of the Wisconsin vote (about six points ahead of its national margin over Stevenson and John Sparkman).

Perhaps because Nixon, as vice president and presiding officer of the Senate, had one foot in the executive and the other beside McCarthy's in the legislative branch, he sensed a useful role for himself in such brokerage—although McCarthy and Nixon, who were often lumped together in the public mind, were not particularly close. Both had come to Washington as part of the big Republican election success of 1946, but Nixon's part in the exposure of Alger Hiss made him a famous anti-Communist nearly two years before McCarthy opened his Red-hunting career at Wheeling, West Virginia, in February 1950.

McCarthy's later excesses caused Nixon several times to try cooling off the senator. While both were in Congress, for example, Nixon advised McCarthy not to call his targets Communists—"say they are sympathetic toward Communist points of view, are fellow travellers, or have Communist-front ties. . . . [A]lways understate your case." This was sagacious advice, if cynically designed to make Red-baiting a little more acceptable. McCarthy ignored it.

Often by insupportable connections, sometimes by uninformed assumptions, the Nixon-McCarthy relationship has been made to seem warmer than it ever was in reality. At the least, Nixon recognized the Wisconsin senator as a reckless and uncontrollable threat, first to the Republican party, then to the Eisenhower administration, finally to both.

But in January 1953, Nixon was no readier than the president to take on McCarthy *mano a mano*. He well understood Eisenhower's reluctance to do so, perhaps because he, too, by attacking the notorious senator, would have risked an open pro- and anti-McCarthy split in the party; and Nixon had the additional problem of trying to retain his own credentials with both the Republican Old Guard, most of them McCarthy backers, and hard-line anti-Communists in both parties.

Besides, Nixon thought McCarthy "personally likable, if irresponsibly impulsive"—an opinion held by many in Washington. And he told Earl Mazo that McCarthy "believed what he was doing very deeply"—a view that the senator's well-known behavior hardly justifies.[7]

Nor did the graduate of Whittier College share what in *RN* he termed "the disdain with which fashionable Washington treated [McCarthy] because of his lack of polished manners." Nixon, after all, fancied himself also disdained by the "fashionable" and the highbrows.

When in 1953 McCarthy attacked a prominent CIA official, the patrician William Bundy, a son-in-law of Dean Acheson, the problem was that Bundy had contributed to an Alger Hiss defense fund. Eisenhower sent Nixon to intervene; both were concerned more about the CIA than about Bundy, and Nixon had a characteristic explanation for McCarthy:

> Joe, you have to understand how those people up in Cambridge think. Bundy graduated from the Harvard Law School, and Hiss was one of its most famous graduates.

It is not hard to hear Orthogonian overtones in that speech. But however Nixon personally felt, he worked out a favorable deal with McCarthy—he conceded McCarthy's committee the *right* to subpoena CIA officials in return for McCarthy's promise not to do it. Nixon's success in thus protecting the CIA was bolstered by the agency's director, Allen Dulles, who told Eisenhower he'd resign unless the administration forced McCarthy to leave the CIA alone.[8]

The CIA deal was accomplished, too, with the aid of the Republicans on McCarthy's investigating subcommittee—Everett Dirksen of Illinois and Nixon's old colleagues from the House, Karl Mundt of South Dakota and Charles Potter of Michigan. With such conservative Republicans, Nixon usually could talk political turkey—party loyalty, patronage, the success of a Republican administration, retaining control of Congress, reasonable restraint in pursuing enemies, especially those whose guilt could not be proven.

For the first year of the administration, Nixon limited himself to the brokerage duties for which he had volunteered at the outset—"putting out brushfires started by McCarthy," he called it in *RN*. He claims, for example, to have talked the senator out of opposing Eisenhower's nominee for high commissioner in West Germany—James B. Conant, the president of Harvard. Conant's crime, in McCarthy's telling, was to have called it inconceivable that any Harvard faculty member could be a Communist.

On the other hand, Nixon assured Dr. Robert Johnson, the director of the U.S. Information Agency, that McCarthy wouldn't prove so terrible, despite his attacks on Johnson's agency, if the director would only understand the senator. This didn't stop McCarthy from forcing the resignation of the head of the Voice of America, Dr. William C. Johnstone, and that of the veteran radio commentator, Raymond Gram Swing. He also imposed a virtual purge of the books in USIA libraries abroad, following the swing through Europe of those "junketeering gumshoes," Roy Cohn and David Schine—two of McCarthy's committee investigators. In late 1953, Robert Johnson himself resigned.

Nixon failed, also, to quell McCarthy's opposition to Charles E. Bohlen, whom Eisenhower named as ambassador to the Soviet Union. "Chip"

Bohlen not only had been at the Yalta conference as an American diplomat; he defended the Yalta agreements, a profound sin in Old Guard eyes. Worse, McCarthy received from the FBI reports that Bohlen might be homosexual. Foster Dulles, hearing the same smear, wanted to drop Bohlen.

Eisenhower, in this case knowing his nominee personally, scoffed at the reports, publicly praised Bohlen and sent Nixon to call off McCarthy. It couldn't be done, although the vice president managed to tone down McCarthy's attacks. Bohlen finally was confirmed, 74 to 13, with the reluctant support of Senator Robert Taft. ("McCarthyism is a kind of liquor for Taft," a friend of his once commented. "He knows it's bad stuff and he keeps taking the pledge, but every so often he falls off the wagon.")

Dulles was still shaky about Bohlen. When he found out that the new ambassador and his wife would travel separately to the Moscow embassy, he told Bohlen they ought to go together.

"For God's sake, why?" Bohlen asked.

"Well, you know," Dulles replied, "there were rumors in some of your files about immoral behavior and it would look better if your wife was with you."[9]

Bohlen flatly refused this outrageous suggestion.

McCarthy's lunges at the administration continued. In March 1953, with no authority beyond his anti-Communist pretensions, he "negotiated" a deal with Greek shipping owners in which they pledged not to deliver cargo to Communist China. Harold Stassen, supposedly the official with authority to make trade agreements, testified to McCarthy's face that the senator's dealings were "undermining and are harmful to our objective."

Eisenhower barely supported Stassen, however, again detailing Nixon, this time with Foster Dulles, to work something out with McCarthy. The public statement they issued was generally interpreted as praising McCarthy and humiliating Stassen—which Stassen probably had not forgotten when it came time for Eisenhower to choose a running mate in 1956.

At the end of 1953, Nixon took McCarthy to Key Biscayne; there, the vice president and William Rogers, then deputy attorney general, again cautioned McCarthy against excess and urged him to look beyond the anticommunism on which he had built his dubious reputation: "You should not be known as a 'one-shot' senator," Nixon advised, again sagaciously as well as cynically. He then told the press that the senator was about to turn his investigative zeal to the subject of Democratic corruption. McCarthy promptly denied it and soon was working the same old turf. And so was Nixon, as a result—still trying to play broker between a nervous administration and the unaccountable senator from Wisconsin.

He did succeed, for instance, in getting McCarthy to rid his committee of its chief investigator, one J. B. Matthews, after Matthews enraged even

Old Guardsmen by threatening to hunt Communists among the Protestant clergy. And when McCarthy demanded in writing that Eisenhower state his position on Western trade with Communist satellites, Nixon managed to get McCarthy's consent to intercept the letter before it reached the Oval Office, where it would have forced the president to give an answer sure to have been embarrassing or unsatisfactory.[10]

Eisenhower himself maintained public silence on McCarthy, even when questioned, in keeping with his lofty view that if the president tangled openly with the demagogue, that would only build up McCarthy's prestige and encourage him to further depredations.

One result of presidential silence was that in February 1954, the Republican National Committee—presumably under Eisenhower's control—officially sponsored Joseph McCarthy on a ten-day national speaking tour in observance of Lincoln Day. (Did someone at the committee have a sense of black humor?) Even under such auspices, McCarthy talked mostly about the Democrats' "twenty years of treason"; still no rebuke came from the White House.

One specific reason the president did not speak out—though it was not known at the time—was his fear that if he pushed McCarthy to the wall, the alley-fighting senator might turn his destructive attention to the sensitive Oppenheimer case. In December 1953, Eisenhower had taken note of information that suggested to him that Dr. J. Robert Oppenheimer—the primary architect of the atomic bomb, most eminent of the nation's physicists—might be a security risk. Sensitive to his own and Nixon's strictures on the Democrats for supposedly harboring such risks, Eisenhower ordered a "blank wall" to be erected between Oppenheimer and classified information. In 1954, as a result, a special board began a hearing on Oppenheimer's appeal against the government's suspension of his access to security information.

Nixon, without having been asked, had defended Oppenheimer in 1950 against charges that the scientist had held a prewar meeting of Communists in his house at Berkeley (see chapter 2). In the spring of 1953, as the new vice president, Nixon had again defended Oppenheimer. Republican members of McCarthy's Senate investigating subcommittee, inspired by an accusatory article by Charles J. V. Murphy in the May issue of *Fortune,* were then considering opening an inquiry into Oppenheimer's views and activities.

That probe never took place; Senator Karl Mundt said that it was dropped when "we got some pretty high assurances that [the subject] would not be neglected" by the new administration. McCarthy himself later said his committee dropped the Oppenheimer case because he had "assurances from top administration officials that this matter would be gone into in detail."

Those assurances came from Vice President Nixon, who knew Mundt well and was doing his best to keep McCarthy in check. Nixon could not actually have known that an administration security investigation was forthcoming; Eisenhower was not to order that blank wall for another seven months. No doubt Nixon understood that letting McCarthy loose on Oppenheimer and the atomic bomb would be a lurid carnival that might force the Eisenhower administration into unwanted action; and, anyway, Nixon already had demonstrated his own confidence in the physicist's loyalty.

During the subsequent Oppenheimer security hearings in 1954, Eisenhower wanted desperately to keep McCarthy out of the matter, for fear that the senator would smear American scientists generally. "We've got to handle this so that all our scientists are not made out to be Reds," the president told Hagerty. "That goddam McCarthy is just likely to try such a thing."[11]

McCarthy, by then, had found a new but dangerous victim to torture— the U.S. Army, the institution that had nurtured Dwight D. Eisenhower, and to which the president still felt great loyalty. Picking on the army, however, was not in itself McCarthy's fatal error. That came only after he took up the matter of Major Irving Peress, an army dentist who had received promotion even after he had refused to answer a loyalty questionnaire. Once a member of the American Labor party, Peress invoked the Fifth Amendment rather than testify before McCarthy. He had nevertheless requested and received an honorable discharge.

That infuriated the risible McCarthy and set off the chain of events— which needs only to be summarized here—that led to his downfall. He summoned Peress's commanding officer, General Ralph Zwicker—who had landed with Eisenhower's forces in Normandy on June 6, 1944—and hectored the general unmercifully, as lacking "the brains of a five-year-old child" and "not fit to wear that uniform." Zwicker, McCarthy charged, was "shielding Communists."

Outraged in his turn, Secretary of the Army Robert Stevens forbade Zwicker to testify further. McCarthy promptly called Stevens himself before the committee. Enter Nixon; he had to intervene, as he pointedly observed in *RN,* because "Eisenhower was away on a golfing vacation." (Eisenhower's biographer, Stephen Ambrose, says the president was on a speaking trip to California.)

In any case, Nixon arranged a meeting in his Capitol office with Stevens, John Adams (the army's counsel), Jerry Persons (the White House congressional liaison officer), William Rogers, Senators Knowland and Dirksen, and Taft's representatives. Out of this meeting came a luncheon the next day in Dirksen's office, where Stevens became a lamb among wolves—McCarthy, Dirksen, Mundt and Potter.

Over a meal of fried chicken, Stevens agreed that he and army subordinates would testify. McCarthy promised to treat army witnesses respectfully. But when the luncheon group met the waiting press, McCarthy did all the talking. The army would testify as demanded, he said—not mentioning his part of the bargain. Naively, Stevens did not call attention to the omission.

Later, McCarthy boasted to a reporter that Stevens could not have surrendered more "abjectly if he had gotten down on his knees." That afternoon, Bill Lawrence of the *New York Times* dutifully called McCarthy. Lawrence had been given what he called "the sewer beat"— keeping up with the Wisconsin "bullyboy"—but had managed to maintain an amicable relationship with him.

"Well, Joe, it looks to me like you got your pound of flesh," Lawrence said. "But you weighed your hand as well."

McCarthy replied: "Bill, have you ever thought you'd like to be a general?"

"Good God, no, Joe. Why?"

"Well, if you want to be a general, I can fix it. I'm running the army now," McCarthy said.[12]

No wonder the press dubbed the occasion "the chicken luncheon" and no wonder Nixon and others had to talk the embarrassed Stevens out of resigning. When Eisenhower returned, he asked Nixon to work with Stevens, Adams and Persons on Stevens's attempt to explain his supposed surrender. They wrote the Stevens statement, Nixon claims in *RN,* while the president, "probably to relieve the tremendous anger he felt, practiced chip shots on the South Lawn."

But Eisenhower—with the Oppenheimer hearings heavily on his mind— still said nothing publicly to demonstrate his anger, except for a mild press conference statement (Nixon claims to have been the author of some of its ideas and language) warning that in opposing communism, "we are defeating ourselves if either by design or through carelessness we use methods that do not conform to the American sense of justice and fair play."

Finally, it fell to Nixon, at Eisenhower's direction, to make a belated public stand for the administration against McCarthyism and its progenitor—not least because McCarthy finally had become a target for previously cautious Democrats. Adlai Stevenson had remarked acidly that the party of Lincoln was "divided against itself, half McCarthy, half Eisenhower." Such pungent criticism pushed the administration to dissociate itself from McCarthy.

The speech the president instructed Nixon to make—as Nixon took care to point out in *RN*—actually was the one "Eisenhower himself had purposely avoided for the last two years." Even so, when Nixon addressed the nation on television, on March 13, 1954, his strongest condemnation was not of McCarthy personally but of "reckless talk and questionable methods."

He wrapped up his criticism, moreover, in a singularly unappealing figure of speech that called upon the Nixonian penchant for battle imagery:

> I have heard people say, "After all, we are dealing with a bunch of rats. What we ought to do is go out and shoot them."
>
> Well, I agree they are a bunch of rats. But just remember this: When you go out to shoot rats, you have to shoot straight, because when you shoot wildly, it not only means that the rats may get away more easily—but you make it easier on the rats. Also you might hit someone else who is trying to shoot rats, too. So, we have to be fair—for two very good reasons: one, because it is right; and two, because it is the most effective way of doing the job.

William Ewald thought with good reason that that passage disclosed a "black *id.*" The whole speech was classic Nixon; he managed to preserve his own Communist-hunting credentials while suggesting that McCarthy had botched the job, without actually condemning him.

As both the Army-McCarthy and the Oppenheimer hearings continued, Eisenhower tried to maintain his silence about McCarthy, although he frequently expressed anger in private. Finally, he was goaded into taking a strong public stand, which substantially contributed to the demagogue's downfall.

Floundering in his own excesses, McCarthy had demanded the names of all army personnel involved in the Peress case. When the president told Secretary Stevens to comply, the unappeasable McCarthy threatened to subpoena White House personnel too. But that was too much for Eisenhower; he informed congressional leaders that he would not "allow people around me to be subpoenaed, and you might as well know it now . . . my people are not going to be subpoenaed." (In 1958, he did allow Sherman Adams to testify voluntarily to a congressional committee.)

Eisenhower then ordered Defense Secretary Charles Wilson to withhold any and all documents, communications and "reproductions" concerning executive branch employees' official discussions, because it was "essential to efficient and effective administrative that [such employees] be in a position to be completely candid in advising with each other on official matters."

At last McCarthy had been denied the meat on which he fed—the power to subpoena documents and witnesses. Swinging wildly in response, he urged federal employees to ignore Eisenhower's order and report to *him* on "graft, corruption, communism and treason." At this effrontery, Eisenhower exploded, if only in private; even so, McCarthy's appeal availed him nothing.

In *RN* Nixon does not even mention Eisenhower's sweeping assertion of presidential power—"the most absolute," historian Arthur Schlesinger, Jr., later wrote, "to that day in American history." Not too many years before, of course, Representative Nixon had been demanding that Harry Truman's aides testify before the House Un-American Activities Committee; so it's not clear what, at the time, he might have thought of Eisenhower's stance.

The president's far-reaching claim of executive privilege nevertheless was one of the strongest lessons and precedents to be impressed upon Nixon during his service in the vice presidency. Eisenhower made his order stick, and it still was sticking twenty years later when President Richard Nixon also invoked executive privilege—by then regarded as traditional and all but unquestionable—as the centerpiece of his Watergate defense.

Leonard Garment, once Nixon's legal partner and then his assistant in the White House, wrote in 1987 that one reason President Nixon had not destroyed the incriminating White House tapes was his "confidence that [the tapes] were securely protected by executive privilege." That confidence clearly was born of Eisenhower's long, frustrating struggle with Joe McCarthy, culminating in 1954 in his decision to withhold so much from Congress, including "reproductions"—which the Nixon tapes certainly were.[13]

There was a vital difference. In the Watergate matter, the Supreme Court upheld the general principle Eisenhower had laid down, but further held that such executive privilege could *not* apply when it might serve not just to protect confidential details about "official matters" but also—as in Nixon's case—to withhold evidence of a possible crime.

Watergate was far in the future as the McCarthy drama drew toward its close, McCarthy himself proceeding doggedly, blindly, to his destruction. He did not, however, wade seriously into the Oppenheimer case, perhaps because he was too preoccupied with his investigation of the army. When James Reston disclosed in the *New York Times* the charges against the physicist and the fact that the security hearings were being held, McCarthy merely ranted that the action was "long overdue." He did not return to the subject.

Unaccountably, Richard Nixon did. On the last day of Oppenheimer's testimony in the hearings, which had become public knowledge, the vice president gave an off-the-record report on his recent Asian tour to the American Society of Newspaper Editors—including his subsequently famous remarks on intervention in Indochina (see chapter 4.) In a question period, he was asked for his views on Oppenheimer and replied that he had been familiar with the physicist's record since his own years on the House

Un-American Activities Committee. Oppenheimer, he said, had been "co-operative, impressive and responsive" to the committee. He had seen, he went on, the full Oppenheimer file; and though it presented a difficult problem, "on the evidence I have seen, Dr. Oppenheimer in my opinion is a loyal American." If "he is not subject to blackmail," he should have the right "to work for the government."

As with his remarks on Indochina, so experienced a politician as Richard Nixon could not have expected his views on Oppenheimer to remain off the record. Two days later, he was identified as the "high administration official" who had spoken up for Oppenheimer.* Nixon did not deny it—a brave act for an administration official in the McCarthyite atmosphere of Washington in early 1954.

Nevertheless, on June 2, the *Times* disclosed that Dr. J. Robert Oppenheimer, the head of the wartime Manhattan Project that had built the atomic bomb, one of the most prestigious scientists in the world and a high-level adviser to the Atomic Energy Commission, had been officially barred from security clearance.[14]

Meanwhile, McCarthy's investigation of the army, in mostly televised hearings, finally was exposing to the watching public his ranting cruelty as well as the emptiness of his charges—an early demonstration of the extraordinary power of live television. Essentially a poseur and an overbearing bully, McCarthy could not survive the searing scrutiny of the camera, the impact of the image in the living room.

On December 2, 1954, nearly two years after Eisenhower and Nixon took office, the Senate censured Joseph McCarthy—technically for his abusive conduct toward witnesses and his insulting behavior to other senators, but not least for his indefensible treatment of General Zwicker. Vice President Nixon presided over the censure session, but was not required to vote.

Save for the president's strong assertion of executive privilege, neither he nor Nixon ever did do much more than preside over McCarthy's slow self-destruction—though Nixon had taken some political risks to control the damage McCarthy was doing and might have done. Neither president nor vice president ever disavowed McCarthy for anything other than tactics they considered counterproductive and threatening to the administration.

Even long after McCarthy's downfall and death, Eisenhower clung to his policy of silence. As his memoirs were being drafted, he struck out page

---

*Dr. Oppenheimer may not have returned Nixon's regard. Fawn Brodie wrote that Dr. Eugene Pumpian-Mindlin had quoted Oppenheimer to her as considering Nixon "the most dangerous man I have ever met," after discussing nuclear weapons with the vice president. *Brodie,* p. 322 and p. 540.

after page of detail on the McCarthy struggle that his writers wanted to include. He explained that "after having used for the two years of 1953 and 1954 silence as my strongest weapon to defeat him" (a dubious proposition), he did not want to give McCarthy's memory "far more prominence than I ever did give him in my own mind."[15]

Undoubtedly, Eisenhower really believed his silence had defeated McCarthy, but Nixon's conclusion, following McCarthy's censure, seems to me to stand well for his and the president's attitude at the time: "McCarthy's intentions were right, but his tactics were, frankly, so inept at times that he probably did our cause more harm than good."

As for Joe McCarthy, he quickly became a battered and pathetic figure, deserted by former friends and derided by some who once had trembled before him. He died of drink and hepatitis on May 2, 1957, a shattered hulk of a man whose monument is a word coined from his name that stands for slander and calumny.

"He regarded himself as betrayed," wrote George Sokolsky, a columnist who admired McCarthy. "He particularly felt that he was betrayed by Vice President Nixon, whom he had always trusted." If so, it must have been because the vice president had presided over his disgrace in the Senate; it's hard to see what else Richard Nixon did to earn the obloquy of a man who destroyed himself, with little help from Nixon or anyone else.[16]

Vice presidents, unfortunately, are neither fish nor fowl; Richard Nixon, like his predecessors, could not be either a real mover and shaker in Congress—although the Constitution made him the presiding officer of the Senate with the authority to break ties—or a major power within the executive branch, although he was nominally the second highest official in the land.

When Nixon sought in 1953 to bring Senate Republicans together at lunch with cabinet members, the party's Senate leaders, jealous of turf and prerogative, forced him to desist. After Nixon went to Moscow and debated Nikita Khrushchev, Eisenhower repeated to his staff a point he had made before: "The vice president is not a part of the negotiating mechanism of government."

Unlike most vice presidents, however, Nixon made the best of what he had. "He didn't just sit there and stew," Robert Finch recalled years later. Not only did Nixon work to educate himself in global affairs, he worked to build the Republican party—something Eisenhower rarely bothered to do—meanwhile collecting as many chits as he could. One year Nixon appeared in twenty-five states, another in thirty-one, speaking, fund-raising, recruiting and supporting candidates, helping the party machinery to run more or less smoothly. That was not only political money in the bank for a young politician's future; it gave Nixon more clout than most vice presidents achieve and some status within the administration as its political point man.

The death of Robert Taft in 1953, the gradual withdrawal of Thomas Dewey from active politics in the fifties, and Eisenhower's illnesses and disinclinations opened to Nixon plenty of political running room; using it adroitly, he became by the late fifties virtually the national Republican party leader. Even before that, Eisenhower himself "showed a certain humility about political issues," Dr. Arthur Burns, the chairman of the Council of Economic Advisers from 1953 to 1956, recalled in an interview. But Eisenhower considered Nixon "an expert" on such matters.

Burns himself—who was later appointed by President Nixon to chair the Federal Reserve Board, and by President Reagan as ambassador to West Germany—regarded Nixon in the Eisenhower years as having "a fine analytic mind" and as "a damn cool and very able political analyst." Nixon's estimates of the political consequences of administration actions were "thoroughly honest," Burns thought, and were expressed "clearly and objectively."[17]

Burns didn't know at the time or later that Nixon secretly resented—so he told Earl Mazo—being considered an "expert" mostly on politics, while his views often were disregarded on other matters. Like the clown yearning to play Hamlet, Nixon wanted to be more than "just a pol."

He was too astute to let such inner frettings be known. "Dick felt his way at first," Jim Hagerty observed to Mazo in the late Eisenhower years, when the vice president had become the obvious leader for the 1960 presidential nomination. "One of his great strengths is that he knows when to keep quiet. . . . When he did speak, he spoke on things he knew about. Gradually, as he developed . . . his judgment became more and more respected."

Burns described Nixonian discretion somewhat differently. The vice president, he said, "spoke up" frequently at cabinet meetings but usually to support the president or someone else—never to oppose Eisenhower. As Burns remembered, Nixon rarely "proposed" anything but spoke most often in response to others' ideas—in sharp contrast to the brash Nelson Rockefeller, who as an official in the Eisenhower administration sometimes "got in trouble" by proposing too much too often.[18]

Arthur Burns also tagged Nixon as a "poor administrator." As late as 1957, the vice president had a staff of only eight people—half what the junior senator from California had rated in 1951—crowded into inadequate quarters in the old (now the Russell) Senate Office Building. Even with such a reduced work force, Burns observed:

> He could not handle them efficiently. . . . I would write him a letter
> and then I might get two replies to the same letter, sometimes no

reply and sometimes a reply that had nothing to do with me or what I had written about. Friends of mine who corresponded with Nixon had similar experiences. . . . So I kept wondering, if Nixon couldn't manage an office of eight or ten properly, how could he possibly manage our enormous government where the President needs to have superb managerial skills? Eisenhower, by contrast, was an extraordinary manager. . . . It was a weakness [in Nixon] I detected early, and a conclusion I never had reason to change.[19]

It was also a conclusion, Burns feared, freighted with warnings for the future. (By the time Nixon left the vice presidency, he had a staff of five assistants and more than a dozen clerical helpers.)

Even so, as legislative and political fixer, presidential stand-in and unofficial party leader, Nixon was far more active in his eight years as vice president—aside from his six major trips abroad, to fifty-eight countries and the Virgin Islands, Puerto Rico, Wake Island and Guam, totaling 159,232 miles traveled—than can be briefly recounted. Of tasks too numerous and varied to detail, a sampling may suggest the whole:

He persuaded the powerful Pat McCarran of Nevada to call off a Senate filibuster against an Eisenhower immigration bill. Across the Capitol, he managed to get Old Guardsman Dan Reed of New York, the chairman of the House Ways and Means Committee, to go along—kicking and screaming—with Eisenhower's tax program.

That was at the outset of the administration; in its last years, Nixon chaired a cabinet committee on economic stability and growth—a real committee, but one also designed to give him a defensible administrative role to boast about as a presidential candidate. (One of the committee's recommendations was rejected by the conservative Eisenhower—the kind of "government control of prices and wages" that president Nixon proceeded to impose in 1971.)

In between, the vice president supported innumerable Republican candidates, picking up chits from their friends and supporters even when they lost. He sought insistently to broaden Republican appeal to moderates and minorities, and to present more attractive Republican candidates of whatever ideological hue (save, of course, identifiable "leftists").

He helped persuade Representative Kenneth Keating of New York to give up a safe House seat to run in 1958 for the Senate—a risky move designed to help Nelson Rockefeller win the New York governorship on the same ticket. In 1959, he stage-managed the overthrow of Joe Martin, the ancient House Republican leader and Nixon's one-time benefactor; and he was the administration's spokesman and lead campaigner in 1954, 1956 and 1958.

On Capitol Hill, Nixon backed with varying degrees of success administration positions on social welfare, civil rights and foreign aid—the last a subject to which he was particularly devoted. He also was a key figure in persuading Republicans to tolerate if not embrace Eisenhower's Korean truce. Nixon put in many hours, too, as a foot soldier in Eisenhower's determined war against the Bricker Amendment, which—as far as anyone understood it—would have limited presidential treaty-making powers.

Opposing Bricker called for some dexterity; as a senator in 1950, Nixon had been a sponsor of an earlier, similar Bricker Amendment. When John Bricker of Ohio reintroduced the amendment in 1953, it had sixty-two sponsors, including forty-four of the forty-seven other Republicans in the majority; that looked unbeatable (only sixty-four votes were then required for Senate passage of a constitutional amendment) but Eisenhower immediately declared war on it.

Working both sides of the street, Nixon sought long and hard for a substitute that would satisfy both the president and the amendment's Old Guard sponsorship—not to mention his own political needs. That proved impossible and the vice president, recognizing the inevitable, then followed his leader and worked against the amendment until its narrow defeat in February 1954.

Which of these three stands represented his real view? He never said, but the likelihood is that his place in the executive branch led him ultimately to take a more presidential view of the matter than he had as the junior senator from California.

(In 1960, when Lyndon Johnson of Texas was campaigning for vice president as John Kennedy's running mate, he frequently regaled the reporters traveling with him—often including me—with stories claiming that he, the Democratic Senate leader in 1954, actually had found the votes to defeat the Bricker Amendment "for Ike." LBJ probably was right about the head count, but he couldn't have done it had not the prestigious Eisenhower proved an uncompromising warrior against the amendment.)

Nixon also was active in getting the support of the Reverend Martin Luther King, Jr., for Eisenhower's 1957 civil rights bill, even after Congress had weakened it. King also pledged to begin "a massive Negro voter registration drive" that the civil rights leader thought would produce many new Republicans. King's promise improved Nixon's hopes for substantial black support for his own presidential candidacy in 1960.

The vice president was among the first Eisenhower administration officials to take seriously the early Soviet space successes. He became a strong advocate within the administration of setting up a civilian space agency, in response to the launching of the Sputnik satellites. Eisenhower at first resisted but finally consented to what became the National Aeronautics and Space Agency. It was to be President Richard Nixon who welcomed back to earth the astronauts NASA sent to the moon in 1969 (at President

Kennedy's instigation) but—as we shall see—the Nixon administration was not otherwise helpful to the space agency.

Vice President Nixon also was an eloquent pleader for expanded student, professional and cultural exchanges—particularly, after his escape from rioters in Caracas—with Latin American nations.

> In the next ten years, our greatest external danger will not be military but economic and ideological [he told Mazo in 1959]. If we have to choose in allocating funds between military programs and the economic, information and other nonmilitary programs, I would put the emphasis on the nonmilitary programs.

Occasionally, Nixon was handed a plum—for instance, the 1956 trip to Austria to be seen welcoming Hungarian refugees to the "free world." It was he who was allowed to dazzle the 1954 governors' conference with Eisenhower's vast interstate highway proposal—which Nixon projected to the delighted governors at $5 billion yearly in federal money for the next decade.

Thus to be associated with the most popular and successful of Eisenhower's domestic programs was a boon that fell to Nixon because he had strongly endorsed the highway proposal in the cabinet—in typical terms. "Earl Warren," he pointed out, "got the reputation of a great liberal because he built schools and roads" in California, thus providing the most desired forms of government largesse. The cabinet paid close attention to that kind of political wisdom.

Nixon's admirers contend that his most important nonlegislative, non-political role was as chairman of the president's committee on government contracts—a body charged with eliminating discrimination against minority groups on work done under federal contract. With a staff of twenty-five, the committee reviewed such contracts—as many as five thousand a year— and processed complaints of discrimination by the contractors.

This was a vital task that Nixon performed ably. Unfortunately, his committee had no enforcement powers save moral persuasion, which in economic matters as in war has its limits. But Nixon was widely credited with strong and effective leadership of what could have been a toothless "for show" committee. The complaints registered with the committee mounted over the years, attesting to its effectiveness, and it became a forerunner of later, more powerful federal antidiscrimination and affirmative action approaches—some sponsored by President Richard Nixon.

Nixon suffered, of course, numerous slings and arrows of outrageous fortune during his vice presidency. In 1958, for instance, when he was apprehensive about the economy, he and Secretary of Labor James Mitchell—a frequent ally—proposed that taxes be cut. They got nowhere, and

Majority Leader Lyndon Johnson taunted Nixon: "You and Mitchell got on that high horse, and here Eisenhower and [Secretary of the Treasury] Bob Anderson rode off and left you."[20]

Again, in late 1959 or early 1960, Dr. Arthur Burns, who had returned to academic life, phoned the vice president to predict, accurately, that the economy was slipping into recession; that bode no good for Nixon's forthcoming presidential campaign. Acting on Burns's advice, Nixon urged stimulative action, but was thwarted once again by the economically conservative president and his advisers.[21]

Robert Finch, Nixon's campaign director in 1960, reminded me that "a hell of an increase in unemployment in the last sixty to ninety days" before the 1960 election (from 5.5 percent in September to 6.1 percent in October and November) damaged Nixon in key states. That, Finch and others believe, was a decisive factor in his loss of the presidency to John Kennedy. Nixon was "ticked off," Finch said, at Robert Anderson because the treasury secretary refused his advice and took the view that "the pump didn't need to be primed"—which may well have cost the Republican party the presidency in 1960. In general, the vice president resented Eisenhower's cautious economic policy more than any other—which may have contributed to his own more adventurous economic management a decade later.

That suggests something about Richard Nixon that was to be important in his presidential campaigns and in his presidency. He was *not* a doctrinaire economic conservative like George Humphrey, Anderson or Eisenhower himself; and because he was not, he found nothing sacred in a balanced budget and nothing reprehensible in federal action to stimulate the economy. Unlike orthodox Republicans, Nixon did not lay claim to inflexible economic "principle." He could be flexible and he could learn from circumstances.

Administration policy also contradicted presidential candidate Nixon's wishes on the troubled subject of Castro's Cuba. Castro was not yet proclaiming himself a Communist in 1960, but he appeared to be moving closer to the Soviet Union. Nixon desperately wanted some kind of action beyond the reduced sugar quota for Cuba that Eisenhower authorized in July.

But the president adamantly opposed other public or military moves (although he urged the CIA to recruit and train the secret Cuban exile force that, within a year, President Kennedy would send to the Bay of Pigs). Nixon had to fight the 1960 election as the representative of an administration that *appeared* to be taking no strong steps against Castro.

The ubiquitous LBJ also was a thorn in Nixon's side—though it was Nixon who had arranged for Eisenhower to visit Johnson in hospital after the latter's near-fatal heart attack in 1955. That courtesy didn't keep the ingenious majority leader from booby-trapping Nixon politically whenever he could—for example, when he rigged a Senate vote on raising the interest rate on veterans' home loans to force Nixon, the presiding officer, to break the tie. Nixon did, loyally voting the unpopular administration and Republican position *for* the increase in interest rates.

When Nixon once referred impermissibly to Earl Warren as "a great Republican chief justice," Eisenhower was enraged—though not, of course, publicly. Ann Whitman recorded in her diary that during the 1954 election campaign, the president also called Nixon to the White House and told him to calm down his "indefensible" rhetoric about the Democrats' alleged softness on Communism. It was not helping Eisenhower win the Democratic votes he needed in Congress.

In 1959, when Khrushchev—Nixon's opponent a few weeks earlier in the so-called kitchen debate—came to Washington, Eisenhower assigned Henry Cabot Lodge, the ambassador to the U.N., as the Soviet leader's tour guide. The choice was generally interpreted as a slight to Nixon, only one of many he suffered in the vice presidential years.

Some wounds were self-inflicted. During one of the recurrent Formosa-Quemoy-Matsu crises with Communist China, for example, in 1958, the *New York Times* published a "leaked" story that of five thousand letters to the State Department on the issue, 80 percent were critical of administration policy. Already fearing a Republican election setback that fall, Nixon decided to respond. He rejected, reasonably enough, the idea that "the weight of the mail rather than the weight of the evidence" should determine American foreign policy. But he went one damaging step further to mention "the patent and deliberate effort of a State Department subordinate [the undetected leaker] to undercut the secretary of state and sabotage his policy."

The implication of disloyalty, the word "sabotage" and the implicit threat to State Department personnel seemed to make a mountain of a molehill and to be both unnecessary and improper—an instinctive reversion, critics thought, to the unsavory tactics of innuendo that many thought a vice president and presidential candidate should eschew.

One of Nixon's worst setbacks came in the second-term struggle for the chairmanship of the Operations Control Board, an important organ of the National Security Council, which was supposed to oversee the carrying out of NSC decisions approved by the president. The chairmanship had been held by Foster Dulles's undersecretaries, first Beetle Smith, then Herbert Hoover, Jr. When the latter prepared to resign as undersecretary after the 1956 elections, Nixon (and his backers) sought the chairmanship to boost Nixon's ability to portray himself as Eisenhower's experienced and powerful right-hand man.

What ensued was primarily one of those ferocious Washington-insider struggles of little interest to a nation going about its business. But it was a major preoccupation of the capital for weeks. Fierce bureaucratic in-fighting flared between State Department traditionalists and Nixon's tough political operators—not least himself. Dulles finally had to take this arcane matter directly to the Oval Office to get it settled in favor of his new undersecretary, Christian Herter.

The president later softened the defeat for Nixon by saying at a news conference that he knew of no other vice president who had been given such "opportunities to participate in difficult decisions, conferences and every kind of informative meeting." Eisenhower's decision was not a criti-cism of Nixon, the president insisted; "as a matter of good governmental organization" it would not have been proper to give a vice president a "position in the executive department."

That he could not be a full participant in either the legislative or the executive branch probably was the heaviest cross Nixon had to bear. And it was in his only constitutionally defined role, as presiding officer of the Senate, that he took on one of Washington's most feared dragons—the customs and traditions of that body, specifically its devotion to unlimited debate, the filibuster.

Unlimited debate, in a legislative body, has the obvious virtue that it can prevent the action of a hasty or vindictive or demagogic majority; one member, as long as he or she can keep talking, can prevent the rest from acting. Robert Taft of Ohio did exactly that, in one of his finest hours, when the Senate moved enthusiastically in 1946 toward approval of Harry Tru-man's exasperated demand that striking railroad workers be drafted into the armed forces.

Unlimited debate also can "slow down the steamroller." That is, for "educational purposes," it can extend debate until issues have been so thoroughly explored—or discovered, or abandoned—that a majority in favor of a proposal amends, extends or restricts it in ways that majority was not prepared originally to do. Senator Wayne Morse of Oregon, a frequent and skilled filibusterer, insisted that he never used unlimited debate to prevent an ultimate vote but only "so that the Senate may be apprised of what is involved in the issues."

That's a distinction without much difference, because such an "educa-tional" filibuster often has been used to hold the Senate hostage, in effect: unless this amendment or that restriction is accepted, the filibusterers will not let the majority pass anything.

As an old Senate reporter and a defender of the rights of individuals and minorities against impassioned majorities, I consider unlimited debate in the Senate, on balance, a useful instrument that ought to be preserved. There's no doubt, however, that the practice is often out of place—in the fifties, for instance, when the minority of Southern Democrats, together with some conservative Republicans, frequently misused the filibuster to prevent action on, and thus passage of, needed and justifiable civil rights legislation. (Admittedly, the filibusterers didn't think such legislation needed or justifiable; nevertheless, they were acting to frustrate a demonstrable majority.)

The Senate's rules were on their side. Rule XXII, in effect, permitted unlimited debate; it provided that cloture—shutting off debate—could be imposed only by a two-thirds vote of the Senate's ninety-six members, or (before the admission of Alaska and Hawaii in 1959) sixty-four senators. Thus only thirty-three could sustain a filibuster indefinitely. The eleven former Confederate states alone had twenty-two senators, of course; they needed only eleven other conservative Democrats or Old Guard Republicans to prevent cloture on civil rights bills. Usually, more than eleven were easy to find, since most senators hesitated to impose cloture on others, against the day when *their* state or *their* interests might need the protection of unlimited debate.

After World War II, as the nation became more and more conscious of the evils and indignities of segregation, "civil rights" became a popular concept outside the South. Pressures on Congress for rights legislation rose steadily—particularly from non-Southern states like New York, with large black populations and numbers of black voters.

Senate Southerners were forced to resort frequently to the filibuster, to stave off such legislation. But their obvious intent—to kill civil rights bills without letting them come to a vote—made it more difficult for conservative non-Southerners to support either the civil rights filibusters *or* Rule XXII; to do so risked appearing to oppose the civil rights tide itself. Rule XXII became an arch-villain for blacks and for many white liberals.

Senator Richard Nixon, campaigning for the vice presidency in 1952, had stated plainly his opposition to Rule XXII; just as plainly, he had put his opposition in the context of civil rights. On October 19, while speaking in New York with its big pool of black voters, he asserted the need for rights legislation but pointed out that it "cannot pass . . . as long as the filibuster exists in the Senate."

If Dwight Eisenhower were to become president, Nixon pledged that night, "We are going to have performance on civil rights, not just promises," because Eisenhower "is going to have a vice president who opposes the filibuster"—a signal that as presiding officer of the Senate, Nixon would try to put an end to Rule XXII, or significantly modify it, perhaps by parliamentary ruling.

No doubt this was a bid for black votes as much as an intellectual and ethical position against civil rights filibusters or the concept of unlimited debate. But it's a politician's business to appeal for votes; civil rights legislation, moreover, *was* needed, and Nixon was entirely correct in identifying the filibuster as a major barrier.

The problem was what, if anything, he could do about it. When the Republican Eighty-third Congress convened in early January 1953, he had resigned from and been replaced in the Senate; but he was not sworn in as vice president until January 20, *after* a challenge to Rule XXII had been disposed of. Two years later, when the Eighty-fourth Congress took office in January 1955 with the Democrats having regained control, the filibuster issue did not arise.

After Nixon's reelection to the vice presidency, however, he tried hard to redeem his 1952 promise—again, undoubtedly, with his eye on black and liberal political support, just as the Southern Democrats who *opposed* civil rights bills were trying to serve the interests of their white constituents, as they perceived those interests. (Southern blacks then were prevented from voting in great numbers.)

The heart of the matter, in the parliamentary rather than the political sense, was that the Senate's conservatives and traditionalists regarded it as a "continuing body"; since only a third of its members was elected every two years, with two thirds going over from one Congress to the next, the Senate's rules, in this long-established view, also were continued in force from Congress to Congress. That meant that Senate rules could be changed only as provided in the Senate rules—so thirty-three senators, under Rule XXII, could filibuster to death any proposed rules change including any modification of Rule XXII itself.

Much passionate senatorial debate was expended on the question of the "continuing body" in those years when Rule XXII, whatever its general virtues, was blocking civil rights legislation. It was against the theory of the "continuing body" with continuing rules—the most cherished idea of true traditionalists as well as of those who were more interested in thwarting civil rights bills—that Richard Nixon prepared to move in 1957.

If his motive was only to bid for black votes for the party of Lincoln, and for himself four years in the unpredictable future, Nixon took a long-odds risk. The day before Congress opened, when he disclosed his intention to three Old Guard stalwarts—Knowland, Styles Bridges of New Hampshire and Leverett Saltonstall of Massachusetts—these conservative traditionalists denounced him angrily. Columnist Joseph Alsop wrote that the four "came as close to blows as men can without using their fists." The Old Guard formed the base of Nixon's support and career, and he seemed to be betraying it.

Nor did Nixon find support in the White House. Eisenhower had never been as enthusiastic as his vice president for civil rights legislation, and had been pained by the Supreme Court's school desegregation decision in *Brown v. Board of Education* in 1954. The president also knew that the executive branch was well advised to keep hands off internal congressional matters.

Eisenhower therefore told Nixon to decide the issue for himself. Probably only from Mitchell, Brownell and Rogers in the administration and from Senate liberals—mostly Democrats and a few Republicans—could Nixon expect support. Nevertheless, on January 13, 1957, when the Eighty-fifth Congress convened under Democratic control and Clinton B. Anderson of New Mexico—an anti-filibuster senator—moved for the adoption of new Senate rules, Presiding Officer Nixon held against precedent that the motion was in order.

He had confounded "continuing body" theology and Old Guard sensibilities. If Nixon's ruling prevailed, the old rules—including XXII—would be held to have expired with the Eighty-fourth Congress. New rules then could be adopted, including a modified cloture rule making it easier to shut off a filibuster. If anyone filibustered to prevent new rules from being adopted, cloture could be imposed by a simple majority—owing to the expiration of Rule XXII under Nixon's ruling.

That ruling was appealed, of course, and on January 14 the Senate not unexpectedly voted by 55 to 38 to table Anderson's motion—in effect rejecting Nixon's parliamentary opinion. That vote not only raised the question whether in any circumstances there was even a Senate *majority* for cloture; it also showed the force of the Senate's traditional view of itself, even against the powerful political pressures for civil rights legislation.

The vote made clear, too, that the vice president had been tilting at a windmill. It's doubtful that he gained enough in the good opinion of blacks and liberals, the latter usually his implacable enemies, to offset the anger of Old Guard Republicans—spurned lovers—and to make up for his humiliating personal defeat. A politician so realistic must have expected such a rebuff, so the conclusion seems warranted that personal conviction— either *for* civil rights, or *against* unlimited debate, or both—to some extent impelled Nixon's ruling. Else, it was quixotic.

In 1959, remarkably and even less effectively, he tried again, perhaps because the 1960 election was nearing. Or perhaps—ironically, in view of his own campaign efforts—he had new hope because the 1958 congressional elections, a Republican disaster, had expanded the Democratic majority in the Senate by thirteen seats, to a total of sixty-two, including more liberals and civil rights supporters. On the other hand, the departing Eighty-fifth Congress, despite Rule XXII, had passed what then appeared to be a substantial civil rights bill. So the necessity for limiting debate seemed not quite so urgent.

In 1959, too, the wily majority leader, Lyndon Johnson was reinforced and ready. Johnson had worked out a compromise with the Southern faction—the base of his extraordinary powers in the Senate. The compromise provided for a modified Rule XXII, permitting cloture by two thirds of senators *present and voting,* rather than of all the ninety-six.

But Johnson's compromise also incorporated a formal statement that the Senate was a "continuing body"; and it would make the cloture rule apply to rule changes as well as to legislation. That would be the end of liberal hopes for a rule requiring a simple majority vote for cloture.*

Again, Old Guard Republicans advised Nixon against radical rulings; this time, he agreed *not* to hold in order a motion for new rules. Therefore, when a liberal motion to adopt new rules was offered the next day, the vice president held that it would have to be debated under the *existing* rules. Then, vainly, he tried to rule that a majority could cut off debate on the motion, despite any existing rule to the contrary—including Rule XXII.

Nixon could neither explain nor defend this muddled position—in effect, that the old rules, except Rule XXII, still applied. On January 9, the liberal motion was voted down, 60 to 36; then Johnson's compromise, making it slightly but not significantly easier to impose cloture, was adopted, 70 to 22.

Nixon again left the chamber embarrassed, and if a champion of civil rights demonstrably an outgeneraled one. The campaign promise of October 19, 1952, had not been redeemed—but Nixon had tried, bravely if none too wisely or skillfully.

In retrospect, what was in that era considered Nixon's most notable service in the vice presidency—his carefully correct vice presidential performances during Eisenhower's three major illnesses—had only one real significance: these episodes led to the historic Eisenhower-Nixon agreement on presidential disability, later adopted by John Kennedy and Lyndon Johnson, and an important forerunner of the Twenty-fifth Amendment to the Constitution.

The agreement, drafted by Eisenhower himself, provided that the president, in the event of his inability to serve, would turn over his powers and duties to the vice president, if able to do so. If he was not so able, the vice president would have the sole power, after appropriate consultations with cabinet and Congress, to declare the president unable to serve and to take over the powers and duties. In either case, the president himself would decide when to reclaim those powers and duties.

Nixon never really was an "acting president," as some journalists and supporters claimed for him after Eisenhower's heart attack in 1955, operation for ileitis in 1956 and mild stroke in late 1957. In all three instances, the president soon was back in effective charge of things—in the case of

---

*Over the years, with the disappearance of the one-party South, and of civil rights as a legislative issue, together with a general loosening of Senate traditions, the cloture rule has been watered down so that only three fifths of senators present and voting can shut off debate.

the stroke, in only a few days. During the president's longest recovery—forty-eight days from his heart attack in Denver on September 24, 1955, until his return to Washington—Foster Dulles and Sherman Adams, with Eisenhower's blessing, were more nearly in charge than the vice president.

At Eisenhower's direction, issued immediately after his heart attack, Nixon did preside over regularly scheduled, routine NSC and cabinet meetings. He also signed some ceremonial documents "on behalf of the president." But when the vice president visited Eisenhower in Denver, two weeks after the heart attack, he found Sherman Adams in residence and in charge, handling all liaison with government officials and agencies in Washington.

Adams's presence in Denver had been arranged by Dulles, who had overriden the vice president's desire to be at the president's bedside. Nixon could hardly protest, since his own highest priority was to avoid even the appearance of trying to seize power.

When Nixon did visit the president, Eisenhower handed him a letter specifying that Dulles would speak for him at a forthcoming foreign ministers' meeting in Geneva. Dulles, the letter said, had Eisenhower's "complete confidence." And to Nixon's face, Eisenhower said that Dulles—not Vice President Richard M. Nixon—"must be the one who both at the conference table and before the world speaks for me with authority for our country."

Nixon could accomplish little more than to arrange for cabinet members, one by one, to make the pilgrimage to the bedside in Denver. When Dulles made the trip, a copy of his memorandum of conversation with Eisenhower went *only* to Sherman Adams.

This was more than a bureaucratic turf fight. From September to late February 1956, it was widely assumed that a victim of a serious heart attack could not run for reelection to the presidency a year later. Dulles and Adams represented the Eastern, more or less liberal Eisenhower Republicans, who were not ready to turn over the party and the nominating convention to Richard Nixon and—they feared—to the Old Guard they had fought so determinedly in 1952.

Nixon, on the other hand, and however he tried to guard against the appearance of power-grabbing, was being urged on by some of his own close supporters and by Old Guardsmen like Styles Bridges, who wired: YOU ARE THE CONSTITUTIONAL SECOND-IN-COMMAND AND YOU OUGHT TO ASSUME THE LEADERSHIP. DON'T LET THE WHITE HOUSE CLIQUE TAKE COMMAND.

Nixon knew things didn't work that way for vice presidents. He never even contemplated trying to take power, or seriously to contest for it with Eisenhower's designees. He stayed in his office on Capitol Hill, he called on cabinet officers rather than summoning them when he needed to see them, and he presided over those NSC and cabinet meetings from the vice president's accustomed chair, not the president's—which remained empty.

At the cabinet session on September 30, Nixon urged those present constantly to remind the public that it was still Eisenhower's administration at work. Upon adjournment that day, Secretary Dulles—one of Eisenhower's appointed protectors—moved an expression of appreciation for Nixon's conduct. Everyone applauded, perhaps sincerely.

Following the same pattern after the operation and the stroke, Nixon managed the considerable feat of appearing to be filling in for Eisenhower as necessary, without giving the impression that he was moving improperly or eagerly to take power. After the president's stroke in 1957, Nixon did discuss the possibility of declaring him incompetent to serve, which would have required the vice president to take over. But that conversation was initiated by Foster Dulles, at a time when Eisenhower's determination to go immediately back to work caused the secretary of state to fear that the president's judgment might be impaired. Nixon agreed on the question of judgment, but both men were well aware of—Dulles even mentioned—the "Wilson problem."

President Woodrow Wilson, when all but incapacitated in 1919, had fired Secretary of State Robert Lansing for appearing to move in on Wilson's presidential powers. Neither Dulles nor Nixon wanted even to raise echoes of that event, and the subject was dropped when both saw that Eisenhower's judgment was *not* impaired—only that his speech was slightly affected.[22]

In terms of general public acceptance, Nixon's finely balanced conduct in these times of trial paid off; he was later able to cite his performances during Eisenhower's illnesses as evidence of his experience, his "readiness" to be president, and his "maturity." These plausible claims were to be major themes of his 1960 presidential campaign.

Other repercussions of Eisenhower's heart attack were much less favorable. While it was being assumed that Eisenhower could not run again, the attention of Republicans was forcibly focused on the question of who would replace him. Nixon was the obvious front-runner; a Gallup poll showed him leading Earl Warren, 28 to 24, with Dewey and Stassen far back. That tended to arouse the fears of those who opposed Nixon, for personal or political reasons, or both.

Once Eisenhower announced that he *would* seek a second term, his suspect health drew sharp attention to his likely running mate—Richard Nixon again—as a man more likely than most vice presidential candidates to succeed to the Oval Office. Late in 1956, Adlai Stevenson, again the Democratic nominee, put the problem delicately but with saber-toothed political point: "Every piece of scientific evidence that we have, every lesson of history and experience, indicate that a Republican victory . . .

would mean that Richard M. Nixon would probably be President of this country within the next four years."

That had actuarial validity; up to then, seven vice presidents had taken office following the death of a president—just over 20 percent of them all. In popular opinion, Eisenhower's heart attack had raised the distinct possibility of an eighth. This mightily concentrated the minds of the many Americans who were passionate opponents of Richard Nixon. And to an extent, varying over several months, it influenced the thinking of the one man whose patronage Nixon could not afford to lose—Dwight D. Eisenhower.

While spending much time at his Gettysburg farm in the later stages of his recuperation, Eisenhower constantly pondered the question whether to run again. Since he actively considered retirement, he also had to think about a successor. Once he made up his mind to run—probably a good deal earlier than he let on—the question of his health forced him to do what he had not done in 1952: think about a running mate capable, if necessary, of moving into the Oval Office.

Speculation about a successor was nothing new for Eisenhower, who had never committed himself to a second term; in the winter of 1953, in fact, he wrote a friend that "I shall never again be a candidate for anything. This determination is a fixed decision." To his brother Milton at about the same time, he suggested that Lodge, Brownell, Nixon, Stassen, perhaps Milton himself, all were or could be of presidential stature.

A year later, disgusted with McCarthy and the frustrating Old Guard Republicans, he reviewed with Jim Hagerty (who shrewdly believed Eisenhower would run again, despite his protestations) the possibilities as he then saw them. These were a strange lot indeed—Herbert Hoover, Jr., Representative Charles Halleck of Indiana, William Rogers and Nixon. Eisenhower's favorite, however, was Robert Anderson, then the deputy secretary of defense, though a lifelong Texas Democrat.

He rated Anderson "just about the ablest man I know," Eisenhower told Hagerty. "He would make a splendid President." Time and again, in the years ahead, Eisenhower was to tout Anderson for president, particularly to Anderson himself. The Texan always refused, usually on grounds that he did not want to be president—in which he showed better judgment than in his later business affairs. In March 1987, the same Robert Anderson—by then seventy-seven years old—pled guilty to federal indictments for tax evasion and illegal banking operations.

While still recuperating at Gettysburg, Eisenhower's speculations even included Thomas E. Dewey, the bête noire of the Old Guard, who had twice led the Republican party to presidential defeats, and whose political activities had greatly slacked off in the fifties. Eisenhower, who seemed to have little sense of the difference in qualities needed by a president and those required for a presidential *candidate*—perhaps because he was one of those rare souls who had both—thought Dewey could be resurrected. Dumbfounded, Hagerty diplomatically set him straight.

The president then talked of George Humphrey, Warren, Brownell, Sherman Adams, Milton Eisenhower and—as usual—Robert Anderson. Humphrey, Brownell, Adams and Anderson, he said, were "mentally qualified," whatever that means. What about Nixon? he asked Hagerty. The press secretary, an astute political analyst, said he thought Nixon "on his own" could not be nominated in 1956.

The question of a successor finally became moot; after a series of tests that resulted in a favorable medical prognosis, Eisenhower announced on February 29, 1956, that he would run for another term. If that solved one problem, it only emphasized the necessity for the right running mate, for the reason that Stevenson was so pointedly to give.

Eisenhower already had taken steps to widen his options beyond Nixon. On the day after Christmas 1955, he had summoned the vice president to the Oval Office and made him one of the most bizarre proposals in American political history: Nixon could strengthen his chances for 1960 (five years off!) by relinquishing the vice presidency and gaining administrative experience in any cabinet position he wanted, except that of secretary of state or attorney general. The president then suggested the Department of Defense (although later he told Foster Dulles he thought secretary of commerce would be about right). Politically cockeyed though it was, this offer reflected Eisenhower's belief in the advantages of administrative experience in a large organization.

Nixon was stunned by this unwanted Christmas present. Aside from the fact that the offer was unenforceable unless Eisenhower ran again (which was not certain at the time), Nixon knew that such a move would *not* strengthen but probably ruin him politically. The public, and the press that informed it, cared nothing about administrative experience; they would see only a demotion. They would see that if Nixon was not again to be Eisenhower's vice president, it must be that Eisenhower did not want to risk making him president by succession.

It is impossible to believe that Eisenhower did not understand this, too—or it would be, except that the unreality of some of his speculations on a successor (*Dewey! Charlie Halleck!* Years later, Arthur Burns told me that at one point Eisenhower wanted to propose Harry F. Byrd, Sr., of Virginia) raises the question whether the president's great prestige and popularity had caused him to lose sight of (if he ever knew) the practical political problems less fortunate men faced in trying to win an American political party's presidential nomination.

Nixon, as he related in *RN,* believed at once and understandably that Eisenhower, egged on by some on his staff, feared that Nixon would be a drag on the ticket if chosen again, and wanted to drop him. And Nixon was right.

A group led by Adams *had* shown the president polls that suggested Nixon would cost him three or four percentage points in a race with Stevenson. And Eisenhower, deeply conscious of his own weakened health, genuinely did worry whether Nixon was "ready," or ever would be, to replace him. But the president, ever concerned to play the nice guy, did not want to *order* Nixon off the ticket.

Even when Nixon asked him point-blank if he believed the Republican ticket would be stronger with another vice presidential candidate, Eisenhower gave no direct answer. Nor did Nixon directly reply to the extraordinary cabinet offer—if that's what it was.

At their next meeting, Nixon must have felt a chill sense of déjà vu. During the fund crisis of 1952—the traumatic experience that seems never to have been far from Nixon's consciousness in the Eisenhower years—he had sensed the great general at the other end of the telephone line waiting for him to resign from the ticket. Now, in the Oval Office, the president repeated his advice that Nixon should move to the cabinet, and seemed to wait for Nixon's reply, just as he had in 1952. Nixon's description in *RN* of his reaction was so nearly the same as his reaction four years earlier that it could have applied to either situation:

> I fully accepted that I was his to choose or his to dismiss. But I did not feel that my getting off the ticket would be the best thing for him or for the party, and I was not going to offer to do so.

Or best for Richard Nixon, he might have added. In any case, Nixon was right again. In March, twenty-three thousand voters wrote his name on the Republican primary ballot in New Hampshire—a message to Eisenhower, even if stimulated by Styles Bridges, who had masterminded the write-in campaign. Later in the spring of 1956, Nixon also got more than thirty thousand write-in votes in Oregon. Still later, 180 of the 203 Republican members of the House endorsed him for renomination.

If Eisenhower didn't know, Nixon and party leaders like Chairman Len Hall did, that within the Republican party Richard Nixon had his own powerful constituency. With the aid of Victor Johnson, a Nixon loyalist on the staff of the Republican National Committee, the vice president had in his pocket by April 1956 pledges of support from eight hundred Republican delegates to the forthcoming national convention. He lacked only the one pledge he most needed.

For Eisenhower to "dump Nixon," therefore, even into the cabinet, risked alienating a major Republican constituency; as in 1952, Eisenhower would split his party if he rid himself of the one man its powerful conservative wing regarded as its link to an administration it neither understood nor much liked. Even after his heart attack, the popular Eisenhower's personal victory probably would not have been as endangered as might have been the case in 1952; but a split would weaken his party and his ability to govern in a second term.

The Nixon question hung fire for months, with the press hounding Eisenhower at his weekly news conferences for an answer to the obvious question: now that he was running again, did he want Nixon on his ticket or did he not? In vain the general tried to picture this as a decision for the Republican convention; but no one, least of all the political press, could believe that.

Eisenhower repeatedly insisted on his high admiration for, and complete satisfaction with, his vice president: "If anyone ever has the effrontery to come in and urge me to dump somebody that I respect as I do Vice President Nixon, there will be more commotion around my office than you have noticed yet." But just as doggedly he contended—shades of the fund crisis again—that the decision was up to Nixon: "The only thing I have asked him to do is to chart out his own course, and tell me what he would like to do."

All the while, however, Eisenhower was wracking his brain for a suitable substitute. He did not want Knowland or any Old Guardsman—or any senator, for that matter. He *did* want Earl Warren but knew Warren would not give up the chief justice's chair for the vice presidency. Warren probably would have been Eisenhower's choice for the "top spot" (since he couldn't persuade Anderson), if the president had decided not to run again.

Eisenhower also toyed with the remarkable idea of asking Ohio's conservative Democratic governor, Frank Lausche, to turn his coat and run for the vice presidency as a Republican. Eisenhower and even Chairman Hall were particularly intrigued with this idea because Governor Lausche was a Roman Catholic. Hall—"one of the greatest politicians I've ever known, a Republican Jim Farley," Bob Finch characterized him—actually predicted that if the Republicans didn't run a Catholic in 1956, the Democrats would in 1960—probably young John Kennedy, he said—"an attractive guy."

Hall, at Eisenhower's direction ("be very, very gentle"), and his deputy, Robert Humphreys, presented the Lausche idea to Nixon, thus increasing pressure on the vice president to accept the cabinet offer. Hall said later that he "never saw a scowl come so fast over a man's face. [Nixon] was so uptight . . . he just stared at the ceiling."

The Lausche plan came to naught but Eisenhower *personally* offered second place on the 1956 ticket to his perennial favorite, Robert Anderson—though Anderson had just failed on a diplomatic assignment in the Middle East. The president added the lure that this would lead to the presidency for Anderson in 1960. Anderson refused again, pointing out that as a Democrat for Eisenhower, he would have little appeal to "a lifelong Republican in Kansas"—precisely the Republican, he perhaps knew, who was most devoted to Richard Nixon.[23]

Nothing worked to dislodge Nixon from the prospective ticket, and still the reporters pressed the president for an answer. None came. Nixon was kept cooling his heels, like an unwanted caller in an anteroom. Bryce Harlow, for one, remembered that Nixon was "upset" by this treatment, and it is not difficult to see why.

After his talk with Hall and Humphreys, sometime in February, Nixon could have been in no doubt that Eisenhower was searching for an alternative. All the fears and doubts—the paranoia—of the fund crisis were evoked: once again, for no specific fault of his own, he was in danger of banishment, ruin; once again, those he had thought friends were turning on him.

After the trauma of 1952, he may even have *expected* that he would have to suffer it again. "In politics," he had decided just four years before, "most people are your friends only as long as you can do something for them, or to them." Eisenhower's evasions in 1956 can only have confirmed that judgment—and that bitterness; and the "dump Nixon" threat has to be ranked with the fund crisis as perhaps the two most destructive traumas of Nixon's early public *and* personal lives.

He had been thinking seriously, even before Eisenhower's transparent cabinet proposition, of leaving politics. In *RN* he recalled that he was tired of bearing the burden of Democratic and liberal criticism (though he did not mention that he had dished out as much in return, and sometimes first) and did not want his growing daughters to think their father "the perennial bad guy of American politics." He was tired, too, of "hard partisan campaigning" but knew that Eisenhower would continue to demand that he do most of it.

Bob Finch believes Nixon also feared long before the post-Christmas conversation that the president might not choose him a second time as the vice presidential candidate. Finch recalled that Nixon assumed he would practice law again; and one reason he actively sought foreign travel while vice president was to qualify for what he thought would be a lucrative practice in "foreign commerce."[24]

In that mood, and with the harsh memory of the fund crisis ever in mind, Nixon took Eisenhower's "chart out his own course" remark as the last straw. He drafted an announcement that he would not run again for vice president—just as, after the Checkers speech, he had written a telegram of resignation. But when Nixon told Vic Johnson of the national committee what he had done, Len Hall and Jerry Persons promptly appeared to talk Nixon out of releasing his statement. In neither case can it be supposed that

Nixon was serious about quitting; in both, he was advertising his exasperation and resentment.

At a news conference on April 25—four months after the president's strange "offer" to shift Nixon to the cabinet, and two months after announcing his own candidacy—Eisenhower was asked if the vice president had yet charted out his own course. The president replied that "he hasn't reported back in the terms in which I used the expression."

Nixon decided the time had come once more to force the issue. As he tells it in *RN* (again, in words that might have applied to 1952):

> The more I thought about it, the more I was convinced that I could not get off the ticket without hurting Eisenhower more than helping him. I knew there would be no way to explain my leaving the ticket that would convince large numbers of party workers that I had not been dumped. These people were more my constituency than Eisenhower's and if they felt I had been treated badly they might decide to sit out the election.

The next day—April 26, 1956—Nixon asked to see Eisenhower and told him he would be "honored" to run with him again, though he still protested politely that he "didn't want to do anything that would make you think I was trying to force my way onto the ticket if you didn't want me." But he was at least forcing the president to reach a decision.

Eisenhower, though he had been exploring every conceivable alternative possibility, wondered blandly why Nixon had taken so long to make up his mind. Then he called Hagerty and told him to present his 1956 running mate to the press immediately. "And you can tell them" he added, finally, and as if he himself had not put Nixon through his long and humiliating agony, "that I'm delighted by the news."[25]

That would have been the end of it except for two unexpected factors. Eisenhower's ileitis operation on June 8 reignited speculation about his health and consequently doubts about Nixon as his successor—perhaps Eisenhower's own doubts.

Then an *opéra bouffe* attempt by Harold Stassen to drive Nixon off the ticket kept the matter alive until the convention. Did Stassen remember the McCarthy ship deal of 1953, when he had been humiliated because Nixon and Dulles failed to support his condemnation of McCarthy's meddling? No doubt. But in the end, showing the first signs of the political ignominy into which he was to sink, Stassen had little choice but to second Nixon's uncontested nomination.

The only thing serious about Stassen's effort was that Eisenhower did not immediately put a stop to it. That caused the bruised and suspicious Nixon to worry that Stassen might actually be acting as a secret agent for the president. If so, and there's no evidence that he was, Eisenhower picked the wrong instrument in the erratic Stassen, and was still underestimating or ready to ignore Nixon's personal strength within the Republican party. But the timely and overwhelming endorsement, in late spring, of Nixon by House Republicans, soon caused Eisenhower to disavow Stassen's effort. It was going nowhere anyway.

Why had Eisenhower—not Nixon—waited so long to make up *his* mind? One reason might have been that during Anderson's Middle East mission—mid-January to mid-March—Eisenhower still hoped to inveigle him onto the ticket. Possibly, too, with his admiration for good administration, he had noticed, as Arthur Burns had, that Nixon ran an inefficient office. If so, the cabinet proposal made some sort of sense, but not much.

While the question of Nixon's renomination remained unsettled, Eisenhower told Bryce Harlow that he wanted the vice president to move to the cabinet because he "hadn't run anything" or even been a "corps commander." Harlow, who claimed some credit for talking Eisenhower into accepting Nixon on the ticket again, thought this judgment might be correct; but he knew it was "politically impractical" to shift a vice president to the cabinet.[26]

But there were deeper reasons for Eisenhower's attitude. As general and president, for instance, he often had been reluctant to fire anyone. In the fund crisis of 1952, the "dump Nixon" episode of 1956, later in the Sherman Adams scandal, he wanted the problem child to decide for himself to go away; failing that, he wanted someone else to do the dirty work.

The president *was* deeply concerned, of course, that he might not live through another term. He much preferred to think of Anderson or Warren replacing him, rather than Nixon, because he had genuine—if not necessarily justified—doubts about his young vice president.

That Nixon was not an intimate of the president meant little; few in the administration were. Nor, on the other hand, do the occasional letters of praise Eisenhower sent his vice president count for much; they were *pro forma,* from an administrator careful about such detail. It probably *is* significant, however, that in a private diary entry Eisenhower listed Nixon only ninth among sixteen "somewhat younger" people in his administration, with no approving comment on his qualifications.

To numerous associates, the president had referred to Nixon as immature—on exactly what grounds, he never specified. Perhaps he agreed with Foster Dulles that men in their forties were too young to have "mature judgment." Frequently, too, he said that Nixon was "too political," and several times he did tell Nixon to tone down campaign rhetoric linking the Democrats to the Communists. But the fact is that Eisenhower *used* Nixon as the administration's political spokesman and hardball player. That allowed the president to maintain the highroad and his preferred role as Mr. Nice Guy.

On several occasions, Eisenhower also stated the view that Nixon, though good at summarizing and analyzing others' ideas, was not himself much of an innovator. The Eisenhower speech writer Emmett Hughes, not a Nixon admirer, recalled that the president had told him he'd "watched Dick a long time, and he just hasn't grown. So I just haven't honestly been able to believe that he *is* Presidential timber."[27]

Owing apparently to such reservations, as late as 1960, when Nixon had the presidential nomination locked up, Eisenhower still was urging—fruitlessly—his old favorite, Robert Anderson, to step in and run. "I'll quit what I'm doing, Bob, I'll raise money," he pleaded. "I'll make speeches. I'll do *anything* to help. Just tell me I'm at liberty."[28]

In addition to his doubts about Nixon's qualifications, Eisenhower in 1956 apparently did not much *like* his vice president—Nixon's inner fear come true. The vice president's obvious ambition and opportunism, his lack of real bonhomie, his intensity, his occasional false and Heepish humility contrasted with flashes of political savagery, the sense that his public persona concealed some other man—none of this made Richard Nixon easy for *anyone* to like (save perhaps those few who knew him most intimately).

Since the fund crisis, moreover, there had been between him and Eisenhower a coolness that never really had been overcome by either. The president was "not fond" of Nixon, Harlow recalled, though Nixon admired Eisenhower and wished for a warmer relationship; Harlow thought Nixon just did not know how to achieve it.

Even Bob Finch, looking back from 1987, although he insisted that there had been no "hostility," called the Nixon-Eisenhower relationship "cool and dispassionate." One reason was that "Ike always carried himself professionally"; he was not "effusive, like a politician." In Finch's view, the Nixon-Eisenhower relationship warmed up only years later, after Julie Nixon married Eisenhower's grandson, David.

Charles Jones, an oil tycoon who was one of Eisenhower's chosen "gang" of personal friends, and who was close enough to call him "Ike" even in the White House, told Nixon—who took care to include the story in *RN*—of a comment he had made to the president's face in early 1956:

> Ike, what in hell does a man have to do to get your support? Dick Nixon has done everything you asked him to do. He has taken on the hard jobs that many of your other associates would have run away from. For you not to support him now would be the most ungrateful thing that I can possibly think of.

On other pages *RN* is peppered with purported quotes from Eisenhower, or Nixon's own observations, that do little to enhance the general's reputation as a "nice guy" or a great president—as if the author is slyly paying back, without quite admitting it even to himself, an accumulation of slights, indignities and rebuffs.

From a 1956 conversation, for instance, in which the president directed Nixon to make a speech in answer to Stevenson, Eisenhower is quoted as follows: "If you have to praise me, that will be okay. I, of course, will be a little embarrassed by that but I know you have to do it to answer." At another point, Nixon writes: "Eisenhower spent the first months of the [1954] campaign at the Denver White House. After a few hours of work in the morning he would golf in the afternoon."

Thus, a book written long after Eisenhower's death, and paying fulsome homage to him, constantly needles him, too. Eisenhower could be, after all, and despite his great charm and consideration for those he liked and admired, a singularly ungracious man.

On election night in 1956, as news of his landslide rolled in, he felt nothing for the crushed Stevenson but irritation that the Democratic candidate did not concede as soon as the president had expected. "What in the name of God is the monkey waiting for?" he demanded. "Polishing his prose?" When Stevenson finally appeared on the television screen, Eisenhower walked out of the room, telling others to stay "to receive the surrender."

Averell Harriman, a wartime colleague who served his country in more positions and for as many years as Eisenhower, was in the latter's ungenerous view, "a complete nincompoop. He's nothing but a Park Avenue Truman." Of Sam Rayburn, who gave him patriotic, bipartisan assistance as the Democratic Speaker of the House, Eisenhower reflected in retirement: "That fellow would double-cross you."

Harry Truman, who had made Eisenhower chairman of the Joint Chiefs and NATO commander, and who had offered to step aside so that he could have the Democratic presidential nomination in 1948 (but who also attacked Eisenhower harshly in the 1952 campaign), was a special target of the general's contempt. "The man is a congenital liar," he once remarked—only a sample of many graceless comments on Truman.

Nixon noted in *RN,* for another example, that when he suggested that former president Truman be invited to take part in a bipartisan rally for the support of the mutual security program, "A cold, hard look came over Eisenhower's face and he said that he would not appear on the same platform with Truman no matter what was at stake."

Eisenhower could be churlish, too, about Franklin Roosevelt, the man who had chosen Eisenhower over George Marshall to command the World War II armies in Europe. As president and in his books, Eisenhower publicly defended the Yalta agreements Roosevelt had accepted; but to Republican congressional leaders, on January 25, 1954, he remarked that "our commander-in-chief didn't have to be so indiscreet and crazy" at Yalta.[29]

At least one Democrat perceived something of all this in the popular Eisenhower: "I could understand it if he played golf all the time with old Army friends," John Kennedy observed in July 1959, "but no man is less loyal to his old friends than Eisenhower. He is a terribly cold man. All his golfing pals are rich men he has met since 1945."[30]

To what extent Richard Nixon may have suffered personally from this unpleasant side of Eisenhower's generally cordial disposition, he does not report in any of his writings. The president did say to him in 1956, in what seems an egregious insult, that Nixon would be better off in the cabinet, but "if you calculate that I won't last five years, of course that is different."[31]

Dwight D. Eisenhower was a proud man of great self-confidence, and one who believed rightly that he had done much for, hence deserved much from, his country and his party—a party that was, in his eyes, inexplicably backward, recalcitrant, infuriating, primarily because of its stubborn, conservative Old Guard.

Perhaps, then, a final reason for Eisenhower's attitude toward Nixon in 1956 was that he did not so much underestimate as *resent* Nixon's high standing with the Republican right wing. If Nixon was so valued *by* them, wasn't he basically one *of* them? Why couldn't he bring them more nearly to Eisenhower's support? If Nixon alone could keep the Old Guard in line in an election year, didn't that make him a potential if unspoken *threat* to Eisenhower's prospects—to his *due*?

In that light, it seems possible that Eisenhower realized all along, at least in the back of his mind, that he had no good alternative to Nixon—that not even Anderson or Warren or Lausche could bring the united Republican political support he needed, grubby and distasteful as the need might be. Indeed, Chairman Len Hall's polls made exactly that point.

A skilled *personal* politician throughout his career, Eisenhower often expressed his disdain for *professional* politicians; surely it irritated him that among men he thought of real quality, such as Anderson, he could find no one who could be substituted for one he considered to have mere political appeal.

If Eisenhower realized, or feared, moreover, that it would be politically dangerous to dump Nixon for someone he preferred personally, it was almost as if he were being blackmailed into running with him again. Eisenhower's sense of himself, his high-mindedness, his natural dominance, the honor he thought due him, all would have been profoundly offended—perhaps enough so that for four long months in 1956, years before it happened to anyone in the Watergate affair, this proud and sometimes ungenerous man could keep the vice president of the United States, his loyal subordinate, "twisting slowly, slowly in the wind."

Nixon had to nurse his bitterness in 1956 largely within himself—his natural instinct anyway—because the reelection campaign was largely his responsibility. No one expected anything but that he would have to carry the load for Eisenhower; and once the convention and the Stassen nuisance were out of the way, he could get down to it. At a news conference in Ohio, the vice president stated the problem, which was "different from that in 1952. . . . [Then] we were giving people the reasons to throw out a group, and now we are giving them reasons to keep an Administration in."

The basic reason to do that, Nixon suggested, was Dwight D. Eisenhower himself—a man, he was to repeat over and over, whose administration had brought "peace and prosperity and progress to America," and a man "whom every American can proudly hold up to his children as one who has faith in God, faith in America, and one who has restored dignity and respect to the highest office in the land." (Nixon used the "hold up to his children" passage so often that reporters traveling with him called it "the weight-lifting act.")

As Nixon well knew by then, he and Eisenhower had not succeeded in making the Republicans a majority party; the ticket needed additional "swing votes" from Democrats and independents if it was to win again. So his partisan appeals had to be muted in favor of praise for "the greatest leader of the atomic age" and "a man who ranks among the most legendary heroes of the nation." Only when Stevenson proposed a nuclear test ban—a goal in which Eisenhower had not let the public know that he was himself interested—did Nixon relax into his old slashing style. Stevenson's "catastrophic nonsense," he declared, played "dangerous politics with American security."

Otherwise, the hit-and-run, take-no-prisoners Nixon of earlier campaigns—especially 1954—was seldom to be seen. In that congressional campaign of two years before, with Eisenhower off the ticket and far above the battle, the loss of both Houses of Congress had seemed all too likely. To prevent such a defeat, Nixon had raced about the country at the highest pitch and the lowest level of his political career.

"To sum it up bluntly," he had said at Milwaukee on June 26, 1954, in what was essentially his campaign theme for the year, "the Acheson policy was directly responsible for the loss of China. And if China had not been lost, there would have been no war in Korea and there would be no war in Indochina," where the French were nearing final withdrawal.

This intrusion of foreign policy into the electioneering was not only a false analysis; it distressed—because it might bring retaliation in Congress—the sitting secretary of state, who had not quite managed, as promised in 1952, to liberate Eastern Europe, unify Korea, or "roll back" communism anywhere. But the Nixon of 1954 had raced and ranted on, taking his lead from Republican officials who, like him, did not realize that the tide was turning—not just against Joe McCarthy, who was being brought low by the army hearings—but against the McCarthy-like tactics Nixon still was employing.

In forty-eight days of campaigning in 1954, Nixon visited ninety-five cities in thirty-one states, made 204 speeches—three to six a day—and held more than a hundred news conferences. Attack, attack, was his style, "K-1, C-3"—Korea, communism, corruption and controls—his substance, as if he were still trying to "throw out a group." In fact, he was desperately trying to hold control of Congress, and thus supported anybody labeled Republican.

When it was protested that Clifford Case of New Jersey was "too liberal," Nixon replied: "We've got to get forty-eight seats in the Senate. Let's get that through our heads." He worked as hard for Case, who won, as for any other Republican.

In 1954, in what the phrase-making Stevenson called his "ill-will campaign," Nixon had seemed to blink at nothing. In Van Nuys, California, on October 13, for instance, and many times thereafter, he told spellbound listeners:

> When the Eisenhower Administration came to Washington ... we found in the files a blueprint for socializing America. This dangerous, well-oiled scheme contained plans for adding $40 billion to the national debt by 1956. It called for socialized medicine, socialized housing, socialized agriculture, socialized water and power, and perhaps most disturbing of all, socialization of America's greatest source of power, atomic energy.

Reporters, of course, pointed out that this was figurative language and that actually there was no "blueprint." That didn't deter Nixon from telling and retelling an effective campaign story. He also used so many figures, so confusingly, for the number of security risks he claimed the Democrats had hired and the Republicans had fired that he could be pinned down to nothing but obfuscation. And always there was the not quite libelous implication that the Democratic party and the Truman administration's leaders had been not quite Communists—just blind or sympathetic or subservient to them.

"McCarthyism in a white collar," Stevenson declared.

In 1954, it was all for nothing, unless the Republicans might have done *worse* without Nixon's shrill campaign. They did badly enough as it was,

losing eighteen seats and control of the House, four senators and control
of the Senate. Eisenhower never again controlled either—and neither did
President Richard Nixon from January 1969 to August 1974, or any
Republican president until Ronald Reagan's overwhelming 1980 election
cost the Democrats their accustomed control of the Senate for six years.

Nixon's lurid 1954 campaign was one good reason why there was so
much opposition to his renomination in 1956, when he obviously would
be a possible successor to Eisenhower in the White House. The Roman
Catholic weekly, *Commonweal,* expressed a typical view in an editorial in
1956:

> He cannot seem to get it into his head that there are some things
> one cannot do if political life is to go on peacefully after an election
> is finished. One can criticize, slash hard, accuse opponents of
> stupidity, blindness, inefficiency—any number of things. But it is
> impossible to imply that one's opponents deliberately betrayed the
> interests of the United States, and then expect to be able to work
> with these men after the campaign is over as if nothing had hap-
> pened.

Nevertheless, Eisenhower wrote Nixon a "Dear Dick" letter, reprinted
in *RN,* in the last stages of that vitriolic 1954 campaign:

> Whenever my burdens tend to feel unduly heavy, I admire all the
> more the tremendous job you have done since the opening of the
> present campaign. . . . Whatever the outcome next Tuesday, I can
> find no words to express my deep appreciation of the contribution
> you have made. . . . Please tell Pat that, too.

These were mere words. After the president's retirement, he deleted
from his memoirs a passage that praised Nixon's 1954 campaign. Milton
Eisenhower had protested its inclusion. "The fact is," Dwight Eisenhower
then told his son John in a memorandum, "that I've never had the opportunity to read the texts of Nixon's talks [in 1954]. It is possible that their
content is something of which I would not approve." That was a decade
after those "talks" had been made on Eisenhower's behalf.[32]

Nixon's conduct in 1954 made it difficult for him to focus the 1956
campaign entirely on Eisenhower, the great leader. In 1956, Nixon himself
was being judged too closely—not only as a man who might have to take
over the presidency, but as one who might well establish in the coming four
years an unshakable grip on his party's 1960 presidential nomination.
(Eisenhower, of course, would be prevented by the Twenty-second Amendment from serving more than two terms.)

Nixon could not escape knowing that he was under harsh scrutiny, which gave him another good reason for sticking to the political high road in 1956. By then, too, some political reporters were using wire recorders to get a verbatim record of what candidates might say at the smallest whistle-stop. Reporters who used the new technology in covering Nixon in that campaign—Bill Blair of the *New York Times,* for example—could see that the vice president was well aware of this new check on political excess.

He by no means succeeded in substituting the so-called new Nixon for the old model in the minds of his detractors; by making so sharp an about-face, he may only have enhanced his reputation for facility and deception. But had he repeated his head-hunting performance of 1954, he might well have damaged himself irreparably.

Stewart Alsop, an astute political observer of the period, theorized that Nixon really was a changed man after 1954, not least because the presidency had become a real possibility for him and thus he thought it politically necessary to meet a higher standard of conduct. Alsop also speculated about an incident arising in 1954 from one of Nixon's most celebrated and criticized remarks.

In the "shooting rats" speech replying to Adlai Stevenson and mildly rebuking Joe McCarthy, Nixon had thrown in what appeared to be an aside—actually one of his calculated innuendoes: "Incidentally, in mentioning Secretary Dulles, isn't it wonderful, finally, to have a secretary of state who isn't taken in by the Communists, who stands up to them?"

There was no need to speak Dean Acheson's name in *that* sentence. Not unnaturally, the words caught the attention of Philip Watts, a banker and former State Department official, who had been a friend of Nixon's since he had been secretary to, and Nixon a member of, the Herter committee in 1948. Watts was "the only really passionate anti-McCarthyite who was close to Nixon."

The morning after the vice president's speech, Watts demanded to see him.

> He wasted no time in telling Nixon what he thought of the remark. The implications . . . were wholly specious, he said—he had worked for Dean Acheson, and it was disgraceful to imply Acheson had been "taken in by the Communists." Moreover, if Nixon wanted the respect of honorable men, he should promptly abandon his habit of making his points by indirection, especially by the sly debater's trick of the rhetorical question.

Nixon listened unhappily and cited Acheson's stand in the Hiss case to justify his innuendo. But Watts told Alsop, "I think he thought about what I said."[33]

If so, it did not affect Nixon's rough campaign in the summer and fall of 1954; the Watts incident had occurred in March. But that year *was* a kind of low-water mark for Nixon; he never again campaigned as harshly, and though the old Nixon of innuendo and other debater's tricks sometimes reappeared, like a stutter or a facial twitch, the move toward a higher road in his political style was noticeable.

In the general election campaign of 1956, however, it did not much matter whether there was a new Nixon or just the old in disguise. The Stevenson-Kefauver campaign looked tired and defeatist, distinguished only occasionally by Stevenson's oratory—itself faded in comparison to that of 1952. Eisenhower had become, in any case, a national father figure. Even his heart attack may have been an asset, in that the possibility of his death or retirement had dramatized for voters how much they liked Ike and wanted to leave tiresome affairs of state to him.

I was working as a reporter for the *Winston-Salem Journal* in 1956, and once asked my publisher's wife, Mrs. William Hoyt, who had expressed her intention to vote for the president: "Doesn't it bother you that he's had a serious heart attack?"

Mrs. Hoyt drew herself up. "Young man," she said, only partly in jest, "I'd vote for Ike if he were *dead.*"

So it went across the country. The Eisenhower-Nixon ticket—even with the Suez and Hungarian crises exploding in the last days of the campaign— waltzed to victory by more than nine million popular votes. But as if to emphasize that this was a personal victory for Dwight Eisenhower, the Republicans failed even on his coattails to recapture Congress.

Despite the presidential victory, the party was plainly in bad shape. In 1952, Republicans had held 199 House seats, 47 in the Senate, and 25 governorships; by 1960, as a consequence of elections in the Eisenhower years, there were to be only 153 Republicans in the House, 35 Republican senators, and 14 Republican governors.

In February 1960, a Gallup poll found only 30 percent of American voters who called themselves Republicans, against 47 percent who confessed to being Democrats. That meant, Nixon pointed out in *Six Crises,* that to gain the presidency that year, a Republican candidate would have to win virtually all the Republicans, more than half of the independents (23 percent of the electorate) *and* five to six million Democrats.

Eisenhower, who might have been elected forever, undoubtedly could have won against such odds, but what would happen to the party's presidential hopes when he had to bow to the Twenty-second Amendment? That was not an encouraging question for any Republican, but for Richard Nixon in 1956 there was ample consolation: a winner again on Eisenhower's shoulders, he was still vice president, with four precious years in which to extend his leadership of the Republican party, lock up for himself its "top spot" in 1960, and build the kind of record that would give him a chance at the prize he had come to covet above all.

As vice president, Nixon chafed under his own lack of power, which mocked his impressive title. He suffered the humiliations of low status in supposedly high office, too, and the crowning indignities of Eisenhower's efforts to dump him from the ticket in 1956, and his lack of enthusiasm for Nixon's presidential candidacy in 1960.

All this had its corrosive effect—on Nixon's dark sense of himself against the world, on his inner anger at those less deserving than he who seemed to receive greater rewards. He nevertheless took from the experience of the vice presidency a seething desire to prove himself, perhaps even *to* himself, and at least one profound impression: *the idea of the presidency as a virtually imperial office for asserting the nation's interests around the globe.*

It was an office, no close observer of Eisenhower in action could fail to see, in which an incumbent with the will could find the means to do almost anything he might want in the world—even destroy, not just defeat, an enemy nation. One man, with the CIA at his disposal, could arrange *in secret* for minor spy adventures or great technological feats like the U-2 overflights or political strokes such as the overthrow of governments; and the same man could employ the armed forces *openly* to shore up perceived American interests, as in Eisenhower's deployment of the fleet in the Straits of Taiwan and of troops in Lebanon.

That man, at will, also could withhold American power, as from the French in Indochina, or unsheath it, as against the British at Suez. He could boldly challenge the other powers, as Eisenhower had in ignoring the Geneva accords to set up the Republic of South Vietnam; or temporize when necessary, as in the abandonment of the Hungarian freedom fighters in 1956; or offer sweeping peace proposals like the so-called Open Skies plan.

All that could be done by the president of the United States, without much hindrance save from a sluggish bureaucracy, and as long as public opinion could be molded to his support. Where he could not absolutely control, the president still could have the greatest single influence, as upon the military budget. No one in the world had more power than he to influence, if not to decide, the ultimate question: War or peace?

Nixon saw, of course, that no such power existed, even in the presidency, for the domination of domestic affairs. Congress, the courts, the states, the interest groups—all had their means of slowing or diluting or directly frustrating even a leader as popular as Eisenhower. Domestic problems, moreover, usually required a president to be more of what Nixon felt he could never be and did not want to be: a "buddy-buddy boy," constantly involved in personal, direct dealings with other people—members of Congress, for example, or important constituents.

These surely were among the reasons directing Nixon's intellectual interests, in his vice presidential years, toward the chessboard of foreign policy—a more remote and impersonal field upon which he could engage his *intelligence* more than his *personality,* in rather abstract games less demanding of the human give-and-take in which so introverted a man felt uncomfortable and disliked. Foreign policy, too, was the area in which a president's power to order things done as he wanted them done was the least checked, the most nearly imperial, and could be the most rewarding.

Sometime during eight years of learning and subservience in the Eisenhower administration, Richard Nixon determined to have that kind of power for himself. The hardworking and ambitious Whittier College graduate who had avoided the lash of his father's tongue and longed to earn his "saintly" mother's approval, hence perhaps her love, whose doubting sense of himself had been further eroded by the betrayals of the fund crisis and the ignominies of the vice presidency—this strange and inward man, who so seldom allowed the world a glimpse of his real face, came to *need* the power of the presidency.

What else could erase the past, make him whole against the wounds and slights of a savage world, perhaps even bring about through his efforts the peace on earth which at last would earn his mother's love? Only the power he had glimpsed through Eisenhower—that rewarding power for which Richard Nixon would suffer anything.

6

★

"If Only ..."

★

KENNEDY ELECTED PRESIDENT

—Headline, *New York Times,*
November 9, 1960, First Edition

KENNEDY APPARENTLY ELECTED

—Headline, *New York Times,*
November 9, 1960, Late Edition

In 1958, Vice President and Mrs. Richard Nixon were so threatened by mob violence during their Latin American tour that President Eisenhower sent four companies of Marines to the Caribbean to guarantee their safety. Walter Lippmann called that "a diplomatic Pearl Harbor"; but in American politics, it was more nearly a Normandy landing.

"For the first time," Nixon recalled in *RN,* "I pulled even with [John] Kennedy in the Gallup Presidential trial heat polls."

The next year, Nixon visited Moscow and engaged Nikita Khrushchev in a round of debates so rancorous that the outspoken Soviet leader called him "an unprincipled puppet" of Joe McCarthy and "a son of a bitch."

So the trip had been, wrote James Reston in the *New York Times,* "the perfect way to launch a campaign" for the White House.

To have been spit upon in Caracas and to have taken on the top Communist in Moscow indeed may have been just what Richard Nixon needed to catapult himself into what turned out to be the closest presidential election of modern times. If so, the ironies are great, for Nixon had not even wanted to go to Latin America on a trip he expected to be a bore; and though he did seek the Moscow trip, it proved a far cry from the total diplomatic coup for which he had hoped.

The vice president's Latin tour was occasioned by the inauguration of Arturo Frondizi as the first elected president of Argentina following the overthrow of the dictator Juan Perón in 1955. That the trip, at such a moment, was considered routine suggests how little Washington—characteristically—understood the peoples south of the Rio Grande. Even the well-traveled Nixon apparently knew little more.

That was the first serious error in what became a string of them. All across the region, autocrats like Perón, Rojas Pinella of Colombia, Perez Jiménez of Venezuela, even Batista in Cuba, either had been overthrown or were under heavy pressures from their populations. In the spring of 1958, popular democracy, in one of its periodic Latin American revivals, was releasing passionate political energies across an entire continent, including those of the region's committed Communists—about 360,000 of them, at best estimate.

These relatively few Communists found many less radical Latinos tired of traditional gringo dominance of the hemisphere and resentful of the "Colossus of the North" that had supported or tolerated so many dictators. Allen Dulles, reflecting CIA complacency, had told Nixon to expect no trouble; in fact, the vice president was walking into a bearpit and did not know it.

His first stop was scheduled for Uruguay—another error—in disregard or ignorance of the fact that Montevideo had become a center of Communist activity in Latin America. At the time, moreover, only 4.2 percent of Uruguay's farm owners controlled 56.4 percent of the land—which actually was the *best* land-distribution ratio in any Latin nation.

In his usual zeal to mingle with the people on the streets and in the marketplaces—and perhaps with his peculiar eagerness for "battle" and confrontation—Nixon himself made the next serious error. On trips abroad he always wanted to "get outside the embassy," Herbert Klein recalled. So in Montevideo he insisted on an unscheduled visit to the university and a debate there with the Communist leader of the Communist-dominated student union.

Nixon "won," but the occasion aroused other Communist leaders in Latin America. Milton Eisenhower, the president's brother and a relatively well informed student of Latin affairs, was separately traveling in South America at the time and later wrote:

> I am convinced that the Vice President unwittingly set the stage [for his later troubles] when he was in Montevideo . . . first because he had outwitted the Communists and other extremists and they sought revenge; secondly, conditions for an insulting attack were favorable; and third, since Nixon was a leading political leader of the United States, he was an ideal target.[1]

These "Communists and other extremists" had no trouble tapping into the latent—or often overt—anti-*norteamericano* sentiments of Latin America, a region disadvantaged in virtually every respect, when compared to the U.S. In educational levels, for only one example, the disparity was particularly telling.*

Economic recession gripped most of the region and it had become evident that private investment from the U.S. and elsewhere—the Eisenhower administration's nostrum—was not bringing the prosperity Washington had predicted. Peru, in particular, bitterly resented administration proposals to reduce American imports of Peruvian lead and zinc by 20 percent, in order to protect the American mineral industry, and the "dumping" of a huge American cotton surplus on the world market. Cotton was Peru's primary export, and Nixon could expect a sour welcome there.

In a rare display of foresight, American officials had left Chile off Nixon's itinerary—mostly because of anger there at American proposals to revive the tariff on copper, when the world price had dropped from forty-six to twenty-five cents. But in Peru, anti-American sentiment caught up with the vice president.

Arriving in Lima nine days after his Montevideo debate, he repeated his earlier confrontational tactic by going to speak at San Marcos University—another error in judgment, made against the advice of its rector, the city's police chief, most American officials, and despite the boasts of Communist leaders that they would stop him. Backed by a mob of two thousand demonstrators, on May 8, 1958, they did.

Nixon nevertheless jumped out of his car, approached the mob, and tried to get another debate going. When someone threw a rock that broke one of Secret Serviceman Jack Sherwood's teeth, even the combative vice president had to give up. But as his open car drove away, he stood up, shaking his fist, and shouted "Cowards!" at his tormentors.

He was spat upon when he returned to his hotel. Sherwood seized the man who did it and the infuriated Nixon kicked the "weird-looking character" in the shin. "Nothing I did all day made me feel better," he confessed in *Six Crises.*

This is a moment in which it's hard to know what to make of Nixon. Being spat upon would infuriate anyone, and Nixon's well-aimed kick is

*A United Nations study showed that 7.3 percent of American males over 25 had completed a college education, 25 percent of males under 25 had finished high school and only 12 percent of the whole male population had less than a primary education. Chile led the Latin nations in all three categories; but only 3.4 percent of its over-25 males had a college education, only 19 percent of its under-25 males had a high school degree and fully 21 percent of all Chilean males had less than a primary education. In a *really* poor country, Haiti, 92 percent of males had less than a primary education; in another, Nicaragua, the corresponding figure was 84 percent.

not only understandable; that he gave way to the angry impulse makes him seem more human, less tightly controlled. On the other hand, kicking someone who is being held by a third party is scarcely a bold or admirable act; and both this moment and Nixon's imprecations on the crowd at San Marcos belie his insistence—repeated so often that he seems almost to be trying to convince himself of its truth—that he is always cool and under iron control in a crisis.

He had challenged the mob at San Marcos University, he explained in *Six Crises,* because he had calculated quite deliberately that to avoid it "would not be simply a case of Nixon being bluffed out by a group of students, but of the United States itself putting its tail between its legs and running away from a bunch of Communist thugs."

If he actually did so pragmatically cerebrate such a decision, Nixon also seems to have projected a geopolitical rationale upon his own characteristic urge to do battle, perhaps to confront his own fears of lacking, or being thought to lack, manliness and bravery. Worse, he confuses himself with his country—of which he was merely a representative, and one not required by his office or his mission to confront angry mobs.

Much worse awaited the Nixon party in Venezuela. There, anti-Americanism was more political than economic. The nation had just rid itself of the dictator Marcos Perez Jiménez—upon whom Foster Dulles's State Department had conferred a Legion of Merit medal in 1954. After being deposed, Perez Jiménez and his hated police chief, Pedro Estrada, had fled to the U.S., where they were granted asylum. Their departure had made it possible for a number of exiled Communists and other extremists to return to Venezuela.

Nixon nevertheless insisted on going to that country as scheduled, despite the CIA's discovery of an assassination plot. His decision was still another mistake, though Nixon had been assured of adequate security by the unelected interim government. As even cursory inquiry should have disclosed, that government was too weak to deal effectively with radical elements and probably did not even know how dangerous the situation was.

At the airport, both Nixons were spat upon repeatedly by a mob of young demonstrators, and the playing of "The Star-spangled Banner" was drowned out by hundreds of voices shouting, *"¡Fuera! ¡Fuera!"* ("Out! Out!"). In the streets of Caracas, mobs ambushed the official motorcade several times—the worst incident lasting a terrifying twelve minutes, while Nixon's limousine was rocked and stoned and the Venezuelan police literally did nothing to stop the attack. Only the six-man Secret Service detail, very likely saving the vice president's life, prevented his car from being overturned. The traveling party barely escaped to the American embassy.[2]

Then came the most serious error of all. Eisenhower dispatched a force of Marines to the Caribbean, in case the Nixons had to be evacuated from

South America. That well-intended precaution not only dramatized a stunning embarrassment for the U.S. in its own hemisphere; but most of Latin America saw the arrival of the Marines as one more Yankee intervention—an unwarranted exercise of gunboat diplomacy.

Mr. and Mrs. Nixon generally conducted themselves in these ordeals with as much dignity and courage as possible, and it would be too much to say that Nixon brought the trouble on himself, or that American insensitivity to its neighbors was entirely responsible. Still, if State Department officials *and* a man who prided himself on his knowledge of global affairs had been more aware of the Latin American mood, and if Nixon had stuck strictly to official talks, luncheons, receptions and so on, the trip really might have turned out to be the bore he had expected.

Nixon himself seemed to sense that. After his return, he told the National Press Club "that the Communists spearheaded the attack. But you have to remember that they had a lot of willing spear-carriers along with them." That recognized, at least obliquely, the depth of anti-American sentiment, rather than Communism per se, in the Latin America of the late fifties.

As Luis Alberto Sanchez put it (in Spanish) in a *cuaderno,* or loose-leaf publication, of September/October 1958:

> The protests against Nixon activated many others who resented the policy of the U.S. State Department in Latin America over the previous sixteen years. Democrats, Communists and pro-Communists as well as fascists joined together in protest during the Nixon visit. . . . The U.S. overemphasized the strength of Communist participation. And those who confused the protests with a broad protest against imperialism committed an error: what was going on was a protest against the errors and vacillation of *U.S.–Latin American policy.* [Emphasis added.]

But in *Six Crises* Nixon abandoned his press club theme and wrote that the violence he had confronted in Latin America "unmasked the ugly face of Communism as it really was." In *RN,* years later, he repeated what he had told a press conference in Lima:

> It would be very dangerous to ascribe the riots to the fact that after ten years of repressive dictatorship the people did not know how to exercise restraint in enjoying their new freedom. These mobs were communists led by Communists [*sic*] and they had no devotion to freedom at all.*

*Why he used a capital "C" for Communist leaders and the lowercase "c" for their supposed followers, I decline to speculate. It seems of a piece with his suggestion to Foster Dulles, a week or so after his return to Washington, that the U.S. use body

The Nixon party returned to Washington to an enormous welcoming reception, featuring the president, the cabinet and Senate Majority Leader Lyndon Johnson. This turnout confirmed again what had long been apparent—that "standing up," whether to crooks and bullies or to mobs and threatening nations, is a much-admired quality in American politics, as in John Wayne movies—and never mind the underlying causes of the confrontation, or even the likely result.

Having stood up to being "stoned in Caracas"—as he liked to quip— proved a political asset that Nixon was sorely to need, and soon.

His continuing and indefatigable work in the muddy trenches of local and state Republicanism (in those years there scarcely could have been a Republican county chairman who did not owe Richard Nixon a favor or fidelity) and his claim (however specious or disputed) to sit at the right hand of Eisenhower, seemed to have made his nomination for president in 1960 almost a certainty. But that was precisely why, according to *RN*, Tom Dewey urged Nixon to stay out of the 1958 congressional campaign:

> I know that Ike won't [lead the party], and I know that all those old party wheelhorses will tell you stories that will pluck your heartstrings, but you're toying with your chance to be President. Don't do it, Dick. You've already done enough, and 1960 is what counts now.

Nixon, too, knew that 1958 would be uphill. Eisenhower's frugal budget policy had divided his party and shaken public confidence. So had his apathetic response—as pictured by the Democrats and widely believed—to Soviet space successes. Cartoonist Tom Little of the *Nashville Tennesseean* had drawn a captionless cartoon that caught the public mood: Sputnik flying above the earth's curve—followed by a golf ball.

Farmers were convinced that the administration's attitude toward them was symbolized by its dour and unpopular secretary of agriculture, the Mormon elder, Ezra Taft Benson. A recession, starting in late 1957, pushed up unemployment to more than five million in 1958; Democrats charged that Eisenhower's tight-money retrenchment was responsible. The economy's upward turn in 1958 came too late to help and was obscured, anyway, by the repercussions of the Sherman Adams scandal.

So in the language of a later time, Nixon looked out on a bad political "scene" in 1958. All polls confirmed that, but he decided to lead the Republican congressional and gubernatorial campaign anyway—"be-

---

language to indicate its preferences in Latin America: a formal handshake for dictators, an *abrazo* for "leaders in freedom."

cause," he wrote in *RN*, "it had to be done and because there wasn't anyone else to do it."

Was Nixon influenced also by his taste for confrontation, and perhaps by the secret conviction that he alone could pull out a victory for his party? Maybe, but the fact was that he had made himself the party's leader, and if he was to parlay that into a presidential nomination in 1960, he had to carry its flag in 1958. The necessity was real but it cost him dearly.

Four years after Joe McCarthy's downfall and on the heels of Adams's forced resignation, Nixon could rely on neither of the prime issues on which the Republicans had returned to power in 1952—anticommunism and anticorruption. He could not focus the campaign, as he had on Eisenhower in 1956, on a president who was constitutionally ineligible to run again. He could try to nullify Eisenhower's limp civil-rights stand by pointing to the Democrats' segregationist Southern governors and senators, but as the leader of a conservative party he could not really exploit the civil rights issue. With an eye on his 1960 prospects, he even hesitated to attack labor, a traditional Republican target.

Thus boxed in, Nixon reverted once again to cut-and-slash tactics, denouncing Democratic criticisms of the Eisenhower defense program as "rotgut thinking." This relatively innocuous phrase instantly evoked an outcry: Tricky Dick, the old Nixon, was back. The vice president never uttered the words again and demoted the staff member who in an internal memorandum had first used the phrase.

Bad luck, bad circumstances and bad politics dogged Nixon and his party in 1958. In Indiana, a traditional Republican bastion, the party was split and still warring. In Ohio, Republicans foolishly threw themselves on their swords in vain support of a right-to-work initiative. Even in Nixon's home state, intraparty warfare produced disaster.

"Bull" Knowland, fecklessly trying to take position from which to challenge Nixon for the 1960 presidential nomination, startled the nation by announcing his retirement from the Senate in order to run for governor of California. But California already had a Republican governor—Goodwin Knight, Warren's successor—who wanted another term and was not "scared out" by Knowland's grab at his office.

Nixon tried to broker the affair, but too late to talk Knowland into staying in the Senate. So Nixon told Knight he could support him only for the Senate—trying, in effect, to arrange a peaceful swap of offices. Kyle Palmer of the *Los Angeles Times,* still the kingpin of California Republican politics, was willing to cooperate in this strategy—he may well have originated it—to make the most of a bad situation. He shut off money and support for another Knight gubernatorial campaign.

That left Knight little choice but to run for Knowland's Senate seat, which he did not want, while Knowland ran for Knight's governorship, for which he was not fitted. This well-publicized disarray looked like a prescription for disaster in the nation's largest state—and on Richard Nixon's turf.

On foreign policy matters, Nixon suffered the cruelest blow of all—repudiation first by Foster Dulles, then by Eisenhower himself. Seeking an issue, *any* issue, Nixon seized in October on a statement by the Democratic Advisory Council that was critical of administration foreign policy; in response, he compared Eisenhower's achievements with what he called "the sorry record of retreat and appeasement" in previous Democratic years and the "defensive, defeatist fuzzy-headed thinking which contributed to the loss of China and led to the Korean War."

Nixon the old campaigner, on old familiar ground, then produced one of his classically pointed formulations: "In a nutshell, the Acheson foreign policy resulted in war and the Eisenhower-Dulles policy resulted in peace."

Actually, congressional Democrats, led by Sam Rayburn and Lyndon Johnson, had been reasonably supportive of administration foreign policy; so, in the presidential tradition, had Harry Truman himself. Democratic support in Congress still was needed. Dulles, therefore, told a news conference the day after Nixon's remarks that "I would hope both sides would calm down" about foreign policy.

Feeling his oats as party leader, Nixon pushed Dulles into a further statement acknowledging the need for a reply to the advisory council. But Eisenhower then told *his* next news conference that "foreign policy ought to be left out of partisan debate. . . . America's best interests in the world will be served if we do not indulge in this kind of thing." Apparently he had forgotten his own indulgences in 1952, such as his trip to Korea.

For perhaps the only time in his vice presidency, Nixon publicly challenged the great man—gingerly but unmistakably. Eisenhower's responsibility was one thing, he said, but his was "the responsibility for carrying the weight of this campaign" and therefore he would "continue to answer the attacks."

Eisenhower was not so lame a duck as to accept that. He telegraphed the vice president directly:

> Both political parties have taken a common stand for a number of years on the essential foundations of a foreign policy. Both of us are dedicated to peace, to the renunciation of force except for defense, to the principles of the United Nations Charter, to opposing Communist expansion, to promoting the defensive and economic strength of the free world through cooperative action, including mutual aid and technical assistance. . . . in my view

these, with rare exceptions, should not and do not lend themselves
to political argument.

Nixon dropped the subject until, a week later, he echoed the Eisenhower
telegram in a speech in Baltimore:

> There is no war party in the United States. All Americans want
> peace. There is no party of surrender in the United States. . . .
> There is only one party of treason in the United States—the Com-
> munist party.

In effect, after so many campaigns, Richard Nixon was saying good-bye
to perhaps the one issue with which he had been most associated in the
public mind. He was never to return to it in the ferocious style of his earlier
campaigns. After the election, he was asked in London by a BBC interviewer whether it was true that Eisenhower had "gently rebuked" him.
"Yes, as a matter of fact," Nixon conceded, "it is true."[3]
That could not have been an easy admission. The realist in Nixon surely
knew that by 1958, the old effectiveness of the Red issue was tainted and
fading; he had to go on to subjects more relevant to changing times.
Nevertheless, he had been forced to abandon what might fairly be called
the basic theme of his early career. After the indignities of 1956, with their
echoes of the soul-searing fund crisis of 1952, and when Nixon was carrying the 1958 campaign all alone, to have had the ground—old familiar
ground at that—cut from under him by the man whose interests (as well
as his own) he was trying to serve, certainly added to Nixon's paranoia and
mistrust even of those supposed to be his friends, as well as his rising stock
of resentments against Eisenhower.
He was left, moreover, in midcampaign with little more than determined
optimism, perhaps born of desperation, but no less empty for that. He kept
predicting a surprise Republican victory that would come as voters, including Democrats, realized—in Nixon's repeated words—"Why take a
chance on a change?" All Republican candidates and spokesmen, he decreed in a telegraphed circular on October 19, "should radiate optimism."
He took his own advice quite literally.
Two years later, as a *New York Times* reporter, I was covering the
campaign of the Republican vice presidential nominee, Henry Cabot
Lodge. I observed to Ed Terrar, a political operative traveling with the
Lodge campaign, that Lodge's most effective applause line ("No one is
going to take over the United States and no one is going to take over the
world") seemed to be almost meaningless rhetoric.
"That's nothing," Terrar said. "You know what Nixon's best line was
in 1958?"

I confessed I did not know.

"He'd just say, toward the end of a speech: 'Their campaign is going *down* and our campaign is going up!' That didn't mean anything either, but it never failed to get 'em up and screaming."

Terrar's story is a commentary on the substantive content of electoral politics in America. At the time, however, such cheerleading was about all Nixon could do. Besides, Herbert Klein, Nixon's press secretary, recalled that the vice president's personal optimism, confounding his usual realism, was genuine. For some reason, Klein told me, Nixon really believed there would be a Republican upset—until, late in the campaign, Klein and Bob Finch checked key states and were told flatly that the party would be "clobbered" in most of them. A Connecticut poll at the end of the campaign dashed Nixon's last hopes.

The outcome was worse than he could have feared—fifteen lost seats in the Senate, forty-six in the House, nine governorships down the drain—a Democratic landslide. The Democrats' popular margin in House elections had risen from a million votes in 1956 (when Eisenhower had headed the Republican ticket) to more than five million. Nixon could claim fairly to have aided Republican senatorial victories in only five of the nineteen instances in which he had tried, and in only three gubernatorial contests.

Dewey's fears were realized. Nixon's national reputation as a campaigner and a winner had been badly damaged; some pundits wondered whether, without the anticommunism issue, he might be just another Republican politician rather than the party's best hope for the future. Meanwhile, the man some regarded as the *Democrats'* best hope, John Kennedy of Massachusetts, had been reelected to the Senate by an impressive margin.

Undoubtedly, the California results were the most cutting. Predictably, as a result of Senator Knowland's clumsy grab for "Goody" Knight's governorship, both major Republican candidates were beaten—Knowland by a Democrat whose career was to haunt Richard Nixon, Attorney General Edmund G. ("Pat") Brown.

After such a setback in his own state, it was small comfort to Nixon to be the sole remaining major figure (with Earl Warren neutralized on the Supreme Court) in the California Republican party—particularly when it was widely assumed that such a self-serving and cynical politician as he was supposed to be somehow must have rigged the whole affair to kill off both Knowland and Knight, his putative party rivals.

In fact, Knowland had precipitated the mess, surprising even the ubiquitous Kyle Palmer and bringing to a sad end his own political career, as well as Knight's. Nixon could hardly have influenced Knowland to stay in the Senate, given Knowland's motive for leaving it—to compete with Nixon for the 1960 presidential nomination. It is true that either Knowland or

Knight as governor might have battled Nixon for control of the California convention delegation in 1960, and their twin defeats did avoid such an internal struggle. On the other hand, though, the riven California Republican party and a new Democratic governor did not bode well for Nixon's chances to carry his home state in 1960.

Equally threatening personally were the returns from the second largest state, New York. An attractive, able and obviously well financed Republican had defeated the incumbent Democrat, Averell Harriman, for a governorship that in less than a half century had been a stepping-stone to the White House for Grover Cleveland and both Roosevelts, to two Republican presidential nominations for Tom Dewey, and one Democratic nomination for Al Smith.

The first successful Republican—there weren't all that many—to whom Nixon telephoned on election night was New York's governor-elect, Nelson A. Rockefeller. The next day, the press labeled Rockefeller the "real winner" in 1958, and made him overnight into what had not existed before: a promising Republican presidential alternative to Richard Nixon—who was, according to the press, the year's "real loser."

In his phone call, Nixon said all the right things to his new rival (for whom he had campaigned). Rockefeller was not so gracious. On a postelection vacation in Venezuela, the scene of Nixon's humiliation earlier in the year, the governor-elect told an inquiring reporter: *"No tengo nada que ver con Nixon"* ("I have nothing to do with Nixon").

No doubt Nixon stored that in his capacious political memory, for future attention. In 1968, when president-elect Nixon was choosing his cabinet, it was so generally assumed that Nelson Rockefeller would be part of it that William Safire asked why not *David* Rockefeller for Treasury, but answered himself: "No, you can't have two Rockefellers in the Cabinet."

" 'Is there a law,' Nixon asked without changing expression, 'that you have to have one?' "[4]

But score-settling was for the future. To Earl Mazo not long after the dark election day of 1958, Nixon confided the wisdom of a man hardened to the cyclical and cynical ways of politics:

> There's no question but that a person in politics is always hurt when he loses, because people like to play winners. But the one sure thing about politics is that what goes up comes down, and what goes down often comes up.

Nixon's visit to the Soviet Union the next year quickly demonstrated that truth—while repeating the lesson of the mob attack in Venezuela— that Americans like a man who is willing to "stand up."

The vice president had only the innocuous assignment of opening the

American National Exhibition in Moscow; his supporters nevertheless promoted the idea that in any talks with Premier Khrushchev he might break or loosen the Soviet-American Cold War deadlock—then well symbolized by a hopelessly snarled Big Four foreign ministers' meeting in Geneva.

How this triumph was to be achieved by a vice president renowned for his anticommunism was undetailed—for example, by the Republican and pro-Nixon *Herald Tribune* of New York, whose editors proclaimed that a "ceremonial visit has now become a diplomatic mission of the first importance."

Before Nixon's departure, however, Dwight Eisenhower undercut this unrealistic vision—and his vice president—twice. First, he told a news conference that Nixon "is not a part of the diplomatic processes and machinery of this country. . . . [H]e can impart information but he is not negotiating anything." Nixon, in other words, was just vice president, not the real thing.

Next, in private and only a few hours before Nixon's departure on July 22, 1959—his head stuffed with details of Soviet-American relations after some typical iron-butt cramming sessions—Eisenhower told the vice president that an exchange of state visits already had been arranged with Khrushchev. If Nixon had had high hopes for some diplomatic achievement in Moscow, they were thus deflated at the start of his journey; the Soviet leader would be in Washington in a few weeks and could deal with the president directly.

Then Eisenhower publicly announced Khrushchev's American visit only two days before Nixon was to *return* to Washington—obviously taking the public edge off the vice president's venture behind the iron curtain. Worse, Eisenhower said in his announcement that before Nixon's departure, the vice president had been told about the planned Khrushchev visit in this way:

> I told him and I said, "So that you will not be astonished or surprised or feel let down by your government, should [the subject of the Khrushchev visit] be opened up by the other side, you are not, yourself [*sic*], and of course will not open this subject."

That sounded more like a general to a lieutenant than a president to a constitutional officer—much less to his supposed partner and heir, as Nixon supporters liked to picture their man. And it left in shreds the idea of a "diplomatic mission of the first importance."

The Moscow visit itself produced mostly a series of debates—Nixon's favorite form of confrontation—with the blustery, emotional Khrushchev. But their most striking exchange was not mentioned in *Six Crises,* at a time when Nixon still was seeking votes in Puritan America; it was fully detailed only in *RN,* written after his retirement. The occasion was the first private meeting between the two principals, in Khrushchev's Kremlin office.

Just before Nixon's departure, Congress—ignoring the American failure to help Hungarian freedom fighters during the uprising of 1956—had observed the annual ritual of passing the so-called Captive Nations Resolution. Taking immediate exception to this symbolic anti-Soviet act, Khrushchev in his best earthy style declared: "This resolution stinks. It stinks like fresh horse shit, and nothing smells worse than that."

Thoroughly briefed as always, Nixon knew that the Soviet leader had been in his youth a pig breeder.

"I'm afraid the chairman is mistaken," Nixon replied. "There is something that smells worse than horse shit. That is pig shit."

Khrushchev had to admit this delicate point, but maintained and even escalated his attack. Fawn Brodie has suggested that the Soviet leader may have reminded Nixon of his father, Frank Nixon—hotheaded, loud, quick to argue, abusive, but (as the vice president later wrote about the Soviet premier) "at times almost seductively charming; at other times . . . boorish and obtuse." Khrushchev, Nixon observed, had "a keen mind and a ruthless grasp of power politics"—and that, too, on a larger scale, was not unlike Frank Nixon.

The most celebrated jousts with Khrushchev took place while Nixon was visiting the American exhibition; unexpectedly, Khrushchev accompanied him and the two clashed first in an American model television studio. There, Khrushchev—still harping on the Captive Nations Resolution—got so much the better of their substantive exchanges that Nixon was forced lamely to fall back on the claim that the U.S. was ahead of the Soviet Union in color television technology. At one point, as if he were a schoolyard debater, he insisted to Khrushchev (as the Soviet leader understood from the translation): "You don't know everything!"

Herbert Klein told the vice president that reporters were interpreting this exchange as a Khrushchev victory, and that television footage would be transmitted from the model studio to the U.S. Klein recalls that he deliberately led the official party toward the American exhibition's model kitchen, hoping for still another debate and a Nixon recovery.

William Safire, later my *New York Times* colleague but then a press agent representing the kitchen's builders, watched as Nixon emerged from the television studio, "sweating profusely, knowing that he had 'lost,' and anxious to find a way to make a comeback." Safire, eager to help a man he admired, believes that his shouts and signals led the official party to the kitchen.

However the combatants got there, in their third confrontation of the day (the first had been the opening salvos in Khrushchev's office), Nixon was in better form—"superb," Safire thought—and handled "the debate with dignity as well as tough-mindedness."

It was in the kitchen that two famous photos were taken: one by Safire, who used a press photographer's camera, that showed Nixon and Khrushchev leaning on a railing at the kitchen exhibit, with Leonid Brezhnev (then virtually unknown) standing next to them; the other depicting Nixon's long finger poking into Khrushchev's chest—pure gold in American politics.[5]

The photos from the kitchen more than offset any American political damage Nixon might have suffered from the exchange in the television studio. Later during his Moscow visit, he became the first American to address the Soviet people on Russian television. On his way home, he stopped over in Warsaw, where an enormous crowd of Poles turned out to give him an enthusiastic welcome—demonstrating, Nixon wrote in *RN,* "not only their friendship for the United States but also their detestation of their Communist rulers and Soviet neighbors."

The crowd—Jacob D. Beam, who was the American ambassador to Poland in 1959, recalls a "mass of people" all along the five miles into the city from the airport—was doubly a tribute because, as Beam recalled, the Polish government had waited until the last possible moment to announce the time and route of Nixon's arrival. Riding in the motorcade with a deputy foreign minister, Beam saw that the official was upset by the unexpected size of the turnout.

Nixon thought at the time that he had lost his "kitchen debate" with Khrushchev, so he got a "great lift" from his welcome in Warsaw. In embassy conversations, Beam got a favorable impression of the vice president, though Nixon showed no interest in Warsaw's main diplomatic attraction—the private talks American representatives had been having there with Communist Chinese emissaries, beginning in 1955.

Beam was able, however, to give the vice president a good preview of what he would face the next day in a private conversation with the Polish leader, Wladyslaw Gomulka ("a mean tyrant, the worst of all of them"), who never before had met with a Western leader. Nixon later felt he had done well in his meeting with Gomulka. Therefore, Nixon "inclined very favorably toward me," Beam recalls, and a decade later, Beam became President Nixon's personal choice for the plum of the Foreign Service—the ambassadorship in Moscow—despite the opposition of an influential Nixon supporter, Senator J. Strom Thurmond of South Carolina.[6]

That final outpouring of the crowds in Warsaw was the only substantive gain of the trip, but the kitchen photos as well as press coverage of Nixon's confrontations with Khrushchev gave the vice president a domestic political triumph. Indeed, said *Time,* Richard Nixon in Moscow was "the personification of a kind of disciplined vigor that belied tales of the decadent and limp-wristed West."

"Disciplined vigor" had been not much in evidence when Nixon returned to the American embassy after his long first day's debate with Khrushchev. As Ambassador Llewellyn "Tommy" Thompson later confided to close friends, the vice president's supposedly iron self-control obviously had been shaken under the pressure of the day's events. As many another might have done, he soothed his nerves that night with liquor—too much of it.

That, of course, was not known to the enthusiastic American public. Before Nixon's trip, the Gallup poll had found Kennedy leading him, 61 to 39, in a presidential trial heat—a margin greater than any Eisenhower had held over Stevenson. Just *after* the trip, the gap closed to 52 for Kennedy, 48 for Nixon. By November 1959, Nixon had moved ahead, 53 to 47.

Adlai Stevenson wrote to the journalist Bill Baggs that the big welcome-home reception Nixon received in the U.S. "fills me with a feeling that must be nausea and wonder about the new image of the American hero to inspire our little boys." That was only egghead carping; Caracas and Moscow, Stevenson the politician conceded, had made Richard Nixon "a formidable candidate" for president in 1960.[7]

Never mind that little useful had been accomplished in Latin America or Moscow, and much damage done. Richard Nixon had faced the mob in Venezuela and shook his finger at the Soviet dictator. That was what counted. That was what Americans admired. He had stood up and fired back, and was therefore confirmed in the public mind as an anti-Communist, a strong leader, a "stand-up guy." He was ready to be president.

Even so, and despite the great advantages Nixon had derived from his years at hard labor within the Republican party, it remains something of a political mystery that he was not more seriously challenged in 1960 by Nelson Rockefeller, the highly touted governor of New York.

"To this day," Bob Finch, Nixon's campaign director in 1960, reflected a quarter century later, "I don't know why Rocky didn't run in 1960." He pointed out that Rockefeller probably could have defeated Nixon at least in some of the northeastern state primaries. "Rocky could buy and sell New Hampshire," Finch reflected. "He could pay for a mailing without denting his wallet."

But Rockefeller didn't do any of that, announcing early in the year that he would not be a candidate. Perhaps he correctly interpreted Nixon's hold on party workers as unshakable, or perhaps he overestimated it and lacked the knowledge of politics outside New York to challenge the more experienced man. Different Rockefeller associates can be found to assert each theory.

Neither in 1964 nor in 1968, when the New York governor was a far more active candidate than he was in 1960, did he show a sure grasp of national politics and the Republican party. The conclusion seems fair that Rockefeller, for all his political dominance in New York, never quite mastered the arcane business of a nationwide run for president, and never gathered around him the staff that could make up for his own deficiencies in that business.

In 1960, he probably knew, moreover, that even if Eisenhower had no great enthusiasm for Nixon, the president had even less for Nelson Rockefeller. One reason was that the ever-enthusiastic Rockefeller, while serving in the Eisenhower administration, frequently "got in trouble" with the president, as Arthur Burns observed, by proposing too many new ideas and departures, rather too bumptiously for a junior man. Nixon had never made that mistake.[8]

In 1959 and 1960, as Nixon's only conceivable rival, Rockefeller was nevertheless a factor to be considered in the battle for the presidential nomination. One of the continuing issues was the adequacy of Eisenhower's military budget; liberal opinion generally, including that of most Democrats and such "modern Republicans" as Rockefeller, was that American military power had been allowed to fall behind that of the Soviet Union, particularly in the new field of ballistic missiles (the so-called missile gap*).

Eisenhower knew better, owing to photos taken over the Soviet Union by the U-2 flights; but he couldn't say so and preserve necessary secrecy. When the U-2 piloted by Francis Gary Powers was shot down in May 1960, the secret of the flights was abruptly ended (as were the trans-Russia flights themselves, and a pending summit conference that had offered what probably was the best chance ever for a nuclear test ban treaty between the superpowers). Still, Eisenhower continued to be hounded by the issue and could not persuade critics that American military forces were not only adequate but, as he insisted, "awesome."

Rockefeller also had annoyed the president by calling for a national civil defense program that Eisenhower thought was both useless and too expensive. On June 8, 1960, Rockefeller angered him again by calling for a $3.5 billion increase in the Pentagon budget to answer the missile gap.

The next day, with bizarre timing, the ebullient governor called Eisenhower to ask the president's opinion on whether he should change his mind and become an active candidate for the Republican presidential nomination. Ann Whitman, Eisenhower's and later Rockefeller's secretary, made a record of the conversation.

*The theory held by many of Eisenhower's critics that the Soviet Union had more nuclear-tipped missiles than the president had been willing to build. Eisenhower knew from secret U-2 reconnaissance flights that the "missile gap" did not exist. But Kennedy repeatedly raised the issue in 1960.

After lecturing the governor on military spending, Eisenhower cautioned him against becoming either "on again, off again, gone again, Finnegan" or a "lone wolfer—a LaFollette." But his main point was that Rockefeller's chances were remote.

Ever optimistic, Rockefeller nonetheless announced that he was available for a draft—which, of course, in the usual way of presidential "drafts," never materialized. Eisenhower didn't like that kind of brashness, felt betrayed by Rockefeller's insistence on spending increases and had developed a consuming dislike for Emmett Hughes, his own former speech writer, who had become a close adviser to Rockefeller.

Nevertheless, the president knew a New York governor was not to be dismissed lightly, particularly one with Rockefeller's resources in those days before campaign spending limitations. The president still did not consider Nixon a strong candidate, and the idea inevitably occurred to him—as to many another Republican—of a Nixon-Rockefeller ticket.

Rockefeller wanted none of that, however, and Nixon—after eight years of playing second fiddle and being at Eisenhower's whim—certainly did not again want to be beholden to anyone, or even to be considered so. He wanted to be on his own, prove that he could win and handle the biggest job of all.

Understanding the ambitions of neither contender, Eisenhower on July 19, 1960, called Gabriel Hauge, his former economics aide; Hauge had written him to say that only a Nixon-Rockefeller ticket could hope to defeat the strong team—John F. Kennedy and Lyndon B. Johnson—the Democrats had nominated. Eisenhower told Hague he'd tried in vain to persuade Rockefeller to take the second spot, and believed there was only one way he would do so.

Then he put forward the phantasmagoric idea, concocted by his speech writer, Malcolm Moos, that Nixon should guarantee that he would serve only one term as president, in return for Rockefeller's agreement to be his running mate. Then Nixon would step aside and Rockefeller could be the Republican candidate in 1964. Eisenhower did allow that "Dick" might not like this scheme—certainly an understatement. The call to Hague demonstrated again that Dwight Eisenhower's ideas about presidential politics for ordinary mortals tended to soar toward the wild blue yonder.[9]

Nothing came of this one, but it shows the president's continuing uneasiness about Nixon—his chances to win, his ability to do the job if he did. But Nixon—though restive about the economy, the military budget, Cuba and some other issues—at least appeared to give Eisenhower's record the general support the president thought it deserved.

As the Republican National Convention got under way in Chicago, a platform was being written under Nixon's direction that Eisenhower was ready to approve. But the vice president suddenly flew to meet Rockefeller at the latter's Fifth Avenue apartment in New York. On July 22, 1960, they issued a joint statement reflecting more liberal and more popular views than the president's on several issues—most importantly, "increased expenditures" for the military (then, unlike now, a "liberal" issue).

Nixon thought he was guaranteeing Rockefeller's support for the Republican ticket—apparently forgetting that Eisenhower's was more important. Rockefeller thought Nixon's agreement would guarantee inclusion of their "Pact of Fifth Avenue" in the platform—apparently not realizing that it repudiated not only Republican administration policy but also the hero of World War II. But Eisenhower, well aware that he still would be president until January 20, 1961, had no intention of tamely surrendering on an issue about which he perhaps felt more strongly than any other.

The president immediately pushed Nixon hard to keep the Fifth Avenue statement out of the Republican platform. Nixon quickly acquiesced, devising compromise platform language and lamely explaining to Eisenhower that Rockefeller had made the pact public without Nixon's consent. (A likely story: Why had so political an agreement been reached, if not to be made public?)

Nixon proceeded without further event to the nomination, went through a show of deliberation about a running mate, then designated Henry Cabot Lodge, upon whom—as Herbert Klein told me—he had decided long before the convention opened. Eisenhower, as might be expected, had hoped Nixon would choose Robert Anderson. But Lodge was an early media star; Nixon knew that Americans had enjoyed watching him, as Eisenhower's ambassador to the U.N., denounce the Soviets on television. Lodge was another who had "stood up" to the Communists and his appeal apparently overrode the fact that the patrician New Englander was the epitome of the Eastern Establishment.

The Pact of Fifth Avenue had finished Rockefeller in Eisenhower's esteem. But neither the pact nor the choice of Lodge quelled his doubts about Nixon. The president deeply desired a Republican victory, primarily as a vote of approval on his own eight years in office; but he never overcame his concern that Richard Nixon might be too partisan and too lacking in stature to achieve or justify that victory. Sooner or later Eisenhower's ambivalence was bound to damage Nixon politically, and on the morning of August 24, 1960, it did.

In the crowded Indian Treaty Room of the old State, War and Navy Building next door to the White House, Charles Mohr of *Time* magazine— later a distinguished correspondent for the *New York Times,* conspicuous for his front-line work during the war in Vietnam—rose to ask a question late in a regular Eisenhower news conference. Supporters of Richard Nixon, and Nixon himself, Mohr began, claimed that the vice president "has had a great deal of practice at being President."

Mohr and everyone else at the news conference, including Eisenhower, knew that Nixon's vaunted "experience" would be a repeated claim in his coming presidential campaign against Kennedy of Massachusetts, the Democratic nominee. Could Eisenhower, Mohr asked, give an example of Nixon's influence on administration policies?

Not really, the president responded. The vice president had attended meetings "and when he has been asked for it, expressed his opinion in terms of recommendations as to decision. . . . Mr. Nixon has taken a full part in every principal discussion." But "there is no voting," Eisenhower said; and the president alone made the decisions.

Mohr persisted. He understood that the power of decision was the president's but "just wondered if you could give us an example of a major idea of his that you had adopted in that role, as the decider and final—"

"If you give me a week," Eisenhower interrupted, showing his irritation, "I might think of one. I don't remember."

It was doubly unfortunate for Nixon that the news conference had reached its thirty-minute limit. With the usual "Thank you, Mr. President!" Jack Bell of the Associated Press, the senior wire service correspondent present that day, cut it off; there could be no follow-up or explanation. Reporters with afternoon deadlines ran for the phones, Eisenhower's last curt answer ringing in their ears.

At the start of the 1960 presidential campaign, therefore, the word went out to the nation that President Eisenhower would need a week to think of a "major idea" that might have been contributed to his administration by the supposedly "experienced" Richard Nixon, the candidate of Eisenhower's own party.

As soon as the devastating political effect of his remark dawned on him, or perhaps when his irritation at the question had subsided, Eisenhower called Nixon to apologize; but the damage was done and it was considerable. A week later the president visited Nixon at Walter Reed Hospital, where the candidate was recovering from a knee wound that had become infected. Not surprisingly, "there was some lack of warmth," Eisenhower later told Ann Whitman, who recorded the remark in her diary.

The short-fused Eisenhower still may have been smoldering about the Pact of Fifth Avenue when he met the press that August 24. On other grounds, as already detailed, and like many other Americans, he was certainly uneasy about Nixon—though he vastly preferred his vice president to Kennedy, whom he disdained. He may even have been influenced still by the 1952 fund crisis, during which Nixon had spoken rudely to him and forced Eisenhower to financial disclosures he did not want to make.

The "give me a week" remark might simply have been thoughtless or politically naive; but on August 24, Eisenhower's wary attitude toward Nixon underlay whatever ire remained from the Pact of Fifth Avenue. So did his pride in controlling his own administration, and his regret that he soon would have to relinquish his power to lesser men—not that, in questionable health as he was, Eisenhower wanted to stay in the White House. But there was just no one but Anderson and a few others he thought worthy to take his place.

Even so, and whether or not deliberate, Eisenhower's press conference remark reflected remarkable carelessness about Nixon's political interests, therefore Eisenhower's own. At his command, Nixon had been the most active vice president in history. From that thankless office, he had made himself the Republican party's choice for the presidential nomination—the first vice president since Martin Van Buren in 1836 to take that huge step up—and thus the man who would have to see to it, if anyone did, that Eisenhower's work would not be undone.

Eisenhower had hurt Nixon personally and politically, but a week earlier, during a quick campaign foray into the South, the vice president had hurt himself worse—physically as well as figuratively.

It was not that Nixon spoke out candidly on civil rights in a speech at Greensboro, North Carolina. His tenure in the vice presidency, particularly his Senate rulings against the filibuster, already had made his moderate views on that subject clear. But as the sizable crowd pushed and shoved in Greensboro, Nixon had banged his knee painfully against a car door. The accident was to prove fateful; but he thought little of it at the time, and two days later, on August 19, 1960, he traveled to the South again.

The *New York Times*'s ranking political reporters were on precampaign vacations, so I was assigned to cover Nixon's second trip, to Atlanta and Birmingham. I well remember the immense and enthusiastic—and integrated—crowd that greeted him at Five Points in Atlanta. This reception tended to confirm Nixon's high hopes both to build on the Republican gains Eisenhower already had registered in the once Democratic South and to increase the Republican share of a black vote that had been heavily Democratic since the New Deal.

On the flight back to Washington that night, the knee injured in Greensboro began to pain Nixon enough so that the next day he called in Dr. Walter Tkach, a White House physician. Tkach sent him to Walter Reed Hospital, where a serious infection—hemolytic staphylococcus aureus— was diagnosed. Nixon had to spend two weeks in the hospital at the outset of his campaign, just as his momentum had begun to build; and that meant the sacrifice of several trips he had planned, in order to fulfill his ambitious—if foolhardy—undertaking to visit all fifty states.

The two wasted weeks at Walter Reed were not improved by Eisenhower's "give me a week" gaffe, nor by the president's apologetic visit. While languishing in hospital, moreover, Nixon received the unwelcome news that his friend and supporter, Dr. Norman Vincent Peale, he of "the power of positive thinking," had signed a statement questioning whether a Roman Catholic president would dissociate himself from the influence of the Church. Nixon feared that this would taint his campaign, however unfairly, with anti-Catholic bigotry—though he thought, with much reason, that it was in fact the Catholic Kennedy and the Democrats who were exploiting the Catholic issue *among Catholics.*

The injured knee caused a further problem more serious than the missed weeks of campaigning. When Nixon was ready to go again, in an effort to redeem the lost time, he sped up his travel schedule—hitting in a frantic first week, in this order, Baltimore, Indianapolis, Dallas, San Francisco, Portland, Vancouver, Boise, Grand Forks, Peoria, Saint Louis, Atlantic City, Roanoke, Omaha, Des Moines, Sioux City, Minneapolis and Saint Paul.

Coupled with the lingering effects of a serious infection and a bout of flu in Saint Louis, followed by a second campaign week as hectic as the first, Nixon's efforts exhausted him and caused him to lose weight. Worse, his frenetic schedule brought him into Chicago mentally and physically in poor shape for his first televised debate with John Kennedy.

The Nixon campaign already had made a crucial miscalculation in its debate strategy—even aside from the basically mistaken decision for the vice president to appear with Kennedy. "A majority" of his advisers, Nixon wrote in *Six Crises,* had decided that the television audience would *build up* during the four scheduled debates, with the largest number of people watching the last one. Since it was believed that Nixon would show to best advantage in discussing foreign policy, the Nixon strategists succeeded in having the *fourth* debate restricted to that subject. The first would deal with domestic issues.

In the event, the largest audience tuned in for the *first* debate. As noted, about eighty million viewers saw the candidates on that occasion; only about sixty million tuned in for the fourth debate on Nixon's preferred topic. Nixon claimed in *Six Crises* to have disagreed with the "majority" on this decision; but he had gone along with his advisers anyway.

This story is open to question, since he also related that at another advisers' meeting in the last week of the campaign "everyone in the room" thought he should make a speech on the religious issue, but "I voted 'no'—and since I was the candidate, this was of course a 'majority' vote." He could have vetoed the debate strategy in the same way, if he'd disagreed strongly enough.

But he didn't veto it, and that huge audience—the biggest for a political event since the Checkers speech in 1952—saw a worn-down, thin Nixon not yet recovered from his hospital stay and exhausted by the intensive travel schedule he'd subsequently followed. Nearly two days of rest in Chicago had not much helped. Dr. Malcolm Todd, the campaign physician, told him after the debate, "You looked weak and pale and tired tonight on TV because, in fact, you *are* weak and pale and tired."

Dr. Todd put Nixon on a two-a-day milkshake regimen, but that was too late to make up for one of the crucial facts of the first debate: Nixon's shirt collar appeared a couple of sizes too large, emphasizing the gaunt neck and the pallid face with its inevitable beard shadow, inadequately camouflaged with something called "Lazy Shave." Kennedy, in sharp contrast, looked tanned, fit and relaxed, cool by comparison to the haggard Nixon sweating under the lights—and perhaps under the pressures of the high-stakes debate.

Many people thought Kennedy even had the better of the substantive exchanges. Dr. Arthur Burns (who later regretted that he had advised Nixon to debate and "finish off that nice young man from Harvard") was one of them:

> In his first eight-minute pronouncement, what Mr. Kennedy said in substance was: we have a wonderful country, a beautiful country, a great tradition, and our task is to make our country more beautiful, more wonderful still. . . . When Mr. Nixon responded by tackling specific issues such as agriculture, and citing statistics . . . I knew he had lost the debate then and there.[10]

That does not much resemble what either candidate actually said in his opening statement, except that Kennedy did issue a more generalized challenge to Americans to "do a better job" and Nixon did respond with more specific points about advances in economic growth, school, hospital and highway construction, wages and the like. Nixon also dismayed his backers by suggesting *four times* in his opening statement that he and Kennedy agreed on goals and differed only on means.

Kennedy, moreover, seized in the opening exchange an advantage inherent in his challenger's position as against Nixon's status as an official of the Eisenhower administration. As Nixon himself wrote in *Six Crises,* he had to defend the Eisenhower record; that gave *Kennedy* the advantage of the attacker that Nixon the debater so highly prized, which he had exploited all the way back to his debate with Jerry Voorhis fourteen years earlier. Without that familiar advantage, Nixon might well have felt disarmed; with it, Kennedy stayed largely on the offensive.

On the other hand, as pointed out earlier, a group of *radio* listeners, uninfluenced by television images, told Ralph McGill of the *Atlanta Constitution* that they "unanimously thought Mr. Nixon had the better of it."

Nixon wrote in *Six Crises* that "as far as the arguments were concerned," he thought he'd had a slight edge.

But the arguments hardly mattered. Not many today remember anything said in the first debate, and few did even a week later. "Only what they looked like" had mattered, David Halberstam observed in a detailed account of the occasion. "All the insecurities and doubts and inner tensions of Nixon," Halberstam added, were disclosed in his sweating face by "that brutal, relentless, unsparing camera."[11]

Whether Nixon's state of mind was more the problem than his physical condition and appearance is debatable. Halberstam and others picture Nixon as not only gaunt and exhausted but in a state of near–nervous collapse—a description that relies heavily on the testimony of Ted Rogers, Nixon's television adviser, other campaign aides and Don Hewitt of CBS News, the producer for the debate (now the highly successful producer of "60 Minutes").

Halberstam suggests, for instance, that Nixon was too apathetic or exhausted to do his usual iron-butt cramming before the debate. If so, Nixon's *debating* performance did not reveal such lack of preparation— and in *Six Crises* he claimed to have studied more than a hundred possible questions for more than five hours on the day of the debate, in addition to having used "every spare minute" for study in the week before.

In his debilitated condition, however, playing for the highest stakes of his life, and confronting the relaxed and confident Kennedy—virtually a symbol of the Franklins Nixon envied, and with whom perhaps he secretly feared he could not compete—it would not be surprising if Nixon lost some of his self-control and poise, and if that loss were sometimes visible to the television audience.

My own recollection of the first debate—reinforced by watching it again in 1987 at the American Museum of Broadcasting—is that Nixon *looked* terrible but performed rather well. He correctly pointed out in his opening statement, for example, that Kennedy's vaunted new programs "seem to be simply retreads of the Truman administration"—not then as admired as it later became.

At the time of the debate, I was in New York, traveling with Lodge, Nixon's running mate; and I came away from the television screen— underestimating what I had *seen* as against what I had heard—with the impression that the debate had been a dead heat. When I boarded Lodge's press bus the next morning, the gloomy demeanor of his aides quickly disabused me of that idea.

In Chicago, at the conclusion of the debate, Mayor Richard Daley, the Democratic boss, buttonholed Leonard Reinsch, Kennedy's television adviser, and demanded:

How many of these debates do we have? Buy the time for more
if you don't have any free ones. These debates will make Kennedy
President.

In Hot Springs, Arkansas, where the eleven Southern governors were
holding their annual conference, Luther Hodges of North Carolina passed
around the draft of a telegram of support for Kennedy. Before the debate,
only Hodges himself was willing to sign; afterward, nine other Southern
governors added their names.

In the next week, it became apparent from public and press reaction that
Kennedy had scored heavily; and in hindsight it seems quite clear that
Kennedy probably could not have won his narrow victory on election night
without the leveling effect of that first debate. That effect, in my judgment,
was primarily the result of Nixon's unprepossessing physical appearance
and manner, contrasted with Kennedy's ease and attractiveness, and *not*
because of a nervous collapse by Nixon—not, at any rate, one visible to the
audience.

But there were other reasons, deriving from the *political* fact that Nixon
never should have debated at all. Kennedy was not as well known and was
widely considered the less mature and experienced candidate; merely appearing on the platform with the vice president and debating him on equal
terms was enormously to Kennedy's advantage in dissipating this idea. For
that reason, had Kennedy lost on debating points to a healthy and rested
Nixon, the Democratic candidate *still* might have come out ahead politically.

Since Kennedy also had that all-important edge of being able to attack
eight years of Eisenhower, forcing Nixon on the defensive as soon as the
debate began, the vice president had nothing to gain and a great deal to
lose.

After the fact, in *Six Crises,* Nixon took the position that he really had
had no choice but to debate. Congress had lifted the "equal time" provision, making the debates legally possible; Thruston Morton, the Republican national chairman, had guardedly agreed that the party's nominee
would debate "under the right circumstances." The public was eager to see
the show and Nixon worried, he wrote, that if he refused he'd be accused
of fearing to defend the administration's record; he did not suggest, but it's
obvious, that he also would have been charged with fearing to debate
Kennedy.

Certain of Nixon's political and personal *dis*advantages also argued *for*
debating. His was decidedly the minority party, and to win he had to
persuade Democrats and independents to give him their votes; the debates
would attract a huge audience of all political hues, giving him a chance to
reach voters who might not ordinarily be inclined to vote for or even listen

to a Republican. By the same reasoning, the debates offered opportunity for a smiling Nixon to refute the Tricky Dick image from which he well knew he suffered.

But still . . . presidential debates were unprecedented in 1960; Eisenhower surely would have refused to give Stevenson such a forum even in 1952, when neither held the office. The skies did not fall on Lyndon Johnson or Richard Nixon himself when they refused to debate in 1964, 1968 and 1972. Morton had no power to commit the Republican candidate in 1960; and, besides, public debating is one thing a president never has to do. Nixon could and should have refused to put his campaign at such unnecessary risk for so little possible gain; and whatever damage he suffered as a result could not have been as severe as that he suffered by giving Kennedy equal status before the nation.

The truth probably is that as a skilled debater on the Whittier College team and as one who had made a successful political debut in debate, Nixon—at least before that infected knee and the frantic weeks of catching up—probably had expected, with Arthur Burns, that the debates would "finish off that nice young man from Harvard."

Stewart Alsop observed that the object of debating teams is to win by scoring points on an opposing team—*presenting*, not necessarily having, the best case. Team debaters, moreover, have to take the positive or the negative and argue *either* with the same skill and knowledge, a process that does not much emphasize the merits of an issue. As Alsop saw it:

> Nixon's first great triumphs centered around debating—debating made him a big man on the Whittier campus, and debating got his name and picture in the august *Los Angeles Times*. In the course of my reporting I have collected a vast anti-Nixon dossier. Ninety-eight percent . . . consists of examples of tricky debating techniques. . . . He used them, one suspects, simply because he was trained in their use.[12]

Thus, in agreeing to debate Kennedy, Nixon not only had reason for confidence; perhaps he was influenced once again by his desire for battle, to prove himself. The misjudgments—of audience size for the first debate, of the unintended leveling effect of appearing with his challenger, of the importance of "image" for *television* viewers (rather than debate judges)—nevertheless were egregious.

In the final three debates, Nixon—profiting from Dr. Todd's milkshakes and the lessons of Chicago—came off at least even and may have had the better of it on substance. The audiences were substantially smaller, however, and nothing could redeem the gaunt, unattractive Nixon "image" that remained; nor could his relative *debating* skills tarnish the picture established in Chicago of a cool, competent, more attractive Kennedy, capable of meeting the vice president on even terms.

From those four debates, virtually nothing of the issues discussed remains either in the public mind or in the pages of history—with one curious exception that's worth recalling. On October 20, the day before the final meeting (limited to foreign policy questions), the vice president was surprised to read in the newspapers a militant Kennedy statement that could only be interpreted as calling for American aid in "overthrowing Castro":

> We must attempt to strengthen the non-Batista democratic anti-Castro forces in exile, and in Cuba itself, who offer eventual hope of overthrowing Castro. Thus far, these fighters for freedom have had virtually no support from our government.

Nixon described himself in *Six Crises* as enraged by this, particularly after he confirmed that Kennedy had been briefed by the CIA, on Eisenhower's instruction, about Cuban affairs (on July 23, 1960, at Hyannis Port, Massachusetts). Nixon assumed that the briefing must have included secret information about the Cuban exile force then being trained by the U.S. (in Guatemala) for action against Castro. So Kennedy, he concluded, not only was "jeopardizing the security of a United States foreign policy operation" but was "advocating what was already the policy of the American government," as if no such policy existed.

Eisenhower, however, did not allocate substantial funds—thirteen million dollars—to the exile force until August 18, well *after* the Hyannis Port briefing. Until then, there was no *certain* plan. Writing after Kennedy's death, Arthur Schlesinger, Jr., asserted that Kennedy had not learned of the exile army's existence until November 17, *after* the election. The hard-breathing statement of October 20, Schlesinger wrote, had been concocted by aides and issued without the candidate having seen or cleared it—although, he added, "in all probability Kennedy *would have approved the text*" with only minor changes (emphasis added).[13]

If Kennedy had wanted to soften or repudiate the statement after his aides had issued it, he could have done so; but he did not, letting it stand as published. It was plausible, then, for Nixon to assume that his opponent had unfairly exploited his CIA briefing. Even so, the Nixon response, made during the October 21 debate, remains hard to understand or justify.

He concluded that to protect the secret of the covert army in Guatemala, "I must attack the Kennedy proposal to provide such aid as wrong and irresponsible because it would violate our treaty commitments." That is just what he did; yet Kennedy's proposal was, in fact, the Eisenhower administration's policy, and one that Nixon claimed personally to have fought for within the administration's secret councils.

Even those who understand that a national leader cannot always tell the whole truth may question whether a presidential candidate, speaking to a national audience, should have lied about a vital foreign policy question— particularly when, in so doing, he deliberately misstated what his own policy would be, and when he seemed to be discrediting what he knew to be the secret policy of the administration he represented. It's hard to see how his reasoning—that "the covert operation had to be protected at all costs"—could justify a candidate in so seriously deceiving a nation in the process of choosing a president.

What else might Nixon have done? When the subject arose in the debate, as the timing of Kennedy's statement made inevitable, he could have protected the exile-army plan and still have played reasonably straight by taking something like the following position: that Kennedy, in a political forum, was demonstrating his lack of maturity and experience by recommending a serious foreign policy step possibly involving American lives, and *before* he was in a position to have all the information and advice necessary for making such an important decision.

Nixon then could have gone on to reflect his campaign position on Cuba—a policy of economic, political and diplomatic "quarantine."

That, of course, would not have been the "whole truth" or as strong a statement as Kennedy's call for action. But it would have protected the covert operation; politically, it would have retained for Nixon the "high road" on the issue (James Reston and Walter Lippmann had criticized Kennedy's statement) without tying his hands if he won the election; and it would have reemphasized Kennedy's supposed immaturity. Most important of all, it would have circumvented the direct lie about his own view.

Neither, though, does Kennedy's conduct here warrant much defense. Having grabbed headlines with a crowd-pleasing call for getting tough with Castro (even if he didn't personally approve such an important statement, which is hardly to his credit), he defended that call in the nationally televised debate, then—two days *after* the debate—backed away. He contended in a second statement, sparked probably by Reston's and Lippmann's criticisms, that he had "never advocated" intervention in Cuba, but only wanted "the moral power of the American government" arrayed on the side of "the forces of freedom" there.

Again, Nixon hardly can be blamed for thinking that Kennedy first got the benefit of anti-Castro sentiment, then changed his position because of "the vehemence of the editorial criticism, particularly from columnists and papers generally friendly to him." The episode left Kennedy, however, with the public image of being stronger and tougher than Nixon in opposition to Castro. So the ironies are remarkable: Nixon's secret policy, when publicly advocated by Senator Kennedy, was regarded by the vice president as a flagrant bid for votes, and as dangerously irresponsible; and when that same policy was secretly *adopted* by President Kennedy, it led him within three months to fiasco at the Bay of Pigs.

Kennedy survived that early disaster of his new administration; but it's as clear as anything can be about the close and disputed election of 1960 that Richard Nixon did not survive his misbegotten decision to debate his lesser-known opponent. Whether it was Kennedy's greater physical and stylistic appeal to viewers in the first debate, or the leveling effect—or both—there's no doubt that John Kennedy "won" the debates, a crucial part of winning the presidency.

When Len Hall asked Nixon at Key Biscayne after the election why he'd agreed to the debates, Nixon "simply looked up at the sky, his eyes closed, his face drawn and tense," and did not answer. He may have been thinking of that automobile door in Greensboro, as a principal object upon which his presidential hopes had been shattered. Or maybe he was thinking about all the Franklins like John Kennedy, who'd had things easy while Dick Nixon had had to work like a dog for everything he had in life.[14]

Defeat, it's said, is an orphan; but victory has a thousand fathers. Kennedy's narrow victory in 1960 certainly had many fathers. Nixon had not been wrong, for instance, when still in his hospital bed he saw political trouble for himself in Norman Vincent Peale's signature on a Protestant statement expressing the concern whether a Roman Catholic President could be free of the Vatican's influence.

That Peale was identified in the press as a Nixon friend and supporter was bad enough, suggesting that the Republican campaign was trying covertly or through intermediaries to stir up an anti-Catholic vote against Kennedy. Nixon could at least try to do something to dampen that idea, and on Sunday, September 11, two days after he left the hospital, he appeared on television—"Meet the Press"—to say:

> I have no doubt whatever about Senator Kennedy's loyalty to his country and about the fact that if he were elected president he would put the Constitution of the United States above any other consideration. . . . I have issued orders to all of the people in my campaign not to discuss religion, not to raise it, not to allow anybody to participate in the campaign who does so on that ground, and so far as I am concerned, I will decline to discuss religion.

To this position he steadily adhered, as even Fawn Brodie, one of Nixon's severest critics, concedes: "Although [Nixon] stood to benefit from an increasing anti-Catholic groundswell, he continued to denounce bigotry where he saw it and to insist that his followers leave the religious issue alone." Later in the campaign, Nixon also refused an endorsement from the Reverend Billy Graham, another friend, and a more renowned and influential cleric than Peale. Graham had joined Southern Baptists in a "no Catholic for president" statement.

Brodie did remark that Nixon "could not attack [Kennedy's Catholicism] lest he appear a bigot." That's true, but it gratuitously suggests something which may be true but for which there is no evidence—that Nixon *would* have exploited anti-Catholic sentiment if he could have done so with political safety.[15]

It can be and has been argued that Nixon secretly inspired anti-Catholic attacks while publicly and piously denying that he was doing any such thing. But there's no evidence for that either. And it's only a myth of the 1960 campaign, not borne out by the record, that Nixon purposely repeated at every stop his pledge not to talk about the Catholic issue—thus reminding his listeners of it without actually "raising" the subject. He could not avoid, of course, answering reporters' frequent questions on the subject, usually with repetitions of his pledge—a fact that is no doubt the source of this particularly enduring Tricky Dick legend.

Early in the general election campaign, moreover, Kennedy himself had virtually stamped out anti-Catholicism as what Schlesinger called "an intellectually respectable issue"—though, the historian noted, ugly religious mutterings continued as "a stream of rancor underground."[16]

The young senator's Democratic primary victory over Hubert Humphrey in heavily Protestant West Virginia had convinced wavering Democratic leaders that a Catholic on the ticket would not be an automatic loser. Once nominated, Kennedy attacked anti-Catholicism head on. In a forthright appearance before a hostile Greater Houston Ministerial Association on September 12 (the day after Nixon's statement on "Meet the Press"), he effectively dispelled the notion of undue Vatican influence on a Catholic president. He also called on the Protestant ministers—and all Americans—to set aside religious prejudice and judge him as an American.

The confrontation with the Houston ministers attracted wide and favorable attention and became a crucial event of the campaign. Kennedy's religion remained a major factor in the 1960 election—in my judgment *favoring* Kennedy. Indeed, it was primarily the Democrats who kept the matter in the public eye—for instance, by their wide circulation of the text of Kennedy's Houston statement.

Democratic leaders repeatedly emphasized the position that Kennedy himself had taken—"I refuse to believe that I was denied the right to be president on the day I was baptized." And from my own reporting of that campaign, I clearly remember Lyndon Johnson, Kennedy's running mate, reciting in every speech, in dramatic tones, the story of Kennedy's brother Joseph's combat death in World War II "when nobody asked him what his religion was."

Just as he could not attack Kennedy's religion, Nixon could do little or nothing about the *Democrats'* emphasis on his opponent's religion—although theirs was a tactic that had three calculated consequences detrimental to Republican prospects:

First, it tended to shame voters who might have had vague anti-Catholic feelings, but who could be appealed to on the basis of fair play—thus holding down the potential anti-Catholic vote, the virulent possibilities of which few denied.

Second, Democratic reiteration of the theme of fair play also aroused the sympathy of voters who otherwise might have supported Nixon on grounds other than religion, but who feared that their votes would be needed to overcome the anti-Catholic sentiment the Democrats were denouncing.

Finally, and most important, the tactic energized Catholics—including those who were Republicans or independents—to turn out *for* a coreligionist and *against* anti-Catholicism, to prove once and for all that no reason existed for fear of Catholics in high office. Many Catholics who supported Kennedy might well have voted for Nixon for ordinary political reasons, in the absence of the Democrats' shrewd appeal for fair play and against bigotry.

This was deliberate strategy, calculated by Kennedy and his staff as far back as his unsuccessful bid for second place on the Stevenson ticket in 1956. They had prepared then and widely distributed a document that continued throughout the following years and into 1960 to provide political underpinning for the Kennedy primary and general election campaigns. It read, in part:

> The Catholic vote is far more important than its numbers—about one out of every four voters who turn out—because of its concentration in the key states and cities of the North. . . .
>
> If [a Catholic candidate] brought into the Democratic fold only those normally Democratic Catholics who voted for Ike, he would probably swing New York, Massachusetts, Rhode Island, Connecticut, Pennsylvania, and Illinois—for 132 electoral votes. If he also wins the votes of Catholics who shifted to the Republicans in 1948 or earlier, he could also swing New Jersey, Minnesota, Michigan, California, Wisconsin, Ohio, Maryland, Montana and maybe even New Hampshire—for a total of 265 electoral votes.

Those big blocs of electoral votes also had been on Kennedy's mind when he led with Paul Douglas of Illinois the Senate opposition to efforts in 1956 to reform the electoral college. Their target was a hybrid constitutional amendment that would have ended the prevailing system by which all of a state's electoral votes were awarded to the winner of its popular vote. That winner-take-all system was the keystone of the strategy detailed in the later Kennedy staff memorandum.

Because the winner-take-all system survived the Senate debate, the memorandum's prediction of good results from a Catholic on the Democratic ticket proved substantially correct—though overly optimistic. A postelection analysis by the Simulmatics Corporation concluded that because of increased Catholic support, Kennedy won six states that he otherwise would have lost: Connecticut, New York, New Jersey, Pennsylvania, Illinois and New Mexico, with a total of 132 electoral votes.

Anti-Catholic voting, on the other hand, cost him—if the Simulmatics analysis was correct—ten states that, as a Democrat, he otherwise might have won: Tennessee, Florida, Oklahoma, Montana, Idaho, Utah, California, Oregon, Virginia and Washington, with a total of 110 electoral votes. Thus, in the Simulmatics accounting (which necessarily included some elements of speculation), the Catholic issue yielded Kennedy a net of 22 electoral votes—a substantial part of his winning margin of only 33 (over the 270 required). His net gain may well have been larger, since it is by no means clear that he could have carried California and Florida had he not been Catholic.

Religion, in any case, cost Kennedy more *states* but won him more electoral votes than would have been the case had he been a Protestant. These results tended to confirm Richard Nixon's preelection expectation, as he described it in *Six Crises* (written *after* the election): "I believed that Kennedy's religion would hurt him in states he could afford to lose anyway and that it would help him in states he needed to win."

As noted in chapter 6, the Republican chairman had predicted to Eisenhower early in 1956 that the Democrats would put a Catholic on their ticket, if not that year then in 1960. Len Hall even foresaw that it would be John Kennedy. Other analyses agree with Simulmatics that the Democrats got a lift from the Catholic issue they so assiduously kept before the public.*

None of these postelection analyses proves, as is sometimes argued, that "the Catholic vote elected Kennedy." It certainly helped him, but the popular vote margin was so close—49.7 percent for Kennedy, 49.6 for Nixon, as counted—that virtually any definable group that had supported the winner could claim to be responsible for his victory.

According to the Gallup Organization's figures, for example, Jews went

---

*The Gallup Organization, for instance, calculated that 78 percent of Catholics supported Kennedy, as against only 51 percent for Stevenson in 1956—the latter figure, of course, influenced also by Eisenhower, Stevenson's immensely popular opponent. But the Gallup study found that 62 percent of Catholics who had voted for Eisenhower in 1956 switched to Kennedy in 1960, while only 3 percent of Catholics for Stevenson crossed the other way to Nixon four years later.

from 75 percent Democratic in 1956 (against Eisenhower) to 81 percent in 1960 (against Nixon). In the same period, the Democrats' score among blacks rose from 61 to 68 percent.[17]

Thus, Catholics, Jews and blacks, at least, each have a statistical basis for claiming that *they* provided Kennedy's hair-thin margin of victory. All would be correct in making that claim; but that really means only that Kennedy would have lost had not *all* these groups moved more heavily into the Democratic column than in 1956. That Catholics provided an indispensable segment of his support, however, lends a certain point to Kennedy's midcampaign quip: "Do you realize the responsibility I carry? I'm the only person standing between Nixon and the White House."[18]

It could well be argued, however, that the person standing between Nixon and the presidency really was Richard Milhous Nixon. It was Nixon who agreed to debate, who chose to accept his staff's recommendation that the crucial first debate be devoted to domestic affairs and who failed even to buy himself the right-size shirt before that event.

It was Richard Nixon who chose Henry Cabot Lodge as his running mate—a choice that seems doubly questionable, in view of the apprehensions about Catholic voting Nixon later claimed to have felt, and in light of actual election results. Nixon might have picked, say, Secretary of Labor James Mitchell, a Catholic to whom he was close, and who might have blunted, at least partially, the effect of a Catholic on the Democratic ticket. That same year, Kennedy's choice of his rival, Johnson, was paying off with the Texas senator's favorable impact in the South, where Kennedy was an object of suspicion.

It was Richard Nixon, too, who made a fatal error that dashed what had been his high hopes for *increased* black support, with the result already noted—that his actually *decreased* share of the black vote also was indispensable to Kennedy's victory.

As a Southerner, I had not failed to note the many black faces in the huge crowd that had turned out for Nixon at Five Points during his visit to Atlanta on August 19. That mixed crowd was evidence to me—and Nixon staff men, that day, were pointing it out to all—that Nixon could expect to do well not only in the South but among black voters everywhere. His activities as the chairman of Eisenhower's committee to insure nondiscrimination in federal contract jobs, his publicized rulings against the filibuster in the Senate, his support for the civil rights bill put forward in 1957 by the Eisenhower administration—all recommended him to black voters.

The Reverend Martin Luther King, Jr., had volunteered, as one consequence of the civil rights fight, to lead a voter registration drive among blacks, which King thought would produce many new Republican voters. Nixon also could count on the latent sympathies of some black voters for the party of Abraham Lincoln and emancipation—blacks' historic political home, from the Civil War to the New Deal.

He did not, however, jeopardize his hopes to run strongly among Southern *whites* by too open an appeal to blacks; the Nixon position on school desegregation, for example, was a sort of gradualism calculated to alienate neither whites nor blacks. In August, he insisted to his Greensboro audience that "law alone, while necessary, is not the answer to the problems of human rights." Still, he was considerably more forthcoming about the civil rights of minorities than Eisenhower ever had been.

Thus, the black vote provided something of a battleground between the candidates, and an important one, owing primarily to the concentration of black voters in big Northern cities—New York, Philadelphia, Detroit, Chicago—where they could have strong influence on their states' major blocks of electoral votes. Nixon's hope was not so much to win a majority of the black vote as it was to hold down the big black majorities Kennedy was sure to win in those states. Nixon might then win the states' electoral votes with a combination of white and black votes.

In 1960, to urban blacks as to those in the South, the Reverend King, with his program of nonviolent rights advocacy, had become a revered national leader; so on October 19, 1960, when King and about fifty other blacks were arrested for sitting in at a segregated restaurant in Atlanta, national publicity resulted and blacks everywhere were concerned.

Most of those arrested soon were released but King was given a four-month prison sentence on an old charge of driving without a license. The immediate outrage in the black community—and among many whites, including some in the South—made King's incarceration an issue in the presidential campaign.

"In retrospect," Nixon observed in *Six Crises,* the incident "might have been better handled" by his campaign. In an often overstated book, this is classic understatement. Nixon's account, moreover, is piously misleading.

Robert Kennedy, who was his brother's campaign manager—Nixon wrote—"realizing the tremendous political potential of King's misfortune, wasted no time in calling the judge in the case." When pressed by Herbert Klein for comment to the press, Nixon said, he told Klein:

> I think Dr. King is getting a bum rap. But despite my strong feelings in this respect, it would be completely improper for me or any other lawyer to call the judge. And Robert Kennedy should have known better than to do so.

That forced Klein to tell the press that Nixon had "no comment" on King's predicament, a response—Nixon conceded in his book—"widely interpreted by Negro leaders both North and South as indicating that I did not care about justice in the King case." Nixon insisted that he had tried in vain to have the White House issue a public promise to have the Department of Justice inquire into whether King's constitutional rights had been infringed. But neither Nixon nor his friend, Attorney General William Rogers, had the clout to persuade the indifferent Eisenhower to make the statement. Nixon's presidential campaign let things go at that, as the story is told in *Six Crises.*

In 1987, Herbert Klein described Nixon's reaction to the King incident quite differently. Klein told me that Nixon's staff, recognizing "the tremendous political potential of King's misfortune," naturally wanted to do something to demonstrate their candidate's concern. Nixon himself vetoed any such action, Klein said, because he feared it would "look like he was pandering" to black voters.

William Safire, who had signed on as a junior member of the Nixon staff, gave a somewhat similar account in 1987. He was writing in praise of Jackie Robinson on the fortieth anniversary of the great black athlete's entry into major league baseball, breaking one of the strongest racial barriers in American life. By 1960, Robinson—an articulate graduate of UCLA—was nationally celebrated, wielded influence among many blacks not much less than King's, but had dared the opprobrium of the black establishment by supporting Richard Nixon for president.

When Martin Luther King was jailed, Robinson—in Safire's account—flew to see Nixon, catching up with him at a "midwestern hotel." The campaign had been moving by train in a reversion to old-style whistle-stopping. Safire, a friend, took Robinson to Bob Finch, the campaign director: "Finch ran him in to see the candidate himself. Ten minutes later [Robinson] came out, tears of frustration in his eyes. 'He thinks calling Martin would be grandstanding,' Robinson reported. 'Nixon doesn't deserve to win.' "

Robinson remained a Republican but "pulled out of the campaign . . . and never supported Nixon again."[19]

Perhaps from misunderstanding, Nixon in *Six Crises* even botched the facts about the Kennedy campaign's quite different response. It was John Kennedy himself who moved first—but not to approach the judge in the King case. Urged on by Harris Wofford and Louis Martin, his civil rights advisers, and Sargent Shriver, his brother-in-law, Kennedy telephoned *Mrs. Coretta King* to offer his sympathy directly—and without having consulted Robert Kennedy or the rest of his staff.

When Robert Kennedy heard of his brother's action, he was at first dubious about its political effect; then, either because he was angry at the incident itself or had decided that if the die was cast, as much as possible might as well be made of it, *he* called the judge and demanded bail for

King—which soon was granted. These communications, astutely publicized by the Kennedy campaign in a pamphlet distributed only in black churches, electrified a black community that had been lukewarm about the Democratic candidate.

The Reverend Martin Luther King, Sr.—well-known as "Daddy" King—even told his congregation in Atlanta that he'd never thought he could vote for a Catholic, and had been supporting Nixon; but after the call to his daughter-in-law, Kennedy "can be my President, Catholic or whatever he is. . . . I've got all my votes and I've got a suitcase, and I'm going up there and dump them in [Kennedy's] lap."

"Imagine Martin Luther King having a bigot for a father," Kennedy remarked to Schlesinger. "Well, we all have fathers, don't we?"[20]

As Safire put it, the King incident and Nixon's unwillingness to "pander" or "grandstand" became one of the many "if onlys" in the closest presidential campaign of modern times. Without doubt, it substantially increased Kennedy's share of the black vote, upon which Nixon at first had placed such hopes; and as already noted, that increase was one—not the only—crucial factor in Kennedy's victory.

In *Six Crises* Nixon never conceded the importance of Kennedy's gesture of concern for King. He did not concede, either, the probable truth—that in his eagerness to do well in the Southern states and among white voters generally, he had miscalculated the net effect of his silence and Kennedy's call on the strategic black vote. Robert Kennedy and other advisers would have urged their candidate to do nothing too, for the same reason, had not Wofford, Martin and Shriver persuaded him to do what John Kennedy called "a decent thing."

That's understandable; some white voters, Southern or otherwise, certainly *would* have thought in 1960 or even later that Nixon was "pandering." But such risky decisions are what politics demands; in this case, Kennedy's snap judgment proved more profitable politically than Nixon's caution. And, at least in today's perspective, most Americans probably would consider Kennedy's call ethically preferable to Nixon's silence.

In *Six Crises* Nixon recalled that, two days after the election, he was driven from his house in Washington to his office in the Capitol by John Wardlaw, his chauffeur, a black who was "one of the finest men I have known." Emotionally, Wardlaw blurted out:

> Mr. Vice President, I can't tell you how sick I am about the way my people voted in the election. You know I had been talking to all of my friends. They were all for you. But when Mr. Robert Kennedy called the judge to get Dr. King out of jail—well, they just all turned to him.

Nixon could only assert the uncomfortable truth: "When an election is this close, John, no one can say for certain what caused us to lose." Then he went one questionable step further: "If there was any fault involved . . . it was mine for failing to get my point of view across."

Whether his silence, in fact, had conveyed to blacks and liberals his *real* "point of view," or had misrepresented it for political purposes—in either case, that silence had not been admirable, and its political cost was immense.

As the campaign moved into its final days, the strongest political voice in America was at last ready to thunder. Never wholly happy with the idea of Dick Nixon as his successor, Dwight Eisenhower was wholly *un*happy at the thought that instead it might be John Kennedy—"the young genius," as Eisenhower acidly referred to him, or sometimes "the young whippersnapper."

"I'll do almost anything to avoid turning the country over to Kennedy," he told Benjamin Fairless of U.S. Steel.[21]

Eisenhower was still so prestigious that he almost certainly could have been elected a third time had he wished and had he been constitutionally eligible. The president was aroused, moreover, by Kennedy's attacks on his administration—a boy aspiring to manhood, in Eisenhower's view—and was ready to strike back, hard. His ambivalence about Nixon was lost in his eagerness to thwart Kennedy and vindicate his own record.

On October 31, he entertained Nixon, Len Hall, Hagerty and some of his speech writers at lunch in the White House. What more could Eisenhower do to help? was the subject. With Hall, the president already had agreed to expand his originally planned schedule, adding upstate New York, downstate Illinois and Michigan.

"Nixon never gave him a straight answer," in William Ewald's account of the luncheon. "He tightened, and in effect turned Eisenhower's offer [to do even more] down." After the luncheon, the angry president complained to Hall: "Goddammit, he looks like a loser to me!"[22]

Hall himself described Eisenhower hunching his shoulders and bending his head in imitation of a withdrawn Nixon. "When I had an officer like that in World War II," Eisenhower said, "I relieved him."[23]

In *Six Crises* Nixon did not mention this luncheon conference or Eisenhower's offer; but after Eisenhower's death, in *RN,* he gave a full account of the October 31 luncheon, attributing his attitude to last-minute telephone calls from Mamie Eisenhower to Pat Nixon, and from Dr. Howard Snyder, the White House physician, to Nixon himself.

Both callers, Nixon wrote, urged that he not allow Eisenhower to take on more campaigning because of the strain it might put on his heart. Mamie Eisenhower, Nixon added, told Pat Nixon that the president "must never know I called you"—presumably an explanation for Nixon's failure to include this story in *Six Crises,* while Eisenhower was alive.

In the later *RN* account, Nixon does not picture himself as uptight or avoiding a straight answer. Despite Eisenhower's arguments—"at first he was hurt and then he was angry," Nixon wrote—"I stood my ground," insisting that the president should limit his campaigning. Nixon did not explain why he could not tell Hall, if not Eisenhower, about the telephone calls.

Dr. Snyder died on September 27, 1970, many years before this exculpatory story appeared in *RN.* Mamie Eisenhower died in 1979, not long after it was published.

Bob Finch, Nixon's friend, cited to me this same reason—Nixon's worries about Eisenhower's health—to explain why the president did not campaign more in 1960, and why Nixon did not "feel let down" by Eisenhower's relative inactivity. Finch may have been taking his cue from the account in *RN.*

The campaign speeches Eisenhower did make were vigorous and effective; reporters could see that he presented a strong physical appearance. So, with due respect to the *RN* version, it seems as likely that after his years of chafing and bitterness in the vice presidency Nixon in 1960 simply did not want to be further beholden to a benefactor he had come to resent.

Nixon believed by October 31 that Kennedy's campaign had "peaked"—a favorite Nixon usage—and would lose ground in the final eight days. Polls, the testimony of reporters covering both campaigns, and crowd response to both candidates suggest Nixon may have been right—at least that he had reasons for such optimism.

Nixon believed, too, that his own campaign was moving up, toward a peak right when he wanted it, on Election Day, November 8. The tide had turned, he believed, during his midwestern whistle-stop tour, during which he had hit harder than ever at Kennedy's supposed immaturity and inexperience. As that trip began, Bryce Harlow had bluntly advised him:

> You're not coming across . . . you're making convincing stump speeches but where's Dick Nixon? You're not in 'em. There's no vibrance, no emotion. People don't feel you in the campaign. Lose your temper . . . bang your fist. Show you care, that you're emotionally involved.[24]

Harlow thought Nixon took his advice; and he believed that the campaign "perked up." Besides, by October 31, Nixon was not totally rejecting Eisenhower's help; the president had been scheduled all along for final-week speeches in Philadelphia, New York, Cleveland, and Pittsburgh. But he wanted to do more and could have done more, and Nixon prevented that.

It's fair speculation that he wanted Eisenhower's help but feared that if the revered general expanded his activities, Eisenhower would get the credit for the victory that, by the end of October, Nixon believed soon would be his anyway. Nixon surely wanted to be seen as having won the presidency in his own right, and not owing to an Eisenhower blitz; he was tired of being obscured by Eisenhower's giant shadow—so tired that he made another mistake in judgment, to limit the president's campaigning.

As it happened, despite Eisenhower's disappointment at not being given more to do, he plunged fiercely into the appearances he was allowed to make, fired up by his contempt for Kennedy and armed with some of Harlow's most vitriolic prose. ("I write nasty stuff," Harlow told me years later, savoring the memory.)

In these gloves-off speeches in major cities, where holding down expected Democratic majorities was crucial, the president was partisan and political to a degree he rarely had permitted himself. His vigor added to his usual charisma, and his audiences loved his apparent rebirth—for example, at a rally at the Westchester Airport in New York on November 2, when he took acid note of Kennedy's slogan, "Let's Get this Country Moving Again."

"Now I have heard complaints about the country not moving," the president said. "Of course you can move easily—you can move back to inflation, you can move back to deficit spending, you can move back to the military weakness that allowed the Korean War to occur . . . no trouble at all."

In Cleveland two days later, he bored in on Kennedy's supposed inexperience, his criticism all the more effective because of his own unmentioned military glory:

> More money, they say, will be saved by military reorganization.
> . . . Now where did this young genius acquire the knowledge,
> experience, and the wisdom through which he will make vast
> improvements over the work of the Joint Chiefs of Staff?

What might a few more such effective Eisenhower appearances in strategic locations have done for Nixon? Carried Illinois, perhaps, or Texas, perhaps another state; he might have clinched the victory Nixon expected—or perhaps not. No one ever will know, because of that October 31 luncheon at the White House when, in my judgment, Richard Nixon decided he could win without additional help from a man to whom he already owed so much—not all of that help welcomed by the recipient.

Even if Nixon did believe, at that point, that he would win, his decision was still mistaken; it's when an opponent is on the ropes, ready to go down, that the knockout punch is most needed. If Nixon felt that he had the election won on October 31, he still should have sent in the Republicans' strongest campaigner to lock up the expected victory.

Nixon's failure to bring in a bellicose Eisenhower can hardly be seen except as another of those "if onlys" that were to plague Nixon in the long years of his defeat and abnegation. He was to emerge from the 1960 defeat not only thus burdened, but with a reputation for bullheadedness—"trying to be his own campaign manager," running the campaign out of his own head and instincts, listening too seldom to the good advice of his party and staff.

It was he, for example, who insisted on flying to Alaska two days before the election, for no better reason than to fulfill his pledge to visit all fifty states—although he was considered to have little chance to carry Alaska and might have done better to return to Illinois or Texas, states he *had* to win. In fact, he carried Alaska, and Herbert Klein pointed out that in the last days of the campaign, Nixon actually picked up five points in some polls; but he didn't pick up enough electoral votes.

It was in 1960, also, that Nixon's dependence on H. R. ("Bob") Haldeman began to affect his conduct, with other aides as well as toward the public. Haldeman was the perfect defender of Nixon's desire to "do it all" for himself, and to share credit with no one—a desire that led naturally to a growing isolation of the candidate from friends and advisers. Haldeman—ostensibly only the campaign "tour director"—knew how to fend off unwanted advice, and how to make himself an indispensable guardian at the door of the candidate's introversion.

Haldeman's latent instinct for power and how to get it, and Nixon's instinct to prove that he needed no one, melded into a combination with long consequences. In 1960, the immediate effect was to shield Nixon from the kind of political give-and-take that might have steered him away from some of his mistakes, and that would have helped create a more cohesive and dedicated staff. Haldeman was not a man to tell the boss he was wrong, and as the campaign went on, he saw to it that few others had the chance to do so.

Nixon's animus against the press became more noticeable, too, as did his bitterness and anger at what he thought was the shabby treatment he had endured in the Eisenhower years. Temper flare-ups almost caused the resignations of veteran staff men like James Bassett and Ted Rogers.

William Ewald, eagerly joining the campaign in October to write speeches, was in only one meeting with the aloof candidate himself; but once, by happenstance, he saw an ominous event—a raging Nixon demanding to know the name of a reporter who had annoyed him: "Get me the name. . . . We're going to get that guy!" By election day, Ewald had become as ambivalent about Nixon as Eisenhower had been.[25]

Bob Finch still insists loyally that 1960 was "one of the greatest presidential campaigns," fought out by "two good protagonists . . . two young candidates at the peak of their powers." Many observers might dispute another Finch judgment: "Whatever dark side [Nixon] showed later, he was a good candidate in 1960."

On top of other misfortunes, the economy turned decisively down, a body blow to the party in power, and one Nixon had foreseen and tried to prevent.

In fiscal 1959, Eisenhower had run up a budget deficit of almost $13 billion. In January 1959, for fiscal 1960 (then running from July 1, 1959, to June 30, 1960), the president—stung by the election in 1958 of so many "people that I would class among the spenders"—sent Congress a budget calling for a $100 million *surplus*. The Democrats controlling Congress tried to out-pennypinch him and the budget debate produced, in fact, a $269 million surplus.

A turnaround in federal expenditures of that magnitude in one year—a swing from a $13 billion deficit to a $269 million surplus—throttled the economic expansion that had begun in April 1958. It became the shortest expansion of the postwar years, and in April 1960—just as the presidential campaign was moving to center stage—the economy began to slide, not to be halted until 1961.

For Nixon, the timing could not have been worse. When Arthur Burns, as earlier noted, warned the vice president of impending recession, Nixon tried but was unable to get the administration to "prime the pump" by loosening credit and increasing military spending. Eisenhower was dead against the latter; Treasury Secretary Anderson and Raymond Saulnier, the chairman of the Council of Economic Advisers, Burns said, were "stonewalls of resistance" to the former.[26]

The budget was not the only economic problem. The Federal Reserve Board had kept money tight since the end of 1956. In 1959, moreover, the Fed raised the discount rate from 2.5 to 4 percent—a dramatically high level thirty years ago—and did not lower it until June 1960, *after* the economy had turned down. As a result, unemployment climbed sharply from 5.5 percent to 6.1 percent in October and November, 1960—the crucial months of the election campaign.

The economy is an "if only" that cannot be blamed on Nixon, who since 1958 had been urging an expansionary policy. But it was another reason for his defeat. Twenty-four years later, as if permanently burned by the downturn of 1960, Nixon publicly warned Ronald Reagan—then rolling to a landslide over Walter Mondale—that the economy might defeat him, too.*

---

*Nixon told Nick Thimmesch, a syndicated columnist, that though Reagan "looks unbeatable" he should be concerned because of "a growing minority of experts who

Still another factor, about which Nixon literally could do nothing, helped sink his 1960 campaign—the unexpected voter appeal that John Kennedy developed. Kennedy's "cool" campaign style, after a relatively slow start, produced hot enthusiasm. His crowds became larger and reporters judged their enthusiasm to be more spontaneous than usual; they noted numerous "leapers" and "jumpers," often women, trying to get better views of the candidate.

After the prim fifties, even Kennedy's rumored feats as a "womanizer"—only later to be detailed—seemed exciting rather than disqualifying. He was a certifiable war hero; and, like Eisenhower's disdain, the early opposition of Harry Truman and other old-timers actually enhanced his generational appeal to younger Americans. His youth and "vigah"—though he actually was not in the good health his appearance usually suggested—was an attractive contrast not only to the gaunt Nixon of the first debate, but to the settled, elderly, somewhat sour facade of the late Eisenhower administration, which aptly symbolized the fifties and an era coming to an end.

Arthur Schlesinger, the Adlai Stevenson loyalist who became an unabashed Kennedy admirer in 1960, tried later to describe what was happening:

> By mid-October one began to feel that the real Kennedy was coming over. . . . Even the Stevensonians were responding to his wit and resolve. Young people in particular felt, in many cases for the first time, a connection with politics. Wildly cheering crowds surged around him as he crisscrossed the country. One has an unmistakeable feeling when a campaign catches fire: it happened to Stevenson for a time in 1952 but not in 1956. It was plainly happening to Kennedy in the third week of October, 1960.[27]

During that surge, which Schlesinger was not alone in remarking, experienced reporters who had traveled with Kennedy or covered some of his appearances were speculating from such crowd reaction that he was pulling away from Nixon, heading for a landslide. Even Bryce Harlow, the most dedicated of Republicans, who remembered the Democratic candidate as a ne'er-do-well young congressman, had a sobering glimpse of the new Kennedy appeal.

---

believe we are going to see . . . higher interest rates and unemployment creeping up a bit." He knew from experience what that could do to the party in power, and in 1987—just before the stock market's "Black Monday" on October 19—he again warned that if the economy turned down, "any jackass" on the Democratic ticket could win the presidency in 1988. Michael Dukakis belied this prophecy.

On one of the last hectic days of the campaign, Nixon had flown from Alaska at 10 P.M. to speak the next morning in Wisconsin; that afternoon he conducted in Detroit a four-hour nationwide "telethon." This grueling television effort, after such exhausting travel, was by common consent one of his most effective appearances. Harlow, pleased with Nixon's skilled performance, was hurrying to catch a campaign bus when he saw on a television monitor "Jack and Jackie waving at a crowd somewhere."

Harlow was stunned at the couple's magnetism. "Good God," he thought, almost involuntarily, "how can you run against *that*?"[28]

Yet, at that very time, Kennedy was physically exhausted and mentally drained, as Nixon was, by their long coast-to-coast competition. When an aide told the Democratic candidate that he could watch Nixon's telethon in an adjoining room, "utterly weary, Kennedy waved him away." That could have been only hours before his television image so impressed the usually unflappable Bryce Harlow.[29]

On election night, November 8, 1960, as a junior reporter for the Washington Bureau of the *Times,* I was sent to the New York newsroom to write the paper's story about the gubernatorial elections taking place in various states, in the shadow of the Kennedy-Nixon campaign. A relatively low-level assignment that nevertheless allowed me to be in the center of the newsroom and the excitement as the returns came in.

James Reston, the *Times*'s "Washington Correspondent"—as the Washington Bureau chief then was called—was writing, as *Times* tradition demanded, the lead presidential election story. (Later, in 1964 and 1968, as Washington Correspondent myself, I wrote the presidential leads—a distinction I cherish.) There's no need here to repeat the familiar story of that night of nearly breathless suspense in 1960; but what happened in the *Times* newsroom may not be so well known as what was happening in the vote-counting rooms across the country.

"Scotty" Reston's early-edition leads reflected the pattern of the Eastern returns—Kennedy moving out front early to an advantage that began to look insurmountable as the hours wore on. Well before midnight the huge banner headline at the top of page one proclaimed: KENNEDY ELECTED PRESIDENT.

But the East was not all of America, and the later the hour, the less certain the result appeared; reporters who had predicted a Kennedy landslide began to look puzzled. To the surprise of virtually every political analyst, Nixon won Ohio with its twenty-five electoral votes; Virginia, Kentucky, Tennessee and Florida fell into his column.

Midwestern Republican heartland delivered Indiana, Wisconsin and Iowa . . . and as the night progressed, it became apparent that

virtually every prairie state, from North Dakota to Oklahoma
would be [Nixon's] and that he would capture every one of the
Western mountain states except Nevada. . . . [H]e defeated
Kennedy in . . . Washington, Oregon and Alaska.[30]

That last-minute flight to Alaska suddenly seemed less quixotic than it
had a few days earlier—or would, after the election. In the *Times* newsroom, Turner Catledge, the amiable Mississippian who was managing
editor—a man who knew national politics as well as where the bodies were
buried in the *Times* building—experienced what he later called "one of the
most nerve-racking nights of my life."

Catledge began prowling the newsroom in shirtsleeves, a scowl on his
usually cheery face. Still the returns came in, and still Kennedy's popular
vote lead kept ebbing. In the early morning hours, the Democratic candidate still had not clinched an electoral-vote majority, with California,
Illinois and Minnesota undecided. Nixon—with a weeping Pat Nixon
beside him—went on television to make a sort of concession ("if the present
trend continues . . ."). But if all three of those states went Republican, *he*
would win.

At a moment of such suspense, "I found myself wishing," Turner Catledge remembered, "that a certain midwestern mayor would steal enough
votes to pull Kennedy through"—not a serious wish so much as a desperate hope that Mayor Daley of Chicago or *something* would vindicate that
early *Times* headline.[31]

I was keeping up with the gubernatorial returns, the presidential election
and Catledge's nervous pacing. He literally stopped the presses, hoping for
some decisive returns. None came. About 2 A.M., I saw Catledge pause at
the national news desk—a crowd gathered around him; there was a hasty
conference with Reston and others. Catledge made a short punching gesture with his right arm and turned away, his scowl deeper. In a few minutes
a new edition was rolling off the press, carrying a new page-one banner:
KENNEDY APPARENTLY ELECTED.

I was impressed with the responsibility resting on the managing editor
of what was then, without challenge, the nation's leading newspaper, and
I admired Catledge's willingness, in newspaper jargon, to "climb down"
when the facts no longer warranted that confident early banner. But I was
even more impressed with what had caused him to act. Numerous hardworking *Times* reporters, including Reston—the class of the breed—were
on the phone to political sources all over the country; the information they
gleaned was helpful, but what really made the difference on that tension-
filled night were the numerous television sets scattered around the *Times*
newsroom.

Television had not been, in the fifties, the ubiquitous source of information—a sort of national nervous system—that it is today; the networks did not even extend their evening news broadcasts from fifteen to thirty minutes until the fall of 1963. But the networks' capacity to collect voting returns had been greatly expanded since 1956—and besides, no election before had generated the public interest shown in the Kennedy-Nixon race. That interest, in turn, had spurred the networks on to greater efforts. As a result, old heads on the *Times* agreed with me that 1960 was the first election year when the print press had to admit that "the tube" was decisively ahead in informing the public.

A newspaper, after all, is a slave to deadlines; and when it's inevitably time to go to press, what can be printed is only what is known at that time. But election-night television has no fixed press time; in a situation as unsettled as that of 1960, television could stay on the air and report every development as it happened. Not only could television follow the curve of events, as a newspaper could not; it was clear to me that the news-covering resources of the great national networks, with their strings of affiliated stations, had developed sufficiently to surpass even those of the mighty *New York Times*.

That night in 1960, as the *Times* began to rely on television coverage, the medium began to demonstrate its vast possibilities. I have had no doubt since then that television had changed journalism forever, as I already knew it had changed politics.

Neither Nixon nor Kennedy, nor practically anyone else, was thinking that night of the future of journalism. Nixon turned in at about 4 A.M.— 7 A.M. in New York—in the Ambassador Hotel in Los Angeles, where eight years earlier he had prepared for the Checkers speech. He was confident of California, knowing that the absentee ballots, traditionally Republican, would carry his home state for him; and he clung to the hope that he might wake up to find that Illinois and Minnesota had made him president.

It was not to be. Nixon slept for two hours, got up to ponder the returns, and knew by 10:30 A.M. (in California) that Illinois and Minnesota were lost. Kennedy had 303 electoral votes, 33 over the minimum, though Richard Nixon had carried 26 states to the winner's 23 (Alabama went for neither). Just over a hundred thousand popular votes, out of about sixty-eight million cast, separated the two major candidates.

"I know," Nixon soon wired Kennedy, "that you will have the united support of all Americans as you lead the nation in the cause of peace and freedom during the next four years."

In his family's compound on Cape Cod, the president-elect accepted victory with the kind of wit that at least half the electorate had learned to appreciate, and which had been part of the sober Nixon's undoing. As Jacqueline Kennedy and her friend, Toni Bradlee—both far advanced in pregnancy—came downstairs that morning, Kennedy took a cigar from his mouth and observed: "Okay, girls, you can take the pillows out now. We won."[32]

"The wonder," the columnist TRB wrote in the *New Republic* on November 21, 1960, just after the election, "is not that a Catholic was elected by a close vote, but that he was elected at all."

That view was widely shared then—by me, for one—and still is, but no longer by me. After much reflection and study, about the event itself and about the two men most directly involved (both of whose presidencies I reported on for the *Times*), what seems most remarkable to me about the 1960 election is that Richard Nixon came so agonizingly close to winning.

Remember that in 1960 only 30 percent of American voters called themselves Republicans, against 47 percent who claimed to be Democrats and 23 percent who considered themselves independents. By Nixon's pre-election calculation, that meant he had to win all the Republicans, half the independents, and as many as five or six million Democrats. Without a national hero like Eisenhower on its ticket, the Republican party was a decided underdog—but Richard Nixon came within a few disputed votes of winning anyway.

Despite all the unfavorable developments of the campaign—Eisenhower's "give me a week" remark, the dubious choice of Lodge, Nixon's knee infection, the first debate, the Martin Luther King incident, the heavy Catholic voting swing to Kennedy, the failure to unleash Eisenhower, the downturn of the economy, Nixon's burden of defending the administration, even his erratic command of himself and his campaign against a charismatic opponent—despite handicaps that would have sunk most candidates, the sometimes-derided, sometimes-despised Nixon, a suspect candidate for a minority party, matched virtually vote for vote the remarkable performance of Kennedy and the Democrats.

Nixon was not "better known" after the first debate. The religious issue helped rather than hurt Kennedy. By election day, the claim that Nixon was "more experienced" carried little weight. No great difference in financing or organization separated the two camps. The major blunders of the campaign had been Nixon's.

What explains, then, the fact that this insecure and embittered man, this introvert withdrawing more and more within himself, a repressed intellectual—as I believe—forcing himself into the fancied mold of a typical middle-class American, so nearly won the presidency of the United States over one of the most attractive candidates ever to seek it?

There's no doubt that Nixon almost won; it may even be that he *did* win. When the electoral votes were tallied officially on January 6, 1961, Kennedy received 303, Nixon 219 and Harry F. Byrd of Virginia (not an official candidate) 15. But electoral votes are decided, generally speaking, by popular votes—although in 1960 it still was possible for individual electors to vote as they pleased. A shift of only 4,480 votes from Kennedy to Nixon in Illinois, where there were plausible charges of fraud, and 4,491 in Missouri—less than 10,000 votes in two states—would have left neither candidate with an electoral majority and thrown the decision into the House of Representatives.*

If an additional 1,148 votes also had been counted for Nixon in New Mexico, 58 in Hawaii and 1,247 in Nevada—still a total switch of less than 12,000 votes—*Nixon* would have had a majority in the electoral college. Any experienced political reporter knows that so few votes could easily have been "swung" in any of those states—probably in *any* state—by various kinds of fraud or error.

Kennedy's popular vote plurality was infirm, too, because of the confused result in Alabama. The Democrats were unpopular in that state that year, mostly for racial reasons, because of the party's advancing liberalism, and owing to Kennedy's religion. So a slate of "unpledged electors" shared the Democratic list with six electors pledged to Kennedy. Democrats who did not want to vote Republican or for Kennedy could vote for the unpledged electors.

Nixon clearly received 237,981 votes in Alabama. Depending on how the vote for the unpledged electors are counted, Kennedy got 324,050 *or* 318,303 *or* 147,295. The reasons are too complicated for brief explanation; but using the first two totals gave him a national plurality of about 118,000 or 113,000 (the figure most often cited). The *lowest* of the three totals** gave Richard Nixon a national popular vote plurality of 58,181.

Republican charges of fraud, moreover, were not merely the fulminations of poor losers. In *Six Crises* Nixon cited a number of cases he said were "sworn to," whatever that means. Fraud, of course, is known to happen in Chicago; but in Republican downstate Illinois, equally strange events can take place on Election Day. The point is not that the election clearly was stolen from Nixon but that it *might* have been, since it was so close. Republicans had ample reason to think it *had* been stolen.

In these circumstances, Nixon quickly found himself under pressure to

---

*The Constitution gives each state, regardless of the number of its members of Congress, *one vote* in such a situation, with a simple majority of twenty-six states required for victory. On January 6, 1961, when the 1960 electoral vote was counted, there were twenty-three delegations controlled by Democrats from northern and border states, six by Deep South Democrats, seventeen by Republicans and four split evenly between the parties. The Deep South delegations, not exactly pro-Kennedy, and the four split delegations would have held the power of decision, making a Nixon victory at least possible.

**The Democratic National Committee actually used that lowest total when determining the number of delegates Alabama rated at the 1964 national convention.

contest the results, even from Eisenhower in their first conversation after the election—or so Nixon claimed in *Six Crises.* Just as obviously, the Kennedy camp did not want its victory marred, or the legitimacy of a new president challenged, in a messy court battle or a publicized and politicized recount.

In the week after the election, the Nixons tried to recuperate at Key Biscayne. They went out to dinner one night, though Herbert Klein recalls that Nixon was in a "very depressed state of mind as the full impact of the loss came on him." Len Hall had flown in to urge Nixon to protest the election results, and Republican investigators were busy studying voting records in Chicago and elsewhere. Both Chicago papers, the *Tribune* and the *Sun-Times,* Klein had been informed, were looking into the considerable possibility of vote fraud by Mayor Daley's redoubtable machine.

On this unhappy evening, the vice president—he would hold that title until noon, January 20, 1961—received word that Herbert Hoover was trying to reach him. Klein took the former president's call at a pay phone in the restaurant. Hoover told him that Ambassador Joseph P. Kennedy, the president-elect's rich and aggressive father, was trying to arrange a meeting between Nixon and John Kennedy.

When Klein relayed this news to Nixon, the vice president snapped out of his funk—"the difference was night and day." Nixon then went to the pay phone, greeting Hoover respectfully: "Hello, Chief."

Without returning the greeting, Hoover repeated "the ambassador's" message. What should I do? Nixon asked. Again Hoover was blunt ("like Sherman Adams," Nixon noted): "I think we are in enough trouble in the world today; some indications of national unity are not only desirable but essential."

This conversation suggested that Kennedy hoped to talk Nixon out of any planned voting challenge; Joseph P. Kennedy's orchestration of events surely had that purpose. After Nixon hung up, he called Eisenhower, who was on one of his frequent holidays in Augusta, Georgia.

Eisenhower readily agreed that Nixon should meet Kennedy—"You'd look like a sorehead if you didn't"—but in a partisan spirit, reinforced by his dim view of the president-elect, he cautioned Nixon to reserve judgment if Kennedy raised the subject of bringing Republicans into a Democratic administration. Eisenhower didn't want Republicans to accept "purely secondary or ceremonial positions" for the appearance of bipartisanship.

Before the Nixon party had left the restaurant, John Kennedy himself placed a call to the pay phone. Again, Klein took the call. Kennedy chatted briefly with him; Klein had done a good job as press secretary in the campaign, he said. He thought his own press secretary, Pierre Salinger, "ought to dress up more." This weighty opinion delivered, he confirmed to Klein that he wanted to talk to Nixon about "the unity of the country."

Klein took the president-elect's Palm Beach phone number; in a few minutes, Nixon called back. Again there was some inconsequential chat before Kennedy said he'd like to fly to Key Biscayne "if it won't interfere with your vacation." Nixon deferentially volunteered to go to Palm Beach instead, "in view of last Tuesday's results."

Kennedy laughed and—no doubt unintentionally—rubbed it in: "No, I have a helicopter at my disposal." Already the great power of the White House was flowing to him, inevitably separating him from the man with whom he had so closely contested for it.

The meeting took place in a detached villa at the Key Biscayne Hotel on November 14, almost a week after the election. Kennedy arrived escorted by a Secret Service car ordinarily used to protect presidents—more salt in Nixon's wounds. The two talked alone, while Salinger and Klein fended off the press outside.

Almost immediately, Kennedy asked his host: "How the hell did you carry Ohio?" His polls, he said, had showed him ahead there, and the loss of that major state had been to him the biggest surprise of the election.

What Nixon may have replied he did not specify in Six Crises. But he might have said what Bob Finch told me years later, that one reason Nixon carried Ohio against most expectations was a radio commercial made on his behalf by Woody Hayes, the Ohio State football coach. In 1960 and for many years before and after, Hayes had status in Ohio not inferior to that achieved in Alabama by Coach Paul "Bear" Bryant (George Wallace once defined an atheist as "anyone in Alabama that don't believe in Bear Bryant").

Ray Bliss, the astute Ohio Republican chairman (later the national chairman who revived the Republican party after the Goldwater debacle of 1964), had persuaded Coach Hayes to record the commercial. Bob Finch regarded its effect in Ohio as one of the master strokes of the campaign.

No wonder, then, that nearly ten years after the campaign of 1960, President Richard Nixon rejected the draft of a rather perfunctory White House letter to Ray Bliss at the time of Bliss's retirement from the national chairmanship. "Too short," Nixon wrote in the margin of the draft. "Warm it up. Refer to Ohio in 1960."[33]

No wonder, either, that Nixon remained a Hayes fan long after both had been forced to the sidelines of the arena. In 1987, former president Nixon delivered one of the eulogies at Hayes's funeral in Columbus, Ohio. He'd met Hayes, Nixon said in that speech, when Senator John Bricker introduced them in 1957 after Ohio State had defeated Iowa, 17 to 13.

"I wanted to talk about football," Nixon told the mourners, in remarks characteristically loaded with sports talk. "Woody wanted to talk about foreign policy. You know Woody . . . we talked about foreign policy."

Unfortunately, Finch's pleasant theory, that Hayes clinched Ohio for

Nixon, does not stand examination, though no doubt he and Nixon believed it. Not only is there no mention of Hayes's commercial in authoritative accounts of the Ohio election; the most often cited reason for Kennedy's defeat is that the state's Democratic governor, Michael V. DiSalle, had sponsored an unpopular tax increase in 1959, thus sparking animosity against his party.

"We have to find a scapegoat," DiSalle bravely remarked the day after the election, "and it might as well be me."

The governor also thought the "religious issue" had hurt Kennedy; if it had, it was not quite as DiSalle thought. One scholarly study of the vote concluded that "(1) Kennedy made a net gain of no more than 1 percent over Stevenson's 1956 vote in the non-Catholic section of the population; and (2) Kennedy probably made a very large gain [over Stevenson] among Catholics [but] it wasn't enough."

Thus, Kennedy, if hurt by anti-Catholicism, still managed to do marginally better than Stevenson among non-Catholics—but could not make a big enough gain among Catholics to carry the state, perhaps because there were not enough of them. Catholics were only 16 percent of the Ohio population in 1960.[34]

At the Key Biscayne meeting in 1960, with Ohio out of the way, the president-elect and his vanquished opponent went on to discuss their poll-takers—Louis Harris and Claude Robinson—and staffs, the difficulties of farm policy, and Nixon's views, after eight years in the Eisenhower administration, of the CIA and the State Department. Nixon suggested splitting the CIA in two—part for intelligence gathering, part for covert and other operations. This was a sound idea that neither Kennedy nor Nixon, as presidents, acted upon.

One reason for Nixon's suspicion of the CIA was that he had come to believe that another of its briefings had contributed to Kennedy's victory. On August 3, Kennedy had asked Allen Dulles about the missile gap and received only an evasive reply. This left Kennedy free to continue charging that the supposed gap existed—a false issue that undoubtedly hurt Nixon. It's unlikely that Nixon mentioned this matter to the president-elect; but the CIA paid for Dulles's caution (if that's what it was) in Nixon's hostility to the agency during his later administration.[35]

Nixon also strongly advised Kennedy *against* recognizing Communist China, admitting it to the U.N. or even adopting a "two-Chinas policy." He did so, Nixon wrote in *Six Crises,* because "admitting Red China to the United Nations would make a mockery of the provision of the Charter which limits its membership to 'peace-loving nations.' . . . [I]t would give respectability to the Communist regime which would immensely increase its power and prestige in Asia."

Kennedy *did* follow this advice, leaving it to Richard Nixon, more than a decade later, to bring China back into the West's idea of the family of nations—although it is not apparent that China was any more peace-loving or less in need of "power and prestige in Asia" than it had been in 1960. The difference, of course, was in the Sino-Soviet split, both doctrinal and geopolitical, to which Nixon paid careful attention while out of office.

President-elect Kennedy—as Eisenhower had anticipated—discussed bringing Republicans into his administration "in view of the closeness of the election." He mentioned Lodge and Ambassador Douglas Dillon—who actually became secretary of the treasury—and "wondered, in fact, if after a few months [Nixon himself] might want to take an assignment abroad on a temporary basis." No doubt to Kennedy's relief, Nixon rejected the idea on grounds that he intended to lead a constructive opposition in the best spirit of the two-party system.

In *Six Crises* Nixon did not mention the possibility of a challenge to the election results (perhaps because when that book was written many Republicans *still* believed the election had been stolen and should have been challenged). Herbert Klein, however, later told me that Nixon assured the president-elect early in the conversation at Key Biscayne that he would not bring a political or legal challenge; and he never did.

Bob Finch believes that Nixon would not do so as "a matter of faith" in the presidency. He "so revered the power of that office," Finch told me, that he feared a recount or a challenge would damage it. "He knew you couldn't play games with the presidency of the United States."

Besides, Finch conceded, there were practical problems: ballots not available for recount, no way to prove many allegations of fraud, legislatures not to be convened in time to hear challenges, Democratic control in Texas and Illinois, the two states most at issue. In *Six Crises* Nixon wrote that "it would take at least a year and a half to get a recount in Cook County [Chicago], and . . . there was no procedure whatever for a recount in Texas."

Klein, however, believed "many cases" of fraud could have been proved, as did Hall, Republican Chairman Thruston Morton, and many other party leaders. Even Nixon, in Klein's recollection, thought he might have won *some* challenges in court action.

Whatever he thought about the legal possibilities, a man like Richard Nixon, who frequently felt himself slighted and mistreated, and whose suspicious nature bordered sometimes on paranoia, surely shared the general Republican view that fraud had deprived him of the presidency. At a pre-Christmas party the Nixons gave in December 1960, he greeted some guests by saying: "We won but they stole it from us."[36]

Elmer Bobst remembered that at about the same time "Pat's Irish blood was boiling." But Nixon himself was "calm and quiet" and insisted that "I will not give this nation's enemies an opportunity to downgrade democracy and to say that our elections were fraudulent." Bobst's affection for the Nixons probably colored his memory of a remark that in his telling sounds a little too stilted.[37]

Klein, too, insisted that Nixon would not pursue a challenge primarily because it would "do too much damage to the country." This seems to me all the more plausible because, even though a legal challenge probably could not have reversed the election's outcome, by vigorously pursuing the vote-fraud charges, Nixon *could* have caused a huge national and international uproar, seriously questioned Kennedy's legitimacy, and increased his own popularity in the Republican party—at least in the short run.

No doubt for Republican consumption, Nixon described himself as having made a serious examination of the possibility of an election challenge after his return from Key Biscayne. But the reasons Finch and Klein gave for his decision—the same reasons Nixon himself set out in *Six Crises*—suggest that it was more an instinctive than a calculated decision.

The highly partisan Bryce Harlow, who had a low opinion of Lyndon Johnson's probity and felt certain that Texas, at least, had been "stolen" for the Kennedy-Johnson ticket, buttonholed Nixon just after the election. He insisted that the vice president had a "responsibility" to fight and assure the nation of an honest election.

"Bryce," Nixon replied, "it'd tear the country to pieces. You can't do that."

Kennedy privately viewed Nixon with some scorn (which was exactly what Nixon would have expected from any Franklin). The urbane Democratic candidate had been annoyed early in the campaign when Eric Sevareid, the CBS News correspondent and commentator, declared in an article in the *Boston Globe* that "the 'managerial revolution' has come to politics and Nixon and Kennedy are its first completely packaged products."

Sevareid wrote that these two "tidy, buttoned-down men" had no real convictions about anything except the primacy of their own ambitions. He had known such men as a college student, concluding: "I always sensed that they would end up running the big companies in town but I'm damned if I ever thought one of them would wind up running the country."

Kennedy seems not to have minded the description so much as having been lumped like "two peas in a pod" with his opponent. "With contempt," Kennedy had remarked of Richard Nixon: "He has no taste."[38]

Fawn Brodie noted with approval that to John Kenneth Galbraith, Kennedy once claimed that he "felt sorry for Nixon because he does not know who he is, and at each stop he has to decide which Nixon he is at the moment, which must be very exhausting."[39]

This was a good if not particularly original insight into Nixon from a man who more clearly knew who he himself was—though not always: the

Kennedy who supported Nixon against Helen Douglas, who was reluctant to condemn Joe McCarthy and who exaggerated his claims to have written *Why England Slept* and *Profiles in Courage,* may not have known himself so well as the Kennedy who ran for president in 1960 seemed to. Kennedy, moreover, had had the advantage of a quite different upbringing and life experience, but still had his own calculations, maneuverings, dark spots and tasteless moments—particularly with women—to answer for.

Was Sevareid really so wrong in seeing Nixon and Kennedy as alike in some fundamental ways? Both, as candidates, *were* to a great extent "packaged products"—the first real television candidates, the first to be presented as desirable items, like any other products designed to tempt consumers. Both had been heavily influenced by their fathers, not necessarily for the best. Both were ambitious, though driven by different demons. The record does not necessarily suggest, moreover, that either was a man of more "conviction"—in the laudatory sense in which Sevareid was using the term—than the other.

Kennedy's campaign pledge to end racial discrimination in housing "with a stroke of the pen" was ignored, once he was in office and under the gun of presidential politics. So were many of the workers to whom he'd promised an increase in the minimum wage. I well remember, from my days as the *Times*'s White House correspondent, James Reston's dismay, on a Saturday night in 1961 in Hyannis: he had joined me for dinner at the Captain's Table restaurant, after having had a private conversation with the president at the Kennedy compound nearby.

"I asked him what was his vision for the country, what kind of country he wanted it to be when he left office," Reston related, as Pierre Salinger played the restaurant piano not far away. "He looked at me rather oddly, and then he finally said, 'I haven't had time to think about that yet.' "

Nor does serenity in knowing one's self, appealing as that is in any personality, guarantee achievement—sometimes quite the opposite. It surely could be said of Dwight Eisenhower and Ronald Reagan, presidents not usually admired by Kennedy fans, that they were serene within themselves. As for Nixon's lack of "taste," a more fitting and relevant word might have been "grace."

John Kennedy usually had both in abundance and Nixon did lack both—with the result, certainly, that Kennedy was a more attractive and likable man than the rival he derided. That does not prove that Kennedy was the *better* man. History will judge the presidencies of each, but the bare records of Kennedy's "thousand days"—admittedly an unfinished odyssey—and of Nixon's *first* term do not necessarily favor the former.

Arthur Schlesinger, Jr., speculated that in the last weeks of the 1960 campaign voters began to have qualms about Kennedy because he seemed *too* remarkable:

It was almost as if the electorate were having sudden doubts whether it really wanted so intense a leader, so disturbing a challenge to the certitudes of their existence; it was as if the American people commenced to think that the adventure of Kennedy might be too much and that they had better fall back to the safe and familiar Nixon.

Aside from the question whether the "American people" ever act on such concerted perception, this thesis strikes me as overstated. For one thing, Nixon's more mechanistic analysis of late campaign events—that the momentum generated by the Kennedy campaign "peaked" too early, just as Nixon's was beginning to gather speed—seems at least as plausible and less romantic.

For another, to anyone who covered that campaign or who studies its record objectively, there's little evidence that John Kennedy offered "so disturbing a challenge to the certitudes" of American existence that voters finally turned away from him. The record seems to me to show, instead, that on foreign policy the campaign was waged in the context of Eisenhower's 1958 rebuke to Nixon, quoted earlier; and that on most issues the candidates differed too little from each other to suggest that life with Kennedy, rather than Nixon, would be a dangerous adventure to be shunned. As Abby Wasserman described the campaign in a meticulous summary she prepared for me:

> Both . . . spoke ringingly about U.S. responsibility as leader of the free world. Both characterized the decade's crucial issue as Freedom vs. Slavery (Communism). . . . During the debates the candidates spoke at length of the Cold War and U.S. leadership in the fight against Communism, and it is in this context that they debated policy in Cuba, Indochina, Quemoy and Matsu. [Both] spoke of Africa, Asia and Latin America as areas of the world needing more attention from the United States because they were particularly vulnerable to the appeal of Communism.

Differences on domestic issues were more pronounced but they were essentially the differences between Truman and Dewey, Eisenhower and Stevenson, post–New Deal Democrats and Republicans. When Kennedy announced his domestic legislative program, his primary proposals—a minimum wage increase, for instance, and a program of medical care for the aged—were worthy but scarcely radical; they had been political issues since the Truman administration. His urgent appeals to "get this country moving again" undoubtedly stirred many voters, particularly younger ones; but this hardly was so daring an approach that Americans finally were too apprehensive to accept it.

Schlesinger nevertheless had a point. Kennedy linked himself more closely than Nixon did, for example, to Martin Luther King and the disturbing—to many Americans—civil rights movement. He frequently drew alarmed attention with his "missile gap" charges—though after the election, the gap turned out to be nonexistent, as Eisenhower had insisted all along. Harry Truman made a point of Kennedy's youth; so later did Eisenhower, both inadvertently suggesting that he was an upsetting force in American politics.

So with his own emphasis on youth ("a new generation of Americans, born in this century"), his more attractive personality and his more ringing calls for "leadership" (Nixon, after all, necessarily had to defend the old leadership of Eisenhower), Kennedy *did* appear a more challenging figure—hence more romantic—than Nixon, who *did* seem "safe and familiar" by comparison.

On election eve, in one of Kennedy's best phrases, he shrewdly defined the race as "a contest between the comfortable and the concerned." And for millions of voters the young senator's "magic" was more than youth, good looks, wealth, intelligence and wit; it lay also and perhaps most importantly, as Schlesinger noted, in "the hope that he could redeem American politics by releasing American life from its various bondages to orthodoxy."[40]

Rather than this "magic" having been so powerful as to frighten some Americans away from it, however, the more plausible conclusion is that approximately half of the sixty-eight million who voted never felt it. Those millions did not consider themselves in bondage to orthodoxy or, if they did, had no longing to be freed from it.

This, in my judgment, is more nearly the reason why Nixon the graceless, Nixon the calculating, though ill-concealed by his alternating masks of piety and bonhomie, came so close to defeating—perhaps really did— the "magic" Kennedy. Those who voted for Nixon sought no liberation from restraints they never felt. They wanted *more* of the same as they understood it: more of the economic affluence, political stability, social conformity and military security that formed the even surface of the fifties—more of Eisenhowerland, from which they took Richard Nixon to be in direct line of descent.

As the Key Biscayne meeting broke up on that November day in 1960, neither Nixon nor Kennedy, so recently locked in bruising struggle, was likely to have been thinking of such abstractions; but Kennedy had more reason, nevertheless, to feel gratitude to Nixon than scorn for him. Whatever Nixon's inner feelings about his just due, whatever his motives for not challenging the election returns—mixed, no doubt, as motives usually are—his decision was both personally unselfish and profoundly in the interests of the country and of the president-elect.

That decision might even be considered graceful, and it's fair to wonder if Kennedy had the grace to tell him so.

The presidential campaign of 1960 is the most famous of modern times—save perhaps Harry Truman's upset victory in 1948. Among other distinctions, the 1960 election put the first Roman Catholic president in office and was the last in which more than 60 percent of eligible voters went to the polls. Though John Kennedy did not begin to make a powerful national impression until well along in the campaign, and may have been declared the victor only because of vote-counting chicanery, his journey into romantic immortality began in that dramatic autumn.

On the other hand, his ultimate triumph over the most determined and defiant of Orthogonians also pegged Richard Milhous Nixon, nearly fatally, as a loser—ironically *because* he had come so close to winning. Humiliating though it would have been for Nixon, a more decisive defeat might have spared him much criticism and cruel analysis. A big and indisputable victory for Kennedy could have been taken by many as evidence of a "Democratic year" or perhaps of an unbeatable opponent, so that no Republican candidate could have thwarted the forces working against him.

As it was, Kennedy's narrow margin gave every Republican license to believe, as Jackie Robinson did, that if only his or her advice had been taken, his strategy followed, his recommended statement made, Nixon would have won. Every controversial decision Nixon had made became subject to the postelection, often hostile, second guess. If only he hadn't debated, chosen Lodge, spurned Martin Luther King—if only, if only. . . .

The narrowness of his defeat left Nixon, too, to brood over the questionable decisions and strategies of his campaign. Perhaps worse, he had come near enough to sense virtually within his hands the great power that by 1960 was the passion of his life, only to see it snatched away by the kind of privileged and advantaged man who represented in his person Nixon's worst nightmares of his own inadequacy.

He even had to put the official stamp on his own defeat. The Constitution requires that the vice president of the U.S. preside over the joint congressional session at which the electoral votes for president are counted officially. So on January 6, 1961, shortly after noon, Nixon took to the rostrum of the House of Representatives with a man who hated him, Speaker Sam Rayburn, and the official count, conducted by one Democratic and one Republican "teller" from each house, proceeded to its inevitable end.

Alabama's votes were tallied first—five for John F. Kennedy, six for

Senator Harry F. Byrd, Sr. With a rare flash of humor, Nixon announced that "the gentleman from Virginia is now in the lead." But the foreordained result was Kennedy 303, Richard M. Nixon 219, Byrd 15.

Nixon thus became the first vice president since John C. Breckinridge of Kentucky, who in 1860 had been one of the three candidates against Abraham Lincoln, to be forced to confirm and announce the victory of an opponent. Nixon did the job without notes but with considerable magnanimity:

> This is the first time in one hundred years that a candidate for the presidency announced the result of an election in which he was defeated. . . . I do not think we could have a more striking and eloquent example of the stability of our constitutional system and of the proud tradition of the American people of developing, respecting and honoring institutions of self-government.
>
> In our campaigns, no matter how hard fought they may be, no matter how close the election may turn out to be, those who lose accept the verdict and support those who win. . . .
>
> It is in that spirit that I now declare that John F. Kennedy has been elected president of the United States. . . .

Members of both houses and both parties gave him a standing ovation—appreciation perhaps as genuine as any he had received in fourteen years in Washington. Even Sam Rayburn shook his hand and—Nixon claimed in *Six Crises*—called him "Dick."

Fourteen days later, as Washington lay paralyzed after an unexpected snowstorm the night before, Kennedy was inaugurated at noon. I was still a junior reporter; and that cold January 20, my *Times* assignment was to cover the day's activities, not of anyone coming in, but of the vice president going out.

I made my way through the snow to Nixon's house in northwest Washington—that was before vice presidents were given official residence at the old Naval Observatory off Massachusetts Avenue—and soon was joined by Don Irwin of the *New York Herald Tribune.* We stood flapping our arms and stamping our feet on the cleared sidewalk until Nixon himself, seeming in good spirits and for once taking pity on the press, invited us in. Mrs. Nixon gave us coffee and cheese from an enormous wheel of excellent cheddar some admirer had sent the vice president.

Irwin and I were the entire press party covering a man who had had a planeload of reporters and photographers following him just two months earlier. That tells as much as anything about the ephemerality of power in Washington. Vice President Alben Barkley had warned Nixon about that eight years earlier, when Nixon succeeded him, and the leaders of the

Eisenhower "crusade"—not unlike the men Kennedy now was bringing to Washington in their places—were setting out to remake the world.

"The hardest part about leaving the vice presidency," the old veep told Nixon, "was losing my car. One day—I'm met by a car, a chauffeur, and a Secret Service man. The next day I'm completely on my own."

Others recall from January 20, 1961, Kennedy's bellicose speech or Robert Frost fumbling with his manuscript; I have my own vivid memories of that snowy inaugural day. One is the sight of Styles Bridges, Everett Dirksen and other Republican worthies in Nixon's official escort committee, as they came up the sidewalk to his house, looking uncomfortable in top hats and morning clothes—the uniform Kennedy had decreed for his inauguration.

Another memory is of the long drive to Capitol Hill. Herb Klein, dutiful to the last, drove; Irwin and I sat in the back seat. In front beside Klein, Rosemary Woods, Nixon's devoted secretary, wept through every moment of the drive.

On the inaugural platform, also looking uncomfortable in morning (mourning?) clothes, Nixon was no more than an onlooker as first Lyndon Johnson, then Kennedy, were sworn in, their breath steaming in the cold. Nixon said little in *Six Crises* about his thoughts on this occasion, or later at a luncheon Admiral Lewis Strauss gave at the 1925 F Street Club for the highest officials of the departing Eisenhower administration.

Years later, in *RN,* Nixon elaborated on a drive he took to the Capitol that night, while the Democrats were celebrating victory at the various inaugural balls. Outside the Rotunda, on a balcony looking west along the snow-covered Mall to the Washington Monument stark against the night sky, Nixon stood alone in the cold for about five minutes, reflecting on his years in Washington, in public life—the arena. Then he started back to his car, but "suddenly stopped short, struck by the thought that this was not the end—that someday I would be back here."

Not many people in Washington that night would have agreed. The next day, my *Times* story about the vice president's last day in office was buried far back in the paper, under an insignificant one-column headline, unnoticed beyond the heraldings of another new era in Washington.

Elmer Bobst, concerned as ever, arranged a week's postinaugural vacation for the Nixons on Eleuthera in the Bahamas, with their old friends Roger and Louis Johnston of Whittier, and Bebe Rebozo, the Key Biscayne banker with whom Nixon had developed a close friendship.

Bobst anchored his yacht, *Alisa V,* just off the island. Every day he and Nixon talked about the future—Nixon apparently uncertain, Bobst positive that his friend should practice law in the East and rebuild his political strength. Bobst strongly urged Nixon to ignore the pleas of Republicans who already were pushing him to return to California and run for governor in 1962. Down that road, the older man insisted, there was nothing to gain and everything to lose. Nixon frequently said he didn't much like the idea either.

If Elmer Bobst took that for an answer, he knew less than he thought he did about a man whose life's experience would always draw him back to the arena.

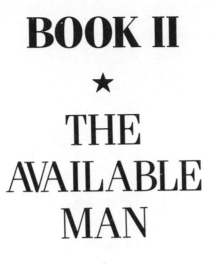

BOOK II

★

THE AVAILABLE MAN

★

7

★

Tides

★

I do not want to get into a debate . . . with
a chronic campaigner like Mr. Nixon.

—President Johnson, November 4, 1966

Richard Nixon was in Dallas on November 21, 1963, the day before the
fatal shots were fired at President John Kennedy. Though Nixon was on
business for Pepsi-Cola, a lucrative client he had brought to the Nixon,
Mudge law firm, he called a press conference—one of a number since he
had proclaimed his "last" in 1962.*

An unreconstructed partisan though a newly minted Wall Street lawyer,
Nixon speculated to attending reporters that unrest over the civil rights
issue might make Lyndon Johnson of Texas a "liability" as Kennedy's
running mate in 1964. Taking note of an ugly demonstration against U.N.
ambassador Adlai Stevenson in Dallas a month earlier, Nixon also urged
the city's citizens to give President Kennedy "a courteous reception" the
next day.

Nixon left Dallas on November 22 just as Kennedy entered it, so he did
not hear the news of the assassination until he was in a taxicab between
Idlewild (now John F. Kennedy) Airport and his New York apartment.
He was as stunned as everyone else, but one of his first moves, when he
reached home, was to take advantage of old associates to learn the details;
he called J. Edgar Hoover.

---

*For reasons given in the Preface, I have chosen not to include a detailed account of
Nixon's California gubernatorial campaign in 1962.

"Was it one of the nuts?" he asked the FBI director.

"No," Hoover said, "it was a Communist."[1]

In his memoirs, Richard Nixon has surprisingly little to say about America in the sixties, that turbulent period of social upheaval at home and an unpopular and unsuccessful war abroad, and the decade during which Nixon staged one of the most remarkable comebacks in political annals.

In *RN* he disparages Lyndon Johnson's Great Society for "its inclination to establish massive federal programs," discusses in detail how he treated the civil rights issue in his speeches, refights Vietnam and notes laconically:

> Another widespread concern during the period was the general tone of American society and the growth of permissiveness. Psychologists, preachers, and parents worried as traditional standards of social and sexual behavior were flouted or abandoned. I felt that to a large degree these excesses reflected the malaise of affluence. In some cases, however, they represented a real change in American culture.

This hardly evokes the decade in which Nixon returned from political ruin to the center of the arena, and to a place on a national party ticket for the fourth time in sixteen years.* Rather, he writes almost as if he had accomplished the redemption of his hopes in a vacuum.

The sixties, as Nixon hardly suggests, saw the flowering and decline of the civil rights movement, together with the "long, hot summers" of racial rioting in American cities; the sexual revolution that followed the widespread use of "the pill" by women; the invasion of middle-class America by drugs; the rise of rock music; the counterculture of "flower children," hippies, yippies and dropouts; consciousness-raising toward a powerful "women's liberation"; and the peace and student movements growing from a war that called into question the effectiveness and responsiveness of the American political system.

Less dramatically, the sixties also saw "the environment" become a national passion and consumer protection an active political issue. Almost invisibly, the decade marked the real beginning of both the nuclear arms race—with President Kennedy's decision in 1961 to build five thousand

---

*Ultimately Nixon ran on five national tickets, a feat that only Franklin Roosevelt has matched. FDR's first national campaign was for the vice presidency in 1920, when the Cox-Roosevelt ticket lost. Twelve years then passed before Roosevelt began his phenomenal record of four consecutive presidential victories; thus his five national campaigns encompassed twenty-four years and four presidential victories. Nixon ran on five national tickets, four of them winners, in only twenty years; but he won the White House for himself only twice, in 1968 and 1972.

Minuteman missiles—and of nuclear arms *control,* with the same president's decision to enter into the Limited Test Ban Treaty in 1963.

In the sixties, moreover, revolt seemed to be sweeping across the world—revolt against power, against authority, against institutions, against politicians, against custom, against "the system," even against more abstract qualities like sham, hypocrisy and pomposity.

In the largely affluent U.S., the individuality after which Western peoples have unceasingly aspired had been inundated by the postwar era's triumphs of technology and production. Americans were living in beehive apartments or sprawling anonymous suburbs, often at the mercy of giant, impersonal corporations and distant, unresponsive labor unions. Their cities had grown nearly to ungovernable proportions, with accompanying diminution, degradation and frustration of those who tried to move and breathe within their limits.

There had been other changes. The great advances of medicine, the vast strides of technology, had largely insulated people against nature, their oldest, worthiest and most consistently challenging opponent; a loss of natural experience and of earned self-awareness was bound to result. How to measure one's worth became a growing, if usually unrealized problem, in a world in which the prime challenge was to fit oneself like a cog into the smooth and indifferent machine of society. It was little wonder that so many young Americans—with so little of what they could see as useful or rewarding work available to them—sought to find meaning in their lives or relief from custom and obligation, in sex, drugs and "dropping out."

Developments of such magnitude and so alien to the apparently sedate American society of the fifties—Eisenhower's era, in which Richard Nixon had first come to national prominence—could not help but affect the *political* atmosphere in which Nixon continued to strive. It was in that atmosphere that the much-derided "Tricky Dick" managed to make himself an apostle of traditional values, social stability and national purpose—perhaps the most remarkable achievement of a man of whom the commentator TRB had expressed the widely shared opinion that he was "without a spiritual home, ready to twist any circumstances to his advantage, devoid of any genuine commitment to either liberalism or conservatism but trying to feel at home wherever the tides of circumstance happen to lodge him."[2]

The tides of circumstance were at their least predictable in the sixties. When Nixon moved east in 1963 after his supposedly catastrophic loss in California, for example, he believed he had no chance for the presidency in 1964—or perhaps ever—and therefore he had no intention of seeking the Republican nomination that year; and anyway, John Kennedy's reelection seemed assured. Then came Kennedy's assassination, an event all but unbelievable to a generation of Americans who had come to exalt the presidency beyond all rational limits, and to whom Kennedy seemed to lead the untouchable life of a young emperor.

Saddened like most of the nation and wondering about the future, the Nixons attended the Kennedy funeral services in Washington. But for a man so steeped in politics, and so linked to the infrastructure of the Republican party, it was impossible for long to put aside speculation about the political consequences of the death of a president.

Nixon quickly and correctly concluded that the new President Johnson, whom he knew so well, would take charge forcefully and make himself the Democratic candidate for 1964; less presciently, he also thought that Johnson, with his Texas background and his overweening ego, might prove a more vulnerable candidate than an incumbent Kennedy would have been. That inevitably raised the question whether the man whom Kennedy had defeated so narrowly in 1960 might be able, after all, to make another bid for the Republican nomination. Before the Kennedy funeral weekend was over, numerous old political associates as well as Nixon himself had concluded that he should at least remain open to the new possibilities of post-Kennedy politics.

Nixon had assets. He was the nationally known "titular leader" of the Republican party, its most prominent spokesman on foreign affairs, and a man who had *almost* won the presidency. It's even possible, as Bob Finch speculated to me years later, that as "the deification" of John Kennedy proceeded in the years immediately after his murder, Nixon actually profited from having been so closely involved with Kennedy in the 1960 election. The two had become linked in the public mind, Finch believed.*

The first Gallup poll published after Kennedy's death had Nixon narrowly out front for the Republican nomination, 29 to 27 percent for Senator Barry Goldwater of Arizona, with 16 percent for Nixon's old running mate, Henry Cabot Lodge (then the American ambassador to South Vietnam). Rockefeller—the only announced candidate at the time—brought up the rear at 13. Undoubtedly, Nixon's lead was more nearly "name recognition" than true public preference.

But numbers of that kind—apparently signaling no other dominant contender—could only tempt a professional like Richard Nixon. In January 1964, he told reporters he would "make any sacrifice" to enable his party to nominate "its strongest man." No one who could read between the lines doubted that he was expressing a willingness to be that candidate, without bluntly announcing a candidacy.

In fact, a "waiting strategy" already was taking shape in Nixon's head: he would play for a deadlock between Goldwater on the right and Rocke-

*Such a Kennedy-Nixon link in the public mind seems plausible to me, but Herbert Klein, for one, disagreed in a later interview.

feller on the left, in the expectation that the party finally would have to turn to Richard Nixon in the center.

Polls continued to aid this strategy, consistently ranking Nixon above the other Republican possibilities. More help came from Nixon's usual willingness to go anywhere and do anything for just about any Republican who would run for any office—on which frequent occasions, the former vice president unfailingly and rather cynically preached the party unity he fully expected to be torn apart in the Goldwater-Rockefeller struggle.

On the face of it, Nixon's waiting strategy seemed to make sense. Goldwater, the right-wing conservative hero, and Rockefeller, the liberal governor of New York, were on a collision course that inevitably would split the party. The retired Eisenhower, never much of a party man or a professional in presidential politics (save in his own campaigns), was looking on more or less helplessly from his Pennsylvania farm. In an American election, moreover, when there are identifiably left- and right-wing candidates, they will ordinarily lose out to one who is as clearly in the center—and the farther left or right, as Rockefeller and Goldwater were perceived to be in the Republican spectrum of 1964, the better for the center.

The bad blood between the Rockefeller and Goldwater factions, moreover, was political, personal and historical, stemming not just from ideological differences but also from the long record of defeated moderate-to-liberal (or "me-too") Republican presidential candidates, from Alf Landon in 1936 to Richard Nixon in 1960. Only Eisenhower's two victories had broken the ignominy of all those losses—and in Eisenhower's campaigns, had not Nixon been instrumental as the "centrist" link between what were then thought of as "the Eisenhower-Dewey liberal" and "the Taft conservative" wings of the party?

By 1964, the gulf was unbridgeable. Even geography played a part. The Goldwater movement was a Southern and Western response to the postwar dominance of the party by "Eastern internationalists" like Eisenhower, Dewey, the *New York Herald Tribune* and Nelson Rockefeller. So the party split was real in 1964—or was going to be.

Nixon, however, was wrongly—though conventionally—predicting the consequences of the impending split. Neither he nor any other center-to-left Republican, and few national political reporters, had recognized in 1963 and early 1964 the power with which a determined army of conservative activists was moving the Republican party toward a Goldwater nomination, rather than toward the centrist compromise that seemed so expectable.

The Goldwater movement was built not on primary-state victories but on mastery of the nonprimary states; and in 1964, a majority of the delegates was still to be had in those states—a good thing for Goldwater, whose hip-shooting candor did not lend itself to winning contested primaries. Most of the press, however, and the more liberal or centrist Republicans

were focused on the publicized primary states, giving Goldwater's dedicated underground army very nearly a free hand in other, more important
states. To some extent, this reflected differing objectives: Goldwater parti-
sans, like their hero, were first concerned to win the nomination and
transform their party, while their antagonists were more concerned about
building the national vote-getting power to win the presidency.

That a canny professional like Nixon shared liberal blindness toward
Goldwater's growing power within the party, and liberal fixation on the
primary states, can only be explained, however, by his rearoused lust for the
presidency. In nourishing his preferred strategy, Nixon did not recognize
reality—which was not impending deadlock but the Goldwater movement's
power. In that light, the waiting strategy—though apparently the best
available to the loser of 1960 and 1962—was ill-conceived, a political error
potentially as serious as Nixon's mistaken decision to run for governor of
California.

In 1964, his denials that he was an active candidate, or planned to be,
deceived few political experts and none of his potential opponents—but they
did convince the public. A business friend in New York—call him Fred—
recalls that during this period he and Nixon took an overnight flight to
London. When Fred made a trip to the toilet, he encountered a reporter for
Time, who asked him at which hotel Nixon would be staying in London.

Fred refused to say and returned to his seat to ask Nixon what was going
on. Nixon explained that the *Time* reporter had been assigned to follow
him as a potential presidential candidate, and had been promised an interview in London. Fred was astonished.

"Are you thinking of running for president?" he asked.

"What do you think?" Nixon said. "Should I?"

The two had had "a few martinis to put ourselves to sleep," Fred
remembers. Perhaps emboldened by the drinks, he replied that, as a friend,
he thought Nixon would be "crazy" to run. Nixon had begun to make
money at last, he was getting to know his young daughters, his family was
leading the good, affluent life in New York. Besides, Pat Nixon didn't want
her husband to return to politics because she liked to be able "to shop at
Bloomingdale's and not be recognized." Why on earth would Nixon even
think about running again?

Nixon's tongue, too, may have been loosened by the martinis.

"Because I know the fucking Commie mind," he said with some vehemence. "But they don't know mine. I really think I could do something.
I really believe I could make a contribution to peace."*

This may well have been only a rationalization for Nixon's reawakened

---

*Fred, who did not want to be publicly identified, later wrote Nixon a friendly letter
repeating his sound advice. I have a copy of that letter and notes of my interview with
Fred.

ambition to be president and his newfound hope that it might be possible even in 1964. Or it may have been a somewhat tipsy adversion to the high-minded desire—as he later described it to Leonard Garment in Elmer Bobst's poolhouse—to dedicate his life to "great purposes." The quest for peace, indelibly associated with Hannah Nixon's Quakerism, was high among those purposes.

Either way, Nixon disclosed his true intention: even in 1964, and at whatever personal and family sacrifice, he aimed to be president of the United States. Perhaps momentarily cast aside, usually concealed even from friends like Fred, that consuming desire had been set in motion again by the tides of circumstance that resulted in John Kennedy's death.

But Nixon not only had underestimated Goldwater's strength, and over-estimated that of Rockefeller (whose divorce and remarriage to a divorced woman undermined fatally his national political hopes); Nixon also played his own hand poorly, even more so than he had in California, failing to control and discipline his rekindled ambition.

A real waiting game probably still would have failed, given the power and fanaticism of the Goldwaterites, but at least it would have been honest. As it was, Nixon visibly tried to reinforce his "availability" without openly declaring his candidacy; that performance, particularly within his own party, only recalled Tricky Dick and invited the derision of opponents. ("He's sounding more like Harold Stassen every day," Barry Goldwater remarked at one point; after the events of 1956, that comparison must have stung.)

Nixon first let a contrived write-in effort for him go forward during the first primary, in New Hampshire—where Lodge, who remained mute in faraway Saigon, unexpectedly won with a virtually spontaneous volunteer effort, leaving Goldwater, Rockefeller *and* Nixon (in fourth place) decidedly embarrassed. Nixon operated more cautiously thereafter; as later primaries unfolded in Illinois, Pennsylvania, Massachusetts, Texas and Indiana, he traveled abroad and formally stayed out of the race—though pointing to his "availability" at every opportunity.

In Nebraska, however, where Goldwater was expected to win, the newspaper publisher Fred Seaton—formerly Eisenhower's secretary of the interior and one of Nixon's strongest supporters in 1960—pushed another write-in campaign on behalf of the man Seaton described as the only Republican capable of debating President Johnson on foreign policy issues.

At a news conference in Omaha a few days before the primary, Nixon a little too eagerly conceded that he was ready to run against Johnson if the Republican convention turned to him. And as the returns came in, they seemed to suggest that the convention might; Goldwater, who was alone on the ballot, ran poorly with only 49.5 percent, while the Nixon write-in was a solid second with 31.5 percent.

The Nebraska primary was the only event of Nixon's efforts for the 1964 nomination that, more than a decade later, he chose to mention in *RN;* he called it "an astonishingly strong showing." It was, however, misleading; the results obviously encouraged Nixon to ignore the advice of counselors and the evidence of polls, so that three days later he ran head on into disaster in Oregon.

Earlier, he had allowed his name to remain on the ballot after that state's officials had listed him as a candidate, though he did not intend to campaign. A Nixon victory in Oregon would have embarrassed Goldwater and Rockefeller, perhaps overshadowed Nixon's losses of 1960 and 1962, and might have made Nixon's availability credible to his party. But there was too little time, between Tuesday in Nebraska and Saturday in Oregon, to mount a campaign, as a professional should have known. Nixon tried anyway and finished a sorry fourth in a state he had swept against John Kennedy in 1960.

Goldwater's narrow victory over Rockefeller in the following primary in California clinched the 1964 Republican nomination, because he had built a virtual majority among delegates from nonprimary states. When no single opposing candidate decisively defeated him in the primaries, his hold on the convention was cemented.

A victory for Rockefeller over Goldwater in California *might* have damaged the Arizonan sufficiently to have salvaged Nixon as a centrist alternative. When the second Mrs. Rockefeller gave birth to a son on the final weekend of the hotly contested primary, however, the renewed publicity about Rockefeller's divorce and remarriage contributed heavily to his defeat. That put an end to any faint chance remaining to him or to Nixon.

Even then, though what Nixon actually did remains controversial and depends on who tells the story, he does not appear to have given up on what was, in effect, his second reach for the presidency. To some extent, of course, he was acting by then in the widely shared conviction that if Goldwater was indeed nominated, he would suffer overwhelming defeat in November. Nixon's actions suggest, however, that he was more nearly seeking the nomination for himself than merely trying to deny it to Goldwater.

The evidence is strong, for example, though he has denied it, that he tried and failed to push Governor George Romney of Michigan into running as a late "stop-Goldwater" possibility who might open the way for a compromise nomination. When Governor William Scranton of Pennsylvania finally did make a late entry, and desperate Republican moderates began to fall in behind him, Nixon—as late as June—again pointed to himself as the available compromise between the right (Goldwater) and the left (now Scranton): "If the party leaders turned to me, then I would undertake the responsibility of the nomination."

When Scranton phoned Nixon—who was on another trip to London— to tell him of his decision to run, Nixon was not encouraging.

"Watch out for the old man," he said.

"You mean Ike?" Scranton asked.

"Yes." Nixon no doubt was remembering the "give me a week" remark in 1960.

Eisenhower, indeed, failed to give Scranton firm backing. By then, the only conceivable stop-Goldwater strategy, however forlorn, would have been support for Scranton. But by then, Nixon's head-counters were trying to convince him that Goldwater had the nomination locked up; Nixon, too, must have realized that, in his head if not in his heart. The Scranton effort, with or without Nixon, could go nowhere. There was no alternative to Goldwater. By the end of June, Nixon, the hardheaded political calculator, finally had overcome the unrealistic and none-too-well-informed dreamer he had been in early 1964, after the disorienting event of Kennedy's assassination.

Recovered, like a man from a binge, Nixon promptly let his supporters know that he wanted all efforts on his behalf stopped at once. Then he arranged with Goldwater's triumphant managers to speak at the national convention *after* Goldwater's nomination—thus reassuring them against the possibility of a last-ditch Nixon demonstration, and giving Nixon a chance actually to play the role of party unifier that he had claimed to be playing all through 1964.

As he wrote of this general period in *RN:*

> I had finally come to the realization that there was no other life for me but politics and public service. Even when my legal work was at its most interesting, I never found it truly fulfilling. I told some friends . . . that if all I had was my legal work, I would be mentally dead in two years and physically dead in four.

"Politics and public service," for a man who had been for so long at his level of the game, could only culminate in the presidency—the brass ring. And this "realization"—probably never since his vice presidency far from Nixon's consciousness—was only enhanced by the return of realism in 1964. It was more to improve his long-term prospects for the presidency than for any immediately practical purpose that Nixon turned to all-out support of Barry Goldwater.

If Goldwater was sure to be nominated, in Nixon's view, he was just as sure to suffer resounding defeat against Lyndon Johnson. The president had ably portrayed himself as the right man to complete the unfinished work of John Kennedy, who was in 1964 a nearly sainted figure; passage of the Kennedy tax and civil rights bills (the latter over Goldwater's nay vote) under Johnson seemed to justify Johnson's claim.

Besides, as experienced political analysts knew, most Americans believed Johnson had earned a term of his own. The country, moreover, was not likely in November 1964 to choose a *third* president in just over a year. In all probability, Nixon himself had been saved by the failure of his waiting strategy from what would have been a third straight major defeat and the certain end of his presidential dream.

Goldwater's excesses—he already had proposed to sell the Tennessee Valley Authority, make Social Security voluntary and give military officers authority to use nuclear weapons—could only make his ordained defeat the more devastating. So there would be pieces to be picked up after the 1964 election: a shattered party would need to be reassembled, reinvigorated and led back into contention; Republican congressional delegations, about to go down with Goldwater, would need to be rebuilt in 1966; and the case on the home front and abroad would have to be made against Lyndon Johnson—who, having served only a year of Kennedy's term, would be eligible to run again in 1968.

Who better to take on any or all of those tasks than Richard Milhous Nixon, the self-identified party unifier and the indefatigable party worker, the perceived heir to Dwight Eisenhower, the most familiar domestic politician and the most experienced foreign policy spokesman of the Republican party? And if he could successfully perform such selfless work for the party, who was more likely to be its *next* presidential nominee, four years in an apparently promising future?

First, however, Nixon had to erase any lingering memory or suspicion that he had tried to stop Goldwater; the Southern and Western Republicans who had nominated the Arizona senator, after all, would continue to dominate the party internally, even after the expected defeat of their idol. Nixon had to emphasize, moreover, his already impressive credentials for party loyalty—whether to the party of Eisenhower or the party of Goldwater.

So, on July 14, 1964, almost as soon as Nixon landed in San Francisco for the Republican convention, he told the press that Goldwater would be an acceptable nominee and insisted with a grandly mixed metaphor that no matter what happened in the fall campaign, "I, for one Republican, don't intend to sit it out, take a walk."

Nixon's speech to the convention, introducing Goldwater after the senator's first-ballot nomination, was a carefully crafted party-unity appeal, lustily cheered by the Goldwaterites, glumly heard by shell-shocked moderates and well suited to Nixon's personal aims. After the incorrigible Goldwater shook hands with him on the rostrum, however, the new nominee promptly undid whatever good Nixon might have done for him.

First, to thunderous approval from ecstatic supporters, he dismissed his Republican opponents: "Those who don't care for our cause, we don't expect to enter our ranks in any case." Then, he further transported his enthusiasts with the memorable declaration that "extremism in the defense

of liberty is no vice; moderation in the pursuit of justice is no virtue."
Goldwater delegates went wild with a joy that seemed almost bloodthirsty
to those of us watching in awe from the press tables.

It was magnificent, but it was not politics. The Goldwaterites were
cheering a moment that had destroyed whatever small chance their champion had had to win the presidency—and whatever semblance of party
unity his nomination had spared.

Thus, even before Goldwater left San Francisco's Cow Palace for his
defiant, doomed campaign, the tides of circumstance were sweeping him
into a downward spiral. From the coming disaster, like Ishmael floating
on his coffin, Richard Nixon only "would escape alone to tell thee"—not,
in his case, of past tragedy but of future triumph.

As a good Republican and a professional office-seeker, Nixon could not
have been pleased by the Goldwater nomination and campaign; in *RN* he
described himself as "almost physically sick" as he listened to the nominee's fatal acceptance speech. As a practical politician with an eye to his
own prospects, however, he went to work at once to support Goldwater
and all other Republicans, to keep the party intact if possible—and deeply
in his debt.

Concentrating on assistance to endangered Republican candidates—of
which there were many—Nixon swept through thirty-six states in the fall
of 1964, tireless as usual, and earning the gratitude of Goldwaterites who
seemed quickly to forget his prominent preconvention availability. Not
incidentally, he also piled up credits locally and nationally as a Republican
who would work as hard for the party in its hour of disaster as in its
moments of glory. This performance was in sharp contrast to that of
Rockefeller and most moderate Republicans, who kept as far from Goldwater as they could, as if to resist contamination.

Thus, Nixon began to make his way back as *the* Republican leader even
before Election Day of 1964 left Goldwater defeated in all but five Deep
South states. Republicans also lost two Senate seats that year, thirty-eight
in the House, and upward of five hundred in state legislatures—a result
fully as calamitous as all serious analysts had foreseen.

Nixon lost no time in testing his status. Two days after the November
election, in Nelson Rockefeller's home city, he called a press conference—
long his chosen forum, the debacle of 1962 notwithstanding—and blasted
Rockefeller as a "party divider" and "spoilsport" who had failed to work
hard enough for Barry Goldwater and the party. In cold political terms,
the charge was true enough, though perhaps overstated. (For Rockefeller's
private reaction, see chapter 1.)

But Nixon had a larger aim than merely scoring points on a past and
possible future opponent. He laid further claim to the esteem of the Gold-

waterites, and pointed out that one who had sat on the sidelines had no
claim to national leadership. By easy implication, one who *had* fought the
battle *was* entitled to that leadership, though Nixon had no need to say so.
His campaign performance had spoken for him and his first tangible reward was not long in coming.

In January 1965, at a meeting of the Republican National Committee
in Chicago, Nixon helped maneuver Dean Burch, Goldwater's handpicked
national chairman, out of the office, clearing the way for the election of Ray
Bliss of Ohio (as noted, a prime engineer of Nixon's victory over Kennedy
in that state in 1960). The switch was mainly a symbolic move to show the
public that Goldwater's right-wing stance was not permanent Republican
doctrine. Goldwater was not amused, but after his own landslide defeat
recognized the necessity for Burch's removal.

The defeated nominee thereafter introduced Nixon before the committee
as the man "who worked harder than any one person for the ticket" in
1964.

"Dick, I will never forget it!" Goldwater exclaimed (forgetting, apparently, his earlier Stassen comparison):

> I know you did it in the interests of the Republican party and not
> for any selfish reasons. But if there ever comes a time I can turn
> those into selfish reasons, I'm going to do all I can to see that it
> comes about.

That was the rich political fruit of Nixon's hardheaded, brilliantly calculated, if belated, accommodation to the political facts of the year 1964—
Goldwater's certain nomination and inevitable defeat. The Goldwaterites,
who still would dominate the Republican convention in 1968, had heard
their champion virtually pledge his support to the man who had worked
harder than any other for the hopeless 1964 ticket.

But Nixon understood that whoever might be nominated for president
in 1968 would have no chance to win the election without a strong and
rejuvenated—*united*—Republican party behind him; that was the first
necessity of his ambition, hence of his strategy. He would take the lead in
building such a party because, as he put it in *RN:*

> I believed that whoever did would gain a significant advantage in
> the race for the 1968 presidential nomination. This enabled me to
> reconcile the paradox of having to help my Republican competi-
> tors—Rockefeller, Romney, and Reagan. I felt that if the base of
> the party were not expanded, the 1968 nomination would be
> worthless. If the party were expanded by the victories of others,

I thought I had a good chance of benefiting from its greater strength.*

Few opportunities to elect Republicans arose in the off-year 1965. Nixon traveled repeatedly, however—abroad to build his expertise as a foreign policy spokesman, in the fifty states as an unflagging partisan, fund-raiser and speaker at party gatherings. He was "available" in a different sense from 1964—available to help any Republican who needed help, to take part in any party program that needed a "draw," to speak out on any issue where a strong Republican voice needed to be heard.

Nixon's most successful foray was a hard-hitting, one-day sweep through Virginia (which holds odd-year state elections) for the Republican gubernatorial candidate, Linwood Holton. Nixon's help was vital to Holton's surprising capture of 38 percent of the vote in Harry F. Byrd's former Democratic stronghold. This showing later helped make Holton (in 1969) the first Republican to win the governorship of Virginia in the twentieth century; he turned out to be one of the state's best. The gains of 1965 also led on to the Old Dominion becoming something like a two-party state. Nixon came in for a good share of the credit.

His one serious error in 1965 stemmed from his usual routine support for Republicans, this time for one Wayne Dumont, the party's gubernatorial candidate in New Jersey, another state that holds odd-year elections (see chapter 1). Dumont had urged the firing of Eugene Genovese, the historian, then a professor at Rutgers, who had said he would "welcome" a Vietcong victory in Vietnam.

When Nixon defended Dumont's position on the firing, he appeared to critics to have reverted to the old Nixon, circa Helen Douglas. In fact, he probably had been swayed less by anti-Communist sentiments than by his post-1964 determination to go anywhere and do anything to support Republicans—whether liberal, conservative or in-between—in order (he said) to maintain the two-party system, but also (he did not say) to rebuild his own party for 1968.

Nixon rather typically tried to turn the Dumont misstep (Dumont lost the election) into a personal asset; he insisted in a commencement address at the University of Rochester in 1966 that his political effort on Dumont's behalf actually had been a selfless attempt to defend academic freedom (!) "from its own excesses." Whatever the effect of this rather strained explanation, the episode probably hurt him most among Democrats and independents, who were little inclined, in any case, to approve of a man who

---

*Ronald Reagan did not win public office until 1966 but owing to an effective nationally televised speech he had made for Goldwater in 1964, he was immediately considered the new conservative leader.

had exposed Alger Hiss and savaged Adlai Stevenson—which is to say that the Dumont matter did not hurt him much, because Nixon's focus at the time was mostly on making himself indispensable to *Republicans*.

Nixon did become the principal national spokesman for his party; among other things, he kept the pressure on Lyndon Johnson to escalate the war in Vietnam. When Johnson ordered an air strike on the North in retaliation for an attack on American forces at Qui Nhon, Nixon declared that it was not enough and called for sustained bombing. It was "no time for consensus government," he said. "It's a time for leadership."

Nixon proved himself, moreover, the party's most willing laborer and its most effective fund-raiser. Between the 1964 and 1966 campaigns, he claimed in *RN,* he "logged 127,000 miles visiting forty states to speak before more than 400 groups. [He] helped to raise more than $4 million in contributions"—political chickenfeed now, but not in the sixties.

By mid-1966, the Gallup poll gave Nixon a lead of almost two to one over Lodge, then his strongest competitor for the 1968 nomination. Consequently, a volunteer group headed by Peter Flanigan and Maurice Stans raised sixty thousand dollars to finance a Nixon campaign that year to elect Republicans to Congress. Both men favored Nixon for president and both understood that success for Nixon, the party leader, in 1966 was indispensable to Nixon, the presidential aspirant, in 1968. Not surprisingly, both men were later to be prominent in the Nixon administration.

The Republican Congressional Campaign Committee added thirty thousand dollars to the Nixon kitty. These funds not only enabled him to stump the country in 1966; the campaign thus financed gave him all but official status as the top Republican leader, instead of the party's "titular head"— Goldwater. Other leaders, such as Romney, Rockefeller and Reagan, were preoccupied by their own state campaigns.

Perhaps as important, Nixon's 1966 congressional campaign gave him reason to call back many of his volunteers, advance men and other loyalists from 1960 and 1962, together with new admirers from his dogged efforts for Goldwater in 1964. In effect, a new Nixon campaign team was taking shape, being tried out and streamlined for 1968, though ostensibly it existed only to elect members of Congress in 1966.

Nixon's approach that year was simple but sophisticated. He reasoned that the Goldwater debacle had caused the defeat of numerous Republican candidates in states and districts where the party usually won—with the result, Nixon liked to say, that Congress had become "a toothless old lapdog of Lyndon Johnson." But any Republican who had survived in 1964 with Goldwater at the head of the ticket probably could take care of himself in 1966. So Nixon concentrated on historically Republican congressional districts where in 1964 Democrats had been elected to first terms on Johnson's coattails—or, more precisely, in Barry Goldwater's wake.

Nixon was busy with the obligations of his law practice during much of 1966—when, for instance, after weeks of preparation, he argued the *Hill* case before his old antagonist, Earl Warren, and the Supreme Court (see chapter 1). His immediate political staff consisted only of Patrick Buchanan, whom Nixon had hired away from the *St. Louis Globe-Democrat,* as a speech writer and researcher. Increasing assistance from Leonard Garment and Tom Evans, another law partner, and John Sears, a young associate at Nixon, Mudge, helped Nixon find the time, nevertheless, for extensive and effective campaigning.

One major issue that year was civil rights, particularly in the Southern states, where both the Eisenhower and the Goldwater campaigns, as well as Nixon's in 1960, had given Republicans cause to believe they could make substantial gains. But progress in the South, if gained by playing openly to white segregationist sentiment, would cost Republicans dearly elsewhere. The man who had sought in 1957 and 1959 to put an end to anti–civil rights filibusters in the Senate, but who had refused to "pander" to Martin Luther King in 1960, did not shrink from the contradiction.

In a nationally distributed newspaper column he was writing in the midsixties, Nixon laid down the obvious position for his party:

> Southern Republicans must not climb aboard the sinking ship of racial injustice. Any Republican victory that would come from courting racists, black or white, would be a defeat for our future in the South and our party in the nation.

Abraham Lincoln's political heirs could take no other stance, historically or practically; but that seemingly balanced phrase, "black or white," slipped in so righteously, was a calculated Nixonism: Republicans need not be reluctant to stand against "black power" advocates or black demands that in white eyes went too far. Between the lines, it could be read that even a degree of white backlash, if not white support for segregation, could be cautiously exploited.

Nixon repeated this carefully rigged approach in appearances across the South—with an important addendum for strictly local consumption. The national party should publicize its support for civil rights, he said, but it could not "dictate" to state Republican parties that they take the same position, because the state parties had the political necessity to work out locally acceptable positions on that or any issue. Nixon vowed to campaign for a strong two-party system in any state in the country "whether or not I agree with the local Republicans on every issue."[3]

Any Southerner could read that. Richard Nixon was willing to let Southern Republicans deal in their own way with the race problem, no matter what he himself believed, or said in other states. Diversity, he made clear, was acceptable—a position that would be remembered when he came South looking for delegates in 1968. A "Southern Strategy" for that year already was evolving; yet it would be hard to charge that Richard Nixon had opposed, or was opposed to, civil rights.

The other major issue of 1966 was Vietnam—a subject that Nixon, after visits to that country in 1964, 1965 and earlier, was as well equipped as any Republican to address. His position was solidly established even before the 1966 campaign opened—and perhaps as far back as 1954 and the Dienbienphu crisis. The war was necessary, he insisted, to halt Communist aggression in Asia and to avoid a bigger war if "South Vietnam is lost and Southeast Asia is lost, and the Pacific becomes a Red Sea."

Here was domino theorizing on a global scale. And apparently because Nixon believed it, and in order to lay out a sound Republican political position, he consistently accused President Johnson of doing *too little* to prosecute the war and talking *too much* about ending it by negotiation.

In a speech in New York in January 1965, he had called for the naval and air bombing of North Vietnam and urged air and sea power to "quarantine" the war and prevent reinforcement and resupply of Vietcong forces in South Vietnam. Perhaps remembering Eisenhower's teachings in 1954, however, or in view of changing public opinion—or just as an older and wiser man—Nixon never advocated the use of nuclear weapons.

Later in 1965, on "Meet the Press," he commented that Lyndon Johnson's "continued talk . . . suggesting that we only want peace, that we want to negotiate, has the effect of prolonging the war rather than bringing it to a close." Johnson, he said, ought instead to make it clear to all that "our objective is a free and independent South Vietnam with no reward and no appeasement of aggressors." Nixon was not reluctant to say that he was for military victory rather than negotiated peace; even a decade later, in *RN,* he quoted both these statements from 1965.

Disaffection for the president and the Vietnam War was increasing (although few if any Republican candidates openly *opposed* an anti-Communist war that year). In part to counter dovish criticism from within his own party, to which Johnson was more sensitive than generally supposed, the president had announced at the end of September a meeting in Manila, to be held three weeks before the election. President Thieu of South Vietnam and other allied leaders from Australia, New Zealand, South Korea, the Philippines and Thailand would attend.

Columnist Richard Nixon immediately and acidly inquired whether Johnson would go to Manila on "a quest for peace or a quest for votes." It was a good question from one who had ample reason to appreciate Johnson's political agility; and Johnson reacted like a man whose hand had been called. He warned that votes for Republicans in November would cause the nation to "falter and fall back and fail" in Vietnam. Nixon, knowing that the Democrats were giving Johnson more grief on the war than the generally supportive Republicans, fired right back:

> The Republican party has not failed America. The only failure is President Johnson's. He is the first president in American history who has failed to unite his own party in time of war.

When the Manila "summit" ended on October 25, 1966, Johnson, Thieu and the other leaders ("my prime ministers," Johnson liked to call them) issued a communiqué ostensibly offering a route to peace. American and allied troop withdrawals from Vietnam would come within six months, if North Vietnam also withdrew and ceased to support the Vietcong in the South, so that the "level of violence" might subside.

Nixon saw in this offer, which obviously was unacceptable to Hanoi—it would leave the Saigon government in power and isolate the Vietcong— proof that the well-publicized, well-timed show in Manila had been staged primarily for the polls and the voters in the U.S. Fearing that Johnson would follow up with Texas-sized claims of a major step toward peace, perhaps swinging an otherwise-lost election to the Democrats, Nixon reacted strongly.

Only five days before election day, he issued a lengthy analysis of the Manila communiqué (which, in tribute to his recovered position of national leadership and international expertise, the *New York Times* published in full). "Communist victory," Nixon declared, "would most certainly be the result of 'mutual withdrawal' if the North Vietnamese continued their own support of the Communist guerrillas."

If, moreover, the communiqué meant that American withdrawal was linked to the level of Vietcong combat efforts, "then we have offered to surrender a decisive military advantage." The Vietcong could lie low for a while, the Americans would withdraw, and the guerrillas could reemerge with Hanoi's support and no one but the South Vietnamese army to oppose them.

Johnson's grandstanding, if that's what it was, had backfired. Much of the press took a cynical view of the Manila summit; hawks called the communiqué "surrender on the installment plan," and doves found it did not go far enough to end the war.

Johnson may have recognized that he had overplayed his hand. No doubt he was tired from an Asian trip that included visits to South Vietnam and South Korea. Perhaps what, in typical Johnsonian imagery, he later told Doris Kearns about his attitude toward the war was more to the point:

> I knew from the start that I was bound to be crucified either way I moved. If I left the woman I really loved, the Great Society, in order to get involved with the bitch of a war on the other side of

the world, then I would lose everything at home . . . but if I left
that war and let the Communists take over South Vietnam, then
I would be seen as a coward and my nation would be seen as an
appeaser and we would both find it impossible to accomplish
anything for anybody anywhere on the entire globe.[4]

Whatever it was that moved him, at a White House news conference on
November 4—a Friday before the elections on Tuesday—Lyndon Johnson
slipped out of control almost as badly as Dick Nixon had four years earlier,
on the morning after his defeat in California. When a reporter asked
Johnson to comment on Nixon's criticism of the Manila communiqué,
"something inside him seemed to break" (as Nixon wrote, not unsympa-
thetically, in *RN*). Startled reporters scribbled furiously as the president
delivered an unprecedented rebuke to a former vice president:

> I do not want to get into a debate on a foreign policy meeting in
> Manila with a chronic campaigner like Mr. Nixon. It is his prob-
> lem to find fault with his country and with his government during
> a period of October every two years. If you will look back over his
> record, you will find that to be true. He never did really recognize
> and realize what was going on when he had an official position.
> . . . You remember what President Eisenhower said, that if you
> would give him a week or so he would figure out what he was
> doing.
>   Since then he has made a temporary stand in California, and you
> saw what action the people took out there. Then he crossed the
> country to New York. Then he went back to San Francisco, hop-
> ing that he would be in the wings, available if Goldwater stumbled.
> But Goldwater didn't stumble. Now he is out talking about a
> conference that obviously he is not well prepared on or informed
> about.

Johnson defended the Manila communiqué, claiming that it made clear
that the U.S. and its allies would stay in South Vietnam, only "so long as
our presence is necessary" to protect that country's territory and put an
end to the fighting. Then he turned again to Richard Nixon, as harshly as
before:

> They know that and we ought not try to confuse it here and we
> ought not try to get it mixed up in a political campaign here.
> Attempts to do that will cause people to lose votes instead of
> gaining them. And we ought not have men killed because we try
> to fuzz up something. When the aggression, infiltration and vio-

lence cease, not a nation there wants to keep occupying troops in South Vietnam. Mr. Nixon doesn't serve his country well by trying to leave that kind of impression in the hope that he can pick up a precinct or two, or a ward or two.

The new, restrained, post-1964 Nixon knew a political windfall when he saw it, and just how to respond.* If the president had taken the low road of personal attack and invective, his victim would be above that sort of thing. Without any high-level advice or consultation, while flying with Buchanan from New York to a speech in Waterville, Maine, Nixon made up his mind to reply in sorrow rather than in anger—to be firm in his position but reasoned, low-keyed, even forgiving.

He said he was "surprised" at Johnson's attack but would "continue to speak out." He expressed respect for "probably the hardest-working president in this century" (did Eisenhower, at Gettysburg, heed *that*?) but called for discussing the issues "like gentlemen." Then he made the hard political point that dramatized Johnson's intemperance, Democratic party divisions and Nixon's own new stature:

> Let the record show that all over the world I have defended the administration's announced goal of no surrender to aggression. I have defended it in the capitals of the world and here at home against members of the president's own party.

What could have been more reasonable? What could so deftly have turned the tables on a president without showing disrespect for his office? What could have served Nixon's own interests more effectively, or those of the Republicans he was seeking to elect? Not since the Checkers speech had Nixon more effectively seized the moment.

Eisenhower (apparently not offended) chimed in with a defense of Nixon as "one of the best-informed, most capable and most industrious vice presidents in the history of the United States" (an encomium that the sensitive Nixon, remembering the indignities of 1956 and 1960, must have read with bittersweet amusement).

The Republican Congressional Campaign Committee immediately handed Nixon a thirty-minute television slot that had been made available to it by NBC for Sunday afternoon, November 6. That same day, he was the guest on ABC's "Issues and Answers." On both programs, Nixon stayed prominently on the high road, repeated his criticisms of the Manila

---

*On May 4, 1990, at a seminar of Johnson administration veterans, John Gardner, the former secretary of HEW, recalled that LBJ had said of the "chronic campaigner" remark: "I shouldn't have made that crack about Nixon. That was dumb."

communiqué and argued for a Republican Congress. (He also used the congressional committee's half hour to try to lay to rest the Wayne Dumont episode with a ringing defense of "the principle of the right to disagree, the right to dissent.")

Then, daring to evoke the daunting memory of his own "last press conference," he even extended a sort of absolution to Johnson, as if from one sinner to another:

> I think I understand how a man can be very, very tired and how his temper then can be very short. And if a vice president or a former vice president can be bone weary and tired, how much more tired would a president be after a journey like yours?

One can almost hear Johnson's teeth gnashing. Elsewhere, the response to both television appearances was strongly favorable; later surveys credited them as important to the sweeping Republican victory that followed, two days later.

All that year, Nixon had been predicting such a victory, using optimism—as in 1958—to stir up enthusiasm among party workers and regulars. But in 1966, resting on a firmer basis, optimism paid off.

Nixon had predicted a Republican pickup of forty House seats; the actual gain was forty-seven. Exactly as he had forecast, the party captured three additional Senate seats. He had claimed that six governorships would go Republican; *eight* did. Only for state legislatures did optimism overstate the case, and that was hardly noticeable; the party won 540 seats against Nixon's prophesied 700.

Among the 1966 winners were some promising new Republican names—Ronald Reagan for governor of California (over Pat Brown, the conqueror of Nixon in 1962), Spiro T. Agnew for governor of Maryland, Edward Brooke, a black, for senator from Massachusetts. There were some old familiar ones, too—notably George Romney, returned to the governorship in Michigan, and Nelson Rockefeller, overcoming divorce and the loss of the presidential nomination in 1964 to win his third term as governor of New York.

On election night, as the great news rolled in, Nixon called them all, congratulating all victorious Republicans of every stripe—even Rockefeller and Romney, probably his most dangerous rivals for the presidential nomination in 1968. Nixon knew that the *party's* victory, far outweighing anyone's individual election, had been the first requisite to his own hopes for the presidency.

It was, in fact, one of the great party victories of the postwar—or any—era, in the context of Goldwater's presidential debacle only two years earlier. But it was a greater victory for Richard Nixon, the well-known loser of 1960 and 1962, the overeager fumbler of the 1964 primaries.

As calculated by Warren Weaver, Jr., of the *New York Times,* of the 66 House candidates for whom Nixon had campaigned, 44 won; of the 86 Republican candidates for all offices that he helped, 59 were elected—a batting average of .686. More important, as he later pointed out in *RN,* "for the first time in ten years, I was identified with a smashing victory." And this time, there was no Eisenhower to take the credit.

Nixon's party knew who had been the chief instrument of its comeback; and he knew that 1966 had taken him well down the road to the Republican presidential nomination in 1968, perhaps even to soul-satisfying victory over the man who had called him a "chronic campaigner."

"I enjoyed listening to the 1966 election returns," Nixon wrote in *RN,* adding the considerable understatement: "There was a lot for me to celebrate."

In the year of Richard Nixon's third reach for the presidency, the sixties came to climax. Nineteen sixty-eight was a year of repeated shocks to what remained of American certainty, of brutal blows to Americans' perceptions of themselves and their country, of devastating challenges to old ideas of authority and value. The long, bloody struggle in Vietnam seemed more and more senseless; worse, it appeared endless. Social upheavals in France and Mexico suggested that "the revolution" of a new generation, the sense of things coming apart, was not just an American but a worldwide phenomenon. Yeats's "The Second Coming" was much quoted: *The centre cannot hold; mere anarchy is loosed upon the world.* *

From the events that made 1968 a year of disillusion and disorientation, many were directly relevant to the presidential drama also played out that year:

> *January 30:* During a supposedly agreed truce for the first day of Tet—the lunar New Year in Indochina—fifty thousand Vietcong and North Vietnamese troops launched a coordinated offensive. Thirty provincial capitals in South Vietnam were attacked simultaneously; major battles erupted in Saigon and Hue. From January 28 to February 3, 416 Americans were killed and 2,757 were wounded. Over 100,000 South Vietnamese homes were damaged or destroyed and property damage was estimated at more than $173 million.
>
> The extent of the offensive startled even the Johnson administration. The biggest shocker to ordinary Americans, however, was the brief occupation by Vietcong forces of several buildings in the Ameri-

---

*After Secretary of Defense Robert McNamara announced the Johnson administration's decision to build a partial defense against a nuclear missile attack in 1967—a decision in which McNamara only reluctantly concurred—he sent me without comment a copy of "The Second Coming." I sent him back Yeats's "Lapis Lazuli," a greater poem, and one that has a different but not unrelated outlook.

can embassy compound in the heart of Saigon. The occupation was not important militarily but it was devastating psychologically; extensive television news coverage of the embassy battle soon reached home screens in the U.S., with strong and depressing effect on civilian morale.

Just the previous autumn, General William C. Westmoreland had spread the good news that light could be seen at the end of the tunnel. Westmoreland now called the Tet offensive a "military defeat" for the Vietcong (who, indeed, were all but wiped out as a fighting force by American counterattacks); but support in the U.S. had been fundamentally impaired—particularly by the piercing of the embassy compound—for the war the North Vietnamese were well able to continue. That support was never to be restored.

"What the hell is going on?" the usually imperturbable Walter Cronkite of CBS News was quoted as saying. "I thought we were winning this war."

He was not alone in that mood. Senator John Stennis of Mississippi, the influential chairman of the Armed Forces Committee and a strong supporter of the war, called the attacks "embarrassing" and "humiliating to the Johnson Administration"—"a victory of surprise" if not "in a military sense."

If Hanoi lost the battle, Tet was ultimately to win the war. Never before had Americans, save perhaps for Southerners in 1865, had to face such devastating defeat as the traumatizing impact of Tet now foretold.

February 29: The President's National Advisory Commission on Civil Disorders (a polite name for the black rioting that had wracked American cities in 1967 and 1968) reported that the nation was "moving toward two societies, one black, one white—separate and unequal"; and the cause, the commission said, was not a Communist or any other kind of conspiracy. It was the "white racism" of ordinary Americans. Much money and effort would be needed to reverse the situation but the report concluded that there was "no higher priority for national action and no higher claim on the nation's conscience."

The Kerner report (named for the commission's chairman, Governor Otto Kerner of Illinois) moved some Americans, disturbed most and infuriated many. But its recommendations, in fact, were *not* the nation's highest priority, or likely to be; instead, Vietnam—bloody and unwinnable—appeared to be soaking up the resources needed to bring black and white Americans into some semblance of an orderly and decent society. Generations that had known the patriotic fervor of World War II and the social complacency of the fifties could hardly comprehend what was happening.

April 23: Dissent from the war—protests and demonstrations of all kinds—was commonplace by the spring of 1968. But it flared into a new dimension when black and white students paralyzed Columbia University in New York.

Erupting from a protest against the university's plan to build a gymnasium opposed by blacks in Harlem, the Columbia demonstrations quickly turned into a general student strike joined by numerous women from Barnard College. Seizing and occupying campus buildings, including the office of President Grayson Kirk of Columbia, the students shut down the university for a week, until a thousand New York policemen, wielding nightsticks, forcibly evicted them on April 30. One hundred thirty-two students, four faculty members and twelve policemen were injured in the recapture; 707 persons were arrested.

The Columbia episode seemed to have lit a fuse; similar student turmoil erupted, that spring, on campus after campus—including such hallowed halls of ivy as Princeton, Stanford and Cornell. What had happened, many Americans wondered irately or sadly, to Harold Teen and Andy Hardy, to the beer parties and Saturday-afternoon football that had symbolized college life in the fifties? Calls for "law and order" took on a new emphasis.

June 29: American deaths in Vietnam reached 25,752—9,557 of them in combat in the first six months of 1968, or 138 more than had been killed in all of 1967.

August 20–21: An old menace reminded the nation that there was more to worry about than Vietnam, race riots and rebelling students. Soviet tanks and more than two hundred thousand Warsaw Pact troops rolled into Prague to crush the Czech movement toward "communism with a human face." The political casualties included Alexander Dubček and other Czech Communists who had tried in the hopeful "Prague spring" to liberalize their party and nation; they lost their positions and their battle, the Czech populace its new freedoms.

Lyndon Johnson was another victim; he had been scheduled to fly to Moscow to open arms control talks with the Soviets, on the same day the Warsaw powers invaded. Their action forced him to cancel his trip and an initiative he had hoped would salvage his administration's reputation.

August 25–31: In Vietnam in that week alone, 408 Americans were killed, and Americans claimed to have killed 4,755 Vietnamese. Since

1961, American casualties totalled 27,508 killed and 171,809 wounded.

Before 1968, even as the many other upheavals of the sixties developed, most Americans had thought of their nation as a mostly finished work—rich, secure, free—requiring only a little tinkering now and then, a Supreme Court decision or a legislative act, to trim its ragged edges. The year 1968 took away what remained of that illusion and supplanted it with a sense of all but irresistible tides of change, the order of things imperiled.

Against that backdrop of shaken faith, rejected values and weakened institutions, a president had to be elected. In such a time, Richard Nixon—no matter his new standing among Republicans—seemed at first glance an unlikely prospect.

He was, after all, a two-time loser in big-time politics, the political product of the bygone ages of Stalinism and McCarthyism, a nationalist hawk who denounced draft resisters, appealed to old-fashioned patriotism and preached an unchanged American exceptionalism. Nixon's idea of student activism was the cheering section at a college football game, and his frequent calls for law and order sounded suspiciously like code words for a crackdown on blacks and other demonstrators. Nixonian innuendo also could make the "peace movement" appear the naive victim of foreign influences.

As for social developments like the sexual revolution, the counterculture and rock music, Richard Nixon—well over thirty, sobersided, uptight and hard-nosed—remained indisputably a "square." He was out of the past, "the old politics," in a time in which the apparent future seemed to be struggling to rid itself of history.

Amid so much upheaval, however, some of it real and permanent, some of it illusory and passing, much also was unchanged, in some cases hardened in place. Many Americans cried out for the return of stability, respect for authority, the primacy of traditional values. Not all were alienated by the war—but many were by kids with long hair, students burning draft cards, blacks marching in the streets, young girls shouting obscenities at police officers, college boys "smoking dope" and hippies "shooting up."

Black rioting in the cities and the rise of the black power movement brought particularly hostile responses—the so-called white backlash. White ethnic groups felt themselves threatened in their hard-won social and economic status; and they deeply resented the fact—as they saw it—that too much was being "given" to the blacks too quickly.

Hadn't these sons and daughters of immigrants "got ahead" in the unadmitted but ferocious class struggles of American society through hard work, sacrifice, patience, patriotism, persistence? Blacks should make it, if at all, in the same way, they believed, deprecating the Kerner commission's idea that slavery, segregation, economic change and skin pigment—much less "racism"—had imposed long-term handicaps on American blacks that the lowliest immigrants had not suffered. Even Lyndon Johnson, who had pushed the Civil Rights Act of 1964 and the Voting Rights Act, telling Congress in his Texas accent that "we shall overcome!" seemed to be backsliding if not backlashing.

"Freedom is not enough," he had told the Howard University class of 1965, in one of the great presidential speeches of the twentieth century:

> You do not take a person who, for years, has been hobbled by chains and liberate him, bring him up to the starting line of a race and then say, "You are free to compete with all the others," and still justly believe that you have been completely fair. Thus, it is not enough just to open the gates of opportunity. All our citizens must have the ability to walk through those gates.

In 1966, nevertheless, he had complained at a news conference that blacks should realize that they were only 10 percent of the population, that by explosions of violence they were jeopardizing gains already made, that most Americans believed in peaceful progress for blacks and that he had done all he could to see that "equality was given." Blacks therefore ought to "cooperate with constituted authority." Those views were widespread and strongly held among whites in 1968, and still are.

Blacks might see "constituted authority" as the corrupt city regimes that brutalized them, or the draft that sent them to Vietnam and left white middle-class youths in college; blacks might wonder why equality had to be "given" to them when it was the unquestioned right of others. But plenty of whites in every region and city, not just the South, put Johnson's complaint in harsher terms; some reacted to black activism with political fervor, some with violence.

"Hippies"—the term applied scornfully to almost any white protester, radical or eccentric—were almost as disdained, even as despised, in middle-class America as the most demanding blacks. Blacks, it was sometimes conceded, *might* have some real grievances; hippies only flouted the values by which many Americans—particularly ethnic Americans—had lived, as well as worked and prospered.

Through marijuana, sex and obscenity, hippies mocked accepted morality; by "dropping out and turning on," they thumbed their noses at the work ethic (and often at the parents whose allowances supported them); by their demonstrations and protest marches, they defied the authority on which society depended for order. Hippies burned bras and the flag, actually and symbolically.

To those millions of Americans who viewed the scene of the sixties with disquiet, fear, bewilderment, anger or disgust, Richard Nixon had much to offer. If he was out of another era, it was one to which those Americans longed to return; if he was not "with it," neither were they; and if he wanted quiet streets, traditional values and American victory in a foreign war, so did they.

In early 1968, however, Nixon was by no means the clearest political beneficiary nor exploiter of such sentiments. For some, that dubious honor belonged to the volatile George Corley Wallace of Alabama. After losing his first race for governor, Wallace had sworn he would never be "outniggered" again, and in 1963 he had "stood in the schoolhouse door" in vain but politically fruitful protest against the integration of the state university.

Having installed his wife Lurleen to succeed him as governor of Alabama, Wallace made no secret of his plans to run for president on a third-party ticket in 1968, to capitalize on white backlash and on orthodox Americans' resentment of draft resisters, "longhairs," antiwar protesters and what many considered the breakdown of law and order.

"If I ever get to be president," Wallace liked to say, in one of his most celebrated campaign routines, "and any of these demonstrators lay down in front of my car, it'll be the last car they ever lay down in front of."

Ignorant but shrewd, a man of vulgar but irrepressible vitality, imagination and energy, Wallace once told me that his political success was owing not least to his understanding of "the uses of defiance." That was one thing that made him formidable in 1968.

No one save his most fanatical supporters in the South—Alabama bumper stickers proclaimed it "Wallace Country"—believed he could be elected president; the confident Wallace himself must have had his doubts. But his would be a campaign of defiance that might take some Southern states away from the Democrats, might win enough popular votes to change the major-party outcome in some other states, and might yield enough electoral votes to deny any other candidate the necessary majority. That would throw the election into the House of Representatives (something that had happened only twice before, in 1824 and 1876), and no one could predict what might happen there.

Wallace knew, too, how to touch his shabby cause with an ersatz moral gloss. With unerring instinct, he could arouse latent racial antagonism while appealing to common sense and Christian duty; with vivid oratory he lamented the vanished righteousness of another day and painted every discontent and complexity of contemporary life in terms of a plot against that American icon, "the average man": "Why, you can't even walk in the shadow of the White House in Washington, D.C., lessen you got two police dogs with you."

These gifts of the "Alabama Gamecock," as he liked supporters to call him, were widely known and feared. A consensus, could one have been had, probably would have held that Wallace was most likely to damage the Democrats (his own party nominally, though he contended in his piny-woods style that "they ain't a dime's worth of difference in the two parties anyway"). This plausible theory held that he would win Alabama and other usually Democratic Southern states, and that elsewhere, ethnic voters and "hard-hat" union men, usually Democrats, would desert to his backlash banner.

The Democrats, however, had greater political troubles than George Wallace. The war in Vietnam and the president who was seen as its implacable proponent had divided the country into antagonistic camps. Despite Lyndon Johnson's brilliant performance following Kennedy's assassination, his liberal political achievements and his landslide victory over Goldwater, the president's public standing had largely vanished by 1968. His vanity, his overbearing manner, occasional crudity, glowering presence and reputation for crafty maneuvering had made him too nearly an object of fear to permit him the popularity with which he had begun in the White House.

Johnson's unlimited faith in federal action, moreover, made him precisely the wrong kind of president to cope with an age of revolt, a time when people striving to retain their individuality were beginning to question smothering if benevolent authority administered through overpowering institutions.

A man who could play upon American government as if it were an organ made for his hands, and who for a while made it function more smoothly than had any president of modern times, Lyndon Johnson naturally came to represent personally what the disillusioned saw as government unresponsiveness to public opinion, its indifference to attitudes—such as opposition to the war—widely held, and its apparently unchecked powers.

Because of his campaign pledges in 1964 not to do what, in fact, he later did do in Vietnam, and because of the desperate tactics he was driven to against those he publicly sneered at as "nervous Nellies"—but secretly feared—Johnson and his "credibility gap" also became symbols of evasion, half-truth, deception and expedience. Those were the qualities that most outraged those young Americans who judged politics in the sixties not by its pragmatic achievements nor by the precedents of the thirties, but by its moral content and popular origins.

As the months passed, however, it was the war, "LBJ's war," a war that couldn't be won or justified, alienating millions of Americans, dividing the country, sapping its resources, leaving the president's visionary "Great Society" mostly to wither on the budgetary vine, making Johnson himself virtually a prisoner in the White House—it was "the bitch of a war on the other side of the world," more than any other cause, that brought his giant's downfall. Of what other president had so many protesters so often chanted such a cruel refrain:

> Hey, hey, LBJ!
> How many kids
> Did you kill today?

As 1968 opened, however, few doubted that Lyndon Johnson would be the Democratic nominee. I had stated this case with unfortunate force in a *Times* column for October 31, 1967:

> One of the questions most frequently asked . . . these days is whether there is a real possibility that the Democratic party will repudiate President Johnson next year and nominate Robert Kennedy.
>
> Once this possibility is downgraded with suitable historical references, the next question follows as the night the day: Well, then, isn't it possible that Johnson will withdraw?
>
> This wistful proposition can be demolished with some confidence. It is about as likely, assuming his good health, that Lyndon Johnson will quit the White House and go back to Texas as it is that Dean Rusk will turn dove, Dick Nixon will stop running, or J. Edgar Hoover will retire.

Antiwar forces, mostly Democrats who saw Johnson's basic weakness despite the powers of his office and his apparent dominance of their party, nevertheless sought an alternative. This "dump Johnson" movement, led by the liberal activist Allard Lowenstein, signally failed in its major effort—to recruit Senator Robert F. Kennedy of New York, at last an avowed opponent of the war, to lead an insurgency against Johnson.

Robert Kennedy and the president detested and—in different ways—feared each other. Kennedy believed that if he ran against Johnson, he would be seen as acting out of personal animosity, as trying to regain the presidential office lost to the Kennedy family and taken by Johnson. Robert Kennedy thought such an insurgency would set off civil war within the Democratic party, and feared also that if he led it, the damaging reputation he already had for ruthlessness would be enhanced.

This was not an imagined problem. When Lyndon Johnson decided in 1964 to take no member of the cabinet as his vice presidential running mate, his scarcely disguised aim was to throw Attorney General Robert Kennedy over the side without appearing to have focused on him alone. LBJ had no intention of putting Kennedy on his ticket, in any case.

But when he explained his decision in a White House luncheon with Douglas Kiker of the *New York Herald Tribune,* Philip Potter of the

Baltimore Sun and me, Johnson produced a poll showing that Kennedy had a "cop image," owing to his pursuit of organized crime figures and what was widely seen as his vendetta against Jimmy Hoffa, the Teamsters Union leader. The cop image would damage the ticket, Johnson believed; or perhaps he was only trying to justify his decision to pass over Bob Kennedy. But the image was real.

In 1968, Kennedy probably shared the nearly universal view that an eligible president, even an unpopular and embattled one, could not be denied renomination by his own party. Not since James G. Blaine took the Republican nomination away from President Chester A. Arthur in 1884 had it happened—and Blaine lost the general election to Grover Cleveland.

Liberal Democrats' failure, despite repeated efforts, to dump Harry Truman in 1948 provided a recent and cautionary example of the difficulties involved in denying renomination to an eligible president. As Truman had known, the man in the White House simply had too much power over his party.

Lowenstein failed also to persuade several others to take on Johnson: General James Gavin, John Kenneth Galbraith, Senator George McGovern of South Dakota. Finally, he found his man in the unlikely person—so it was thought in Washington—of Senator Eugene McCarthy of Minnesota, who announced his decision to run for president on November 30, 1967.

Once almost a protégé of Senate Majority Leader Lyndon Johnson, McCarthy had been angered when Johnson passed him over and chose Minnesota's other senator, Hubert Humphrey, for vice presidential running mate in 1964. McCarthy was a good hater, but he was not in 1968 motivated entirely by revenge; he had become a bona fide opponent of the war and soon saw that he had been fortunate to be left out of Johnson's presidential orbit. His decision to challenge Johnson and the war—he insisted to skeptical reporters—had been reached on principle rather than on the belief that he actually could win the presidency.

Principle really was at work, at least in part. Undersecretary of State Nicholas deB. Katzenbach had told a Senate committee in November that the Tonkin Gulf resolution Johnson had sponsored in 1964 was "the functional equivalent of a declaration of war." Upon hearing that, McCarthy stalked angrily from the hearing room and told E. W. Kenworthy of the *New York Times:* "It's got to be taken to the country."

McCarthy declared himself concerned also by Americans' seeming inability to change the war policy through established political channels, by the power of unresponsive political institutions and leaders and by the growing tendency of young people to move outside those channels into street demonstrations and other forms of resistance—a dangerous trend in a democracy, suggesting that it was failing.

He hoped, the Minnesotan said in his announcement of candidacy, "that this challenge . . . may alleviate to at least some degree this sense of political helplessness and restore to many people a belief in the processes of American politics and American government."

From the start of his campaign, therefore, McCarthy moved on a different course from the one expected of Robert Kennedy. The latter's opposition to Johnson was just as real, but it was based more nearly on specific issues—the war, the problems of race, poverty and children, violence in the streets. Kennedy wanted to *use* the power of government to deal with these and other issues. McCarthy wanted to restrain that power.

McCarthy was, besides, a Roman Catholic intellectual with a distant manner and a hard eye for fools, an Irishman who knew how to bear a grudge and resented what he called "political Catholics" like the Kennedys. He had not been a leading senator or a heavyweight politician and was not at first taken seriously—perhaps even by himself. A renowned, rather cynical wit, he replied when asked if he thought he might be committing political suicide, that it would be more nearly an execution. Later, in cold and snowy New Hampshire, when asked if he felt a groundswell of support for his candidacy, he said it was only a "frost heave."

And so it was, at first; in late 1967 polls, he had the support of only 17 percent of Democrats. A serious if not compelling poet, something of a mystic and an indifferent campaigner in the usual glad-handing sense, McCarthy was not an instant hero to every dissenter from the war. To I. F. Stone, the wise and perceptive "radical" journalist, McCarthy gave "the uneasy feeling that he really doesn't give a damn." Stone was not alone in that view.

McCarthy's mere presence in the race nevertheless encouraged Republicans to think they might be able to defeat a divided Democratic party in the general election. They had no lack of horses for the race—notably square-jawed Governor George Romney of Michigan, an avowed candidate; the new party star and old movie hero, Governor Ronald Reagan of California; the liberal perennial, Governor Nelson Rockefeller of New York, who professed to be standing aside in favor of Romney; and indisputably, if somewhat surprisingly, Richard Milhous Nixon—the goat of 1960 and 1962 turned hero in 1966, the "chronic campaigner" who had stumped the country so often that his was one of the most recognized, although not revered, names in America.

After Romney's reelection in 1966, the governor had surged ahead of Lyndon Johnson in the polls, 54 to 46; he led Nixon for the Republican nomination by 51 to 42. But by 1968, Romney had all but talked himself out of contention.

On his first precampaign swing in 1967, a tour through Alaska, some of the mountain states, Arizona and New Mexico, the big national press entourage attracted by a front-runner began to wonder if Romney's square jaw was not attached to a blockhead. His speeches were unremarkable; but in each of five news conferences in six days, he proved not only unable to define a coherent position on Vietnam, but also seemed to become more confused, and confusing, with each effort.

How, reporters asked themselves and each other, could a man so easily disconcerted under questioning, and so quickly goaded into intemperate or inexplicable statements, expect to make presidential policies—even if he *could* shape them effectively—understandable to the public?

Then, in August 1967, on a Detroit television program, Romney disastrously reinforced this pejorative impression. Asked about inconsistencies in his numerous statements about Vietnam, the governor replied:

> Well, you know when I came back from Vietnam [two years earlier], I just had the greatest brainwashing that anybody can get when you go over to Vietnam. Not only by the generals, but also by the diplomatic corps over there, and they do a very thorough job. And since returning from Vietnam, I've gone into the history of Vietnam, all the way back into World War II and before. And, as a result, I have changed my mind. . . . I no longer believe that it was necessary for us to get involved in South Vietnam to stop Communist aggression.

Romney finally had taken a clear stand disputing the supposed reason for waging the war. But this declaration, which might have brought him strong support from antiwar groups, was mostly lost in the furor over the incautious "brainwashing" remark. The admission that he *could* have been "brainwashed"—a term from the Korean War, associated with robotlike acceptance and repetition of foreign propaganda—was not only unpresidential; it encapsulated reporters' sense of Romney as a bumbler, which they had no doubt passed along to the public, with or without intent. His statement brought him only ridicule, the one thing no candidate needs.

The *Detroit News* demanded that Romney withdraw from the presidential race to clear the way for Rockefeller. The same editorial noted that Romney's trip to Vietnam had been two years before the television interview, and that the governor had *supported* the war throughout the interval. In a speech at Hartford in April 1967, for example, Romney had declared that "our military effort must succeed"—moving Lyndon Johnson, no doubt with 1968 in mind, to compliment the Republican governor publicly on his "strong endorsement of the fundamentals" of Johnson's policy!

"How long," the *News* asked sarcastically, "does a brainwashing linger?"

The word did earn Romney minor cult approval in the antiwar movement, which regarded support for Johnson's Vietnam policy as a sort of *national* brainwashing. But who wanted a president who could be "brain-washed" and then not recover for two years? Romney immediately dropped sixteen points in the Harris poll; he had dealt the probable death-blow to his own presidential candidacy, though in his pontifical fashion he vowed to continue the race.

Rockefeller had financed much of the Romney campaign and was Romney's most prominent supporter—with the result that Romney was widely considered a mere stalking-horse for the New York governor. Romney himself was too messianic to have played such a role deliberately; but Nixon, for one, never believed Romney had the right combination of qualities to win the nomination, and saw Romney's floundering campaign both as a nonstarter that Rockefeller ultimately would have to take over, and as a welcome setup that would give Richard Nixon an easy opponent to knock over in the early primaries.

Rockefeller, traumatized by the vicious opposition of the party's right wing in 1964, portrayed himself as anxious for someone else to carry the liberal banner in 1968. He issued frequent bulletins insisting he was not a candidate—in fact, did not even want to be president. Few political leaders, certainly not Nixon—who knew something about the presidential obses-sion—took the governor seriously.

After the debacle of 1964, when he had been so roundly booed at the Cow Palace in San Francisco, the ebullient Rockefeller had fought back to win his third gubernatorial term in New York. He obviously had the means, the experience and the name recognition, however unfavorable within his own party, to be a strong candidate. No matter what he said, therefore, he could not be dismissed; and Governor Spiro T. Agnew of Maryland opened late in 1967 a "draft Rocky" campaign. Rockefeller ostentatiously gave it no public support.

Ronald Reagan, who had launched himself into political prominence with his nationally televised speech on behalf of Barry Goldwater late in the 1964 campaign, had defeated Pat Brown in 1966 to become governor of the most populous state. No one holding that office could be dismissed either, especially one with Reagan's charm and Hollywood glamour.

He declared himself, however, only a "favorite son," in order to keep control of the large California delegation. The favorite-son device, how-ever, forced Reagan to leave his name in the running for the Oregon primary; he said he couldn't swear he was not a candidate—as required to get off the ballot in that state—and still keep his favorite-son campaign honest. This decision set political heads to nodding cynically.

When it became known that F. Clifton White, the bow-tied Machiavelli of Goldwater's nomination, had shifted his considerable talents to Reagan, and after the handsome governor proved himself a top crowd-pleaser and fund-raiser outside California—in Wisconsin and South Carolina, for ex-

ample—political buffs generally considered him a real contender, not just
a favorite son. After all, Reagan was Goldwater's natural heir, without
Goldwater's fatal candor and disdain for political realities.

Inevitably, the idea arose of a "dream ticket": Rockefeller and Reagan,
two renowned campaigners joining the two most populous states, East and
West, left and right. No one ever quite said which would be at the top of
the ticket, and the dream went nowhere—which is where perfect political
dreams usually go. Neither governor wanted any part of the other, or of
such a deal. It had been mostly a liberal Republican inspiration anyway,
an effort to get the monkey of conservative opposition off Rockefeller's
back.

But with George Romney largely discredited, talk in the two wings of
the party about Rockefeller and Reagan put the major remaining possibility, Richard Nixon, right where he always wanted to be—in the center.

8

★

Shocks

★

We are a great country, an unselfish country, and a compassionate country. I intend to make that my basis for running.

—Robert Kennedy's last speech,
June 4, 1968

Not long after the news of the Tet offensive (which began on January 30, 1968) had spread across the U.S., I sat in a room of the New Hampshire Highway Hotel in Concord with other reporters, in a political bull session with Eugene McCarthy. Most of us still gave him little if any chance to unseat Lyndon Johnson or even to run well against him in conservative New Hampshire.

Johnson had not allowed his name to go on the ballot there, but his surrogate, Senator Tom McIntyre, was active on the president's behalf, along with most New Hampshire regular Democrats. They were waging an intense and well-financed write-in campaign and had predicted incautiously that McCarthy would get less than 10 percent of the primary vote.

"What do you think this new Vietcong offensive will do to the campaign?" someone asked McCarthy.

Offbeat as always, he had just come in from playing in a local ice hockey game and was—I wrote of that motel-room encounter—"dropping his sizzling sentences like pats of butter on a red-hot griddle." But neither his wisecracks nor his sometimes acid manner could conceal the fact that he was a shrewd political judge.

"Give it three weeks," he said. "Time to sink in. By then it could make the difference."

. . .

In October 1967, a Gallup poll put Richard Nixon far ahead of his presidential rivals among Republicans—42 percent to Rockefeller's 18, 14 for Reagan and 13 for Romney. For the first time, moreover, Gallup also found Nixon ahead of President Johnson, 49 to 45.

Paradoxically, that lead, narrow as it was, and considering Johnson's obvious political difficulties, actually suggested Nixon's major—some thought insurmountable—handicap: his "loser's image" from 1960 and 1962. A poll defeated no one at the ballot box; and it was only good for the day it was taken—witness Romney's decline. Richard Nixon needed to defeat a live opponent in a real primary.

At a Republican governors' conference in Palm Beach that October, influential governors seemed torn between accepting Nixon as a potential nominee and warning that he had been and still might be a loser. A "draft Rockefeller" movement to stop Nixon, the moderate John Love of Colorado warned, would be "a destructive thing"—but he prefaced the statement with a cautious proviso: "If Nixon wins the first two or three primaries. . . ."

Nixon recognized his problem. At the Palm Beach conference, his operatives encouraged Governor Tim Babcock of Montana—thought to be a Reagan leaner (though secretly he was committed to Nixon)—to say that he'd accept Nixon on the national ticket if the former vice president could win the first two primaries. Thus, both Love and Babcock (left and right, more or less) planted the idea that a few primary victories could bury the reputation of Nixon, the centrist, as a loser.[1]

Polls convinced Nixon and his advisers that unless he made some horrendous blunder he could crush Romney in New Hampshire. Reagan's favorite-son strategy would keep him out. Rockefeller, still Romney's professed backer, could not enter against his own supposed candidate. It would be one on one, Nixon versus Romney; so New Hampshire appeared to be the place where the loser's image could be erased.

Romney's own polls showed Nixon with an insurmountable lead in New Hampshire—64 to 13, in late December 1967. So even Romney probably would not have competed in that state, which would vote on March 12, had his fortunes not declined so precipitously. His desperation strategy was simply to do better than expected in New Hampshire, which might create a sense of momentum for his campaign, while sustaining Nixon's reputation as a loser.

Loudly proclaiming himself a 5-to-1 underdog, Romney therefore plunged into New Hampshire in January with the fervor of an evangelist— which in many ways the Mormon governor was—and the energy of a young bull. But Nixon, in his disciplined new style, did not even allow his name to be entered in the primary until an hour or so before the deadline, and did not go personally to the state until February 1.

Long before that, Romney was roaming New Hampshire from one end to the other, shaking hands and invading pool halls, cafés, factories, church meetings and living rooms. He even managed finally to put out a reasonable position on Vietnam, calling for an "internal settlement" between Saigon and the Vietcong's National Liberation Front, and the ultimate "guaranteed neutralization" of Vietnam.

Romney also began to savage Nixon as a "me-too" candidate whose "glib" evasions could not hide the fact that his Vietnam policy was "no more than a blurred carbon copy of the discredited Johnson policies for ending the war." Frequently, too, he spoke of the "Johnson-Nixon policy of more and more military escalation."

Nixon reacted cooly. Relying on extensive and efficient organization, he disdained Romney's challenges to debate, passed almost contemptuously over Romney's Vietnam speech, ignored the governor's attacks and—after he finally joined the race personally—moved along serenely from planned stop to planned stop, speaking largely in generalities. He made leisurely trips to other states, and as if he were already the nominee directed his remarks not at Romney but at the state of the nation and the "new leadership" he said it needed and deserved.

Meanwhile, a Rockefeller write-in campaign had developed and Rockefeller—never too surefooted in national politics—helped it along, thus further damaging Romney, when he conceded to reporters on February 24 that he'd accept a draft in "the unlikely event. . . ." Rockefeller's secret strategy, however, was to stay out of the primaries—to avoid reawakening right-wing ire left over from 1964—at least until Oregon in May.

The ill-considered statement about the possibility of a draft was the next-to-last straw for George Romney. The bluff governor then was confronted on February 26 with depressing news from Fred Currier, his preferred polltaker. Not only was Nixon still far ahead in New Hampshire, Currier reported; he actually had *gained,* despite all Romney's hail-fellow campaigning.

Romney had no realistic alternative but to withdraw, both to spare himself humiliation on March 12, and to keep a pledge he had made to moderate Republican governors a year earlier, that if he found he could not win the nomination, he would clear the way for a moderate who might—presumably Rockefeller. On February 29, as gracefully as possible, George Romney dropped out.

Thus, almost at the last moment—as Romney also intended—Nixon was denied the smashing, knockout victory he had hoped would end forever his loser's image. He still hadn't personally beaten anybody at the polls; there were no numbers, no ballot count, no percentages to boast about. Romney, moreover, was no longer in the race, which meant the more formidable Rockefeller had a clear track to enter.

Romney's withdrawal, however, was less spectacular than developments in Vietnam and in the other party. Not only was McCarthy's campaign against Johnson bearing out his motel-room prediction that the Tet offensive eventually would make a difference; on February 9, the powerful voice of Robert Kennedy delivered what I termed, in a column in the *New York Times*, "the most sweeping and detailed indictment of the war and of the Administration's policy yet heard from any leading figure in either party."

Kennedy maintained his refusal to run against the president, but Tet plainly had moved him to sharpen his criticism:

> Half a million American soldiers with 700,000 Vietnamese allies, with total command of the air, total command of the sea, backed by huge resources and the most modern weapons, were unable to secure even a single city from the attacks of an enemy whose total strength is about 250,000.

On March 5, just before the filing deadline in Massachusetts, Lyndon Johnson ordered that his name not be entered in the primary there, just as it had not been in New Hampshire. That meant that Eugene McCarthy, running officially unopposed in a state where write-in voting had been made difficult, would win all of Massachusetts' seventy-two delegates to the Democratic National Convention.

Johnson and his campaign manager, James Rowe—an astute Democratic veteran with credentials back to the New Deal—were prepared, in fact, to stay officially out of *all* the primaries, a decision that would cost them only about four hundred of the more than twenty-five hundred delegates. They thought it good politics to picture the president as too busy running the war and the country to run in primaries; and anyway it would have cost about half a million dollars—a lot of campaign money in 1968— to be sure of subduing McCarthy in liberal Massachusetts. Johnson's decision nonetheless handed McCarthy a state delegation without a fight and the seeming distinction of having "scared," or at least maneuvered, the president out of Massachusetts.

On Sunday, March 10, my column in the *Times* asserted: "Slowly, perhaps not quite surely, but with increasing momentum, American public opinion seems to be moving to the conclusion that the war in Vietnam is a creeping disaster that military means cannot salvage."

Among the "straws in the wind" adduced to support this conclusion was a Gallup poll taken in March, in which for the first time a plurality of respondents (49 percent) said they believed the deployment of American troops in Vietnam had been a mistake. That was a substantial increase from December ("the last moment of euphoria before the Tet offensive"). Sixty-one percent, moreover, thought the U.S. and South Vietnam were losing the war, or making no progress toward winning it.

Other "straws": Robert Kennedy was reported to be "reconsidering" whether to run for president. Senate debate was provoking more criticism—the conservative Senator Harry F. Byrd, Jr., of Virginia asking, for example, "Is not now the time for a reappraisal of our policies and objectives?"

Nelson Rockefeller, long a hawk, also had said at a news conference that "what we need is to find moderate solutions. . . . [T]o reach for a gun or to call in the military isn't necessarily the best solution."

But perhaps the most significant straw was Richard Nixon's new tactic of reminding his audiences that he had been part of a Republican administration that ended the Korean War by negotiation. Nixon rarely said anything without a keen sense of what his audience wanted to hear.

The Republican front-runner had even declared in New Hampshire in early March that if elected he would "end the war and win the peace." Nixon did not specify then, nor ever throughout the 1968 campaign, how he would accomplish this dual goal. Nor did he, as some in the press wrongly reported, mention "a secret plan" to end the war. What he did say, however, was a far cry from the Nixon of 1966, when he had attacked Johnson for talking too much about negotiation and not enough about military victory—the goal Nixon had been espousing as far back as 1954.

McCarthy, moreover, had been expected by local political experts to win no more than 10 percent of New Hampshire Democrats' votes. But on the weekend before the primary, the same experts were saying that he might win as much as 25 to 30 percent.

Even in ignominious defeat, George Romney of the other party had had much to do with McCarthy's rise; after Romney withdrew on February 29, the political press had turned its attention from the suddenly uncontested Republican primary to the Democratic battle. Partially as a result, the McCarthy effort—he was the only Democrat actually campaigning in New Hampshire—was transformed in the headlines from a hopeless run into a dramatic challenge to the president and the war.

On Saturday night, March 9, just over a month after Tet and with the New Hampshire primary to be held on the following Tuesday, Washington's power structure—and much of the nation's—settled down to enjoy the annual dinner and satirical stage show of the Gridiron Club. Before the main course could be served, early editions of the *New York Times* appeared, with the lead story that General William C. Westmoreland had called for 206,000 more troops for Vietnam. Word of that blockbuster exclusive quickly began to spread among the white-tied diners, whose hosts were the leading figures of Washington journalism.

Having become the *Times*'s Washington Bureau chief, I took a certain newspaperman's satisfaction in seeing our competitors leave their turtle soup and scramble around to match our story—not easy at about 10 P.M. on Saturday. Like many other Americans, however, I was greatly disquieted by the story itself, which I had approved before it appeared.

Only months before, Westmoreland, Ambassador Ellsworth Bunker and other impressive voices had assured the nation that victory was in sight. Now the administration was considering a request that would increase by 40 percent the size of the American command. How many more lives were yet to be poured into the vast killing grounds of Indochina?*

By then, the fabled Children's Crusade had come to New Hampshire—literally thousands of high school and college students from all over the nation getting haircuts, putting on neckties and replacing blue jeans with skirts in order to be "clean for Gene" McCarthy, their new antiwar hero.

They rang doorbells and collared voters all over New Hampshire—canvassing for the antiwar candidate in enthusiastic and effective numbers never before seen in that or any state, carrying their idealism, the McCarthy message, and their disdain for the hated Johnson to every corner of the state. One of McCarthy's stated goals had been to channel the energies of the young into constructive political action, rather than leaving it to explode in street demonstrations; in New Hampshire, at least on that score, he clearly was succeeding.

Senator McIntyre, Governor John W. King and other Johnson representatives felt the heat of the Children's Crusade and responded none too generously. There would be "joy in Hanoi," their radio commercials blared, if Johnson lost; a vote against the president, in fact, would not be so much a vote for Eugene McCarthy as for Ho Chi Minh. This response was in line with Johnson's frequent strictures on those who wanted to "bug out" or, in his Texas usage, "tuck tail and run."

McCarthy's response to that motel-room question about Tet, however, had been only a few days off the mark. On March 12, 1968, he rolled up 42 percent of the New Hampshire Democratic vote against the president of the United States and the party hierachy of the state—a psychological victory almost as stunning as that of the Vietcong at Tet.

Johnson actually had won with 48 percent, and as a write-in candidate at that. In the major city of Portsmouth, however, McCarthy had 66 percent of the vote to less than 30 for the president. In Keene, Nashua and Dover—also cities, by New Hampshire standards—where Johnson had been expected to smash him, McCarthy won more than 40 percent of the vote. Only in Manchester, the largest city in the state, did he run poorly.

All over New Hampshire, Democratic turnout was heavier than in 1964.

---

*In the end, mercifully, the huge reinforcement was not carried out. About eleven thousand more troops soon were sent, and in April twenty-four thousand reservists were mobilized, with perhaps ten thousand ultimately going to Vietnam.

That reflected high interest in the Johnson-McCarthy campaign, and the increased participation of independents, most of whom voted against the president. Johnson's vulnerability on the war issue had been exposed dramatically, and speculation rose immediately that had Robert Kennedy challenged him, rather than the lesser-known McCarthy, the president would have suffered actual as well as "moral" defeat.

McCarthy's showing diverted attention from, though it could not conceal, the Republican primary. Running all but unopposed save for the unimpressive Rockefeller write-in—which got no further support from the governor—Richard Nixon captured an extraordinary 80 percent of the vote. He ran up huge totals in the New Hampshire cities and swept the rural and upstate vote.

"That," Nixon pointedly told the press, "will impress those who have been waiting to find a winner."

"There was no competition," said Rockefeller, just as pointedly.

Nixon surely had the better of *that* exchange. If he had not quite destroyed his loser's reputation as he had hoped, he had taken a long step toward doing so. He could draw comfort, moreover, both from the intraparty battle that had erupted among Democrats, and from the evidence that Lyndon Johnson was in deep political trouble—a fact that was helpful to Nixon even among Republicans: the weaker Johnson seemed, the less they would worry that Richard Nixon had been a loser in 1960 and 1962.

If McCarthy and Nixon were the stars of the moment, for two other major figures of American politics—Robert Kennedy and Nelson Rockefeller—New Hampshire changed everything.

By staying out of the race until McCarthy had demonstrated the potential of an antiwar candidacy, Kennedy had given himself the worst of two worlds. First, he had allowed McCarthy to earn the credit for taking on the president, when to do so seemed hopelessly quixotic, and for gaining a moral victory over Johnson in New Hampshire. It was McCarthy who had sensed that millions of Americans wanted to vote against the war and who had been willing to give them their chance to do so.

Now the nation's young people, who had looked to Kennedy both as antiwar leader and as his brother's heir, had flocked to support McCarthy instead. Many believed the Minnesotan was playing a role that had been destined for Robert Kennedy—who had failed it: "I'm going to lose them," Kennedy said of young people, "and I'm going to lose them forever."[2]

Second, if Kennedy decided to run for president after New Hampshire, he would rearouse the "ruthless" image that plagued him by appearing to steal the plum McCarthy had fairly won. Worse, he might succeed only in splitting the antiwar vote against Johnson.

On the other hand, the suddenly important McCarthy campaign made it less likely that Kennedy would be held responsible for dividing a Democratic party that obviously was split already. And as it became more likely that Richard Nixon would be the Republican nominee, it became necessary in Kennedy's mind not only that Johnson should be brought down but that Nixon—whom he held in contempt, as had his brother before him—should be prevented from taking the president's place.

Was not another Kennedy more likely to accomplish both objectives than the relatively unknown and decidedly unorthodox Eugene McCarthy?

Besides, Robert Kennedy was strongly concerned, in early 1968—more than any other candidate or potential candidate—about race relations in America, black riots in the cities, the likelihood of continuing social upheaval. A major reason that he finally decided to run for president, he said in his announcement, was the need for new policies "to end the bloodshed . . . in our cities, policies to close the gap that now exists between black and white, between rich and poor, between young and old in this country."

Some of Robert Kennedy's impassioned defenders, of whom there are many to this day, insist that for all these reasons he made up his mind to run for the presidency on March 5, a week before the New Hampshire primary, and that his announcement was withheld in order not to divert support from McCarthy's effort. But the reaction hardly could have been worse than it turned out to be on March 13, when Kennedy conceded that he was "reassessing" his position, or March 16, when he announced that he would enter the race after all.

Withholding his decision, if that is what he did, made it appear that it was McCarthy's 42 percent in New Hampshire that had changed Kennedy's mind. With Johnson's weakness exposed for all to see, it was easy to believe that ruthless "Bobby" Kennedy had determined to brush McCarthy aside and take over the antiwar movement for his own purposes.

Kennedy tried hard to head off these predictable reactions. In his announcement, he said he admired many of President Johnson's accomplishments, appreciated his kindnesses to the Kennedy family and had "the deepest sympathy for the burden that he carries today." The issue was not personal, he insisted, but consisted of "our profound differences over where we are heading and what we want to accomplish."

As for Gene McCarthy, Kennedy's explanation was elaborate—and tortured. He would actively support McCarthy, he said, because it was "important now that he achieve the largest possible majority next month in Wisconsin, in Pennsylvania and in the Massachusetts primaries."

Kennedy was too late to enter any of those contests. But he said he would run in the California primary on June 4, officials in Oregon and Nebraska would put his name on their primary ballots under state laws, and he left little doubt that he would also enter the Indiana primary.

McCarthy was running in all those states, which raised the question how Kennedy could "actively support" him, in deeds as well as words, by contesting with him for their votes.

Kennedy insisted, nevertheless, that his candidacy "would not be in opposition to [McCarthy's] but in harmony": "My desire is not to divide the strength of those forces seeking a change but rather to increase it. . . . [I]n no state will my efforts be directed against Senator McCarthy."

All this was palpably unrealistic—two Democrats, after all, could not share their party's presidential nomination—but may have been justified tenuously by McCarthy's early insistence that he was running more on principle and for specified purposes than actually to win the presidency. Before their contest was done, both men were to move far away from the protestations of political innocence with which each had entered it.

Kennedy's suggestion that he might run in Indiana, forcing the first possible Kennedy-McCarthy collision, was widely interpreted as a none too subtle effort to force, or perhaps only to invite, McCarthy out of the race. But if Kennedy really thought the Minnesota senator might leave the field to him, he did not know his man (although a high Kennedy adviser already had whispered to me that certain unspecified reasons why McCarthy "should not be president" were known to the Kennedy staff).

McCarthy, in fact, had worked against *John* Kennedy's nomination in 1960, gaining his first national headlines with an eloquent speech in behalf of Adlai Stevenson at that year's national convention. He did not hold the Kennedy brothers in high regard, and he had thought he had Robert Kennedy's assurance that Kennedy would stay out of the 1968 race. Besides, McCarthy's success and sudden notoriety in New Hampshire had diminished his earlier diffidence about his chances to defeat Johnson. All this inflamed his resentment at Kennedy's late entry.

In Green Bay, Wisconsin, on March 16—the day of Kennedy's entry into the race—McCarthy reacted sharply: "An Irishman who announces the day before St. Patrick's Day that he's going to run against another Irishman shouldn't say it's going to be a peaceful relationship." He would not turn down any help Kennedy might give him in Wisconsin, he said, but added that he was "not prepared to deal with anyone."

Later, in his most acidulous manner, McCarthy—without naming Kennedy—spoke of politicians "willing to stay up on the mountain and light signal fires" but unwilling to take part in the battle below. He shrewdly realized, however, that Kennedy's late entry once again gave him the kind of "lonely underdog" role that he had skillfully played in New Hampshire. In fact, he had become a double underdog, battling now not only the president but the supposed power of the Kennedy family.

One hostile reaction to Kennedy's announcement was to his face and from a friend—the reporter Mary McGrory, then of the old *Washington*

Evening Star, and an Irish Catholic who had been considered close to both John and Robert Kennedy. At a news conference after Robert Kennedy announced his decision, she asked if he would stay out of Wisconsin should McCarthy request him to.

"Certainly," Kennedy replied.

"So he [McCarthy] could have the victory for himself," Miss McGrory said, quite audibly. She became a strong McCarthy partisan.

Another liberal journalist, Murray Kempton, enraged at a man he had admired, wrote: "In one day, [Kennedy] managed to confirm the worst things his enemies had ever said about him."

One vitally interested party, Lyndon Johnson, took the news in unwonted good humor. "Some speculate in gold, a primary metal," he said. "And others just speculate in primaries."

Jim Rowe, however, was in no laughing mood. He immediately struck right at the sore spots: "I'm going to watch with fascination Bobby's efforts to convince those former young supporters of his who are now supporting Gene McCarthy that he's neither ruthless nor a political opportunist." Kennedy's campaign, he added, might "destroy the Democratic party for a generation."

These critics had it right—at first. Kennedy's entry *was* deeply resented by many Americans. He *was* regarded as ruthless and ambitious. McCarthy's young army *did* mostly stand by him, often with deep bitterness against the supposed treachery of Kennedy (in splitting the antiwar movement).

Robert Kennedy never entirely shook off any of these problems, and friends believe such reactions wounded him deeply, no doubt adding to the sense of sadness and reflection that seemed to surround him in the spring of 1968. One night on a campaign bus he wrote a note to Al Lowenstein:

> For Al, who knew the lesson of Emerson and taught it to the rest of us: "they did not yet see . . . if a single man planted himself on his convictions and then abide, the whole world would come round to him."[3]

But the first responses to Kennedy soon became irrelevant because of the size and intensity of the crowds he nevertheless drew, and their reaction to his antiwar speeches and his emotional pleas for new approaches to race relations and economic deprivation. His voice and manner recalled his late brother, then still widely revered; and he capitalized recklessly on a capacity to rouse an audience that sometimes verged on the frightening.

Kennedy had promised to take his campaign all across the country and as he did so it quickly became clear that despite the handicaps he had imposed upon himself, Johnson had been right to fear him. Robert

Kennedy was a formidable candidate who touched, as his brother had, something deeply responsive in millions of Americans.

Nothing about that first primary in New Hampshire could have pleased Nelson Rockefeller—probably not even Johnson's setback; for despite his "liberal" reputation, Rockefeller's views on the war were not much different from the president's. As early as his Oregon primary campaign in 1964, he had urged the bombing of North Vietnam—long before Johnson ordered it. Besides, the more Johnson appeared to be in trouble, the less Nixon's "loser's image"—a Rockefeller asset—would trouble other Republicans.

The New York governor had stayed mostly clear of the New Hampshire write-in campaign. But it, too, had brought him grief, netting less than the fifteen thousand votes its sponsors had said they aimed for, and *less than half* the number Rockefeller had won in his official campaign in 1964. Worse, fewer voters wrote in his name in 1968 than had cast write-ins for that "loser," Richard Nixon, in a similarly unauthorized campaign in 1964. If Rockefeller was waiting for a draft, New Hampshire had given no sign that one was likely.

An immediate dilemma confronted him from across the continent in Oregon. There, state officials automatically put on their primary ballot the names of politicians they considered real, even if unannounced, candidates; Nelson Rockefeller certainly would be so designated. To get off the ballot, he would have to sign a statement that he would not accept his party's nomination—which obviously would demolish even the possibility of a draft. On March 13, as he glumly studied the bad news from New Hampshire, he had only until March 22 to decide whether to stay on or swear himself off the Oregon ballot—a hard call.

If he stayed on, becoming in effect an avowed candidate, Nebraska then would put him on its earlier ballot, too. The bitter animosity of the Goldwater conservatives undoubtedly would flare up again, as in 1964; they were powerful in Nebraska. If Rockefeller survived that hazard to win the nomination, the party might well be so split that he would not be able to take advantage of the Democrats' obvious problems.

If Rockefeller took himself off the Oregon ballot, however, a Nixon nomination would be all but assured, and a unified party might well take him to victory in November. With his old rival in the White House for four or eight years, Rockefeller's presidential hopes—hardly perennial as they were—probably would be ended.

Since Romney's withdrawal on February 29, speculation that Rockefeller would move into the race had been mounting. Richard Nixon—a confirmed cynic, with much to be cynical about, in the contemplation of political tactics—was convinced that the governor was coming after him again. On March 15, in Oregon, Nixon moved characteristically to set things up in his favor.

He assured the press that if Rockefeller left his name on the ballot in that state, the governor would have to be the favorite to win its primary, since he had won it in 1964. But if Rockefeller lost in Oregon, he said, Richard Nixon inevitably would be the Republican nominee.

With that kind of buildup, the whole country waited for Rockefeller's expected entry, and he duly scheduled a news conference for March 21, the day before the Oregon deadline. For the occasion, the New York Hilton ballroom was jammed with reporters, photographers, television cameras and the Republican faithful of New York. Governor Agnew of Maryland, still leading a "draft Rocky" movement, had a television brought into his Annapolis office and invited Maryland reporters to watch the great moment with him. A day earlier, the *New York Times* had reported confidently that Rockefeller would run.

The *Times*'s story may have been correct when written—more likely, it had been planted to increase the surprise Rockefeller intended to spring on March 21. He had made a hard appraisal of the Republican situation, Rockefeller said, in opening his news conference, and it had convinced him that a "considerable majority" of the party's leadership wanted to nominate—Richard Nixon!

> It appears equally clear that they are keenly concerned and anxious to avoid any such divisive challenge within the party as marked the 1964 campaign. It would therefore be illogical and unreasonable for me to try to arouse their support by pursuing the course of action they would least want and most deplore.

Americans already had been jolted by Romney's dropout, McCarthy's New Hampshire upset and Robert Kennedy's about-face. Now, with near disbelief, they heard Rockefeller insist that he would not "campaign directly or indirectly" for the presidency in 1968. He would answer any "true and meaningful" draft, of course, but he expected and would encourage no such call.

Was it surrender or strategy? The question arose immediately. Rockefeller certainly was correct that Republican leaders (as distinct from Republican voters) preferred Nixon and shrank from a divisive primary war and another party split. He was right, too, that no unaided draft was likely. In that light, his announcement looked like the kind of realistic adjustment to the national political situation that he had not always been willing to make in the past.

That impression was strengthened when it became known that Rockefeller had not done Agnew, his most public champion, the favor of advance notice of his decision. The Maryland governor, even as statehouse reporters looked on, had been embarrassed and infuriated by the announcement—scarcely the mood in which Rockefeller should want to put his draft leader, if a stimulated draft was in his mind.

Many Republicans and political observers—including me—nevertheless were not convinced that Rockefeller had surrendered to the inevitable. He was anything but a quitter and wanted nothing so much as the presidency. And 1968 was looking more and more like a Republican year.

In my *Times* article for March 22, I quoted a Republican "analyst": "There is no sense risking your Presidential hopes on one lousy primary, if you can avoid it. Rocky managed to avoid it." The "analyst" referred to the Oregon primary, where Nixon already had tried to set up Rockefeller for a showdown the governor was by no means certain he could win. (His operatives said their private polls had Rockefeller ahead in Oregon, but not far enough for comfort.)

In Nebraska, Nixon almost certainly would have defeated him decisively, making a later Rockefeller victory in Oregon even more vital. Even one victory apiece in the two states would have dimmed the idea that Rockefeller was more "electable" than Nixon.

Rockefeller's tactical aim in staying out of the primaries, skeptics believed, was "exposure without infighting." He did not risk defeat by Nixon, who would be deprived of the flesh-and-blood victim he needed finally to dispel his loser's reputation. The governor still could speak out as often as he liked, and be heard on all major issues—on March 21, for instance, he again had backed away from his former hard-line views on Vietnam. His *strategic* goal—to earn a position in the polls as the Republican best able to defeat President Johnson—thus could be pursued at low risk and low political cost.

To prevent Nixon's nomination, moreover, Rockefeller needed to smoke out moderate Republicans who, unlike Agnew, had been unwilling to oppose the former vice president. "A lot of these fellows wanted Rocky to fight Nixon and the conservatives," one Republican told me, "but they didn't want to lay their own necks on the line. Now Rocky has handed the fight over to them and they can either make it or take Nixon."

Nixon had been as surprised as anyone by Rockefeller's retreat, but he quickly praised the governor's tender concern for party unity—then claimed the nomination for himself. Even if he was sincere on both points, his first private response nonetheless was cool, professional and clearly aimed at locking things up: he sent an envoy to Annapolis, where a meeting between Agnew and Nixon was arranged for New York on March 29. The two men hit it off well, furthering the process of weaning the embittered Agnew from Rockefeller, and adding the Maryland governor to Nixon's list of possible running mates.

Then Nixon turned his attention to the Wisconsin primary—and to Vietnam. In Wisconsin, he had a strong organization built by John Mitchell, a new partner at the Nixon, Mudge law firm and a coming man in the Nixon hierarchy. The sophisticated Wisconsin apparatus was directed at once to start holding Republicans in line to vote for Nixon; in antiwar Wisconsin, it was feared, many of them might be tempted by the fact that he was unopposed to take advantage of the state's crossover procedure and vote in the Democratic primary against Lyndon Johnson.

With that possibility much in mind, Nixon himself began work on a new speech on the overriding issue of Vietnam. Rockefeller had softened his warlike stance, Kennedy and McCarthy were in open opposition to the war, and even Johnson, on March 22, had announced the recall of General Westmoreland from the Vietnam command—raising the possibility that the Democratic party split might be influencing the president at last toward a change of course. Besides, Nixon was facing more and tougher questioning about the meaning of his statement in New Hampshire that, if elected, he would "end the war and win the peace." How did he intend to do either?

As an unchallenged hard-line anti-Communist since his exposure of Alger Hiss, Nixon had the maneuvering room to modify his views. The possibility that antiwar Republicans might cross over to Gene McCarthy in Wisconsin gave him immediate reason to do so. But there were two problems: Nixon's own strongly held view that the war was justified and necessary, and his reluctance to drift, as Romney had, into too much debatable detail.

The new Vietnam speech, to which Nixon and his writers devoted two days at the end of March, cautiously developed Nixon's 1968 theme that stronger diplomatic efforts were needed—a sharp contrast to what he had said so often in 1966. He eased away from his former line by stressing the argument that a continuing war in Southeast Asia was not an aid to improved Soviet-American relations. If Moscow could be persuaded of that point, perhaps it would want to bring pressure on what Nixon asserted was its client in Hanoi to accept a negotiated peace. If that could be brought about, Nixon foresaw "a new era in our relations with the Soviets, a new round of summit meetings and other negotiations."*

Thus, ending the war was the key to better relations with Moscow—and Moscow might be the key to ending the war. Nixon also noted the need for Soviet-American cooperation *against* the Chinese.

The speech was planned for national radio on Sunday night, March 31, two days before the Wisconsin primary. But when the White House announced that President Johnson had requested radio and television time for that same night, Nixon canceled his speech. In view of the *New York*

---

*This foreshadowed the approach Nixon actually followed, after he became president.

Times story about the possibility that 206,000 more troops might be sent to Vietnam, and in light of McCarthy's strong showing in New Hampshire, followed by Bob Kennedy's entry into the race, the president surely would have something important to say about the war. That could overshadow Nixon's subtly changed approach.

Who knew *what* Johnson might say? At the time, my earlier conviction about the inevitable renomination of an incumbent president had been shaken by McCarthy and Kennedy; a week earlier, I had even suggested in a *Times* column that no one could be positive, in such a year as 1968 was turning out to be, that Lyndon Johnson would continue to seek reelection.

Despite an external appearance of unity, the Johnson administration was riddled with dissent; officials who loyally kept public silence privately despaired of winning the war and believed that its cost (in money, lives, national unity and deterioration in the nation's relations with other countries) could not much longer be borne. The Tet offensive aroused these in-house dissenters—in the Pentagon, men like Paul Nitze, Paul Warnke and Townsend Hoopes—to greater internal efforts to change the president's course.

That meant changing Lyndon Johnson's mind—blunting his determination that "persevere in Vietnam we will and we must." Again, Tet—by leading Westmoreland to ask for vastly more troops, despite the "victory" he claimed to have won—was crucial.

Johnson understood, perhaps better than anyone, that he could not heavily reinforce the Vietnam command without mobilizing the reserves, raising taxes, cutting back his cherished social programs even further, putting the nation on a war basis—the political consequences of which the country and the administration might not be able to bear. So Johnson, though all tough talk in public, at last was willing to listen, perhaps even to reexamine.

Tet had coincided, too, with the arrival of a new secretary of defense, Clark Clifford, a prestigious lawyer and Democrat who had been prominent and influential in Washington since serving as a principal aide to President Truman. Clifford was a public supporter of the war when he entered the Pentagon; else Johnson would not have asked him to take the job. But Clifford, too, had his secret doubts, and his was to be the decisive role in the conflict for Johnson's mind.

As a member of the President's Foreign Intelligence Advisory Board, a sort of oversight group for the CIA and other intelligence agencies, Clifford had toured Asia with General Maxwell Taylor in 1967; their objective was to persuade allied nations to send more troops to South Vietnam. Clifford was dismayed to find none willing to do so, as he later wrote:

I returned home puzzled, troubled, concerned. Was it possible that our assessment of the danger to the stability of Southeast Asia and the Western Pacific was exaggerated? Was it possible that those nations which were neighbors of Viet Nam had a clearer perception of the tides of world events in 1967 than we? Was it possible that we were continuing to be guided by judgments that might once have had validity but were now obsolete?[4]

Clifford had not forgotten that experience or those questions when he took over the Pentagon on March 1, 1968, and as an experienced political analyst he was acutely aware that domestic support for the war had been falling fast. Johnson, moreover, immediately asked Clifford to chair a high-level task force to review Westmoreland's request for massive reinforcement—not its necessity, but the means by which it could be met, if at all.

Throughout March, the task force discussed the issue, usually in day-long sessions. It was made up of "the men who knew the most about" the war, and they found it impossible to assess *means* without going to ends. Would the new troops enable the U.S. to win military victory? If so, by what strategy? How long might it take?

At last, the dissenters—Nitze was one member of the task force—had a chance to convince a man who was willing to listen, and who would have weight with the president. As the discussions wore on, Clifford found virtually no answers that held out hope for victory anytime soon:

> I could not find out when the war was going to end; I could not find out the manner in which it was going to end; I could not find out whether the new requests for men and equipment were going to be enough, or whether it would take more and, if more, when and how much; I could not find out how soon the South Vietnamese forces would be ready to take over. All I had was the statement, given with too little self-assurance to be comforting, that if we persisted for an indeterminate length of time, the enemy would choose not to go on.

But, he asked, did anyone "see any diminution in the will of the enemy after four years . . . after enormous casualties and after massive destruction from our bombing?" No one did.[5]

Clifford was a good interrogator; more important, he was one of the most eloquent advocates in Washington, and he now began the job of persuading Johnson that the war could not be won within a feasible time limit. War hawks like Secretary of State Rusk, General Taylor and Walt W. Rostow, the president's national security adviser, pressed from the other side. Johnson listened to both, though he usually hated having to decide between his advisers and wanted them to bring him agreed-upon decisions.

Events conspired for the dissenters. The Gallup poll in early March (already cited) found that 49 percent of respondents believed the U.S. had been mistaken to involve itself in Vietnam. That was quickly followed by adverse public reaction to the *New York Times*'s disclosure of Westmoreland's reinforcement request, and by McCarthy's "moral victory" in New Hampshire. Then, as Johnson later told Doris Kearns, came "the final straw":

> The thing I feared from the first day of my Presidency was actually coming true. Robert Kennedy had openly announced his intention to reclaim the throne in the memory of his brother. . . . The whole situation was unbearable to me.[6]

So too had the war become to Johnson's "wise men"—a group of respected former officials—men like Dean Acheson, John J. McCloy, Robert Lovett, McGeorge Bundy. The wise men, some of whom had helped construct the American side of the Cold War along the lines of the Truman Doctrine, had always supported the war in Vietnam. Containment and anticommunism had been main themes of their public lives. Now they came to the White House and told a president who held them in some awe that the war was at a stalemate, victory was impossible and the American people wanted an end to their involvement in Vietnam.

Harry McPherson, a trusted aide to Johnson since the latter's days as Senate majority leader, had been working on a Vietnam speech for the president, full of the usual hard-line statements. But McPherson was one of the inside dissenters; sensing the possibility of change, he prepared an alternative draft developing some of Clifford's ideas. It pledged the president to stop the bombing of North Vietnam above the 20th parallel— confining bombing to the area just north of the Demilitarized Zone at the 17th parallel, where forces most threatening to American troops and installations were concentrated.

McPherson's alternative draft also offered to halt *all* bombing in return for prompt de-escalation of the fighting by Hanoi. This was clearly a bid to wind down the war and negotiate a peace.

In retrospect, it's not so surprising that Lyndon Johnson accepted the alternative draft for the March 31 speech that preempted Richard Nixon's planned radio talk. Johnson, too, was aware of rising congressional and public opposition to the war; on the day he spoke, the Gallup poll showed that his handling of the war was approved by only 26 percent of respondents, and his general conduct of the presidency by only 36 percent.

He also understood the huge political and economic costs of meeting

Westmoreland's reinforcement request. And it mattered to him that men like Clifford, Acheson and Bundy—respected men whose approbation was necessary to a basically insecure president who often concealed fears of his own inadequacy in bombast and defiance—it mattered that these impressive men had turned against the war.

Beneath his combative exterior, moreover, Lyndon Johnson craved "consensus" and hated conflict. His fabled Senate career had been built on compromise; the Great Society promised in his domestic program offered something to every group, every class, every interest. In the White House, Johnson cared less *what* his aides recommended than that they should be in agreement on it.[7]

It was therefore as much a *return* to his deepest instincts as it was a surrender to political pressure that caused Johnson on March 31 to announce that he would stop most of the bombing of North Vietnam in a move toward peace. But whatever shock his new position on Vietnam might have caused was quickly absorbed in his truly remarkable peroration—written by Horace Busby, a former staff assistant, and kept secret from all but a few close associates and Mrs. Johnson:

> With America's sons in the fields far away, with America's future under challenge right here at home, with our hopes and the world's hopes for peace in the balance every day, I do not believe that I should devote an hour or a day of my time to any personal, partisan causes or to any duties other than the awesome duties of this office—the presidency of your country.
>
> Accordingly, I shall not seek, and I will not accept, the nomination of my party for another term as your president.

Literally no one could remember such a climax to such a series of political stunners in so short a time. But the month's earlier shocks had all been tremors compared to Johnson's earthquake on March 31. Even in my semiprescient column of March 24, I had posed Johnson's withdrawal as only the wildest of possibilities.

So closely was his decision held that two of the president's principal campaign advisers—Jim Rowe and Postmaster General Lawrence O'Brien—were advised of his withdrawal only moments before the 9 P.M. speech. Former governor (later senator) Terry Sanford of North Carolina, who had agreed to be a cochairman of the Johnson campaign, had talked strategy with Rowe and O'Brien in the White House on the afternoon of March 31; he flew back to North Carolina that night and was dumbfounded to hear the news when he got off the plane at Raleigh-Durham airport.

Johnson may have been influenced by a discouraging report from

O'Brien on the president's prospects in the Wisconsin primary, delivered on Saturday, March 30; an experienced head-counter, O'Brien told him he could do no better than lose by about 55 to 45 (although the postmaster general actually thought the loss would be about 60 to 40).[8]

Johnson's withdrawal, however, was not a last-minute snap judgment. As early as September 1967, the president and his wife, Lady Bird, had discussed with their close friend, Governor John B. Connally of Texas, whether LBJ should seek a second term. The president's chief of staff at the time, James R. Jones, wrote in a *New York Times* op-ed page article twenty years later that their "unanimous decision" was that "he should not."

Johnson at first wanted to make public this decision in his 1968 State of the Union message in January, but decided not to—Jones recalled—for fear that his legislative program would suffer. Two days before the March 31 speech, Jones and two other members of the White House staff, Marvin Watson and George Christian, were summoned to a long discussion of a possible withdrawal. Christian, the press secretary, agreed with the president that he should not run, while Jones and Watson argued the other side. Johnson appeared to Jim Jones to have made up his mind not to seek another term—even though he had a poll ostensibly showing that he could be reelected over any possible opponent.

The president was worried mostly about Vietnam, but he also pointed out to Jones—who later became a seven-term member of Congress from Oklahoma—that both his father and grandfather had died of heart failure at age sixty-four; LBJ already had suffered a severe heart attack in 1955, and was well aware that he would be sixty-four in 1972, during a second term.[9] (In fact, Lyndon Baines Johnson did die of a heart attack in 1972, at age sixty-four.)

Johnson's doubts about running had been well concealed from the public, however, and almost before he was off the air—as with Rockefeller's earlier refusal to run—debate began as to whether the president meant what he had said. Even though he had declared that he would not "accept" the nomination, his "credibility gap" was so wide by 1968 that many Americans simply assumed that he had some crafty plan up his sleeve. One theory was that he was angling to have a divided Democratic convention draft him, when no other candidate proved able to win a majority.

Johnson's defenders dismissed such notions. They insisted that he should be taken at face value and they propagated a more complimentary reason for his withdrawal—that he was determined not to submit his policy on such a vital issue as Vietnam to the passions and political currents of a Democratic National Convention that would be sure to contest bitterly whatever Vietnam plank it was offered. Rather than risk his control of presidential policy then and later in the election, they insisted, a patriotic president had removed himself from contention.

Jim Jones insisted in his op-ed article in 1968 that Johnson's withdrawal was sincere, and for good. Larry O'Brien, who discussed the matter with Johnson on the day after his withdrawal, also believes that the president meant what he said.[10]

Johnson *may* have hoped secretly for a draft, though he surely meant to keep control of Vietnam policy, and—like all presidents—wanted to pass to his successor an office no weaker than he had found it. But I believe he withdrew mainly because he was physically exhausted, worried about his health, tired of conflict, despairing of consensus and saw no better way out. I believe he knew "that bitch of a war" had diminished prospects for the Great Society, and that therefore he could never win the great public love and approval he deeply desired, and which he believed his expansive social goals should have earned him.

Besides, if removing himself from the presidency proved to be a step toward national reconciliation, not only would that be consonant with Johnson's ever-present desire for consensus; it would be one last thing he could do to show that his selfless service, as he saw it, should bring him love and appreciation—not the bitterness and hatred of his last years in office.

That, at least, I believe, was the mood in which he acted on March 31. Although there's no solid evidence to support the idea, he may have thought, hoped or schemed differently later on—as the campaign wore along, his party reeled toward disintegration, candidates continued to denounce him, and Hanoi's reciprocal moves proved to be less sweeping than he had hoped.

Johnson might have come to some private hope, for example, that scheduled nuclear arms control talks with the Soviet Union could become an instrument for regaining power, as well as popular approval. He might return in triumph from Moscow, to great approbation; and powerful party lieutenants like Connally and Mayor Richard Daley of Chicago, in whose city the convention was to be held, might even engineer his renomination after other candidates failed to win a majority of the delegates.

If Johnson ever did harbor such hopes—which I doubt—they were shattered by the Warsaw Pact invasion of Czechoslovakia on the eve of the Democratic convention. After that, his trip to Moscow had to be canceled—a last disappointment—and nuclear arms control talks went over to the agenda of his successor. At Chicago, to my knowledge, no serious effort to renominate Johnson was made or contemplated by serious persons.

Richard Nixon, upon hearing the news of the president's withdrawal, was as skeptical and astute as usual, putting his finger at once on a major fact of the campaign after March 31: "I'd be very surprised if President Johnson lets Bobby Kennedy have it on a platter."

. . .

Lyndon Johnson *was* confident that Vice President Humphrey, not Kennedy, would replace him as the regular Democratic candidate and would support Johnson's policy on Vietnam. Humphrey had been one of the few persons to whom he had shown a copy of his withdrawal statement before he made it public. And after the vice president did enter the race on April 27, Johnson lieutenants like Connally and Rowe, together with numerous governors and mayors and the regular Democratic party hierarchy, gave him every assistance—though Larry O'Brien, the old Kennedy hand, did defect to the new head of the family. Johnson's support for "HHH," and that of Johnson loyalists, was crucial to Humphrey's eventual nomination.

The day after he announced his candidacy, Humphrey said in a television interview that he would run on the record of the Johnson administration; but then, as if sensing that that record was a major and unavoidable problem, he insisted: "I am my own man." Whether he really was quickly became the central issue of the Humphrey candidacy.

The vice president had been so visibly a part of the Johnson administration, had so roundly praised its works and its master at every opportunity, that in 1968 he had no choice but to take political responsibility for his years of enthusiastic association with those works and that master. How then could he also convince the voters that he was, indeed, his own man?

The question was not whether he would repudiate Johnson and the war; he could not credibly do either and was not hypocrite enough to try. Nor was it whether he would slavishly take orders from Johnson after Johnson officially was gone from power; no one believed that.

The question was whether Humphrey was sufficiently his own man to recognize what the early months of 1968 were making clear: the yearning and the need of the American people for new leadership and a change of direction in Vietnam. If he did recognize the need, could he extricate himself sufficiently from Johnson's teachings and influence as well as his own record to satisfy it? If he could, could he make the public believe in the conversion?

In fact, Johnson's support, which meant that of the party hierarchy and most of its state and local officials, was Humphrey's major asset—to be defied only at his peril. Thus, Humphrey's entry came too late for the vice president to compete in any of the primaries; in fact, he waited from the end of March to the end of April to make his official announcement in order to avoid these public tests.

With Robert Kennedy drawing huge and enthusiastic crowds and leading the polls, Humphrey—who had lost to John Kennedy in the 1960 primaries—feared defeat in such a late-primary state as California (although Kennedy and McCarthy might have split the anti-Johnson, antiwar vote sufficiently for Humphrey to have won a plurality). And the prospect of running against another Kennedy intimidated the vice president. When on Sunday morning, March 31, Lyndon Johnson showed him a copy of the withdrawal statement to be made that night, he told Humphrey: "You'd better start now planning your campaign."

As Jim Jones recalled in his *Times* op-ed article: "Humphrey's facial expression was pathetic at that moment. Shoulders hunched, he said softly, 'There's no way I can beat the Kennedys.' "

Humphrey regained his confidence quickly enough; his strategy, well-designed in 1968, was to seek delegates in the more numerous nonprimary states, and through the party machinery. That tried-and-true route to a presidential nomination—Goldwater's in 1964, in the other party—did have two disadvantages: it tied Humphrey even more closely to Lyndon Johnson, and it forced the vice president to rely on back-room, arm-twisting power politics—what McCarthy's young supporters were calling "the old politics"—against the open "participatory politics" of the primaries in which Kennedy and McCarthy were competing.

But the nonprimary strategy had greater attractions. It not only negated the necessity of running against Kennedy; more important, it was likely to work—at least in winning the nomination. McCarthy, for example, won the Pennsylvania primary on April 23, with 76.5 percent of the Democratic vote, against an unimpressive write-in total for Humphrey (while Nixon, unopposed, was picking up 76.3 percent of Republicans in another write-in campaign). But these were "beauty contests" and did not bind Pennsylvania's big delegations.

It quickly became apparent that *Humphrey* would dominate the selection of the actual Democratic delegates, through the efforts of his regular party supporters, such as Mayor James H. Tate of Philadelphia. McCarthy's more than four hundred thousand primary votes were going to count for little at the convention.

That would have been unexceptionable in the "old politics." But would Democrats who had voted for McCarthy—against the war and against Johnson—stick with Hubert Humphrey in November if in April he deprived McCarthy of the delegates the latter could fairly claim to have won? The new politics of participation and the ease with which the public could be reached by television over the heads of the "bosses" made that a real question in 1968.

For the other candidates—particularly for Nixon—Johnson's withdrawal meant that a prime target had been removed. The president had become so identified with the war, and his overbearing and seemingly unresponsive presence had evoked such echoes of an unchangeable conflict inexorably grinding up lives and treasure, that it had been easy to attack him, and through him, the war—or, in Nixon's case, *instead* of the war.

Humphrey would make a suitable substitute target for Kennedy and

McCarthy, the antiwar candidates, unless he did a complete about-face—in which case Johnson would disown him. But, lacking Johnson's wheeler-dealer reputation and his menacing personality, the amiable vice president had not nearly the same utility for Nixon. The more Johnson had dissembled and appeared inflexible in pursuing the war, the more he was disliked and disbelieved; and the more *he* was disliked and disbelieved, the more the public forgot that it had once disliked and disbelieved Tricky Dick Nixon, too. Humphrey provided Nixon no such cover.

Since it was by no means clear that Humphrey could defeat Robert Kennedy for the nomination, the specter of another Kennedy-Nixon campaign in the fall gave pause to a lot of Republicans who remembered the first one. That also might prove a major factor in the impending renewal of the rivalry between Nelson Rockefeller and Nixon—whose batting average versus the Kennedys was .000.

Rockefeller, too, had seen a new light when Johnson took himself out of the race. It was impractical, after his I-won't-run statement of March 21, for the New York governor to turn around and enter the primaries. But many Republicans thought he would be a better national vote-getter than Nixon and that, as a ranking liberal, he would be in better position to take on Robert Kennedy if that became necessary. Rockefeller, at least, was convinced that Republicans thought that way, and he naturally concurred in such views of his prowess.

These views were agreeable anyway to his never-quenched thirst for the presidency, and he began to reassess his prospects soon after Johnson's withdrawal—never mind the March 21 declaration that he would not run and would not encourage a draft.

But if Johnson's withdrawal was therefore something of a blow to Nixon, the president's move toward peace in Vietnam was even more a boon. The day after Johnson spoke, Nixon proclaimed a "moratorium" on any further statement about Vietnam until the effects of Johnson's partial bombing halt became clear: "In order to avoid anything that might, even inadvertently, cause difficulty for our negotiators, I shall not make the comprehensive statement on Vietnam which I had planned for this week."

Not only could Nixon put away his speech text; but his moratorium was to become a blackout, which he maintained for the rest of his campaign, allowing him to avoid any further explanation of what he had had in mind when he pledged in New Hampshire to "end the war and win the peace."

Johnson had handed Nixon a virtually unassailable position on the most difficult issue of the campaign, and the "chronic campaigner" had known just how to take advantage of it: he insisted that he would not jeopardize current peace talks by any comment of his own, nor would he risk limiting by such comments his own options, if he should be elected and have to deal with a war still being fought. Patriotically and pointedly, throughout the remaining months of both the primary and general election campaign, Nixon held to this refusal to say what he thought *should* be done, or what he *would* do in the future, about Vietnam.

Yet he could hardly be accused of ducking the issue. When Johnson announced on May 3 that Hanoi had agreed to talks in Paris, following the partial bombing halt of March 31, Nixon responded, for example, that "no presidential candidate of either party, should say anything or do anything to destroy the fragile hope that arises today." Who could criticize that?

Nixon even chided his Republican opponents when he could make them appear less circumspect than he in his self-imposed moratorium. Always he held above Johnson and any potential Democratic successor the subtle but clear warning he had coupled on April 1 with his moratorium declaration—that no settlement should "encourage further aggression by its weakness" or succumb to "the temptations of a camouflaged surrender."

Johnson's departure from the race also destroyed the threat of a Republican crossover against the president—if there ever had been one—in the Wisconsin primary on April 2, though Johnson was still on the ballot. Those who believed or hoped he was angling for a draft could find no support in the Democratic returns: McCarthy 412,100, Johnson 253,700, Kennedy 46,500 write-ins. The two antiwar Democrats, one not even on the ballot, had taken over 64 percent of the vote.

On the Republican side, the voting demonstrated that if Rockefeller was going to enter the race after all, he would have a hard time overcoming the momentum the unopposed Nixon was building in the primaries. Nixon compiled a vote that made him look anything but a loser: 79.4 percent of the Republican total, outdoing his New Hampshire performance, and mocking the 11 percent Ronald Reagan picked up in an absentee campaign. A Reagan campaign film, widely shown on Wisconsin television, dramatized his 1966 victory over the same Pat Brown who had whipped Richard Nixon for governor of California in 1962. The film obviously did Reagan little good.

The Wisconsin results and even Johnson's bombshell seemed to fade into insignificance on April 4. That morning, the Reverend Martin Luther King got off a telegram to Attorney General Ramsey Clark, urging that the unprovoked shootings of black students by state policemen at Orangeburg State College in South Carolina on February 8 "must not go unpunished." It was up to the Johnson administration, King insisted, "to bring to justice the perpetrators of the largest armed assault undertaken under cover of law in recent Southern history."

That was King's last appeal for justice. Later on April 4, while standing on a balcony of his motel room in Memphis, he was shot to death. King had come to that old city by the Father of Waters to aid the leaders of a garbage workers' strike—an essentially economic mission suggesting how far King had traveled since his early leadership of the civil rights movement.

That movement had been more nearly an effort to "reform the system" than to change it fundamentally. In the years since, King had perceived that the economic, class and race struggles in America were inextricably entangled. Civil rights legislation offered an empty victory if its supposed beneficiaries were not allowed, or lacked the resources, to participate as equals in the economy.

"We must recognize that we can't solve our problems now until there is a radical redistribution of economic and political power," King had told followers in 1967. The black revolution, he declared, "was forcing America to face all its interrelated flaws—racism, poverty, militarism and materialism. . . . [A] radical reconstruction of society itself is the real issue to be faced."

So thinking, he also had become of necessity an outspoken opponent of the war in Vietnam. The champion of nonviolence denounced the U.S. as "the greatest purveyor of violence in the world today" and insisted that peace in Vietnam—where poor blacks were the cannon fodder of the armed forces—was necessary to racial justice at home.

This was not the kind of talk most whites liked to hear, including the one who occupied the White House. J. Edgar Hoover, the FBI director, was convinced without evidence that King was a Communist; Hoover's efforts to get such evidence through listening devices were fruitless, but they did disclose King's occasional excess drinking and his sexual infidelities.

With this scurrilous material, Hoover did his best to smear and discredit the man he referred to as "the burrhead." The day after King's murder, Attorney General Clark could not even persuade the FBI director to leave a racetrack in Maryland and go to Memphis to head the investigation of a shooting that plainly threatened the domestic peace of the nation. Clark went himself.[11]

King had his critics among blacks, too; as "black power" attitudes became more radical in the face of continuing white resistance, they began to challenge, in some ways to supplant, King's advocacy of nonviolence.

"Violence," declared H. Rap Brown of the newly militant Student Non-Violent Coordinating Committee "is as American as cherry pie." To those who followed black leaders like Brown and Stokely Carmichael of SNCC, Martin Luther King sometimes seemed too nearly a collaborator with the white establishment, reliant on conciliation and reform rather than on the confrontation and rebellion they had come to see as necessary.

It was tragically ironic, therefore, that not only did "the apostle of non-violence . . . become the victim of violence," as Hubert Humphrey sadly noted, but that the murder in Memphis set off a veritable wave of violence all across the country by blacks who no longer shared, or had forgotten, King's belief that "in the process of gaining our rightful place we must not be guilty of wrongful deeds."*

In the week after April 4, racial violence exploded in 125 cities in 29 states and the District of Columbia. Washington, D.C., was among the hardest hit—causing me to write from there in the *New York Times* for April 6:

> Panic threatened this easy-going city this afternoon as fear of black violence spread rapidly across the downtown shopping area and through massive government buildings. . . . The worst of the violence and lawlessness was in a relatively limited part of the city but its effect elsewhere was immediate and remarkable—a graphic demonstration of the power of black groups to shake and demoralize a great city.

By April 14, forty-six persons had been killed nationwide, more than 2,600 injured and over 21,000 arrested. More than 2,600 fires had been set, leading Mayor Daley to order Chicago police to "shoot to kill" the arsonists. Federal troops were deployed in the nation's capital and 55,000 federal and National Guard soldiers were called to duty across the nation. Property damage in losses alone was estimated at $45 million. The apostle of nonviolence not only had become a victim of violence—violence was to be his most immediate memorial.

Not, fortunately, his only one. President Johnson proclaimed Sunday, April 7, a day of national mourning. Johnson and dozens of national leaders, including all presidential candidates, attended funeral services in Atlanta on April 9. Richard Nixon, who had done nothing when King was jailed during the 1960 campaign, was among the mourners at nationally televised services in the Ebenezer Baptist Church. Perhaps a hundred thousand black and white Americans—not including Nixon—marched behind the mule-drawn farm wagon that bore King's body to its grave in South View Cemetery. The American flag was at half-mast at all federal facilities in the U.S. and abroad. Memorial services, marches, rallies, were held everywhere. Schools and businesses—even the stock exchange— closed; in Hollywood, the Academy Awards ceremonies were delayed.

Thus, in death, King received the nearly universal approval of his country, which it had denied him in life. But the final, terrible irony was that

---

*A white man, James Earl Ray, almost immediately was the leading suspect in the shooting. He was later caught, convicted in March 1969 and sentenced to ninety-nine years in prison with no chance for parole before half the sentence is served.

even as he was being extolled, the so-called Martin Luther King riots were generating a new and potent white backlash—hence a heightened disregard for the message he had died in delivering.

Even amid the mourning, moreover, the argument was heard that the marches and demonstrations King had led, and his insistence that people had a right to defy "unjust laws," had tended to make lawlessness and disorder respectable—thus had made more likely the kind of looting and burning and mob action that followed the news of his murder.

That argument exalted order at the expense of truth. Martin Luther King had known, he said in his last speech, that his people had to fight for the "promised land" he had seen beyond the mountain of injustice; he knew, too, that "order" would never get them there. Years before, from the Birmingham jail, he had eloquently answered the charge:

> You may well ask: "Why direct action? Why sit-ins, marches and so forth? Isn't negotiation a better path?" You are quite right in calling for negotiation. Indeed, this is the very purpose of direct action. Nonviolent direct action seeks to create such a crisis and foster such a tension that a community which has constantly *refused to negotiate* is forced to confront the issue. [Emphasis added.]

King had sought desperately and bravely to make the white community "confront the issue" before it was too late, and he had preached with an oratorical power and a moral force unmatched by any American of his time against despair and vengeance by his own people. He knew white recalcitrance and black impatience would bring red skies over America, and it was not his tragedy but the tragedy of those who would not listen that in the savagery and senselessness of life his martyr's death delayed, rather than hastened, his dream—that "the dark clouds of racial prejudice will pass away and the deep fog of misunderstanding will be lifted from our fear-drenched communities."

In response to King's violent death at the hands of a white man (as it was immediately believed), no one could have spoken more eloquently than Robert Kennedy. In the years since another assassin's deed had transformed his life, he had traveled perhaps as long and burdened a journey to understanding as had King himself. Perhaps he knew, too, where such a journey might end; he told Romain Gary, the French writer, that he himself might be killed "through contagion, through emulation" of other murders.[12]

On the night of April 4, Kennedy broke the awful news to a crowd that had been waiting for him for more than an hour in the black ghetto of Indianapolis. Then he spoke quietly:

In this difficult time for the United States it is perhaps well to ask what kind of nation we are and what direction we want to move in. . . . What we need in the United States is not division; what we need in the United States is not hatred; what we need in the United States is not violence or lawlessness, but love and wisdom, and compassion toward one another and a feeling of justice toward those who still suffer within our country, whether they be white or they be black. . . . Let us dedicate ourselves to what the Greeks wrote so many years ago: to tame the savageness of man and to make gentle the life of this world. Let us dedicate ourselves to that, and say a prayer for our country and our people.

After King's funeral, Richard Nixon—still pacing and disciplining himself and his campaign as he had so signally failed to do in 1960—deliberately went into seclusion for more than two weeks. That was a luxury he could afford, with no announced opponent; but it was also necessary, so that he could reassess the new situation and decide how best to cope with it.

Johnson was gone. Rockefeller was coming in. Robert Kennedy might well be the Democratic nominee. Middle-class white backlash had been elevated into equivalent or greater importance than Vietnam—which, in any case, was an issue well covered by Nixon's inspired "moratorium."

He could, moreover, exploit the racial issue in less blatant terms than George Wallace was using, merely by placing more emphasis on his familiar calls for "law and order." In the lurid glow of fires burning within sight of the Capitol, those calls would ring with a new urgency that would be well understood in white America—but about which there need be no taint of overt racism.

Despite all that had happened, therefore, the road to the nomination still looked smooth in mid-April—in some ways, smoother than before. So it proved, although Rockefeller did announce formal candidacy on April 30. In Indiana, where Nixon was a favorite, he polled 508,000 votes on May 7; though he was unopposed, it was not lost on Republicans that the two-time loser ran nearly 200,000 votes ahead of Robert Kennedy's total in the hotly contested Democratic race.

In Nebraska, a week later, Nixon was again in familiar territory and again was unopposed; he took 70 percent of the vote, to 23 for Reagan—the former movie star again did not campaign personally—and scattered write-ins for Rockefeller. So persistent, however, was the Nixon loser stigma that some analysts got more excited over Reagan's "surge" to double his Wisconsin vote than about the winner's 70 percent.

Rank-and-file Republicans, not to mention professionals, read the Nebraska returns more sensibly. Senator Howard Baker, Tennessee's favorite son, promptly announced that he and his delegation were swinging to Nixon. Delegate hunters for the former vice president were roaming other nonprimary states, citing his victories to parry the "Nixon can't win" talk being spread by Rockefeller men, stirring up memories of Nixon's loyalty to Goldwater versus Rockefeller's desertion, touting their candidate as the best man for foreign policy and—always—for law and order.

All those plodding years, before and after 1960, when Nixon had relentlessly plied the state convention and local banquet circuit, when he had campaigned for every Republican who could scrape up a filing fee, and almost single-handedly had led the party back to respectability at the polls in 1966—those hard years began to pay off. Where Nixon delegate hunters could not get actual pledges, they often could work out a favorite-son candidacy or an uncommitted delegation; beyond shutting out Rockefeller and Reagan, many such delegations could be expected, at the convention, to repay all Nixon's past favors.

So it came down to Oregon on May 28 (since favorite son Reagan's name had closed the California primary on June 4 to all other Republicans). The farsighted Nixon had spared no effort in Oregon, making five trips there in six months. His campaign was managed locally by Howell Appling, the knowledgeable secretary of state, and at least a half million dollars was channeled in from national headquarters. Some of Nixon's best operatives came with the money; both contributed to a tight, effective organization. Nixon campaigned extensively in the state in the week after Nebraska, capitalizing on his big victory there, and capped off his Oregon effort with a statewide telethon that drew more than twenty thousand phone calls.

Against this massive and long-planned operation, Rockefeller and Reagan essentially had nothing to offer. Rockefeller's surrogate, Mayor John Lindsay of New York—then still a Republican—and Reagan's television film simply were no match. On May 28, primary day, Nixon could afford to relax at Portland in the Benson Hotel—the scene sixteen years earlier of some of his most traumatic moments during the fund crisis. As if already nominated and elected, he graciously received numerous reporters—so many that those going in passed others coming out.

Even before the polls closed that day, Nixon was in no doubt of his victory and believed that it assured his nomination. In an expansive mood, he listed for David Broder of the *Washington Post* those he was considering as his running mate—mentioning for the first time Governor Spiro T. Agnew of Maryland (a state in the *Post*'s circulation area). To Robert B. Semple of the *New York Times* and me—as we talked to Nixon together— he did *not* mention Agnew. In an off-the-record moment, he did throw out another remark that remains vivid to me.

We had asked him if he might consider Reagan, the glamorous political newcomer, as his running mate.

"Absolutely not," Nixon said, without hesitation.

"Why not?"

"Because he's a know-nothing in foreign policy," Nixon said. "I'd never put him next in line for the presidency."

He had not always been so dubious of Reagan's foreign policy views. After the famous Khrushchev-Nixon debate in 1959, Reagan—then known mostly as an actor—wrote the vice president a congratulatory note and added:

> One thing in particular has long needed saying, namely that "Communism or Marxism is the only system with aggression advocated as an essential part of its dogma." . . . It was almost startling to hear you say this directly to the Russian leaders because I suddenly realized it was a truth seldom if ever uttered in diplomatic exchanges.

Nixon ordered a "special reply" describing Reagan's remarks as "exactly on the beam."[13]

Nixon's operatives, sound politicians that they were, had pictured the combined Reagan-Rockefeller write-in potential in Oregon as a real threat to Nixon; he'd be lucky, they tried to convince people, if he could win 34 percent of the vote—by no coincidence, Rockefeller's winning total in Oregon in 1964. But the most assiduous reporters could find no evidence of such powerful opposition; in fact, there was none.

At dinner in the Benson that night, Nixon could not have been much surprised—no one else was—to learn that he had polled 73 percent of the vote against 23 for Reagan and a dismal, damning 4 percent for the Rockefeller write-in.

Who now, jubilant Nixon men were entitled to ask, had a loser's image?

Rockefeller had yet to realize it, but the fight was over. Nixon had run impressively in the primary states, a showing the more remarkable because there had been no dramatic contests to stimulate a big turnout. Nixon also had more organization, more support and more debts to call in from the nonprimary states; he was more popular within the party and the favorite sons were generally leaning more toward him than to Rockefeller.

The New Yorker could turn in only one direction—to the polls. That had been his real strategy since his April 30 entry, or more probably since his March 21 claim that he would not enter—a statement, Rockefeller later told Agnew, that had taken him "the wrong way at the psychological moment." Agnew, unimpressed by this candor, announced that he would hold Maryland's delegation as a favorite son, in effect denying it to the man he once had hoped to draft for the nomination.

The Rockefeller poll strategy relied on the belief that somehow, mostly by newspaper and broadcast advertising and by Rockefeller's indefatigable personal campaigning, perhaps by a last-minute revulsion against Nixon— by *something*—the public could be convinced and the polls could be made to show that New York's three-time governor was more likely to defeat the Democratic nominee (particularly if he proved to be Robert Kennedy) than was the two-time loser of 1960 and 1962. If that could be done, the delegates to the convention in Miami Beach might yet be persuaded to turn to Nelson Rockefeller—even though many of them would be the same delegates that had booed him viciously at the Cow Palace in San Francisco, only four years earlier.

It was a forlorn hope, hardly worth Rockefeller's considerable invest-ment. He did not see it that way, of course; nothing blinds otherwise sharp-eyed men like the lust for office (witness Richard Nixon in the first half of 1964). Besides, Rockefeller had come from far behind to win reelec-tion in New York in 1966, using much the same strategy of influencing the polls. He was ebullient, an optimist, and the presidency was his Grail; he really believed Nixon could not defeat Robert Kennedy and that he, Rock-efeller, had only to make the Republican party see that, too.

Besides, in Rockefeller's world, there was little that money could not buy, including public opinion. So the plan was drawn up by an advertising agency and the governor approved it, as another man might his household grocery bill. The focus would be on thirteen "Northern tier" states and Texas (though the latter, Rockefeller men apparently did not know, had been all but locked up for Nixon by John Tower, the Republican who had taken Lyndon Johnson's Senate seat in 1961).

These fourteen states were home to 60 percent of the national popula-tion. Advertising would include 377 pages in 54 newspapers in 40 cities, plus 42 television spots per week on 100 stations in 30 cities. The cost: $3 million.[14]

On the Democratic side, Oregon was anything but decisive. With Hum-phrey concentrating on the nonprimary states, Oregon's primary in May, like those earlier in Indiana and Nebraska, became a shootout between Kennedy and McCarthy, the antiwar candidates. Forgotten, by then, was Kennedy's pipe dream, or cover story, of a sort of cooperative Kennedy-McCarthy campaign against Johnson; long gone was McCarthy's cam-paign for principle rather than personal victory. They *had* to run against each other, in the nature of politics, and each wanted to win.

Once his campaign got rolling, Kennedy was expected to swamp McCarthy, so that the nomination was thought to lie between Kennedy and Humphrey. It hadn't turned out that way in the first Kennedy-McCarthy collision, in Indiana. Kennedy won the state handsomely, with 42 percent of the primary vote; his firm grip on the 10 percent of Democratic voters who were black allowed him also to make only slightly veiled law-and-order appeals to the state's numerous conservative whites—capitalizing, in a time of rioting in the cities, on that "cop image" Lyndon Johnson's polltakers had discovered in 1964. In the strife of 1968, it had become a useful image.

But McCarthy was not quite wiped out. He took 27 percent of the vote while Indiana's popular governor, Roger Brannigan, polled 31; originally Brannigan had been a stand-in for Johnson, but by primary day many Hoosiers considered him a stand-in for Hubert Humphrey. Whatever he was, he and McCarthy carried 58 percent of the Democratic vote. Many of the state's political analysts thought that in a two-man race, McCarthy would have gotten a considerable share of Brannigan's support; and it was in Indiana the Minnesotan was first seen clearly as more than an antiwar candidate.

His youthful organization (strong at the bottom, he said, where it mattered) brought computer skills into politics in a way Indiana's supposed "pros" had never seen. His appeal to high-income groups with high educational levels, rather than to the mass of Americans, was unique. So was his campaign against the strong presidency—usually an article of veneration—that he held responsible for the war in Vietnam, American militarism and the unresponsiveness of the federal government. McCarthy, Arthur Schlesinger, Jr., said, was the only candidate running "against the powers of the Presidency."

McCarthy even renounced the kind of ethnic- and interest-group appeals that usually are the staples of American politics. Instead, he said, he sought a response that would not

> be in terms of membership in a special bloc or in a defined group within America; it must be intensely and particularly a personal one in which we call upon everyone . . . to be as fully responsible, and that means as fully political, as he possibly can be. And in so doing we can achieve a genuine unity, first of all a unity of understanding with reference to what our problems are . . . and then a unity of purpose as we seek to accomplish what we judge must be done.

McCarthy left Indiana with his candidacy alive but without having shown that Americans were ready for a candidate who would only "appeal to everyone as a person . . . to pass an intellectual judgment upon what was needed for this country." Nor were they ready in Indiana the following week, as Kennedy scored a more impressive—about two to one—victory in another head-to-head race. The Kennedy juggernaut appeared to be rolling at last.

Elsewhere, Humphrey was hard at work; with the power of the White House largely at his team's disposal, they claimed big delegate hauls in Delaware, Wyoming, Hawaii, Nevada, Arizona and—under unit rules— 49 of 49 in Maryland and 22 of 22 in Alaska. More important, they announced a virtual sweep of the 115 Ohio delegates.

On the eve of the Nebraska primary, Robert Kennedy had rolled in a motorcade through a tremendous crowd in Columbus, leading some Ohio Democrats to dispute the Humphrey claim. The Humphrey leaders stood fast, perhaps remembering that President John Kennedy once had lamented that there was "no city in the United States in which I get a warmer welcome and less votes than Columbus, Ohio."

In Oregon, the shift in emphasis—following the murder of Martin Luther King—from Vietnam to black rioting and law and order proved not to Kennedy's advantage, as it had been in Indiana and Nebraska. On the contrary, Oregon was the state where McCarthy's kind of candidacy found its best reception. He understood that; on the night of his defeat in Nebraska, he called on history to reassure his faithful followers that the real test would come when "we cross the Platte River and set out upon the Oregon trail."

A few days later, in Portland, as I followed Kennedy on a downtown walking tour along Sixth Avenue, I fell in with Dick Tuck—usually celebrated as a clown but also, in those days, an astute political operative for the Kennedys and for Pat Brown of California. Tuck muttered rather disconsolately that Portland was a "lousy place to campaign."

Why?

"No ghetto," Tuck said. "No ethnics."

Portland was then and is now a clean, prosperous, cheerful place, with lovely views over the Tualatin Valley, and brief shafts of sunlight breaking through the customary gray skies of the Pacific Northwest. In 1968, there was a small black community on the east bank of the Willamette River, which bisects the city; rumbles of discontent had been heard there, but the fiery riots in Washington, Chicago, and Cleveland seemed far away. In the whole state of Oregon, only a few thousand black voters were registered.

That same day, in nearby Saint Helen's, Kennedy got his biggest response not from his standard appeals about unemployment in the ghetto and violence in the streets but from a neat piece of homework. He was the only candidate, he told an apathetic crowd standing in the rain in front of the courthouse, who "cared enough to come to Saint Helen's" and who knew that its residents wanted a new road to Portland.

So if Saint Helen's voted for anybody else, he warned: "You'll go bumping along that old highway and you'll remember the mistake you made."

That roused them. But McCarthy, meanwhile, was drawing bigger crowds (for the first time in any state), attacking Kennedy directly ("a spoiled child" too accustomed to getting his way), and taking advantage of the white, middle-class nature of Oregon. His criticisms of the powerful presidency struck home in a freethinking Western state, and an outdoors-loving populace responded to his pleas for environmental protection; McCarthy was the first presidential candidate to make this a standard political appeal.

He even became the first presidential candidate ever to attack J. Edgar Hoover for being too powerful—again an interesting approach to young people and to the state's rugged individualists. And to Oregonians, who were mostly well-educated, he pointed out that Kennedy's backers were "among the less intelligent and the less educated people in America."

Kennedy was infuriated by this graceless remark. But however it sounded in the urban ghettos, it seemed to go over well in Oregon.

On the Friday before the primary on Tuesday, McCarthy was able to book twenty thousand dollars in last-minute radio and newspaper ads—television time was all taken—using funds shipped in the night before from a big McCarthy rally at Madison Square Garden in New York. Angered by Kennedy's focus—after Nebraska—on Humphrey as his major opponent, McCarthy used the ads to call attention to the fact that it was he, not Kennedy, who had first challenged Lyndon Johnson; and he repeatedly demanded a debate—which Kennedy repeatedly refused.

In an issue-oriented state, McCarthy thus appeared to be the candidate who most wanted to discuss the issues. The Kennedy campaign was seen as too reliant on pressure tactics against Oregon Democratic leaders and voters, and on celebrities like the astronaut John Glenn and the pro football star Roosevelt Grier.

The payoff came on primary day: McCarthy 45 percent, Kennedy 39. For the first time in any primary or general election, a Kennedy had been beaten in direct competition. On May 21, during a sidetrip to California, Robert Kennedy had remarked incautiously that "if I get beat in a primary, I'm not a viable candidate." After Oregon, that statement came back to haunt him; suddenly, the supposed juggernaut was off the track, and Kennedy—having been expected to demolish McCarthy—was facing a fight for survival.

Having privately concluded that his opponent in November would be Humphrey, Nixon was celebrating his victory that same May 28 in the other Oregon primary, which assured his nomination. On another floor of the Benson Hotel, Robert Kennedy mulled his almost equally portentous loss. He accepted defeat graciously, but recognized its meaning: suddenly, it had become critical for him to win the California primary a week later. He would withdraw, he said, if he lost there.

In sprawling California, with its ghettos in San Francisco, the East Bay and Los Angeles, and its high proportion of low-income Hispanics,

Kennedy was back on fertile political ground. So, in a different sense, was McCarthy, who could ride in on the tides of publicity from his unexpected Oregon triumph. His witty style and his record of opposition to the war were well suited to the urbane and sophisticated sectors of California— where the campaign phase of the peace movement and McCarthy's own candidacy had begun.

A little more than a year earlier, in March 1967, the liberal California Democratic Clubs had voted to put up a slate of peace candidates to run for the state's national convention delegation, unless President Johnson took action to end the war by that September. He didn't, to CDC satisfaction, and on October 26, at breakfast with Al Lowenstein and Gerald Hill of the CDC, Eugene McCarthy had agreed to become a presidential candidate against Johnson.

So two extraordinary candidates, McCarthy and Kennedy, each brought distinct advantages to the nation's most populous state, and to that climactic Democratic primary. Kennedy had his family name and an emotional, almost mystical bond with minorities and the downtrodden generally. McCarthy had made his historic challenge to Johnson and offered his radical critique of previously unquestioned institutions and assumptions of American life. In a state as near as any to a microcosm of the nation, they were a brilliantly matched, if very different, pair.

It was fitting, therefore, that the lone Kennedy-McCarthy debate took place in California. It was generally considered a draw—though, in practical fact, it yielded a slight edge to Kennedy because it killed the Bobby-won't-debate issue, and because he proved not to be overmatched against McCarthy, his supposed intellectual superior. But the main focus of the campaign was not on the debate but on Kennedy's fight for survival, which he took repeatedly to his favored arena—the ghetto.

Perhaps not before and certainly not again, at least until Jesse Jackson began campaigning for the presidency, has a more emotional response to an American politician been seen than Robert Kennedy received in California. He drew crowds everywhere, but in the ghettos they surged around him alarmingly; children leaped and shrieked and grown men risked the wheels of Kennedy's car just to pound his arm or grasp his hand. Moving through the sleazy back streets of Oakland one day, he repeatedly stopped traffic; for six blocks along East 14th Street, his motorcade could barely creep through the crowds. The scene was repeated, day after day, wherever Kennedy went.

In Hunter's Point, a black slum housed in "temporary" buildings thrown down on the slopes above Oakland Bay for World War II shipyard workers—the sort of place Kennedy called "unacceptable," his all-purpose term of opprobrium—black rioting had occurred and unrest was constant. One quiet black man in working clothes volunteered to me how many votes

Kennedy would get in that neighborhood: "Man, he gonna get 'em all—for the simple reason, that Kennedy administration was the greatest the Negro ever lived under."

"So will you help me on Tuesday?" Kennedy would exhort the swarming black crowds that followed him. "Will you give me your vote? Will you give me your hand? I need your help and I'm coming here to ask for it and if I can get it we'll make a difference here in the United States!"

That was his call in Elmhurst Park, Oakland, but it was the same everywhere—the candidate's emotional fervor, the crowd's passionate response. Still, California is not all ghetto and these scenes did not always play well—on television they could be frightening—in the state's far-flung suburbs and its wealthy city neighborhoods and its sunlit small towns, in all of which McCarthy was an equally appealing figure—cool in a hot and feverish season.

On the last day before the voting on June 4, still capitalizing on his crowd appeal, Kennedy flew from Los Angeles to San Francisco, back to Los Angeles, traveled by motorcade through Watts and Venice to Long Beach, emplaned for San Diego and then returned late to Los Angeles, exhausted. The next day, in a result close enough to honor both candidates, Kennedy took first place, 46 to 41 percent—undoubtedly, the most important primary victory of the Democratic campaign, the one he had to win.

"What I think is quite clear," he said in his victory statement at the Ambassador Hotel,

> is that we can work together in the last analysis, and that what has been going on within the United States over a period of the last three years . . . the divisions, whether it's between blacks and whites, between the poor and the more affluent, or between age groups or on the war in Vietnam—is that we can start to work together. We are a great country, an unselfish country, and a compassionate country. I intend to make that my basis for running.

Then he finished his speech, and started out of the hall through the hotel kitchen. A moment later, Robert Kennedy's campaign was over forever.

9

★

Redemption

★

I'm voting for Humphrey, and I think you
should suffer with me.

—Eugene McCarthy, to California
Democrats, October 30, 1968

In the late autumn of 1968, as a tense presidential election neared its end,
the world was full of speculative rumors about Vietnam. Le Duc Tho, the
chief North Vietnamese negotiator at the Paris peace talks, was mysteriously on the way to Hanoi—via Moscow. An American spokesman, William J. Jorden, conceded "movement" in talks that had been stalemated
since May, though he stopped short of saying "progress"—a diplomatic
hair-split that did nothing to quell rising international curiosity.

The day Jorden spoke—October 16—Vice President Hubert Horatio
Humphrey, the Democratic presidential candidate, was campaigning in St.
Louis. After a slow start, plagued by antiwar demonstrators who lumped
Humphrey indiscriminately with their arch-villain, President Lyndon B.
Johnson, the vice president's frenetic campaign was beginning to pick up
speed and support. The main reason was that on September 30, in a
desperation speech at Salt Lake City, he had made a carefully hedged
statement that, if elected, he would halt the bombing of North Vietnam "as
an acceptable risk for peace."

That was about as little as he could have said to open some distance
between himself and Johnson, but it nevertheless took some courage to say
it. Humphrey had acted against the advice of several pro-Johnson and
pro-war advisers and despite his not unreasonable fear that a vengeful,

still-powerful president would repudiate him if he ventured off the White House line on Vietnam.

The Salt Lake City speech served its purpose, however; it substantially quieted the demonstrators who had been drowning out Humphrey's traditionally liberal speeches with choruses of "Dump the Hump!" Thereafter he began to move up in the polls.

On October 16 in St. Louis, Humphrey was about to speak in a gymnasium-auditorium at the Christian Brothers College High School when he was summoned to the locker room to take a phone call from President Johnson. When he picked up the receiver, Humphrey found himself in a four-way conference call with the president, George Wallace of Alabama, the racist demagogue running on the ticket of his jerry-built American Independence party, and Richard Milhous Nixon, the former vice president of the United States and for the second time the Republican nominee for president.

Incredibly to many who remembered his defeat for the presidency by John Kennedy in 1960, and for governor of California by Pat Brown in 1962, Nixon not only was the Republican candidate; he was the acknowledged front-runner, leading by 40 to 35 over Humphrey in a Harris poll on October 10. Wallace was third at 18. And that was *after* Humphrey's political resurrection in Salt Lake City, when he had trailed Nixon by 43 to 28, in a Gallup poll that had Wallace at 21.

Nixon took the Johnson conference call at the tomblike old Union Station in Kansas City, while a large crowd—the kind his advance men, led by John Ehrlichman, seldom failed to drum up—waited for him to make his patented stump speech. As he listened to the president, the Republican candidate was as apprehensive as Humphrey, in St. Louis, was hopeful; both had good reason.

The inconclusive Paris talks had opened in May after Johnson had announced on March 31, 1968, a partial halt to the bombing of North Vietnam—excluding only the 10 percent of its territory that lay directly north of the Demilitarized Zone or "DMZ," the supposedly neutral belt that divided North and South Vietnam at the 17th parallel. Little progress had been made in the talks, causing Johnson to tell the Veterans of Foreign Wars at Detroit on August 19 that he would make no further concessions.

"We have made a reasonable offer and we have taken first a major step," the president said. But Hanoi, he insisted, had not responded to his further offer to stop *all* bombing in return for "prompt de-escalation" by the other side.

The October hints of "movement" in Paris nevertheless had led Humphrey to hope and Nixon to fear that, at the climax of the presidential campaign, the shrewd and partisan Johnson was about to stop all bombing of North Vietnam. That could hardly fail to boost Humphrey's campaign, particularly since he had called for such a move on September 30; and Nixon knew a bombing halt might destroy his remaining lead.

But the president had no such news for the candidates on October 16. He told them instead that he could not yet announce a complete halt to the bombing or any real progress in the peace talks, despite Jorden's statement in Paris. He did *not* tell them what is now known—that by October 14, *two days earlier,* the president could inform high administration associates like Secretary of Defense Clark Clifford that an "understanding" *had* been reached with North Vietnam.

It called for the U.S. to stop the bombing completely. The Saigon government of South Vietnam then would be allowed to take part in the Paris talks, there would be no "indiscriminate shelling" of South Vietnamese cities, and Hanoi would not so violate the DMZ as to endanger American forces in the South.

Thus, the trouble was not with Hanoi, as Clifford later disclosed, but that

> the cables *from Saigon* were stunning. The South Vietnamese government, suddenly and unexpectedly, was not willing to go to Paris. First one reason, then another, then still another were cabled to Washington. As fast as one *Saigon obstacle* was overcome, another took its place. . . . I felt that *Saigon* was attempting to exert a veto power over our agreement to engage in peace negotiations.[1] [Emphasis added.]

Nguyen Van Thieu, South Vietnam's president, obviously saw in the "understanding" the ultimate likelihood of a North Vietnamese takeover in the South, the death of his regime—perhaps literally his own death. But if he could hold out until the hawkish Nixon was elected, perhaps the war could be continued long enough to weaken North Vietnamese forces; and the Thieu regime, behind a continuing American shield, might be able to strengthen itself enough to remain in power when the war finally ended.

Johnson, of course, said nothing in the conference call about Thieu's intransigence; to complain about that would have given Nixon reason to charge that the president was selling out an anti-Communist ally in Saigon. Johnson only insisted that no breakthrough had occurred, and that the American bombing could not yet be stopped.

So when Hubert Humphrey came out of the Christian Brothers High School locker room, I and others in his press entourage could see the disappointment on his expressive face. He told the waiting crowd only that he could say nothing lest his words be misinterpreted and damage the prospects for peace. Undoubtedly, this was wary recognition of Richard Nixon's standard campaign position on Vietnam—that nothing should be said by any candidate that might complicate or set back the Paris negotiations or the overall chance for peace.

As Nixon, in *RN,* tells the story of the October 16 conference call, he asked President Johnson for "some assurance that [Johnson] was still insisting on reciprocity from the Communists for any concessions on our part." Johnson told him—accurately—that in return for a complete bombing halt he was insisting on serious talks, North Vietnamese observance of the DMZ and no rocket or artillery attacks on South Vietnamese cities. The president did *not* say that Hanoi already had agreed to these requirements.

The next day in Johnstown, Pennsylvania, and later in Rochester, Nixon carefully did not disclose what the president had told the candidates. He did hedge against his strengthened suspicion that Johnson was edging toward an announcement that he would halt the bombing of North Vietnam, on terms to which Nixon could not plausibly object: "If a bombing halt," he said, "can be agreed to in Vietnam . . . one which will not endanger American lives, and one which will increase the chances for bringing a peaceful and honorable solution to the war, then we are for it."

This apparently calm and studied reaction concealed the Republican candidate's near-panicky apprehension that LBJ—Nixon's old nemesis in the filibuster rulings of a decade earlier, the man he thought responsible for the theft of votes in Texas in 1960 that might have cost him the presidency then—was about to blast his hopes once again.

Besides, Dr. Henry Kissinger—though at the time a trusted "consultant" to the Johnson administration—was setting early the course of duplicity for which he later became notorious. Years later, in *RN,* Nixon confirmed that in 1968 Kissinger was feeding inside information about the Paris talks to the Republican campaign. Bryce Harlow, Nixon also wrote, was picking up similarly privileged information from a source "whose credibility was beyond question" and who insisted that Johnson thought he could "pull out the election for HHH" with a bombing halt.

Nixon believed, from the reports of Kissinger and from Harlow's informant, that Johnson was on the verge of a deal with Hanoi, and was driving hard to consummate it before November 5—and that was true. If Johnson succeeded just as the election came to a climax, nothing might be more devastating to Richard Nixon's smooth, bland and well-organized campaign, which had carried him through a chaotic year almost without a misstep.

Not only was a war-weary people anxious for an end to the killing in Vietnam and the dissension the war had caused at home; peace—even apparent peace—would undercut Nixon's repeated charge that the Democratic administration was unable to end the war it had begun and expanded in Southeast Asia. A breakthrough at Paris might galvanize the independents and bring Democrats by the thousands back into the fold that many would consider deserting only in protest against a hated and seemingly endless war.

But for two crucial weeks after the conference call of October 16, no announcement came from the White House. Expectations continued high; on October 26, Nixon even took the risky preventive step of telling the public essentially what Kissinger and Harlow had been telling him— though of course naming no names. Then he added his own touch, a classic example of his special talent for blending savagery and piety: "I am . . . told that this spurt of activity is a cynical, last-minute attempt by President Johnson to salvage the candidacy of Mister Humphrey. This I do not believe."

With that first sentence, however, he had seen to it that a lot of voters *would* believe it. Still, day after day, as the campaign moved inexorably toward Election Day, there was no announcement of breakthrough, bombing halt, cease-fire. The possibility remained—any day, any hour, the word could be flashed that could kill Nixon's hopes.

Probably no other two weeks in the years since his move to New York in 1963 had been more nerve-racking for Richard Nixon, or more important to his long, patient, coldly calculated third reach for the presidency that, in October 1968, lay all but within his hands.

Nixon's confidence that his nomination had been assured by his victory in the Oregon primary on May 28 had been amply justified by events. Robert Kennedy's assassination a week later only tightened Nixon's grip on the victory.

Nelson Rockefeller almost immediately thereafter set off on a forty-four state, sixty-thousand-mile delegate hunt—backed by his saturation ad campaign—in which he tried without much success to assume Kennedy's place in the hearts of the poor and the minority groups. He picked up some support—most notably that of Governor Raymond P. Shafer of Pennsylvania—but scarcely shook Nixon's established lead.

Ronald Reagan, whose favorite-son victory in the California Republican primary had been obscured by Kennedy's murder on the same night, nevertheless became an avowed candidate (surprising practically no one) during the Republican National Convention at Miami Beach, August 5–8. His declaration only improved Nixon's hold on the center. Reagan from the right, mostly among the Southern delegations, and Rockefeller from the left and the major urban states, tried mightily but could not break Nixon's primacy in a party he had served so long.

One measure of the Nixon campaign's smooth professionalism was a willingness to cooperate with Rockefeller's forces in devising a platform plank on Vietnam that, without repudiation of the war, promised "de-

Americanization" and an effort for a "fair and equitable" negotiated settlement. Any Republican candidate, after all, would need to distance himself from an unpopular war; Humphrey, the likely Democratic nominee, had been so damaged by association with Johnson and Vietnam that he could hope to reclaim some part of the antiwar vote only if his opponent was a hard-line hawk also identified with the war.

Nixon, sure that he would be that opponent, was not about to show himself as that hawk, thus possibly giving Humphrey an escape route. Nixon had seen the political necessity to soften his position on the war at least since March, when the address in which he intended to do so had been preempted by Johnson's withdrawal speech.

On the other hand, the right-wing Reagan forces were prepared to challenge a Vietnam plank they considered too dovish, and in a floor fight on that issue they might have been able to cut into Nixon's control of the convention. Nixon himself, moreover, had for so many years expressed hard-line anti-Communist and pro-war views that he had to avoid the appearance of abrupt change. As recently as the New Hampshire primary, he had called the American commitment to Saigon "the cork in the bottle of Chinese expansion in Asia."

He could hardly be seen as a Republican candidate willing to pull that cork; so the expertly drawn Vietnam plank had to be just dovish enough to make Humphrey look like the hard-liner without opening Nixon to the charge of "flip-flop," and just militant enough to avoid a Reagan challenge on the floor. Nixon and Rockefeller lieutenants cooperated to produce such a plank, which could serve either—but not Reagan—in the fall campaign.

Throughout the convention, nevertheless, Rockefeller as well as Reagan claimed to be making inroads into Nixon's "soft" political support. Even Senator Everett Dirksen of Illinois, the honey-throated platform chairman, said that though Nixon appeared to have the nomination "buttoned up" he might begin to slip if he didn't win it on the first ballot.

In the end, however, the Nixon head-counters were vindicated; his support was by no means "soft" enough. When the roll call on the first ballot reached New Jersey, for example, he had 384 votes—precisely the number Nixon agents had predicted to Senator Clifford Case, the state's favorite son. Such accuracy was one reason why Case, a liberal Republican holding out for Rockefeller, could not keep the delegation in line; eighteen of the forty members broke to Nixon in anticipation of his first-ballot victory.*

---

*"Case did not give up easily or gracefully," Nixon recalled in *RN*. "As I watched him on the [television] screen, I thought of the work we had done together in the House and how my campaigning for him in 1954 had helped to win him his Senate seat by a bare 3,000 votes. . . . [O]ur relationship would never again be the same."

Wisconsin gave Nixon the votes he needed for a majority of 667. The final first-ballot tally was Nixon 692, Rockefeller 277, Reagan 182, and 182 for "others"—favorite sons left holding the bag, notably Governor James Rhodes of Ohio.

Some Rockefeller strategists said at the time that the New Jersey breakout to Nixon was the most damaging development of the convention. Other analysts thought the harder blow had been struck by Agnew of Maryland. On August 5, Agnew had ended his favorite-son status, swung the Maryland delegation to Nixon and was rewarded by being named to make the principal nominating speech—national television exposure for a little-known governor, from a small state! Few suspected that even bigger recognition for Agnew was in store.

A more general blow to the Rockefeller candidacy—and thus to stop-Nixon efforts—was the failure of the governor's polling strategy. A week before the convention opened, on Monday, July 29, the *Miami Herald* stunned early arrivals with the final preballoting Gallup poll: Rockefeller 36 to 36, a dead heat with Humphrey, and Wallace at 21—but *Nixon* 40 to Humphrey's 38 and Wallace's 16.

On the evidence of the poll, Nixon took votes away from Wallace; he had, moreover, risen to his lead over Humphrey from a 35 to 40 deficit in July's Gallup poll. Though his edge over Rockefeller (when both were matched against Humphrey) was not great, it was more than enough to shatter the governor's claim that he was the more electable of the two.

A later Harris poll gave Rockefeller a slim advantage; he beat Humphrey 40 to 34 while Nixon lost to HHH, 36 to 41. But that could not undo the damage already done to Rockefeller; the differences in the two polls merely confused the issue, a net advantage to Nixon since they did not establish conclusively Rockefeller's supposedly greater electability. The polltakers also severely embarrassed each other, and the contradiction between their findings never has been explained satisfactorily.

In retrospect, it seems clear that even more important had been Nixon's ability to rebuff Reagan's efforts to cut into the Southern delegations. They were mostly pledged to Nixon but many of their hearts belonged to the glamorous conservative hawk from California—the underlying fact that had led Dirksen to warn Nixon that he needed to win on the first ballot. The Illinois senator feared that the South ultimately would turn to Reagan, and Nixon's relatively narrow margin on the first ballot—25 delegates over a bare majority—suggests that Dirksen's apprehensions were not far off the mark.

Nixon's major assets among Southerners were the revered Barry Goldwater and the almost equally influential Senator Strom Thurmond of South Carolina, the apostate Democrat, former Dixiecrat presidential candidate, and anti–civil rights leader. Thurmond, a general in the army reserves, also was one of the ranking Republicans on the Armed Services Committee. Nixon had clinched Thurmond's support (though Thurmond, too, pined for Reagan) by promising strong national defense measures, including an anti–ballistic missile defense—a promise he was to find hard to keep.

Thurmond, won over by such promises, worked indefatigably to swing Southern delegations to Nixon, then to hold them against Reagan; for, despite their visceral inclinations, Thurmond and many Southern Republicans feared Reagan would be "another Goldwater" as a national candidate.

"If it hadn't been for Strom and Goldwater putting the heat on," Clifton White, Reagan's delegate-hunter, told Jules Witcover, "Nixon never would have gotten the South."

The fact remained that it was Richard Nixon who had forehandedly lined up Thurmond, Goldwater and such other Southern Republican stalwarts as Tower of Texas, Representative James C. Gardner, the Republican candidate for governor of North Carolina, and Clarke Reed, the Mississippi state chairman. Nixon characteristically had gone to Mississippi to campaign for Reed, for example, when Reed had run a nearly hopeless campaign for governor in 1966; Reagan had ignored Reed's plea for help.

Nixon himself played shrewdly to Southern interests. The *Miami Herald* got hold of a tape recording of one meeting between Nixon and Southern delegates at Miami Beach, and the transcript the newspaper printed disclosed some of the main themes of Nixon's "Southern strategy":

"I am not going to take [for my running mate], *I assure you, anybody that is going to divide this party"*—which meant that the Southerners need not fear a dove or a liberal like Mayor John Lindsay of New York or Senators Mark Hatfield of Oregon and Charles Percy of Illinois, all of whom were being touted in the press.

"I don't believe you should use the South as a whipping boy, or the North as a whipping boy"—which, in answer to a question on busing children for the integration of schools, emphasized Nixon's expressed opposition. In general, the line eased chronic Southern paranoia about "persecution" from Washington.

"I think it's the job of the courts to interpret the law and not make the law"—which meant no more Earl Warrens.

On May 31, in Atlanta, Nixon had assured assembled Southern state chairmen that he would send patronage south through the party machinery. Together with his earlier refusal to insist that state party platforms conform to national party positions, these themes assured his support in the South, even among Republicans who lusted in their hearts for Ronald Reagan.

Besides, there was a fundamental flaw in the Reagan-Rockefeller stop-

Nixon scheme. If they ever had been able to do it, one of them then would have had to accept the other, and neither had any intention of doing so. Even if some of the Southern delegates for Nixon had faltered, therefore, Everett Dirksen's warning and Clifton White's claims may have been overstated. Either Rockefeller or Reagan probably would have gone along with Nixon, somewhere down the line, rather than swallow the other. That's the advantage of being in the middle.

Norman Mailer, all too briefly turned reporter in 1968, attended Nixon's only news conference during the convention and later painted a memorable prose picture of the "chronic campaigner," as he appeared to the novelist's eye. By his own admission, Mailer had been a severe critic; but he suspected that Nixon's comeback from disaster in 1962 meant that "either the man had changed or one had failed to recognize some part of his character from the beginning." Or both, a reader might conclude from the following:

> He had taken punishment, that was on his face now, he knew the detailed schedule of pain in a real loss, there was an attentiveness in his eyes which gave offer of some knowledge of the abyss, even the kind of gentleness which ex-drunkards attain after years in AA. As he answered questions, fielding them with the sure modest moves of an old shortstop who hits few homers but supports the team on his fielding (what sorrow in the faces of such middle-aged shortstops!) so now his modesty was not without real dignity. Where in Eisenhower days his attempts at modesty had been as offensive as a rich boy's arrogance, for he had been so transparently contemptuous of the ability of his audience to *witness* him, now the modesty was the product of a man who, at worst, had grown from a bad actor to a surprisingly good actor, or from an unpleasant self-made man—outrageously rewarded with luck—to a man who had risen and fallen and been able to rise again, and so conceivably had learned something about patience and the compassion of others.[2]

The convention was briefly upset when Nixon surprised it with the choice of a relatively unknown figure as his running mate—a border-state governor with a reputation for supporting civil rights but cracking down on civil disorders. Spiro Agnew pleased the South (as Nixon had pledged that his choice would) but left the liberals in the big Northern states dissatisfied. In fact, Nixon chose the Maryland governor mostly as a man reasonably acceptable to all factions, and as one who would not outshine the top of the ticket; under Eisenhower, Nixon had had enough of standing in the shadows.

Once a brief, vain challenge to Agnew from George Romney was out of the way, Richard M. Nixon, for the second time in eight years, accepted the Republican presidential nomination. His acceptance speech was delivered with professional aplomb to a convention that, if not wildly enthusiastic about him, was reasonably content, unified and confident of victory.

Little notice was taken in the hall or in the garish hotels of Miami Beach of the black rioting that had erupted a few miles away, across Biscayne Bay in Miami. The National Guard had to be called out to quell the looting, firebombing and sniping. This outbreak was scarcely even a distraction to celebrating Republicans and went unremarked by their presidential nominee.

It foreshadowed, however, the far more extensive disorders that three weeks later were to surround a convention that hardly could have been less content, unified or confident.

The Democrats convened on August 26 in Chicago—a city torn by strikes, besieged by young antiwar demonstrators and fearful, from Mayor Richard Daley on down, of a catastrophe the mayor and his police were determined to prevent. Exactly *what* they feared still is not clear—that the city's hot, sprawling ghettos might erupt again, that antiwar protestors might invade the convention and bring it to a halt, more likely that either the ghettos or the marchers or both would create so much disorder in the city that the convention would be overshadowed, its nominees damaged, and the city's reputation blackened.

The last of these fears came all too true—but only with the aid of what later investigators aptly termed a "police riot" directed at the antiwar protestors. The determined Daley and his outraged police—hard-hats in uniform who could not abide young girls shouting obscenities and young men smoking pot—made their own worst nightmare come true.

The convention itself—the last to be held in the cramped, noisy, inadequately cooled Stockyards Arena, where Franklin Roosevelt, Dwight Eisenhower and Richard Nixon had been nominated in earlier campaigns—was suspenseful mostly on the subject of Vietnam. To most of those present, the nomination seemed a foregone conclusion, though a step the convention would take only reluctantly.

Hubert Humphrey had entered no primaries and was widely derided both as a back-room candidate—and, as suggested, Lyndon Johnson's lackey. Many of those at the convention doubted that he could beat Richard Nixon in the fall election; but, indisputably, Humphrey had the delegates. Could he keep them? The question was often heard, and the best answer was another question: Who was going to take Humphrey's delegates away?

McCarthy had continued his campaign, though the heart and heat seemed to have gone out of it, and out of him, after Robert Kennedy's death. But McCarthy's apparent loss of interest was only one reason why, despite substantial popular strength, he had no chance to be nominated. He had never quite been a party regular: in 1968, he had challenged the party and its leaders directly and openly, and his unorthodox campaign had appeared to the Humphrey-Johnson delegates and to those of the party hierarchy as a radical threat to their power and position.

McCarthy also had appeared contemptuous of some of the most powerful American political institutions, even the presidency itself, and most Democratic party leaders were not contemptuous of such things. McCarthy's irreverence only added to their determination not to support a man they so deeply mistrusted and with whom they doubted they could work. If the alternative was to nominate Humphrey, a man they understood even if they feared he might lose, so be it.

The late entry of Senator George McGovern of South Dakota provided essentially a surrogate candidacy for some bereaved Kennedy supporters. McGovern, staunchly antiwar though having turned down Al Lowenstein's early entreaty that he run, was earnest and respected, but he was not Robert Kennedy. Nor was he backed by all Kennedy's followers.

The clownish presidential bid of Governor Lester Maddox of Georgia was so inept that he had to announce his withdrawal before the balloting began, charging that the Democrats were a party of "looting, burning, killing, and draft-card burning. . . . I denounce them all." Few wept to see Maddox go.

In these circumstances, the ghosts of Robert and John Kennedy and the name of their living brother, Edward, seemed to dominate the Stockyards Arena and the downtown hotels. Many Robert Kennedy followers believed that had he lived he surely would have been nominated; there well may be more today who in the merciful passage of time *still* believe that, and who are convinced that Kennedy would have beaten Nixon in the general election and changed the history of the country.

A good example has been provided by William Manchester, the journalist and author of an account of John Kennedy's murder, *Death of a President,* first authorized, then opposed, by Jacqueline Kennedy. In a review of a book called *Robert Kennedy in His Own Words,* published in 1988, Manchester observed, without evidence:

> There can be little doubt that had [Robert Kennedy] been spared, he, not Hubert Humphrey, would have been the Democratic nominee in 1968, and that Bob would have defeated Richard Nixon. The Vietnam War would have been swiftly ended, and money for Latin America would have been spent not on guns, but to stimulate land reforms.[3]

Whether Robert Kennedy could have defeated Richard Nixon and acted thereafter as Manchester suggested can never be known. On the question of his being nominated instead of Humphrey, however, some evidence does exist and plausible conjecture is possible; but it leads to the more likely conclusion that, even had Kennedy escaped Sirhan Sirhan's bullets in the Ambassador Hotel, the Democrats would have nominated Hubert Humphrey anyway.

Kennedy had planned to win as "the people's choice." But the hard blow of his defeat in Oregon dimmed that prospect; his subsequent victory in California redeemed it only narrowly. In all, Kennedy had won fewer primaries, five, than Eugene McCarthy, six; and only 30.6 percent of the total Democratic primary vote to 38.7 percent for McCarthy. That, of course, was due in part to his having made a later entry into the race—but his late entry, in fact, would have remained one of his biggest problems.

At the time of the California primary, some reconciliation with McCarthy was conceded by Kennedy to be a necessity in his final drive for the nomination. That appears now, as to many observers it did then, to have been a vain prospect.[4]

In April, a Gallup poll had depicted *Humphrey,* not Kennedy, as the second choice of McCarthy backers, by 42 to 31 percent, with 27 percent undecided. As the campaign turned bitter in its later stages, it's highly unlikely that Kennedy's prospects improved among impassioned McCarthy followers—or that they would have after the California primary.

At a caucus of the important California delegation in Chicago, McCarthy himself was asked if he would support "another person who has similar views"—presumably the latecomer George McGovern. With the palpable bitterness to which he had become more and more prone, McCarthy recalled that "during the New Hampshire primary I was asked whether I could support Senator Robert Kennedy if he should become the nominee and his views were the same as mine. I said I could. . . . I have been waiting for them to say the same thing about me."

"They" never had done so. Besides, McCarthy's willingness to support Kennedy had been stated *before* Kennedy entered the race on top of McCarthy's success in New Hampshire—the event that remained at the root of Kennedy's inability to placate McCarthy and his supporters.

The animosity ran both ways. Even Kennedy's murder could not bring most of his backers into McCarthy's ranks, so harsh had their rivalry become. Theodore C. Sorensen, the lawyer and speech writer who had served first John and then Robert Kennedy, said openly at a South Dakota political dinner in July that those who had followed Kennedy should support *neither* Humphrey nor McCarthy.

It's well-nigh inconceivable, therefore, that either Kennedy or

McCarthy would have stepped aside at or before the convention and helped or allowed the other to win the nomination. So Humphrey's delegate total would have remained a significant, probably insurmountable, barrier to a Kennedy nomination.

On June 4, two days before California and Kennedy's murder, *U.S. News and World Report* put the delegate count at 1,020 for Humphrey, 357 for Kennedy, 247 for McCarthy—and 998 uncommitted or locked up by favorite sons, most of whom would ultimately back Humphrey. On the day the 1968 convention opened, Humphrey could claim 1,480 votes on the first ballot; only 1,312 were required for nomination. Most head-counters found Humphrey's claim plausible; *Newsweek* had counted 1,279 delegates solid for or leaning to him as early as June 4. In the event, Humphrey was nominated on the first ballot with 1,760¼ votes.

Just how a living, hard-campaigning Robert Kennedy would have overcome Humphrey's strength and the White House and party power behind it—particularly with McCarthy dividing the antiwar forces—is hard to see. Larry O'Brien, perhaps the most experienced of Kennedy's delegate-hunters, was one who was not persuaded that it could be done.

After Kennedy's loss in Oregon, O'Brien had hurried to New York—where the state's delegation was to be put together on June 18—to assess the situation there. Even though Kennedy was a senator from New York, O'Brien found him in worse shape for delegate strength in that state than expected. O'Brien calculated that even if Kennedy won California, he could not gain a majority at the convention unless he could "peel off" delegates already pledged to Hubert Humphrey. They would have been hard to peel, because being pledged to Humphrey at the time was not much different from being pledged to Lyndon Johnson; and whatever the state of Johnson's public popularity, he still wielded formidable power within the party.[5]

O'Brien was not alone in his doubt. As the convention approached, six regional coordinators for Kennedy tracked every delegate. Their tally sheets were not public, of course; but a decade after Kennedy's death, Dick Tuck asserted that "their best-kept secret was that Bobby didn't have enough delegates to win the nomination."[6]

Robert Kennedy himself was too hardheaded to have had much confidence in his chances. He planned to appear extensively on television and to barnstorm the nation after California, demonstrating his undeniable public appeal; and he did hope to convert some Humphrey delegates. But those were long shots. Any hopes he had for rapprochement with McCarthy were even less realistic and perhaps the product of Kennedy's lingering guilt at his own failure to perceive in 1967, as McCarthy had, that a move against Johnson would find a significant constituency.

The president, of course, would have been the last and most formidable holdout against the nomination of Robert Kennedy—not only because of their political differences but because of that long-standing belief, and fear, that Robert Kennedy had meant from the first to "reclaim the throne." Johnson was Kennedy's visceral enemy. And it was Johnson who provided—in the Vietnam plank he caused the Democrats to adopt at the Chicago convention—perhaps the strongest argument against the idea that Robert Kennedy would have been nominated had he lived.

The platform committee was dominated by Johnson and chaired by Representative Hale Boggs of Louisiana, a committed Johnson man. But the committee also included a significant minority of McCarthy and Kennedy-McGovern antiwar members; and even some Democrats supporting Humphrey wanted a Vietnam plank that would put some distance between him and Johnson's apparently fixed, bankrupt policy of fighting on. The best evidence is that Humphrey, too, wanted such a plank, but was powerless to do much about it.

This presented an opportunity but also a delicate political and linguistic problem—the drafting of a proposal that Johnson and thus Humphrey would not repudiate as too dovish, but that would be just dovish enough to open the necessary distance between the president and the nominee. In addition, the compromise effort had to be made without Humphrey's open support; the spectacle of the vice president and potential nominee working with the doves for an alternative Vietnam plank surely would have caused Lyndon Johnson to turn on him in Texas wrath.

A suitable plank was a forlorn hope, but for a while it seemed possible; and compromises were worked out on such arcane matters as whether Vietnam was torn by a "civil war," as against the president's insistence that South Vietnam was the victim of "external aggression." Humphrey was not personally involved in these negotiations; but he knew about them and his own platform draftsman, David Ginsburg, actively tried to work out the necessary language.

In the end, no compromise proved possible on the root question of an "unconditional" halt to the bombing. The proposed compromise wording on that issue was delicate and restrained, meeting Ginsburg's approval: "Stop the bombing of North Vietnam. This action and its timing shall take into account the security of our troops and the likelihood of a response from Hanoi."

That does not appear to be promising much. Johnson already had ordered, in March, a halt to the bombing of North Vietnam except for the territory just north of the DMZ. The compromise plank thus contemplated an unconditional bombing halt only in that remaining 10 percent of the North, with bombing continuing as necessary in the South.

Hubert Humphrey never got—or made—an opportunity to accept or reject this compromise worked out on his behalf; and what happened next may have cost him the election. Johnson got word of what was going on, demanded to see the proposed compromise and ordered it torn up, with a rewritten version to be adopted without revision: "Stop all bombing of North Vietnam when this action would not endanger the lives of our troops in the field; this action should take into account the response from Hanoi."

The words are not much different but the meaning has been drastically changed, from an unconditional bombing halt to a conditional one, to take place only when Johnson had assurances from Hanoi that Hanoi had not previously been willing to give. The president's old, familiar policy had been transmitted directly into the platform on which Hubert Humphrey would have to campaign. Thus given its marching orders, the platform committee adopted Johnson's version, 65 to 35, virtually without debate, along with other language entirely agreeable to the president.

After a spirited debate on the convention floor, the Johnson plank, rather than one offered by the doves, was adopted by about two to one, with Humphrey's concurrence and the support of his delegates. That was compelling evidence as to whether Humphrey, at that time, *really* was his "own man"; and it left little doubt that Johnson, not the putative nominee, controlled the convention.

Most "Humphrey delegates" were party loyalists and party workers, many the political creatures of the mayors and governors and state chairmen who had sent them to Chicago. Many of these delegates, moreover, supported the war and Johnson's policies not only because their leaders did, but because they were emotionally patriotic, sincerely anti-Communist and not given to questioning national policy, particularly on complex foreign policy matters.

Among such delegates, even a determined Humphrey probably could not have found enough independent souls to have formed a majority coalition with the McCarthy-McGovern delegates on the Vietnam issue; that never will be known, but it was not in Humphrey's nature to take such a formidable risk. Had he tried and failed, a wrathful Johnson might well have moved to prevent Humphrey's nomination by pulling back delegates from states in which the president could exert control—perhaps even becoming again a candidate himself.

Here was a paradox. Johnson's public support was weak, but within the party convention, made up as it was of loyalists and workers, his hierarchical position was powerful. In just such a situation in 1948, Harry Truman had forced his own renomination. Lyndon Johnson might have been able to do it, too. Humphrey feared so, at least, and it can be argued that even an unpopular incumbent with the powers of the presidency at his disposal could be a stronger candidate than a perceived surrogate and yes-man.

Johnson conceivably might have *preferred* to run, even to run and lose, if the alternative was to be repudiated by his party's convention and its nominee on the crucial issue of the war. His chief of staff at the time, Jim Jones, later disclosed that in March, when Johnson had withdrawn from the race, the president had a poll that convinced him he *could* win if he chose to run; no doubt that involved some wishful thinking, but Johnson still might have believed it in August.[7]

Had Robert Kennedy lived to argue the case in his emotional and appealing way, the dove showing in the platform fight no doubt would have been improved. That would only have intensified Johnson's opposition and the risk to Humphrey in differing with the president. The outcome of the platform fight, as it was, suggests as strongly as anything can that Robert Kennedy—perhaps *especially* Robert Kennedy—could not have broken Johnson's control of the convention, and might have brought Johnson out of retirement to assert that control in person.

The living, breathing Edward Kennedy—a year before his career was dashed by the Chappaquiddick incident—was another matter. He did not bear the onus of having chosen to oppose the party leaders and the president, as Robert Kennedy and Eugene McCarthy had, and he was somehow perceived to be less strongly opposed to the war than his brother had been; at least he was not so powerfully on record. Some Democrats thought even Lyndon Johnson could have accepted him for the sake of Democratic victory. No one really knew about that, however, and it was the Kennedy name and the Kennedy legend—augmented tragically but dramatically by the second assassination—that really accounted for a "draft Ted" movement that suddenly blossomed amid the doubts about Humphrey's ability to win.

Edward Kennedy did not attend the convention—purposely—but even before it opened, his name was constantly heard, either as the subject of a possible draft for the presidential nomination, or as the best man to be Humphrey's running mate. Humphrey conceded—despite what he was saying implicitly about his own weakness—that Edward Kennedy would "add great strength to the ticket." A Harris poll specified that the Kennedy name might bring that ticket as many as five million votes.

He was everyone's favorite for vice president and many, nominally including even Gene McCarthy, apparently were willing to go along with a presidential draft—although some believe McCarthy's offer was not genuine. McCarthy did meet, during the convention, with Stephen E. Smith, Edward Kennedy's brother-in-law and an astute political manager for the Kennedy brothers, and he did tell Smith that he would withdraw his own candidacy and support Edward Kennedy; but he said also that he was *not* willing to nominate Edward or to call publicly for a draft—which lessened the effect, if not necessarily the sincerity, of his offer. In the end, McCarthy's intention was never tested.

No greater tribute than the various "draft Ted" efforts could have been paid to the power of the Kennedy name in 1968. The emotional impact of the assassination of the two older brothers, the lingering—if largely imagined—glamour of "Camelot," the obvious vote-getting abilities of the clan, all were powerful. So was the widespread fear among Democrats that Humphrey, burdened as he was with Johnson's war, could not win in November.

So Edward Kennedy, thirty-six years old, a senator only since 1962, who had been elected to that body mostly as President Kennedy's youngest brother, and who had not yet become—as he later did—a leader of the Democratic liberals, succeeded without effort to a position among the delegates that Robert Kennedy probably could not have matched at that convention.

As early as July 26, Edward Kennedy had rejected, in a statement about as conclusive as he could make it, the suggestion that he take second place on a Humphrey ticket. His reasons, he said, were "purely personal"—an understandable position in view of his brother's death, and one that quieted draft talk for the moment.

But as doubts about Humphrey's electability began to spread, and the Republicans' nomination stimulated Democrats' antipathy to the idea of archenemy Richard Nixon in the White House, "draft Ted" activity resumed and spread to the presidential nomination itself. The California delegation, led by Assembly Speaker Jesse Unruh and once committed under the unit rule to Robert Kennedy, was out front in the movement; other "draft Ted" leaders at the convention included former governor Michael V. DiSalle of Ohio and, in effect though in private, Mayor Daley of Chicago—who shared the convention's doubts about Humphrey.

Daley had titillated the convention by not immediately throwing the support of Illinois to Humphrey; unknown to the delegates or to the press, he had called Edward Kennedy on Saturday before the convention opened on Monday, and urged him to seek the presidency. Kennedy gave him no encouragement but did not turn him down decisively. Draft talk continued to escalate, particularly after word of the Smith-McCarthy meeting began to seep through hotels and the convention hall.

In view of Daley's call to Edward Kennedy, some believe that the mayor would have supported *Robert* Kennedy's nomination; Robert did mean to try hard for the mayor's backing, telling associates that it could be "the ball game." But it would have been difficult for a regular Democrat like Daley to have repudiated President Johnson and Vice President Humphrey, in effect. It would have been even harder to have pushed them to support the man who had most seriously challenged and threatened them—as Robert Kennedy had but Edward had *not.* Daley would have been abandoning party regularity itself, thus undermining the idea upon which his own power rested.

Late on the night of August 27, before the presidential nomination the next day, James Reston of the *New York Times* reached Edward Kennedy, on Cape Cod, from a telephone installed in the *Times*'s working space on the convention floor. While the delegates whooped and howled a few feet away, Reston questioned Kennedy about the draft movement. As a result, I was able to write in the *Times,* on Reston's information, that Kennedy

> apparently was not at first averse to a Presidential draft, but refused to give it positive blessing for fear that it would result either in his being drafted for vice president or in damage to his prospects for the Presidential nomination in another year. Mr. Daley, on the other hand, might well have lent formidable weight to a Kennedy draft, had he had assurances that [Kennedy] would state his willingness to accept.

The inconclusive talks between Steve Smith and McCarthy, Kennedy's reluctance to cooperate openly with a draft, and Daley's refusal to proceed without that cooperation, ultimately doomed the effort—which never went far enough to cause Lyndon Johnson to disclose how he would regard a candidacy by Edward Kennedy.

On August 28, Kennedy issued a Sherman-like refusal to be drafted for anything. Daley then threw all but six of Illinois's delegates to Humphrey, and the latter's nomination—not the least of the milestones on the way to the political redemption of Richard Nixon—came off on schedule.

> CHICAGO, August 28—While a pitched battle between the police and anti-war demonstrators raged in the streets, the Democratic National Convention nominated Hubert H. Humphrey for President tonight, on a platform reflecting his and President Johnson's views on the war in Vietnam.

That lead in the *Times* was perhaps a bit long; but into it I crammed the two elements that were to haunt the Democrats' campaign from beginning to end: violence in the streets, and the connection of the party and its candidate to the least popular war in American history.

Over several days, at the moment of Humphrey's and his party's greatest exposure on national television—by 1968 the major instrument of national politics—they had had to share the screen with terrifying scenes of protesters surging through Chicago's streets, only to be repelled and in many cases savaged and teargassed by the maddened Chicago police. When the National Guard arrived, carrying army rifles and riding in army jeeps and trucks, audiences everywhere saw what looked like, and many viewers must have thought was, a revolution being put down by the armed forces.

"Like millions of other Americans watching television that night," Richard Nixon recalled in *RN:*

> I did not want to believe my eyes. . . . Television magnified the agony of Chicago into a national debacle. I knew, of course, that the impact of Humphrey's nomination would now be seriously undermined. He would have to spend his entire campaign trying to patch up the divisions in his party.

The spectacle from Chicago not only tore apart the already reeling Democratic party; the street violence and counterviolence reinforced the fears of many in the nation and turned them toward the political right. The convention's aura of bloodshed and rebellion clung to the Democrats for at least the vital first month of the campaign, making all the more effective among middle-class voters Richard Nixon's repeated calls for "law and order"—not to mention George Wallace's strident campaigning against "longhairs," hippies, radicals and "the bloc," his favorite code word for black voters. (Blacks were not much involved in the Chicago antiwar protests, but many white Americans thought they were. By midsummer 1968, blacks were almost automatically associated in the national consciousness with "violence in the streets.")

On the other hand, to strongly antiwar voters and those repelled by the force used against the Chicago protesters, the televised struggles surrounding the Democratic convention emphasized the unresponsiveness of the administration and its supposed willingness to impose its policies by force and brutality. Thus, it was that the Democrats became the party of violence in the streets *and* the party of police repression.

By extension, Hubert Humphrey was condemned for the same sins. What he found within himself to say about the struggle in the streets that formed such a lurid background to his acceptance speech only added to his troubles:

> Rioting, burning, sniping, mugging, traffic in narcotics and disregard for the law are the advance guard of anarchy. . . . [V]iolence breeds counterviolence and it cannot be condoned whatever the source. . . . [W]e do not want a police state but we do need a state of law and order.

Adopting something like Nixon's rhetoric could not save Hubert Humphrey from those damning pictures on the screen. Other Democrats were not so restrained. Senator Abraham Ribicoff of Connecticut, not previously known for defying authority, dared to say in an otherwise unexceptional nominating speech that with George McGovern as president, "We wouldn't have these Gestapo tactics in the streets of Chicago!"

Amid the chorus of cheers and boos that followed from the floor and the galleries, well packed with Chicago municipal workers and party loyalists, Mayor Daley himself leaped up from his seat just below the podium and shook his fist at Ribicoff. Then he cupped his hands around his mouth and shouted angrily. How many in the television audience lip-read his words will never be known; the words were inaudible in the uproar of the Stockyards Arena but those who did read Daley's lips knew that the mayor of Chicago had shouted at the senator from Connecticut: *"Go fuck yourself, you son of a bitch!"*

Ribicoff had reached his finest hour. He leaned over the podium and replied to the mayor directly: "How hard it is to accept the truth!"

None of that helped Hubert Humphrey, nor did his blubbery tribute, in his acceptance speech, to Lyndon Johnson: "Tonight, to you, Mr. President, I say thank you . . . thank you, Mr. President!"

For what? journalists wondered, no doubt in company with many viewers. Largely at Johnson's insistence, the convention had left Humphrey to run on Johnson's platform for Johnson's war, on Johnson's policy that was hated by so many, on a Vietnam plank that actually could be interpreted as more hawkish, because it was more specific, than the one Richard Nixon had painstakingly worked out with Rockefeller at Miami Beach.

Even Nixon the hard-liner had known that he could not run in open support of Lyndon Johnson's war, and even Ronald Reagan the harder-liner had accepted that fact of political life, and the consequent Republican platform. But Hubert Humphrey, the Democratic nominee, left Chicago committed to "Johnson's war"—a position to which one of his campaign managers, Senator Fred Harris of Oklahoma, could pay only minimum tribute. Humphrey, he said, "could live with it."*

But he couldn't, not for long. From the moment HHH, as he styled himself, entered upon his campaign, hecklers trailed him, derided him, disrupted his speeches, dominated the news of his movements, made his political life miserable, and ingrained upon the public consciousness their viciously effective slogan: "Dump the Hump! Dump the Hump!"

Particularly dismaying was Humphrey's appearance with Edward Kennedy on September 21 atop the marquee of the Jordan Marsh department store in downtown Boston—a city that was ordinarily a Democratic stronghold. Kennedy's presence with Humphrey in that city should have assured a successful rally and one of the bright moments of the Humphrey campaign. Instead, a storm of boos and catcalls had come down on Humphrey *and* Kennedy as their car first edged through the big crowd in narrow Washington Street. A mean and ugly sound, the booing rose and fell as they appeared on the marquee, and throughout their attempted

*Later, as a senator and a presidential candidate himself, Fred Harris—who had hoped to be Humphrey's vice presidential running mate—became an outspoken opponent of the war in Vietnam.

speeches—despite their repeated pleas for elementary courtesy, fair play and regard for free speech.

Kennedy probably never had been booed before, certainly not in Boston, and was visibly shocked. Humphrey by then had been through it all, and fought back vainly.

"Your actions here are going to disgust the American people!" he shouted from the marquee.

"Bullshit! Bullshit!" the hecklers chanted in response.

Humphrey tried to tell them that their actions were only helping Nixon and Wallace; but they paid no heed. He tried to rally their support for the nuclear nonproliferation treaty, usually a favorite of the antiwar movement; they only shouted "hypocrite!" in return. Nothing availed; and though Humphrey struggled gamely on, the desired effect of a campaign speech—to evoke the enthusiasm of the faithful—was lost in the heckling.

So it was at virtually every stop. Humphrey's campaign literally was being ruined—not just because he was prevented from arguing his case, but because, on the one hand, the aura of violence and revolt continued to surround him, angering and disgusting middle-class Americans; while, on the other hand, his persistent backing for the war kept antiwar voters from drifting back to his support.

Whether Humphrey understood it or not, the (mostly) young people who were destroying his campaign were practicing a sort of "moralized politics," springing from opposition to the "immoral war" in Vietnam (and the military draft it made necessary) and to the Johnson administration, which insisted upon prosecuting that war, seemingly at any cost. This actually was a *non*political attitude, reflecting a rigid moral interpretation of human affairs. The protesters could not tolerate a man like Humphrey, who backed a position they deemed inarguably immoral, or one like Edward Kennedy, who did not support the war but gave his political backing to a man who did—one who, indeed, had been among its progenitors.

To these impassioned moralists, a "war criminal" on Vietnam—which is what they considered Johnson and Humphrey—could not be a peace-lover on another issue, such as nuclear nonproliferation. They saw little difference, in moral terms, between Humphrey and Nixon, or Wallace for that matter; if anything, Humphrey was worse because he bore some responsibility for the administration perceived to have started and maintained the war.

So the hecklers cared little if their disruption of the Humphrey campaign helped other candidates. What mattered to them was that their scorn and contempt for "the Hump"—and by proxy for Johnson—should be openly and freely expressed. A placard in Washington Street read: A LESSER EVIL IS STILL AN EVIL. They would not put aside their moral rectitude for any "lesser evil" and they would shout "sellout!" at Ted Kennedy when *he* appeared to do so.

Hubert Humphrey, in September 1968, literally had no place to hide from these moralists in politics, these modern puritans of peace. His rhetoric, the "old politics" of his nomination, his connections with Johnson, the war, and "the bosses," even his windy boasts about his liberal past, when set against his present position—all branded him in their eyes as the kind of political manipulator that they most despised, unprincipled and cowardly. As they saw it, I wrote in late September, while trying to explain a more caustic view than my own, Hubert Humphrey had "no real standing of his own; he seems to be the weakling puppet of the White House, the tool of the labor bosses and the Southern governors, a burnt-out case who left his political manhood somewhere in the dark places of the Johnson Administration."[8]

At the end of the month, Humphrey had had enough. An emotional man who for most of his career had bathed in the adulation of the crowds to whom he loved to speak, he was several times reduced nearly to tears by the hatred and intolerance he had to face every day. Even Lyndon Johnson could have done him no more harm than his antiwar opponents were doing—as in the Boston protests—and mostly on television for all to see.

Democratic leaders like Fred Harris, Jesse Unruh of California, Larry O'Brien and George Ball—who had just resigned as Johnson's ambassador to the U.N.—were urging Humphrey to put some space between himself and Johnson on the war issue. Ball even brought assurances from Averell Harriman, Johnson's negotiator in Paris but always a partisan Democrat, that Harriman would not object to a call for a bombing halt.

Harriman's judgment on the bombing halt question proved correct, but he may have been more emphatic and eager for Humphrey to ease his opposition because he could not abide the idea of Richard Nixon, a man he had long despised, as president of the United States.[9]

At Salt Lake City on September 30—a day or so after several hundred militant students at Reed College in Portland walked out on the Democratic nominee, chanting "End the War!"—Humphrey made his carefully hedged statement that, if elected, he would halt the bombing of North Vietnam "as an acceptable risk for peace." He would do so, he said, "because I believe that it could lead to success in the negotiations and a shorter war; this would be the best protection for our troops."

That directly refuted Johnson's insistence that a bombing halt would endanger the lives of American soldiers. But in the next sentence, Humphrey veered back toward the White House line; he would place "key importance," he said, on North Vietnam's willingness to "restore the Demilitarized Zone." Was that a precondition or just a sop to Johnson?

It didn't seem to matter to the demonstrators; as if by magic they began to drop or soften their attacks on Humphrey—apparently not seeing that, in the moral terms they preferred, Humphrey was "selling out" Lyndon

Johnson, the man most responsible for his nomination, and abandoning his own past support for the Johnson policy.

What did that matter? After Salt Lake City, what made the difference to those who had so tormented Humphrey was that the hated Johnson had been at least in part repudiated and the Democratic nominee finally had crossed the line, his Rubicon, to oppose—if gingerly—a major part of the "immoral war" that was at the center of the moralizers' political consciousness.

Less ideological Democrats, who had merely doubted Humphrey's ability to win on Johnson's platform, were reassured that he had stated his own slightly differing position. Liberal money began to flow back into Humphrey's empty bank accounts; rank-and-file Democrats began to work for his election.

The day after his declaration of semi-independence, Humphrey declared in Nashville that he would run thereafter as the Democratic candidate and "leader of my party"—not as vice president (and not, the implication was, as Lyndon Johnson's man). A few days later, his inhibitions dropping with the rise in his prospects, he declared that he was for a bombing pause with "no periods, no commas, no semicolons."

From September 30 until Election Day, Humphrey began to campaign as if a load literally had been thrown off his shoulders; the heckling and demonstrations that had ruined his public appearances declined rapidly; and he began to bring his familiar wordy zest to the kind of lunch-bucket politics at which he and his party excelled.

"What did Nixon ever do for St. Louis?" Humphrey bellowed hoarsely at a downtown rally in that city. "What did he do for the country?" (an adaptation of a famous Lyndon Johnson line from 1960: "What did Dick Nixon ever do for Culpeper?"—then a whistle-stop town in Virginia). But Humphrey never let his audiences forget what the Democrats had done for the country—Medicare, aid to education, Social Security, eight years of good economic times and so on.

"What political party brought you, Mr. Businessman, more prosperity than you've ever enjoyed?" he cried at Evansville, Indiana. "If you're the head of a corporation, you owe it to the stockholders to vote Democratic because the profits show it!"

What Humphrey was doing *in* Indiana was a mystery, because he was given no chance to win there; but when Senator Birch Bayh said in his introduction that the Democrats were the party of "tomorrow and tomorrow and tomorrow" (another borrowed line), Humphrey raved on for an hour about the glories of *the past* in a stump speech bristling with all the Democratic clichés of the past four decades.

He was at last in his element, willing to speak anywhere at any length, grubbing for every vote, clutching at any straw, preaching indefatigably the gospel of his political life, as his campaign slowly began to move; and of such performances as that in Evansville, I was moved (or something) to write:

> The veins stand out in the high forehead; the voice grows fuzzier and reaches an ever-higher pitch; the fist pounds the podium; and in each of the stumping, sweating speeches, scorn is heaped on "Richard the Chickenhearted" in measure to equal the fulsome tribute paid every Democratic achievement since the bank holiday.

How much Humphrey himself, or that kind of campaigning, had to do with the improvement in his fortunes is problematic; but his Salt Lake City speech relieved the dilemma of those many Democrats who wanted to vote neither for Richard Nixon nor for the war policies of Lyndon Johnson, and thereafter Humphrey's national poll score rose significantly.

It needed to; just before he finally broke free on September 30, the Gallup poll showed that he had slipped far behind Nixon—43 to 28—with Wallace at 21, and only 8 percent of respondents undecided. At about the same time, Harris found Nixon 41, Humphrey 31, Wallace 21. In a three-way race, either poll signaled disaster for the Democrats.

By October 10, however, in the resounding echoes of Salt Lake City, Humphrey had risen 4 points to 35 in the Harris poll, with Nixon at 40 and Wallace down to 18. The election had begun to look like a contest.

Humphrey could gain, for another reason: his Republican opponent had made little effort to boost his own standing in the polls. No wonder. The day after Labor Day, Nixon had led Humphrey by 12 points, 43 to 21 (with Wallace at 19 and 7 percent undecided).

But even before this evidence of his lead, at a planning meeting at Mission Bay on the Southern California coast after the smoothly run Miami Beach convention, Nixon and his top advisers had made their fundamental strategic decision—basically, to wage a "holding" campaign. The Nixon team gambled correctly on a divided Democratic convention and a divided Democratic party afterward; the contrast with their own unified party and efficient campaign, they calculated, should add enough points to Nixon's beginning strength to cement victory in a three-way race.

Nixon and his men also banked on a huge initial electoral college advantage. Twenty-one smaller states that cast 117 out of the needed 270 electoral votes looked safe for the Republicans. These states—such as the Dakotas, Indiana, Colorado, New Hampshire—needed little attention from the national campaign; in fact, only one of them, Washington, defected to the Democrats.

In the privacy of the Mission Bay meetings, the Deep South was virtually conceded to George Wallace, as were a few states to Humphrey. Nixon personally devised for his campaign the list of fourteen states where maximum effort was to be concentrated—New York (43 electoral votes), California 40, Pennsylvania 29, Illinois and Ohio 26 each, Texas 25, Michigan 21, New Jersey 17, Florida 14, North Carolina 13, Missouri, Virginia and Wisconsin 12 each, and South Carolina—which Strom Thurmond liked to boast he had carried on four different tickets—with 8.*

Out of these 298 electoral votes, Nixon aimed to win at least the 153 he needed—more if possible—to add to the 117 of his "safe" states, for a bare electoral majority of 270. He thought all fourteen target states "winnable," though he put New York on the list more nearly because it was the largest, and some effort there seemed necessary. Of the other thirteen, California, Florida, Ohio, Virginia and Wisconsin had been won by Nixon over John Kennedy, who had carried the other eight by margins small enough to be considered "reversible" in 1968. If Nixon could carry his five again (112 electoral votes), and add, say, Pennsylvania and Texas (54), as well as his twenty-one safe states (117), he would be just over the top (283).

Nixon had learned from his defeat eight years earlier. He was not after a landslide, he had no intention of running in all fifty states and he reasoned that as a front-runner it was more important for him to avoid mistakes—like the snub of Martin Luther King in 1960—than to take risks in pursuit of an overwhelming victory. That kind of play-it-safe game plan no doubt would have pleased his friend, Coach Woody Hayes of Ohio State. But it also bore within it the seeds of "Deweyism"—the possibility that a defensive "do-nothing" campaign might be vulnerable to an upset on the order of the favored Thomas E. Dewey losing to Harry Truman in 1948.

The confident but cautious Mission Bay meetings designated three primary issues—Vietnam, crime and civil disorder, and inflation—and seven states in which to concentrate the candidate's personal efforts—New York, California, Pennsylvania, Ohio, Illinois, Texas and Michigan. They cast 210 of the needed 270 electoral votes. Even subtract New York (43), where victory was not likely, but carry the rest and add the safe states, and an electoral majority (284) would result.

Spiro T. Agnew, Nixon's almost unknown (nationally) running mate, was to operate mostly in the border states and the upper South, and was charged primarily with carrying Maryland and Tennessee; this reflected Nixon's concern about George Wallace. For much of the campaign, indeed, Nixon was more worried about Wallace than about Humphrey—not that the Alabama demogogue could win the presidency, but that he might

---

*Thurmond had won in his home state as a Democrat for governor and for the Senate, as a write-in candidate for governor in 1946, as Dixiecrat candidate for president in 1948 and as a Republican for the Senate in 1964.

take enough votes away from Nixon, the more respectable law-and-order candidate, to let Humphrey win some of the border states and the upper South, even the presidency, with a plurality. Or it might be just as fatal to a Republican if the Wallace candidacy were to deny anyone an electoral majority and throw the election into the Democratic House of Representatives.

Late in the campaign, Nixon proposed to Humphrey that they endorse a proposal that if the election went to the House, the delegations there should vote for the candidate with the largest popular vote—or, as Nixon put it in *RN* "that the winner of the popular vote should get the support of the loser." Humphrey replied that he would "stand by the Constitution." (Nixon's idea merely appeared to allow popular opinion to rule, and there was nothing secret about it; nevertheless, it suggested what the nation was later to see in Watergate—an impatience with constitutional procedures and a willingness in some cases to circumvent them.)

Nixon doubted that Wallace could win any of the Northern industrial states, despite his strong law-and-order appeal to blue-collar union men. But the danger in those states was different: that Democratic voters who said they were opting for Wallace in 1968 ultimately might defect from him and cast a traditional vote for Humphrey. If that happened, the Democrats, however down and out in September, could win these states that Nixon needed. Thus, *Nixon* could be *helped* by a strong Wallace performance in the North, detracting from Humphrey's potential.

In the age of television, however, Nixon could hardly preach against Wallace in the South and for him in the North, as these threats seemed to demand; and it's unlikely that he would have done so openly anyway. In *RN* Nixon asserts that when Wallace was left out of the sampling, polls showed "his votes came to me on more than a two-to-one basis, especially in the South. Therefore it was essential that I keep the Wallace vote [in that region] as low as possible."

That proved, in some states, to be mistaken. Apparently relying on such polls, however, Nixon used his own more respectable but unmistakable law-and-order rhetoric to win potential Wallace voters for himself. His primary emphasis always was on what his audiences mostly wanted— tough law enforcement. Nixon rarely mentioned specifically the improvement of police personnel, techniques, working conditions or even salaries; and he took no note at all of what specialists in the subject were saying— that real progress in improving American police work was being made under the leadership of the one official Nixon never failed to attack, Johnson's attorney general, Ramsey Clark—who Nixon pictured as "soft on crime."

Nixon's law-and-order line frequently included attempts to claim the issue for himself, at the expense of Wallace, whom finally he attacked as

vigorously in the North as in the South. In a televised panel show from
Atlanta, he took a direct shot at Wallace, turning one of the feisty governor's most famous routines back on him:

> We need politics at home that will go beyond simply saying that,
> "Well, if somebody lies down in front of my presidential limousine,
> it will be the last one he lies down in front of." Now look here.
> No president of the United States is going to do that, and anybody
> who says that shouldn't be president of the United States.

Later, to a blue-collar audience in industrial Flint, Michigan, a Wallace
stronghold, Nixon made the powerful argument that no third-party or
independent presidential candidate ever has been able to overcome, in a
nation that has erected two-party politics into something like a religion:

> Do you want to make a point, or do you want to make a change?
> Do you want to get something off your chest, or do you want to
> get something done? Do you want to get a moment's satisfaction
> by your vote of protest, or do you want to get four years of action?

In other words, why waste your vote on a candidate who can't win, just
to "Send 'em a Message"—Wallace's slogan? Why not vote for a candidate
who could win election and actually do something about law and order,
civil and racial disturbances, school busing—all the middle-class anxieties
to which Wallace so blatantly appealed, to which Richard Nixon also
appealed, but more subtly?

It was an effective approach and, as it began to sink in, many an American voter, no matter how disaffected, did what voters usually have done:
they began to desert the third-party candidate, the man who couldn't win.
It's a circular phenomenon, one that helps give American politics its
relative stability—and therefore it's strong tendency to maintain the status
quo. A non-major-party candidate looks like a loser, just because he is *not*
a major-party candidate; therefore, since few people want to "waste" their
votes on a candidate they believe can't win, an independent or a third-party
candidate *becomes* a loser—perception turning into reality.

In all American history, only two third-party presidential efforts out of
more than thirty have won over 20 percent of the popular vote: the Whig-
Americans in 1856, and the Progressive (Bull Moose) party, led by Theodore Roosevelt in 1912. In this century, other than TR, only Robert
LaFollette in 1924 and Wallace in 1968 took more than 10 percent of the
vote as third-party candidates.

In 1968, as the campaign wore on, organized labor also played a large
role in sinking Wallace. Worried about heavy rank-and-file support for the
Alabama governor, union leadership began to attack his record in office,

particularly Alabama's low ranking in manufacturing jobs and per capita income, its miserly educational expenditures and its high illiteracy rate. Slowly, surely, as the election neared, Wallace's early support, over 20 percent in many polls, began to erode—a process, as we shall see, that was not entirely favorable to the other "law and order" candidate.

Wallace helped bring about his own decline with his maladroit choice on October 3 of General Curtis LeMay, a political naïf and an evangel of the nuclear bomb, as his running mate. Wallace introduced LeMay in Pittsburgh at perhaps the nadir of all news conferences; in a war, the general then remarked, "If I found it necessary I would use anything we could dream up . . . including nuclear weapons if it was necessary." Even racists can be turned off by easy talk about dropping nuclear bombs: after that, Wallace saw to it—too late—that little more was heard from his running mate.

The same could hardly be said of the Republican vice presidential candidate. As planned, Nixon himself astutely avoided damaging campaign mistakes. But as the weeks passed, it began to appear that he might have made a major error at the outset—an error named Agnew. The inexperienced and not exceptionally bright governor was given to verbal gaffes—he called a reporter a "fat Jap," remarked that "if you've seen one ghetto, you've seen them all" and referred to "a Polack." He even said, in apparent seriousness, that "some of my best friends are Jews."

When he claimed that such remarks were only "locker-room humor," Homer Bigart reminded him in an article in the *New York Times* that "locker-room humor should never be equated with running for vice president of the United States." Senator Thruston Morton of Kentucky, a former Republican national chairman, after brief exposure to Agnew, labeled him succinctly "an asshole."[10]

Agnew's worst transgression came early. In a breakfast session with reporters, he accused Humphrey of being "soft on communism." Having believed Agnew to be a relatively moderate governor of Maryland, I thought this was a slip of the tongue; but when I questioned him on the phrase, he obviously had no sense of its contemporary connotation, or its association with McCarthyism. He even enlarged it to "squishy-soft." At a later news conference, Agnew backed down, conceding that he hadn't realized the political history of "soft on communism"; but he never regained in the campaign, or with me, what little stature he once had.

The Democrats knew an open target when they saw one. As one Agnew blooper followed another, Democratic media men put a television ad on the air that began with a card reading SPIRO AGNEW FOR VICE-PRESIDENT. The words stayed on the screen while on the sound track there was nothing but loud and prolonged laughter. Then came the punch line: THIS WOULD BE SERIOUS IF IT WASN'T SO FUNNY.

The Democrats were particularly eager to emphasize Agnew because he looked so weak in contrast to Senator Edmund Muskie of Maine, the Democratic vice presidential candidate. Muskie impressed voters and particularly the press with his dignified demeanor, his knowledge and his obvious ability. It became a campaign cliché to refer to the lanky Muskie as "Lincolnesque"; and since he was what Agnew had called "a Polack," he also brought ethnic strength to the Democratic ticket.

Muskie's performance in 1968 made him the early favorite for the presidential nomination in 1972, even before 1968 was over. Humphrey, ever eager for a claim to make, took to praising his running mate so lavishly that Muskie sometimes seemed to be at the top of the ticket; some polls suggested he should have been.

Richard Nixon had had a taste of the same medicine in 1960, when frequent suggestions had been heard that his running mate, Henry Cabot Lodge, was more "presidential" than Nixon himself. One of his motives in choosing the less impressive Agnew in 1968 had been to prevent that from happening again; and in *RN*, he remarked pointedly that the public and press "infatuation with Muskie could not have pleased Humphrey, but he had to acknowledge and use it." Nixon knew all about making the best of things that couldn't be changed—perhaps his own choice of Agnew.

Muskie was, however, one of the few advantages the ill-financed Humphrey campaign could boast. In sharp contrast to Humphrey's frenetic and indefatigable campaigning—much of which appeared to be waste motion—Nixon's schedule of public appearances was remarkably easygoing, reflecting his lead in the polls and his deliberately low-keyed, often remote campaign. By design, he never came close to losing control of his schedule and therefore of his physical and mental energies, or his judgment, as he had during his nonstop campaigning in 1960.

Few reporters experienced in presidential elections ever had covered such an apparently leisurely campaign; those who remembered the haggard, hustling Nixon of 1960 were astounded by the contrast. The well-turned-out Nixon of 1968 made only a few appearances a day, spent long hours secluded in hotel suites, and retreated to Key Biscayne on the weekends, ostensibly to prepare himself for the next week's campaign—in reality because his holding strategy did not require him to dash around the country in search of votes. In his near-fanatical determination to avoid mistakes, he even abandoned his once-frequent news conferences.

When he did appear in public, Nixon placed himself almost exclusively in circumstances he and his staff could control. The big rallies that looked spontaneous on television were stacked with handpicked crowds guaranteed to whoop it up for the unspecific set-piece political speech Nixon invariably delivered. Before he spoke, he and Mrs. Nixon would materialize onstage in a handsome and carefully arranged tableau, to a roaring welcome.

Soon, as if the adulation of even these arranged crowds slaked some thirst in his soul, Nixon would lunge eagerly at his audience, flinging his arms high above his head, his fingers extended in the V-signs politicians had adopted from Churchill, his familiar jowly face split wide in what no one could doubt was a victory smile. Mrs. Nixon smiled patiently and waved often.

These rallies were primarily for Republican morale and get-out-the-vote purposes—though reporters began to wonder if they were not also necessary balm to Richard Nixon's ego. For somewhat more specific campaigning, an expert media team provided Nixon frequently with controlled television appearances in different television markets; these also featured cheering, if smaller, audiences, and were staged most often in a question and answer format.

In these "telethons," a panel of local voters—screened to keep out anyone too hostile—asked him about his views. Usually, Nixon could give long-prepared answers in a lofty and statesmanlike, often quite effective manner. Reporters were shunted away to separate studios where they could watch him on screen, but not question him.

The television time was paid for by the well-financed Nixon campaign—then the most expensive in history—and few of the questioners put embarrassing inquiries to him. It was a masterly new political concept, enabling Nixon apparently to let himself be questioned freely, while running little risk of a hostile inquiry, a damaging answer or some other mistake.

This kind of campaign predictably frustrated and angered the reporters trying to cover it—though they did not suffer from the usual early-morning baggage calls and exhausting one-day coast-to-coast tours of most presidential campaigns, or for lack of food and liquor provided by the efficient Nixon minions. That Nixon held few genuine news conferences—to which reporters always feel entitled—was a particular irritation to his traveling press corps. They believed, as reporters do, that they represented the public and therefore had something like "a right" to question a man who might well be the next president.

Ray Price, Frank Shakespeare, Harry Treleaven and other Nixon aides had spent many hours watching television clips of past Nixon appearances, culled by Shakespeare (a CBS executive on leave to the campaign) from CBS News files. They concluded that Nixon appeared at his best when at his most spontaneous—a conclusion that led them to the innovative technique of filming their candidate answering questions from a live audience, when he was less conscious of the cameras than of the questioners.

The latter, Ray Price insists, were not chosen only to ask easy questions; he and other aides wanted Nixon at least challenged, if not savaged. The telethons were an effort to show the nation more nearly the *real* Nixon, Price argues, than the glad-handing candidate who worked the airport crowds and delivered the set-piece speeches. Reporters saw it just the other way around—as a contrived means of selling Richard Nixon by television.[11]

Nixon's aloof unavailability to reporters, and his exploitation of television question and answer sessions beamed directly to the public, in which experienced reporters could play no part, as well as their sense that he was a "packaged candidate" being sold to the public like a marketable commodity, profoundly increased whatever dislike the press had held for him when his campaign began. The mutual antipathy of reporters and Nixon was to be of large consequence in his White House years.

Two decades after the 1968 campaign, I mentioned to a pair of journalists who had covered it that I was writing a book about Richard Nixon. Almost immediately and simultaneously, they recalled with rather bitter amusement a "typical Nixon" incident from the first night of his New Hampshire primary campaign.

That night, he promised reporters at a party that he would be easily available and planned to keep the press well informed. But the very next morning he slipped off secretly for a television-taping session with some New Hampshire voters selected by the local Nixon committee; no reporters were present. The taped question and answer session was later excerpted into Nixon television spots—another new campaign technique he frequently repeated in 1968. To have had reporters present, Pat Buchanan blandly explained, would have "inhibited" the questioners—not to mention, of course, the answerer.

On the other side of the coin, in a 1968 luncheon conversation with John Osborne of the *New Republic,* a journalist much respected by other reporters, Bryce Harlow threw at him the surprise question: "Why do you hate my guy [Nixon] so much?"

Evasively, Osborne replied, "I don't know." Then he apparently realized that, not having denied the proposition, he had inadvertently admitted it.

"You've trapped me," he told Harlow. "I'm profoundly embarrassed." And under pressure he conceded: "The press corps calls [Nixon] 'the cardboard man' because we can't see past the facade of the candidate. I've never met the real Richard Nixon."

The avuncular Harlow, who got along well with the press, said he understood. "He's smarter than you bastards. He's like Old Betsy the cow, except he don't let down his milk until he wants to. You fellows fester because he controls it and you don't."[12]

Nixon's aloof and technically innovative campaign was not above some strident touches of the "old politics"—the tried-and-true technique, for example, of extravagantly promising what people wanted. He pledged in Texas to support the oil depletion allowance, the F-111 fighter plane (built in Fort Worth) and to "keep America first in space" (Houston, take note). In Tennessee, he praised the TVA and the Oak Ridge National Laboratory. In North Carolina, textile workers heard him vow to "rectify" the problem of imports, and in Pennsylvania steelworkers got the same promise. All those states were on his or Agnew's target lists.

Nor did the statesmanlike Nixon of the telethons entirely eschew old-fashioned political billingsgate, when (rarely) on the old-fashioned hustings. During an October whistle-stop tour of Ohio, he accused Humphrey of "buying the people's votes with the people's money" and of "a lackadaisical do-nothing approach to law and order." The vice president, he declared, had "spent four years in obedience school."

Again and again, Nixon returned to the law-and-order line: "For four years Mr. Humphrey has sat on his hands and watched the United States become a nation where fifty percent of American women are frightened to walk within a mile of their homes at night." Plainly, as the election approached, Nixon saw votes slipping away from George Wallace and was determined not to let them leapfrog the other law-and-order candidate on the way to Hubert Humphrey.

He was none too restrained in exploiting the issue. On September 25 in Denver, he claimed that in Washington, D.C., "bus drivers have to carry weapons." In fact, District of Columbia law specifically prohibited them from doing so, and the D.C. Transit Company said it would fire any driver who did.

Nixon was not above a little florid patriotism, either. "The American flag isn't going to be a doormat for anybody when we get in," Nixon declared to a Minneapolis audience packed with schoolchildren bused in by his hardworking handlers. He also had a few standard laugh-lines, Nixonian to the core, that usually brought down the house: "It's one thing to give 'em hell but it's another thing to give 'em Humphrey!"

Among his best applause-getters were some rather obvious generalities. "When you're on the wrong road, get off it and take a new road!" he exhorted his audiences, usually with one of his Lawrence Welk gestures, and the crowds shrieked back as if he had recited the Gettysburg Address. Then the clincher: "Let's not send in the old team for the new job!" Pandemonium.

In still another new campaign technique, Nixon reserved his most thoughtful speeches for a series of radio addresses, not so widely heard as his carefully arranged "telethons" were seen, but serving a useful purpose (for him, at least). The speeches put on the record his views on the most serious issues of the year, without anyone being able to question him directly and immediately about those views.

On October 24, in one of these radio talks, Nixon charged the Kennedy and Johnson administrations and the Democrats generally with having produced "a gravely serious security gap," allowing the Soviet Union to forge ahead in various types of weapons. The Democrats had evolved, he said, "a peculiar, unprecedented doctrine called 'parity' " which, in the real world, meant relative superiority for the Soviets, at least in "commitment and will." And that would mean that in a few years the U.S. would be "irretrievably" behind in the most crucial areas of national security.

The speech was highly reminiscent of John Kennedy's "missile gap" charge against the Eisenhower administration—and candidate Richard Nixon—in 1960. Then, the charge had provided a winning issue, and it's plausible to wonder if Nixon, with his long memory, was trying to turn the same weapon back on the Democrats. Kennedy's missile gap had been nonexistent but that was not disclosed until after his election; Nixon's security gap was nonexistent, too, but Hubert Humphrey nailed it before it could get off the ground.

Humphrey's staff had long expected such a charge and had prepared a rebuttal in advance. The day after Nixon's speech, the Democratic nominee was ready with some convincing facts—for instance, that "today we have three times as many strategic nuclear weapons in our strategic alert force as we had at the end of the [Eisenhower] Administration, including a fifteen-hundred-percent increase in numbers of ballistic missiles."

Among other things, Humphrey pointed out correctly that, so far from having forged ahead in "ballistic-missile multiple warheads," as Nixon had charged, "the Soviets are at least two years behind us in simple multiple warheads, and these have already been made obsolete by our technology."

This exchange is worth noting for a number of reasons other than its possible aping of Kennedy's 1960 tactic. It appeared to contradict Nixon's much-discussed assertion in his acceptance speech at Miami Beach that "an era of negotiation" now had to replace the "era of confrontation" between the Soviets and the U.S. In nuclear terms, the rejection of "parity" and the call for "clear-cut" superiority could only mean that, if elected, Nixon planned to achieve a first-strike capacity.

That, I wrote in the *Times* for October 27, was well beyond the economic means "of any sane nation," and the mere attempt to achieve it would be highly threatening to the other superpower, enhancing the prospect of war. Surely such an effort had no place in an "era of negotiation."

The radio speech echoed, moreover, as nothing in his campaign had done, the "old Nixon" of hard-line anticommunism. For me, in private, it was the decisive event of the campaign; though I strongly believed the Democrats deserved rebuke at the polls for bringing on and maintaining the American war in Vietnam, I could not vote for a candidate who proposed to seek the infinitely dangerous chimera of "clear-cut" nuclear superiority. So it may have been for other Americans, since the security-gap exchange appears to have been an important element in Humphrey's rising public support in the last weeks of the campaign.

In the White House, as it happened, Nixon abandoned the idea of nuclear superiority and entered into the first major arms control agreements on the general basis of nuclear parity between Moscow and Washington. Might Humphrey's swift and effective rebuttal and the general view that he had won the exchange with his opponent have had something to do with Nixon's important change of approach? Did it "make Nixon think again about the automatic salability of the 'hard line' " and the relative strength of the superpowers?[13]

Or did the Miami Beach acceptance speech represent Nixon's real view, while the later radio talk was merely a bid to capitalize politically upon Cold War fears reawakened by the Warsaw Pact invasion of Czechoslovakia earlier in 1968? Perhaps Nixon himself could not have resolved such subtleties of motivation.

The security-gap exchange was the nearest the candidates of 1968 came to a face-to-face debate. Nixon steadfastly refused to take on Humphrey—which was why Humphrey called him "Richard the Chickenhearted"—on the ostensible grounds that equal-time requirements would force the inclusion of Wallace. The major parties, Nixon insisted, should not give Wallace such a platform.

This had surface plausibility, but the real reasons for Nixon's refusal were the possibility, in such a high-noon shootout, of the fatal mistake he was determined not to make, and the risk that, even if no such mistake occurred, Humphrey might be seen as the victor. Nixon's was also the reluctance of any front-runner to give such free national exposure to his opponent—particularly one like Humphrey, who was too strapped for funds to afford the kind of television time Nixon was buying routinely. Who can doubt, moreover, that Nixon's traumatic memory of the first Kennedy-Nixon debate in 1960 was at work?

Humphrey screamed constantly for a debate, and even offered to split the cost of paid time, but Nixon was adamant, calling debates "kid stuff." Besides, even in paid time, he argued dubiously, Wallace would have to be included. Meanwhile, Republicans and conservative Democrats in Congress managed to stall legislation that would have made a two-candidate debate clearly possible. Undoubtedly, Humphrey gained on the "Chickenhearted" issue—but not, perhaps, as much as Nixon might have lost by giving Humphrey the national debate platform, and risking some damaging setback. Besides, as noted, debates are irrelevant to a president's duties.

On October 23, the *New York Times* ran a long story on the front page under my byline and the headline POLITICAL OBSERVERS CAUTIOUS ON VICTORY BY NIXON. Four days later, the paper's off-lead was another of my campaign roundups, headed: HUMPHREY SURGE IS OFFERING AIDES A HOPE FOR UPSET. These typically restrained *Times* headlines described a situation transformed since the chaotic Democratic convention and the days of Richard Nixon's seemingly insurmountable lead in the polls.

But those "cautious" observers were not hedging their bets because they thought Hubert Humphrey's obviously improved reception since the Salt Lake City speech actually presaged victory. Richard Nixon still held an ample lead in the polls—43 to 31 over Humphrey in a Gallup poll just published, with Wallace at 20 and 6 percent undecided. The state-by-state surveys of the *Times* and other news organizations still pointed to an almost certain Nixon victory. Humphrey's improved position, however, made a number of cautionary factors suddenly more prominent, at least in the minds of politicians and journalists.

High among them were the presence of George Wallace as a sort of loose cannon in the race; the memory—still cogent in 1968—of the late Truman gains that had so astonishingly upset the supposedly unbeatable Dewey only twenty years earlier; and ample empirical evidence that the voters were not particularly enthusiastic about *any* of the presidential choices offered them. That meant that the support of the front-runner, in particular, might be none too solid. Voters can change their minds, after all, right up to the moment of casting the ballot.

The Wallace conundrum was not that anyone expected him to win; nor did many believe he would throw the election into the House, though that remained a possibility. What was really uncertain was the effect Wallace's popular vote might have in major electoral-vote states. It could be dramatic; under the winner-take-all system, an extremely small plurality of the popular vote, even 34 percent, could swing all of New York's 43 electoral votes to a single candidate in a three-way race. A huge popular majority for Nixon in Nebraska, on the other hand, would bring him only five electoral votes.

Ohio, Pennsylvania, Michigan, Texas, for example, in all of which the race was beginning to look closer than expected, might be swung by even a small Wallace popular vote, from one major-party candidate to the other. And that was possible even if, as historical precedents and organized labor's counterattack suggested, the Wallace vote fell off in the last week or two of the campaign.

Humphrey had not yet shown in the polls that he was making the kind of steady gains Truman had achieved—and the "experts" had ignored—in 1948. In that election, however, one out of seven voters still had not made a final decision as the last two weeks of the campaign began. If that were to be the case again, something like ten million votes were still to be won on October 23, 1968; and if these uncommitted voters decided in favor of a challenging Democratic underdog, instead of a supposedly sure-thing Republican, in roughly the same strong proportion as they had in 1948, 7.5 million would vote for Hubert Humphrey.

As for crowd enthusiasm, none of the candidates—save Wallace among blue-collars and rednecks—could generate much. Nixon's big audiences were too obviously drummed up and dressed up by efficient advance men; and despite Humphrey's sweating, shouting efforts, the crowds that turned out to hear him were neither outsize nor rousing.

Later, the Democrats put on their traditional last-week rally in the New York City garment district, usually a highlight of presidential campaigns. But when Humphrey made his entrance

> riding in an open car, those waiting on [Seventh] Avenue could see only his big moonlike apparently disembodied head sailing along above the crowd, his arms waving beatifically, his smiling face a little too glassy, as if he were about to fall from his perch. . . . [His] arrival stirred little more excitement than had the speakers before him.

Or so I saw it that day. And when Humphrey thumped and shouted through his usual speech praising the Democratic party and damning Richard the Chickenhearted and promising peace and prosperity, I had no sense of anyone really listening.

> The cheers went up routinely and in the proper places, as if the candidate were holding up cue cards; confetti swirled down in the pale sunlight, and there was the usual array of placards. . . . The only thing missing was passion.

Humphrey's aides and enthusiasts nevertheless professed to see evidence of a Truman-like surge, and there was enough substance to their claims to give pause to more objective observers. Increased campaign contributions were easing, though not ending, the Democrats' financial plight. One result was that a new television blitz was being planned, to feature supposedly hard-hitting spots—like the Agnew laugher—rather than the loquacious presidential candidate himself.

"There is no doubt about the upsurge," said Humphrey's national chairman, former governor Sanford of North Carolina, as he counted seventy-seven thousand dollars in small contributions that had arrived in one mail delivery, following a Democratic broadcast seen by seventeen million viewers. "The only question is whether it's enough."

Too, the rising popularity of Senator Muskie, as opposed to the unimpressive Agnew, was another cause of Democratic optimism, though few could cite an example of a running mate pulling a losing ticket to victory. More important was polling evidence that Democratic congressional and state-office candidates were running strongly in a number of important states—the kind of "reverse coattail effect" that had been important in the Truman victory and could help Humphrey mightily.

Antiwar Democrats, moreover, were continuing to drift back to the Humphrey ticket, post–Salt Lake City, and even Eugene McCarthy, his aides let it be known, was readying an endorsement for his old antagonist. McCarthy, they said, was waiting only to find an occasion and a formula that would not appear to his most ardent followers as a surrender to party pressure and the "old politics."

The expected McCarthy statement and Democrats' continuing hope that President Johnson would yet be able to announce good news from the Paris peace negotiations raised the further hope that something like a united Democratic party—minus hard-core Wallacites—might yet confront Richard Nixon on Election Day.

Nothing, meanwhile, not even Humphrey's born-again campaign after his separation from Lyndon Johnson in Salt Lake City, had shaken Nixon out of his standard refusal to give details of his plans for dealing with the war in Vietnam. But as the gap between the candidates narrowed, Nixon— who harbored no illusions about anyone's political motives—continued to expect the wily Lyndon Johnson to pull some trick out of his extensive bag in an effort to make the nation believe that the president was about to put an end to the war.

Nixon's campaign, in time-honored style, exuded confidence in victory; but the increasing sharpness of his attacks on Humphrey suggested that he, too, was uneasy, and feared that Johnson was about to make a damaging move. Nixon denied at the time that he was trying to counter such a move in advance, but in *RN* he later made no bones about that:

> The only way to prevent Johnson from totally undercutting my candidacy at the eleventh hour was for me to make public the fact that a bombing halt was imminent. In addition I wanted to plant the impression—which I believed to be true—that his motives and his timing were not dictated by diplomacy alone.

Johnson fired right back at Nixon's "ugly and unfair charges." But Nixon's inside informants, including Kissinger, still insisted that a bombing halt could come at any time. So it was too much to expect that Richard Nixon, with so much at stake, and so near the end of his long quest, would not take what steps he could to protect himself—particularly since a bombing halt would be

> the one move [he wrote in *RN*] that I thought could determine the outcome of the election. Had I done all this work and come all this way only to be undermined by the powers of an incumbent who had decided against seeking re-election?

But Vietnam was not the only matter worrying the Nixon camp; belatedly, top aides and Nixon himself realized that they might have fallen prey to a degree of "Deweyism"—that his top-lofty, above-the-battle campaign, waged as if he already were president, like Dewey's, had given his opponent the opportunity to go on the attack and command the headlines and the evening news broadcasts, from which voters got sometimes irrevocable impressions.

This belated recognition helped account for Nixon's hard-hitting late whistle-stop through Ohio, his renewed emphasis on law-and-order, a sharper edge to his descriptions of Humphrey ("the fastest, loosest tongue in the nation . . . who would rather switch than fight, rather spend than save, rather talk than mind his tongue on sensitive international matters"), and even for his decision to appear, for the first time in two years, on one of the network question and answer shows, "Face the Nation" on CBS. Given this rare opportunity (in 1968) to quiz Nixon, the reporters were tough on him; though making no gaffes, Nixon appeared stiff and uncomfortable—particularly in trying to explain his involuted charge of political cynicism against the president.

In another of his radio speeches, Nixon hedged again—more circumspectly this time—against Johnson's expected peace move. He warned against wasting or lightly playing "the highest trump card in our negotiators' hand" (a bombing halt), but added:

> My view is this: If the bombing can be ended in a way that will save American lives rather than costing American lives, and if the president determines that these conditions have been met by the North Vietnamese, then I will support his order to stop the bombing.

That left Nixon situated to go either way. He could support the president, or if any announced agreement appeared not to meet his criteria, he had a position from which to denounce it patriotically. With this speech, Nixon had done about all he could do to soften the shock of whatever Johnson might announce.

Then, with little more than a week to go, the Gallup poll hit Nixon hard from another direction. Humphrey had made a real and sizable gain at last, moving up five points from 31 to 36. This was at the expense of Wallace, who slipped to 15, while Nixon himself gained a point to 44; but that was small comfort to a front-runner seeing himself standing virtually still while his principal opponent closed in. It was disconcerting, moreover, to see Wallace defectors moving all the way to Humphrey, despite Nixon's tough law-and-order stance.

The news was bad from the important state of Texas, too. Governor Connally, whom Nixon had hoped to claim for his own, and who actually had done a little early work for him in disgust at the Democrats' botched convention, came out for Humphrey, along with Connally's bitterest in-state enemy—the liberal Senator Ralph Yarborough. Connally apparently had felt the heat of the Humphrey surge as well as the grip of Lyndon Johnson's hand.

Voter apathy was another problem. In North Carolina, a Nixon target state, polls showed strength declining for all three candidates, with the pool of undecided voters as big as the support for any one candidate. In the border states, a sharp rise in undecided voters also had been recorded. Did this mean that the Truman-Dewey syndrome of late-deciding voters was at work again? That idea could hardly calm Nixon's newly aroused fears.

Antiwar Democrats still were moving back to Humphrey, and when Gene McCarthy finally made his announcement of support for the ticket, voting Democratic would become for them even more permissible. Frequent disagreements between the Gallup and Harris polls, Gallup consistently showing Nixon farther ahead than Harris, also cheered the Democrats. If the polls couldn't agree, maybe they were both wrong; maybe Humphrey never had been in such bad shape as Gallup and Harris once had made it appear.

Against this kind of speculation, the hard arithmetic of the election still did not favor Humphrey—quite the opposite.

Of the eight major electoral states, Illinois was considered all but hopeless for the Democrats (reflecting, no doubt, Mayor Daley's lack of enthusiasm for Humphrey). If Humphrey carried all seven of the other majors, they would yield him only 201 of the 270 electoral votes needed for victory. Finding the other 69 votes would be far from easy—and even coming that close presupposed the unlikely: that Humphrey could carry seven of the "Big Eight" states.

Few analysts believed he could do it. Nixon still was the heavy favorite in California and Ohio ("Wallace is killing us," a high-ranking Ohio Democrat told the *Times*), led in Pennsylvania and appeared to be running at least even in Texas. If Humphrey lost California, or any two of the Big Eight states, plus Illinois, he could not hope to make up their electoral votes elsewhere.

Still, there was no question anymore but that Humphrey was moving up. On October 29, Eugene McCarthy—pushed, finally, by Nixon's ill-conceived "security gap" speech—made it official, if grudgingly: "The position of the Democratic candidate falls short of what I think it should be," he said. But Humphrey had "a better understanding of our domestic needs" than his opponent, and was more likely to cut back the arms race and reduce military tensions.

To this day, McCarthy is criticized by some Democrats for not having backed Humphrey sooner, and the suggestion sometimes is made that had he done so the Democrats would have won the election. The latter may or may not be the case, but if it is, the blame attaches at least equally to Humphrey himself and the Democratic establishment of the time.

Who can point to any real effort at Chicago, on the part of the nominee or of the establishment that supported him, to compromise with or accommodate the obviously critical McCarthy faction, as coalition strategy normally would have required? Johnson dictated the war plank of the platform and, at the last minute, Humphrey refused to join McCarthy's people even in supporting abolition of the unit rule that had so deprived the challenger of delegates honestly won in the primaries.

What, moreover, did Humphrey—the self-proclaimed as well as the official leader of his party—do after Chicago to earn the backing of a man who had opposed the war and Lyndon Johnson so strongly, the support of whose constituency was so vital, and whose point of view had received so little accommodation or comfort at Chicago?

The Salt Lake City speech? Effective as it was politically, it did not even offer unconditional cessation of the bombing, it went further than Johnson had done in reserving the right to resume, and it made no concession to the coalition government that was the cornerstone of McCarthy's Vietnam policy.

Party unity and conciliation, in short, run along a two-way street; in traditional politics it's up to the party leader—who in this case was the man with the most at stake—to begin walking on his side of it. Hubert Humphrey never did. McCarthy not only endorsed him in the end; he made a graceful appearance on Humphrey's final telecast, again urging antiwar Democrats to support Humphrey, who had done little to deserve such help. Had McCarthy done more, and done it earlier, he would have been acting from a degree of generosity—not his long suit in any case—and selflessness that no one had a right to expect.

After McCarthy's endorsement, there was one more tangible thing that could be done to help Humphrey's campaign. On October 31, not quite a week before the election to be held on November 5, Lyndon Johnson finally did it.

Making a nationally televised appearance early in the evening, the president announced that he had ordered all bombing of North Vietnam halted, and that agreement had been reached with Hanoi that Saigon would be "free to participate" in expanded talks to begin in Paris the day after the election. The National Liberation Front could take part, too. Therefore, Johnson said, "we expect . . . prompt, productive, serious and intensive negotiations in an atmosphere that is conducive to progress." Clark Clifford, the secretary of defense, immediately announced that the arrangement had his support and that of the Joint Chiefs of Staff, and that adequate assurances of good intentions had been received from Hanoi.

Had this favorable news come too late to boost Humphrey over the top?

And what had happened in the crucial two weeks since October 16, when in that conference call to Humphrey, Nixon and Wallace, Johnson had said he could not make such an announcement?

In Clifford's words, on October 16, "the South Vietnamese government, suddenly and unexpectedly, was not willing to go to Paris." And for those two long weeks, when the election perhaps hung in the balance, Saigon successfully had stalled Johnson, Hanoi and the agreement that essentially had been worked out with North Vietnam as early as October 14, when Clifford first learned of it.

That day in Saigon, Ambassador Ellsworth Bunker had put a proposed joint communiqué, detailing the arrangement, in front of President Nguyen Van Thieu. Thieu was surprised at an agreement he had thought Hanoi would never accept—but he was not surprised that the Johnson administration had acquiesced. Thieu had long feared that the Americans, when it suited them, or when they felt sufficiently pressed by the war, would find a way out at the expense of his Saigon regime. Humphrey's Salt Lake City speech had both heightened Thieu's fear and made him wary of Humphrey as a potential president.

When Thieu, backed by his National Security Council, balked at Bunker's proposed communiqué—ostensibly because it permitted the NLF to go to Paris on something like equal terms with his own delegation—Johnson was forced to make the October 16 conference call to the presidential candidates.

Intense negotiations between Washington and Saigon, Washington and Hanoi, with the Paris delegations chiming in and Soviet diplomats putting pressure on the North Vietnamese representatives, followed this first setback.

Moscow was playing the game of American politics, too; the Soviets realized that a bombing halt would help Humphrey, and they then held the well-known anti-Communist, Richard Nixon, in disdain—an irony, in view of the fondness for him later developed by the same Soviet leaders.[14]

Not a few in Johnson's inner circle believed that Thieu also wanted to influence the Nixon-Humphrey election, by preventing, not agreeing, to the bombing halt. In this view, the South Vietnamese president calculated that he could get a better deal from Nixon in the White House than from either Johnson or Humphrey. And the way to put Nixon there was to deny Humphrey the bombing halt.

Johnson, too, had political motives—though Rusk and others in the administration assert that these motives were secondary to his desire to end the war before he left office. He did want to stop the bombing on suitable terms and for sufficient returns from Hanoi; but he also wanted to stop it in time to aid Humphrey's chances, and he believed that aid would be the more powerful if Saigon were a party to the agreement. Partisan Democrats like Averell Harriman in Paris and Clark Clifford at the Pentagon also were eager to help Humphrey defeat Nixon.

For its part, Hanoi first tried to exploit the tensions between Saigon and Washington for greater concessions. Once that failed, the North Vietnamese signaled that they were prepared to wait for Johnson to straighten things out; they disengaged, for instance, most of their troops from American forces in Vietnam.

On October 27, with campaign time running out, Johnson again pressed Thieu, through Ambassador Bunker; and on October 28, Thieu apparently agreed to a joint communiqué that made no specific mention of NLF participation in the Paris talks, though it did not rule it out, and was not intended to. The agreement of American military authorities to the arrangement was secured—Johnson insisted on that—and he ordered preparations for a national television speech on October 30.

Then Thieu struck again. He objected to an NLF presence in Paris, though he had known perfectly well when he first agreed to the communiqué that it tacitly approved NLF participation in the talks. Johnson's planned speech for October 30 was canceled, but in Paris the American negotiators informed the North Vietnamese that the exasperated president was at last prepared to go ahead without Thieu.

He did so, announcing the bombing halt on Thursday night, October 31—two long weeks after Thieu's resistance had prevented Johnson from saying the same words to the nation, when those words would have given Hubert Humphrey's campaign the biggest lift it could have had, perhaps all the way into the White House.

Had Johnson then, at the last moment, still given Humphrey enough help to win the election? Nixon certainly had reason to fear it. Yet he could hardly denounce an agreement the Joint Chiefs endorsed, and after his many protestations that the president was the best judge of when appropriate concessions had been made by Hanoi. At a huge Madison Square Garden rally on the same night that Johnson announced the bombing halt, Nixon could only say that neither he nor Agnew would do anything to "destroy the chance of peace. We want peace."

But as word of the bombing halt swept across the nation, it seemed to give a new push to the late Humphrey surge. Nixon could do nothing but make the best finishing kick he could, and on Friday, November 1, he took off for Texas. Even this was questionable, since after Johnson's bombshell Nixon's best hope might lie in a low turnout that would favor the front-runner, backed by the more disciplined Republican voters. To reporters following him to Texas, Nixon appeared dispirited; but in Fort Worth, nevertheless, he lit into Humphrey: "I am the one that stands for a stronger U.S.," he cried, "and Mr. Humphrey for a weaker U.S.!"

Still, he stepped cautiously around the bombing halt. "Peace is too important for politics," he insisted.

It was possible, that Friday, to sense that Nixon—in one of his own phrases—had "peaked" and that, late though it was, the announcement of the bombing halt marked the downward turning point for him. Back in New York, Pennsylvania and Ohio, Hubert Humphrey was racing around in full cry, a happy warrior at last, with the smell of victory in his distended nostrils. Even Al Lowenstein, the original "dump Johnson" agitator—the effort implied dumping Hubert Humphrey, too—finally had endorsed Johnson's vice president and one-time loyalist.

Then, once again and this time publicly, Nguyen Van Thieu came to Richard Nixon's rescue. On Saturday, November 2 (U.S. time), three days before the polls opened, Thieu issued a statement that Johnson's announcement had been "unilateral," that in Saigon's view the cessation of the bombing was not justified by appropriate concessions from Hanoi, and that therefore his government "deeply regretted" that it could not take part in the talks. The South Vietnamese National Assembly that Thieu controlled quickly voted by acclamation to condemn Lyndon Johnson for his "betrayal." Richard Nixon was back in business.

Thieu was a devious politician but he may not have been acting entirely on his own, or without stimulation. Prominent Republicans—notably Mrs. Anna Chennault, the Chinese-born widow of General Claire Chennault of Flying Tigers fame, a frequent dabbler in Republican politics and the cochairwoman (with Mamie Eisenhower) of the Nixon-Agnew National Advisory Committee—were urging Thieu through back channels to hold out against the bombing-halt agreement, assuring him that he could get a better deal from Nixon than from Humphrey. After Humphrey's September 30 speech, Thieu believed this anyway and hoped for a Nixon victory.

Dean Rusk remembers that at the end of October, American intelligence agents were reporting on Mrs. Chennault's efforts; others that Rusk remembered—years later—as being cited in the reports included "high-level Nixon campaign officials . . . Spiro T. Agnew, and two Republican senators." President Johnson recalled that Republicans were assuring Thieu that "a Nixon administration will be more friendly to Saigon than the Democrats . . . stick with us and we will stick with you."[15]

Rusk's memory is no doubt largely correct; the bumbling Agnew and the two senators may have been involved with Mrs. Chennault. It's hard to believe, however, that the intelligence reports could have been right that "high-level Nixon campaign officials" were involved. To the extent that such officials knew about Mrs. Chennault's unofficial diplomacy—they eventually learned about it from the White House, if not before—they were horrified. Obviously, it would be fatal for the Nixon campaign to be connected with an effort to delay a bombing halt, possibly a peace settlement, for domestic political purposes.

When Thieu had come to Washington in the summer of 1968, Mrs. Chennault tried to arrange a meeting between him and Nixon. The Nixon aide who read her letter reacted as if it were a rattlesnake, urging Nixon that "this not be done for any reason and under no circumstances." Such a meeting would be "dangerous in the extreme and injurious to our Vietnam position—that is, to U.S. national interests." In the last days before Johnson's announcement of the bombing halt, Mrs. Chennault tried constantly to reach "high-level Nixon campaign officials," including John Mitchell, by telephone. None of them, alerted no doubt by White House inquiries, would accept her calls.[16]

It's possible that the Nixon campaign only cut off Mrs. Chennault *after* her activities became known to the administration and that she had acted, before that, at least with the tacit consent of campaign officials or of someone authoritative. But this seems far too great a risk for a campaign built on the principle of taking no risks; the possibility of a damaging disclosure, on balance, seems to outweigh anything that might have been gained. Besides, urging Nguyen Van Thieu to reject the bombing halt was preaching to the converted.

In any case, according to Rusk, the administration had no evidence that *Nixon himself* had had anything to do with whatever private approaches might have been made to Thieu. That was a primary reason why both Johnson and Humphrey eventually decided *not* to make public a charge that, if circulated at the last minute, could have ruined Nixon's chances.

Both Rusk and Clifford, highly respected men in the Johnson White House, counseled against making that charge. And when Johnson eventually called Nixon and asked him directly about Mrs. Chennault's activities, Nixon convinced the president that she had had no approval, advice or assistance from Richard Nixon or his official family.

But when Nguyen Van Thieu rejected the bombing-halt agreement—whatever and whoever, other than his own instincts, might have caused him to do it—he nonetheless handed Nixon a reprieve. The impetus to Humphrey's campaign produced by the bombing halt could not be reversed; but Thieu's public rejection gave Nixon the opportunity to picture Johnson as the one who had acted for domestic political purposes. Nixon lost no time.

On October 31, before going on television, Johnson had called Nixon to inform the Republican candidate of what he was about to do. In *RN* Nixon states flatly that, in this private call, "Johnson explained that he had not been able to persuade Saigon to agree to the provisions of the bombing halt, so that South Vietnam would not be joining in the announcement."

This seems incredible. It was not until November 2 that Thieu publicly attacked the bombing halt. If Johnson told Nixon of Thieu's resistance *two days earlier,* he was handing him the information on which he could base a charge that Johnson had acted prematurely, before a "faithful ally" and perhaps American troops had been sufficiently protected, and for the domestic political purpose of helping a Democrat win election to the White House.

After Thieu made public on November 2 his refusal to join the agreement (*not* after Johnson's October 31 phone call), that's exactly what Nixon did, though not personally. That afternoon, November 2, aboard the Nixon campaign plane on its way to Los Angeles from Texas, Bob Finch told wire service reporters (contradicting Nixon's later statement in *RN*) that, from what Johnson had said in his private call to Nixon on October 31, "we had the impression that all the diplomatic ducks were in a row."

Translation: but they weren't, so Johnson had moved to halt the bombing before he had the consent of all parties, in order to help Humphrey win the election.

Nixon could hardly have had the impression that "all the ducks were in a row" if Johnson had told him that Thieu was holding out against the agreement. And if Johnson had done so, Nixon need hardly have waited two days to have Finch insinuate, if not directly charge, that Johnson had acted prematurely and for domestic political purposes.

The next day, Sunday, November 3, Nixon appeared on NBC's "Meet the Press" (another sign that Deweyism had been abandoned) and insisted that Finch was speaking only for himself—though in *RN* he was to write, "I asked Bob Finch to put the word out to newsmen that the prospects for peace were not as advanced as Johnson's announcement might have made them seem."

Even at the time, reporters on "Meet the Press" treated Nixon's insistence that Finch had acted on his own with the disbelief it deserved. On the air, Nixon then conceded that after Johnson's phone call he had assumed, as Finch had said, that Saigon was a party to the agreement. Why would Johnson have accepted it otherwise?

> The only *quid pro quo* we got from the bombing pause, at least publicly, was the right of South Vietnam to attend [the Paris talks]. Well, now, if you played your trump card for the right of South Vietnam to attend and then did not know that South Vietnam was going to attend, you'd be giving away the card for nothing.

That seems so self-evident that Nixon's claim in *RN* to have been informed by Johnson of Thieu's resistance cannot be accepted. Johnson surely expected, as ultimately happened, that Thieu would be forced to come around, particularly after the election; there was no reason whatever for LBJ to have disclosed to the Republican candidate the damaging fact that Thieu was not yet "on board" at the time of the public announcement.

After Thieu himself made that clear, Nixon intimated on "Meet the

Press," as Finch had to the wire services, that either the president had been deceived or that he had acted prematurely to benefit Humphrey. That was about all Nixon could have done, short of the impossible step of opposing the bombing halt.

On this disputed note, the campaign was all over but for the voting. Humphrey finished strongly—for instance, at a huge rally in Houston on November 3, featuring Lyndon Johnson, John Connally and Ralph Yarborough on the same stage. Few Texas political buffs ever had expected to see such a sight, more exciting to some than Frank Sinatra acting as emcee.

Then Humphrey was off to Los Angeles, where he got a rousing welcome from the same ghetto residents who had poured into the streets for Robert Kennedy in June. Humphrey closed his campaign on Monday night with a lively national telecast—McCarthy taking part by telephone and Muskie on hand—and then a bibulous all-night party that properly capped off a vigorous, if not particularly effective, campaign.

Nixon, as befitted his reserved conduct all year, concluded more sedately with another of his prearranged telethons, also from Los Angeles, featuring relatively soft questions, statesmanlike answers and—finally—a blooper. In one answer, he spoke of "getting down to the nut-cutting," realized what he had said, and quickly added "as they say." No one seemed to mind this mild bit of scatology; Agnew, had he not been exiled to the safe state of Virginia, might have defended it as "locker-room humor."

Even the telethon suggested, however, that Nixon was no longer taking his victory for granted. A highlight of it was David Eisenhower reading a tribute from his grandfather—then in Walter Reed Hospital—to Nixon's "statesmanlike conduct" in refusing to criticize or exploit the president's bombing halt, even though Eisenhower suggested that Johnson might have "acted hastily, perhaps seeking to influence the election." No one could criticize Nixon for words he assuredly had put in Dwight Eisenhower's mouth; and no doubt the general's willingness to help, even from a hospital bed, salved some old wounds for his former vice president.

"In the circumstances," Eisenhower was further quoted, Nixon's response "must have taken extreme self-restraint." So it had, but the Eisenhower statement itself was evidence that he had found other ways to get the message across.

The final polls suggested that the Johnson-Humphrey message of peace in Vietnam had reached farther and hit harder. On the day before the election the *New York Times* published a state-by-state survey that predicted for Nixon, once so far in the lead, no more than a bare-bones victory—29 states with a total of 299 electoral votes. Nine states with 77 votes were forecast for Humphrey and 5 with 45 votes for Wallace. Seven with 117 votes were considered too close to call.

The public opinion samples brought even worse news for Nixon. Gallup, after picturing the Republican candidate with a safe lead throughout the campaign, found him on the last weekend barely ahead of Humphrey, 42 to 40, and within the margin of error; thanks no doubt to the bombing halt, Humphrey had gained 6 points in the final week. Was it going to be Truman and Dewey all over again?

Worse, Louis Harris polled a day later and found Hubert Humphrey— who had not been able to make himself heard above the booing and heckling in September—running ahead at last, 43 to 40, after one of the most amazing comebacks in political history. Even Richard Nixon must have feared that after five years of virtually unremitting effort, and despite the glowing prospects of September, he was going to be a loser again.

He was, at the least, to go through the election-night agonies of 1960 all over again. As the votes were being counted in 1968, Nixon separated himself from his family, giving his wife and daughters a suite to themselves in the Waldorf-Astoria. In his own, he allowed only a few of his closest associates to come in from time to time. They included Murray Chotiner, who had been with him from the beginning, twenty-two years earlier in California's Twelfth District.

Though Nixon was a loner in any case, these arrangements suggest that, perhaps subconsciously, he did fear a repetition of his earlier defeat. And, almost incredibly, as the night of November 5, 1968, wore on indecisively, turning slowly to the morning of November 6, once again the election came down to the same states that had decided it against him eight years earlier—Illinois, Texas and Missouri.

Some who saw Nixon that night testify that he went through it with relative calm, though he must have been seething inside. At one point, Humphrey actually forged ahead of him in the popular vote; states Nixon had counted on, Pennsylvania in particular, failed him; early returns from Illinois and Ohio, states he had to win, shook him.

By the small hours of November 6, however, it was apparent that of the three candidates only Nixon could win a majority in the electoral college, and that if he won Illinois he would win the presidency. Believing from his own information that he had won that state, he became "irritated," he recalled in *RN,* because Mayor Daley would not release the final count Nixon thought would cement his victory. He ordered Bryce Harlow to call Larry O'Brien, Humphrey's campaign manager, in Minneapolis, where Humphrey was watching the returns:

> Bryce, lay it on the line. Don't fool around. Tell O'Brien to tell Hubert to quit playing games. We've won Illinois, so let's get this thing over with.

Harlow reached O'Brien's suite, Nixon recalled, "but either [O'Brien] was not there or would not take the call."

O'Brien had been too busy to speak to Harlow, a good friend despite political differences. Some time after the election, however, O'Brien encountered Harlow casually and asked what he had been calling about on election night.

"Nixon wanted you to tell Hubert to concede," Harlow said.

Twenty years later, when he told me his version of Harlow's call, O'Brien—a man of considerable political punctilio—was still outraged. He considered it a breach of manners and procedure for a winning candidate to urge the loser to concede, and so it seems even to the layman. Nixon's instructions to Harlow again suggest his inner uncertainty.[17]

No wonder. It was 8:30 A.M., November 6, after a long night in which Humphrey came strikingly close to denying Nixon an electoral majority, before ABC news—on the basis of its vote projections—called Nixon the winner in Illinois, making his victory, if not yet official, a certainty. After a few handshakes and congratulations with aides, he went down the hall to his family in the other suite. After a while, he wrote in *RN:*

> I sat alone with Pat, and she told me it had been a terribly difficult night for her. The speculation by the commentators about Illinois had driven her to tears. Waves of nausea had swept over her as she feared that we would have to experience a repeat of the outrageous frauds of 1960. When I told her it was all over, she asked emotionally, "But Dick, are we sure of Illinois? Are we completely sure?"
> I answered, very firmly, "Absolutely. The votes are in, and there is no way that it can be turned around at this point." Then I held her, and she burst into tears of relief and joy.

It's hardly to be wondered that Mrs. Nixon was so distraught at what must have seemed at the time so nearly a repeat of that earlier traumatic election night. And it seems reasonable to suppose that in recounting her anxiety, Richard Nixon also was suggesting his own.

The 1968 election also turned out to be too close for any one factor to have been necessarily decisive. Nixon lost Pennsylvania and its 29 electoral votes, for example, because Humphrey carried Philadelphia with too large a margin to be overcome elsewhere in the state; and that happened not least because the proportion of black voters in Philadelphia, voters Nixon made no effort to win, had risen in eight years from 28 to over 34 percent.

"I am not going to campaign for the black vote at the risk of alienating the suburban vote," Nixon had told Thatcher Longstreth, a leading Philadelphia Republican. "If I am President, I am not going to owe anything to the black community." In a campaign designed to be mistake-free, that was a big one. Nixon's share of a substantially increased black vote dropped nationally from 32 percent in 1960 to 12 in 1968.[18]

A mistake, yes; but was it more than that? Eight years earlier, Nixon had refused to "pander" to Martin Luther King and had suffered a grievous loss of black votes. In 1968, he had made a decision not to risk suburban votes or indebtedness to the "black community." These were not openly antiblack decisions but political calculations.

Yet, the "mistakes" of 1960 and 1968 are consistent with each other, and with his conduct toward the Southern delegations before the 1968 convention and his law-and-order tactics afterward. They force the question of whether Nixon subconsciously disdained black voters, hence any overt effort to win them, despite his generally good civil rights record and his vice presidential efforts to change the Senate filibuster rules. His later conduct in the White House did nothing to dispel such suspicion.

Nixon's loss of Pennsylvania was aided, too, by voters defecting from Wallace—who, despite all Nixon's efforts, were Democrats moving mostly to Humphrey. The same phenomenon cost him Michigan, where once the law-and-order issue had seemed so dominant, and where Nixon had delivered his strongest attack on George Wallace. By election day, Wallace got only 10 percent of the Michigan vote, though polls in mid-October had given him 16 percent. Miscalculation of Wallace's effect and how to counter it in these key states—admittedly not an easy thing to do—was another Nixon problem.

On the other hand, New Jersey and Ohio defectors from Wallace went *to* Nixon in sufficient numbers for him to carry those states. Similarly, normally Democratic Tennessee and sometimes Democratic Kentucky also went to him, mostly because Wallace cut deeply into what might have been Humphrey's strength.

Once again, Lyndon Johnson helped save Texas for the Democratic party, more by forcing the brief alliance of Ralph Yarborough and John Connally behind Humphrey than by any ballot-box manipulation. A huge increase in Hispanic and black voter registration also helped Humphrey.

Illinois, which Nixon so firmly believed had been stolen from him in 1960, probably went for him in 1968 because Mayor Daley was not sufficiently motivated to carry it for Hubert Humphrey. It was Humphrey who made the mistake in Illinois, by insufficiently reassuring Daley—though Humphrey knew the mayor had feared he could not win and had wanted to draft Ted Kennedy.

Of all the influences that produced the outcome in 1968, however, none could have been more powerful than the two-week delay, from October 14 to October 31, in Lyndon Johnson's announcement of the bombing halt in Vietnam. As in 1948, huge numbers of voters had not made up their minds until the last weeks and days of the campaign—or changed their minds then; in Illinois, for example, a survey showed 17 percent of the electorate still undecided on November 1.

Nixon's big lead in California, his home state, had shrunk to one percentage point by the last weekend of the campaign. In Michigan, a *Detroit News* poll found Humphrey—immediately after the announcement of the bombing halt—gaining a virtually incredible seven points over the previous weekend. A *Buffalo Courier-Express* poll of eight western New York counties found a Nixon advantage of seven points reduced to one in the final survey.

In the end, Humphrey lost the popular vote by just over half a percentage point, only half a million votes. The electoral-vote count was not quite so close, due to the winner-take-all system within the states: Nixon 301 (two less than Kennedy's winning majority in 1960), Humphrey 191, Wallace 46.

Yet, in the poll most favorable to him, Humphrey had trailed by 40 to 35 on October 20, and by more in the Gallup sample. While it can't be known precisely how many voters switched to him, or made up their minds to vote for him, because of the bombing halt, it seems entirely reasonable to assume that had it been made public two weeks earlier, it could have added a half-million votes to his total. Cast in the right states—Illinois and Missouri, for example, which totaled 38 electoral votes and were carried for Nixon by only 135,000 and 20,000 respectively—those votes would have denied anyone an electoral college majority and thrown the election into the House of Representatives.

There, with each state casting only one vote, Hubert H. Humphrey might well have been constitutionally elected president of the United States. In the Ninety-first House, convening in January 1969, there were 26 Democratic delegations to only 19 Republican, with five tied between the parties (Illinois, Maryland, Oregon, Texas and Virginia). Five of the Democratic delegations would have been under Wallace's influence, since he had won a plurality or a majority of their states' popular votes.

No one can know for sure what would have happened in such a situation when all of the wheeling and dealing, logrolling and vote-swapping was concluded. What does seem indisputable is that the delay in announcing the bombing halt elected Richard Nixon to the presidency. In the end, Nguyen Van Thieu helped put the man he wanted in the White House, and Averell Harriman's prediction was to come true: the war in Vietnam would go on for another four years. The bombing would begin again and another 27,000 Americans would die before the war finally was lost, and the effort abandoned.[19]

Nixon the loner had spent most of an unnerving election night by himself, waiting once again for the returns from the same states on which everything had depended in his first presidential campaign. After his appearance at the Waldorf to claim victory on the morning of November 6, and after an informal lunch in their Fifth Avenue apartment with his wife and daughters, he again sought solitude in his library. There, he recalled in *RN,* he put on the record player one of his favorites, the rather bombastic score from "Victory at Sea" by Richard Rodgers.

> I . . . turned the volume up high. My thoughts meshed with the music. The battle had been long and arduous. We had suffered reverses and won victories. The struggle had been hard fought. But now we had won the final victory.

In "politics and public service"—that peculiarly demanding calling of which Nixon knew "there was no other life for me"—final victory is elusive, perhaps impossible. In less exalted moments, no one understood that better than Richard Nixon; he had lived that truth himself.

On the day of his redemption from defeat and humiliation, the long years of adversity, the endless plodding from party dinner to party dinner, the countless speeches and news conferences vindicated at last—on that day, when he had struggled to the most cherished goal of his fifty-five years, the saintly mother and the glowering father at rest in the hard-earned triumph of the son, who could blame him if he did not dwell on the trials his election foretold?

In the satisfaction of the moment, in the sounding brass of Rodgers's music, with his biding dream come true, no wonder Richard Nixon forgot, for once, what his life had taught him—that "the one sure thing about politics is that what goes up comes down, and what goes down often comes up."

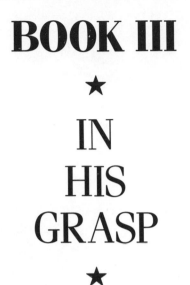

BOOK III

★

IN
HIS
GRASP

★

Richard Nixon had it within his grasp to be
our greatest post–World War II president.

—Elliot Richardson at Hofstra,
November 19, 1987

10

★

Pragmatist

★

We've got the reputation of . . . building a
wall around the President. The fact is that he
was down under the desk saying "I don't
want to see those fellows" and we were trying
to pull him out.

—John Ehrlichman

The day after the election of 1968, November 6, was "a day for visiting
the sick and burying the dead," Eugene McCarthy remarked. "It's gray
everywhere—all over the land."

It was not, of course, a gray day of such lamentation for President-elect
Richard Milhous Nixon. With his wife and daughters and seven assistants
he flew that evening to Key Biscayne, where for nearly twenty years, win
or lose, he had gone to recover from tough campaigns.

This time he stopped over in Washington to visit Dwight D. Eisenhower
in his bed at Walter Reed Hospital—family homage to the patriarch, as
well as the new order of Republicanism paying due respect to the old,
whatever the differences of the past.*

That night in Key Biscayne, in a house rented from John Kennedy's old
party-going chum, Senator George Smathers of Florida, Nixon slept for
nine hours. The next day, as far as the world knew, he got down to the
business of forming a new administration.**

*David Eisenhower, the old general's grandson, and Julie Nixon were to be married
on December 22, 1968.
**The austere Nixon and the carousing Smathers had been freshmen senators together
in 1951, and had remained good friends, though Smathers was a Democrat. The
Smathers house in Key Biscayne was next door to one owned by their mutual friend,
Bebe Rebozo.

Actually his staff did. "There is a lot of newspaper copy about . . . bulging briefcases and his staff and doing a lot of work," John Ehrlichman recalled years later.

> All baloney! What generally happened in Key Biscayne was that [Nixon] went over to his house, which was on the west side of the island; we went to a hotel on the east side of the island and never the twain met. We did have a couple of meetings . . . but basically [staff members] were left on our own to compose the government.[1]

No doubt remembering his meeting with the victorious Kennedy in 1960, Nixon put in a call to Hubert Humphrey, inviting him to Key Biscayne. Humphrey, like George Romney—but unlike most of Nixon's other major opponents—was no Franklin of old blood or big money, or both. At Whittier College, it's altogether likely that Hubert Humphrey— the depression-era pharmacist's son—would have been an Orthogonian. When Nixon called, Humphrey was about to leave for the Virgin Islands for losers' therapy in the sun, but readily agreed to stop off in Florida.

The actual meeting of winner and loser, on November 8, took place near Miami at the Opa-Locka Coast Guard Station, since Humphrey was still vice president and his party was traveling in a government plane. After the two had talked privately, Nixon—with shaky grammar but perhaps to balance off one of the most galling moments of the past—told Humphrey before a crowd that had gathered at the airstrip: "I recall in 1960 after losing a very close election, President-elect Kennedy called on me when I was in Florida, and history repeats itself, so I know exactly how you feel."

He probably did. As Kennedy had made an offer to him in 1960, he even suggested, *pro forma,* the U.N. ambassadorship for Humphrey. Just as with Nixon and Kennedy, the loser declined but pledged his support. Appearing to be as ebullient as usual, Humphrey assured the audience that "I'm going to want [Nixon's] presidency to be an effective presidency because as he succeeds, we all succeed."

Ehrlichman recalled, however, that when the two former opponents privately "went into the operations building to make up . . . Humphrey cried. He was very emotional about the whole thing." The stoic Nixon, so often a loser himself, was not likely to have understood *that.*

Nixon had had a purpose in bringing John Ehrlichman along to Opa-Locka. A Seattle land-use lawyer with a prosperous practice awaiting him, Ehrlichman had been in 1968 a highly effective "tour manager"—"the best job in a political campaign . . . barring none," Ehrlichman later called it. He had traveled with the candidate, headed the corps of advance men who arranged rallies and speech appearances, and oversaw the traveling party:

We would set the schedule with [Nixon's] approval; we'd set the trips; advance men would go out and do the job. When the time came, Nixon would appear at the airplane door and wave and go down and work the fence and do what he was scheduled to do, and get back on the airplane and we'd button him up and go on to the next place.

Ehrlichman, forty-three years old in 1968, had been so effective as tour manager that he was one of only a handful of aides Nixon took to Key Biscayne. Ehrlichman, however, though he had been an advance man as far back as the Nixon campaign of 1960, did not consider himself entirely partisan or committed; politics to him was only an interesting sideline, or so he thought, and he intended to go back to his law practice.

Getting wind of this, Nixon arranged for Ehrlichman to ride back with him from Opa-Locka to Key Biscayne. When he asked what his former tour manager, obviously a first-rate staff man, would like to do in the government, Ehrlichman said "nothing"—though he conceded that some-day it would be nice if Nixon "in a weak moment" nominated him as a federal judge.

The president-elect countered right then, offering to appoint Ehrlichman attorney general. That imposing offer struck the young lawyer, in his own words, as "ludicrous," and he again refused. So Nixon proposed that he serve for a year as White House counsel, adding baldly, as Ehrlichman recalls it: "Then you can go back and get very rich practicing law because everybody will want to hire you because you are the president's friend."

Without comment on this realism, Ehrlichman concedes that he was "sort of intrigued with the idea of seeing how the White House operated from the inside and that seemed like a pretty good position from which to do it." So he accepted, went to work in the Hotel Pierre transition head-quarters in New York, and eventually moved to the White House as one of Nixon's premier assistants.

In recounting, years later, how he came to be hired, Ehrlichman may have been somewhat flippant. The episode tells much, however, about Nixon on the eve of his presidency. He clearly wanted Ehrlichman's ser-vices but, if Ehrlichman's important role in the administration began as casually as he describes it, had little idea how to use them. Perhaps more important, it was the second time Nixon had gone out of his way to talk Ehrlichman into taking a responsible position the Seattle lawyer did not at first want to fill.

Ehrlichman had done "a little part-time scheduling"—an understate-ment—for Nixon during the latter's ill-fated race for governor of Califor-nia, and was in the Nixon party on the morning of the famous "last press conference" in 1962. Nixon's disastrous performance, Ehrlichman did not fail to notice, came "after a night of drinking and sleeplessness" and he began to wonder if Nixon might not "be his own worst enemy."

Two years later, at the Republican National Convention that nominated Barry Goldwater in San Francisco, Ehrlichman again was in Nixon's temporary entourage. After Nixon's well-received speech of reconciliation to the convention he gave a party in his suite. As Ehrlichman, a straight-arrow Christian Scientist, recalls the occasion, Nixon "got pie-eyed, which cut across the grain as far as I was concerned."

So when Bob Haldeman, Ehrlichman's friend from college days and his main link to Nixon, had invited him into the 1968 campaign, Ehrlichman hung back. Haldeman urged him to come to New York and talk to Nixon himself. Eventually, Ehrlichman did:

> I leveled with [Nixon]. I said . . . "I have a feeling that you are highly susceptible to alcohol. I'm not interested in coming away from my practice and my family and going out and beating my brains out if this is going to be a problem."
>
> [Nixon] got very serious with me; he said he thought I was right. He made me a very solemn pledge that it would not be a problem. He asked me to come and help him and I was persuaded. . . . [H]e kept that promise, all through that campaign. He was very fit; drinking was not a problem.

Aside from Ehrlichman's courage in opening such a confrontation with a presidential candidate, it cannot have been an easy charge for a presidential candidate—or anyone—to hear. Nixon's acceptance of it, at least in Ehrlichman's telling, suggests, first, that he, too, feared he had a drinking problem.

But *denial* is usually the problem drinker's immediate response to such an accusation; so Nixon's acquiescence also suggests that in 1968 he was not by any means an alcoholic or a secret binge drinker. That he kept his pledge "all through that campaign" further suggests that he was able, almost on demand, to keep full control of himself; that in turn conforms to his well-established reputation for iron self-discipline.

Ehrlichman, however, deliberately used the qualifying phrase "all through that campaign," that is, 1968. Though he never was aware of Nixon drinking in the White House, he was uneasy about the president's weekends at Key Biscayne, where little real work was done and the ever-present Bebe Rebozo acted not only as untiring listener but as bartender. In Ehrlichman's view, Rebozo in the latter role was kept all too busy; Ehrlichman did not, however, during his White House tenure, regard alcohol as a real problem for the president.[2]

Another Nixon drinking episode of some importance, probably unknown to Ehrlichman, was talked about by others. On the night after Vice President Richard Nixon's famous "kitchen debate" with Nikita Khrushchev in Moscow in 1959—an exchange Nixon knew to be fraught with meaning for his personal future, and believed to be important to American-Soviet relations—he returned to the American embassy and drank too much, rather obviously seeking relief from tension.*

That incident makes Ehrlichman's later diagnosis seem all the more sensible:

> Physiologically, this fellow has a disability. . . . One drink can knock him galley west if he is tired. Even if he is not tired, about two and a half drinks will do it. So he is much more susceptible than a lot of people I've met. . . . [H]e simply has to watch it.

A rather similar view is expressed, but more gently, by Ray Price, a respected Nixon aide since 1967, a principal speech writer during the White House years, a close personal associate even after those years. Price strenuously objected in an interview to the idea of Nixon as a "problem drinker"; he conceded, however, that when Nixon was tired—"particularly if he'd had a sleeping pill"—one drink or "even a beer" could make him appear drunk.[3]

This is by no means reassuring. Few persons are more likely, more often, to confront tension and stress than the president of the United States; and few need more sorely to keep wits and judgment clear. Nor is it comforting to think of a president who might just have had a tense confrontation with, say, the leader of the Soviet Union, being knocked "galley west" with one stress-relieving martini.

Nixon himself had warned in *Six Crises:*

> The most dangerous period in a crisis is not in the preparation or in the fighting of a battle, but in its aftermath. This is true even when the battle ends in victory. When it ends in defeat, in a contest where an individual has carried on his shoulders the hopes of millions, he then faces his greatest test.

Hugh Sidey, the *Time* magazine columnist and an intimate of most presidents since Kennedy, once had a telephone call from Nixon during which Sidey concluded that the president had been drinking, "since he

---

*This incident was observed by a diplomat who told it in confidence to a close friend, an eminent journalist, some time later. The journalist, an equally close friend of mine, told me the story—identifying the diplomat—long after Nixon left the White House. I repeat it here because I regard both sources as unimpeachable and because the incident is thirty years old.

couldn't talk very well." But Maurice Stans, Nixon's secretary of commerce and fund-raiser—and, it should be said, a devoted admirer—has insisted that Nixon "was highly disciplined in his personal life, as evidenced by his very limited drinking, nonsmoking, regular exercise, and exemplary personal and family behavior."

Stans was questioned about a book in which Alexander Haig, Nixon's last national security assistant, said he sometimes had to act as president when "Nixon was drunk."

"I can't believe that," Stans replied. "I've seen Nixon on a number of informal social occasions where it would have been very easy for him, as for other presidents, to take three or four drinks, but his habit was almost universal to take one and carry it around all evening or as long as other people were drinking. . . . Haig may have seen him on one occasion or another when for some reason he seemed not responsive, but I didn't."

Nixon's old law school professor, Kenneth Rush, later to become his deputy secretary of state, then deputy secretary of defense, "never saw President Nixon take more than one drink. . . . I know that [these drinking stories] are false." Bob Finch could say that "from personal knowledge [drinking] was no problem during the 1960 campaign, or while I was close to him when he was president."

Price similarly asserted that there was never a time, during his many years in close association with Nixon, when he saw drinking affect Nixon's performance. He dismissed as "fiction" the famous account of a drunken president in *The Final Days,* by Bob Woodward and Carl Bernstein.

These witnesses, Nixon admirers all, of course may have seen only what they wanted to see, or what Nixon allowed them to see. But Robert Stripling, who knew Nixon well and saw him often during Nixon's service on HUAC, now is an outspoken critic. He remembers that Nixon had "no capacity to drink . . . two or three drinks would make him drunk."

On the other hand, Ehrlichman, the Christian Scientist and teetotaler, charged during the Watergate hearings that many members of Congress frequently were affected in their duties by too much drinking. He may have seen in Nixon what he feared to see—and, at that, concedes he never saw it in the White House.

All that granted, the Nixon passage quoted from *Six Crises* takes on new overtones when related to Ehrlichman's diagnosis. Given their tense precampaign exchange, it seems all the more remarkable that when Ehrlichman, barely a year later, once again demurred at serving Nixon, the president-elect once again met his objections and brought him around. Aside from Ehrlichman's obvious abilities—many persons are able and most would be eager to work for a president—it's reasonable to suppose that Nixon valued, at least accepted, Ehrlichman's demonstrated willingness to level with him, a quality Nixon knew from the Eisenhower years always to be in short supply in any White House.

Bryce Harlow's experienced assistant, Kenneth BeLieu, pointed out the obvious, that "when they play 'Hail to the Chief,' give a twenty-one-gun salute, and everybody stands up when you come in the room, and nobody ever tells you to go to hell, you lose touch with reality." Nixon knew that better than most incoming presidents, but BeLieu believed he, too, ultimately "lost touch with reality."

That was later. It may well be that the president-elect, as he prepared for the White House in 1968, himself feared what Ehrlichman called a "disability" enough so that he wanted to keep at hand a man whose mere presence would remind and warn him of it—one who might, indeed, be expected to do so directly, if necessary. If Ehrlichman agreed to stay on, clearly it would have to be on the same basis with which he had joined the staff a year earlier.

In staffing a new administration, Bob Finch has said, "it may be necessary to use the talent that have done a good job in the campaign. But that same group can't be allowed to totally exercise the responsibilities of governing." The job is more difficult than commonly understood, in Ken BeLieu's opinion, because "the normal political campaign does not produce people that are necessarily the right ones for administering the government properly."

From lengthy Washington experience in the Pentagon for the Kennedy and Johnson administrations and as a Senate committee staff director in the fifties, BeLieu regarded Haldeman and Ehrlichman, for example, as "bright young men" who "didn't understand government"—didn't even know "how to spell Defense Department." Harlow told BeLieu they'd been rewarded with their important jobs "because they helped Nixon get elected." This led the irreverent BeLieu to conclude that the two young aides at least knew "how to use a sunlamp to disguise heavy whiskers."

BeLieu was not overly surprised at their emergence because he had come to believe that "most politicians are administrative idiots. . . . [U]sing military terms, they've never commanded over twenty-five or thirty people at the most." In his view it may not be "possible for a man to go through all the hurdles necessary to become president and become a good administrator at the same time."

That truth has become even more apparent since Nixon's election in a campaign that featured the most shrewdly conceived use of television up to that time. A president's lack of administrative experience and skill is only one of the problems for the American system created by the widening divergence, television-born, between what it takes to get elected and what is required for governing.

Slogans and "sound bites," for example, are effective in winning votes. Later sloganeering may help a president maintain his popularity. Both results are important to any president but will be of little help in making hard policy choices, in putting the right person in the right spot, or in dealing with foreign adversaries. The likelihood, however, is that in the era opened by extensive television coverage of politics—and advanced by Nixon's adroit use of the medium in 1968—presidents are going to be accomplished in slogans and sound bites, whether or not they lack experience, judgment or courage.

In 1968, Nixon had not known exactly what to do with Ehrlichman in the new administration, and by the latter's testimony had mostly left his highest assistants alone at Key Biscayne to "compose the government." He was far from uninterested in staffing and organization, however, and had more specific ideas and plans of his own than Ken BeLieu was likely to have known. Bryce Harlow, recalling the transition from candidate to president, said that Nixon "had it all planned" and could say confidently "here's what we're going to do."

His experience as vice president had been "terribly valuable," in Harlow's opinion, particularly because he had been the first vice president "really used by the president"—a plausible claim (see chapters 4 and 5). Those eight years, certainly, had left Nixon pretty sure of some things he would not do in the White House.

He had no intention, for example, of tying himself up with scheduled meetings that would cause him to lose control of his time. Eisenhower regularly held a meeting with congressional leaders on Tuesday, a news conference on Wednesday, a cabinet meeting on Friday and a number of other set pieces. Nixon considered this kind of routine a waste of presidential time.

He also planned to hold few cabinet meetings, Harlow recalled, because he had found those in the Eisenhower administration "ineffably boring." For two hours every Friday, sitting opposite the president, Nixon had had to conceal his boredom and his irritation at what he considered the waste of everyone's time, not least his own. After Eisenhower's heart attack, things had gotten worse; the Eisenhower cabinet members and Nixon were under instruction not to raise subjects so controversial that they might upset the president.[4]

Nixon had urged Eisenhower, after his stroke in 1957, to cut down on his attendance at meetings. At first the president complied but, as Nixon recalled—rather disdainfully—in *RN:* "Within a few months he was again attending every meeting and allowing the discussions to ramble on as if it were his duty to be bored for his country as well as to lead it."

Such recollections led Nixon, when he became president, to the notion that he would have a virtually autonomous cabinet, composed of men who would "run their departments" and not bother the president about matters that did not interest him.

There were quite a few such matters, as Ehrlichman learned, because

Nixon had "a very narrow range of interests . . . he's not the sort of fellow that you'd find fascinating as a next door neighbor."

> If you are willing to talk to him about the things that he's interested in, he's fascinating. But if the conversation at the party turned to something that he wasn't interested in, he might go home or go upstairs and take a nap or go for a walk around the block because he is simply not able to get involved in things that he's not interested in.

Ehrlichman detected something of a pattern in Nixon's interest, or lack thereof, in domestic matters. "Passion issues," Ehrlichman thought—busing and school integration are prime examples—engaged him because they called on his political skills and knowledge. Less emotional questions, such as revenue sharing, were too technical or administrative to catch his interest, though he dutifully dealt with them.[5]

Nixon certainly did not propose to be bored in his own administration, as he had been in Eisenhower's. Even before he was elected, he had insisted to the journalist Theodore White: "This country could run itself domestically without a President. All you need is a competent Cabinet to run the country at home. You need a President for foreign policy."[6]

That idea lasted only a few months—until Nixon predictably found cabinet and subcabinet officers making policy pronouncements he could not accept, particularly on segregation issues at Health, Education and Welfare, at Housing and Urban Development—where in Ehrlichman's words, "[Secretary George] Romney was off saving the world"—and at Transportation, where "[Secretary John] Volpe was saying some funny things about air bags" as safety devices in automobiles.

It was for such reasons that Nixon soon began taking back the "delegations of absolute authority that had been rather frivolously handed out in transition time. . . . [T]hat caused a good deal of heartburn out in the Cabinet."

Relations ultimately became so strained between president and cabinet that a "rump session" of department heads convened in Romney's conference room to discuss economic problems they had been unable to raise in regular cabinet meetings—which, as Ehrlichman describes them, had become "more and more perfunctory." The White House got wind of the meeting, Nixon sent Ehrlichman over to be "a skunk at a garden party," and the result was that the rump session, too, was "sort of perfunctory."

From the cabinet members' point of view, of course, White House staff dominance caused more than heartburn. It left them uncertain of administration direction and policy. Long after Ehrlichman's presence squelched the cabinet's rump session, Nixon's second secretary of agriculture, Earl

Butz, realized that when Haldeman or Ehrlichman would "call and say 'this is what the President wants,' you soon had to ask, 'is that Ehrlichman or the President speaking?' You were never quite sure."

Even before being sworn in, Nixon also decided quite deliberately to have no one speaking for him or empowered to describe policy in his own words, as Jim Hagerty had been able to do when he was press secretary in the Eisenhower administration. One reason was that Nixon believed himself to be "the best communicator of his policies and that he as President was best able to move the country in the directions that he was trying to move it," Bob Haldeman recalled. "When we got to important stuff, Nixon charged into the press room . . . and articulated what he wanted to say the way he wanted to say it."

There were other reasons to have "no Jim Hagerty." Nixon not only thought Hagerty had had "too much impact" on policy through his power to enunciate it; with his long memory and talent for grudges, he had not forgiven Hagerty personally for not "cleaning up" Eisenhower's "if you give me a week" remark about Nixon during the 1960 campaign.[7]

No doubt Nixon recalled also the Indochina flap of 1954. It had been Jim Hagerty who had questioned him sharply, while attempting to control the damage Nixon had done with his suggestion that the U.S. send troops to Indochina if the French withdrew (see chapter 4). Hagerty was no longer around to be paid off, but Nixon was symbolically evening some old scores.

The Hagerty precedent also suggests why Nixon did not appoint his long-time associate, Herbert Klein, to be the White House press secretary, but instead installed Ronald Ziegler to be a sort of wind-up spokesman—one who would say only what he was told to say, and not that if he could avoid it. Klein had a good reputation with, and a wide acquaintance among, reporters and editors; and Nixon feared he might develop a power center of his own, as Hagerty had, in the press office. So Klein was shunted upstairs to the nominally higher ranking but less visible, less crucially involved, job of general oversight and promotion of the administration's press and public relations.

Nixon also wanted no back entrance into the Oval Office he looked forward to occupying. He had seen the power Ann Whitman, Eisenhower's secretary, had developed through her ability to get visitors into the president's presence without clearance from the official appointments secretary. He knew too that "Missy" Lehand had had much the same unofficial control of presidential time in Franklin Roosevelt's administration.

Often himself denied access to Eisenhower, Nixon well recalled that Miss Whitman would let Harlow or Hagerty in to see the president virtually at will; and that Foster Dulles would drive up to the South Lawn entrance without an appointment, to be ushered right in by Miss Whitman.

As with the Hagerty precedent, Nixon was in some sense reacting to old wounds; but he also aimed to prevent Miss Whitman's kind of informal control of the president's time and presence. A congenital loner, he wanted the Oval Office to be more nearly a barricade against a demanding world, and was determined to make it so.

That gave Bob Haldeman, appointed by Nixon to head the staff during the transition, an opportunity he quickly seized. Inevitably, rivalries were developing anyway, as Bob Finch realized,

> between the old and the new—those of us who had been with Nixon a long time and had gone through the 1960 campaign and the new group that came in in 1968, the Haldeman-Ehrlichman group. In their eyes they had done what we couldn't do in 1960. . . . It was the "old and new guard" kind of thing.

At the Hotel Pierre transition headquarters in New York, after the early organization meetings in Key Biscayne, this rivalry had a most startling consequence: Haldeman "cut off the hands" of Rosemary Woods, Nixon's faithful personal secretary, who for so long had served him in victory and defeat (and who in my presence had wept all the way to the Capitol on the cold day of Kennedy's inauguration in 1960).

Haldeman not only took full control of access to the president, he also arranged the White House staff so that Miss Woods would be relegated to a basement office far from the portals of power—all with the president-elect's acquiescence. Whatever qualms Nixon may have felt about this treatment of a faithful and deserving colleague, it removed the possibility that Miss Woods would provide back-entrance access to him. It also signaled the arrival of a new flow of power, based on the 1968 campaign team, in the Nixon hierarchy.

At about the same time, Bryce Harlow—an older, more relaxed man—was using much different methods to ease out Ray Bliss, the chairman of the Republican National Committee during Nixon's 1968 campaign and the architect of his surprise victory in Ohio in 1960. Bliss did not want to resign—"the news almost broke his heart"—and Harlow "virtually forced the president to see him" at the Pierre.

Nixon, "as considerate as he could be," offered Bliss an ambassadorship to the Netherlands or to Australia (both of which the old pol wisely refused) and explained that he was replacing him only because Bliss had been a "nuts and bolts" chairman when what was required was "someone who can drive home the issues, attack the Democrats." A decade earlier, Vice President Nixon no doubt had reasoned similarly when he supported Charlie Halleck for the House Speakership against Nixon's former benefactor, Joe Martin (see chapter 2).

Harlow's gentler approach, he recalled, "really fussed Haldeman. To him it showed an indecisiveness and lack of requisite toughness." Before long, Harlow and Arthur Burns, the two most experienced men on the White House staff, noticed that they were being excluded from certain meetings to which, as senior counselors, they should have been invited.[8]

Nearly twenty years after Haldeman's coup against Rosemary Woods, Bryce Harlow still termed himself "appalled" at Nixon's willingness to permit it. Shortly after Haldeman's move, Harlow had seen her refuse to speak to the president-elect, in an elevator at the Pierre.[9]

Another witness, who understandably does not wish to be named, recalled that Miss Woods, when informed of her fate, had yelled at Nixon in his Pierre office: *"Go fuck yourself!"*

"I'm sure it's the only time in her life she ever said that word," the witness insisted.*

Bob Haldeman had earned Nixon's confidence in three major campaigns but actually was appointed "assistant to the president" rather than "chief of staff." In 1968, however, Haldeman had been acknowledged as campaign chief of staff; so, no matter what his official title, the "chief" designation stuck in the White House, too—and in reality.

Haldeman and Ehrlichman often were considered by the outside world to be twin terrors—the "Germans" who had erected a "Berlin Wall" around Nixon. The two were indeed friends from college days in California, and formidable operators; but they were by no means twins in manner, role or relationship with the president.

The more relaxed and occasionally disheveled Ehrlichman, a burly man with thinning hair and a face that could break into a smile as well as the scowl that later became his television trademark, never equaled Haldeman in official status. Ehrlichman achieved his high standing because of his strong management of Nixon's domestic council, and his willingness to exert the power of a favored presidential aide, including unpleasant tasks from which Nixon recoiled. Ehrlichman maintained, however, a certain degree of independence and skepticism in his relations with Nixon—and in his regard for his own eminence—undoubtedly a reason why he was not as close to the president as was Haldeman and, for a time, Charles Colson.

Haldeman was without peer in his influence on Nixon, and in the confidence the president had in his loyalty and discretion. Even Henry Kissinger, whose public presence made him appear so dominant within the White House, seems to have feared falling from grace with the chief of staff. Haldeman, though he could be friendly in private, had a coldly efficient presence that his crew cut and his sharp eyes emphasized. A meticulous

*Notes of a confidential interview are in the author's possession.

administrator, a zealot for procedure, even his smile could appear menacing, as if he were enjoying the prospect of cutting someone down—although the latter perception may have been mostly in the eye of the beholder. Even if so, Haldeman knew how to use his capacity to strike fear into those who answered to him.

He has succinctly described his own White House role:

> I was the closest person to the President in the first term—physically I spent by a wide margin more hours with him than anyone else did, both alone and with other people. I worked with him on the total range of duties of the Presidency as contrasted to everybody else who worked with him who was working in one area or another but not in overlapping areas.

Ehrlichman told me that Nixon and Haldeman were virtually "joined at the hip"—linked in a "true marriage." The relationship, Ehrlichman believed, was based on "real supplementation" by Haldeman, a true believer in Nixon's destiny since sometime in the fifties. Haldeman provided necessary counterbalances for the weaknesses he, better than anyone else, saw in his man—weaknesses he understood and anticipated.

Haldeman realized, for example, that Nixon lacked physical stamina, and erected a White House organization that largely prevented the president from having to work or make decisions when he was tired. He was well aware, too, of Nixon's reclusive tendencies and factored this into the White House administrative structure. He had a sharp sense of how Nixon's mind worked, and tried to keep the president in circumstances that best served his needs and preferences.[10]

> Was Nixon irresolute? Haldeman would be his backbone, hiring and firing, saying no, demanding staff performance with icy firmness. When Nixon was reticent, Haldeman persuaded him to do the necessary public things. When Nixon's energy flagged, Haldeman shielded him from the necessary demands that would sap his strength.[11]

Haldeman was not a sycophant, despite his belief in Nixon's greatness. The staff chief did not hesitate to disagree with the president when he thought Nixon was wrong, and he frequently disregarded some of the president's more impulsive or petulant orders. He usually thought Nixon right, however, sometimes on issues about which Ehrlichman or others disagreed—in which cases, Haldeman saw that Nixon's wishes were carried out. In his eyes, the president came first.

Haldeman's function worked two ways—up to the president, down to the staff:

Better than most summarizers, Haldeman could effectively put forth an absent or inarticulate aide's point of view. Each of us, telling Haldeman what we thought about a given matter, would be certain that our point of view would get to the Old Man "with the bark off," reduced to essentials and put persuasively—without the tone of voice or added comment that would undercut it in transmission. That was Haldeman's greatest talent, his most important contribution.[12]

Nixon, for his part, had full confidence and trust in Haldeman, and confided in him extensively—though Haldeman, for the most part, stayed out of substantive issues and concentrated on the administrative, logistical and political aspects of Nixon's White House. Nixon's dependence on Haldeman became virtually total, and he did little without the knowledge of his staff chief—which makes it all the stranger that the two men had no social relationship at all, on the residential side of the White House or at Key Biscayne or San Clemente. One good reason, perhaps, was that Pat Nixon did not like a man she correctly perceived to have more influence and effect on her husband than she did.[13]

Haldeman has insisted that he controlled access to the president only as Nixon wanted him to (the Rosemary Woods episode tends to confirm that idea), and only to suit Nixon's peculiar work methods and personal attitudes. The problem, as Haldeman saw it, was

deciding how to time and work out the seeing of the President by people in a way that suited the President. . . . [T]here was not a delegation to me or anybody else as to who could and who couldn't see the President or when they could or anything else. . . . [I]t was how do I get in the people the President wants gotten in today?

Haldeman disputed the idea that Nixon did not want to see people and did not want to hear views that he disliked. "He very strongly wanted to hear what the people that didn't agree with him felt, but he didn't want to hear it from unknowledgeable people."

Whatever all that may mean, the net effect was a considerable isolation of the man in the Oval Office; Haldeman and Ehrlichman, in Harlow's critical view, "ran a taut ship." Haldeman conceded the point, but added that it was "the President [who] did the screening."

The pontifical George Romney, Nixon's old antagonist, and his choice to be secretary of HUD, was a particular thorn. Ehrlichman recounts this typical Nixon reaction to a Romney request for an appointment: "I don't want to listen to him. He comes in here and he bends my ear and he wastes my time, and he whines a lot because I don't see him enough. I don't want to hear all that."

If this suggests a certain disdain for his own appointees, Nixon—the political thinker, the realist, the world traveler, the veteran of more than two decades in national affairs—undoubtedly felt it. James R. Schlesinger, who was in the Bureau of the Budget, then director of the CIA, then secretary of defense under Nixon, recalls a cabinet meeting during which Nixon whispered something irreverent in Schlesinger's ear and added: "But I can't say *that* in front of *these* clowns"—meaning the cabinet members he had appointed.

Schlesinger also noticed that at cabinet and other meetings Nixon not infrequently would silence long-winded remarks from one of the "clowns" with some sarcastic or cutting—but never personal—remark. Ehrlichman provided an example, again featuring the hapless Romney:

> [Romney] would raise his hand and begin to discuss, and Nixon would say, "George, I'm terribly sorry but I've got an NSC meeting that I've got to get ready for. I wish I could extend this meeting. Why don't you write me a memo on this?" He'd then get up and run out of the room as fast as he could go.

In James Schlesinger's view, bolstered by such demonstrations, Nixon was "intellectually impatient" with men he generally considered less than his equals in intelligence.[14]

Haldeman and the other senior staff members had planned a staff system in which five equal assistants would serve the president, all of whom would be available to him at any time, for whatever tasks might be needed. But the only one among these planners with real White House experience, Bryce Harlow, pointed out to Haldeman that "there is no such thing as five equal assistants to the president. There will be one who will be more equal than the others."

This was prescient, particularly since it was Haldeman who became *primus inter pares*—and the main lightning rod for Nixon's reclusive habits. Haldeman welcomed the assignment:

> Especially when congressmen or a senator or some other normally self-important individual did not get to see the President, it was better for him to go away thinking that that S.O.B. at the door kept me out instead of thinking that the S.O.B. on the other side of the door didn't want to see me.

Haldeman's four senior colleagues, in the beginning, were Ehrlichman for domestic policy development; Henry Kissinger as national security adviser; Harlow for congressional relations, with some reach into Ehrlichman's turf; and Daniel Patrick Moynihan as urban affairs counselor—and also, in Haldeman's judgment, "the House Democrat and the inside gadfly to poke at us in the political sense."

Moynihan's appointment was, to an extent, the fruit of Nixon's rather uncharacteristic desire to bring Democrats into his administration. Richard Nixon was nothing if not a partisan Republican; he also had a long memory for those, including not a few Democrats, who had offended him. Haldeman noted that Nixon had "a remarkable ability to keep most of them pretty well catalogued, and they were clear in his mind."

Haldeman insisted, however, that Nixon had the professional politician's ability to make a distinction between a real enemy and a *pro forma* opponent: "He did not view someone who was not for him as being an enemy. He only viewed someone who overtly and actively carried out a role of an enemy as being an enemy."

Nixon had, for instance, "a strong personal regard" for Hubert Humphrey but a "very limited respect for Humphrey's ability." Despite Nixon's old Senate rivalry with Lyndon Johnson, he and Johnson "got along extremely well," and Johnson was "respected and in some ways liked" by his successor. John Kennedy, on the other hand, "was neither respected nor liked" by Nixon—any more than Nixon had been by JFK.

Nixon recognized, however, as most presidents have, a certain utility in being able to present his administration as bipartisan—at least not exclusively partisan. He had been for years, as he knew, the one Republican most disliked by Democrats. In 1969, moreover, he had to cope with the fact that both Houses of Congress were strongly Democratic; he was the first new president since Zachary Taylor in 1853 whose party had not also carried at least one House. Conciliation across party lines obviously was in order.

Far from being the acid partisan seen by public opinion, Nixon gave Bryce Harlow a special mission to cultivate congressional Democrats. He asked Harlow for a list of the congressional leaders and the chairmen and ranking minority members of all committees in both Houses, promising to telephone each one. "We are going to get along and get things done together," the new president insisted, as Harlow recalled:

> He was quite sincerely counting on them to cooperate. Now, we're talking about some thirty-one committees, two members apiece to be called—sixty-two calls by a man who hardly had time to go to the john, plus a score of other leaders. He had to make some eighty calls to do this project. Each call would take at least five minutes, that is four hundred minutes, which is about seven hours. He did exactly that. He called them all. They all were flattered . . . and promised to cooperate as best they could.

Harlow was less enthusiastic about a breakfast meeting with Nixon and the new postmaster general, Winton "Red" Blount of Alabama. Blount had accepted a thankless job only after Nixon promised to help him make the post office more efficient; so at the breakfast Blount outlined plans to "depoliticize" the postal system. Aghast at the loss of Republican patronage he foresaw, Harlow warned Nixon that if he supported Blount's proposals, he'd be "committing hara-kiri."

"I know it," Nixon replied, but pledged Blount his backing anyway. Harlow soon was confronted by H. R. Gross of Iowa, the cantankerous ranking Republican on the House Post Office Committee. "That son of a bitch [Nixon]," Gross complained, "takes away all the job opportunities Republicans have been crying for for a generation."[15]

Nixon also surprised members of his Domestic Affairs Council by coming out vigorously for home rule for the District of Columbia: "I've always been for that," he declared. He had resided, after all, in the voteless District from 1947 through 1960—longer than he had lived as an adult in California or New York. The experience apparently outweighed the obvious fact that the District was heavily black and Democratic, so that home rule would do little for Republicans.[16]

Predictably, in the spring of 1969, Harlow had to pour oil on troubled Republican waters. Not least because of Nixon's bipartisan gestures, Republican senators waxed wroth "because they hadn't gotten their political appointments." Harlow got through "this bath of acid" by calling a meeting and convincing the assembled Republican senators that "we don't have as many jobs to parcel out as collectively you want."

Nixon, after offering Humphrey the U.N. ambassadorship, though expecting to be rebuffed, offered the same post to Sargent Shriver, President Kennedy's brother-in-law. Shriver made demands that, according to Nixon in *RN*, he could not accept. Cyrus Vance, formerly Robert McNamara's deputy at the Pentagon under Lyndon Johnson, was sought for undersecretary of state; but Vance refused.[17]

The new president also hoped to bring John Connally of Texas into the administration—and eventually did, but only after Connally later turned Republican. Nixon tried hard but in vain to recruit Democratic Senator Henry "Scoop" Jackson of Washington for secretary of defense, since he and Jackson were mostly in accord on national security issues; Jackson ultimately refused on partisan rather than ideological grounds.

Harlow remembered that the new president spent two hours talking with George Meany, the head of the AFL-CIO, traditionally the backbone and bankroll of the Democratic party. Senator Edward Brooke of Massachusetts and Whitney Young, Jr., of the Urban League evaded Nixon's efforts to bring a high-ranking black into the administration. Later, James Farmer, the former director of the Congress on Racial Equality, accepted an appointment as assistant secretary of HEW.[18]

The selection of Henry Kissinger as national security adviser did put a "non-Nixon" person, but not a Democrat, on the White House payroll. Kissinger had been closely associated with Nelson Rockefeller, and as the White House staff was being formed, Haldeman recalled, "nobody on the Republican side . . . ranked higher than Nelson on Nixon's adversary list, except maybe his brother David." But the president, as will be seen, had other reasons for seeking out Rockefeller's foreign affairs adviser.

Nixon succeeded in landing a real, live, identifiable Democrat only in the case of Daniel Patrick Moynihan. Moynihan, an Irish Catholic, had served in the Kennedy and Johnson administrations and was a witty and convivial academic, a Harvard professor who with his Irish verve and storytelling "entranced" the distinctly non–Ivy League Nixon. Moynihan was a sort of "court jester," Harlow thought—a "consummate courtier," in Elliot Richardson's opinion. Nixon himself wrote in *RN* that he found Moynihan's "thinking refreshing and stimulating . . . free of professional jargon and ideological cant"—not to mention the rote anti-Nixonism common to other Democrats.

Moynihan did bring the new administration something of the desired bipartisan cast, though many other Democrats were not amused at his participation in a Republican administration. That was merely partisan; in a broader sense, Moynihan had some solidly un-Republican ideas about welfare and urban affairs, areas in which Nixon and most of his staff, as well as the Republican party generally, were neither expert nor deeply interested—hence could use Moynihan's guidance.

Before accepting Nixon's appointment, for example, Moynihan exacted agreement that Nixon would seek welfare reform and would "put the issue of drugs on the agenda of American foreign policy." Nixon fully intended to change the welfare system anyway, but Moynihan powerfully influenced the way he tried to do it; and the Nixon administration, perhaps more than any since, proved to be highly effective in combatting drugs.[19]

Moynihan, however, was not given free run of the urban affairs field. Nixon had appointed Arthur Burns, formerly Eisenhower's chairman of the Council of Economic Advisers, as a counselor to the president, though it generally was understood that sooner or later the avuncular economist was to be named chairman of the Federal Reserve Board. While in waiting, Burns devoted much of his time to urban affairs, coming frequently into conflict with the brash and more liberal Moynihan.

On the day after his inauguration, Nixon—as Burns recalled it—offered him the position of White House chief of staff. This conflicts with Nixon's statement in *RN* that he had named Haldeman to that post during the transition, and with Haldeman's claim that the title "evolved" from his duties. But memories often clash on such matters; and in any event Burns refused what he took to be Nixon's offer. He felt that "running the White House staff was a task for a young man with different interests."

Nixon took the older man into the cabinet room, that January 21, and showed him a chair that already bore a plaque with Burns's name and the title of counselor. Burns tried to protest but Nixon would have none of it. Thereafter, he kept setting up meetings for Burns, giving him assignments, until Burns was more or less co-opted into the White House staff structure.

"He handled me then and there with extraordinary skill," Burns observed years later, but added dryly: "He wasn't always that skillful."

One reason Burns, then a professor at Columbia, had to be persuaded into the Nixon White House was a sense of unease the economist felt about the president himself—a man he otherwise liked and mostly admired. In June 1968, before the Republican convention had nominated Nixon, at a luncheon in his apartment, the candidate had assured Burns that he could only be "a one-term President." Burns was astonished.

> "Why?" I asked him. His answer was, "As President, I will have to do so many unpopular things that I almost certainly could never be re-elected. And second, these will be difficult years and I will be thoroughly exhausted at the end of those years and probably could not carry on physically."

Burns took this to mean that Nixon was bent on far-reaching reforms, whatever the political cost. On January 20, 1969, however, from his seat on the inaugural platform, as Burns watched Nixon come down the Capitol steps to be sworn in, he thought he saw "an arrogant expression on his face and it troubled me greatly. I wanted to see an expression of humility."[20]

The next day, Nixon's first in office, Burns said, the new president's "whole manner . . . was such that I arrived at the conclusion that he was already running for a second term." In view of Nixon's earlier claim that he would be a one-term president, Burns's hopes for extensive reforms quickly faded.

Nixon explains in *RN* that he deliberately brought Burns into the White House and gave him some responsibility in urban affairs because "I thought that his conservatism would be a useful and creative counterweight to Moynihan's liberalism." Haldeman cited this intent as a good example of Nixon's "concept of adversarial relationships on a constructive and friendly basis."

> There was an intentional conflict set up there and a play of forces within the operation. We worked that within all aspects of policy and operational development with my role being that of an honest broker . . . getting both sides or all sides of adversarial positions presented, weighed and considered properly . . . rather than the

development of a policy intentionally starting from a preconceived
viewpoint to arrive at a preconceived destination.

This sounds well-planned and effective. The actual working of "adversarial relationships," however, only confirmed Arthur Burns in what he
had come to believe from observing Nixon a decade earlier—that President
Eisenhower "was a great and orderly manager" but Richard Nixon never
was. As Burns saw it, Eisenhower "never played administration officials
against one another," but Nixon frequently did.[21]

To John Ehrlichman, the Burns-Moynihan "adversarial relationship"
was "oil and water," Moynihan with a staff of liberal "young Turks" versus
Burns and "a bunch of conservative young fellows," each with ill-defined
lines of authority in an administrative nightmare of "ideological animosity": "It got to be the game of who talked to the President last. . . . As
quickly as Burns walked out, Moynihan would come in and undo everything that Burns had done."

Stephen Hess, Moynihan's scholarly deputy, saw the rivalry differently.
The competing Harvard and Columbia professors, he thought, both were

> men of great knowledge and wisdom and they built strong staffs.
> We fought it out quite honorably for the President's mind and soul
> . . . and in 1969 I felt that I was in worthy combat. . . . We won
> what we cared about most, which was the Family Assistance Plan.
> That was the first time a President had ever proposed what would
> have amounted to a guaranteed annual income for poor families.
> . . . I think the Burns people's major priority may have been
> revenue sharing. They won on that one.

However "enchanted" Nixon was with Pat Moynihan, however loyal to
Burns and however committed in principle to "adversarial relationships,"
he quickly tired, Ehrlichman recalled being told by the president, of "these
two wild men on the domestic side . . . beating me up all the time." He
soon wanted "a more orderly way."

Nixon's ultimate means of resolving this conflict was to replace both
Burns and Moynihan with an enhanced urban affairs staff structure, over
which Ehrlichman was to preside. To do so, the president first had to be
rid of Moynihan, a problem he solved by kicking him upstairs into a more
anomalous staff position with a cabinet seat; then he had to oust William
McChesney Martin, the Federal Reserve Board chairman he had inherited,
so that Burns could be installed in Martin's place.

Ehrlichman, rapidly becoming a troubleshooter, persuaded Martin to go
quietly. Nixon gave Martin "a grand state dinner," Ehrlichman recalled,
"and all his old pals got invited and the President said wonderful things

about him and gave him the gold watch, and on he went"[22]—which is the way of power in Washington, or anywhere else, but which again tells much about Richard Nixon as president. Essentially, he had removed the Moynihan-Burns conflict from his presence, not by direct, firm action but by arranging for the principals to be shifted to where they would have to stop beating him up all the time.

Steve Hess—now a senior fellow of the Brookings Institution and the author of many works on politics and the presidency—sees this in retrospect as a natural process: two bands of "itinerant intellectuals," who had done their conceptual jobs of putting together a Nixon program, were replaced by "lobbyists and wily bureaucrats" who could push that program through Congress.

It's possible, however, to see in this episode the shades of a president who had not wanted personally to fire Sherman Adams a decade earlier (see chapter 5), and of a vice president who had studied that president intensely and who, himself, had maneuvered Meade Alcorn into delivering the final blow to Adams.

Herb Klein, perhaps as a member of the "old guard" from 1960 and before, when he had been Nixon's perennial press spokesman, saw something else in the occasion. "Soon after Burns and Moynihan left," Klein observed, "the White House changed distinctly and became an organization where hardball replaced political philosophy as the major consideration."[23]

Richard Nixon came to the presidency in January 1969, after nearly twenty years of national campaigning. In every election year since 1952, excluding only his run at the governorship of California in 1962, he had crisscrossed the nation for his party, in good times and bad, triumph and defeat. Perhaps no president ever entered the White House with a more copious education in the political attitudes of the American people.

All of Nixon's years in the arena, moreover, had been spent in the shadow of Franklin Roosevelt's New Deal and its successor administrations. Except for Eisenhower's eight years, Democratic presidents had occupied the White House since 1933, and the Democratic party had dominated Congress for most of those years (it still was to do so, during Nixon's presidency.)

Nixon was therefore the *political* product of two conflicting forces—just as he was *personally* heir both to "saintly" Hannah and her Black Irish husband, Frank Nixon. The rightward tug of the party he had served for so long and the ambitions he followed within it, as well as his innately conservative instincts, had not let Nixon become, like some Republicans, a thinly disguised New Deal liberal. But his political realism, formed in so many national campaigns during the New Deal era—perhaps bolstered by depression-era memories of poverty, and his resentment of the privileged and powerful—would not allow him to be a "standpat" Republican, either.

Elliot Richardson, who had been in Eisenhower's department of HEW, recalled at a conference at Hofstra University, in November 1987, that Vice President Nixon had saved a program of federal aid to education Richardson had helped develop by "an extraordinarily skillful performance" at a cabinet meeting—"the only cabinet meeting I've ever attended where anything was actually decided."

I recall that same education bill being frozen in the House Committee on Rules in 1960 by a combination of Southern Democrats and Republicans. I was covering the legislation for the *New York Times,* so I called Herbert Klein and asked him if Nixon the presidential candidate was going to do anything to rescue a measure important to his campaign. Within an hour, Klein called back to say that Nixon would get the bill out of committee; and he did, by changing some Republican votes. The bill still lost on the House floor, primarily due to Republican opposition led by the minority leader, Charles Halleck of Indiana—whom Nixon only recently had backed to replace Joseph Martin.

"I would rate Eisenhower as basically more conservative than Nixon," said Bryce Harlow, who served both presidents. "Deep down Ike was a hard conservative as compared with most people, including Robert Taft."

Nixon was by no means such a conservative. He was located nearer the center than either flank of the political spectrum—certainly the center of the Republican party. He nevertheless brought with him to his great new office, if not a detailed program, some well-developed attitudes. On the day he was sworn in, as Ehrlichman recalled, "Richard Nixon had a pretty well articulated sense of direction, on the domestic side as well as the foreign policy side."[24]

It was not, however, either an ideological or a programmatic sense. Garry Wills, in his brilliant *Nixon Agonistes,* identified Nixon as what might be called a "classical liberal"—one who regards the marketplace as the universal testing ground of achievement and success, where an individual must stand alone to succeed or fail by his own ability, effort and ingenuity. Wills's book was subtitled *The Crisis of the Self-Made Man;* twenty years after its publication, the idea of Nixon as self-made man seems more relevant than ever.

To locate Nixon on the larger historical and philosophical spectrum (of which there's little evidence he is even aware) is not my purpose here, although Wills's analysis strikes me as explaining much about the man. My concern, rather, is with the contemporary political awareness and outlook that Nixon's practical experience had given him by the time he became president.

He had been elected as a centrist—in the Republican primaries between Ronald Reagan and Nelson Rockefeller, in the general election between George Wallace and Hubert Humphrey. A centrist, I believe, he was to remain. The direction his political sensibility pushed him to follow in the White House was basically pragmatic—a vector formed not only by the pressures of left and right but also by those of the necessary and the possible, as perceived through the prisms of his experience and personality. For the latter, Wills's insight is invaluable.

Nixon the Republican certainly did not believe, as Lyndon Johnson had, that the federal government could or should be the major instrument for coping with, or solving, the problems of American society. In fact, in his first years in office, Ehrlichman pointed out at Hofstra, Nixon and his aides went to "a lot of time and effort dismantling the rather useless machinery" (as they saw it) of some of Johnson's Great Society programs.

Unlike, however, his newest party rival—Ronald Reagan—Nixon did not delude himself that government had no, or at most a minimal, role in promoting the welfare of the American people. With the lesson of Barry Goldwater's landslide defeat so recently before him, and Reagan's rise to national power far in the future, Nixon was reaffirmed politically in his chosen position near the center—from which, of course, he could and did move temporarily left or right as seemed to him necessary or expedient.

Nixon belonged to an older tradition than either Johnson's or Reagan's; he walked more nearly in the political footsteps of the party that had given birth to his own—the socially conservative but economically venturesome Whigs. Before disappearing in the pre–Civil War years, to be replaced by the more militantly antislavery Republicans, Whigs had stood against Andrew Jackson's emphasis on executive power and "equalitarianism" but *for* Henry Clay's "American system" of public works and internal improvements (roads, canals and the like), together with strong currency and credit to further the nation's industrial development. Whigs were "industrialists, bankers, 'go-ahead' businessmen, and conservative farmers" willing to use government as necessary in their and the nation's interest.[25]

The first Republican president, Abraham Lincoln, formerly a Whig, retained Whiggish views except on emancipation. During his administration, for example, he supported establishment of the land-grant colleges and passage of the Homestead Act. Nixon's view on the allocation of resources and the distribution of power resembled these antecedents more than the core attitudes of the modern Republican party that had elected him.

Like most in that party, Nixon did believe it was necessary "to deemphasize people's expectations of the federal government," and "move functions and resources back to the local levels as much as possible"—an attitude, Ehrlichman recalled in his Hofstra remarks, that was "in full flower . . . the first day he sat down to be president."

But Nixon did *not* want to turn away from what he recognized as the federal obligation to maintain the national well-being and standard of living, and he was too much a political realist—all those losing Republican campaigns had left their scars—to think that the public wanted a restoration of Herbert Hoover's America, or would support a president who did.

"I was determined to be an activist President in domestic affairs," he recalled in *RN,* adding characteristically that he told the first meeting of his Urban Affairs Council: "We don't want the record written that we were too cautious." Despite much bravado in his speeches about defying public opinion, Nixon was never indifferent to what would be said or thought about him—nor should any president be.

One document, in particular, exposes Nixon's sensitivity on this point, and the rather cynical reason for it. Charles Colson, one of his aides, had reported on the wide distribution of a printed booklet that included a Nixon speech and others delivered at the dedication of the Woodrow Wilson Center for scholarly research. The president returned Colson's memo to Haldeman with irate handwritten notes in the margins:

> H—This completely misses the point. It isn't the Center but the speech we want to build up. What happened to my idea of a mailing of the *speech alone*—with a letter explaining its historic significance, eloquence etc. [Emphasis Nixon's.]

Then, as if a furious second thought had seized him, Nixon scribbled in the margin again:

> H—This is typical of our failures. . . . We mail a *mass* of material—without the covering memo which will get people to think of the speech itself. 1. No one who gets the mailing will read the speech. 2. Anyone who does will miss the point. 3. It is what someone says *about* a speech, not the copy, which means something.[26] [Emphasis Nixon's.]

What Nixon called his "activist" approach was illustrated by the development during his administration—from the inspiration of the Burns team—of the special- and general-revenue-sharing program that lasted until its demise in the Reagan administration. Revenue sharing relied upon the federal government to do what it did best (and what most Republicans usually like least)—raise revenues. These revenues then were passed back to cities and states to do what *they* were supposed to do best—provide public services.

Under Nixon's revenue-sharing program, moreover, those services were mostly of the localities' own choosing, rather than being dictated by Washington in New Deal–style categorical grants. Not incidentally, and not surprisingly, revenue sharing brought the Nixon administration the strong political support of many governors and mayors, including some Democrats and notably Nixon's old rival, Governor Nelson Rockefeller of New York. All welcomed the money *and* freedom from federal control.

Revenue sharing nevertheless was "very low on [Nixon's] list of legislative priorities," Ehrlichman confessed. Domestic issues—particularly those that did not arouse the passions of the voters—simply were not his main presidential interest. Nixon *understood* those issues and their importance, he told Pat Moynihan, but he was not passionately *interested* in them.

Moynihan was given to understand, however, that Nixon held it as a guiding principle that he had to pursue a strong, or "liberal," *domestic* policy—which his years of campaigning had convinced him that most of the American people desired—if he was to have the political leeway to conduct a strong, effective *foreign* policy. Acting on that principle, Nixon was willing to promote some policies even a Democratic administration might have followed, so that he could use the political capital thus acquired to support the activist role in foreign affairs that he was determined to play.[27]

No apprentice of Eisenhower's could have failed to absorb the lesson, moreover, that national security and a powerful role in world affairs demanded a strong economy at home; hence no president could successfully mount an activist foreign policy, or aggressively assert the national interest abroad, if the American economy was weak or constantly struggling. With his interest in what otherwise was a dry subject stimulated by its direct connection to his plans for foreign policy, Nixon spent much of his time as president, and developed a considerable expertise, on the domestic economy.[28]

He already had shown himself willing to rise above Republican economic orthodoxy when the second half of those potent political twins, "peace and prosperity," was threatened. In 1959, on the advice of Arthur Burns—scarcely a flaming liberal—he had urged Eisenhower and Secretary of the Treasury George Humphrey to "prime the pump" to head off what Burns warned was a coming recession (see chapter 6). Nixon's election prospects for 1960 would be endangered by recession, so he had good reason to call for action; but expediency is sometimes sound politics.

Eisenhower and George Humphrey, both traditionalists who refused to believe that deficit spending might strengthen the economy, could not be moved. The resulting recession was a major factor in Nixon's defeat by John Kennedy, and in his continuing political and economic education. Of the unemployment that rose by 452,000 in October 1960, he later wrote in *Six Crises:* "All the speeches, television broadcasts, and precinct work in the world could not counteract that one hard fact."

This episode, more perhaps than his depression-era upbringing, left its mark. Before his inauguration, Nixon asked Herbert Stein to describe the economic problems facing the new administration. Stein, who was to be a member, later chairman, of the President's Council of Economic Advisers, said the main problem was inflation.

"But remember," Nixon replied, "we must not have any increase in unemployment."

Normally, that's more nearly a *Democratic* concern. Stein believes Nixon's economic policies "suffered . . . in many respects" from his fixation against unemployment.

Like Stein, however, Nixon also had a typically Republican and well-justified attitude toward inflation, which by 1969 had been stimulated by the war in Vietnam and Lyndon Johnson's reluctance to raise taxes until he had to. In his determination to attack Johnson's inflation, Nixon achieved balance in the first budget of his administration. It turned out, however, to be his last balanced budget—in fact, the last balanced budget *any* administration has achieved, up to 1990.

In effect, therefore, Nixon's *political* experience, not the least of which was his recognition of the nation's long fealty to New Deal liberalism, and his deepest desire—to conduct a strong and effective foreign policy—conspired to assure an "activist" domestic program.

Just as in the struggle between Moynihan and Burns, however, other and more conservative tendencies within the new administration's ranks demanded to be heard. It was in the nature of Nixon's pragmatism that he also tried to accommodate those opposed to a liberal domestic policy—particularly since they were led by a man who was to become, in the early years of the administration, one of its most powerful figures.

Nixon had kept his unnecessary but politically effective campaign promise to fire the Johnson administration's attorney general, the liberal Ramsey Clark. Clark's replacement was to be Nixon's law partner and campaign manager, the bond attorney John Mitchell. The taciturn Mitchell had no experience either in law enforcement or in other Justice Department concerns, notably civil rights—but he had had no experience in campaigns either, and most observers believed he had turned out to be a brusquely effective and sensible political manager.

In a postelection meeting, he obliquely apologized to Ramsey Clark for Nixon's attacks, saying that they had been merely "a simplistic way to personalize the crime issue." Nixon actually held Clark in high esteem, Mitchell insisted, and would apologize personally if Clark would only take the initiative by saying that he realized Nixon's attacks on him had not been meant personally.

"I guess that judgment should be left up to third parties," Clark replied, in his deceptively mild manner.[29]

Nothing more was heard of an apology from Nixon, and the incident seems to be one of the few on record when John Mitchell let himself appear "soft." A forceful man, relentless in his advocacy, blunt to associates and in his public statements, in the months after the new president took office Mitchell was considered the strongman of the administration. He seemed to exemplify the kind of tough, no-nonsense attitude that Nixon most admired.

On a letter from Robert W. Thayer, Jr., of Stockton, New Jersey (received at the White House in February 1971), for instance, Nixon underlined for approval the assertion that "certain historians put Lincoln down as a gentle man when, in reality, the man himself was tough as hell." Nixon aspired to that kind of historical appraisal; and as long as he saw Mitchell as just such a tough guy, Mitchell had his confidence and his ear.[30]

Mitchell's fundamental counsel to the new president, though narrowly conceived, had the strength that it reflected major elements of Nixon's election victory and comported with many of Nixon's own political resentments and attitudes: Your constituency is made up of the Republicans who supported you in 1968 and the people who voted for George Wallace but might be convinced to vote for you in 1972. Those are the people who will reelect you, if anyone does, and therefore the people who need to be cultivated and whose views need to be favored by your administration.

Mitchell's chief opponents were Moynihan and Bob Finch, Nixon's old, close friend and protégé, his campaign director in 1960. The lieutenant governor of California in 1968, Finch had been Nixon's first choice for vice president at Miami Beach; he had refused with an emotional declaration that he and Nixon would be accused of something like nepotism. Thereafter, given virtually his pick of the top jobs, Finch chose to head HEW, center of some of the most controversial programs of the day—including, fatally for Finch, school desegregation.

As a newcomer to the Nixon circle with an Ivy League background and a Democratic history, Pat Moynihan—though a skilled bureaucratic infighter—could not hope to match the well-established Mitchell's influence on Nixon. Finch might have, but he wavered between his largely liberal instincts and his personal devotion to the president—a hesitation that only reinforced the general indecision he soon displayed. Mitchell moved swiftly past Finch in effective influence, if not in Nixon's personal regard.

Besides, Mitchell's advice appeared to be more solidly based in political possibility. Finch wanted to expand the Republican party in a new direction, attracting blacks, young people, moderate liberals who felt the Democrats had swung too far left; but that was speculative, problematic. Nixon himself had little confidence that blacks ever could be lured back to the Republican party or that "libs" could be persuaded to support him. It may also have weighed with the president, even subconsciously, that Finch had managed for him a losing campaign in 1960, while Mitchell had steered him to the victory of 1968. As noted earlier, Finch himself was well aware of such a division among Nixon's aides.

Southern leaders like Strom Thurmond and Clarke Reed, the aggressive Mississippi Republican chairman, also had legitimate claims on a president they had done much to nominate and elect. Nixon's campaign, moreover, had been in essence a *conservative* effort—though centrist in the context of his Republican opposition. If he wanted, overall, to have an activist domestic program, he nevertheless needed to placate the Southern and conservative claimants on his policies.

That fitted *Mitchell's* strategy; and in 1968, school desegregation in the South was one of the major issues a new president could not avoid. Fifteen years after *Brown v. Board of Education,* only 5.2 percent of black children in the Southern states were in "unitary"—or actually unsegregated—school systems, a far cry from the Supreme Court's call for "all deliberate speed" toward desegregation.

White society in the South still was largely determined to resist anything but the most token and technical versions of "unitary" school systems; yet the federal courts had made it clear in many decisions that state-ordered and state-supported (de jure) segregation was unconstitutional. Something had to give—either Southern whites would be allowed successfully to defy the federal courts, or Southern schools would have to be desegregated in fact as well as in pretense.

Richard Nixon had never been passionately involved with the race question. He had grown up in the near-rural suburbs of Los Angeles, where in his youth few black faces were to be seen. In later years, he liked to claim that his had been an integrated household, with blacks and Mexicans often at the dinner table. No doubt Hannah Nixon allowed no discrimination, but it's not clear where the blacks who supposedly shared her family's hospitality might have come from.

A. C. "Ace" Newsom, once the mayor of Whittier, and an acquaintance of Richard and Pat Nixon, described the town as having few minority groups even after World War II: "We had no Negroes [living in Whittier] at all. We had one or two Negroes that came to work. We had a shoeshine boy at a barber shop."

There also was what Newsom called "Jim Town . . . out between Whittier and Pico Rivera." But he said it was safe to assume that Richard Nixon had had "fairly little contact with minority groups" while he grew up in Whittier.[31]

Nixon, in fact, could hardly have been keenly aware that a race problem existed until he went to Duke law school, in segregated Durham, North Carolina. Race was not an issue of great public importance in any of his local, state or national campaigns before 1956. In that year, Eisenhower's popularity swept everything before it, despite the general's refusal to endorse the *Brown v. Board* decision and his old-fashioned assumption of white superiority.

As Nixon's 1960 presidential campaign approached, however, he did hope to win black support; and his unavailing efforts, as presiding officer of the Senate, to break the filibuster rule were not unrelated to that hope. His prospects among blacks in 1960 were good, in fact, until John Kennedy reacted in support of Martin Luther King when the black leader was jailed in Georgia.

In 1968, partly as a result of 1960, Nixon assumed that blacks would largely support his opponent, and made little effort to sway them (see chapter 9). His "Southern strategy," anchored on the support of Strom Thurmond of South Carolina, certainly did not suggest a strong effort to desegregate Southern schools—though, in the North, Nixon had sought to give the impression that he was committed to civil rights.

In fact, just as his campaign looked North and South at once, Nixon was of two minds on the issue—"anti-segregation but . . . also anti-busing." He not only opposed but was angered by court decisions that he saw as requiring "racial balance" rather than the "desegregation" he thought the only legitimate goal of judicial action. He believed busing orders were designed to achieve racial balance—thus were not protection for the constitutional rights of blacks so much as an infringement on the constitutional rights of those opposed to sweeping remedies for de jure segregation.

Nixon had made this view of constitutional questions clear in his campaign, not least because the public largely shared it, at least as regards busing. In April 1970, a Gallup poll found an eight-to-one majority of whites *and* blacks opposed to that means of achieving racial balance.[32]

Nixon was determined, nevertheless, to enforce the law. To what extent this reflected his personal view cannot and need not be determined, because he had no real choice. Even Eisenhower, in the famous Little Rock case, had been driven to uphold a federal court order, and the necessity was embedded in the presidential oath. Besides, how could a president who had been elected, to a great extent, on his pledge to reestablish law and order, *not* support the judgments of the federal courts? The new president recognized, moreover, that in some instances the courts had been driven to what he considered "extremes"—busing, as the clearest example—by the intransigence, ingenuity and shortsightedness of Southern whites in resisting less drastic remedies, in seeking at all costs to cling to essentially segregated schools.

The school desegregation question became one of the most emotional and divisive issues within the early Nixon administration. Nixon's Southern strategy campaign had produced the widespread belief that he would in some crafty way continue to curry favor with the white South, Thurmond's constituency, at the expense of blacks and civil rights. But there was another side to the Southern strategy, not widely realized in 1969 or later.

Nixon's very detachment, his lack of emotional involvement in racial issues, enabled him to deal with Thurmond, Reed, Senator James O. Eastland of Mississippi, Representative Otto Passman of Louisiana, and other Southern resisters on a basis of respect and trust; that was impossible for liberals—particularly Southern liberals—who were deeply committed to civil rights for blacks.

The Southern white leaders, as the detached and analytical Nixon was able to see them, were not bigoted "segs"; they were honorable men, victims of history, confronting a problem that most Americans did not have to face, at least in such intense degree. For Nixon, solving the desegregation problem was not so much a moral imperative—as it was for liberals—as a matter of cool analysis and effective politics.

By treating Southern white leaders with personal respect and giving their point of view genuine consideration, Nixon in his Southern strategy had earned respect and consideration from them for his own policies—and, importantly, the acknowledgment that they were not being treated by Washington as outcasts, even outlaws.

In all these conditions, it's not surprising that the new administration developed, in its domestic policies, something of a split political personality, not unlike Richard Nixon's own—a persistent streak of something suspiciously like liberalism cutting through its basic conservatism. But in his approach to foreign affairs—his supreme preoccupation—the new president suffered no such divisions or ambiguities.

As he looked out at the world from his new office, Nixon was neither Whig nor Republican, much less isolationist or liberal; he was Jacksonian in his belief in executive power, Gaullist in his determination to exercise that power personally, Machiavellian in his willingness to manipulate and maneuver to advance American interests, and purely Nixonian in what others might have considered a grandiose ambition rather than a "great purpose"—to achieve a lasting "structure of peace."

Nixon's preference for a strong hand in foreign affairs while, as he vainly hoped, a "competent cabinet" ran the country's domestic business, had been building since his seminal service on the Herter committee in 1947. The experience in foreign affairs he gained from his extensive travels as vice president had generally been considered one of his strengths against Kennedy in 1960. In the ensuing decade, as Nixon continued his travels and rebuilt his career, he came to be widely acknowledged as his party's most expert and experienced spokesman on foreign affairs.

More than that: In his travels, Nixon had consistently sought out heads of state, foreign ministers, party leaders. Some saw him—for example,

Charles de Gaulle, who had had his own experience of being out of power; but many had no time for a mere former vice president, a leader of the opposition party in the U.S.—a two-time loser regarded as having little if any political future.

My late colleague Drew Middleton, who for a time in the sixties was the *New York Times*'s bureau chief in Paris, remembered Nixon showing up in that city and, characteristically, calling a news conference. Middleton attended but not too many other reporters, French or American, did; and Nixon had little to say because few French officials had been willing to talk to him.

When the news conference was over and the reporters were leaving, Middleton noticed Nixon lingering alone in the room. Impulsively, Middleton invited him to dinner "if you have nothing else to do." Remarkably, Nixon didn't, and the two men passed a conversational evening in one of Middleton's favorite restaurants—talking, of course, about foreign affairs.

In those years, Nixon often was on his own as he traveled the world. Alone, doggedly talking with anyone who would give him the time, choking back his sensitivity to slight, always learning and listening, Nixon frequently found himself in the offices of lower level officials who lacked the standing to snub him. As the years wore along, however, just as happened to Nixon himself, some of those on whom higher authority had fobbed him off got themselves elected president or prime minister, or appointed foreign secretary.

Few of them, certainly not Richard Nixon, forgot those downscale meetings in Kuala Lumpur or Algiers or wherever. When he came to the White House in 1969, he was not only widely and personally acquainted among the world's leaders; with many, he shared a bond of hard, sometimes humiliating experience.

Some U.S. diplomats shared the same bond. Graham Martin, for example, Lyndon Johnson's ambassador to Thailand, incurred the displeasure of Secretary of State Dean Rusk and was relieved of his post. But Martin had given Nixon red-carpet treatment when the out-of-office lawyer visited Bangkok. So when Nixon finally reached the White House, he resurrected Martin for the embassy in Rome and later made him ambassador to South Vietnam—the last one the U.S. was to send to Saigon.

But more than his experience shaped Nixon's interest in foreign affairs when he assumed the presidency. He knew from his years of apprenticeship to Eisenhower that it was in the conduct of foreign affairs that a president could have his most important effect, while operating most nearly without hindrance from Congress, the press, even public opinion.

"The place where you can do something is in foreign policy," and Nixon knew it, in the opinion of his old law school teacher, Kenneth Rush, later to become both deputy secretary of state and deputy secretary of defense in the Nixon administration.

> You can tackle the farm problem or the trade deficit or the monetary structure but it's like attacking a pillow—you push in here and it comes out there. In foreign policy you have the fate of the country at stake.

That was what Nixon craved—the sense of dealing at the highest level, risking disaster on a scale less likely in domestic matters, playing as an equal among leaders like de Gaulle and Chou En-lai, with his country's fate in his hands. He often told intimates that it would take a genius to wreck the American economic system, but it wouldn't take much to cause serious problems in foreign policy.

Like a basketball player in the last seconds of an undecided game, he "wanted the ball." The sports analogy is not idly chosen; Richard Nixon, a competitive man who wanted to compete with the best, saw world affairs as the "fast track"—a phrase he often used—on which he aimed to run.[33]

Nixon knew also, from his years in the Eisenhower administration, that a president's substantive authority in foreign affairs (to set policy, target foreign aid or use military force) was greater than it was in domestic matters. He understood, too, that a president had the advantage that he was assumed to *know* more about foreign affairs than anyone else—any member of Congress, for example, or any opposition leader—because of his greater involvement and because he was believed to have more sources of intelligence and information.

Therefore it was harder to thwart or even contest a president acting as the nation's leader in the world. In the battered but not shattered postwar aura of "bipartisan foreign policy," moreover, it was widely supposed that "politics should stop at the water's edge"—that even the other party should support, in the main and as a matter of national unity, a president's leadership.

Richard Nixon himself, before 1953 and after 1960, had seldom honored that dictum, although he had shrewdly pictured his self-serving "moratorium" on discussion of Vietnam in 1968 as exemplifying it. Nevertheless, in practice, the persistent notion of a bipartisan foreign policy usually reinforced a president's power to conduct foreign affairs. An opposing party or politician could be made to suffer politically—Vice President Nixon, in the fifties, had been an expert at the tactic—if they appeared to be undercutting the president.

Besides all that, for a man so profoundly engaged for so long in politics, Nixon was not deeply versed in *national* problems. Joseph Sisco, a high State Department official, discovered that Nixon had a "monumental dis-

interest in domestic policies," considering them "a bore." And after his
first meeting with the president-elect at the Hotel Pierre, Pat Moynihan
"could not get over the things that Nixon said that he didn't know."

Moynihan, probably not entirely in jest, told Steve Hess, "I would have
bluffed it," rather than admit to such lack of knowledge. Hess was not
surprised. He had served in the White House under Eisenhower, knew
Nixon as vice president, had been one of his closest aides during the
ill-fated campaign for governor in California in 1962 and understood that
the president-elect was "really consumed by international affairs."

In January 1969, Nixon may also have been driven by a certain sense
of crisis more general than the war in Vietnam. Gerard Smith, who was
to be his arms control negotiator, got the impression that the new president
thought that during his administration there'd be something like a "last
chance" to effect a far-reaching arms arrangement with the Soviet Union.

Nixon thought it would be a last chance, in Smith's recollection, because
he believed the Soviets were moving full speed ahead in an arms buildup,
while he doubted that Congress—weary of the draining war in Vietnam
and aware of public disaffection with the military—would provide the
appropriations that would allow the U.S. to keep up or catch up, much less
regain the lost military superiority of the fifties and early sixties.[34]

Ray Price has pointed out that by the time Nixon took office,

> the Russians had built their military strength to a point at which
> the American strategic advantage was all but gone. [He] set out
> to create a new "structure of peace" that could hold Soviet ambi-
> tions in check within the constraints of what was politically possi-
> ble and militarily credible.

That was challenge enough even for Richard Nixon.

American-Soviet relations were therefore, in Sisco's words, "the number
one item on the agenda"; and Nixon saw the world primarily in terms of
managing the American-Soviet relationship, containing Soviet power and
making possible at least an uneasy peace.

Events decreed, however, that American-Soviet relations had to wait. In
1969, any new president's attention would have been forcefully directed to
the one overriding element of American foreign involvement—the war in
Vietnam. The war dominated everything—budgets, public interest, partisan politics, congressional relations, the attitudes of foreign powers, the
upheavals in American society. The most corrosive American experience
since the Depression, that war necessarily demanded Nixon's primary
focus, whether he wanted it that way or not.

He had no specific plan to "end the war and win the peace"—except the
idea that Moscow might be persuaded to help, and the vague and inaccu-

rate notion that he might emulate what he thought was Eisenhower's threat to use nuclear weapons to end the Korean War. Nixon's campaign promise had been mostly political rhetoric. According to Haldeman, he nevertheless set himself to make good, by the fall of 1969, on his pledge to end the war.

Nixon was heavily influenced by his belief that the Soviets would put pressure for peace on their Vietnamese allies, in return for better relations with the U.S. Nixon believed, moreover, that he could not abruptly withdraw American forces from Vietnam without giving an impression of weakness and therefore jeopardizing his intent to "normalize" relations with China; and he saw that "normalization" as the key to his hopes for a new and smoother relationship with the Soviet Union—his "main mission," Leonard Garment termed it, to which "everything else was subordinated."

Amidst the problems of putting together a new administration, Nixon remained a detached loner. Shortly after he took office in 1969, a group of editors from the Washington newspapers, then the *Post* and the *Evening Star,* were invited for lunch at the White House. Nixon, not untypically, did not appear but sent word that he'd receive the journalists later in the Oval Office.

Nixon was standing alone when they were ushered into an office that Nicholas Blatchford of the *Star* remembered as bare even of books in the bookcases. The atmosphere was stiff, cold, almost silent. Finally Nixon tried to break the ice, gesturing at some flags along the wall. The flags, he said, were the only things "they let you take with you when you leave."

Blatchford blurted: "Look, you just got here. Don't talk about leaving!"

Nixon approached, grasped both of his arms, and said something warm—Blatchford, years later, could remember only that the new president appeared to be grateful for what he had said. He regarded Nixon's suggestion about the flags as perhaps "a prophetic thing."

Though acknowledged as what Lyndon Johnson liked to call "the leader of the free world," Nixon was often at a loss for personal or conversational ease. "Cocktail party conversation," the witty Kissinger observed in a speech at Hofstra, "is not a subject for which President Nixon will go down in history."

The president and Mrs. Nixon once entertained the White House press corps at dinner in California, an unusual occasion. For the most part, Nixon engaged only in uncomfortable small talk with those at his table, and would not remark upon substantive matters. Many silences resulted. At one point, obviously looking for something to say, Nixon praised some decorations in the Mexican restaurant where the affair was held.

"But Dick," Mrs. Nixon said. "They're plastic."

Muriel Dobbin of the *Baltimore Sun,* who was at the Nixon table, saw the president's "face darken"—the only time, she told me later, she ever saw this cliché actually happen to anyone. She took it that he thought Mrs. Nixon was "trying to put him down" in front of the press, and she never forgot his acute lack of ease in what was supposed to be a relaxed evening.

Kenneth Rush, Nixon's old professor, had many conversations with the president—"about the economy and foreign affairs"—in Nixon's so-called hideaway in the Executive Office Building next door to the White House. "He always talked business," Rush recalls. "He never wanted to talk trivial stuff."

Foreign affairs offered this repressed, introverted, driven man—at last and gratefully posted in the White House, above grubby human trivia, the personal give-and-take of day-to-day politics—a chessboard upon which to play out his ideas, test his conceptions, in something like the "splendid isolation" the presidency is supposed to confer, but so seldom does. On the foreign affairs chessboard, Nixon as president could do much of what he wanted without entangling himself in confrontations with Congress or his party or the ubiquitous "enemies" he supposed were all around, or even—as he managed to arrange things—the State Department he disdained. The chessboard did not demand an intimate human connection with other people.

Foreign affairs lent themselves to "game plans," to outlines on the ever-present yellow legal pads upon which Nixon liked to scrawl while alone in his hideaway, or in the Lincoln Sitting Room at nights, before the blazing fire that was one of his fetishes (even in an air-conditioned room). Fully detailed foreign policy schemes could be cerebrated in solitude, or in conversation with an equally focused intellect, without boring committee meetings or difficult confrontations with lesser minds, by a president who knew the world, knew its leaders, knew what he wanted to do.

These plans then could be carried out by directives and messages and "signals," through "back channels" only a president could establish, in the secrecy that well suited the inward-looking, mistrustful man whom life and politics had made of Richard Nixon. And secrecy itself could be justified to the public and Congress more nearly in foreign affairs and "national security" than in any other fields.

For Nixon, in fact, secrecy was a high principle—congenial not only to his guarded personality but to his perception of the world. No matter how open the society he represented, his primary dealings—with the Soviet Union, the North Vietnamese, the Chinese—had to be with closed societies. Secrecy was necessary, he was convinced, if he was to maintain credibility with the leaders of those nations; and credibility was necessary if he was to negotiate on even terms and not be pilloried in domestic politics for doing so—as he himself once had castigated Dean Acheson and his "cowardly college of Communist containment."

After Nixon left the White House, he proposed ten primary rules for his successors, among which was Number Three: *Always remember that covenants should be openly agreed to but privately negotiated.* At the Hofstra conference, my former *Times* colleague, C. L. Sulzberger, described Nixon's method as "open diplomacy secretly arrived at."

If, for example, Nixon had announced his intentions toward China, Kenneth Rush believed (in what might have been Nixon's own thoughts) that

> you would have had the old upsurge of emotions about Taiwan.
> . . . The Congress and the press would have started to debate, emotions would have been aroused, and nothing would have been accomplished.

The secretary of state—his old friend, William Rogers, a loyal counselor even in the fund crisis of 1952—was shut out of that particular secret, an exclusion that the undeniable need for discretion hardly seems to justify. Nixon's fear was that if the secretary knew, word would spread through the State Department and be leaked to the press; the free hand he believed he needed would be lost.

As we shall see, that was not the only denigration of patient Bill Rogers perpetrated by his supposed friend. As Joseph Sisco reflected:

> The humiliations—and they were numerous—heaped on [Rogers] have scarred him indelibly. . . . He was not as ineffective a secretary of state as our press made him out to be. He was a man of eminent good sense and wisdom. . . . The experience he went through . . . should not have happened to any individual whether as the head of a corporation or the secretary of state.

As Nixon had told Theodore White, however, he believed that "no secretary of state is really important. The president makes foreign policy." In his determined view, an old and loyal friend could be no exception.[35]

And it was only a chessboard maneuver for Richard Nixon, minding the long-ago counsel of Syngman Rhee, to encourage "adversaries" to consider him a madman who could not be predicted.

"They obviously think I'm nuts," Nixon once said to Michael Raoul-Duval, one of his White House aides. "That's what I want them to think."

Ample testimony, including his own, documents that Nixon came to the White House with a visceral mistrust of the sprawling federal bureaucracy—particularly those sections of it dealing with foreign affairs.

This attitude was spawned no doubt during the Eisenhower administration, when he had felt himself scorned by a snobbish State Department establishment more in sympathy with Alger Hiss and Dean Acheson than with Tricky Dick Nixon. Later, when out of office, as he pursued his extensive private travels, he had thought he received precious little help from the "cookie pushers" in the State Department and the Foreign Service.

The new president had little more use for the Central Intelligence Agency, even if it was the favorite target of the antiwar movement. He regarded the CIA less as a hawkish center of derring-do and American imperialism than as a haven for Ivy League intellectuals pushing one-worldish schemes in the guise of intelligence analysis.

There was something to this latter view. Allen Dulles originally had recruited many of the CIA's personnel—persons like William F. Buckley, Jr., William Sloane Coffin and Cord Meyer—from the Ivy League colleges, where a sense of noblesse oblige joined a strong strain of Establishment anticommunism. During the Kennedy administration, McGeorge Bundy, then the national security adviser, told me that there were "more liberal intellectuals per square foot" at the CIA than anywhere else in government. Not the secret operatives, perhaps, but many of the analysts poring over rail timetables, production figures and trade statistics fitted Bundy's approving description—and Nixon's idea of Franklins. He was convinced, moreover, that the CIA had favored and helped Kennedy in 1960 (see chapter 6).

Primarily, Nixon wanted no such powerful personality as Allen Dulles's brother Foster intervening in the foreign relations he meant to conduct himself. More than that, however, his long experience taught that within any bureaucracy much inertia, even stagnation, is inevitable; officials with protected jobs and fixed views are not easily moved, and no small part of the bureaucrat's art is to thwart policies not "on all fours"—as he is apt to say—with his own views.

Helmut Sonnenfeldt, who served on Nixon's national security staff, had moved there from the State Department, and understood the president's fears on this point. "There's nothing a bureaucracy knows how to do better than to take a decision that goes against its own recommendations," he recalled from his Foreign Service days, and "in its implementation, transform it into what the bureaucracy wanted in the first place."

One of the oldest and most solidly grounded clichés of the Washington establishment—which remains valid through all changes of administrations—is that "where you stand depends on where you sit." Translated, this means that designated "experts" on, say, India—they sit at the India desk—are likely to stand for India's interests as much as for their own country's.

As Sonnenfeldt put it, in terms of an issue that arose after the Nixon years:

> The Latin American bureau in the State Department is going to have a lot of sympathy with how the Argentines look at the Falklands. The European bureau and the rest of us who have spent our lives putting together NATO are going to have a lot of sympathy with the way the British look at the Falklands.

The Latin bureau, in fact, might have called the islands the "Malvinas," as the Argentines do. Many department officials had such regional biases. Some were "Arabists" hostile or indifferent to Israel. Some, like Sonnenfeldt, were "Europeanists." Others were committed to Taiwan, or were deeply opposed to the "Chicoms" in Peking.

In the Johnson administration, for example, these latter—with the considerable aid of Secretary of State Dean Rusk, whose views had been shaped when he was an Asian desk man in the Kuomintang period—had been able to block Johnson's private desire to open discussions with Communist China. Despite his sometimes imperial behavior, LBJ's working method was to act on agreed-upon "consensus" positions; and he probably did not have the self-confidence, in foreign affairs, to override such veterans as Rusk. Richard Nixon ultimately bypassed them.

Such entrenched bureaucratic blocs were likely to throttle or limit Nixon's policies, if he tried to move in directions they feared or disapproved. Once experienced bureaucrats got wind of such departures, the most common tactic was to leak to the press, stirring up opposition, which might form into powerful coalitions or move Congress to countering action. Or, in dozens of other ways, skilled bureaucrats could simply resist "implementation"—the actual carrying out of policy supposedly dictated by a president.

Resentment and resistance from the bureaucracy was particularly predictable as the Nixon administration took office. Since the days of the New Deal, and not withstanding the depredations of Joe McCarthy, the government had been dominated by liberal Democrats, few of whom admired Richard Nixon any more than he did them. Even in the Eisenhower administration, in Nixon's judgment, not enough had been done to bring Republicans and conservatives into the permanent government he now had to work through; and the eight intervening years of the Kennedy and Johnson administrations had made things worse. But Nixon did not intend to be frustrated by internal opposition, as he knew Eisenhower often had been.

Harry Truman had remarked presciently, as he was about to turn over the White House to General Eisenhower: "He'll sit right here and he'll say

'Do this! Do that!' And nothing will happen. Poor Ike. It won't be a bit like the Army."[36]

Sixteen years later, Nixon assumed the presidency with more than his share of personal insecurities; but these seem to have contributed to his strengths as well as to his weaknesses. For one thing, as his entire career had demonstrated, he was an uncommonly driven man in his desire for greatness, achievement, recognition; but these are more nearly the drives of someone uncertain of his own worth, eager to prove that worth to himself, than of a man comfortable in his identity.

Nixon's insecurities—the resulting sense that he had to work harder, learn more than others—ironically led him to the intensity of analysis, the conviction that his goals were the proper goals, and the determination to achieve them, that marked his foreign policy–making. A man more secure in his personality—Eisenhower, for example, later Ronald Reagan—probably would have been more willing to share authority and take the advice of others, and less concerned that his ultimate authority would be diluted, his aims deflected by lesser visions.

Nixon's confidence in his ability to deal with the nation's foreign interests seems the obverse of insecurity, even if it was, in fact, the consequence of it. In his untiring pursuit of achievement and advancement, he had become "intellectually self-confident enough," Elliot Richardson observed, "to be sure that he could learn enough about any substantive issue, hold his own on it and do so effectively, and that he could manipulate people and situations to his own ends even though the actors were people of some independent strength."

Nixon's conception of foreign policy as the primary function of the president allowed him to see his office as what he most wished it to be—a center of near-absolute power from which men like Roosevelt and Truman had reshaped the world. Nixon wanted that kind of power—he was, Richardson concluded, one of only a "handful" of people in Washington "over the last thirty years [who] really have had an overriding desire to exercise power."

Power would bring Nixon vindication; what he would do with it would show the Franklins of the world that the grocery boy from Whittier had achieved more than all of them. Only power could enable him to reach those "great purposes" of which he had spoken to Leonard Garment in Elmer Bobst's poolhouse long ago, to which he had said he would dedicate his life—purposes befitting the son of Hannah Nixon.

But Richard also was the son of dark and brooding Frank Nixon. He was a dark and brooding man himself, who saw no reason why the pursuit of "great purposes," any more than the pious expression of righteous sentiment, should foreclose savage action when it became necessary. "Morality," to him, was an ambiguous concept; a seemingly immoral or cynical act, such as bombing a city, could have a "moral goal," just as seemingly moral acts could have immoral consequences—if a president did nothing, for instance, because he was legally restrained, while a people or a nation suffered for his inaction.[37]

Ray Price stated a proposition undoubtedly absorbed from Richard Nixon: "The worst thing a president can do is to be so paralyzed by propriety that he shrinks from bending the rules when the nation's security requires it."[38] Nixon was never so paralyzed, certainly not by propriety. In his somber vision, only a president had both the means and the necessity to achieve great purposes, and if they were great enough he could not suffer conventional moral and ethical ideas to thwart either. In the awful solitude of power, Lincoln had drenched the nation in blood to restore its unity. Franklin Roosevelt, in the struggle against the monstrous evil of Nazism, had called forth a primal power by which it might destroy itself. Truman had unleashed that power in the name of peace.

All, in Richard Nixon's saturnine appraisal, had done what "great purposes" demanded, what great men thus were justified in doing. If all had paid in pain and loneliness and opprobrium for the measure of greatness their necessary deeds had earned them, they had been right nonetheless. Richard Nixon had paid in the same coin for what he already had achieved, and knew its cost as well as anyone; but he was determined to stand in history with its greatest figures, and he was willing to pay far more.

Nixon may have exaggerated the problems he would face, as well as the potential for achievement in his new role; but the effect on his approach to foreign policy–making was profound. To make the American side of the chessboard exclusively his, to keep the great power he coveted from being diffused and wasted, he aimed to move the pieces around the board without the usual interference from a meddlesome Congress, an irresponsible press, the uptight military men in the Pentagon, above all from the striped-pants bureaucrats in the State Department "fudge factory" and the tiresome, time-consuming procedural rites they thrived upon, often without substantive results.

Nixon was determined upon a closely held, narrowly focused procedure, with foreign policy–making centered in, and if possible limited to, the White House—and few outside it knowing what he was doing or going to do. That way, equally few would be able to oppose the judgments and decisions he believed himself amply prepared and officially entitled to make. To erect and carry out such a remarkable scheme, Nixon found his instrument—in some ways the perfect instrument—in the unlikely person of Nelson Rockefeller's foreign affairs adviser, Dr. Henry A. Kissinger of Harvard.

In 1968, Kissinger was a powerhouse waiting to come on line—a respected intellectual, a rising academician and the author of the influential *Nuclear Weapons and Foreign Policy,* with experience (about which little is known) in the intelligence community of the fifties. Twice—in 1964 and 1968—the Harvard professor had sought high government office in the entourage of his patron, Rockefeller. But twice Rockefeller the presidential candidate, hence Kissinger the foreign policy counselor, had missed out— one reason, perhaps, that Nelson Rockefeller made Kissinger a cash gift of fifty thousand dollars, largesse of dubious propriety, coming as it did soon after Kissinger went to Washington in 1969.

In the Kennedy administration, Kissinger had been neither fish nor fowl but an occasional foreign policy consultant, a status that frustrated rather than satisfied him. Late in the Johnson administration, again as a consul- tant, he had played a more important role in negotiations to end the war in Vietnam. In this capacity, he had won the confidence of important administration officials, including Averell Harriman, Johnson's chief nego- tiator in Paris.

Kissinger does not mention this latter service in his memoirs, nor the cat that Nixon let out of the bag in *RN*—that while ostensibly still a Rockefeller loyalist and officially a consultant to the Democratic adminis- tration in power (cleared by it for all secrets), Kissinger had fed inside information on the Paris talks to the Nixon campaign.

Instead, Kissinger claimed in *White House Years* that he was asked for, and gave (to John Mitchell), not information but only his expert opinion that Hanoi would agree to a bombing halt before the election. Nixon wrote, however, that "during the last days of the campaign, when Kissinger was providing us with information about the bombing halt, I became more aware of both his knowledge and his influence."

This apparently clear contradiction of Kissinger's bland account sug- gests that Kissinger used his access to Johnson's negotiating team to angle for a high position in the future administration of a man he had formerly disdained (Rockefeller, Kissinger wrote, considered Nixon "an opportun- ist without . . . vision or idealism"; and he conceded that "in 1968 I shared many of these attitudes").[39]

Nixon leaves little doubt that it was Kissinger's help during the cam- paign that earned him the president-elect's favorable attention and an offer to become his assistant for national security affairs. This may tell much about both men—supporting, for example, what a senator said of Kissinger to Ken BeLieu:

> Henry would have made a good broken-field runner in football. He
> could look one way and drift another. Before anyone knew it, if
> someone tried to tackle him, he was gone.

The same senator, clearly not an admirer, thought Kissinger had "one of the most brilliant minds in Washington. He also has the greatest ego and every time his mind competes with his ego, it loses."

When the sharp-eyed Kissinger answered the summons to the Pierre Hotel in late November 1968, he saw at once that Nixon was "painfully shy" and nervous. He got an immediate taste, as well, of Nixon's indirect methods of dealing with people. Even on the main question—would Kissinger join the new administration?—he observed, "Nixon's fear of rebuffs caused him to make proposals in such elliptical ways that it was often difficult to tell what he was driving at." John Mitchell, in Kissinger's account, had to intervene at a second meeting before Nixon unambiguously offered the national security post.[40]

Kenneth Rush later saw the same phenomenon in a different light. Though Nixon's old friend and professor, Rush was approached about joining the administration—at first, as ambassador to West Germany—not by the president but by Peter Flanigan, an assistant. This, Rush believed, "was in accordance with Nixon's custom of having one of his assistants initially approach a prospective presidential appointee to avoid the undue pressure involved in the president's making the first approach directly. . . . He is a sensitive and considerate man, contrary to what many people might think."

In the light of later events, Kissinger's insight seems the more acute, particularly since Rush is a Nixon loyalist. Nevertheless, the contrast suggests how differently Nixon could be perceived by different people in different circumstances, even when he was acting in much the same way. Both Kissinger and Rush, moreover, may have been right—the insecure Nixon no doubt *was* on his guard against a Harvard intellectual's rejection; and Rush is by no means alone, among Nixon associates, in finding him a sensitive and considerate superior.

He leaned over backward, for example, to avoid firing or even wounding Bob Finch and John Mitchell, two friends who proved unsatisfactory in office. Though, as shown, he often bypassed and humiliated Bill Rogers, Kissinger is witness in *White House Years* to the real agony Nixon seemed to suffer in thus treating a friend who stood in the way—Nixon feared—of his cherished foreign policy designs.

Ray Price, moreover, insists that he "never worked for or with anyone so personally considerate" as Richard Nixon. Arthur Burns was startled to receive, in 1986, an unsolicited letter from Nixon, thanking him for being, as Burns described it, "one of the few who never sugarcoated" what he said to a president.

"He didn't have to [write that letter]," Burns said. "I can't do anything for him anymore."[41]

Nixon's elliptical approach to Kissinger, as noted earlier, resulted in a political coup; the recruitment to the new administration of a man from the liberal Rockefeller camp as well as the academic world. As in his search for Democrats, Nixon wanted to give his administration the appearance of a broad range of support and interests. Kissinger filled the bill, and the relief many liberals felt at his appointment was palpable; perhaps the hated Nixon would not be so bad after all, at least in foreign policy.

Though not quite as these liberals hoped, Kissinger *was* ideally suited for the kind of foreign policy management the new president envisioned, as well as to deal with the numerous peculiarities of Richard Nixon. "I had a strong intuition about Henry Kissinger," Nixon said in *RN,* and well he might have.

In the first place, though Nixon remarked on the contrast of "the grocer's son from Whittier and the refugee from Hitler's Germany, the politician and the academic," Kissinger was *not* a "Franklin"; he was as much a self-made man as Nixon—a point that counted.

Not that Kissinger was a man of humility. His celebrated wit included the remark that it would be all right to call him "Excellency," and he once told an audience standing in a room at the West German embassy, "I don't mind if you kneel." Such derision of arrogance actually may have *suggested* arrogance, rather than the self-deprecation with which Kissinger was credited.

In the second place, Kissinger was at least Nixon's intellectual peer, probably his superior, and his knowledge of foreign affairs, if more academic, was even more encyclopedic. On that level, the two men hit it off immediately. Richardson, early in the administration, saw and talked with Kissinger "several times a week"; in his view Nixon

> enjoyed very much . . . the opportunity to talk with Kissinger about all his foreign policy ideas and to explore the implications of various possible approaches to dealing with the problems of Vietnam, arms control, and so on. Kissinger's intellect, background, knowledge and conceptual capacity were ideally adapted to his serving as an interlocutor with Nixon.

In the third place, Henry Kissinger was a natural courtier, of old-world deviousness, who understood from the start that he had a "constituency of one" and who was willing to spare no effort to woo it. That cannot have been easy; indeed Kissinger ultimately grew tired of "excruciatingly long conversations" with Nixon, as he described them at Hofstra, that often roamed back and forth over the same ideas and information. Kissinger nevertheless adapted himself to this Nixonian method of reaching policy decisions; Kissinger was nothing if not adaptable to power.

"Richard Nixon was like a cow," John Ehrlichman inelegantly said of the president's conversations—which often turned into monologues:

> He would chew his cud over and over on a subject and turn it over and chew it some more, and turn it over and chew it some more. ... Probably you'd grunt at the right times or make some comment or other.

When the existence of the White House tapes was later disclosed, Kissinger told Ehrlichman that "we are going to look like perfect fools when those tapes come out." Historians, he feared, would believe Nixon's listeners were "acquiescing" in everything the president said, including "the most outrageous stuff."

Ehrlichman reassured him that it would be understood that "far from acquiescing, our minds were probably drifting off to other things."

Another major asset for Kissinger in his relations with Nixon was the fact that their substantive ideas ran along much the same lines. Kissinger, too, believed the war in Vietnam could not be summarily abandoned without unacceptable damage to the American position in the world, and he, too, considered relations with the Soviet Union of the highest priority. Both men had a balance-of-power concept and a geopolitical view of the world; and, like Nixon, Kissinger wanted to establish principles, a "structure" for American foreign policy, as well as a formal management system, to replace what both thought were the ad hoc procedures and decisions, born more often of external crises than of planning and forethought, typical of the Kennedy and Johnson administrations.

Kissinger's nature was as secretive as Nixon's, and he believed as strongly as the new president that secrecy was essential to the successful conduct of foreign policy. Nor did he feel himself bound, any more than Nixon did, by conventional precepts of "morality" or duplicity in seeking an effective foreign policy; if the ends were useful, the means were justifiable.

Above all, however, Henry Kissinger shared Nixon's desire for power and his willingness to use it—as the shrewd Nixon may have discerned; it takes one, they say, to catch one. That meant that Kissinger was as eager as the president to gather all the elements of foreign policy–making within the White House. On the fundamental points of who would manage foreign affairs in the Nixon administration, and how, Nixon and Kissinger understood and reinforced each other.

Though in 1968 a relatively untried academic more eager for power than experienced in its exercise, Kissinger also was to show himself as adept as his new principal in the Byzantine ways of bureaucratic maneuver and personal advancement. Before the new administration was under way, Kissinger the broken-field runner already had demonstrated his swivel hips, accomplishing much of what Nixon wanted before anyone knew it or tried to tackle him.

Under the president-elect's instructions to create the kind of foreign policy structure Nixon envisioned, Kissinger submitted a memorandum of organization for the National Security Council and its subgroups that sharply shifted power from the State Department to the White House— and greatly enhanced the powers of the president's national security adviser.

The memorandum proposed that Kissinger should both set the agenda for NSC meetings and chair the review committee that decided which of the papers coming up from the bureaucracy, setting out various options, would go to the president; the other members of the review committee were to be subcabinet officials. Both functions formerly had been exercised by the so-called Senior Interdepartmental Group, which was under control of the State Department.

One of the major consequences of Kissinger's proposal would be to exclude the secretary of state and other concerned cabinet officers from early influence on foreign policy decisions—or even on what decisions had to be made. In Kenneth Rush's view, the arrangement was

> a very clever way of keeping the secretaries from participating in the decision-making process until it reached the National Security Council, by which time the President had pretty well made up his mind. It was . . . very cleverly designed to try to keep the President in direct control.

Roger Morris,* at Hofstra, described the Kissinger proposal as "a coup d'état." The plan, not surprisingly, was approved by Nixon as soon as he read it. At a meeting the next day—December 28, 1968—at the Key Biscayne house, he disclosed the new arrangement to his major foreign policy associates, including Secretary of State–designate Rogers, and a former colleague in the House, Secretary of Defense–designate Melvin Laird.

"Like so many meetings in the Nixon administration," Kissinger recalled, "the Key Biscayne session had its script determined in advance." Before any substantive discussion could develop, Nixon announced that he had approved the reorganization already; that assured there would be no objections to his face, from his subordinates around the table. Instead, a

---

*Morris was a member of Kissinger's NSC staff in the early years of the Nixon administration. He is the author of what will be a four-volume biography of Nixon.

titanic bureaucratic struggle ensued in Washington, as the State Department sought to prevent its own emasculation.[42]

For at least two reasons this was a fight the department could not win—which was clear to Kissinger, with his understanding of Nixon's intentions. This confidence had enabled him, in the first place, to make such an audacious foray into State Department turf; later, it encouraged him to stand fast. For one thing, the State Department struggle appeared to be in defense of the status quo and the department's usual prerogatives, both of which Nixon was determined not to continue. More important, the president was intent on taking control of foreign policy, and no one in the department—not even Secretary Rogers—could change *him*. Kissinger had given him the means.

Rogers, in fact, did not literally lead the fight, though he made known his subordinates' vigorous opposition. His unwillingness to provide vigorous leadership in a cause he suspected was hopeless was another reason, though none was needed, why the State Department could not win.

The new secretary, like Kissinger, was aware of Nixon's desire to manage foreign policy from the White House—though he probably did not fully grasp how far Nixon intended to carry his plans. Rogers, in fact, had accepted his own appointment *despite* his understanding of Nixon's aim. He was, moreover, a neophyte in foreign policy—a former attorney general, a prosperous corporate lawyer, whom Nixon wanted at State primarily for two reasons: because he believed Rogers was a tough and skilled negotiator, and because his old friend did *not* know much about foreign policy, hence would be less inclined to resist a subordinate role.

The day before he was inaugurated, Nixon signed a National Security Decision Memorandum putting the Kissinger reorganization into effect. The new scheme was made public on the president's first day in office—the same day his "manner" persuaded Arthur Burns that he already was running for reelection. Kissinger the newcomer had won his first and one of his and Nixon's most important battles.

In *White House Years* Kissinger denigrated the importance of the formal directive and the organization it authorized, on grounds that the State Department still was adequately represented in foreign policy–making and—more important—that under *any* bureaucratic system of management the president intended to be the dominant figure, therefore inevitably would have been. Nor was the reorganization, Kissinger wrote, perhaps with tongue in cheek, a vast new grant of power to the national security adviser.

No doubt the literal details of the policy-making apparatus mattered little more, in view of Nixon's determination, than Kissinger claimed they did; Nixon would have had his way in any case. But Kissinger's reorganization got the job done for Nixon at the outset; and Kissinger conceded that the system he had devised later made it easier for the president to plan policy without hindrance from the rest of the government, and to conduct the secret negotiations—as in the cases of China, Vietnam and SALT I —that policy often demanded.

That old government hand, Ken BeLieu, came to see it as "a mistake on Nixon's part to let Henry short-circuit" established consultative processes:

> If the machinery of government is not used, you open yourself to a lack of data, lack of advice, and are apt to develop a mentality that only looks at one area of the information. Therefore the decisions may be tainted.

In general, BeLieu's point is well taken, but his judgment sounds perilously close to bureaucratic justification for endless and often unproductive consultations. Nixon wanted none of that and lost no time in demonstrating his intentions. The day after his inauguration, he instructed Kissinger to telephone Henry Cabot Lodge, the newly appointed negotiator with the North Vietnamese in Paris, to change—without State Department clearance—Lodge's negotiating instructions along Nixon's preferred lines.

At the president's first meeting with the Soviet ambassador, Anatoly Dobrynin, on February 17, the secretary of state was not present; Henry Kissinger was. In March, Nixon went so far as to have Kissinger inform Dobrynin that Secretary Rogers, in a talk with Dobrynin, had not outlined *Nixon's* views on Vietnam negotiations, but Rogers's own.

As for the national security adviser, Kissinger quickly put the bureaucracy to work on projects that enhanced his own ability to advise the president, and kept it from pushing forward matters with which Kissinger and Nixon did not want to deal. In his first month in office, Kissinger ordered at least thirty-five different studies on thirty-five different international problems.

BeLieu offers an example of how Kissinger seized upon his enhanced position, and guarded it against all comers. After a meeting between Nixon and the influential Democratic chairman of the Armed Services Committee, Senator Richard Russell of Georgia, with Kissinger, BeLieu and Bryce Harlow also present, the president said: "Ken, you and Bryce come back and we'll have a nightcap and discuss some of the things we have been talking about."

Harlow and BeLieu escorted Senator Russell to his car and returned, only to be met by Kissinger at the door to the Oval Office. "The President and I have something to talk about," he said. "Good night." And that was the end of Nixon's invitation.

"Juxtaposition to the President was Henry's strength and he fought to keep it," BeLieu noted.

Kissinger's claim that the reorganization did little to enhance his position is obviously disingenuous. As Joseph Sisco described one of Kissinger's functions under the new dispensation:

> Any of the papers that developed options ultimately came to Henry Kissinger's desk as part of the overall review. He basically decided how these papers were presented to the President, if they were presented at all. A number of times, he wrote critiques of them and indicated whether a formal meeting of the National Security Council was necessary or desirable.

That's power. And when Kissinger's memorandum became the basis for the administration's way of making foreign policy, he gained the immense internal prestige of an early and major bureaucratic victory. That advertised his close relationship with the president and his unprecedented primacy over the secretary of state; conversely, it tabbed Rogers as weak and a loser, demoralizing many in the State Department and encouraging the aggressive Kissinger and the manipulative Nixon to override or ignore Rogers and the professional diplomats.

Nixon did assign Rogers responsibility for the Middle East, an area about which Kissinger at first was not well informed. Nixon wanted the secretary of state to have "his own little niche," in the opinion of Joseph Sisco; and it may have been that the president was sensitive to public opinion in keeping Kissinger, a Jew and a German, out of affairs involving Israel. Whatever the reason, "Henry resented this; there wasn't any question about it," as Sisco saw; but exclusion from the Middle East was only a small and temporary setback for the national security adviser (see chapter 16).

The psychological effect of Kissinger's victory enabled him quickly to become very nearly Nixon's *only* foreign policy adviser, one of unparalleled influence. His frequent access to the Oval Office, shrewdly exploited, helped make that perhaps inevitable. But earlier occupants of his post had gained no such preeminence; Kissinger, in fact, had written his own passport into Nixon's presence and favor. His triumph in the preinaugural warfare within the administration clearly opened the way for his extraordinary later emergence.

Nixon's first presidential news conference—on January 27, 1969, in the East Room of the White House—found him at his best. Well prepared, as relaxed as he ever would be, and aware of the inclination among White House reporters to accord a "honeymoon" to a new president, Nixon appeared confident and statesmanlike as he answered fifteen questions in impressive detail.

No doubt the moment was one of some satisfaction for him; by 1969, televised news conferences had become a recognized hallmark of the presidency, eagerly awaited by the press and the politically interested public. Holding his first, in the deferential presence of those persons he believed most consistently opposed to him, with the nation watching on all three networks, put a stamp of authenticity upon his arrival perhaps more tangible than the oath he had sworn. More than any earlier action, Richard Nixon's first news conference announced that he was president at long last; the lengthy, lonely pursuit of his most cherished goal had ended in victory.

Among other matters, that day, Nixon retreated from his campaign pledge—hotly challenged by Hubert Humphrey—that the nation would regain nuclear "superiority" over the Soviet Union. He seized, instead, upon the word "sufficiency" (offered in a question by Edward P. Morgan of ABC news) as better defining his view than either "parity" or "superiority."

Helen Thomas of United Press International, the senior wire service reporter present, ended the news conference with the traditional "Thank you, Mr. President!" Herbert Klein, the new administration's "director of communications," a title he had contrived for himself after the press secretary's job he really wanted went to Ronald Ziegler, then followed the reporters out of the East Room.

On the White House portico, the affable Klein encountered Mary McGrory, a columnist for the *Washington Star* and one of the more talented writers in the political press corps, whose liberal views and low regard for Nixon were well known.

"Your man was great," Ms. McGrory told Klein. "He handled everything well, and I was encouraged by what he said about Vietnam and arms limitation—'sufficiency.' Maybe he's different now that he's president."

Klein, on the other hand, was relieved because if Mary McGrory had approved Nixon's performance, it must have been good; on the other hand, he was disturbed by her suggestion that a "different" Nixon had emerged.

"When one looks at the history of Nixon and his relations with the press," he later wrote, " 'new Nixon' comes out almost like code words. I lived through 'new Nixon' after 'new Nixon.' " Klein knew that whatever improvement of relations with reporters might result from still another Nixon, even a President Nixon, it would be short-lived; sooner or later the "old Nixon" would reappear in the eyes of the press, that much the worse for having even briefly led reporters astray.[43]

Klein regarded Nixon and the press as having "a love-hate relationship," because though each basically disliked the other, each also invested in the other an intense interest and maintained an unrelenting scrutiny of the other's activities and attitudes. That may suggest jealous and obsessive lovers; in fact, there was little love between Nixon and the press at any time—except for those few political reporters (Nixon estimated them at less than 35 percent of the total) whom he wrote in a memo to Haldeman "actually do live by the decent ethics of the top-flight press men—wire service men, etc., *and those few who are basically on our side.*"[44] (Emphasis added.)

This suggests that Nixon made little distinction between reporters who he thought possessed "decent ethics"—presumably, those who were truly unbiased—and those who were "on our side." Readers may find it difficult to discern an ethical difference between reporters biased against Nixon and those biased *for* him, but Nixon had no difficulty in that regard; his scorn, animosity and—it is not too much to say—malevolence were directed at the former and, even in the White House, could not long be repressed.

Reporters, he told Haldeman in the same memo

> have a fetish about fairness, and once they are caught being unfair, they are very sensitive about it and try to compensate it from time to time. On the other hand, they have no intention whatever to be fair whenever they are able to get away with unfair coverage.

Nixon did not seem to suspect a deliberate press "conspiracy" against him so much as to believe that reporters, in some unspecified but herdlike way, mostly thought and acted as one—against him. Quoting a friendly older reporter "who now spends most of his time around the Press Club bar," the president wrote in another memo to Haldeman, most reporters' "whole objective in life is to bring us down." Neither Nixon nor the bibulous informant explained why or how this uniform impulse had been reached (although the latter did concede and Nixon noted that "some of them may not even be aware that they are reporting in a prejudiced way, but their feelings are so strong that they cannot really hide them").

Consequently, Nixon instructed Haldeman, the White House staff "should treat [reporters] with the courteous, cool contempt which has been my policy. . . . The greatest mistake we can make is to try to do what [President] Johnson did—to slobber over them with the hope that you can 'win' them. It just can't be done." The word "slobber" is written in Nixon's hand over a less expressive verb.[45]

Even praise in the press was suspect. Early in the administration, Pat Moynihan called Nixon's attention to a favorable column by James Reston in the *New York Times,* and reported that he had spoken to Reston and to me, adding: "When these matters are laid out [probably concerning the Family Assistance Plan], responsible and intelligent men come forward with a strong and favorable impression." Nixon scribbled on the edge of Moynihan's memorandum: "Good job! (But don't expect them to *remain* good!)"[46]

The origins of the Nixon-press hostility have been many times analyzed, but not in my judgment conclusively. Bela Kornitzer, an early and sympathetic biographer, provided a bit of evidence that Nixon's attitude might even be traced to his Black Irish father. Frank Nixon volubly disliked the press for reasons not recorded, a fact with which Dick Nixon grew up; later, after one of his early political victories, when reporters gathered at the Nixon house in Whittier, Frank urged his son to throw them all out.[47]

Some theorists trace the ugly relationship to the Hiss affair, though in fact much coverage of young Congressman Nixon in that episode was favorable (and sought by himself); and since he concedes in *Six Crises* that publicity about the case made him a national figure, it could hardly have been all bad. Some reporters, from the early years of his career, did view Nixon sourly as a sort of junior-league Joe McCarthy, owing not only to the Hiss case but to his California campaigns against Jerry Voorhis and Helen Douglas. In both races, however, Nixon's overall press coverage was more favorable—particularly in the paper that then counted most for him, the *Los Angeles Times*—than most candidates in hard-fought campaigns could expect.

More likely, the bad seeds of the relationship sprouted most potently from the fund crisis of 1952—an episode that embittered Nixon for life. Not only did he get his first real taste of hard and unfavorable, potentially fatal press coverage, an experience he regarded as unfair and never forgot; he also considered himself betrayed and abandoned by those he had thought friends, and he felt himself to be struggling virtually alone for his political life and personal honor.

Herbert Klein, in his long, close association with Nixon, saw the fund crisis as having had "an impact on him which made him feel that he could listen to advice but basically he had to depend upon his own wits."[48]

It seems plausible that Nixon's sense of betrayal extended to a press that, up to then, had been generally friendly, and a basic contributor to his success. The *New York Herald Tribune,* for example, had delivered the first really hard blow against him. After the Checkers speech, the supreme political effort that saved him, was reviled and jeered by many reporters and commentators, he came to believe that he could count only on opposition and hostility from a press that was essentially an enemy too.

The anti-Communist jeremiads of 1952 and 1954 then earned Nixon real, not imagined, hostility from many in the press; he responded in kind. The long, humiliating ordeal of Eisenhower's "dump Nixon" dalliance in 1956, as it appeared in the newspapers, could only have added to his sense of persecution—that "they" were out to get him.

In 1960, in the campaign against Kennedy, Nixon and many on his staff became convinced (they probably were predisposed to believe) that a cabal of reporters—Bill Lawrence of the *New York Times,* Sander Vanocur of NBC, Phil Potter of the *Baltimore Sun,* among others—was working to

harass and embarrass him during news conferences. Most of these reporters would admit that they personally favored Kennedy; the late Bill Lawrence, whom I knew well, made no secret of his close association with the
senator—too close, I thought then and now. All would insist, I have no
doubt, that their personal preference did not affect their professional coverage.[49]

But Nixon was sure—and Klein agreed—that these reporters were gang-
ing up on him. After September 21, 1960, when members of the supposed
cabal questioned him sharply at a news conference in Springfield, Missouri,
Nixon refused to meet with the press again, though there were *seven weeks*
to go before the election—a petulant and unpolitical decision that Klein
believes worsened the campaign's press coverage and was instrumental in
Nixon's defeat.[50]

At the famous "last press conference" in California in 1962, the pent-up
bile of at least a decade spewed out of a defeated and hung over Nixon.
Thereafter, however, in one of his all but patented acts of will, during all
the years of his comeback, he managed to repress—though he never lost—
his hostility to journalists. He knew he had to repress it; and his relentless
appearances in news conferences everywhere he traveled and his tireless
willingness to be interviewed by reporters local or national, singly or in
groups—not to mention the considerable skill with which he learned to
handle these encounters—were indispensable to his political recovery.

In his 1968 campaign, carefully pacing himself as he had not in 1960 and
exercising iron self-control in statements and appearances, Nixon avoided
serious conflict with the press—though political reporters resented his
copious use of the contrived "telethons" at which they were unable to
question him. That year, as in all those of his public life, however, Nixon's
calculated presentation of himself contributed to the conviction of skeptical reporters that he was—in John Osborne's memorable phrase—a "cardboard man" trying to appear to be something he was not.

In this, the reporters were essentially right, even Ray Price conceded.
What they did not understand, he insisted to me, was that Nixon was not,
in the usual political pattern, pretending to be *better* than he was but, with
a necessary eye to the mass of voters, was making himself appear *less*—less
intellectual, less introverted, less detached, less concerned with high policy
than with Main Street interests. The cardboard facade that reporters so
suspected, Price argued, hid a more genuine and impressive person rather
than concealing a lesser man.[51]

Particularly if that were so, it might have been supposed that in the
White House—enemies vanquished, the prize in his hands at last—Nixon's
hostility toward the press would abate because he could afford to relax and
take a more generous view of critics. Instead, his attitude toward the press,
toward "enemies" generally, hardened almost into paranoia.

Perhaps it was because he was all the more in the public eye, therefore subject as never before to harsh press comment on his least important moves and his least significant words. Perhaps he knew there was more to lose, hence feared there was more to guard against, more enemies to fend off. Or perhaps his new power and the institutional prestige that now surrounded him deluded him into the belief that he could strike back, as he had long wanted to do, with impunity.

Or it may be that all of this overly complicates a simpler attitude rooted in Nixon's withdrawn personality, his admitted lack of the "buddy-buddy" sensibility. Lou Cannon, an astute correspondent for the *Washington Post* who covered the White House during some of the Nixon years, "was told that Nixon was so upset about [holding] press conferences that he would throw up beforehand."

Cannon's colleagues conventionally believed Nixon "hated and loathed" reporters but Cannon was not so certain:

> I think he couldn't face people very well and that we were a manifestation of that. He wasn't inimical to the First Amendment in any theoretical sense. I think that some of us in the media may be oversensitive. After all, why should we be different? Who did Nixon love? Maybe we were hated, but mostly we were just there and we forced him into personal experiences that he didn't like.

Nixon certainly could not "face people very well" and the press unquestionably posed "personal experiences that he didn't like." It was "the media," for an obvious example, through which any politician had to reach the people; hence it was the media that in the first instance forced an introverted, cerebral man into the extraverted and hortatory exercises of the politician.

Perhaps as important, the very nature of the reporter's trade must have offended not only Nixon's belief in secrecy but his view of his presidential responsibilities: a reporter's business was to publish information; a president's—in Nixon's view—was to keep information in his own hands until it was useful to make it public.

The existence and persistence of reporters forced Nixon to deal with questions that he did not want to answer, or was not ready to answer, or believed should not be answered at all. Reporters' inquiries complicated the already daunting problems of an opening to China or a withdrawal from Vietnam. And when reporters published information Nixon did not want published, either through a leak or by hard digging, they could damage or destroy the most intricately conceived policy. At the least, they could complicate the necessary tasks of making policy and of maintaining a president's standing and credibility.

Even so judicious a man as Ray Price, once a distinguished journalist himself, came to share this view that uncontrolled information was dangerous. The worst problem for any president, in Price's view, is not that information leaks but that people then misunderstand and misinterpret it—because a leak is seldom complete, rounded, or a properly developed and timed delivery of information. Price's experience, which after 1965 was linked to Nixon's and reflected it, had taught him that no matter what "gets out" from the White House to the public, someone will "use it against the president," deliberately or by misunderstanding.[52]

No doubt; but taken to its logical extreme, this view would result in *no* White House information reaching the public unless and until a president decided to make it public—and then only in the form that he permitted. It's possible to sympathize with the view that in some abstract way this might best serve a president and his policies; but so might many powers that, wisely, presidents have not been granted, and shouldn't be.

Presidents, even with the best of intentions—history has demonstrated many times—are not necessarily the best judges of their own policies, or even of the national interest. The strongest of checks and balances is an informed public. So long as American democracy sustains the First Amendment, no president can control information, and none should be able to, though all will try—in what they perceive as the nation's best interest, or perhaps only in their own.

Lou Cannon's insight—persuasive to me—has the twin virtues of simplicity and generosity, and cuts through endless arguments about whether the press did or did not treat Nixon fairly in one or another situations, with this or that result—all of which demand subjective judgments that vary with their makers. But Cannon's point does not preclude what I also believe was the lasting effect of the fund crisis—not just on Nixon's attitude toward the press but on the greater reclusiveness of his personality after that shattering experience.

However he came by his hostility, Nixon in the White House—and consequently those closest to him—devoted extraordinary amounts of time and concern to the press, particularly television, which by 1969 was the major force in politics. Nixon was certain, for one thing, that even on trivial subjects the press—in some uniform instinctive fashion he seemed not to question—gave him more critical coverage than it had his predecessors, particularly John Kennedy.

Nixon demanded, for example, that Haldeman provide him "a complete rundown" on press coverage of his appearance at the 1970 Gridiron Club dinner. "I recall," he wrote in justification of the request,

> each time Kennedy appeared before the Gridiron there were reams
> of columns with regard to the effectiveness of the appearance, even

though on at least one occasion I recall it was somewhat of a bomb.
. . . [C]heck to see what our "friends" in the Gridiron do with
regard to [my] appearance.[53]

The supposed love affair between the press and John Kennedy was
always a thorn in the side of Nixon and his aides. Reporters, in the opinion
of Kenneth Rush, would "cover up" for Kennedy, "no matter what.
Everybody knew about his sexual peccadilloes but nothing ever came out
about it in public while he was President." On the other hand, as Rush saw
it, the "liberal" and the "establishment" press (generally seen as the same
thing in the Nixon administration) "developed a hatred for [Nixon] that
was unbelievable." Rush "ran into it all the time"—though he does not
specify how or where or when.

The important thing here is what was perceived by Nixon and those
around him, because that is what they acted upon. Though it cannot
change these perceptions about the press, or the unhappy consequences,
the truth is that no such general effort to protect Kennedy existed in what,
admittedly, was the relatively unaggressive White House press corps of his
time (I was the correspondent of the *New York Times*).

It's unquestionably true that the rank and file of those reporters, many
of whom were still covering the White House when Nixon arrived, *liked*
Kennedy better than they liked Nixon—not least because we perceived
that Kennedy, unlike Nixon, liked *us.* More important, Kennedy was
killed *before* the two most disillusioning (hence liberating) experiences
undergone by the American press in modern times—Vietnam and Watergate.

After Vietnam, later compounded by Watergate, reporters' trust in presidential probity and veracity was badly shaken, for the good reason that
much presidential lying and duplicity had necessarily been exposed—as
much by events as by any diligence on the reporters' part. Primarily for
that reason, though to a lesser extent because of the mutual mistrust
between many reporters and Nixon, Kennedy *did* receive more favorable
coverage than Nixon later was to have—no question about it. JFK was
more attractive and likable, qualities to which reporters, like anyone else,
responded favorably.

It was, however, Nixon's primary misfortune not to suffer some wholesale, vaguely "liberal" press instinct to do him in, but to come to office at
a time when the president and the White House no longer were held in the
respect that once had been palpable among Washington journalists. Had
Franklin Roosevelt served after Vietnam, he probably would not have been
spared press mention of his disability or photos of his leg braces and
wheelchair—as, in fact, he was during his long tenure.

Jimmy Carter, who had no pre–White House history of warfare with the national press, was president after *both* Vietnam and Watergate, and he unhappily endured press coverage at least as critical as that Nixon received—more so in some respects.*

As for the supposed cover-up of Kennedy's sexual affairs, which now seem so brazen, neither I nor any White House press colleague whom I've asked knew much about them, certainly not enough to write a story. We knew *something*—rumors, innuendo, Kennedy's prepresidential reputation for womanizing, all kinds of sniggering suggestions—but not the kind of documented fact that reporters of "decent ethics" insist upon before publishing a story.

One of the most strongly pursued "scandals" of that time was "John's other wife"—a never-proved report that Kennedy had had a secret marriage annulled before his marriage to Jacqueline Bouvier. Every news organization in Washington vainly sought this story about the first Roman Catholic president, to the point that Kennedy finally had to issue a formal White House denial.

I cannot imagine, moreover, any reporter, whatever his political views, who would not have written, had he known and been able to prove, so sensational a story as that the president of the United States was fornicating in the White House with the girlfriend of a Mafia chieftain.[54]

Nixon's dislike for the press certainly was returned by numerous reporters. Hugh Sidey, who later developed considerable respect for Nixon's presidency, remembers from the vice presidential years in the fifties seeing something like my own first view of him—"that hunched figure trying to skulk off down the back ways of the Senate." Sidey and other reporters "just didn't like [Nixon]. The feeling was mutual and [we] could sense it."

In the White House, in Sidey's recollection as in mine, Nixon was "remote and still bitter and vindictive," though he "recognized that he needed the media and tried to use it as much as possible." Nixon's obvious attempts to manipulate, sometimes to intimidate, the press naturally did not improve reporters' feelings about him; and even after his major accomplishments as president, Sidey noted, the press continued to dislike "his manner, his style, the person."

I was well aware of, and to some extent shared, this attitude but never saw it as anything like a press crusade to "get Nixon." As a columnist, I wrote many critical articles about him—some of them, in retrospect, overstated and rather righteous. My prime motivation, I believe, always was disagreement about his policies, particularly on Vietnam and civil liberties; but the fact that I found him no more appealing as a personality than did most reporters may have affected my view subconsciously.

---

*After he left office, Carter told me that he, Nixon and Johnson had been considered "outsiders"—nonestablishment figures—and hence all received poor coverage from a press that felt these presidents somehow did not belong in the White House.

Because Nixon was not likable, the press tended to exaggerate his political machinations and personal pretensions; in his case, these were seen as his basic *persona* rather than as the curious appurtenances of public life shared by all politicians. Such a story as the following would have been attributed to a genuine lack of sincerity rather than to quick political footwork:

When Nixon visited Samuel Goldwyn, who was terminally ill, to present him with a Presidential Medal of Freedom in a private ceremony, he made the old Hollywood producer a schmaltzy speech about the wholesomeness of his films. It was 1972 and Nixon was up for reelection; Goldwyn tugged at Nixon's coat and the president bowed to hear his whisper: "You'll have to do better than that if you want to carry California."

Nixon hastily ended the ceremony and left the room.

> Sam [Goldwyn] junior showed him to the door. In the foyer, Nixon asked, "Did you hear what your father said?" Sammy had, but to avoid any embarrassment, said he had not. The president's shoulders drooped in relief. "He said," Nixon boomed, " 'I want you to go out there and beat those bastards!' "[55]

It's true that John Kennedy probably would have been amused by the old man's rebuke; he was unusual in his ability to laugh at himself. Nixon had little of that quality; and his opportunistic bombast, had the story been known at the time, surely would have been seen as evidence of incurable duplicity.

As for the Nixon-press love-hate relationship, surviving like a noxious weed into the White House years, my judgment is that considerable responsibility lay with both sides. But Nixon had the better opportunity to improve the relationship, as Herb Klein seemed to admit:

> Had the President . . . accepted the press evaluation that there was a "new Nixon" and followed through in kind after that first press conference, many of the later troubles . . . might never have happened. A more open give-and-take relationship with the media would have made the White House more sensitive to public perceptions.
>
> The White House did not accept the concept of openness and gradually we drifted from an atmosphere of mutual working arrangements to an unproductive bully attitude toward the news media. The problem stemmed not from a lack of attention to the media but more from obsession with it.[56]

As the Nixon administration got down to business in 1969, Bob Finch, the new secretary of HEW, reflected that with "both Houses of Congress and a good portion of the press" in opposition, President Nixon "had to exercise great care." At that time a friend as much as a counselor, Finch believed he need not worry on at least one score: there would be no embarrassing verbatim accounts to leak out.

Finch was sure of that much because of what had happened when Nixon returned from the postelection Key Biscayne meetings and was invited to the White House for transition talks with Lyndon Johnson. Finch had accompanied the president-elect, and while Nixon conferred with Johnson, Joseph Califano—then a principal assistant to LBJ—showed Finch around the historic premises. Among other things, Califano mentioned a "hand-initiated" audio taping system Johnson had installed in the cabinet room, the Oval Office, "and maybe one other place."

Finch told Nixon about this presidential device. Nixon replied at once: "Get rid of it. I don't want anything like that."

He did not know, then, what with typical pragmatism he later advised his would-be successors: "A President always has to be prepared for what he thought he would never do."[57]

11

★

Channels

★

If the summit meeting takes place, you will
be able to sign the most important arms control agreement ever concluded.

—Henry Kissinger to Richard Nixon,
April 24, 1972

Sometime during the interregnum between Richard Nixon's election and
his inauguration, Morton Halperin suggested to Henry Kissinger that
Nixon could save time and effort by adopting the arms control proposals
Lyndon Johnson had planned to put before the Soviets. The Joint Chiefs
of Staff reluctantly had "signed off" on those proposals, overcoming their
traditional hostility to serious arms negotiations. Halperin, a holdover
from the Johnson administration, thought it might be difficult to get the
chiefs to agree again, on a different arms plan.

Kissinger offered the suggestion to Nixon—or so he later told Halperin.
But the new president wanted to make his own strategic arms appraisal.

"Don't worry about the chiefs," he told Kissinger. "If necessary, I'll
overrule them."

When Kissinger passed along Nixon's reply, Halperin observed, with the
wisdom of long experience in the federal bureaucracy: "It's not that easy."[1]

Though Richard Nixon is credited with the first major arms control
treaty with the Soviet Union, it was the *Johnson administration* with which
the Soviets first agreed to enter negotiations, and in which the Joint Chiefs
of Staff were first persuaded to support such a treaty. Those may have been
the *real* breakthroughs.

The Joint Chiefs in the sixties formed (and still do) a powerful but inertial body that moved, if at all, "like a glacier, only in one direction, and that was hard to change." Nor did the chiefs, for most of the Johnson administration and during its postwar predecessors, take arms control seriously.[2]

The subject was assigned to a low-prestige staff unit that produced formal reports routinely including demands for on-site inspections and other provisions that the chiefs were confident the Soviets never would accept. The chiefs' faith, after all, was in the acquisition, not the relinquishment, of weapons; they also held religiously to the doctrine that *quantity* in arms might someday perhaps be limited (disarmament), but *quality* should never be restricted.

In 1967, all three armed services were supporting deployment of a ballistic missile defense (BMD), which required the development of more weapons; naturally, the chiefs backed the idea. To most members of Congress, moreover, missile defense seemed a persuasive idea. Even if millions were killed in an atomic or nuclear attack, might not millions of others be saved? Not to mention installations and industries. Besides, to build a BMD would keep up with the Soviets or get ahead of them, depending on which intelligence report you read. And it would spread a lot of juicy contracts around the military-industrial complex—of course including the districts and states of many members of Congress.

Congressional opinion—to which President Johnson, the old majority leader, was particularly sensitive—became a major force for a BMD. The most effective opponent was Robert McNamara, Johnson's coldly efficient secretary of defense, who was not treasured by the chiefs, upon whom he kept a restrictive rein. No great affection for McNamara was felt in Congress, either.*

He was not then recognized as the seminal thinker he was among the emerging class of international nuclear strategists and analysts. The defense secretary had realized, however, that in the early sixties he and President Kennedy had bought a larger strategic force of Minuteman missiles than was necessary. That stimulated a responsive Soviet missile buildup so extensive that it threatened to force the U.S. into a new round of this particularly lethal arms race. Its "mad momentum" had to be brought under control, McNamara tardily saw, both to avoid nuclear war and to permit better American-Soviet relations.

McNamara doubted, too, that a BMD would work, since it could be defeated by an opponent launching more warheads and dummies than could be properly identified and intercepted. More than twenty years later,

---

*Johnson, with his gift for crude imagery, once told me that in dealing with Congress, McNamara "couldn't find his ass with both hands."

that remains the unresolved weakness of missile defense technology, even after billions have been spent on President Reagan's so-called Strategic Defense Initiative (SDI).

Equally or more important for McNamara was the fear that an American BMD would cause the Soviets to believe the U.S. was pursuing nuclear superiority. He was years ahead of his time in understanding that such superiority was neither attainable nor useful; but he was convinced that if the Soviets thought the U.S. was seeking it, they would too—thus continuing the "mad momentum" he feared.

McNamara grasped what few others then did: that a successful BMD would *not* be purely defensive, but would threaten the side that did not have one. If deployed by either superpower, even a partially successful BMD would limit the ability of the other's strategic forces to *respond* to a nuclear attack—therefore threatening its all-important ability to *deter* such an attack. In later years, Richard Nixon was to point out in reference to Reagan's SDI that if two men are fighting with swords, and one of them picks up a shield, the *defensive* shield will give the one who has it an *offensive* advantage. He can attack with a higher degree of impunity to his opponent's sword. (As will be seen, that was an understanding Nixon had not always shared.)

Deploying a BMD therefore would have two consequences (now as well as then): First, such a defensive deployment would cause the other side to build up its *offensive* forces in order to overcome its adversary's defense; second, the other side would try to match its opponent's *defense,* too, which in turn would cause the first deployer of a defense to build up its offense as well.

So if the world escaped war while all this happened, the *balance* of forces might well come out the same—but at a dangerously higher level, and despite great expenditure on both sides.

Toward the end of 1966, nevertheless, American intelligence had concluded that a much-debated defense ring—called "Galosh"—that the Soviets were building around Moscow, at first thought to be against aircraft, was a genuine BMD. Conceivably, Galosh was the core of a *national* ballistic missile defense.

This conclusion increased pressure on Lyndon Johnson to authorize an American ABM—an acronym for antiballistic missile used more or less interchangeably with BMD. Congress, the Joint Chiefs, much of the public, and Republican leaders like George Romney—who for a while seemed a better bet than Richard Nixon to be the presidential nominee against Johnson in 1968—all strongly favored deploying a missile defense.

McNamara insisted, however, that the proper response to Galosh was improvement in American *offensive* arms; and since 1962 the U.S. had been working on a qualitative advance that looked like just the thing—"multiple, independently targetable reentry vehicles," or MIRVs, multiple warheads on a single missile, each warhead able to be independently launched at a different target. MIRVs might overwhelm a Soviet missile defense.

McNamara still hoped to avoid a new round in the arms race; the Soviet defense system appeared to be a long way from operational, and MIRV had not passed the point of no return in the slow process of developing a new weapon. But Johnson had to have a political escape from the pro-BMD pressures that Galosh had intensified.

On December 6, 1966, the intense McNamara persuaded LBJ to accept a two-pronged policy—beginning procurement for a missile defense, but with no final decision on deployment, coupled with an effort to begin arms limitation talks with the Soviets. So in January 1967, Johnson asked Congress to appropriate funds for a defense, but said that he would defer decision on BMD deployment until it could be determined whether the Soviets would agree to arms control talks.

With that single stroke, LBJ tried (fruitlessly, as it turned out) to soften the "warmonger" image Vietnam had brought him within the peace movement of his own party, to suggest to the Soviets that a failure to enter talks would cause him to go ahead with BMD deployment and to thwart temporarily his congressional and Republican critics.

The Soviets, however, would not sufficiently cooperate with McNamara's strategy. Even after he personally argued the case against missile defense to Premier Aleksei Kosygin at the minisummit in Glassboro, New Jersey, in June 1967, Kosygin clung stubbornly to the idea of BMD as purely defensive; or perhaps Secretary of State Dean Rusk was correct in his belief that the premier "had not been fully briefed" on arms control, had no instructions from the Politburo, and was therefore unable to respond.[3]

Even after Glassboro, the Soviets continued to reject all proposals for arms talks. Moscow may well have seen such talks as an American scheme to preserve American offensive advantages while limiting the Galosh missile defense; at one point during his debate with McNamara, Kosygin had seemed to think the U.S. was interested only in limitations on defensive arms.[4]

Johnson had little choice after Glassboro. In 1967 he was holding open the possibility of seeking reelection; and in January 1968 his annual budget message would provide his last chance before the election to make more than a rhetorical start on missile defense. Some form of deployment, he told McNamara, would have to be announced—and that became all the more certain when in the late summer of 1967 the People's Republic of China unexpectedly exploded a hydrogen device—a test quickly detected by American intelligence.

Seizing on Johnson's reluctance to overrule him altogether, McNamara disclosed in a speech in San Francisco in September 1967 that the U.S. would deploy a "thin" missile defense, called "Sentinel," against the possibility of a *Chinese* attack. Sentinel also would provide some protection against an accidental missile launch from anywhere—but it was *not,* McNamara insisted, the first step in the kind of "thick" nationwide system that would threaten the Soviet deterrent force and cause Moscow to react with an offensive buildup. He and Johnson had approved Sentinel— McNamara did *not* say—only to delay and if possible to prevent the more destabilizing deployment of a "thick" system.

Three months later, the U.S. in effect dropped the other shoe. John S. Foster, the Pentagon's director of research and engineering, announced that the development of MIRV was proceeding rapidly toward deployment—which was necessitated, Foster said, by new Soviet offensive and defensive missile deployments. MIRV would be used, if necessary, to saturate Soviet missile defenses, thus complementing Sentinel with an improved American offensive capacity.

The calculated decision to deploy the limited Sentinel defense, together with the MIRV announcement, appear to have been important factors in swinging Moscow toward the arms control talks McNamara wanted. His antidefense lecture to Kosygin at Glassboro also may have had more impact in Moscow than was known at the time.[5]

Probably of equal or greater importance was Johnson's turn toward negotiations rather than escalation in Vietnam, announced at the same time as his withdrawal from the presidential race, on March 31, 1968. His retirement made more likely the election of hard-line Richard Nixon— Romney had flunked out. Nixon was not then considered a proponent of arms control and certainly not of withdrawal from Vietnam. Better deal with Johnson, the Soviets may well have reasoned, while it's still possible.

On June 24, 1968, the Senate decisively rejected a move to deny funds for Sentinel deployment. Three days later, the Soviet foreign minister, Andrei Gromyko, declared in Moscow that his government was ready for talks on limiting offensive and defensive arms. And after only three more days, on July 1, at ceremonies for the American signing of the Nuclear Non-Proliferation Treaty (on which Moscow and Washington had continued to cooperate), President Johnson announced that both nations had agreed to enter arms negotiations.[6]

In that traumatic year of the murders of Robert Kennedy and Martin Luther King, and that wrenching summer of the turmoil in Chicago at the Democratic National Convention, Johnson's announcement was salutary. War and rioting for once were matched in the headlines by hopeful words about peace. Some believed the arms talks might be Johnson's reentry vehicle into the presidential race.

Meanwhile, the president's compromise of December 1966 had not been cosmetic; in his agreement with McNamara, Johnson had envisioned a "serious" proposal for arms control talks—not another of the Joint Chiefs' ritual plans designed to be rejected. The president made it clear to them that he wanted a "hard" proposal to restrict the arms race and did *not* want to hear about the difficulties of reaching it. Fortunately, the development of such a proposal was facilitated by improvements in satellite photographic techniques, the mainstay of "national technical means" of verification.* This enabled drafters to get around the chiefs' usual insistence on on-site inspections.

On July 31, 1968, the Johnson administration's arms control plan— already approved by the chiefs—could be laid before a high-level group known as the "Committee of Principals." The first *serious* American effort for arms control, the proposal did not envision *reductions* in arms on either side; it left ample room for the *qualitative* improvement in weaponry deemed so important by the chiefs; but what the plan did envision was far-reaching for the time:

> 1. A limit on ballistic missile defense deployments, at an equal level to be negotiated.
> 2. A freeze on offensive strategic weapons (ICBMs).
> 3. A ban on mobile strategic offensive systems and on mobile BMD launchers.
> 4. Verification by national technical means with no demand for on-site inspection.
> 5. No numerical restrictions on MIRVs.[7]

Both Washington and Moscow, after much haggling, agreed to say on August 21 that Johnson and Kosygin would open strategic arms limitation talks on September 30, or thereabouts, in the Soviet Union. But on August 20, Warsaw Pact tanks rolled heavily into Czechoslovakia, putting a drastic end to the "Prague spring," to Lyndon Johnson's hopes to make a historic beginning in arms control—and to any lingering thoughts anyone may have had about his reentering the presidential campaign.

The invasion caused so much outrage in the U.S. and most of the world—notably, as we shall see, in China—that Johnson had to cancel the scheduled talks on the eve of their announcement. Why then had Moscow taken an action that Dean Rusk likened to "throwing a dead fish in the face of the president?" In addition to their perceived need to quell the

---

*Mostly satellite observation of the other nations' terrain and deployments, together with electronic monitoring of telecommunications, computer technologies, and other such wizardry. High-resolution photography greatly improved the capabilities of satellite observation.

Czechs, the Soviets probably gambled that if they agreed to announce the arms talks at that particular time, their consent might mollify the world's and Johnson's predictable reaction against the Czechoslovakian invasion.[8]

However that may be, Johnson's arms control tragedy—in retrospect, hardly less profound than his fatal involvement in Vietnam—was final only for him. The arms control stage was empty only for the moment; Johnson's sad departure left it set and lighted for the accession of Richard Nixon to the presidency.

In his inaugural address, a few months after Johnson's peacemaking hopes were dashed, Nixon had expressed his belief that the "era of confrontation" between the superpowers had to give way to an "era of negotiation." In actual practice, however, neither he nor Kissinger wanted to move too quickly to improve American-Soviet relations. They needed to get control of government machinery and make a comprehensive review of American military and strategic capacities; and they could not quickly brush aside the continuing American and world reaction against the crushing of "communism with a human face" in Czechoslovakia.

As early as Inauguration Day, however, and even before that, the Soviet Union—having done by then a complete about-face—privately and publicly let it be known that the strategic arms limitation talks originally scheduled with Johnson could go forward anytime the new president was ready. On February 17, 1969, the Soviet ambassador, Anatoly Dobrynin, met with Nixon to inform him that negotiations on a wide range of issues, even at a Nixon-Brezhnev summit, were possible.

Significantly, at the express wish of Richard Nixon, Secretary of State Rogers was not present for this meeting. Nixon seized the occasion, instead, to inform Dobrynin that on matters of special and sensitive interest, the ambassador should talk to Henry Kissinger rather than to the secretary of state.[9]

As for negotiations with Moscow, Nixon was deliberately noncommittal; a summit, he suggested to Dobrynin, required careful preparation. During the interregnum, he and Kissinger had resolved not to be rushed into talks before they could set up their policy of "linkage"—a plan, as Nixon described it in *RN,* "to link progress in such areas of Soviet concern as strategic arms limitation and increased trade with progress in areas that were important to us—Vietnam, the Mideast and Berlin." The implicit suggestion is that arms limitation was more nearly a Soviet than a Nixon "concern."

Domestic politics, of course, forced Nixon to focus primarily, not on dealings with Moscow, but on the overriding problem of finding a way out of the war in Vietnam. He also wanted to solidify relations with the European allies before turning to Moscow. Just a week after Dobrynin's summit proposal, the president took off for an eight-day round of talks in Western Europe.

SALT was not, therefore, high on Nixon's original list of priorities. Neither he nor Kissinger believed deeply in arms control per se; neither did Secretary of Defense Laird or—as we have seen—the Joint Chiefs of Staff they had inherited from the Johnson administration. Kissinger saw arms limitation primarily as a means to what he considered more important ends.

On January 27, at Nixon's first news conference—despite his public acceptance on that occasion of nuclear "sufficiency" rather than "superiority"—he subjected arms control to linkage. SALT, he said, should be pursued "in a way and at a time that will promote, if possible, progress on outstanding political problems at the same time."

To Nixon, arms control at the outset of his administration was primarily a *political* instrument, more than a means of substantial reduction in the dangers of nuclear war. So it remained for him, as for Kissinger—a means, not an end. Just for that reason, however, and rather quickly, SALT became the vehicle for opening the promised "era of negotiation."

Arms talks promised the quickest and best route over which Nixon could move the Soviet Union and the U.S. toward a new superpower relationship that he was not yet calling "détente." SALT had great public support, for one thing; if carefully negotiated, for another, restraints on nuclear weapons obviously would remove some of the dangers of war and some of the sources of American-Soviet suspicions.

Besides, a substantial arms agreement would be an original Nixon achievement dwarfing Kennedy's almost-forgotten Limited Test Ban Treaty of 1963, which had only stopped nuclear testing in the atmosphere. By taking strontium 90 out of babies' milk, while leaving both sides free to build weapons, the LTB had proved more nearly an environmental than an arms control treaty.

As the search for a means of escape from Vietnam dragged on without success and public opposition threatened to turn "Johnson's war" into "Nixon's war," the president also realized (as had LBJ) that SALT might balance his record—the Vietnam warmaker could appear to be a nuclear peacemaker.

It quickly became clear in 1969, moreover, that whatever its earlier attitude, the Soviet Union was anxious for SALT—for good reasons. One was the perennial Soviet desire to achieve "parity" with the U.S.—not just in weapons or trade but in respect, in the world's regard. Moscow, like any parvenu, longed to be accepted, in this case as an equal superpower; and sitting down at the table with the Americans to bargain over the two sides' nuclear arsenals was in itself an act of equality.

Another reason was provided by the Chinese. After they forced a major armed clash on the Sino-Soviet border on March 2, 1969—thirty-one Soviets were killed—such fighting, though usually less sanguinary, became commonplace well into the summer. As will be detailed later, Chinese resentment of the Warsaw Pact's invasion of Czechoslovakia in 1968 was one of many factors in the border fighting, which threatened Moscow with war in the East.

A third reason was the situation in Eastern Europe, Moscow's buffer against the West. Despite or because of the Czechs' fate, Eastern European states remained unsettled in 1969, and Communist parties in Western Europe were no less restrictive than the Chinese. The Soviets felt the heat of the displeasure in the Communist world, exacerbated by long-standing economic difficulties within the Soviet Union itself. An agreement with the West would shore up Moscow's prestige and position with its satellites.

To a greater extent than Washington did, the Soviet leaders—not, of course, unanimously—also wanted arms control for the sake of arms control. McNamara's arguments against missile defense were, by 1969, Moscow's own. Despite the Soviets' ICBM buildup, moreover, they still lagged in technology and in certain vital weapons. The economic failings of the Soviet system—later to become obvious to the world—even then were visible to expert analysts and no doubt made the rising costs of the arms race onerous to Soviet leaders. For all these reasons, in Moscow, with every month that passed, SALT seemed a better idea.

To Nixon and Kissinger, that meant that the Soviets might pay a political price for strategic arms talks—linkage. Preoccupied with Vietnam as the president and his adviser were, and perhaps influenced by—if they did not actually believe—the old American misconception that Moscow ruled its "puppets" with an iron hand, they calculated that the road to extrication from Vietnam ran through the Soviet Union. In return for SALT and a nuclear arms agreement, the Soviets—among other things—might bring pressure on Hanoi to end the war.

Here is an example suggesting that experience is sometimes the worst teacher. In 1953, on his first vice presidential trip abroad, Nixon had made it clear in Indochina that he believed the roots of the anti-French war were in Moscow. Just as the Truman and Eisenhower administrations had, he concluded that the Soviets also had directed the North Korean invasion of South Korea in 1950—ignoring Kim Il Sung's desire to achieve reunification under his rule.

In 1969, with those precedents in mind, Nixon—though he did not believe the war was *entirely* the product of external direction—naturally thought that the Soviets, if they chose, could influence or persuade, with carrot or stick, the North Vietnamese to make peace. In practice, to the new president's disappointment, the Soviets proved to be of little help. In March 1969, Nixon had confidently predicted at a cabinet meeting that the war would be over in a year. But as that year wore along with the search for peace going nowhere, Nixon found himself under rising pressure to get moving on SALT.

In March, honoring his promise to Strom Thurmond, Nixon announced that he was going forward with deployment of a missile defense, Sentinel renamed "Safeguard" and designed to protect strategic missile silos rather than fend off a Chinese attack. This tended to confirm that Sentinel-Safeguard, in Nixon's plans, was the first stage of a "thick" BMD against the Soviets—as Thurmond and other congressional potentates wanted. Nixon asserted, however, his readiness to consider limitations on defensive as well as offensive strategic weapons—though he still announced no decision to enter talks with the Soviets.

On June 11, 1969, Nixon finally let Dobrynin know privately that he would be ready to begin SALT at the end of July—when a decent year would have passed since the subjugation of the Czechs and the collapse of Lyndon Johnson's hopes for arms control. Almost immediately, however, Nixon *publicly* declared—at a news conference on June 19—that the U.S. was going to proceed with flight tests of MIRV; they had been started on August 16, 1968, by the Johnson administration. The point of no return in that threatening weapon's development was rapidly approaching; and the Soviets already were testing their own version—multiple but not yet independently targetable warheads.[10]

By August 14, 1969, when the Senate approved Safeguard by the narrow margin of Vice President Agnew's tiebreaking vote, no Soviet response to Nixon's private offer of June 11 had been received. But the certainty that American missile defense deployment was going forward in the more ambitious Safeguard—almost two years after McNamara had announced the "thin" Sentinel in his San Francisco speech—and that MIRV was nearing deployment must surely have whetted rather than curbed the Soviet appetite for SALT.

These developments, however, may also have caused officials in Moscow to delay actual agreement to arms talks, lest they appear to have been coerced. Nixon's visit to Romania in August 1969 surely displeased the Soviets, and may have further influenced them to delay acceptance of his offer. Kissinger speculated that before the Safeguard vote Moscow did not want to damage the arguments of Safeguard's *opponents,* that it was incompatible with arms control negotiations.[11]

In the summer of 1969, too, Soviet leaders were preoccupied with their border difficulties with China. So it was not until October 25 that spokesmen in both capitals could make the announcement that "negotiations on curbing the arms race" would open in Helsinki on November 17, 1969.

With Safeguard and MIRV proceeding, Nixon appeared to be entering SALT with a strong hand. The linkage he had sought, however, the price he had hoped Moscow would pay, had not materialized—certainly not in the form of Soviet help in reaching a peace settlement in Vietnam.

On November 3, just over a week after the announcement that SALT was to begin, Nixon took to television for his famous appeal over the heads of Vietnam protesters ("And so tonight, to you, the great Silent Majority of my fellow Americans, I ask for your support . . .") and to proclaim—not the settlement with Vietnam that he had promised to achieve—but his determination to fight on in the same old search for an elusive "honorable" peace no one could quite define. The new nuclear peacemaker was still the old Vietnam warmaker.

When SALT finally began in Smolna Palace at Helsinki, neither side put forward actual negotiating proposals. They limited themselves to listing items for an agenda, to working out a schedule in which alternate negotiating rounds would be held in Vienna and Helsinki, and to appraising the other's intentions.

Gerard Smith, the chairman of the American negotiating team, did table for the Americans a list of "Illustrative Elements," primarily designed to elicit Soviet reaction; but he first advised Vladimir S. Semenov, the chief Soviet negotiator, not to take them literally as proposals. The "Elements" show, nevertheless, that the underlying American position still was basically the one the Joint Chiefs had agreed to in the Johnson administration—a freeze on offensive strategic missiles and equal limits to be negotiated on missile defense systems. The Elements did not mention MIRVs.[12]

Thus in the year that had passed—with the Czech drama delaying SALT from October 1968 to January, the Nixon administration holding it up from January to June, and the Soviets from June to October 1969—the fundamental American position had not substantially evolved from that developed for President Johnson. But a high price had been paid by both sides, particularly by the U.S., for the delay.

"The year that was lost between when Johnson wanted to start negotiations and when they actually started was a terrible year to lose," Walt Rostow, Johnson's national security adviser, lamented long afterward.[13]

For one thing, the Soviets had made remarkable additions to their strategic offensive forces—particularly ICBMs. From January 1967, when Lyndon Johnson had first sought arms control talks, to November 1969, when they actually began, Moscow more than doubled its ICBM force from 500 to 1,140, while the number of American ICBMs remained at 1,054; in the same period, total Soviet strategic force levels (ICBMs, submarine-launched ballistic missiles [SLBMs] and manned bombers) also doubled, from 750 to 1,470, entirely owing to growth in strategic missiles, while the American strategic force level actually dropped from 2,280 to 2,235.[14]

By the time the talks got seriously under way, moreover, the *next* generation of Soviet ICBMs—MIRVed, at that—had been planned and settled upon in Moscow. In any government, decisions of that kind, dependent as they are on technology, allocation of resources, lead time and production schedules, are not easily changed. Nor could they have been, except possibly at a high price in concessions that the U.S. showed itself unprepared to make.

More important, though largely unnoticed by the public, American tests of MIRV had been completed and the weapon was ready for deployment. The point of no return that had not yet arrived when McNamara reluctantly called for Sentinel in 1967 rapidly followed the beginning of MIRV flight testing on August 16, 1968; by late 1969, that point had come and gone. As 1970 opened, the U.S. had MIRV—the most "destabilizing" weapon since the ballistic missile itself—ready for operational deployment.

The Soviets, however, had not yet developed an independently targetable warhead even to the point of flight-testing it. The combination of a weapon in hand, a clear lead in its technology and the resulting military "advantage" was irresistible to the Joint Chiefs of Staff and even to the civilian leadership of the Pentagon. Both pressed, of course, for deployment of MIRV; and both predictably opposed any effort in SALT to limit use of the new weapon by either side. No better example can be found of the tyranny of technology over politics.

Unfortunately, the pattern of the arms race already had shown that anything either side could do, in time the other side could and would do, too. No secrets needed to be stolen, no technological miracles passed. The necessary knowledge to match the other side's advantage was available, only waiting to be developed; so most arms race advantages were temporary. With an eye to future consequences, Nixon and Kissinger would have been well advised to consider whether it would be wise to forgo such a short-run gain.

They might also have pondered the fact that an American MIRV was not merely a short-run advantage; MIRV could turn fatally on its originators. The Soviets would match American technology, probably sooner rather than later, and when they did, the greater and more lasting advantage would be theirs. They had built their rocket forces around bigger, heavier missiles, capable of carrying greater payload than those of the U.S.—no particular advantage, if any, for pre-MIRV purposes, but a fact that would allow them ultimately to mount *more* MIRVs on a single missile than the U.S. could.

Sometime in the *foreseeable* future, therefore, MIRVs unrestricted by arms control might threaten the U.S. more seriously than they would the Soviet Union. By loading more and more MIRVs on each of its heavy missiles, the Soviets would be able to overwhelm a missile defense at far less cost than the U.S. would incur in strengthening or "thickening" its defense.*

Nor was this the only problem the U.S. would create for itself if it failed to seek a MIRV ban. The truth, recognized too late in Washington and probably in Moscow as well, was that "no stable agreement to limit offensive strategic arms could exist without stringent MIRV control."[15]

When the negotiations began, as we have seen, the Soviets were increasing the numbers of their missile launchers at a pace that had doubled their number in two years. The U.S., having started earlier on such deployments, was not increasing the number of its launchers at all; so in November 1969, the Soviets had 1,705 ICBM and SLBM missile launchers deployed or under construction, and the U.S. had 1,710 deployed. A primary American purpose in SALT was to stop the Soviets' expansion of their launcher capacity while the two sides were approximately equal.

Through MIRV, however, the U.S. was about to increase significantly its arsenal of nuclear *warheads* mounted on its existing ICBMs. Since it was certain that Moscow would demand a concession in return for limiting its launcher expansion, MIRV would be the obvious "chip" with which the U.S. would be able to bargain.

Thus, again, American interest seemed to demand a MIRV ban—not only to forestall the ultimate MIRVing of heavy Soviet missiles and the resultant threat to American land-based missiles, but to achieve the American purpose of stopping Soviet launcher construction at a point giving each side roughly equal numbers.

But the American military saw only the deployable weapon in hand, as no doubt any military would have. MIRVs not only boosted the effectiveness of strategic missiles; they were a cheaper alternative to building more launchers and missiles. An American missile-launching submarine of the time, for example, could launch warheads against sixteen targets at once; assuming ten MIRVs to a missile, the same boat could attack 160 targets with the same number of missiles.

Opposition to MIRV and support for a ban on the weapon, however, was to be found only in the State Department, which was distrusted in the White House, and in Gerard Smith's arms control agency, which was seen

---

*By the early eighties, as it proved, the Reagan administration was seriously concerned about the so-called window of vulnerability, during which American land-based missiles in fixed silos supposedly could be destroyed by highly accurate MIRVs launched from huge Soviet missiles with the "throw-weight" capacity to carry almost any number of independently targetable warheads. The window of vulnerability, which was (technologically) plausible though (politically and strategically) unrealistic, actually was opened in the failure to ban MIRV in SALT I, before that particular genie got out of the bottle. SALT II, which was never ratified, would have put a limit of ten MIRVs on a single missile, thus locking the barn after the horse was stolen.

by Nixon and Kissinger as infested with Democrats and holdovers from the Johnson administration, and as more interested, anyway, in disarmament than in security. As far as is known, no effective support for a MIRV ban ever was forthcoming from the Nixon White House, although on July 21, 1969, in Nixon's general guidance for the SALT delegation, he wrote that he *might* authorize an effort to ban MIRV. By November, when the talks actually opened, more specific guidance "expressly canceled" this possibility.[16]

On April 8, 1970, an NSC meeting chaired by Nixon considered detailed proposals for the second round of SALT—the first substantive talks—to open in Vienna later that month. Among the options presented for review was a MIRV ban that had been originated in the arms control agency, and developed into specifics by Raymond Garthoff, a key member of Gerard Smith's SALT delegation. Garthoff's proposed ban was to have been verified by national technical means, rather than by on-site inspections—which the Soviets had ruled out specifically in the opening round at Helsinki. Thus, Garthoff's plan *might* have been taken by the Soviets as a sincere proposal at least worth consideration.

The CIA, which was mostly responsible for satellite monitoring, supported national technical means of verification; the Defense Department and the Joint Chiefs, however, ritually demanded that on-site inspections be required. Those who supported this crucial modification at the NSC meeting included two who knew little or nothing about arms control but who had fixed notions of Soviet iniquity—Attorney General Mitchell and Vice President Agnew.

At the time, Nixon—in Gerard Smith's opinion—"must have understood the logic of banning MIRVs" rather than deploying; but the president "may have calculated that ABM limitation was all the traffic would bear, the 'traffic' in this case being the Secretary of Defense, the Joint Chiefs, their supporters in Congress and their constituencies around the country. . . . Whatever his reason, the President accepted the military's position that a MIRV ban required on-site inspection"—in effect, dooming any hope of Soviet acceptance.[17]

Though final, this was not even a technically informed decision. Interagency studies later showed, and Kissinger conceded in a news conference in Moscow on May 27, 1972, that "the capability of cheating against on-site inspection is very great, and the national means of detection are more reliable for the kind of agreement we have made here" (which did not include, of course, a MIRV ban).

The American decision to demand on-site inspections was nevertheless deliberate. The Soviets had insisted at Helsinki and the U.S. had agreed that verification of any agreements reached in SALT would be by national technical means only. Nixon himself had instructed the delegation at Helsinki to retreat behind a demand for on-site inspection if the Soviets themselves raised the MIRV issue. Little consideration had been given, moreover, to the fact that on-site inspections would have to be reciprocal; would the U.S. really tolerate exposure of its own secret arms installations to Soviet inspectors?

Nearly four years after that NSC meeting, at a news conference on December 3, 1974, Kissinger conceded that "in retrospect I wish I had thought through the implications of a MIRVed world more thoughtfully in 1969 and 1970 than I did." But that was long after the failure to achieve or even seriously to seek a MIRV ban in SALT I; and the confession was disingenuous.

The omission of a MIRV ban from SALT I was *deliberate* on Kissinger's part and, as Smith believed, on Nixon's too—although in *RN* the latter does not even mention what was one of the most important decisions of his tenure in the White House. The problem certainly was not Kissinger's failure to "think through" the importance of MIRVs; he is far too intelligent and was by then too well informed for that explanation to be credible.

He once told a congressional group, for example, that without *qualitative* controls on offensive weaponry, *quantitative* limits might not mean much. At one point in 1970 he even told Gerard Smith that he *favored* a MIRV ban "if it could be verified."

Sidney D. Drell, the physicist and now the deputy director of the Stanford Linear Research Accelerator, was a member of a small group of scientists who met regularly with Kissinger to advise him on technical issues. From his recollection of many discussions at those meetings, Drell is convinced that Kissinger fully understood the MIRV issue *at the time.* Morton Halperin, too, recalls that Kissinger understood the MIRV problem "well enough" in 1969.[18]

The problem, instead, was what Gerard Smith suggested: the internal politics of the Nixon administration and the glacial resistance—well understood by Morton Halperin, if not at first by Nixon and Kissinger—of the Joint Chiefs, backed by a more compliant secretary of defense than McNamara had been.

The chiefs had not "signed off" on a MIRV ban during the Johnson administration because SALT proponents believed it more important to negotiate a missile defense. Once the chiefs agreed to seek an ABM treaty, no one had the stomach to take them on for a MIRV ban, too. When the Nixon administration succeeded Johnson's, the chiefs remained in place, and so did the problem of persuading them to go further than they already had.

At the time, there was some justification in the chiefs' collective mind, other than their pleasure in the weapon, for not trying to ban MIRV. Some analysts—Halperin, for one—believed that in a MIRVless world, one in which the U.S. could launch relatively fewer warheads, the Soviets might be able to agree to a treaty banning missile defense *as such,* and still have a makeshift missile defense *in fact.*

They could do this, it was feared, by upgrading the extensive SAM (surface-to-air missile) aircraft defense systems deployed throughout the Soviet Union. The SAM systems might then be able to shoot down the many fewer single-warhead missiles the U.S. could launch if it had no MIRVs. During the course of SALT I, Soviet technicians largely discounted this American fear of a "SAM upgrade," but the threat was considered real in 1969 and for some time thereafter.

Kissinger's problem with a MIRV ban, however, was strictly political and bureaucratic. Knowing of the chiefs' stout opposition, he was not willing to seek their agreement for such a ban because he too considered an ABM treaty more important, believed that the chiefs would not agree to both, and feared that their stand would stir up activity in Congress and on the political right that would kill or eviscerate an arms control treaty.[19]

If, in fact, a choice necessarily had to be made, Kissinger chose correctly, in terms of arms control *and* domestic politics. Manifestly, it was better to have the chiefs support a SALT position including limitations on missile defense than to have them oppose SALT altogether, on grounds that limiting missile defense *and* banning MIRV would endanger national security.

MIRV's main purpose, moreover, was to overwhelm a potential Soviet missile defense. If both sides could be restrained from deploying such a defense, the need for MIRV theoretically would disappear and the possibility of negotiating some kind of restraint on future MIRV deployment therefore might be enhanced. MIRV also was a potential safeguard against the possible future breakdown of an ABM treaty.

If, on the other hand, a MIRV ban *was* agreed upon, but no ABM treaty was reached, missile defenses going up on either or both sides would be more effective and threatening, since MIRV, a prime means of overcoming such defenses, would not be available. The possibility of a SAM upgrade also would become more serious in the absence of MIRV.

But was the choice between ABM and MIRV really necessary? A ban on both obviously was the preferable course toward the most important goal: strategic stability between the superpowers. If missile defenses were strictly limited, after all, the basic strategic justification for deploying MIRV *did* disappear, and it became for the U.S. only one more in a long series of momentary military advantages soon to be matched—overmatched, probably—by the Soviets. That being the case, and in view of the long-term implications of Soviet as well as American MIRVs, should Kissinger and Nixon have allowed internal pressures, in effect, to make their decision not to seek a MIRV ban?

Granted the bureaucratic and political difficulties of overcoming the Joint Chiefs' opposition, and that they might have made impossible the ratification of a treaty they disliked, and even acknowledging the benefits of hindsight, it *still* seems remarkable that Nixon and Kissinger apparently did not make a serious effort *within* the administration—much less at Vienna or Helsinki—for agreement on a MIRV ban. Instead, the proposal they did put on the SALT table was purposely designed to be rejected by the Soviets; thus, to permit the American military to go ahead with a MIRV deployment that Nixon and Kissinger "must have understood" to be ultimately self-defeating.

Pentagon insistence on the deployment of MIRV never wavered. The result was not only a severe threat to American security later raised by Soviet MIRVs on heavy missiles; but by 1972, when a five-year interim "freeze" on missile launchers at then-existing levels was agreed upon— instead of the desired treaty limiting or reducing offensive strategic weapons—the Soviets had built a substantial lead in such launchers.

At that point and during the five-year freeze, MIRVs on American missiles made the Soviet advantage in launchers relatively unimportant. But MIRV could be such an "equalizer" *only* until the Soviets began MIRVing their own larger missiles—which they were doing by 1976. Again, the short-term American advantage had been deceptive, and the failure to put forward a workable MIRV ban in 1969 or 1970 proved a double strategic setback for the U.S., the effects of which still are being felt.

The two sides' inability to agree on how to deal with American "forward-based systems"—aircraft and submarines based in Europe—is often cited as the reason no solid treaty limiting offensive arms could be negotiated in SALT I. But in Gerard Smith's view "it may well be that . . . the real reason was that the United States was years ahead of the U.S.S.R. in MIRV technology." The U.S. was not willing to bargain away that seeming advantage; and the Soviets would not limit their own offensive forces while the U.S. held such a lead.[20]

Here may have been a damaging consequence of Nixon's determination to keep major foreign policy and national security decisions so closely in his and Kissinger's hands. Had they allowed a greater voice to informed officials during internal SALT planning, had they been more willing to listen to expert counsel, the short-sighted, strictly military views of the Joint Chiefs and the Defense Department might not finally have prevailed. When Nixon and Kissinger decided not even to try to persuade the chiefs to support a workable MIRV ban, the issue was effectively closed; there was no real counterweight of opinion.

It is possible that Nixon, at least, did *not* understand the implications of MIRV as well as Gerard Smith surmised; Kissinger comments snidely in his memoir that the president "simply would not learn the technical details [of arms issues] well enough to choose meaningfully," suggesting that Kissinger had to do the choosing for him; and he describes Nixon at the crucial NSC meeting on April 8, 1970, as "bored to distraction" by the discussion of options "only the broad outlines" of which interested him.[21]

It's also possible that Nixon *did* understand the MIRV problem and *did* want to ban the weapon, but found in actual bureaucratic warfare that, as Morton Halperin knew, it was "not so easy" to "overrule" the Joint Chiefs. The president may have lacked the means or the stomach—or both—to change the course of a glacier.

Those are possibilities it is only fair to raise. The conclusion seems to me warranted, nevertheless, that Nixon and Kissinger made a deliberate decision to forgo serious efforts for a MIRV ban with the chiefs, and consequently with Moscow. They accepted the risk of heavy Soviet missiles bearing MIRVs in the future and achieved a less binding agreement on offensive forces than they had originally sought, because they wanted to be sure to bring home from the summit an arms control agreement, however insufficient they might know it to be, to a receptive Congress and applauding voters.

When SALT reopened in Vienna in April 1970 the chairman of the American delegation, Gerard Smith, orally presented the text of the American proposal to ban MIRVs. A highly placed member of the Soviet delegation made notes as Smith spoke; but Raymond Garthoff, on the American side of the table, noticed that after the provision for on-site inspections was read, the note-taker "simply put down his pen."

Later, the man remarked privately: "We had been hoping you would make a serious MIRV proposal."[22]

But not only did the demand for intrusive on-site inspections assure Soviet rejection; the American proposal also specified a ban on *testing* and deployment of MIRV—but not on its production. Testing was easily verifiable but production was not; so it didn't take a Soviet rocket scientist to see that the American scheme to ban testing would prohibit the Soviets even from *developing* MIRV. But the proposal would not necessarily stop the U.S. from *producing* and stockpiling unlimited quantities of MIRVs that could be deployed in some future American "breakout" from an agreement.

It is not clear, however, that the disappointed hope of that particular Soviet negotiator reflected Soviet policy. Moscow's own MIRV proposal was virtually a mirror opposite of the American: it banned *production* and deployment but not testing. That was unacceptable to the U.S. because it would permit the Soviets to develop MIRV; because without a test ban—violations of which could be easily discovered—there would be no way to verify whether or not the Soviets were actually developing it; and because production of a MIRV the U.S. already had developed would have been prevented.

Thus, the Soviets at Vienna appeared no more serious than the Americans were about an effective ban on MIRV; but they had better reasons. Moscow was bound to fear the American ability to develop a stockpile, abrogate a MIRV agreement, and quickly deploy from its MIRV stockpile. And the U.S. proposal to ban testing of a weapon the Americans already were deploying (on Minuteman III missiles) would prevent the Soviets from developing it at all.

Finally, Soviet analysts are not fools; they understood the same fact that concerned Smith, Garthoff and other members of the American delegation who wanted to ban MIRV. The greater size and throw-weight of Soviet missiles meant that the long-term advantage of MIRV would go *to the Soviets.* Just as the American military naturally wanted to deploy what it had in hand, the Soviet military naturally wanted to be able, in future, to match and exceed, if possible, the American deployment.

So it is not at all certain or likely that had the U.S. offered an evenhanded proposal for a MIRV ban, the Soviets would have accepted or negotiated seriously. The sad fact, however, is that no real American effort ever was made to find out what the Soviets were prepared or could have been persuaded to do about MIRV. And the sadder fact is that a compromise that might have suited the interests of both sides *was* available.

If the U.S. had been willing to ban *production* and deployment of MIRV, and if the Soviets had been agreeable to a ban on *testing* and deployment, they might have been able to agree to stop testing *and* production. A production ban would have been hard to verify, which would have laid the greater *risk* on the Soviets; but the U.S. would have had to make the bigger *sacrifice,* in giving up deployment of a developed weapon.

Again, however, no effort was made by either side to explore the possibilities of such a compromise; when Smith's delegation sought permission to do so, the White House—Nixon and Kissinger—refused to authorize it.

The MIRV issue made short work of the first American package proposal put forward at the beginning of the SALT round in Vienna in April 1970—a ban on MIRV testing and deployment, verified by on-site inspections; a freeze on strategic offensive missiles at the existing American level, with *no* on-site inspections; and *one* ABM defense site around each nation's capital (known as the NCA or "national command authority" proposal).

When the Soviets rejected this package virtually out of hand, because of the demanded on-site inspections for the MIRV ban, the Americans were ready with a second package. It offered the one-site NCA plan for missile defense, no limits on MIRV and a complicated plan for *reductions* in strategic offensive forces. No on-site inspections were sought.*

This second package, too, was spotted by the Soviets for a sham. American forward-based forces in Europe that were able to strike the Soviet Union were not limited, and American heavy bombers were held only to their existing level. But the proposal required substantial cuts in the Soviets' area of greatest strength—their land-based missiles. Meanwhile, with MIRV untouched, the U.S. could *expand* its ICBM capacity by adding more independently targetable warheads on the ceiling number of missiles.

These opening American positions had not been "serious"—except in terms of American politics. In that arena, never far from Richard Nixon's mind, the two rejected packages were serious enough. They *appeared* to meet the wishes of congressional and public proponents of bans on MIRV and ballistic missile defense; and the predictable Soviet rejections made Moscow *appear* the opponent and Washington the seeker of arms reductions.

On the single question of missile defense, however, substantial progress was made, at least in Moscow's view. The so-called NCA option, appearing in both packages, would permit the Soviets to retain the Galosh defense they already were deploying around Moscow. They quickly accepted that plan, leaving only the details to be negotiated, and clung to it throughout the further rounds of SALT.

Even here, the Americans had not been entirely forthcoming. The NCA option would sharply limit the Safeguard system the administration actually was building—ostensibly to protect missile sites and the population against a Chinese or an accidental attack, but with the secret expectation of expanding it to a "thick" national defense against the Soviets—as promised to Strom Thurmond in 1968. Official guidance for the SALT delegation in November 1969 made it clear that "the President is committed to the area [continental] defense component of the Safeguard program."[23]

Some in the SALT delegation, having probed the Soviets' intentions at the opening Helsinki round, were not surprised that they accepted the NCA option. Kissinger and Nixon, however, had expected them to demand more than the one site permitted by the NCA proposal. That option had been approved by Nixon only in the expectation that it would be *rejected* by Moscow, and that the Soviets would make a counterdemand for more defense sites.

Nixon and Kissinger planned then to use this Soviet position to persuade the Senate to approve a more extensive missile defense. For that purpose,

---

*Each package also contained a ban on ABM systems but the delegation was instructed to offer the NCA option first; after the Soviets accepted it, the ban was not put on the table.

they knew, effective persuasive pressure would be needed, because the Senate had approved even the limited Safeguard system only by the tie-breaking vote cast by Vice President Agnew.

Soviet arms experts, however, apparently had been convinced by the arguments Robert McNamara had advanced at Glassboro in 1967 against national missile defense, though the Nixon administration had *rejected* that rationale. Thus, the Soviets would not cooperate with Nixon and Kissinger by insisting on an extensive missile defense, as expected.

More, consequently, was to be heard of the ABM issue in SALT; and after several fruitless months of haggling in Vienna over offensive weapons, the U.S. offered in August still another package. This one followed lines Kissinger had preferred all along: a simple freeze on strategic weapons at the level of 1,710 missile launchers, with no annual cuts and no on-site inspections (as in the first package described above), no limit on MIRVs (as in the second), but a major change on missile defense—a choice between *no* sites, or the NCA option of *one* site apiece defending Moscow and Washington.

Whatever Washington had expected, the Soviets—no doubt baffled by this sudden American switch from a proposal already accepted—again promptly chose the NCA, one-site option. But this SALT package foundered, too, on the familiar issue of American forward-based systems, on which the two sides remained far apart.

SALT seemed to be going nowhere, except possibly on missile defense—and even that offered a snag. The U.S. had insisted from the first that there should be a single comprehensive treaty on missile defense and offensive weapons; but by June 1970 the Soviets were talking of either an ABM treaty alone, or such a treaty coupled with some minor agreement to reduce the risk of accidental war.

Probably for domestic political reasons in an election year, Nixon was tempted to accept a separate ABM treaty to be signed at the summit. "On July 11 [1970]," Kissinger recalled, "Nixon specifically told me he would pay this price to get to see the Soviet leaders."

Nixon never gave the order to do so, perhaps because it was not until December that the Soviets formally offered the separate treaty. Kissinger was horrified by Nixon's willingness to pay such a price for a summit, but he wondered later "if the Soviets might have been more tractable during the recent Middle East crisis [in the fall of 1970] if we had accepted [their] proposal and reached an ABM treaty." This assumed the Soviets were at the root of the 1970 Middle East crisis, a dubious proposition (see chapter 16).[24]

Washington continued to insist on the single larger agreement, even after the Soviets in March 1971 presented a draft ABM treaty including no provisions on offensive weapons. Thus stood matters in early 1971.

By then, however, unknown to the American SALT delegation and to anyone in government outside the White House, "back channel" talks between Kissinger and Anatoly Dobrynin, the Soviet ambassador to Washington, had become a second, secret, most remarkable—but not always helpful—level of negotiations.

In January 1971, Kissinger and Dobrynin met in the national security adviser's office to discuss arms control. A treaty to limit or ban ballistic missile defenses was possible, Kissinger told the ambassador; but the American side would insist that the treaty be coupled with a freeze on launchers for ICBMs.

Would the freeze, Dobrynin immediately asked, include ballistic missiles launched from submarines underwater?

Maybe, said Kissinger, but that issue could be left for detailed negotiations between the two nations' official SALT delegations in Helsinki.

The two men again met secretly in February and Dobrynin returned to his question: Would a freeze on ICBM launchers have to include SLBMs or not?

Kissinger replied that the U.S. would be prepared to have it either way. In that case, Dobrynin said, the Soviet Union would prefer *not* to include SLBMs.

Thus, in a casual sentence or two, President Nixon's national security adviser abandoned what had been the American demand for a limit on Soviet SLBMs—a position the U.S. had pressed for almost a year. The official SALT delegation was not informed of this development and it was to be *four months* before its chairman, Gerard Smith, the director of the Arms Control and Disarmament Agency, discovered what Kissinger had given away.

Smith was the most knowledgeable official of the Nixon administration on the intricacies and subtleties of strategic arms limitation. When in May 1971 he finally read the sketchy record of the Kissinger-Dobrynin talks, Smith was particularly shocked to find "no evidence to indicate that this major change in SALT policy was ever considered in advance by anyone except Kissinger—and perhaps not even by him. It may well have been a random answer of a fatigued and overextended man who did not realize the immense significance of his words."[25]

It may well have been. February 1971 was the month of an ill-fated incursion into Laos of South Vietnamese troops backed by the U.S. Kissinger was deeply involved in other secret negotiations with Communist China, through France, Pakistan and Romania. Both Kissinger and Nixon were in suspense as to whether the Laos campaign would halt or delay these secret efforts for a new relationship with Peking. They were deeply concerned, too, with domestic opposition to the administration's handling of the war in Vietnam, which had been fueled anew by the operation in

Laos. SALT was only one of their projects, although by 1971 it was near
the top of their priorities.

Whatever the excuse, Kissinger had handed the Soviet Union a huge
advantage, permitting Moscow to proceed with what by January 1971
American intelligence agencies knew was a substantial buildup of a missile-
launching submarine fleet. The Soviet Union had then almost as many such
boats in operation or under construction as the U.S. had in operation, and
was going for more. The U.S., however, owing to previous commitments
to build attack submarines instead, would have *no* capacity any time soon
for building more ballistic-missile submarines than those already authorized.

Not for six long years, moreover, even under an accelerated program,
would the first of the new Trident missile-launching boats be commis-
sioned.

Kissinger never admitted his blunder, certainly not to the one man he
had to please, Richard Nixon. As far as is known, the president never
learned of it; and for several months, Kissinger himself apparently was
unaware of what he had done.

That was one unwanted but predictable result of the secret negotiations
that peculiarly suited Nixon's and Kissinger's determination to keep foreign policy tightly within their own hands. The State Department, the
SALT delegation and the rest of the national security bureaucracy were
shut out of what the president and his equally secretive aide were doing,
even when—as in SALT—it paralleled and sometimes confounded or ignored the work of the official negotiators.

Similarly, the State Department and Secretary William Rogers had no
idea what was happening in those back channels through Pakistan and
Romania to bring the U.S. and China together. They did not even know
there *were* such channels.

Only Nixon's authority and Kissinger's brilliance served the U.S. in
these channels; sometimes they were not enough. For Kissinger's private
strategic arms talks with Dobrynin, "There were no building blocks, no
analytical work, no strategic analysis in the agencies concerned," Gerard
Smith observed. "There were no Verification Panel* or National Security
Council discussions. There were no consultations with congressional committees or with allies."

In SALT, the back channel was "one American (presumably keeping the
President informed) ranged against the top Soviet political and technical
authorities."[26]

_____
*A high-level administration group supposed to review arms control proposals to and
from the Soviets.

In May 1971, however, Smith was permitted to review what he called the "meager" record of the secret Dobrynin-Kissinger negotiations—which he probably never would have seen had Kissinger understood what that record would reveal to an expert eye. Smith promptly pointed out to Kissinger that he had given away the store; the security adviser tried, however, to portray the record on SLBMs as merely "ambiguous."[27]

It was not ambiguous to Moscow; nor was Kissinger's willingness to exclude SLBMs from the missile freeze a secret from the official *Soviet* SALT negotiators. To the puzzlement of their American counterparts, they several times placed on the SALT record their understanding that the proposed freeze would *not* include SLBMs, without specifying how they had reached that conclusion.

With Nixon's approval, however, Kissinger would not disclose to the administration's SALT negotiators the record of what he had said to Dobrynin. Even Smith, without an official instruction to do so, could not acknowledge what he had learned of Kissinger's giveaway. So a freeze on Soviet SLBMs, though Kissinger had privately renounced it, actually remained the *official* policy of the American SALT delegation; and Nixon himself—unaware of or not understanding his adviser's exchanges with Dobrynin—urged Gerard Smith to push hard for Soviet acceptance of an SLBM freeze. This contradiction must have been puzzling in Moscow.

In keeping silent about his agreement with Dobrynin, Kissinger apparently expected that Soviet insistence on excluding SLBMs from the freeze ultimately would cause the Defense Department, the SALT delegation and other interested American agencies to agree, which would cause Nixon to do so too. As time passed and that did not happen, Kissinger sought to get out from under his own mistake—still without admitting he had made it.

In March 1972, still in secret, he reversed his position from the talks of January and February 1971, at last telling Dobrynin the truth—that the bureaucratic and political situation within the American government made it necessary, after all, that the proposed freeze include SLBMs. Moscow would have to accept what in fact would be a token limit of 950 SLBM launchers on 62 submarines—the extreme "worst-case" level of Soviet expansion capacity projected by American intelligence for the five-year period that by then had been agreed upon for the freeze on ICBM launchers.

The 950 SLBM launchers almost surely exceeded what the Soviets actually were planning to build; so under Kissinger's formula, they could meet American demands for a freeze at that level and still *continue* their SLBM buildup. In sharp contrast, the official SALT delegation, under strict instructions from Nixon, was insisting unsuccessfully on a freeze of Soviet SLBM launchers at their *then-current level*—740 in operation or under construction. That limit would have meant something.

In April 1972, Kissinger secretly journeyed to Moscow and, as usual, not even the State Department or the SALT delegation was informed of his trip, much less his mission. He was under Nixon's specific instruction to seek Soviet help in speeding up the Paris peace talks on Vietnam; he was *not* to talk about SALT unless he could get the Soviets to prod Hanoi toward a settlement of the war. No such progress was made but the aggressive Kissinger talked about SALT anyway, in the highest of back channels.

On April 22, Leonid Brezhnev, the Soviet leader, handed Kissinger a paper that outlined a "new approach" to the SLBM question. Not surprisingly, Brezhnev suggested that the Soviets indeed would accept a freeze at the level of 950 launchers. Armed with the knowledge of Kissinger's statement to Dobrynin that the U.S. would require a freeze on SLBMs as part of the final arms agreement, Brezhnev had added a shrewd further proviso. He *increased* the price of Soviet acceptance of even Kissinger's token freeze.

The U.S. would be limited not to its existing 41 submarines with 656 SLBM launchers, but to 50 boats with up to 800 launchers—*including* those of the U.S.'s allies, France and Britain. The resulting imbalance—950 Soviet but only 800 allied SLBM launchers permitted—would be equalized, Brezhnev's paper explained, by American "forward bases" for submarines in Europe.

The Soviet leader actually was advancing two of Moscow's long-standing aims, a pair of troublesome precedents: not only would the deal take account of British and French forces in American-Soviet negotiations, but the Soviets would be compensated for them and for American forward bases in Europe. The U.S. steadfastly had rejected these propositions in all other exchanges.

Nevertheless, on April 26, 1972, after his return to Washington, Kissinger presented the entire "Brezhnev plan" to Nixon as a major Soviet concession (without disclosing his own role in its origins). This proposal, Nixon claimed in *RN,* was "considerably more favorable than we had expected." It was, moreover, a "freeze" that the official SALT delegation had been unable to negotiate, since it had been instructed to seek a tough limit of only 740 Soviet SLBM launchers.

The 950 Soviet launchers to be permitted by Kissinger's deal with Brezhnev were described by Kissinger as at least 200 fewer than the Soviets *could* build if there were no freeze; nor, he could say, would the agreement hold back any American program to build more SLBM launchers. In fact, none was planned or physically possible during the five-year freeze period.

The airy figure of 200, representing the supposed Soviet concession, shortly was backed by an NSC staff study (directed, of course, by Kissinger) showing that, if unrestrained by agreement, the Soviets *could* build up to as many as 1,170 launchers on 80 submarines, during the five years at issue.

Later, the official NSC estimate of the Soviet potential was adjusted to 1,050—exactly 100 more than the freeze limit Kissinger had agreed to. That not only far exceeded the intelligence agencies' previous "worst-case" projection; even if accurate, 1,050 was a measure of what the Soviets *might* be able to do at the far outer limits of their capacity—not what they actually were going to do, or even planning to do.

If it bothered Nixon that Kissinger, the Harvard professor turned diplomat, had ignored his instructions in order to talk arms control with Brezhnev, the president did not show it at the time; years later in *RN* he confined himself to two characteristic remarks: "I felt we might have missed the last opportunity to see how far the Soviets were willing to go [in pressuring Hanoi] to get the summit" and "I also feared that they would interpret Kissinger's willingness to negotiate [on strategic arms] without first getting a firm Soviet commitment to restrain the North Vietnamese as a sign of weakness rather than a sign of pragmatism."

Actually, Nixon was pleased at the deal Kissinger brought home from Moscow because it included Soviet agreement to a summit meeting in 1972, one at which—his national security adviser told him—"you will be able to sign the most important arms control agreement ever concluded." That was the kind of superlative, proudly recalled in *RN,* that Richard Nixon liked. In the spring of 1972, moreover, in the wake of Nixon's triumphant journey to Peking, Kissinger's promise seemed as near a guarantee of reelection as any president could wish.

Kissinger proceeded to operate as effectively in Washington as he had in Moscow. The after-the-fact NSC study persuaded the Joint Chiefs of Staff that a limit of 950 Soviet launchers was a reasonable deal for the U.S. Kissinger let the secretary of defense, Melvin Laird, know that an accelerated Trident program depended on his support for the Brezhnev deal—support Laird then volunteered. That left only Gerard Smith and William Rogers in a position to object authoritatively—and Rogers was a secretary of state who had been systematically shut out of the back channel, as well as most major foreign policy developments. He had little clout with Nixon and none with Kissinger.

On April 28 and 29, at two meetings of the Verification Panel, with Kissinger in the chair, Smith stated his willingness to accept the general principle of the Soviet proposal but *not* the American inequality in SLBMs specified in the numbers Brezhnev had put forward—numbers, Smith did not then know, that had first been suggested by Kissinger.

Smith also argued the previously standard American positions against inclusion of British and French nuclear forces and "compensation" to the Soviets for American forward bases. But all the SALT negotiator got for his pains was Kissinger's displeasure; others at the meetings were persuaded that the Brezhnev-Kissinger freeze on SLBMs was better than no freeze at all, particularly since it paved the way for Nixon's trip to the summit.

Apparently defeated, Smith alertly volunteered to draft the formal reply to Brezhnev, for President Nixon's signature. Playing a bureaucratic game of his own, he hoped that he might be able through subtle wording to keep open some of the issues about which he was concerned. So the draft he prepared accepted the general approach proposed by Brezhnev but mentioned no specific numbers; and it began by stating: "While we cannot agree with certain considerations expressed in the paper given to Henry Kissinger in Moscow. . . ."

On Monday, May 1, 1972, Nixon met with the NSC to discuss the ballistic-missile freeze as proposed, supposedly, by Brezhnev. Admiral Thomas Moorer for the Joint Chiefs and Laird for the Defense Department spoke in favor of the Brezhnev plan for SLBMs. Rogers, primed by Gerard Smith, made a powerful argument *against* it; then Smith again stated his informed reservations about the 950-limit and the American inequality in SLBMs that would result—this time adding pertinently that these might be singled out by Congress and the press as points of opposition to the overall agreement.

Neither Rogers nor Smith, forceful though they were, had any apparent effect on the president or the others at the NSC meeting, and Smith was about to suffer a more grievous rebuff. Just before the meeting opened, he had been shown the text—derived from his draft—of the Nixon reply that was to be sent to Brezhnev. So after stating his objections to the freeze proposal, he further protested that an "important reservation" (the opening statement that "we cannot agree with certain considerations . . .") had been deleted from his draft. The president of the United States cut him off with a single word: *"Bullshit!"*

Smith, a rather old-fashioned gentleman in his personal manner, later recorded himself mildly as "puzzled by the violence" of this reaction—which to others may appear the more extraordinary for having been expressed in such exalted surroundings. Smith was mystified, too, by the president's further remark that he would be glad to hear from Smith "on matters of substance" but not on irrelevant changes in language; an expression of disagreement, beginning a formal reply from one state leader to another, surely *was* a matter of substance. But the discussion was effectively finished, and Nixon abruptly ended the meeting.

Smith later was told by Al Haig, Kissinger's assistant, that Dobrynin had advised against inclusion of the phrase in the reply to Brezhnev. But the real reason it was excised probably was suggested by Kissinger's angry comment to Smith, as the meeting broke up: the position Smith and Rogers had taken, the security adviser insisted, was "unbelievable." *He* had made the necessary deal for the long-sought SALT agreement and Nixon's trip to the summit, and *they* were trying to block it.[28]

In his later account of all this, Gerard Smith did not elaborate except to suggest that Nixon's acceptance of the Brezhnev proposal apparently had been conveyed to the Soviet leader in some way *before* the *pro forma* NSC meeting, and that therefore Nixon himself probably had cut out the qualifying expression of limited disagreement. But in the light of later knowledge, the meaning of Kissinger's angry words seems clear:

Without inclusion of the SLBM agreement with Brezhnev, there would be no overall strategic arms agreement; without that agreement there would be no summit in Moscow; without a summit, Richard Nixon could not be the architect he wanted to be, of "détente" for the present and a "structure of peace" for the future. More immediately, he could not present himself to the American electorate as a "man of peace," despite the war in Vietnam. Therefore, even considering his opening to China, he might not be reelected later in 1972.

Kissinger, for his part, would not be able to pursue the geopolitical advantages of "linkage" between areas of Soviet concern, such as arms control, and American goals, such as an "honorable" end to the war in Vietnam.

Against those objectives, any numerical disadvantage to the U.S. in missile-launching submarines, or in an overall arms control agreement, was not considered important. To the president's national security adviser, moreover, it was "unbelievable" that the secretary of state and the arms negotiator could not see things quite that way.

Although from the first, Nixon had told Dobrynin that serious exchanges should be sought through Kissinger rather than the State Department, Moscow apparently remained unsure whether to follow this unusual advice. Its stiffly correct diplomats were embarrassed by having to bypass the department and the official SALT delegation.

Perhaps for that reason, Chairman Semenov and other Soviet arms negotiators hinted in early May 1971 to their American counterparts that perhaps a separate ABM treaty could be reached, together with an "understanding" for a freeze on ICBMs, even including a sublimit on heavy missiles—a very different thing from a treaty on offensive strategic weapons. To the Americans, this seemed a significant shift in the Soviet position; but they were getting the word at second hand.[29]

When the delegation reported the apparent shift formally to Washington, moreover, Kissinger was enraged. The new Soviet position had been a subject of talks in the Kissinger-Dobrynin back channel, too; and its appearance in the formal talks seemed to Kissinger evidence of a Soviet lack of good faith and confidence in the secret discussions. He promptly communicated both this view and his anger to the president.[30]

Kissinger claimed in his memoir that Smith and the SALT delegation were being handed "shopworn goods." He and Dobrynin had advanced *beyond* the agreement Semenov was subtly suggesting: that, first, an ABM treaty be concluded separately, and second, a freeze on offensive missiles *then* be negotiated. In Kissinger's view, "once an ABM treaty was known to exist, we would be under irresistible pressure to sign; the minute we had signed, the offensive freeze would evaporate."

If an ABM treaty was reached first, Kissinger feared, Congress might even immediately cut off funds for deploying an ABM system, in which case the Soviets would gain the "ideal outcome"—unilateral American abandonment of its missile defense, with no formal obligation on the Soviets to follow suit or limit offensive weaponry. Therefore, Kissinger argued with Dobrynin for an arrangement "that the offensive limitations could be discussed *before* an ABM agreement was completed." (Kissinger's emphasis.)

Kissinger's later disclosures concerning this contretemps are sometimes astonishing and often disturbing, about himself and about President Nixon. He writes, for example, that even before word of Semenov's suggestions in Vienna reached Washington in early May 1971,

> Nixon was seized by the fear that Gerard Smith, rather than he, would get credit for the seemingly imminent breakthrough of linking offensive and defensive limitations. He had taken enough of a beating on Vietnam and Cambodia *not to succumb* to the human emotion of wanting the credit for the initiatives identified with peace. [Emphasis added.]

If Kissinger meant, as the first sentence seems to indicate, that Nixon *did* succumb to that "human emotion," it must be wondered, first, how a mere ambassador who could not act without a president's express approval could take credit for something achieved at that president's direction and, second, how even to a president under political attack some possible diminution in "the credit" he received could be more important than an agreement of such immense significance, to the achievement of which he supposedly was dedicated.

Nixon's demonstrated anxieties and insecurities may be the answer. But it seems rather more likely that it was Henry Kissinger, at least as much as the president, who was "seized by the fear" that someone else was going to get the credit. In his case, that fear might have been more realistic, and its realization could have had greater personal repercussions. Kissinger, though important, was not yet in 1971 the dominant figure he later became;

and he always was dependent upon, but not always secure in, Richard Nixon's belief in his national security adviser's indispensability.

Kissinger "reassured" Nixon that a breakthrough to a SALT agreement could be achieved by the SALT delegation, rather than in Washington, only if "Moscow made a deliberate choice" to bypass what Kissinger immodestly called "the Presidential Channel"—that is, the secret Kissinger-Dobrynin talks. When Gerard Smith reported Semenov's suggestions to Washington, Kissinger angrily concluded that Moscow had made just that choice—why, he seems unable to say. Kissinger quickly seized on the report from the SALT delegation both to reverse Moscow's choice, if it had indeed been made, and to "bring matters to a head."

In what he records as "a rather blunt conversation" with Dobrynin on May 11, Kissinger suggested that the Soviets were "play[ing] off our two channels against each other" but that nevertheless "the President's tenacity and my control of the bureaucratic machinery would get matters to where we wanted them"—that is, that ultimately the White House, not the SALT delegation, would have the final word, an assertion that seems too obvious to have needed such emphasis.

If Moscow continued what Kissinger saw as its double-dealing, moreover, a "loss of confidence in the seriousness of a private, direct channel" would ensue in the White House, and Nixon's "anger at what [the president] could only construe as a deliberate maneuver to deprive him of credit would be massive."

At this point, though the agreement Kissinger wanted had not been concluded, by Kissinger's own admission he and Dobrynin were "approaching agreement"; they already had settled on the "simultaneity" that was Kissinger's primary demand. The "blunt conversation" with Dobrynin was necessary, therefore, not because the Soviets were *refusing* an agreement but to assure that they concluded it *with Henry Kissinger,* in the channel he and Richard Nixon preferred, rather than in the official negotiations.

All this sharply raises the question, as perhaps nothing else in the Nixon years does, whether there ever should have been a back channel of such importance. How could Nixon and Kissinger have expected there would be no confusion and conflict? Why should the Soviets not have tried, if they did, to play off one channel against another in an administration unwilling to let one hand know what the other was doing?

Even if the Kissinger channel was necessary, why did it have to be kept secret from the Department of State, the official SALT delegation and the rest of the government? Why could it not have been used as a supplement or a last resort? Kissinger himself conceded that, for Chairman Smith, "it was bound to be painful . . . to be excluded from the culmination of years of work." It might be added that if Smith *had* to be excluded from it, he hardly should have been the supposed "chief negotiator."

Kissinger argues that his channel was speedier, more authoritative and direct, and less subject to leaks and external pressures. If so, it also was vulnerable, as we have seen, to a lack of expertise and consultation— resulting, for example, in Kissinger's blunder on SLBMs and the resulting advantage to the Soviets.

Another, in a sense more serious, mistake by Kissinger might have been corrected had he not isolated his negotiations with Dobrynin. On March 10, 1970, the Soviet ambassador asked whether their talks should concentrate on a "comprehensive" or a "limited" arms agreement. Kissinger made no specific answer then, but on April 9 he told Dobrynin that the U.S. would present "several comprehensive proposals" (described above) when SALT reconvened in Vienna. "If, however, the Soviets decided they were interested in a more limited agreement in the interim, we were prepared to explore it as well."[31]

Raymond Garthoff has pointed out that this was a "stunning invitation" for the Soviets to reject the comprehensive American proposals, knowing that "limited" approaches perhaps more to Moscow's liking were not ruled out. That is exactly what happened, and one reason Kissinger's ultimate "breakthrough" resulted in a limited agreement rather than the comprehensive treaty he and Nixon first sought. The American SALT delegation never did learn officially of this Kissinger concession, though some members did from their Soviet counterparts; so the delegation labored in good faith but in vain from April 1970 to May 1971 for the comprehensive agreement the Soviets no longer had an incentive to pursue, and doubted the Americans really wanted.

Throughout SALT, moreover, Kissinger by agreement with Dobrynin, and as a token of "good faith," informed the Soviets in advance of the American position before it was formally put on the table. Thus, the Soviets almost always knew what Kissinger and Dobrynin were telling each other, and what the U.S. would propose, while the American SALT team was kept in ignorance of the back-channel negotiations. Had an American journalist discovered and published what the U.S. was about to propose in SALT, Nixon and Kissinger might well have called for his or her prosecution.[32]

Even the "breakthrough" that Moscow hastened to accept the day after Kissinger's "blunt conversation" with Dobrynin, though probably accelerated by that exchange, was announced in what Kissinger himself called "somewhat convoluted" words of greater vagueness than official negotiators were supposed to allow. Nixon read it to the press on May 20, when it also was announced in Moscow:

> The Governments of the United States and the Soviet Union, after reviewing the course of their talks on the limitation of strategic armaments, have agreed to concentrate this year on working out

an agreement for the limitation of the deployment of anti–ballistic missile systems (ABMs). They have also agreed that, together with concluding an agreement on ABMs, they will agree on certain measures with respect to the limitation of offensive strategic weapons.

The offensive limitations were not defined, and remained to be determined by hard bargaining in SALT. So did the details of the ABM treaty. There would be no comprehensive agreement, as Washington had demanded at first but Kissinger had virtually renounced. Nor would a "decoupled" ABM treaty be concluded without any offensive restraints, as the Soviets had wished; both sides had compromised their proposals—which is what usually happens in successful negotiations.

Kissinger had achieved the breakthrough for Nixon to announce, and thus had opened the way to the summit. Understandably, the national security adviser maintained in his memoir that this could not have been done, or would have been too long delayed, by the formal SALT delegation. No doubt that's correct; for as Kissinger made the necessary compromises in the back channel in 1971 and 1972, Smith and his team labored in Helsinki and Vienna under strict instructions *from Nixon and Kissinger* to stand fast on the comprehensive American proposals of August 4, 1970—proposals the White House knew the Soviets refused to accept.

There was one exception, and it casts doubt on Kissinger's claim that his secret negotiations were necessary. The ABM Treaty, incomparably the most important consequence of SALT I, was arranged by the SALT delegation in April 1972—first in informal conversations, later called the "tundra talks," when the delegations jointly visited Lapland on April 16, the next day in more official talks between the chairmen, Semenov and Smith.

When Leonid Brezhnev handed his proposal on SLBMs to Kissinger in Moscow on April 22, the paper included also the outlines of the ABM agreement the SALT delegation—*not* Kissinger—had worked out: two defensive missile sites for each side, one around the capital of each, the other to guard an ICBM launcher; a maximum of 100 ABM launchers and interceptors at each site, to be deployed in circles within a radius of 150 kilometers.[33]

That was the heart of the final treaty—and it was not developed or even influenced in the back channel. It probably could have been reached years earlier—literally—had it not been for the constant shifting of positions by Kissinger and Nixon in Washington. When Smith, for instance, was allowed—at his insistence—to inquire privately about a total *ban* on ABM systems, the Soviets showed interest, whereupon Washington instructed Smith to drop the idea.[34]

Strangely, Richard Nixon was not elated by Kissinger's "breakthrough." The president's immediate reaction, Kissinger wrote, was "considerable anguish" that he would now have to let Secretary of State Rogers know that negotiations had been going on behind his back. The president's anguish was so great that he finally sent faithful Bob Haldeman to do the dirty work. But the anguish was momentary because the "Presidential Channel" had achieved more than an agreement leading to the summit and an arms control treaty. It had led to—quite possibly it had assured— Nixon's reelection.

Kissinger observed, moreover, that "the May 20 agreement was a milestone in confirming White House dominance of foreign affairs. For the first two years White House control had been confined to the formulation of policy; now it extended to its execution. . . . Nixon judged that, given his conviction and personality *and subordinates,* he could achieve results no other way." (Emphasis added.)

Nixon's principal foreign policy subordinate, of course, was Henry Kissinger.

That does not quite complete the story of SALT I and the "Presidential Channel." Something more had been required than Kissinger's tough talk to Dobrynin, more even than the hard and thankless work of the delegation in Helsinki.

On June 9, 1971, only three weeks after President Nixon had announced the "breakthrough" with the Soviet Union, two tough union leaders met in the White House with Kissinger, at his invitation. The security adviser put his visitors through a lengthy lecture on international affairs—until Thomas W. ("Teddy") Gleason, the president of the International Longshoremen's Association, interrupted: "I don't see why the hell we're beating around the bush," Gleason said. "There's a big grain deal involved. We're against it."[35]

Kissinger at first pretended to know nothing of a grain deal, then conceded the point, and tried obliquely to persuade Gleason and Jay Lovestone, the director of international affairs for the AFL-CIO, to cooperate. Again Gleason interrupted: "Dr. Kissinger, I want to tell you something. We won't let you sell the American people down the Volga or down the Yangtze."

Or, he might have said, sell the American maritime unions down the Mississippi. Both Gleason and Lovestone were fierce anti-Communists; but beyond that, in 1963, President John Kennedy had ordered that 50 percent of all grain sold to the Soviet Union had to be transported in American vessels—a boon to the maritime unions that they fiercely guarded, for reasons of economics as well as ideology.

The order still stood in 1971; and even if Nixon rescinded it, the unions could refuse to load foreign, particularly Soviet, ships with American grain. There was no doubt that they *would* refuse; Gleason himself had told a Maritime Administration hearing in 1964: "Let the Russians go to hell. Let 'em starve."

Kissinger was undaunted by his failure to move Gleason and Lovestone. The next day, the White House removed export controls on a number of items, including agricultural products. Largely unnoticed in the publicity—given instead to what was billed as the end of a twenty-one-year embargo against the People's Republic of China (see chapter 15)—was the president's decision to rescind Kennedy's order of 1963.

The maritime unions, though critical, were moderate in their public response. But Kissinger passed word that found its way into the press that the unions' moderation was a result of his meeting with Gleason and Lovestone. This slippery tactic infuriated the union leaders and George Meany of the AFL-CIO; thereafter Kissinger could make no headway at all in trying to get the unions to accommodate grain sales to the Soviets.

These began in the summer of 1971 and were by no means marginal. Riots in Poland had been caused by severe meat shortages; and Moscow's planners feared more of the same, in the Soviet Union as well as throughout Eastern Europe. By 1971, they had increased the use of feed grains for livestock by 40 percent—but more would have to be imported. That summer, they turned to the U.S. and placed orders for $200 million in grain, about 15 percent of total American grain exports in 1970.

On October 12, 1971, Nixon announced that he would go to Moscow for a summit meeting with Leonid Brezhnev in May 1972—just six months before he would be seeking reelection. But that month Nixon also laid a problem in the lap of a hard-edged aide, Charles Colson, whom the president knew to be a man "who could be called in to take on the rough chores others wouldn't do."

"Henry has been cold-shouldered by Gleason," Nixon told Colson, in obvious concern. Would Colson see what he could do?

Of course Colson would, and he had just the right connection. He got in touch with a "really great" acquaintance, Jesse Calhoon, the president of the Marine Engineers' Beneficial Association. Colson explained that Nixon wanted American union men to load Soviet ships with American grain, and insisted: "We've got to make a deal."

Calhoon had not risen to be president of his union for nothing. If a deal was imperative, he reasoned, Nixon would be willing to pay for it.

"What's in it for us?" Calhoon said.

His instinct was unerring. In further talks with Colson, Calhoon learned that the "breakthrough" of May 20, in which Nixon announced that there would be an arms control agreement with Moscow, had been at least partially the result of an old-fashioned political deal: Nixon and Kissinger had pledged to the Soviets that *in return for the arms agreement, the U.S. would sell wheat to the Soviet Union.*

Now the bill had come due—the Soviets had kept their end of the bargain and the summit in Moscow would virtually assure Nixon's reelection; but those huge grain purchases had to be delivered to the Soviet Union. If they were not, the SALT agreement could fall apart, the summit would be a failure, Nixon's reelection might well be threatened. Calhoon particularly remembered being told that Ambassador Dobrynin had put it bluntly: "There would be no SALT agreement unless the grain deal was worked out."

So Colson had known what he was talking about—Nixon *had* to make a second deal, this one with the maritime unions. Through Colson, the unions proceeded to exact their price.

First, Colson agreed—on Nixon's behalf—to free budget funds that would speed construction of more merchant ships to expand the American fleet and to provide more union jobs. Second, and more important, Colson pledged the president *not to veto* pending legislation that would require half of all American *oil* imports to be carried in American ships.

That, too, would greatly benefit the American maritime unions. But if Nixon allowed the legislation to go through, he would be double-crossing the oil industry, whose costs would be sharply increased; and that industry had raised vast sums for Nixon's campaigns. Even so, the president had little choice but to pay the union price; in the end, however, he was spared having to keep that hard promise by only eight votes in the Senate—the margin by which the oil-import legislation failed to pass.

The union leaders believed Nixon would have vetoed, if he had had to, so they loaded the Soviet ships anyway. They also kept, as did the White House, the secret of their agreement with Colson—largely, Calhoon said, because the unions did not want "to be seen as a friend of the Russians." Their silence enabled the White House to conceal the arms-control-for-grain arrangement with Moscow; and also to announce to the press, in the voice of an assistant secretary of commerce who had helped Colson negotiate, that the unions had not "asked for anything in return for permitting the grain to be loaded on foreign vessels."

In May of 1972, the Moscow summit proceeded with scarcely a hitch, with the signing of the ABM Treaty and the interim offensive arms agreement. In July and August, the Soviets contracted to buy 400 million more bushels of American grain for $700 million; their purchases rose to more than $1 billion by the end of the year, with American credits facilitating the sales.

In September 1972, Teddy Gleason announced his support of Richard Nixon's reelection. Later that fall, however, it became apparent that the Soviets had bought at low prices, depleted American grain stocks and driven up prices to American consumers—leading some to refer to "the great grain robbery" and Kissinger to remark that "the Soviets beat us at our own game."[36]

The ABM Treaty concluded at the Moscow summit made a lasting contribution to superpower arms control and must be ranked as a major achievement for Richard Nixon—though, as we have seen, the necessary groundwork was laid by Robert McNamara and Lyndon Johnson. The Nixon-Kissinger secret operations, moreover, complicated the negotiations unnecessarily.

The ABM Treaty made the idea of strategic defense passé until Ronald Reagan revived it in 1983 in his SDI—and even then the treaty's wording proved a major barrier to the kind of crash effort Reagan unwisely wanted to make, so that he was prevented from locking SDI into long-term American budgets and plans.

Remarkable as the achievement of the ABM Treaty was, it did not include what Gerard Smith, for one, thought possible: a complete ban on ABM systems (which would have prevented the controversy over SDI in the Reagan years). Smith's colleague on the SALT delegation, Raymond Garthoff, also thought an ABM ban could have been achieved. But Nixon and Kissinger insisted on at least one ABM site for each side and apparently expected, before congressional politics made it hopeless, to build a nationwide ballistic missile defense.

The Moscow summit was far less successful in dealing with offensive arms, particularly because the "Interim Agreement" on such weapons signally failed to put any limits whatever on MIRVs—the single most damaging error of the ballistic missile era. Nor did it limit qualitative missile improvements, particularly increased accuracy, or ban antisatellite weapons (ASATs), or affect the development of aircraft and cruise missiles; no one will ever know whether these steps could have been negotiated, since neither side really tried.

The interim agreement was intended to lead on to further offensive-arms restrictions; but both technological and political factors prevented SALT II from achieving as much, later in the decade, as had been hoped; and for a variety of reasons—notably the Soviet invasion of Afghanistan in 1979—the U.S. Senate never ratified the treaty.

SALT I remains a milestone in establishing the concepts of parity and sufficiency—though they have not always been pursued. The Soviets, in particular, did find national satisfaction in SALT I's tacit recognition of their equal standing with the U.S. as a superpower.

More important, the agreements committed both nations to "mutual assured destruction"—the so-called balance of terror—rather than to a deceptive and dangerous reliance on missile defense. As Nixon, after having to give up missile defense, put it in *RN:*

> Each side was leaving its population and territory hostage to a strategic missile attack. Each side therefore had an ultimate interest in preventing a war that could only be mutually destructive.

That remains the case today, despite Reagan's efforts to return to missile defense.

The Moscow agreements of 1972 also were an excellent example of the practical possibilities of Nixon's prescription for American-Soviet relations: moving from an "era of confrontation" to an "era of negotiation." Unfortunately, SALT and the détente it suggested were drastically oversold to Congress and the public in an effort to make Nixon appear as the great peacemaker of the age.

As only one example, in a briefing for members of Congress, Kissinger fancifully described SALT I as "linked organically to a chain of agreements and to a broad understanding about international conduct appropriate to the dangers of the nuclear age." A document called the "Basic Principles of Relations" between the superpowers had been signed at Moscow, but it never represented a serious or binding procedural understanding between the U.S. and the Soviet Union; and the idea that SALT I was part of a "chain of agreements" governing "international conduct" was far-fetched.

Such statements, however, tended to persuade some Americans that the Cold War was over; or, at the least, that the Soviets had agreed to conduct their international affairs in ways congenial to the U.S. When, later in the seventies, these expectations inevitably were disappointed, SALT I was unfairly denigrated; and by the time SALT II was going forward, disillusionment with the effects of SALT I was a distinct factor in the opposition.

To a substantial extent, moreover, the SALT I agreements and the Moscow summit were shaped and rushed into existence to promote Richard Nixon's reelection prospects. Not that exploiting major political achievements for electoral purposes is inherently wrong or at all unusual, or that Nixon's larger ambitions were not worthy; nor is it certain how much more might have been achieved by taking more time, or had Nixon and Kissinger been more interested in arms control per se than in the diplomatic consequences of agreement with the Soviet Union and the political effect in the U.S.

Still, in light of the quarter century of costly, dangerous and fruitless arms racing since the Moscow summit, the SALT I agreements seem to represent missed opportunity as well as a signal achievement.

12

★

Reformer

★

If one considers liberalism as the development and extension of the policies and purposes of Roosevelt's New Deal, the last
liberal President was Richard Nixon.

—Robert A. Solo of Okemos, Michigan, in
a letter to the editor, *New York Times,*
September 6, 1988

The Jefferson Room in the State Department had seen few more extraordinary gatherings: fifteen ordinary Mississippians—nine whites, six blacks,
liberals, conservatives, segregationists, integrationists—having lunch with
some of the highest officials of the federal government, including Attorney
General John Mitchell and Secretary of Labor George Shultz.

It was June 24, 1970. Southern schools were still largely segregated. But
unlike Dwight Eisenhower, his most recent Republican predecessor, President Nixon had said explicitly that *Brown v. Board of Education,* the
Supreme Court's famous school desegregation decision of 1954, was "right
in both constitutional and human terms." In the same statement, on March
24, 1970, he had made it clear that he aimed to enforce the law; court-
ordered desegregation would proceed in the fall of 1970.

In accordance with one essential element of his strategy, nevertheless,
Nixon continued to treat Southern white leaders, whatever their views,
with respect. Another element was to give them public responsibility—and
whatever federal help was needed—for maintaining the peace, while seeing
to it that court orders were carried out. A third was to emphasize the
importance of "quality education" for their states' children, white and
black alike. That could not be achieved or maintained, Nixon argued,
unless the desegregation controversy was settled.

To pursue those purposes, the President's Cabinet Committee on Education had decided to set up advisory committees of local citizens in the affected Southern states. They first tackled Mississippi, historically the most recalcitrant; the June 24 luncheon was an effort to persuade fifteen of the state's reluctant citizens to serve.[1]

At one table, George Shultz was working hard on Warren Hood, the white president of the Mississippi Manufacturers' Association, and Dr. Gilbert Mason, a black physician who was president of the Biloxi NAACP chapter. Shultz was trying to persuade them to accept appointment as chairman and vice chairman of the advisory committee. The labor secretary—later to be secretary of the treasury, then Ronald Reagan's secretary of state—had become de facto leader of the cabinet committee, since Vice President Spiro Agnew, its nominal chairman, wanted no connection with the problem of school desegregation in the South.

Robert C. Mardian, the committee's staff director and the fourth man at the table, was well regarded in the white South as a former lieutenant to Barry Goldwater in the 1964 presidential campaign. Mardian had tried to include Mississippi's two senators and five representatives in the luncheon, but all had shied away, one of them reproaching Mardian: "You've been around long enough to know I'm against desegregation, and most of all against eating with niggers."

That rather well reflected the way things were with whites and blacks in 1970, and not just in Mississippi or the rest of the South.

Neither Hood nor Mason, and none of the other Mississippians, was happy to be at the luncheon, or to have been singled out by "Washington" for what might well be an unrewarding assignment. Whites like Hood could suffer economically, perhaps physically, for associating themselves with desegregation; blacks like Mason might appear as Uncle Toms to their followers, particularly—as the blacks at the luncheon feared—if the state advisory committee turned out to be just another white man's trick to keep the black man in his place.

On the other hand, while the Nixon administration appeared to be going out of its way to accomplish desegregation, white Southerners could see that Nixon was trying to do it with as little dislocation and repercussion as possible—and to do it everywhere, not just in the South. In his first year in office, the president himself—via legal appeals and Supreme Court nominations—had established himself as a friend of the South, and had pledged to treat all sections equally.

Just that morning, Nixon had come out of his usual presidential shell long enough to meet and shake hands with the Mississippians—in itself a demonstration of the commitment to the advisory committee that he then affirmed in a brief statement. He also scored with his politician's memory, saying to one of the more militant blacks, Alvin Fielder: "You're the druggist from Meridian." They had met when Nixon visited Mississippi after the state had been hit by Hurricane Camille in 1969 (the president's recollection probably was bolstered, of course, by efficient White House staff work).

In *RN* Nixon claimed that one of the Mississippi blacks with whom he shook hands was moved to observe: "Day before yesterday, I was in jail for going to the wrong beach. Today, Mr. President, I am meeting you. If that's possible, anything can happen."

That sounds a little pat, like many of the pointed remarks Nixon recalls from strangers; but it was pretty nearly the argument George Shultz made at the luncheon table: If the blacks and whites chosen for the committee could work together, they could make "anything happen," even in Mississippi. To Hood and Mason alike, Shultz argued that if two such respected leaders joined to head the advisory committee, its credibility with both whites and blacks would be enhanced; and that would make more likely the achievement of the committee's purpose—the least possible disruption, as Mississippi moved to a unitary and constitutional school system, and sought "quality education" for all its children. Wasn't it their *duty* to their state and nation to serve?

Mardian thought Shultz was making headway. Suddenly, however, the secretary—whose reputation had been made as a mediator in labor disputes—excused himself from the table and called on the baffled Mardian to follow.

"I learned long ago," Shultz explained when they were alone, "that when parties get that close to a decision, there's only one way they can complete it—by themselves."

So it proved. Left alone, Mason and Hood agreed that they were perhaps the only men in Mississippi who could make the advisory committee work; if they didn't surely no one else could, or perhaps would even try. Before they arose from lunch, the two men shook hands—thus making the Mississippi state advisory committee possible, and perhaps those in the rest of the Southern states as well. Had Mississippi refused, it would have been the more difficult for the administration to win acquiescence elsewhere.

Soon, however, the Mississippi group was followed by similar biracial committees in South Carolina, North Carolina, Georgia, Arkansas, Louisiana and even Alabama—still "Wallace Country" in 1970. And that September, with the vital aid of the state committees under the reluctant but firm leadership of Richard Nixon, after sixteen years of effort and resistance, the root promise of *Brown v. Board* was realized. The Southern states at last put an end to dual school systems.

There's no doubt about it—the Nixon administration accomplished more in 1970 to desegregate Southern school systems than had been done in the sixteen previous years, or probably since. On February 4, 1971, Elliot Richardson—who had replaced Bob Finch as HEW secretary—sent Nixon the figures:

Public elementary and secondary school pupils in the South:
8.6 million white
3.2 million black
11.8 million total

Pct. blacks in schools 50 pct. or more white:
Fall 1968: 18.4
Fall 1970: 38.1

Pct. blacks in all-black schools:
Fall 1968: 68
Fall 1970: 18.4

Pct. blacks in schools 80 pct. or more black
Fall 1968: 78.8
Fall 1970: 41.7[2]

There's no doubt either that it was Richard Nixon personally who conceived, orchestrated and led the administration's desegregation effort. Halting and uncertain before he finally asserted strong control, that effort resulted in probably the outstanding domestic achievement of his administration.

Any number of officials who were engaged in the 1970 desegregation drive testify to the president's personal leadership. Unlike Agnew, Nixon even publicly associated himself in the South with desegregation, addressing a well-publicized meeting in New Orleans of representatives from all the state advisory committees, while photographers recorded the scene.

"It will be politically harmful," he grumbled beforehand, "but it will help the schools so we'll do it."[3]

John Ehrlichman, generally one of the more skeptical of Nixon's former associates, recalled with considerable admiration how in 1970 the president met frequently with Shultz, Mitchell, Finch and others, insisting that they pursue his plans, seeing to it that they did, giving the effort personal leadership as in perhaps no other instance of his presidency (outside of foreign policy).[4]

From the white Southerner's perspective, Harry Dent—a South Carolinian who had moved from Strom Thurmond's staff to Nixon's White House—wrote that the desegregation effort "was successful largely because of the personal attention and direction given it by the president himself."

From the other side of the political spectrum, George Shultz told Dent: "Had they been recording all [Nixon's] words then, they would have a proud record of some of the President's finest moments of leadership."[5]

Paradoxically, Richard Nixon was not a crusader for integration or racial balance; he had never been a civil rights activist; he had repeatedly criticized busing orders and curried favor with Southern white voters and officials in his ambiguous 1968 campaign. In the White House, he even became the first president to send federal attorneys into court to argue for *postponement* of school desegregation already ordered.

In innumerable discussions of the desegregation problem with his aides in 1969 and 1970, Nixon seldom included Robert Brown, one of the few blacks on the White House staff, and supposedly his liaison with the black community. Nor is it recorded that James Farmer, the black assistant secretary of HEW and the former director of the Congress of Racial Equality, played a role in these discussions. Nixon "found it hard to talk with Brown around," and presumably with Farmer.

Twice, in private conversation, the president told Ehrlichman that blacks could never achieve real equality because they were genetically inferior to whites—a belief it would be hard even to infer from his public statements, including those designed to appeal to the white South.[6]

When Nixon settled, moreover, upon a firm civil rights policy for his administration, it was a restrictive one. Edward Morgan, an Ehrlichman staff aide assigned to desegregation problems, once reported in a memo to the president that Herbert Klein had encountered complaints in Dallas and Richmond about "over enforcement" of civil rights laws. In the margin of Morgan's memo, Nixon scribbled wrathfully:

> E[hrlichman]—I want you personally to jump Richardson + Justice + tell them to *knock off this crap*. I hold them personally accountable to keep their left-wingers in step with my express policy—do what the law requires and not *one bit* more.[7]

Time and again, Nixon repeated that formula to those in the White House, Justice and HEW who were involved in desegregation. The letter of the law was to be observed—just that and no more—and with the "lowest possible profile." Local officials were to be cooperated with, not coerced. No one in the administration was to "brag" about any desegregation that was achieved, as if an enemy had been conquered. Nixon's opposition to busing was constantly to be stressed.

In a memorandum for the president on August 4, 1970, Haldeman summed up these points, as they had been discussed in a White House meeting. The memo included Nixon's political judgment on the desegregation effort:

We don't win anything by our actions in the South. We have to do what's right but we must separate that from politics and not be under the illusion that this is helping us politically. . . .

[W]e will get no credit from the Blacks for doing this desegregation and a lot of heat from many of our supporters. The best approach then is quietly to do our job without press conferences or announcements of what our plans are.

Desegregation had had an unpromising beginning in the Nixon administration. When the president and his new HEW secretary, Bob Finch, reported for duty on January 21, 1969, they found that Lyndon Johnson and Finch's predecessor, Wilbur Cohen, had left them an unwelcome present—a Cohen ruling that federal funds for five Southern school districts would be cut off on January 29 unless by then the districts had submitted desegregation plans meeting HEW's tough guidelines. They had not done so.

In his campaign competition with George Wallace for Southern white support, Nixon had declared that "to use the power of the federal treasury to withhold funds in order to carry out" federally ordered desegregation schemes was "going too far." That kind of action "should be very scrupulously examined and in many cases should be rescinded."

Thurmond, in whose state two of the five school districts were located, was at hand to remind the new president of those words. So were other white Southern leaders who had become convinced that, once in office, Nixon would be able to roll back or at least put a stop to further school desegregation. How they came to that conclusion is understandable but, in fact, it was mostly wishful thinking.

Nixon's carefully calculated campaign statements, while lacking specific pledges, certainly had left the impression—as he had wanted, at least in the South—that he would slow down school desegregation. A Gallup poll taken nationally in February 1969 asked respondents for their "best guess" as to how the new administration would push integration. The response was:

> Faster   16
> Not So Fast   48
> About Right   28
> Don't Know   8

But it was quixotic, even for segregationists, to believe that *any* president could go beyond "not so fast" to "stop," much less to "roll back," in view of existing legislation and Supreme Court rulings—particularly *Greene v. New Kent County School Board,* decided in May 1968. That decision all but ruled out the so-called freedom of choice plans favored in the South (and guardedly praised by candidate Richard Nixon), since most such plans had left segregation largely intact. The court ordered desegregation to move ahead rapidly.

Finch, for one, knew the president would have but little choice about that; he had proceeded to recruit two liberal Republican Californians, John Veneman and Leon Panetta, as his undersecretary and chief of civil rights enforcement. Both wanted to push desegregation, as did an HEW bureaucracy largely inherited from two Democratic administrations.

Nixon, probably not yet fully focused on the issue but mindful of his debt to the Southerners, buckled immediately under their pressure to delay the withholding of funds from the five districts. Finch and Veneman talked him into a modification: the funds would be cut off *but* the districts involved could recover them if they submitted acceptable desegregation plans within sixty days. As with many compromises, that left all sides displeased.

On February 13, Finch—urged on by the aggressive Panetta—did cut off funds to three Southern school districts that had not met HEW deadlines. Harry Dent considered this a Pyrrhic victory: "The Southern reaction was so strong and the White House was so upset that the Finch crowd began losing one battle after another."[8]

That was an overstatement, but the central question for the next months of struggle and maneuver within the administration indeed had been raised—what to do about the deadline of September 1969, set in the Johnson administration, when most of the remaining segregated Southern school districts were supposed to submit plans for unitary systems to be achieved in the 1969–1970 school year. Under existing HEW guidelines, federal funds would be cut off for those that failed to submit such plans.

On one side of that issue, pushing to observe the deadline, were Veneman, Panetta and—in the White House—Pat Moynihan and Leonard Garment. Finch was usually with them but often wavered, owing to his great loyalty to Nixon. On the other side, eager for delay, were Attorney General Mitchell, Dent and Mardian, then general counsel at HEW. They had the powerful support of Southern Republicans in Congress, headed by the redoubtable Thurmond, and the Southern states' Republican chairmen. Nixon himself probably was with these latter in spirit, if not in final policy.

This battle reflected the general question of the administration's political direction. If a desegregation delay was granted, that would perfectly fit Mitchell's strategy of holding the support of those, heavily including Southerners, who had voted for Nixon in 1968 *and* adding those who had supported George Wallace; that combination would result in an overwhelming reelection victory in 1972—and, of course, sink Finch's desire to attract blacks and liberals to an expanded Republican party.

Mitchell wanted, in pursuit of this strategy, to abandon administration-ordered fund cutoffs, moving instead to reliance on court orders to accomplish whatever desegregation could not be avoided. If Southerners blamed judges rather than the president for that desegregation, Mitchell's political vision for 1972 still could be realized.

Given this division of forces, Finch's irresolution and the political stakes, it's surprising that the outcome of this ferocious internal battle was not a more conclusive victory for the segregationist South. But as word was leaked that the administration was about to cave in to Southern wishes, a broad counterattack was mounted by Republican moderates—such men as Governor Winthrop Rockefeller of Arkansas—who then exerted considerable influence in the party, hence on the president.

The result was a statement issued July 3, 1969, in the names of Mitchell and Finch, outlining another unsatisfactory compromise. No general year-long delay in desegregation, for which Southerners had hoped, was announced; the document allowed only that "there may be sound reasons for limited delay"—specifically, "bona fide educational and administrative problems" in some districts. These districts might therefore be able to talk themselves into a reprieve; but an effort by the Mitchell-Dent team to specify "community resistance" as a good enough reason for delay was *not* included; there was "community resistance" to desegregation practically everywhere in the South.

Nor did the statement overtly move away from fund cutoffs as an enforcement tool, though it made clear that the Nixon administration wanted to use that tool only as a last resort. The two-thousand-word statement, in the drafting of which Nixon himself took a strong hand, generally suggested sympathy for the difficulties of desegregation but nevertheless pledged the administration to enforce the law. Its basic theme was that the best results would be achieved by an effort "to induce compliance rather than compel submission."

Leon Panetta felt that he could say at a news conference called to explain the statement that "the current guidelines are still in effect." The statement nevertheless appeared to black and liberal leaders as a considerable retreat from desegregation—which is not surprising, since the White House attempted to picture it in just that light, in order to mollify Thurmond and his allies.

A "shocked" National Education Association, for example, happened to be holding its national convention at the time and voted to "insist" that Nixon restore the 1969 deadline—though it had not actually been set aside. Ronald Ziegler replied from Key Biscayne, where the president had gone for the Fourth of July weekend, that the administration was "unequivocally committed to the goal of finally ending racial discrimination in schools."[9]

Few believed Ziegler—not only because of Nixon's campaign positions, but because, in previous months, the Nixon administration had taken numerous actions that were widely interpreted as antagonistic to civil rights for blacks. Nixon had asked Congress, for example, to reduce funds for enforcement of fair housing laws. In some civil rights fields, the administration had appeared to do too little—leading Clifford Alexander, a black Democratic holdover from the Johnson administration, to resign from the chair of the Equal Employment Opportunities Commission with a blast at a "crippling lack of [Nixon] Administration support."

Nor had Nixon been willing to make conciliatory gestures toward blacks. DeWitt Wallace, then publisher of *Reader's Digest,* had written to the president in April to propose a White House luncheon at which Whitney Young, Jr., the black head of the Urban League, would be asked to speak to white businessmen. Nixon noted on Wallace's letter: "E[hrlichman]. 1. Ack[knowledge] warmly. 2. But don't do it."[10]

In June, Mitchell's Justice Department had even attempted to back away from the successful Voting Rights Act, which was expiring. Rather than recommending simple extension of a measure that had worked (all too well, Southern white leaders thought), Mitchell proposed a substitute that would not require Southern states to submit state voting-law changes to the U.S. attorney general for approval. That had been precisely the provision that had been most responsible for moving the South toward open and fair registration and voting—a movement that had added nearly a million blacks to the Southern rolls.*

School desegregation, though an unwelcome item, kept coming back to the top of the administration's agenda. August 11, 1969, for instance, was the deadline for thirty-three Mississippi school districts to submit court-ordered desegregation plans to the Fifth Circuit Court of Appeals. Southern pressures on the administration for delay, particularly from Senator John Stennis, Democrat of Mississippi, intensified as the date approached. Stennis, the chairman of the Armed Services Committee, might dash the president's desperate desire for approval of an anti–ballistic missile defense system (see chapter 11).

That possibility, together with the opprobrium of the South, was too big a risk for Nixon; notwithstanding the July 3 statement, he ordered Finch to go into federal court and seek a delay in the August 11 deadline. The

---

*The restrictive Mitchell version of the Voting Rights Act passed the House, but the Senate passed an extension of the original act. The extension became the final bill. Nixon was urged to veto it because the Senate had added a provision authorizing the vote for eighteen-year-olds, and it was widely believed that the newly enfranchised young people would vote heavily Democratic. Nixon signed the bill anyway, probably to avoid the double onus of appearing to veto the vote for Southern blacks *and* for youths. In 1972, when they first voted, eighteen-year-olds in fact divided their support between Republicans and Democrats.

HEW secretary's basic loyalty to Nixon took over; he obeyed without real protest, sought out Mitchell, and together with the attorney general decided to ask for more time, until December 1, on the fatuous ground that adequate desegregation plans could not be prepared in time.

Actually, completed plans already were on hand in Finch's own office of education, which he and Mitchell well knew; thus, the administration's presentation to the Fifth Circuit was blatantly false. It was nevertheless accepted by that court. For the first time, the federal government had taken a stand *against* desegregation and "the Department of Justice was seated at the table with the South rather than with the NAACP."[11]

If anything had been needed to convince blacks and liberals that the Nixon administration was retreating from school segregation, the shock of the unprecedented appeal in the Mississippi case would have done the trick. Just as convincingly, it made the point in the white South that Nixon really was a friend and ally—as Thurmond, Dent, Clarke Reed and other Southern leaders had promised in 1968.

Nixon tried to put a good face on his action. "There are those who want instant integration and those who want segregation forever," he said at a news conference. "I believe that we need to have a middle course between those two extremes."

Put that way, much of the nation undoubtedly agreed with the president. Taking its own view, the Supreme Court emphatically did not. On October 29, 1969, ruling on an appeal by the NAACP Legal Defense Fund from the Fifth Circuit decision, the high court slapped down the lower court *and* the administration—and all the harder because the decision was unanimous, thus joined in by Nixon's recent appointee, Chief Justice Warren Burger.

"The obligation of every school district," the court decreed, "is to terminate dual school systems *at once* and to operate now and hereafter only unitary schools." (Emphasis added.)

Again, Nixon tried to make the best of it. Asked at a subsequent news conference what would be his policy as a result of the decision, he replied:

> To carry out what the Supreme Court has laid down. I believe in carrying out the law even though I may have disagreed as I did in this instance with the decree that the Supreme Court eventually came down with. But we will carry out the law.

The administration appeared to be acutely embarrassed by the court's rebuff, particularly by Burger's vote. But both the rebuff and Burger's position had been predictable, even inevitable. The law had been clear at least since the *Greene* decision in 1968; the better lawyers in the administration (probably not including Mitchell, who was more opinionated than informed on civil rights law) knew they could not uphold the Mississippi delay in the Supreme Court.

It's not clear whether Nixon—a lawyer himself—understood that; but after his concentration on the issue in the 1968 campaign, in view of the trouble it had caused him as president, and given his capacity for study and concentration, it would be surprising if he actually thought the Supreme Court would accept the administration position (though he and Mitchell undoubtedly expected support at least from Burger).

Whether or not Nixon calculated it, the fact is that once the Supreme Court had overruled the stay that the administration had won in the Fifth Circuit, the president found himself in exactly the position most favorable to his aim: the Supreme Court had *ordered,* in terms that could not be evaded or misconstrued in the South, that desegregation must proceed; but Richard Nixon had been seen by Southerners to do his best to *delay,* even at considerable political cost outside the South.

"The Southern reaction," Harry Dent observed, this time in understatement, "was one of placing the blame on the court and recognizing that Nixon had tried to be helpful."[12]

Had that reaction been foreseen, even sought, in hopes of easing Southern resistance to desegregation Nixon knew was unavoidable? If so—and the question is worth returning to—it was the second time, but not the last, that Nixon had turned the Supreme Court to calculated political ends.

Not long before the Johnson administration left office, the crafty LBJ had made an arrangement with Chief Justice Earl Warren. A controversial figure as much for the Warren Court's decisions on criminal law as for its seminal desegregation rulings, Warren agreed to retire upon confirmation of his successor, rather than at a specified time.

Warren knew Johnson would nominate as the new chief justice the brilliant Abe Fortas, an associate justice whose views were highly acceptable to Warren. The arrangement he made with Johnson gave both men the assurance that if Fortas should not be confirmed as chief justice, Warren would hold the seat and Fortas would remain an associate justice. Johnson could try again, or Warren could stay on, and Warren's old antagonist, Richard Nixon, would not be able to appoint Warren's successor. So great was the antipathy to Warren among conservatives, moreover, that Johnson anticipated most would support even the liberal Fortas in order to be rid of Warren.

All this was overly clever. Johnson's nomination of his longtime political ally and counsel, Fortas, was fiercely opposed in the Senate because Fortas was considered the president's "crony" and a part of the hated Warren court—and also because in a presidential election year Republicans, urged on by their nominee, Richard Nixon, wanted to keep open the possibility that a president of their party, instead of LBJ, might replace Chief Justice Warren.

The Senate opposition to Fortas was led by Robert Griffin, the Republican from Michigan, and naturally by Thurmond, the ranking Republican on the Judiciary Committee. They could not assure Fortas's rejection, however, and Thurmond resorted, finally, to a filibuster. That did make Fortas's confirmation impossible, and he withdrew; but the battle had gone on for so much longer than expected that even Johnson—a president not noted for delicacy—agreed that a replacement for Warren, when and if he actually stepped down, should be nominated by the new president.*

That, of course, proved to be Nixon. Earl Warren, despite his twenty-year political estrangement from his fellow Californian, soon resigned again; and in May 1969 Nixon nominated Warren Burger, then chief judge of the Court of Appeals for the District of Columbia, to replace him. Burger was sixty-two, older than Nixon wanted, but a "strict constructionist" of the kind promised in the 1968 campaign; he had the judicial experience the president also had promised, and he appeared to Nixon and Mitchell to be the best prospect from the disappointingly small pool of Eisenhower's appointees still on the bench.

Besides, Warren Burger had been chairman of the Minnesota Republican party in 1952 and had led that state's delegation, originally for Stassen, when it switched to support Dwight Eisenhower at the Republican National Convention. That had helped make Nixon the party's vice presidential candidate, and subsequently—as Nixon noted in *RN*—Warren Burger had been among the first to send him a telegram of support during the never to be forgotten fund crisis of 1952, when Nixon's career was at stake. Those were credentials that counted with the new president.**

The Fortas affair was not over, however; intensive Republican and press scrutiny of his affairs during the fight over his nomination to be chief justice eventually led to a *Life* magazine story that Associate Justice Fortas—incredibly, for one so experienced in politics—had accepted a twenty-thousand-dollar retainer check from a foundation financed by Louis Wolfson, a stock market operator of dubious reputation (though the impropriety would have been as great, for a Supreme Court justice, had the

---

*Here is an irony of history: Had Vice President Nixon not failed to eliminate or modify the Senate's Rule XXII in 1957 and 1959, and had not Majority Leader Lyndon Johnson thwarted Nixon's intention to do so, then ten years later perhaps no filibuster would have been possible and President Johnson's nominee, Fortas, might have been confirmed. In that case, as will be seen, President Nixon would have been deprived of two Supreme Court nominations.

**Another who wired his support to Nixon during the fund crisis was the young Representative Gerald Ford of Michigan. Twenty-two years later, Nixon nominated him to the vice presidency, from which office Ford succeeded Nixon in the White House.

retainer come from a more reputable source). With the help of additional evidence from Mitchell's Justice Department, and with Earl Warren's sad concurrence, Fortas was forced to resign.*

Delighted to have two openings where only one had been expected, Nixon in August—just before seeking the delay in desegregating the Mississippi school districts—nominated Judge Clement F. Haynsworth, Jr., of Greenville, South Carolina, and the Fourth Circuit Court of Appeals, also a surviving Eisenhower appointee, to replace Fortas. Thurmond had favored another South Carolina judge but readily accepted Haynsworth—a conservative and "strict constructionist" of good family and reputation, who had turned Republican in 1964 in support of Barry Goldwater.

Nixon considered Haynsworth entirely qualified and in just the right mold for a Nixon court nominee. The choice nevertheless was politically calculated—as most presidential nominations are, and should be.

Not only was the open seat that of Fortas; it had been occupied previously by Arthur Goldberg, Felix Frankfurter and Louis Brandeis, so that it had become known as "the Jewish seat." Nixon had determined that it should be the "Southern seat" instead (the only Southerner then on the court was Hugo Black, a liberal who did not represent the South in the sense Nixon intended); and the president's specific instructions to Mitchell had been to find a white Southern judge, under sixty, with strict constructionist views. Clearly the Haynsworth nomination—however strong judicially—was another bid for Southern approval.

Judge Haynsworth appeared likely to sail through Senate confirmation as easily as had Burger. But on November 21, 1969, less than a month after the Supreme Court had overturned Nixon's Mississippi stay, Clement Haynsworth was rejected in the Senate, 55 to 45—the first Supreme Court nominee to fail confirmation since John J. Parker, Herbert Hoover's choice, in 1930. Not insignificantly, Parker too had been a white Southerner, from North Carolina.

No single issue defeated Haynsworth, who went on to long and reputable service on the Fourth Circuit and is widely regarded today as having been worthy of confirmation. Liberal senators' reaction against Nixon's slow-motion policy on desegregation; a debatable conflict-of-interest charge against Haynsworth, in an atmosphere still sensitive to the Fortas impropriety; hard lobbying by George Meany of the AFL-CIO, who regarded Haynsworth with some evidence as antilabor; the rather vague contention that he was anti–civil rights—all played a part.

Birch Bayh of Indiana, the Democratic senator who led the fight against Haynsworth, said at the Hofstra conference nearly twenty years later that the judge had been damaged by his unwillingness to admit an error in

*Wolfson later was convicted and imprisoned for stock market manipulation.

permitting even "the appearance of impropriety" to arise in the alleged conflict of interest. Bayh deprecated the idea that Democratic resentment of the filibuster against Abe Fortas's nomination to be chief justice was a factor; there's little doubt, however, that the rejection of Fortas—before his forced resignation—had cast a long shadow over the Haynsworth nomination.

Griffin of Michigan, who had fought long and hard against Fortas, voted against Haynsworth, too. Griffin was up for reelection in 1970 and may have been trying to blunt the idea that his leadership against Fortas had been purely partisan. Sixteen other Republicans deserted Haynsworth, some perhaps anxious to balance their tickets after the Fortas affair; they included the minority leader, Hugh Scott of Pennsylvania, and the formidable Margaret Chase Smith of Maine.

Nixon himself stood by Haynsworth valiantly, deployed the full power of his administration in the judge's support, refused to hear of withdrawing the nomination, and—characteristically—tried to strike back at "the libs." He instructed Ehrlichman to urge House Minority Leader Gerald Ford to mount an impeachment effort (impeachment must be voted in the House) against the liberal Associate Justice William O. Douglas, who had been accused of sexual and other peccadilloes.

Ehrlichman delivered the message, Ford none too enthusiastically made the effort (to no avail), and the blameless Haynsworth was further damaged by the linkage Washington soon made between Ford's proposal and the confirmation battle.[13]

After the vote against Haynsworth, Nixon was only the more determined to put a Southern conservative on the court—and was well aware that both the October Supreme Court decision in the Mississippi schools case, and the November defeat in the Senate, had made him and his administration more popular than ever in the South. To Dent, the Southern emissary in the White House, he said: "Harry, I want you to go out this time and find a good federal judge *further south and further to the right.*" (Emphasis added.)

Dent found G. Harrold Carswell of Florida, recently given perfunctory confirmation by the Senate to the Fifth Circuit Court of Appeals, and recommended him to Mitchell—which would have meant to the attorney general that Carswell had the support of Dent's patron, Strom Thurmond. In fact, Carswell *did* have that support, as any Southern conservative would have had, as well as the advantage of his recent Senate confirmation. He seemed to fit the campaign bill of particulars, too. Mitchell, too quickly, sent Carswell's name to Nixon; Nixon, too quickly, sent it to the Senate.[14]

Neither they nor anyone else dreamed that a second presidential nominee might be turned down; but as Bayh remarked at Hofstra, Carswell "made Haynsworth look like Learned Hand." Not only did Carswell's critics in the Senate and the press turn up old but serious incidents of racism; the nominee's judicial skills were so lacking that seven of the eighteen judges of the Fifth Circuit (including the distinguished Elbert Tuttle) refused to sign a telegram approving his nomination. The realistic Bryce Harlow told Nixon that even staunch Republican senators were fleeing from Carswell.

"They think he's a boob, a dummy," Harlow said. "And what counter is there to that? He is."[15]

By the end of the battle, even Mitchell and Nixon had been privately convinced by Carswell's record and inept performance in his own defense that he was not an appropriate nominee; Justice Department lobbying on his behalf became noticeably unenthusiastic. But Nixon was stuck with Carswell and thought he had no choice but to try to back him by all possible means—including the unfortunate claim, in a letter (drafted by Charles Colson) to Senator William Saxbe of Ohio, that what was at stake was "the Constitutional responsibility of the President to appoint members of the Court."

Nixon should have known, if Colson didn't, that the president is not "the one person entrusted by the Constitution with the power of appointment." There is no such person, though nearly twenty years later the claim would be made again, during Ronald Reagan's losing battle to place Robert Bork on the Supreme Court. The Constitution only grants a president the power to *nominate,* while giving the Senate the clear power to *confirm* or *reject* a presidential nominee to the Supreme Court.*

Nixon was stuck with Carswell only because of his Southern strategy; it would have been prudent to withdraw Carswell's name, had he not been playing still for political favor in the South. When the Senate rejected Carswell by 51 to 45, Nixon again appeared to have suffered a stunning setback, but the reality was that he had redoubled his political capital in the white South. Nixon moved promptly to be sure of it.

On the night of the Carswell vote, Nixon spent a brooding evening cruising the Potomac with Mitchell on the presidential yacht *Sequoia.* The next day, speaking to the press, the president gave vent to what many who saw him thought was genuine wrath:

> I have reluctantly concluded that I cannot successfully nominate to the Supreme Court any Federal Appellate Judge from the South who believes as I do in the strict construction of the Constitution.

*A decade after the Carswell debacle, Nixon claimed, in *RN,* that "there was a basic Constitutional principle involved, the right of a President to choose his nominees for the Supreme Court." Nobody ever disputed that right, which is considerably different from "the power of appointment" claimed in the letter to Saxbe.

... [T]he real issue was [the defeated judges'] philosophy ... a philosophy that I share, and the fact that they had the misfortune of being born in the South. ...

He would not, Nixon said, nominate another Southerner because any such nominee would be subjected to the same kind of "malicious character assassination." But having already toned down Pat Buchanan's original fiery draft, he omitted the sharpest charge from his remarks—though it remained in the White House text released to the press: "I understand the bitter feeling of millions of Americans who live in the South about the act of regional discrimination that took place in the Senate yesterday."

The president's anger no doubt was real; but was it actually on the South's behalf, or because Nixon had been twice humiliated by the Senate and "the libs"? No doubt both emotions entered into this intemperate statement, and perhaps in his heart the president knew, too, that the Carswell appointment had been a mistake that demeaned him *and* a co-equal branch of government. It marked, almost certainly, the downward turning point in Nixon's reliance on Attorney General Mitchell: the ultimately successful nominee for the Fortas seat, Federal Judge Harry Blackmun of Minnesota, came from a list provided not by the attorney general but by Warren Burger, who was anxious to take the Supreme Court out of controversy.

After the Carswell episode, too, Nixon and his staff took increasing notice of Mitchell's unsteady management of the Justice Department. As the White House more and more often had to intervene in what should have been Mitchell's work, Nixon's affection for his former law partner did not abate; with his publicly unknown capacity for being considerate with such close associates, Nixon knew Mitchell had a worrying problem on his hands—his outspoken and alcoholic wife, Martha. So he made no move to replace his attorney general.

Nixon's reaction, instead, was to move Justice Department problems frequently into the White House, as he was about to do with desegregation—antitrust concerns, for example, later Supreme Court nominations, even some decisions about federal prosecutions. The decisions to move against some municipalities, but not others, for racial discrimination against firemen were made by Nixon personally; he also decided for himself the sensitive policy that segregated "Christian" schools in the South were not to be granted federal tax exemptions. These decisions might have been made anyway; but after the Carswell blunder, Nixon's loss of confidence in Mitchell became predictable.[16]

Years later, Ray Price—whose loyalty to Nixon is unquestioned—told the former president that if he, Price, had been in the Senate, he would have voted for Haynsworth but against Carswell, "a judicial mediocrity who had no business being on the court." With the benefit of hindsight, Price recorded, "Nixon agreed."[17]

Most observers came to that conclusion at the time. Carswell's nomination appeared to be what another Nixon speech writer, William Safire, later termed it: "one of the most ill-advised public acts of the early Nixon Presidency."[18]

Was it? In terms of Nixon's overall reputation, yes. But Harry Dent, dispatched to the South by the president to repeat the sentiments of his angry post-Carswell statement, found that everywhere he went "Richard Nixon was a hero . . . and so were Judges Haynsworth and Carswell." In Dent's experienced political view:

> No action by the president did more to cement the sinews of the southern strategy, although Nixon never meant to have his southern nominees assassinated by the U.S. Senate. The outcome may have strained some congressional relations and peeved the liberal establishment but it considerably improved [Nixon's] standing with southerners and conservatives.[19]

There was little the president thought he needed more, as the second year of his term began, than to "cement" those sinews and improve that standing, because the Supreme Court rebuff of October 1969 had forced his hand. He had no real choice except to move ahead on the desegregation of Southern schools when classes opened in the fall of 1970, even at risk to Mitchell's strategy and to his own reelection hopes. And he was readier to do it than was generally realized.

In February 1970, Nixon appointed the Cabinet Committee on Education—imprudently calling it at first the Cabinet Committee on School Desegregation. To give the group good Southern credentials, in addition to Agnew's *pro forma* chairmanship, Nixon included Winton Blount of Alabama, the postmaster general, and Harlow, who was well known to Republicans to harbor strong reservations about desegregation. Robert Mardian was named staff director—another bow to the South.

Leon Panetta had somehow survived White House efforts to oust him, mainly because HEW undersecretary Veneman threatened to quit if Panetta was fired. Following the Supreme Court's October decision, Panetta had decided to move quickly against all segregated school districts in the South. That was fatal; when word of Panetta's intent reached the White House, it was too much for Richard Nixon, despite his personal reluctance to see his old friend Bob Finch, Panetta's boss, further embarrassed.

Nixon was by then referring to Finch as "poor Bob" and facing up to the fact that, largely because of the pressures of the desegregation struggle within and without the administration, Finch had lost control of his department; again, in his strangely considerate way, Nixon apparently did not blame Finch so much for indecision and ineptitude, but himself for putting Finch in a job that had proved too big for him.

Panetta, who had never been Nixon's man anyway and who would not follow the president's policy once it had been set, was another matter. Panetta was disloyal, one of the worst of political sins, as Nixon saw it, so one morning in February 1970 he abruptly announced during a White House meeting: "I accept Leon Panetta's resignation."

Panetta had not even submitted it; but he was quickly gone anyway, Finch making little effort to save him. Another pacifier had been handed to the South; Nixon told Ehrlichman that firing Panetta, whose desegregation efforts had made his name a red flag in the old Confederacy, was "worth dozens of speeches and statements about integrating the schools."[20]*

A few weeks later, Bob Finch was gone too—moved into an anomalous position as a White House counselor, rather than fired outright, as probably anyone else in his position would have been. Even so, Finch's miserable year at HEW—torn between his instincts and his staff on the one hand, and his loyalty to Nixon on the other—had finished his political prospects in California, where once he had been expected to become governor or U.S. senator.

Finch was replaced by Elliot Richardson; but the focus of action on desegregation had shifted from both the Justice Department and HEW to the White House itself. The conflict between departments was over. Finch basically was out of the game; Mitchell had lost much ground with the president. Richard Nixon and his Cabinet Committee on Education were in charge, and the president was determined to make *his* policy that of the administration, in fact as well as form.

First, that policy had to be set forth. On March 24, 1970, in something like a "white paper," Nixon offered what its principal draftsman, Ray Price, later called "the most comprehensive treatment of school-desegregation issues that had ever been issued by any president." In eight thousand careful words the document reaffirmed Nixon's personal belief that *Brown v. Board of Education* had been correctly decided; and stated succinctly his determination to enforce the law and the Constitution.

The white paper stressed, however, the importance of local leadership in the South. It made careful analysis of court decisions and the current state of the law—including Nixon's conviction that de facto segregation

*Panetta landed on his feet, turning Democrat and winning election to Congress from California. He was still a member of the House and chairman of the Budget Committee in 1990.

resulting from housing patterns was *not* constitutionally forbidden, so that no remedy for such segregation was required in any school district—North or South. Heavy emphasis was laid on the claim that de jure segregation, resulting from deliberate gerrymandering by school boards, existed in the North as well as the South, and would be eliminated *throughout the nation.*

Having thus brandished, however gently and not exclusively at the South, the stick of law enforcement, Nixon also held out the carrot of financial assistance. He pledged to seek $1.5 billion in federal funds to assist school districts in overcoming any problems caused by desegregation—additional faculty and facilities, construction, improved transportation, peacekeeping, and the like. One hundred fifty million dollars was to be made available for the opening of schools in 1970.*

The net effect desired by the president was to leave no doubt that he intended to carry out the mandate of the law—but with minimal coercion anywhere, in the North as well as the South, and with all possible federal assistance to the local leadership that would be required. Crucially, the paper made it plain: he was not pursuing "racial balance" but only desegregation to the extent demanded by law.

This important statement was printed because Nixon believed the matter too complex and legalistic to be briefly discussed on television or in a news conference; besides, a speech might build up more intensity of emotion, pro and con, than he wanted. He might also have shied away from identifying himself with a policy bound to create controversy on the left—for moving too slowly—and on the right—for moving at all.

The long statement also represented a bureaucratic victory for Leonard Garment, one of the few "resident liberals" on the White House staff. The paper's origins had been in a plan for Vice President Agnew to make a speech in Atlanta, echoing one he had made as governor of Maryland, denouncing "agitators" and impatient activists. Pat Buchanan, who had written Agnew's famous Des Moines speech blasting the press, was assigned to draft the Atlanta statement.

Buchanan had just set out his views in a tough memo to the president: "The second era of Re-Construction is over; the ship of integration is going down; it is not our ship . . . and we cannot salvage it; and we ought not to be aboard."

Perhaps aware of Buchanan's reactionary attitude, Ehrlichman assigned Garment to "keep an eye" on the speech text. Though politically at odds, Garment and Buchanan got on well personally; and "they worked all night long in Buchanan's office, shouting at each other, pounding tables . . . fighting . . . on every line of the speech," producing a text that pleased neither but had to go to the president anyway.

---

*Nixon made the requests as promised; but Congress cut the $150 million in start-up funds in half, and did not respond to the $1.5 billion proposal.

Garment, however, sent along a covering memo in which he advised Nixon that the subject was too important to be dealt with in such haste; involved was a "historic issue not to be taken lightly" but needing much more study. That issue, moreover, was too sensitive to be left to Agnew; the president ought to deal with it personally. From the presidential level, he might even be able to influence the direction of the courts—this last an argument bound to appeal to Nixon.

At a White House social function that night, or perhaps the next, in a moment Garment obviously treasured nearly twenty years later, he saw Bob Haleman across the room, giving him a thumbs-up signal. A moment later, Haldeman told him: "You won." Nixon had accepted Garment's ideas; the Agnew speech was off and with it the hotly disputed Buchanan-Garment draft. Garment was assigned with Price and Harlow—under the direction of Ehrlichman—to produce a new text, this one for Richard Nixon.

Garment worked for weeks producing what he called a "black book"—two hundred pages of facts and figures, ideas, staff submissions, texts of decisions, even an analysis by Alexander Bickel, the Harvard constitutional scholar. The black book became the basis of Price's white paper.[21]

The intellectual underpinning of his policy having been laid on the record, the president sent Harlow and Mardian to seek cooperation from governors, school officials and leading citizens in the states to be affected. The idea of the state advisory committees—a proposal backed by aides as different in outlook as Garment and Dent—evolved, and was particularly pushed by Shultz. The committees proved to be the best way to promote Nixon's insistence on local leadership and participation, and became "the key to success."[22]

Dent provides an example. In Alabama, despite George Wallace's hovering presence, Governor Albert Brewer gave the committee complete information about the places where his police expected the most trouble on the first day of school—thus informing the committee members where to concentrate their efforts. Governor and committee pledged to support each other, then held a joint news conference with television cameras recording the scene.

> All over Alabama, citizens saw fellow Alabamians stand with the governor of the state, and together, and commit their energies to a peaceful transition and upholding of quality public education. And the Alabamians heard Craig Smith, Alabama's representative on the national advisory committee, as he said, "Our only clients are the white and black schoolchildren of this state."

Some of the state committees, in addition to extending to desegregation the "cover" of their members' good reputations, helped to negotiate the actual details of desegregation. Dent states, without evidence, that the committees' work prevented "major tragedy" from occurring in Mobile and in Charlotte, North Carolina—both of which were under unpopular court busing orders.[23]

Nixon himself provided the final push in his New Orleans meeting with all the state committee leaders, on August 14, 1970, with the schools' opening day just weeks ahead. Desegregation would occur on that day, Nixon told them, but the federal government was committed to helping ease the difficulties. The real responsibility, however, was local: "You can have good schools, inferior schools, or no schools." That was up to Southerners themselves.

Then, on television, he declared that the Supreme Court had left him no choice, but that its decisions would be carried out in a way "treating this part of the country with the respect that it deserves."

> The unitary school system must replace the dual school system throughout the United States [but] as a result of these advisory committees being set up, we are going to find that in many districts the transition will be orderly and peaceful. . . . And the credit will go to these outstanding Southern leaders.

He was right on both counts. As we have seen from Elliot Richardson's statistics, when Southern schools opened in September 1970, a spectacular advance in desegregation was achieved—largely, in Harry Dent's phrase, "without tensions, bayonets and bullets." A year later, more than 90 percent of black schoolchildren in the South were enrolled in unitary school systems. The state committees and local school officials did get most of the credit, and deservedly so.

Richard Nixon received little credit then, and probably gets less today, for having overseen—indeed, planned and carried out—more school desegregation than any other president, and for putting an end, at last, to dual school systems in the South. It is not hard to see why this achievement, perhaps the most significant of his administration's domestic actions, has been so little recognized.

For nearly two years, after all, the Nixon administration had appeared to be in retreat from desegregation, while actively engaged in courting the Southern white vote. Federal lawyers had been sent into court to delay desegregation, earning proper rebuke from the Supreme Court. Two failed nominations of Southerners to that court, followed by Nixon's sharp denunciation of the "regional prejudice" he said had doomed them, had dramatized the president's Southern strategy even for those not closely following the desegregation issue.

The administration's most visible advocates of desegregation—Finch and Panetta—had been removed. Much of the more positive activity of 1970, including the important formation of the state advisory committees, had received little publicity; rarely for him, Nixon had wanted none. Those who did realize that a historic achievement was coming to fruition in the fall of 1970 generally believed that that outcome was inevitable, the product of court decisions; if Richard Nixon had had anything useful to do with it, his hand had been forced by the courts, he had complied reluctantly, and anyway, why hadn't he done it a year earlier?

Even after black and white children began going to school together in greater numbers than anyone had expected, Nixon made little effort to call the general public's attention to that fact. That would have risked undoing much that had been done—particularly the effect of local leadership and the state committees in damping down traditional Southern resentment against "outside agitators" and "Northern liberals" and "forced integration." Nixon wanted Southerners to feel good about their own achievement of desegregation, not angry toward outsiders who had imposed integration on them.

Too much should not be claimed for him. The retreats and blunders of 1969 could hardly have been in every case part of a deliberate strategy to win the white South; the Carswell nomination, for example, appears to have been more vindictive than calculated. The plea for delay in Mississippi was heavily influenced by John Stennis and his power over Nixon's greatly desired ABM system.

Nixon owed much to Thurmond and other Southern white leaders who had been essential to his election and he was ready to pay off, which he began doing in the first days of his administration. He certainly wanted them on his side again when he ran for reelection in 1972 (as he had every intention of doing, despite his disclaimer to Arthur Burns). And his sympathy for Southern reluctance to desegregate was genuine—as no doubt it was for many Americans who shared Nixon's view.

At the Hofstra conference, Roger Wilkins—nephew of Roy Wilkins and, during the Johnson administration, an assistant attorney general much engaged in civil rights matters—made a vigorous argument that the "worst thing" the Nixon administration did was to make possible the later presidency of Ronald Reagan, with his "grotesque" civil rights policies. Richard Nixon, Wilkins argued, had sent "cultural signals" to Americans that their innate racism was permissible—signals such as his open opposition to busing and his palpable sympathy for segregationists; and this cleared the way for them to vote for and support Reagan when the time came.

On the same platform, Sallyanne Payton of the University of Michigan law school, a black who had handled District of Columbia affairs for John Ehrlichman's Domestic Affairs Council, offered points in mitigation.

Nixon had been a *Republican* needing to pursue a Republican strategy, she reminded the Hofstra audience, and was handicapped by having been elected on "a tidal wave of white backlash." But Ms. Payton conceded Wilkins's point that Nixon had encouraged, in effect, and whatever his intent, "some of the worst elements of the country."

In a later interview with me, she termed the Nixon administration a "symbolic disaster" and pointed out Nixon's "failure to use the symbolic power of the presidency to disavow racism as a premise of American culture."

All that is true. Yet, the indisputable fact is that he got the job done—the dismantling of dual schools—when no one else had been able to do it. Nixon's reliance on persuasion rather than coercion, his willingness to work with Southern whites instead of denouncing them, his insistence that segregation was a national, not just a Southern problem, the careful distance he maintained between himself and the "liberal establishment," the huge political credit he earned in the South with his Supreme Court nominations and his other gestures to the Southern sensibility—particularly local leadership—all resulted in a formula that worked. At least after early 1970, it was Richard Nixon's formula, deliberately conceived, meticulously carried out.

It's true that the Supreme Court had left him basically no choice. But the South had displayed its ingenuity and determination before; in other hands, under other policies, desegregation might have been delayed again, or faked, or—perhaps worse—carried out in 1969 or 1970 with "tensions, bayonets and bullets." Nixon found a way around all that.

It's true, too, that dealing with the desegregation crisis in 1970 was better, for Nixon as well as the nation, than letting the situation continue to fester. So if his effort was highly political—to maintain his popularity in the South and his reelection prospects, even though meeting the requirements of the Constitution and his oath—that hardly tarnishes the result. Lincoln acted "politically" too, when he freed the slaves where he had no power to do so and left them in bondage where he did have the power of emancipation—with one stroke holding the border states in the Union and defining the Civil War as a crusade against Southern slavery.

That comparison is not meant to put Nixon on a level with Lincoln, the greatest of American presidents. But much as Americans might wish the presidency to be a place of moral purity and disinterested public service, it is essentially a *political* office, functioning best in the hands of an astute politician—a place from which to persuade people (in Harry Truman's words) to do what they ought to do without persuasion.

That sometimes may mean that the presidency must be a "bully pulpit" from which leadership is effectively preached, as the Texan Lyndon Johnson did when he told a joint session of Congress in his Southern accent that "we *shall* overcome." It may demand courageous public action, as when Eisenhower defied the nation's most cherished allies, Britain, France and Israel, over Suez in 1956, or when Truman fired General MacArthur to reassert civilian control of the military.

On occasion, however, and more often than the public wants to admit, what public opinion itself requires of a president is that he "row to his object with muffled oars" (as was said of Martin Van Buren). Franklin Roosevelt did that, because he could not move openly, in leading the nation quietly, effectively toward participation in World War II; and Richard Nixon did it in shepherding the South toward desegregation in 1970.

Nixon was not a crusader, a liberator or a visionary. He was a politician who had to enforce the law, and did, with the least possible outcry and upset—to his own prospects as well as to Southern society and national unity. That does not make Nixon a hero; it was only what he was elected to do. It *does* make him a president—for the "great purposes" of 1970, if not for the long future, the right president at the right time.

Richard Nixon was no more an environmental than a racial activist when he entered the White House; he had only a dim view of the environment as a political issue and delegated the subject largely to Ehrlichman. Again, however, he found that he had little choice but to address an unavoidable issue.

The imperative was not court decisions but public opinion—an "environmental revolution," as it was termed by John Whittaker, one of Nixon's primary environmental aides, later undersecretary of the interior, in remarks at the Hofstra conference in 1987.*

This was not a resurgence of the old Teddy Roosevelt–style concern for "conservation" of natural resources in great national parks. It was instead a growing demand that the *quality* of the environment be improved and protected everywhere—that stream water should be clean, forests and species protected, natural beauty preserved, and the air over American cities less polluted.

The *need* for such a movement dated far back into early industrial America but an important modern starting point would be Detroit's profit-driven decision in the early post–World War II years to build bigger cars with bigger engines—cars emitting, therefore, more carbon monoxide and other pollutants. Before long, "smog" became a new word in the American lexicon, and—worse—a choking new cloud over American life.

The first, and perhaps the strongest, catalyzing force of the modern

*Unless otherwise cited, direct quotations concerning the Nixon administration and the environment are taken from tape recordings and the author's notes of the Hofstra conference previously described.

environmental movement was the publication of *Silent Spring* by Rachel
Carson in 1963, with its dramatic and moving disclosures of the effects of
DDT and other pesticides on plants, animals and earth. In direct response
to the newly exposed threat of DDT, for example, the Environmental
Defense Fund, still a major force in national politics, was born on Long
Island.

Other seminal events followed *Silent Spring*—the fight against Con-
solidated Edison's plan to put a power plant atop Storm King Mountain
along the Hudson River, national revulsion against a proposal (endorsed
by that great outdoorsman, Barry Goldwater) to build power dams in the
Grand Canyon, most of all perhaps the oil spill in the Santa Barbara
Channel off California in 1969. As early as Lyndon Johnson's "Great
Society" speech in 1964, he had declared:

> Our parks are overcrowded, our seashores overburdened. Green
> fields and dense forests are disappearing. . . . [O]nce our natural
> splendor is destroyed, it can never be recaptured.

Some substantial legislation was passed in the Johnson years, mainly
under the leadership of Senator Edmund Muskie of Maine. Notably, a start
was made on controlling smog and preventing water pollution; after a hard
fight, and with substantial support from Mrs. Johnson, a highway
beautification bill also became law.

In the 1968 campaign, however, neither Nixon nor Hubert Humphrey—
both men of sensitive political antennae—spoke more than cursorily of
environmental concerns, despite Muskie's presence on the Humphrey
ticket. Obviously, the candidates felt no need to. Nor were they pressed to
speak on the subject by the reporters trailing them.

In 1969, after Nixon told him of a White House meeting with groups
including the Sierra Club, Henry Kissinger asked: "What *is* the Sierra
Club?" Kissinger's ignorance was not atypical at the time. In April 1970,
however, public opinion took a mighty surge forward with the unprecedented success of Earth Day.

The passage of twenty years may have obscured the impact of that event:
ten thousand schools, two thousand colleges and universities, nearly every
community in the nation, took part. Huge crowds turned out for environmental observances—for example, one hundred thousand in New York
city for an "eco-fair" in Union Square. Congress adjourned to permit its
members to attend teach-ins on the environment. All three television networks featured Earth Day events and the Public Broadcasting System
turned over all its daytime programs to the subject.

Immense national interest was now visible. The environment suddenly
rose high on the national agenda; and newly formed groups like the Na-

tional Resources Defense Council could channel that interest into effective pressures on Congress, the executive, the states.

In May 1969, a private White House poll had found only 1 percent of respondents who believed the environment was the most important issue facing the new president. Two years later, as John Whittaker recalled it, another survey found that the figure had increased to 25 percent of respondents; and in the second poll, the environment was surpassed as an issue of concern only by Americans' personal economic worries.

That quickly, a strong new consensus had developed; and "the juggernaut of environmental regulation proved not to be controllable by the Nixon Administration."[24]

After the Earth Day demonstrations, Richard Nixon, pragmatic as always, moved not to flee or thwart but to seize upon that environmental consensus—another instance suggesting that purity of motive is not the only, or necessarily the best, impulse from which a political leader can act usefully. Sometimes, he or she will be more effective when driven by political forces, when scrambling to get out in front of supposed "followers."

At the time, environmental responsibility was scattered among government agencies and only weakly accepted by most. The Department of the Interior looked after water problems; air quality was largely the province of HEW, for reasons of health. So were solid waste and radiological concerns. The Department of Agriculture, ever the friend of the farmer and often his tool, regulated the use of pesticides, mostly in the breach.

After first seeking to shift all these functions to an expanded Interior Department, a proposal that foundered on congressional opposition and intra-administration hostility to Walter Hickel—who had unexpectedly proven himself an aggressive secretary of the interior—Nixon proposed, just two months after Earth Day, to create the Environmental Protection Agency. EPA was to take over the scattered environmental functions of the government, with greater regulatory power; Congress approved Nixon's proposal and the agency opened its doors on December 2, 1970.

One advantage of the EPA was quickly seen. It was originally staffed, of necessity, with personnel from the departments that formerly had exercised what little environmental responsibility anyone undertook. Many of these men and women were dedicated but had been restrained by the policies of higher officials and other administrations. At the new EPA, they found themselves much freer—even encouraged—to exercise the kind of oversight and regulation they thought the job demanded.

As the first EPA administrator, Nixon named an assistant attorney general, William Ruckelshaus, formerly a member of Congress from Indiana and in 1968 a losing senatorial candidate (to the incumbent, Birch Bayh). Ruckelshaus was a good choice, a strong leader who stood up against industry pressures as well as the "go-easy" forces within the administration.

His successor, Russell Train, had been the director of the President's Council on Environmental Quality and was an equally fortunate choice. At least until 1989, when President George Bush appointed the environmentalist William K. Reilly to head the EPA, the two Nixon appointees still were considered the strongest leaders the EPA had had.*

The three-member CEQ, modeled on the older Council of Economic Advisers, had been set up by Congress—which was also feeling the heat—in the landmark National Environmental Policy Act. That legislation also required that federal agencies prepare environmental impact statements on their proposed actions; and this provision proved its worth almost the day it was passed, as activist groups quickly began filing lawsuits that stopped many environmentally hazardous projects—dams, wilderness roads, flood control projects, power plants—that in the past would have been carried out routinely.

The National Environmental Policy Act was a congressional initiative. In 1969, by Ehrlichman's account, this legislation became deadlocked in the Senate, in a jurisdictional struggle between Scoop Jackson of Washington, the chairman of the Interior Committee, and Muskie, the chairman of Public Works. The new administration ultimately threw its weight behind Jackson. (Was Nixon remembering Muskie as Humphrey's greatly lauded running mate in 1968 and worrying about him as an opponent in 1972?) The impasse was broken, and the way cleared for a veritable spate of environmental legislation—including establishment of the EPA.[25]

Nixon also determined upon a major environmental statement, which became the highlight of his 1970 State of the Union message ("Clean air, clean water, open spaces—these should once again be the birthright of every American"); specifically, he proposed a $10 billion clean water plan and suggested new air-pollution regulations. Later, not untypically trying to go Earth Day one better, he proclaimed the period April 18–24, 1971, as Earth Week.

John Whittaker, preparing the pertinent proposals in the 1970 State of the Union message, called attention in a covering press release to the thirty-seventh president's thirty-seven environmental proposals. An aide discovered, too late, that there were only thirty-six. Whittaker consoled himself that no one in the press would take the trouble to count. He was right—which says something about the press but does not detract from the most comprehensive environmental statement any president had made.

---

*A decade after his first term, Ruckelshaus had a less productive second tenure at the EPA under the far more restrictive President Reagan. One reason Nixon's two appointees were able to do more than most of their successors is that they worked during the early rush of public enthusiasm for environmental protection, and when the worst offences could be more easily, if not fully, corrected.

The NEPA had set a pattern of congressional initiative and subsequent administration support. The Clean Air Act of 1970—Muskie was the floor leader—was the most controversial and far-reaching effort to control air pollution ever achieved, and, as later revised, it still is. The hardest-fought of its provisions forced the automobile industry to meet emission standards, over its stringent protests.

The industry did finally and grudgingly propose a level of emissions its spokesmen conceded could be met, over time. The Nixon administration found the industry plan insufficient and sent to Capitol Hill a more restrictive proposal; Congress, to great public acclaim, then approved even tougher standards. The effect of this escalation, however, was that the deadlines had to be postponed repeatedly, as Detroit's laboratories failed to produce the necessary technology to meet the requirements—higher than those sought by the White House—that Congress arbitrarily had imposed.

Other legislation followed in rapid (for Washington) succession: an oil spill law designed to prevent more Santa Barbara incidents (it didn't); an act to give the EPA greater power to regulate and suspend pesticides; an anti–ocean dumping bill proposed by the CEQ; an interesting "noise control" act that, unfortunately, never has been pursued to its potential; and the Coastal Zone Management Act, giving states the power to regulate land and resource uses along their coasts. The only real break in the pattern was Nixon's veto in 1972 of a strong Clean Water Act that would have set federal water quality standards and established a grant program for the construction of necessary facilities.

Whittaker at Hofstra said he and Ehrlichman had warned Nixon that he would be "wiped out" politically if he vetoed the clean water bill. The president did not object to its substance but was angered by congressional add-ons that ran its cost to about $18 billion. He vetoed it—in Whittaker's words—"purely for dollars." To the certain prospect of an override, Nixon replied:

> Let's set up Congress to take the blame for a tax increase. They have overspent the budget on water and these other things, so we will have no choice but to change our position and ask for a necessary tax increase. Let them go home and explain that to the folks.[26]

Ehrlichman and others talked the president out of this proposed vendetta—apparently one of the frequent outbursts, more bluster than threat, to which Nixon was given, and which, unfortunately, more eager aides like Colson sometimes took seriously. Ehrlichman, however, agreed in this instance that, to clean up the waters, Congress was appropriating money that "the Administration did not have." Subsequent events indicated that the money could not be spent, moreover, at the rate for which Congress had appropriated it.

Nixon's veto was overridden as expected, and an assistant attorney general named William Rehnquist came to the administration's budgetary rescue with a legal ruling that the president could impound congressionally appropriated funds—a "godsend," as Ehrlichman called the ruling, but a strange view for a conservative like Rehnquist, whom Nixon later nominated for the Supreme Court and Ronald Reagan chose for chief justice.*

Armed with Rehnquist's ruling and in a constant budgetary battle with the Democratic Congress, Nixon impounded as much as $18 billion of appropriated funds by 1973; the practice had been used by presidents before but not so extensively. In the Budget Reform Act of 1974, Congress legislated a stop to it, and reformed its own budget-making procedures.†

In a conversation with Ruckelshaus (before the Rehnquist ruling) Ehrlichman said that the extra money in the water bill would be impounded. Ruckelshaus said he saw no way to do that, since the funds had been legally appropriated by Congress. He was astounded by Ehrlichman's response: "You mean to tell me you think that if Congress passes something that's clearly against the public interest, the president has to go ahead and enforce that law?"

Ruckelshaus replied, "It's just your opinion against theirs as to what's in the public interest." He recalled that remark some months later as an indication of an imperial view of presidential powers that he thought led inevitably toward Watergate.[28]

Particularly under the leadership of Russell Train, the CEQ—which had no operating responsibility, hence plenty of time to think and plan—also made significant contributions to the Nixon environmental record. Its proposed guidelines for the impact statements required by the NEPA were largely adopted, and it was instrumental in the cancellation of the Cross-Florida Barge Canal, the Tocks Island dam and Sierra Nevada road development. The CEQ also joined in the battles to clean up federal lands and ban DDT, and the ocean-dumping act was one of its initiatives.

All of this was done with Nixon's approval, or at least not against his will—though he was not immune to reaction. When Ehrlichman, to whom Nixon had delegated substantial environmental authority, used it

*One of the odd aspects of modern conservatism is its insistence on expansive presidential powers, as against those of Congress or the courts. This may reflect the fact that Nixon, Ford and Reagan were in the White House for sixteen of the twenty years after 1968; but traditional conservatism *opposes* concentrations of state power in any one branch, office or person.

†Herbert Stein, the chairman of Nixon's Council of Economic Advisers, prepared a defense of impoundment based on the Employment Act of 1946; Stein argued that the act implicitly authorized presidential impoundment of appropriated funds.[27]

to cancel the barge canal, the president immediately came under fire from Florida interests complaining to his friend, Bebe Rebozo. When Nixon asked Ehrlichman to explain his action—which indeed was high-handed for a White House aide—the latter offered to show the president the thick file of environmental objections to the canal; it would ruin the water table, it was destroying wildlife habitat, it couldn't be justified economically and so on.

Nixon immediately retreated from the dismal prospect of reading all that, and satisfied himself by giving instructions that the decision to cancel the canal be explained to Rebozo, so he could defend the cancellation to his Florida friends.

The only environmental matter in which Nixon appeared to Whittaker to take a really personal interest was that of national parks. Whittaker attributed this to Nixon's memory of his youthful poverty and his sensitivity to the cost, for low-income families, of long trips to Yellowstone and Yosemite.

"We have to bring the parks to the people," Nixon said more than once, and Whittaker recalled that when any controversy arose over the divestment of federal land, Nixon's stated policy was: "When in doubt, make it a park."

Had Nixon studied the record of the Cross-Florida Barge Canal, as Ehrlichman suggested, undoubtedly the president would have been most impressed with its lack of economic justification. Cost-benefit ratios were a real concern to him, so much so that the environmentalist-scientist Barry Commoner pointed out at Hofstra that it produced what he considered one of the worst flaws in Nixon's environmental record, the imposition of the Office of Management and Budget's authority over the decisions of the EPA. Bringing cost-benefit analysis to environmental questions meant that unless the economic benefits outstripped the costs of an environmentally sound action, it should not be taken.

Commoner charged that Nixon the politician, sensitive to the public response to Earth Day, had merely "latched on to a motherhood issue" in 1970; and that so far from leading the environmental movement in a positive way, he had proceeded to weaken congressional efforts to write effective laws. Richard Nixon "began the process of . . . putting loopholes into the law," Commoner asserted. One result, he said, was that clean air legislation had removed only 14 percent of pollutants, though it had been theoretically designed to achieve a 90 percent reduction.

Commoner cited a Nixon appearance before the Economic Club of Detroit on September 23, 1971, less than two years after his ringing State of the Union message on protection of the environment. The president had shown his true colors, Commoner said, before an audience that included many automobile executives—and Nixon certainly did stress, in answer to a question, his cost-benefit concerns:

> It is vitally important . . . that more attention must be given to the cost factor as well as to the factor that we are all interested in—of cleaning up our air and cleaning up our water. . . .
>
> [W]hen the Congress, or an administration carrying out the will of the Congress, sets certain standards . . . we must weigh against that: How many jobs is it going to cost? And, if it is going to cost a disproportionate number of jobs . . . then we have to reevaluate the decision. . . .
>
> We are committed to cleaning up the air and cleaning up the water. But we are also committed to a strong economy, and we are not going to allow the environmental issue to be used sometimes falsely and sometimes in a demagogic way basically to destroy the system—the industrial system that made this the great country that it is.

Into these remarks undeniably pleasing to business ears must be factored the occasion: no president was likely to tell the Economic Club of Detroit—or anyone else for that matter—that jobs and the economy were of little concern to him; nor should he. Nixon's criticism, moreover, was not of the environmental issue itself but of its false or demagogic use (though he cited no examples).

Besides, cost-benefit analysis cannot be wholly disregarded even in environmental matters. To use an example Whittaker cited, suppose spending one hundred dollars to clean up 95 percent of an environmental problem would be justified; would it be equally justified to spend another hundred dollars to get at the remaining 5 percent? Perhaps; but surely *the question* is reasonable.

So, to the extent that his case was based on the Detroit remarks, Commoner overstated it; Nixon's answer hardly proved that he understood by 1971 that environmentalism was "a threat to the free market system" (which is not exactly the same as "the industrial system that made this the great country that it is"), or that he had backed away from his 1970 environmental message. The likelihood is that Nixon would have stated the same reservations of personal belief—whether or not justified—a year or two years earlier.

Barry Commoner, a man of outspoken views and formidable knowledge, had a point of view to push, anyway; he stated the candid belief that profit-driven corporate decisions (like Detroit's deliberate post–World War II policy to build bigger cars) were at the root of all environmental problems. In that view, regulatory legislation after the fact, like that signed by Nixon, could never do the job; the only effective way to protect the environment was to give the public a voice in corporate decisions. That was not a procedure likely to be furthered by a president who had pledged, in Commoner's view, not to destroy the free market system. But what president ever did want to destroy it?

Commoner was nevertheless on target concerning Nixon's basic views. Ehrlichman has testified to the president's lack of fundamental personal interest in the environment, and Whittaker conceded that Nixon was "a very strong capitalist" who had the "visceral, gut reaction we have to be careful about how fast we go in being Mister Clean." And to a speech writer, Nixon once remarked: "In a flat choice between smoke and jobs, we're for jobs."[29]

On April 27, 1971, five months before his economic club appearance, Nixon met in the White House with Henry Ford II and Lee Iacocca (then still an executive of the Ford Motor Company); on that occasion he *did* reveal colors much like those Commoner attributed to him. The conversation, secretly recorded by Nixon's later-famous taping system (and edited here only for length), discloses the kinds of pressures businessmen can bring even on the president (as well as the essential illiteracy of much high-level discourse in American political and business life):

PRESIDENT: Whether it's the environment or pollution or Naderism or consumerism [we] are extremely probusiness. Uh, we are fighting, frankly a delaying action. . . . [W]e can't have a completely safe society or safe highways or safe cars and pollution-free and so forth. Or we could have, go back and live like a bunch of damned animals. . . . [A]nd, boy, this is true. It's true in, in the environmentalists and it's true of the consumerism people. They're a group of people that aren't one really damn bit interested in safety or clean air. What they're interested in is *destroying the system.* They're enemies of the system. So, what I'm trying to say is this: That you can speak to me in terms that *I am for the system.*

FORD: . . . Uh, we represent the total automotive [industry], about one sixth of GNP. Now, if the price of cars goes up because emission requirements is gonna be in there . . . safety requirements are in there, bumpers are in there. . . . [T]hat's leaving out inflation and material-costs increases, which are also there. We think that the prices of cars are going to go up from [1972] through '75 anywhere from a hundred dollars to, up to maybe seven or eight hundred dollars in the next four years because of the requirements that are being, that's leaving out the inflation. . . . If these prices get so high that people stop buying cars. . . .

PRESIDENT: Um-hum.

FORD: . . . [T]hey're gonna buy more foreign cars; you're going to have balance-of-payments problems. . . .

PRESIDENT: Right. I'm convinced. . . .

FORD: Granted, the foreign [unintelligible] have got to do the same thing, but they're doing it at a wage rate that's half [unintelligible].

IACOCCA: . . . [W]e have already sunk two hundred and forty million into the safety area. And we have on our cars today a hundred and fifty dollars of, I don't say all gadgetry, 'cause the steering columns, I think, are saving lives, the collapsible column and the like, but the shoulder harnesses, the headrests are complete wastes of money. . . . What we have in safety right now on our books through 1973 into the air bag area is about the four-hundred-dollar level on a car. . . . But [the Department of Transportation] is making speeches right now saying that up till now they've only put eighty dollars on. . . . [Emphasis added.]

At the end of the thirty-five-minute meeting, the president was sympathetically promising to take another look at the problems raised by Ford and Iacocca. Again, too much, perhaps, should not be read into the views Nixon expressed to the automakers. Ehrlichman—the note-taker at this and most other such meetings—came to see the president as a sort of chameleon, adapting himself to the different people with whom he talked, taking on their coloration and tone. He did this, in Ehrlichman's view, because of his constant desire to avoid personal confrontation, argument and unpleasantness.

When Frank Rizzo, the tough-guy former Democratic mayor of Philadelphia, came as a newly minted Republican to seek Nixon's blessing for another run at the mayoralty, Ehrlichman was both impressed at how Nixon "played him perfectly" and shocked at how easily the president dropped into a discussion pitched to Rizzo's sleazily profane level. Rizzo departed happily, believing he and the president were political "soul mates."[30]

Nevertheless, and however he may have overstated his views to placate Ford and Iacocca, Nixon the politician undoubtedly did seize upon the environment as "a motherhood issue," while Nixon the capitalist (Garry Wills's classic liberal, the self-made man) harbored reservations about the cost to business and the possible loss of jobs (a preoccupation with him). Nor would he have been the first president (both Roosevelts and Wilson come to mind) who pushed or accepted useful but limited social legislation in order to preempt more radical measures.

In all likelihood, too, the "group of people" who pushed environmentalism and consumerism ("libs" for sure and probably Franklins) did not appeal to a president who valued hard-nosed realism—which, to him, would have been represented by the Iacoccas of the world, men determined to keep profits up by holding the price of cars down, with as little concession as possible to safety and environmental considerations.

Besides, Nixon's real interest lay in other matters. "A visit to a sewage-treatment plant in suburban Chicago (to show support for a Clean Water Act) somehow didn't make Richard Nixon feel like the leader of the Free World," Ehrlichman observed. "But the point is that President Nixon *did* visit sewage plants and energy generators. . . ."[31]

Does Nixon's personal attitude matter all that much, in light of the results? How much difference is there between an achievement of personal conviction and one of political necessity? If, sometimes, the former might be more sweeping, the latter certainly occurs more often; and as the perfect can be the enemy of the good, too high an aim can sometimes miss altogether.

On the environment, as in school desegregation, Nixon was pragmatist, as well as opportunist. He recognized that he had little choice in the face of the "environmental revolution" but to act; the force of public opinion was too great to resist, as had been the force of court desegregation orders. Presidents are elected to make such judgments, and devise acceptable means of doing the necessary.

Nixon the centrist again chose a middle course—for example, in proposing a permissible level of auto emissions higher than that put forward by Detroit but lower than that approved by a "credit card" Congress (as he sometimes termed it) not then much constrained by budgetary worries. If he established the EPA, he also gave the Office of Management and Budget significant power over it; if he signed environmental legislation, he tried to limit the spending Congress was willing to approve; if he failed to please Barry Commoner, he also displeased the auto industry—the latter unquestionably of more concern to him.

It's hard to suppose that another president would or could have passed up the opportunity the environmental revolution laid before Nixon. It's equally hard to believe, in light of the inherent opposition to that revolution, that someone else in the Oval Office would or could have gone much farther than Nixon did in meeting public demand for action. In fact, no president since *has* gone farther, though Jimmy Carter should be given credit for trying. Richard Nixon, moreover, can hardly be imagined ducking for eight years the acid rain issue, as Ronald Reagan did.

Ehrlichman, a far more enthusiastic environmentalist than his boss, ranks Nixon's response to the environmental revolution second only to school desegregation as the major domestic achievement of his administration. And he believes that no matter what the president's original reservations, Nixon wound up being "rather proud" of his environmental record.

That record, in the view of Charles Warren, an EPA official in the Carter administration, has yet to be improved upon by any president. And in the perspective of two decades, David Sive of the National Resources Defense Council has put it this way: Nixon "was there when it began, he signed all the basic legislation, he appointed some absolutely wonderful people."[32]

That neither overstates nor understates the considerable environmental achievement of a president who answered to political necessity while seizing political opportunity—though he never exorcised his instinctive reservations.

As he wound up that conversation with Ford and Iacocca, Nixon unburdened himself of a final sarcastic blast at environmentalists, consumerists and the like—elitists all, in his eyes:

> PRESIDENT: What it really gets down to is that, uh . . . progress, [unintelligible] industrialization, ipso facto, is bad. The great life is to have it like when the Indians were here. You know how the Indians lived? Dirty, filthy, horrible.
> UNKNOWN: (Laughs)

Whoever "unknown" was, it surely was not John Ehrlichman, the note-taker. Ehrlichman had a considerably higher opinion, and much more knowledge, of Native Americans than Nixon had. Not that the president was entirely hostile; he admired no one more than "Chief" Newman, his old football coach. And as in the cases of school desegregation and the environment, the record of Nixon's administration in Indian affairs tends to confound the personal attitude his remarks to Ford and Iacocca suggest.*

In 1971, for example, Bobbie Kilbrig, a member of Ehrlichman's staff and the Nixon administration's resident authority on Native American affairs, alerted Ehrlichman to the problem of Blue Lake in New Mexico. The U.S. Forest Service had undertaken to lease grazing rights in the vicinity of the lake to white ranchers, and the Taos Pueblo was protesting bitterly. To the Indians of the pueblo, sacred ground was being profaned; their ancient belief was that their gods rose through the waters of Blue Lake itself. The Forest Service and the ranchers were trampling on their religion as well as their rights.

Acting with the remarkable authority Nixon had delegated to him in

---

*After his conviction on Watergate charges, Ehrlichman asked that he be sentenced to do pro bono legal work for Native Americans. He was sent to prison instead, but his plea was widely noted in the press; as a result, after he moved to New Mexico, Indians and Hispanics did seek and receive his help.

domestic affairs, Ehrlichman took up the pueblo's cause and had legislation prepared to stop the Forest Service from leasing the grazing rights. The bill moved quickly through the House, but ran into trouble in the Senate, where Scoop Jackson, the chairman of the Interior Committee, blocked it.

Jackson presented a serious problem because his long service had made him one of the great powers of the Senate, in a time when that meant great power indeed; a Nixon favorite, though a Democrat, Jackson had been the president's first choice for secretary of defense. More important, Jackson's support—like that of John Stennis—was vital to Nixon's hopes for approval of his proposed ABM defense.

Jackson was not personally opposed to Ehrlichman's bill, but Clinton Anderson of New Mexico—another of the Senate's great powers—strongly supported the white ranchers who wanted those grazing rights. In the back-scratching atmosphere of the Senate, not only was Anderson influential with members of the committee on a matter affecting his state; his secretary, Helen Langer, then was involved romantically with the bachelor Jackson (they were later married)—a situation that may have tilted the Interior chairman toward Anderson's position.

Jackson told Ehrlichman that his committee would not approve the Blue Lake bill; he could send it to the floor anyway but the committee's disapproval meant almost certain defeat by the full Senate. Jackson did not want that, as few things are regarded with greater horror by a congressional chairman than to have one of his committee's bills beaten on the floor.

Few things, on the other hand, are less welcome to the White House than to have a presidentially sponsored bill bottled up in a congressional committee. Ehrlichman told Jackson he regretted the conflict but that the White House was committed to the Taos Pueblo; the matter would have to be fought out on the Senate floor.

The trouble was that though the *White House* may have been institutionally committed, *Richard Nixon* personally was not; he knew nothing about the Blue Lake controversy, Ehrlichman having acted on delegated authority. Jackson, moreover, was not an enemy Nixon wanted or needed— indeed, the Democratic senator from Washington, once the chairman of the Democratic National Committee, had been as much an ally of a Republican administration as partisan politics would permit. So Ehrlichman laid the matter on the president's desk with some trepidation.

Nixon heard him out and asked one question: Had Ehrlichman committed the president to the support of the Blue Lake bill? Yes, his aide replied.

In that case, Nixon said, there was no choice; the prestige of the White House would not permit retreat. They would have to fight Jackson in the Senate, win or lose, even on this protest raised by a small group of Indians.

The bill eventually went to the floor, and administration lobbyists did manage to overcome Scoop Jackson's committee. The Forest Service leasing program was stopped; the Taos Pueblo retained its ancestral tribal right to Blue Lake and its environs, hence to its religious beliefs; and Scoop Jackson eventually was mollified, perhaps because he had not really opposed the substance of the bill.

Bobbie Kilbrig also brought to Ehrlichman's attention the matter of Alaska natives' one-hundred-year-old claims to landownership. That state's fifty-three thousand Eskimos, Aleuts and Indians were lobbying hard for payment of these extensive claims; but the Alaskan white establishment—strategically represented in the Nixon administration by Secretary of the Interior Walter Hickel—was resisting just as strenuously. When Hickel, for other reasons, was replaced by Rogers Morton of Maryland, Ms. Kilbrig laid the Alaska matter before Ehrlichman.

After involved negotiations with the Alaska native representatives, a complicated formula of tribal corporations and land allocations was worked out by Ehrlichman and his staff. But Morton, who had arrived at Interior with an open mind on the Alaska issue, was swayed by holdovers from the Hickel regime and opposed the natives' claims. Again using his delegated authority aggressively, Ehrlichman informed the secretary of the interior that the formula he had approved was "what the President wanted."

"Then Morton caved," Ehrlichman dryly recalls.

Before the secretary could discover the truth, Ehrlichman hastily obtained Nixon's actual approval—testimony not only to adept political footwork on the part of a determined White House aide, but to how much one of these powerful, unelected officials can accomplish (not always in the public interest) merely by bold use of the president's name.

White House and Interior Department support had been the missing elements for the Alaska Native Claims Act; once they were behind it, congressional supporters moved it along the hard route to passage in late 1971. The administration proposal was for $500 million paid over twenty years, plus ten million acres of land; Congress proved considerably more generous, granting Alaska natives $962.5 million ($500 million of it in state and federal mineral revenues) and forty million acres of land, together with an arrangement for native corporations to administer all this.

In his memoirs, Nixon does not mention this landmark legislation, which might not have passed without the intervention of his administration. That suggests how little interest he had in such matters; nonetheless, the Alaska settlement happened "on his watch" and to no small extent because of his openness to his staff's urgings.[33]

As these incidents suggest, Ehrlichman and Bobbie Kilbrig stimulated Nixon to much activity concerning Native Americans that was unusual in their experience of the Great White Father. Bruce Willkie, executive director of the National Congress of American Indians, told *U.S. News and*

World Report in September 1971 that Nixon was the only president since George Washington to commit his administration to honoring the nation's usually ignored obligations to the tribes.

One event that evoked Willkie's tribute was a special presidential message to Congress in 1970, in which Nixon declared a new federal policy to recognize the sovereignty of tribes and to strengthen the links between them and their individual members. Before that, the government had sought for years to break or loosen those links and focus Indian loyalties more nearly on the federal government.

Nixon also initiated successful legislation to strengthen tribal governments and tribal economic development. In a period of high Indian militance—the takeover of Alcatraz Island, the second Battle of Wounded Knee—Nixon further responded to perceived political necessity by increasing the budget for the Bureau of Indian Affairs and expanding federal funds for Indian health care.[34]

He could be pushed too far, however, and he was, in 1973, when the Indian activist Russell Means led a messy sit-in at the offices of the BIA in Washington. Documents, furniture, and other facilities were destroyed and Nixon's sensibilities were offended. The BIA sit-in caused the president *not* to do what Ehrlichman thought he had persuaded him he should do, and what Russell Means and his followers probably would have welcomed: abolish the BIA, a target of Native American wrath through the decades.[35]

Nixon was in office at a time when the sixties had released a number of such forces, to which a president was forced to respond, even if he seemed not to do so. The women's movement sparked in the sixties by Betty Friedan and others also was showing considerable strength by the time of his election—which is a major reason why, in his first year in office, Nixon issued an executive order that federal agencies establish affirmative action programs for equal employment opportunities for all employees—obviously including women.

Since his service in the House (1947–1951), Nixon had been a supporter of the Equal Rights Amendment; as president, he also backed legislation to prohibit sex discrimination in educational institutions that received federal funds, to permit bigger tax deductions for child care and to add provisions against sex discrimination to a number of existing programs. One clear initiative of his administration was the expansion of the Civil Rights Commission's authority, to include action against sex discrimination as well as other forms of inequity.

As with the Bureau of Indian Affairs, however, Nixon could see only so far: he vetoed an advanced piece of social legislation that would have provided day care free to poor families and on a progressive fee scale to wealthier households. No doubt a man who remembered his mother, father and brothers all working to keep the Whittier grocery store in business, rebelled internally at what he saw as federal "intervention" in family life.

Nixon's record in bringing women into government was only "average," Bob Finch informed him on April 15, 1971, three years into the Nixon administration. Only fourteen, or 3.5 percent, of full-time "presidential appointments" had gone to women—though that was a better record than the Kennedy or Johnson administrations had achieved at their halfway points. Finch urged that a goal be set for 1972 to double the number of women, from twenty-six to fifty-two, in "high positions"—not all full-time—in the government.

Nixon noted on the memo: "Bob Finch + H[aldeman] 1. This is an excellent job. 2. However I seriously doubt if jobs in government for women make many votes from women."[36]

This might have been rationalization of his reluctance to appoint women; or it could have been hard political calculation; or it conceivably was a view somewhat ahead of its time that women generally wanted effective measures against sex discrimination rather than highly visible "token" jobs in government for a select few.

One woman who might have been expected to receive a high place in the Nixon administration was Rita Hauser, a New York Republican lawyer and an active Nixon supporter. But after the president read a newspaper account quoting her opinion that the Constitution did not bar marriage between persons of the same sex, he exploded to Ehrlichman: "There goes a Supreme Court justice! I can't go *that* far. . . . Negroes [and whites], okay. But *that's* too far!"[37]

Nixon had not come into office as a vocal supporter of affirmative action for minority groups. But we already have seen an ironic pattern of achievements he had not particularly set out to achieve, and here was another— perhaps the first *real* success of any president in affirmative action. As in school desegregation, Secretary of Labor George Shultz was the key figure; in fact, it was the success of Shultz's "Philadelphia Plan" in 1969 that caused Nixon to draw him into the planning for desegregation in 1970.

Shultz devised the Philadelphia Plan—with the help of Arthur Fletcher, an assistant secretary of labor who was one of the few high-ranking blacks in the administration—in response to the long-established refusal of lily-white construction unions to open their ranks to black workers. The unions thus had closed one of the traditional American routes—the building trades—by which generations of immigrants and others had gained greater status and prosperity.

But if the construction unions were engaged in projects financed in whole or in part by federal funds, the Philadelphia Plan required that the contractors involved hire a certain number of minority workers; the unions had to train black youths as apprentices and grant them union membership once they were qualified. If that looked suspiciously like a "quota" plan, which the unions were not slow to call it, Shultz and Fletcher undercut the issue by referring ostentatiously to "goals and timetables," a phrase that since has entered the language of civil rights law.

The Philadelphia Plan may have reminded Nixon of his chairmanship in the Eisenhower administration of a committee to seek fair employment in government contract work. It appealed to him also because it satisfied his usual preference for the middle course: the NAACP wanted much tougher action against the building trades unions, but organized labor, including George Meany of the AFL-CIO, resisted *any* action. Shultz's plan was attractive, moreover, because it did what the Democrats could not do; despite their reliance on the black vote, they dared not offend Meany and his unions, on whom they relied even more for votes and campaign funds.

"The Democrats," Nixon said, "are token-oriented. We're job-oriented."[38]

No doubt the president also was bolstered by John Mitchell, who in 1969 was far more influential than the relatively unknown (to Nixon) Shultz, let alone Fletcher, the black assistant secretary. Shultz won Mitchell's support for the Philadelphia Plan by emphasizing that economic opportunity was more important to blacks—hence its stimulation was more important to the administration—than civil rights legislation, which the attorney general, always attentive to the white South, did not wish to sponsor.

Besides, the Philadelphia Plan could be put into effect by executive order, and that appealed to Nixon's desire to get things done efficiently. He supported Shultz's proposal, even after the unions pushed a bill through the Senate to outlaw the plan. Nixon's strong stand helped persuade the House to reject the Senate bill, whereupon Shultz extended the plan to nine other cities.

The Third Circuit Court of Appeals ultimately upheld the Philadelphia Plan, the toughest affirmative action scheme that any administration had put into effect, and one of the boldest steps of Nixon's tenure in office. Later, however, his support waned—which meant that the plan was enforced less effectively—mostly because the hard-hats in the construction unions came vigorously to his support on the war in Vietnam.

When Paul O'Neill, a veteran of many years in government, later chief executive officer of Alcoa, was assigned to the Bureau of the Budget by Lyndon Johnson in 1964, he began a survey of federal health programs. He found twenty-eight federal departments and agencies administering *more than one thousand separate programs.*

As bad as the inevitable duplication and overlap, O'Neill saw, was the fact that these programs were financed by money collected in taxes from all Americans, but were redistributing that money haphazardly, in many cases unfairly.

On August 8, 1969, O'Neill—by then the deputy director of the Budget Bureau—heard President Richard Nixon denounce the inequitable distribution of federal funds. Nixon used an example from the welfare program: owing to differences in how much matching money the states were willing to put up, a family of four in Mississippi received thirty-nine dollars a month through the federal Aid to Families with Dependent Children (AFDC) program; a similar family in New York received two hundred fifty dollars a month from the same source.

Though an experienced civil servant not much given to political enthusiasms, O'Neill was thrilled to hear Nixon pledge to do something about this and other inequities:

> A third of a century of centralizing power and responsibility in Washington has produced a bureaucratic monstrosity, cumbersome, unresponsive, ineffective. . . .
>
> For a third of a century, power and responsibility have flowed toward Washington, and Washington has taken for its own the best sources of revenue.

O'Neill was hearing an early description of what Nixon called in his more expansive State of the Union message of January 22, 1971, "the New Federalism"; it would bring, he then promised Congress and his national audience, with his taste for the bold stroke and the big slogan, "a Second American Revolution."

No such revolution occurred, nor did Nixon's New Federalism produce anything like radical results. Its most successful effort, a program of general and special revenue sharing with states and cities, was terminated in 1986—a victim of Ronald Reagan's lack of interest and Congress's lack of funds. In more than a decade, however, revenue sharing poured about $83 billion into states and localities, benefiting roughly thirty-seven thousand political jurisdictions at every level; in the process, it did alter federal-state-local relationships, mostly for the better.

The program at least partially answered Paul O'Neill's complaint about inequitable distribution of funds—the size of revenue-sharing grants was determined by a federally prescribed formula—and it eliminated some of the overlap and duplication that had caused O'Neill such distress in 1964. Revenue sharing met Nixon's desire to "reverse the flow" of political power to Washington, sending some of that power back to states and localities in the form of money and responsibility. That helped build the modern Republican party,* and it led to at least one near-miracle:

*Ironically, the basic idea for revenue sharing was conceived by two Democrats: Walter Heller, the chairman of the Council of Economic Advisers in the Kennedy and Johnson the political reconciliation of Richard Nixon and Nelson Rockefeller.

Governor Rockefeller and Mayor John Lindsay of New York City (a Republican who had been reelected on the city's flexible Liberal ticket) then were locked in numerous struggles. Neither Lindsay nor the city offered Nixon much support; so, as John Ehrlichman recalled in some amusement, "the full engine of the White House" was turned against the mayor, thus making something of an ally of Rockefeller.

No wonder revenue sharing then persuaded Rockefeller to abandon his ancient warfare with Nixon—twice the governor's nemesis in presidential politics, and a man he had called a "political gypsy" after Nixon moved to New York and accused Rockefeller of failure to back Barry Goldwater. Revenue sharing, after all, was just what the name implies: the return of substantial federal tax revenues—over $5 billion annually by 1974—to states and localities to do with as local needs demanded, with few strings attached, demanding no complicated forms to be filled out, no new bureaucracies to administer it and minimal accountability to nit-picking officials in Washington.

For governors and mayors caught between rising demand for services and public resistance to taxes, revenue sharing was a bonanza. Governor Ronald Reagan of California, whose political career was based on opposition to government and taxes at all levels, was one of the few who opposed it; that left Rockefeller of New York as what Ehrlichman called the "functional leader" of state and local officials who helped Nixon's loyalists and lobbyists push the plan through a reluctant Congress.

As Nixon entered office, Johnson's Great Society programs and the "long, hot summer" race riots of the sixties had made the nation acutely aware of its urban problems. Though the idea seems quaintly demented now, the anticipated end of the war in Vietnam—no one quite realized in early 1969 how far off that end really was—gave rise to the notion of a coming surplus of formerly war-devoured dollars; what was to be done with this "Vietnam dividend" to prevent it from becoming a "fiscal drag" in the form of a deflationary federal budget surplus?

The Nixon administration discovered soon enough that there would be no Vietnam dividend, owing to the rising costs of entitlements and other programs already in the law. From the president's vacation house in California, in August 1969, flamboyant Pat Moynihan declared to reporters that "the Vietnam dividend is as evanescent as the clouds over San Clemente."

It was apparent, also, that there was a fiscal mismatch between the vast revenues of the federal government and the numerous services required of

---

administrations, and Joseph Pechman of the Brookings Institution. President Johnson rejected their proposal.

state and local governments. That mismatch, if sustained, inevitably meant a continuing transfer of traditionally local tasks to the entity that had the *money* to handle them—the federal government—whether or not it had the *ability*.

Why not cut federal taxes, so local taxes could be more easily raised and the money kept in the states and cities to begin with? Eisenhower had tried that and it hadn't worked. His administration allowed a federal telephone tax to lapse specifically so that the states could pick up the tax and the revenue. Few did because no local politician wanted to be seen converting a federal *tax reduction* into a state *tax increase.* States and localities were eager, however, to accept redistribution of existing federal revenues with no tax increases required of them.

Exactly how to return money, to whom—the states alone? the cities? regional entities?—and under what rules? These questions had to be thrashed out between the Nixon White House—Arthur Burns's staff, primarily—and the Budget Bureau. Ultimately, the program included "special" revenue sharing for six specialized fields—urban problems, rural problems, education, manpower training, law enforcement and transportation—as well as general revenue sharing, which states and cities could spend mostly as they chose. Rockefeller, a champion of the rest of the program, opposed the transportation grants; so on one of the governor's visits to Washington, Paul O'Neill was assigned to change his mind.

As O'Neill later told the story, Rockefeller taught him something about "what a marbled cake federalism and our democracy really is." The budget official explained to the governor at length why the transportation grants (for capital expenditures) were a good idea. Rockefeller listened patiently.

"Paul, you just don't understand," he said finally. "I need to have a subsidy for *operating expenses* for the subway in New York City."

That was a bad idea, O'Neill said.

"Look, you have to understand this," Rockefeller insisted. "If we don't get operating subsidies for the subway (to hold down subway fares), we're not going to be able to get 50 percent of the vote in New York City and if we don't get over 50 percent in New York City, we can't carry the State."

The Nixon administration held out against such subsidies anyway and Rockefeller continued to state the opposition of the second-biggest state— with the result that Congress failed to approve the capital grants for transportation.

The decision to distribute the funds according to strict federal formula settled the matter of equity among the beneficiaries, but still allowed general revenue sharing to be targeted to areas of greatest need—for example, cities with large minority populations. Besides, most potential recipients were too happy to receive no-strings-attached money to worry overmuch about the precise division of the available funds.

Getting the program past members of Congress was harder than putting it together. "We really passed this over their dead bodies," Ehrlichman said. Again the reasons are not hard to find.

Politicians who vote to *raise* revenues, as members of Congress had to do, historically are reluctant to let others *spend* those revenues. But Nixon was asking them to turn over control of vast sums to state legislatures and city councils—bodies for which many members of Congress had little respect, and which were widely felt to be susceptible to irresponsible local pressures.

That objection had some merit. Another, as potent, was less respectable. Revenue sharing meant the end of a kind of Santa Claus game that members of Congress loved to play, and from which they profited politically.

Under the old programs of categorical grants, for which states or cities had to meet federal requirements, a senator or a congressman would get advance word from some politically astute agency that a county in the politician's state or district was about to get federal funds for, say, a new sewage disposal plant. This statesman then could hold a news conference to announce with pride that his untiring efforts had resulted in a great achievement for the folks back home. Sometimes he actually had helped. Even if not, of such fulsome claims many a political career had been made.

Revenue sharing largely put an end to this amiable con game; money distributed annually and automatically by formula did not permit members of Congress to take such credit, as their cries of anguish attested. In fact, one of the most effective efforts to move the program through Congress took advantage of just this change: White House letters went out to each of thirty-seven thousand political jurisdictions, informing each how much it would receive *automatically* under revenue sharing, and urging local officials to bring pressure on senators and congressmen for approval of the program. That made it difficult for members to vote—not just against revenue sharing generally—but against those specifically promised funds.

Nixon pitched enthusiastically into the lobbying effort. He "involved himself frequently," Ehrlichman noted, "virtually on request," in seeking congressional support. "He made it a personal issue," which in the case of revenue sharing was easy, since the president not only was "philosophically attuned" to the program but "saw the political magic" in it.

How much, in fact, the administration and the Republican party benefited cannot really be established. But big-city mayors, generally speaking, were not natural allies of either, nor were urban or minority voters. All of them got a lift from revenue sharing and may have traced it to Richard Nixon and the Republican party. So did heartland states that were naturally Republican and Southern states that were slipping out of the Democratic fold.

Nixon's rapprochement with Rockefeller guaranteed what was likely anyway—that the governor would not oppose an incumbent Republican president in 1972—and improved the shaky unity of the party. It's hard to conceive of a real political *cost* to Nixon or his party, once revenue sharing had been forced past Congress.

Some—mostly liberals—did complain that recipient jurisdictions used the money to build tennis courts or buy armored cars for the police or to lower local taxes, instead of for the social programs or the innovations these critics favored. But to this, Nixon could and did reply that if power was truly returned to local government, it could not then be controlled from Washington; and that most of those receiving funds knew best what they needed.

Despite safeguards, some of the money undoubtedly went for openly or covertly discriminatory uses; but that was inherent in the idea of local control, and was no doubt overbalanced by the nondiscriminatory uses to which most revenue-sharing grants were put. Nixon was charged with trying to increase his own presidential power; and his sponsorship of revenue sharing probably did improve his reelection chances. He may have gained, also, because revenue sharing lessened somewhat the power of Congress; and many of those who "condemned his power-grabbiness were concerned not that the power being grabbed was going to the President . . . but away from them."[39]

Any politically popular program, some with less justification than revenue sharing, is likely to add to the credit of the president who sponsors it. Compared, moreover, to Nixon's impounding of appropriated funds and his secret excesses in other areas, revenue sharing seems a relatively innocent political exercise.

Nixon, strangely enough, never gave it the high priority that might have been expected. Ehrlichman claims that despite Nixon's hard lobbying for the program, he several times had to talk the president out of cutting revenue-sharing funds from the federal budget; Nixon was desperately seeking ways to cut the budget, and the $4 or $5 billion in revenue sharing funds was an annually tempting target that threatened only faraway local activities in which he had no direct or tangible interest.

Since revenue sharing proved to have a shelf life of only a little more than a decade—Reagan, an original opponent in Sacramento, at last had his way in Washington—a postmortem is more than usually possible and useful. On the favorable side, first, of course, were the often important local and state programs carried out with revenue-sharing funds (at greatly reduced administrative costs and with less bureaucratic hindrance), programs that might not otherwise have come to fruition.

In addition, various interest groups—all of which wanted more money for their causes—were stimulated, for better or worse, to greater local activity, a consequence hardly to be regretted in a democracy, even when the specific cause might have been dubious. The assumptions, common in the sixties, of ever-increasing power for federal government and of growing futility at the other levels, also were shaken.

Less favorably, state and local dependence on the federal government may actually have been *increased* by the "free" money revenue sharing sent out from Washington, as local governments came to rely on these funds. The idea of trying to deal with problems mostly by spending more money on them may have been strengthened, too, as federal funds flowed to statehouses, courthouses and city halls.

Finally, Nixon's emphasis on turning power away from the federal government probably provided a logical if unintended step toward Ronald Reagan's far-different "New Federalism"—an effort to reduce the power of government *at all levels* in favor of reliance on the "free market."

Such a link would be ironic, for the Nixon administration was trying to make government *more* responsive to the governed, less distant and isolated from the people. That was what Ehrlichman meant when he said that revenue sharing was "consistent with Nixon's sense of direction and general approach"; it was perhaps the most successful example of his hope to reorder government responsibilities so that necessary services could be performed at the most appropriate level, rather than being concentrated in the Washington bureaucracy.

For this sense of priority and responsibility, primarily, Nixon's revenue-sharing plan—though plainly for him more nearly an intellectual interest than a deeply felt commitment—seems to me to warrant honorable inclusion in his dossier as a reformer. If revenue sharing did not come close to the promised "revolution," it still was a good try at redeeming government from the gathering public opprobrium that was to find its champion in Ronald Reagan.

In the eventual machinations and self-aggrandizing reaches for power that brought Nixon's downfall, he was of course anything *but* a reformer. That only emphasizes the complexity of his character, political as well as personal; and it cannot erase the fact that during his administration Nixon set off or at least allowed what economist Richard Nathan has called a "creative period" of reform and advance. Unfortunately, Nathan conceded, Nixon's later transgressions produced in the public "a tendency not to give credit" even where obviously due.

Perhaps nothing makes this point better than a sweeping Nixonian reform that did *not* become law—creative though the idea unquestionably was, striking in its boldness, far-reaching in intended effect, and for which the president who sponsored it seldom receives appropriate credit.

On April 17, 1971, Elliot Richardson, the secretary of HEW, reported to President Nixon on an "unresolved problem" with Governor Ronald

Reagan's welfare policy in California—a proposal "to have the recipients work off their welfare checks" by doing labor for the state or locality.

Nixon impatiently wrote in the margin of Richardson's memo:

> E[hrlichman]—why haggle over this—I like the idea of working off welfare checks—push Richardson to cooperate to the *maximum* allowed by law.
>
> To extent our welfare reform proposal differs from this concept—change it *immediately*. [40]

The emphasis was Nixon's, and this appears to have been one of what Ehrlichman called his "Alice in Wonderland" outbursts, not really to be acted upon.*

Such attitudes as the one apparently expressed in this note—or, say, Nixon's request for Merle Haggard to sing the derisive country-music song, "Welfare Cadillac," during a White House performance (Haggard stoutly refused)—have led to the widespread belief that Nixon was simply hard-hearted toward welfare recipients and did not really support progressive welfare reforms, proposing them only for political effect.

On December 11, 1970, however, in a memo worth repeating almost in full, Nixon wrote Ray Price the following suggestions for a forthcoming presidential speech:

> Paint a picture of what a terrible mark [welfare] leaves on the child's life. Point out that [Nixon's proposed reform] takes away the degradation of social workers snooping around, of making some children seem to be a class apart. . . .
>
> [W]e have got to find a way to see to it that in the free lunch program children are not separated. Julie [Nixon Eisenhower] does practice teaching at a school which is primarily Negro. She tells me that it breaks her heart every day to see the welfare children who get the free lunch herded into the cafeteria where as a matter of fact they get a nice, warm lunch that is better than those who are not on welfare and the ones who do not get the free

---

*In his oral history, Ehrlichman also referred to what he called "I am the president" instructions, in which Nixon might say, " 'I want all federal money cut off to MIT. Do it now, do it today, there is no appeal. . . .' So you would make a note of that and go out and do nothing. Two or three days later he might say, 'What have you done about cutting off all the federal money to MIT?' and I'd say, 'Well, I haven't done anything about it.' 'Well, I've been thinking about it; it's probably just as well,' he would say." In similar vein, Nixon once wrote Secretary of State Rogers to "direct" that he fire everyone in the embassy at Laos, including the ambassador, by the end of the week. Rogers ignored the letter and he and the president later laughed about the episode. [41]

lunch and bring their lunches eat in the classroom. All of them know, of course, which ones are on welfare and which are not.

I will work in some personal recollections with regard to the depression years when I well remember how deeply I felt about people my age who used to come in my father's store when they couldn't pay the bill because the father was unemployed and how this seemed to separate them from the others in the school. None of us had any money, but those who were in families where there were no jobs and at that time precious poor relief were, in my opinion, probably marred for life. . . .

Point out that the greatest [problem] of the present welfare program is the effect that it has on children, and that the greatest benefit of [his proposed reform] is the fact that it will allow the children of all families in America to stand proud with dignity without being singled out as those who are getting food stamps, welfare, or what have you.

[I]n the depression years I remember when my brother had tuberculosis for five years and we had to keep him in a hospital, my mother didn't buy a new dress for five years. We were really quite desperately poor, but as Eisenhower said it much more eloquently at Abilene in his opening campaign statement in 1952, the glory of it was that we didn't know it.

The problem today is that the children growing up in welfare families receiving food stamps and government largess [*sic*] with social workers poking around are poor and *they do know it.* . . .

[T]his is our chance now to see that every child, at least, will grow up in a family where he will not have the fact constantly thrown in his face that his father never married his mother and doesn't live at home, and that therefore in common parlance he is a bastard and further that he is on welfare, while his school mates can point with some degree of pride to the fact that their fathers at least are taking care of the family and have a little pride. The need for dignity, pride, character to be instilled in those first five years of life is something that could well be [included.]

[W]rite in these human terms if you will.

Nixon could make the claims in this memo because the Family Assistance Plan (FAP) he was proposing would have ended the nation's "great lady" approach to welfare—in which, symbolically, at Christmas a rich woman distributes a basket of food to the poor, while advising them to live moral lives.

This kind of welfare had prevailed for decades in the so-called services strategy by which the poor received Medicaid, food stamps, free school lunches and the like, plus—in the Aid to Families with Dependent Children (AFDC) program—direct payments varying (as we have seen) by the amounts the various states were willing to put up to match the federal stipend.

But the AFDC program banned, in about half the states, payments to families in which the father *was present in the household;* in the other states, if the father lived at home, no payments could be made unless *he was unemployed.* Thus, poor families with a working father residing in the house got no payment at all from AFDC, and the result was obvious: fathers "deserted" their families so that their children could qualify for AFDC payments, which in many states, for large families, brought in more money than an unskilled, uneducated father could earn at a dead-end job.

Since many of the working poor, who received no AFDC help, were white, and many AFDC families were black, a none-too-subtle racial schism had opened, too: working whites resented welfare blacks, on grounds that too much was being "given" to the latter, while in many cases the former had to work for little if any more income.

In FAP, Nixon proposed—to the consternation of his critics and his supporters alike—to replace all that by *direct payments* with a uniform minimum standard in all states, payments for which the "working poor" as well as families with no male breadwinner would be eligible. For the first time in American history, a president was proposing—though he carefully avoided the term—a guaranteed annual income, one for which poor children would be eligible whether or not their fathers worked or lived in the household.

When FAP was first put forward in 1969—in that August speech that aroused Paul O'Neill—the proposed minimum standard was sixteen hundred dollars annually for a family of four; that was raised to twenty-five hundred dollars when the proposal was revamped in 1971. Each state was expected to supplement this amount.

These provisions would have resulted in aid to *three times* as many children as were eligible for AFDC payments. Able-bodied heads of beneficiary families would have been required, in return, to "accept work or training"—save for mothers with preschool children. If parents refused that requirement, only the parent's share of the cash payment would be withheld; the guaranteed income *for children* thus was unconditional.

Nixon had proposed nothing like this in his 1968 campaign; instead, he had denounced the idea of a guaranteed annual income. Polls showed, moreover, that the general public rejected both a guaranteed income and a negative income tax (the device on which FAP was to be based). These ideas, in the common view, would deliver undeserved benefits to shiftless people and immoral women spawning too many illegitimate children. In 1969, as welfare critics endlessly repeated, over 69 percent of welfare births in New York City were out of wedlock.

In view of this public attitude and of Nixon's campaign excoriation, few expected anything progressive from him on welfare—let alone anything as startling as FAP. But as early as April 11, 1969, less than three months after his inauguration, Nixon wrote Ehrlichman in the margins of a memo from Moynihan detailing the costs of FAP: "E—*in confidence* I have decided to go ahead with this program. *Don't* tell Finch + M[oynihan]— et al. But get a plan ready for implementation by 1st of next week."

Moynihan's memo had informed Nixon that the new welfare scheme would cost $1.6 billion yearly as a substitute for AFDC and $3.4 billion for "adult" programs. Nixon's emphasis on not telling "Finch + M—et al." may have reflected fear that these formidable numbers might leak to the press.

In retrospect, ample reasons can be seen for Nixon to have taken the radical approach of FAP. Public and congressional impatience with the existing welfare system, for one thing, had reached such heights that he had to do *something*—in *RN* he termed welfare reform his "highest priority" when he took office. But that same widespread public impatience suggested that mere tinkering—"incremental reform," in the scholarly phrase— might well not be enough even to damp down criticism, much less actually improve a discredited system.

A respectable recommendation for a guaranteed annual income also was available to Nixon when he became president, in a report from a Commission on Income Maintenance (the Heineman commission) appointed by Lyndon Johnson. LBJ had refused to accept the proposal. At a time when Nixon was concerned also about unemployment and recession, the Heineman commission's proposal must have seemed doubly attractive; it would improve the purchasing power of the poor, and thus provide a new stimulus for the economy.[42]

Too, a federal floor under income for the poor would ease the burden of welfare payments on the states, about which Nixon was hearing much from irate governors. In addition, since FAP would include the mostly white working poor as beneficiaries, the program would answer with cold cash the white notion that blacks were getting more out of the government than whites were.

Many critics of the old welfare system—as a *New York Times* columnist, I was one of them—advocated cash payments to replace the services strategy, on the capitalist theory that putting money in the hands of people who had had none inevitably would cause them to want more—hence to work themselves into greater affluence.

Besides, FAP fitted the predilections of the president and his Council of Economic Advisers. Nixon's campaign criticisms of Great Society programs had not focused on their costs but on the idea that they "encouraged dependency, family breakup, idleness, hostility and the development of radical para-government organizations"—this last particularly obnoxious to a law-and-order president. The council thought it preferable to "hand out money and leave the recipients free to spend it. Also [the CEA] thought that [the Great Society] needlessly injected social workers into the lives of the poor." The new president concurred.[43]

"The basic premise" of FAP, Nixon said in *RN*, slightly overstating the case, "was simple: what the poor need to help them rise out of poverty is money."

The work-or-training requirement further made it possible for Nixon to claim "no work, no welfare"—again something of an overstatement. But his insistence, together with the direct cash payments, seemed to validate his protestations to the taxpaying middle class that FAP would provide incentives for welfare recipients to get off the welfare rolls and onto payrolls—in Lyndon Johnson's inelegant but expressive phrase, to become "tax payers instead of tax eaters."

Nixon actually could argue that FAP, however radical it appeared, was in this sense a *conservative* idea (a negative income tax, in fact, was originally the brainchild of conservative economist Milton Friedman); and the president never explicitly conceded that his proposal constituted a guaranteed income for the poor.

Moynihan, in the period of his greatest influence on Nixon, was an early and enthusiastic advocate of the cash strategy. So were members of the Council of Economic Advisers and officials of HEW held over from the Johnson administration; these latter soon convinced Finch, John Veneman and Tom Joe, Veneman's welfare adviser (first in California, then at HEW). The basic FAP plan emerged from HEW; Moynihan became its prime champion in the White House, with Arthur Burns its sharpest critic.*

This formal, cabinet-level recommendation for such a sharp departure— and for such a surprising step to be taken by Richard Nixon—undoubtedly appealed to the president's well-documented love for the big, jaw-dropping gesture. (Who but he, for example, could have proclaimed that the American astronauts' trip to the moon and back in 1969 had made those July days "the greatest week in the history of the world since the Creation"? This hyperbole evoked remonstration even from Nixon's admirer, the Reverend Billy Graham.)

As the quoted memo to Price makes clear, Nixon also brought into the White House—though it was largely unrealized by the public, then and later—a considerable empathy for the poor, arising from his own experi-

---

*Burns fought on all fronts. At one point, he sent Nixon an account of the failure in Britain, from 1795 to 1834, of the "Speenhamland Law," an early version of an income subsidy for the poor. Nixon sent it on to Moynihan, Finch, "Schulz" (*sic*), and McCracken for comment. Apparently they were not sufficiently impressed.[44]

ences. Pushing FAP on him was to some extent pushing an open door, whatever the public may have believed.

Moynihan cleverly played two additional themes that were effective with a president who longed, more than he ever admitted, for the approval of intellectuals and Franklins. One was to draw a parallel between the president and the great British prime minister, Benjamin Disraeli. Intelligent conservatives like Disraeli and Nixon, Moynihan argued, were in the strongest position to carry out the best *liberal* ideas—ideas for which liberals themselves would be unable to muster the support necessary to overcome orthodox conservative opposition.

"Tory men with liberal policies" therefore could not only do what liberals could not do; such Tories could win working-class support for doing it—as Disraeli had for British conservatives, and as Richard Nixon might for the Republican party. Nixon was not slow to accept this argument, much less the identification with Disraeli.

With even more alacrity, he swallowed Moynihan's other point—that FAP by its cash strategy would strike a hard blow at the welfare bureaucracy. Many social workers and assorted "do-gooders," for whom Nixon had little use, those "snoopers" he denounced to Ray Price, would be put out of business if the services strategy was supplanted by cash payments directly to the poor. Nixon personally disliked welfare bureaucrats, more than they deserved, and few of whom he actually could have known; he also perceived that they were usually Democrats, and that the welfare system they served and promoted was a Democratic party construct.

Thus, with FAP, Richard Nixon could not only improve the welfare system; he could do it by substituting a sound Republican and Tory plan for a failing Democratic and liberal program.

Hindsight, the indispensable tool of scholars and journalists, nonetheless suggests that FAP was doomed from the start. At the least it was a very long shot, first and perhaps foremost because it *was* revolutionary—revolutionary in concept (the idea of handing taxpayers' money to many Americans considered by many others to be shiftless and immoral), perhaps revolutionary in practice. The latter possibility worked at first subtly, later openly, against approval.

FAP would have made thirteen million more Americans—so Nixon estimated in *RN*—eligible for federal assistance than were receiving it in January 1969. Sixty percent of the poor would have been brought above what was then the official poverty line, with what social and economic results for the general society no one could be sure.

In the Southern states, whose representatives with their long service and great seniority carried so much weight in Congress, and where the civil rights question already was causing so much unrest—in those states, the gross income of poor persons (many of them black) would have been *tripled*. At Hofstra, Sallyanne Payton suggested that this would have "blown apart" the political structure of the South—and, indeed, the revolutionary dream of Southern liberals always has been to unite poor blacks and poor whites around their common *economic* interests, while the successful strategy of Southern conservatives has been to fan *racial* hostility between these elements.

The economic and probably the political order of things in the South would have been shaken, at the least—a prospect quickly perceived by powerful members of Congress like Russell Long of Louisiana, chairman of the Senate Finance Committee.

Everywhere, the economic upgrading and upheaval FAP suggested was disturbing, intimidating, probably for more people than those who might welcome such a radical prospect. What would guaranteed income mean for employment, social stability, the work ethic, the role of women, the likelihood of the middle class "getting ahead in the world"?

Because of the American public's ingrained Horatio Algerish ideas about the poor and its restrictive views of permissible government action to help them, FAP proponents had to be wary of terms like guaranteed income and negative income tax. Thus, they could seldom label FAP for what it was, or talk realistically about what it would and would not do, and they suffered for some of the arguments they made instead.

Nixon's emphasis on the work-or-training requirement and his frequent references to "workfare," for example—however he might have thought them necessary to sustain his own conservative image and persuade his supporters—backfired with liberals and some intended beneficiaries. Many became convinced that the work feature of FAP was far harsher than it really was, a sort of draft system for the poor; some believed it was "racist" in concept, since so many welfare recipients who would be forced to work were black.

The Nixon welfare reform, in any case, was fundamentally a cerebral proposal, a calculated reform developed by economists, sociologists and government officials. FAP did not come "up from the ranks" as a demand of popular opinion; nor as the proposal of the poor themselves; or even as a long-standing idea—as revenue sharing was—whose political time had come. Hence, FAP never had the kind of popular support that environmental legislation had, at about the same time. Members of Congress were not flooded with mail on its behalf, or accosted on the streets when they went "back to the District."

Not everyone believed, moreover, that Dick Nixon, the familiar hard-liner, really was fully supporting a program of cash for the poor; it seemed too far out of his perceived character. If members of Congress believed that, in proposing FAP, he was just "making a record" and was not really committed, they felt less need to back the plan and less fear that the president would retaliate politically if they didn't.

Besides, just as Nixon had welcomed the opportunity to substitute a Republican welfare system for a Democratic one, Democrats—the political majority in Congress—were unwilling that a Republican president (Richard Nixon, of all people!) should get credit for such a fundamental reform. That kind of change, they felt in a nearly proprietary manner and with some historical justification, could only come from the post–New Deal Democratic party (the reverse of Moynihan's Disraeli argument).

Nixon, in fact, may *have* lost interest as the battle dragged on and other events and causes preoccupied him—though Moynihan insists that the president's efforts never really flagged. In April of 1970, the House of Representatives passed the bill, a considerable achievement for administration lobbyists; but Russell Long's finance committee bottled it up in the Senate, then in November rejected it, 10 to 6. The House again approved in 1971 and again the measure went nowhere in the Senate. Even Nixon, in *RN*, concedes that after the second defeat his heart was no longer in the effort.

"By 1971," he wrote,

> the momentum for FAP had passed and I knew it. . . . [T]here was also the prospect of the 1972 election; I did not want to be in a losing fight with conservatives over FAP in an election year.

He put up no further struggle.

It was not just conservatives, however, who prevented the passage of the most far-reaching welfare reform—one might say *economic* reform—ever proposed by a president. The overriding barrier to congressional approval was a strange but potent liberal-conservative alliance that sprang from the nature of the proposal.

All other criticisms aside, conservatives—Governor Ronald Reagan prominent among them—saw FAP as a further reward for the idle and promiscuous, a leftist scheme even from a Republican president, a new attack on the traditional family and the American work ethic. This attitude was perverse—FAP was conceived to hold families together and to provide work *incentives*—but not unexpected; what took Nixon and Moynihan from the blind side was the resistance of liberals and the poor themselves.

Public sector unions and social-work organizations—the "welfare bureaucracy"—seeing the same danger to themselves that Moynihan had pointed out to Nixon, opposed FAP out of self-interest. Their line of attack—joined with more laudable motives by such liberal groups as the National Council of Churches and such representatives of the poor as the National Welfare Rights Organization—was that FAP was inadequate: its cash payments would be too low to eliminate poverty. Some charged the plan was racist because of its work requirements, despite the vast increase in income it promised for Southern blacks.

The surprising liberal opposition with the expected conservative resistance, together with the fear of unknown consequences bound to accompany any such revolutionary change, could not be overcome. Defeat was made certain by Southern Democrats who feared—with a few notable exceptions like Wilbur Mills of Arkansas, the chairman of the House Ways and Means Committee—another "revolution" in their region to rival that already set off by civil rights laws and court decisions.

Thus died what Nixon called in *RN* "an idea ahead of its time." It was surely that, and a great opportunity missed as well, one that has yet to appear again as a liberal idea from a conservative leader: an opportunity literally to put a federal floor under income in America. FAP, wrote John Osborne of the *New Republic,* was "the best in domestic planning and policy that we have had from the Nixon Administration."[45]

If the Family Assistance Plan would not actually have "eliminated" poverty, as so many liberals argued, it's fair to ask: What would have? And what, in the realm of the politically possible, would have done more to approach that unattainable goal? If FAP would have extended "welfare" to more people, as conservatives angrily charged, it's equally fair to point out that many of the additional recipients would have been blameless children given—as Nixon hoped—a new dignity and a greater chance, as well as money. What would have served the future better than that?

Richard Nathan may have been suspected of loyalism, a failing to which remarkable numbers of former Nixon aides succumb, when he extolled the creativity of the Nixon administration. But Nathan backed himself with specifics—community development grants, the Supplemental Security Income program (the only element of FAP to survive) that guaranteed income to the aged, the blind and the disabled, and a comprehensive health insurance plan—CHIP—that proposed, as early as 1971, to require employers to provide health insurance for their employees. CHIP went nowhere, and in 1988 George Bush still was denouncing the basic idea as socialistic.

To make the point that Nixon was an effective domestic reformer, before Watergate and during the period of his more celebrated achievements in foreign policy, there's little further need for discussion of his lengthy record—though Nathan's list and the foregoing chapter are by no means comprehensive. Either could have cited, for example, the establishment of the Occupational Safety and Health Administration—pleasing George Meany and organized labor but soon a red flag to conservatives. OSHA answered a real need of American workers, however clumsily in some cases—a fact that outweighs Nixon's probable *political* motive of attracting blue-collar voters to the Republican party.

Daniel Patrick Moynihan, nearly two decades later and approaching his third election as a Democratic senator from New York, still was proud to have served in a Republican administration he considered "the most progressive" of any administration of the postwar era. In support of that extravagant judgment, Moynihan ticked off on his fingers the Family Assistance Plan, school desegregation, Nixon's environmental record and his improvements in, and expansion of, efforts to feed the hungry—the uniform application, for example, of the food stamp program in all fifty states and the expansion of the program from $340 million in 1969 to $610 million in 1970.[46]

In 1989, Thomas S. Foley of Washington, then about to replace Jim Wright as the Democratic Speaker of the House, remarked of his many years on the House Agriculture Committee: "The Nixon Administration was most important in advancing the anti-hunger fight in America. You get in trouble if you say a good word about Richard Nixon in Democratic circles but that's the truth."[47]

Like Nathan, Moynihan could have gone on—to pension reform, as well as more funds than ever before for the arts and humanities, abolition of the military draft in favor of the volunteer army we still have, and the renunciation, in 1969 and 1970, of biological and toxic warfare and weapons programs. Even the rudiments of what had been and still is anathema to most American businessmen, Republicans and conservatives: federal planning.

Nixon actually committed himself to a national growth policy—the first president to do so. He established a National Goals Research Staff and advocated a national land-use policy. Within Ehrlichman's domestic policy staff, "planning" on a less institutional basis was standard practice; a "forecast" team, looking ahead to problems and opportunities in the future, functioned regularly. At one point, Ehrlichman even had a group of aides working on a "ten-year plan" for guiding domestic developments—until Nixon heard about it.

"Don't they know I go out of office after eight years?" he complained.

That was the end of the ten-year idea but other forms of planning continued within a White House staff that Ehrlichman believes was better organized for that purpose than any before or since.[48]

Whatever else Nixon was, or may be considered, he was *not* a do-nothing or a turn-back-the-clock president in national affairs. Nor, as we have seen, was he guilty of the frequent charge of indifference to domestic policy. In a tribute to Nixon long after his presidential years, Leonard Garment remarked that this charge was "part animus, part ignorance and pure silliness . . . Like breathing, domestic policy is a central part of the presidential life."[49]

Even the Great Society that Nixon had deprecated remained largely intact, none of its major programs perishing in the Nixon years. This may have been reelection strategy, something in which all presidents indulge, some too heartily. As William Greider, one of the more astute observers of Washington's vagaries, has suggested, Nixon

> let the federal gravy pour and took full credit for it until after his re-election in 1972. Then, safe from the voters, he set about trying to turn off the federal spigots. Too late. Watergate intervened, and we shall never know whether Nixon would have prevailed. . . .[50]

As has been repeatedly suggested, moreover, Nixon usually was a *reluctant* reformer; much accomplished in his administration actually was initiated by his staff or in Congress, or forced by public opinion and the courts. To some extent—as with his real and symbolic olive branches to Southern segregationists, on the way to school desegregation in 1970, and his mixed response to environmental pressures—he set back as well as advanced the causes with which he had to deal.

He was, for example, the president to whom fell the privilege of welcoming the Apollo astronauts home from the first landing on the moon. But he was also the president who set in motion the long decline of the American space program. Under budgetary pressures from his new Office of Management and Budget, Nixon rejected proposed programs for a permanent space station and for a manned exploration of Mars; lack of funds then forced the space agency to cancel subsequent moon landings and abandon the huge Saturn rocket.

Even the space shuttle, which was left to become the centerpiece of the American effort, was underfunded; and the board of presidential science advisers was disbanded. None of the presidents who succeeded Nixon gave much more support to an active space program, but—after the technological triumph of Apollo and the moon landing—the judgment of Jerome Wiesner (formerly President Kennedy's science adviser) seems warranted: Nixon "killed a very important part of the brains of the U.S. government."[51]

But when Nixon's hand was forced legally, as in school desegregation, or politically, as on the environmental issue, or when his interest was aroused, he was a shrewd and effective politician, maneuvering ably toward necessary ends that he had not always chosen for himself, seeking usually the possible rather than the perfect.

Nixon actually had a certain definable domestic vision, a commodity not every president has brought to the White House: he wanted, and to some extent achieved, a government doing what needed to be done for the welfare of the nation, but doing it with a diminished concentration of power in Washington. Though he was not necessarily eager for change or reform, in domestic affairs he was open to persuasion, to public opinion, to political opportunity, to valid pressures—more than most presidents before or since.

This strange and reclusive figure, cynical as he certainly was, darkened by ancient hurts and corrosive ambition, forever on his guard against a threatening world, was not personally an activist or a progressive *man;* but—vastly more significant—in his first term he was both an activist and a progressive *president,* mostly because he had to be.

The element of political compulsion is not to be despised; the American people may want more from the White House than Nixon the man ever promised, but they usually get considerably less than Nixon the president delivered.

13

★

Keynesian

★

[Nixon] was impatient with the dull, pedes-
trian and painful economics of conventional
conservatism. He called that the economics
of three yards in a cloud of dust, whereas he
yearned for the long bomb.

—Herbert Stein

President Nixon usually assigned the drafting of economic speeches to
William Safire—not because Safire was an expert on the subject but because
he wasn't; Safire had not even studied economics in college. Nixon's sound
assumption was that a nonexpert could write a clearer explanation of
presidential economics than anyone deeply versed in "the dismal science."

On Thursday, August 12, 1971, Safire was alerted to keep his weekend
free; and the next morning he was told to pack a bag and report to a White
House helicopter pad. He and Herbert Stein, a member of the Council of
Economic Advisers, shared a car to the pad, on their way to an unknown
ultimate destination—unknown, at least, to Safire.

Stein knew more. "This could be the most important weekend in the
history of economics since March 4, 1933," he confided.

"We closing the banks?" Safire asked.

Stein, a wit to match the speech writer, chuckled at this irreverence:
"Hardly. But I would not be surprised if the President were to close the
gold window."

Safire had no idea what the gold window was. On the helicopter, however, when a man from Treasury asked him what was going on, Safire
repeated Stein's remark. The Treasury man "leaned forward, put his face
in his hands, and whispered, 'My God!' "[1]

It's well known that on August 15, 1971, President Richard Nixon placed the American economy under wage and price controls—the first president to do in peacetime what no Democratic liberal, much less a Republican, ever had come close to doing except in war. Here was a long bomb indeed—government controls on the economy from a supposedly conservative president who had learned to dislike and distrust such controls during brief, low-level World War II service in the Office of Price Administration.

It may not be so well remembered that on that same August 15, Nixon took an even more radical step: he "suspended" the convertibility of the dollar into gold, leaving the dollar and the rest of the world's currencies to be valued against each other—supposedly only temporarily—rather than against the fixed price of the gold in American vaults.

So on that August 13—Friday the 13th—Safire, Stein, the shocked Treasury man and the highest economic officials of the administration were on their way to Camp David, the presidential retreat in Maryland. Two notable absences might have been remarked upon:

No one, from the secretary on down, had been invited from the Department of State; nor had Henry Kissinger, the ubiquitous White House national security adviser. Economics was neither Kissinger's passion nor his strength: of more than one hundred forty policy reviews completed on his order in the first three years of the Nixon administration, only one dealt with international monetary policy. Nixon's distaste for the "fudge factory" overrode the plain fact that the State Department had a strong interest in—perhaps even some wisdom to contribute to—the international economic situation.

That remarkable weekend—even the understated Stein considered it "one of the most exciting and dramatic events in the history of economic policy"—was something like an "economic summit," out of which came the "New Economic Policy" announced in the president's speech of August 15, 1971. (That Lenin once had proclaimed a New Economic Policy was an irony that escaped Nixon's men until Safire discovered it too late for a change.)[2]

His own NEP momentarily slaked Nixon's thirst for bold gestures and startling announcements. It also produced two of the most adventurous, even radical actions of Nixon's tenure. Yet the new policies did not consist of impulsive gestures or wild gambles; they were the calculated actions of generally conservative men—George Shultz, Stein, Paul Volcker (then undersecretary of the treasury for monetary affairs) and Nixon himself—taking what they saw as logical and necessary, if not welcome, next steps in a long battle against inflation and a deteriorating American economic position in the world.

Of those involved in the summit decisions, only Secretary of the Treasury John B. Connally might have been considered reckless—or at least not fundamentally hostile to controls. Connally in 1971 still was nominally a Democrat, the former protégé and Texas political retainer of Lyndon Johnson. Though sharing Nixon's predilection for dramatic action, Connally was not in *favor* of controls so much as indifferent to economic ideology *opposing* them; he liked to echo an old Johnson story: "I can play it round or I can play it flat; just tell me how to play it."[3]

In 1968, Nixon had hoped until the last weekend of the presidential election that Connally would support him instead of Humphrey (see chapter 9). Subsequently he appointed Connally as a member of the Ash commission, which recommended upgrading the Budget Bureau into the Office of Management and Budget—a major administrative reform Nixon carried out with little fanfare. Connally impressed Nixon with his work on the commission and his eloquent defense of its conclusions; and the president then named him to the Foreign Intelligence Advisory Board, one of Washington's lesser-known but more prestigious bodies.

When in December 1970 the resignation of David Kennedy gave Nixon a chance to bring Connally into the cabinet as secretary of the treasury, the president jumped at it. He still wanted a "top Democrat" to give him more "stroke" with the Democrats commanding Congress; and anyway, Republican Senator John Tower of Texas wanted Connally, a potential opponent for 1972, taken out of state politics. As a member of the cabinet, moreover, Connally surely would help Nixon carry Texas in a reelection campaign. But there were even stronger *personal* reasons for the appointment.

Nixon inordinately admired the handsome, articulate and decisive Connally, in much the same way that Eisenhower, a decade earlier, somehow had seen greatness where few others could in another Texas Democrat, whom *he* appointed secretary of the treasury—Robert Anderson. A self-made Orthogonian like Nixon, Connally exemplified power, toughness, capability, in the way Nixon aspired to do but never quite believed he did. Connally was physically attractive, too, another quality Nixon may have envied. John Connally, it's not too much to say, was a sort of *beau idéal* for the basically insecure man who had made himself—mostly by indomitable will—president of the United States.

"Only three men in America understand the use of power," Nixon told Arthur Burns. "I do. John Connally does. And I guess Nelson [Rockefeller] does."[4]

Such a remark seems self-reassuring rather than self-assured, but it accurately reflected Nixon's opinion of Connally. It's not surprising, therefore, that as Eisenhower had tried to promote Robert Anderson (instead of Dick Nixon) to be his successor in the White House, Nixon also sought in various ways to make John Connally (instead of Spiro Agnew) the next president, even before the Texan became formally a Republican.

"Every Cabinet should have at least one potential President in it," Nixon believed (an ironic notion in the light of his dismay at Eisenhower's offer to demote Vice President Richard Nixon to the cabinet after 1956). Connally would be the one in the Nixon cabinet; and he himself may have accepted the Treasury appointment and the party switch it implied in the hope of replacing Agnew on the Nixon ticket in 1972. Nixon probably encouraged him in that hope.[4]

Primarily because neither a Republican convention nor a Democratic Congress was likely to accept an apostate Democrat for the vice presidency, Nixon was no more successful in setting Connally up to be president than Eisenhower had been with Anderson. But owing to Nixon's admiration, as well as his own self-confident forcefulness, Connally promptly became the leading member of the Nixon cabinet as well as the administration's most decisive voice in economic policy.

Connally found a major problem on his desk when he took over the Treasury Department—and "took over" is the right expression for his advent. Before he joined the cabinet, for instance, the so-called Troika— the secretary of the treasury, the director of the budget, and the chairman of the Council of Economic Advisers—met regularly to discuss administration economic policy over breakfast. Paul McCracken, the council chairman, acted as host at the Cosmos Club, of which he was a member. When Connally arrived, he immediately and unasked "took over" as host; thereafter the Troika's breakfast meetings were held in the secretary's private dining room at the Treasury.[5]

Even Connally, however, could not by forcefulness alone deal with that major problem he found awaiting him—the imbalance of American payments, which threatened to result in a potentially disastrous outflow of gold. The nation was spending more abroad—for imports, for instance, in foreign aid, and especially for the defense of Europe, Japan and Korea— than it was earning from exports and foreign investments. Other nations were accumulating large sums of dollars that—under the international financial system in force since World War II—the U.S. was pledged to redeem on demand *in gold* at thirty-five dollars an ounce.

This pledge was the guarantee of stability in international trade and finance; the dollar was backed by gold, and most other currencies were backed by the dollar. By 1971, however, the U.S. had nowhere near enough gold at Fort Knox to redeem all the world's dollars at that price; and the supply it did have—$18 billion against about $36 billion in potential dollar claims abroad—was shrinking, as occasional redemptions were demanded.

In May 1971, the dollar's appearance of soundness had been shaken by a rush of money into West German marks and other European currencies, driven by higher interest rates abroad and by the widespread belief that a long series of deficits in the American balance of payments had weakened the dollar in fact if not in policy. Whistling bravely past the graveyard, American officials continued to insist that the dollar was as strong as ever—although gradually rising inflation and the war in Vietnam had *increased* the payments deficit.

Thus, the international financial system rested on a shaky basis that was getting shakier: in order not to cause "a run on the bank," other nations tacitly agreed not to demand American gold for their dollars, although they no longer trusted the dollar and held more of them than they wanted; but no one could be sure that some other nation, or others, might not go to the American "gold window" and start a run, or even draw out *all* the gold. In effect, the dollars foreign nations held were backed mostly by trust in each other—a weak reed to lean on in the financial world—rather than by an adequate American supply of gold at thirty-five dollars an ounce, or even by a universally trusted dollar.

If the U.S. withdrew its backing for the world's currencies by refusing to redeem dollars in gold, not only would the dollar itself decline in value but all currencies, the dollar included, would "float"—that is, their value would be determined by supply and demand in the market, and against the value of other currencies. This would suit free marketeers—a description more or less fitting most of the Nixon economists—who thought currency values *should* be determined in the market, and who believed that fixed exchange rates caused undesirable interference with trade and capital movements.

But to devalue the dollar would be to raise the price of imports—which would be inflationary. American exports would be stimulated, of course, but to the disadvantage of competitors—particularly in agriculture. All that might help the balance of payments, but the end of gold convertibility would suggest to the world that the U.S. was not really fighting inflation, had little concern for price stability and had failed in its "great power" obligation to stabilize currencies and trade throughout the world.

Besides, the dollar backed by gold was a shibboleth of business and political conservatism; conventional wisdom held that the necessity to maintain fixed exchange rates forced governments to avoid inflationary policies and to watch expenditures. For the U.S. to abandon gold convertibility had long been considered unthinkable.

By 1970, however, the U.S. was taxing interest Americans earned abroad, in order to limit the outflow of overvalued dollars into foreign investments. A cap on lending to foreigners by American banks also had been imposed; both were efforts to support the fixed exchange rate forced by gold convertibility. Businessmen thus found *themselves,* not just the government, paying to support a fixed exchange rate—which, businessmen being businessmen, Herbert Stein reflected, "did much to convince the conventional conservatives of the virtue of free exchange rates."[6]

Numerous American industries, moreover, were greatly disturbed about rising competition from Japan, with which in 1971 the U.S. already was running a trade deficit not helped by the strong dollar. Import quotas were being talked about; but to free marketeers in and out of the government, allowing the value of the dollar to decline against the yen was preferable to protectionism. That meant, finally, refusing to redeem dollars in gold.

A floating and devalued dollar was no more expected from the Nixon administration—a Republican administration—than wage and price controls on the American economy. In the beginning, moreover, little had suggested that Nixon's domestic economic policy ever would have to confront the question. When he was inaugurated on January 20, 1969, the inflation rate was 5.5 percent and unemployment stood at only 3.3 percent.

Twenty years later, in view of hard intervening experience, those statistics might seem to suggest something near the best of all possible worlds; but at the time, for Richard Nixon and his economists they meant something else. These numbers conveyed to the world no *appearance* of economic crisis demanding strong action by a new president; yet, inflation was too high for comfort, and the wage-and-price trend looked ominously upward. Something would have to be done *even if* no public demand for action existed—every politician's nightmare—and even if the Democratic Congress, still in the lingering grip of a Great Society mood, wanted *less* unemployment and *more* government spending.

The new president, who did not consider himself an expert in economics, was not champing at the bit to turn back inflation; his experience of recession as the perceived cause of his defeat in the 1960 presidential campaign had been too traumatic. After that, Nixon had gone to see William McChesney Martin, the chairman of the Federal Reserve, and blamed Martin to his face for the tight-money policies that Nixon believed greatly responsible for his loss to Kennedy.[7]

Consequently, as he took office, Nixon had set his sights on high employment rather than price stability; that was not only a personal preference resulting from 1960 but a political judgment, probably correct, about what the American people preferred. This attitude, moreover, was the major element in Nixon's basic economic policy—a field in which he believed the public was little interested, except in hard times, and unsophisticated. Dour Republican economic conservatism based on a balanced budget and low inflation was not, in his view, a winning position; he saw no "mileage" in it.

Nor was Nixon, in the traditional Republican manner, in league with big business. Its leaders in 1964 and 1968 plainly had preferred Scranton or

Rockefeller for president, and Nixon—with his considerable capacity for holding a grudge—had not forgotten that they had not welcomed him to New York in 1963. He respected Wall Street's power but was prepared to get along without its favor—relying, instead, on his sense of his high standing on Main Street. Business leaders who wanted to raise federal revenue by, say, eliminating the home mortgage tax deduction, or to hold prices down by inducing unemployment among ordinary Americans—the people Nixon considered his constituency—found no warm welcome in his White House.

Still, Nixon was a Republican, dependent to some extent upon his party and obliged, to that extent, to observe its canons. Perhaps more important, he remembered grimly the disillusionments of his months with the Office of Price Administration in World War II. If John Connally was not set by economic ideology *against* controls, Richard Nixon certainly was not disposed to be *for* such unfair and inefficient interference—in his view—in wages and prices.

Because of the pragmatism the two men shared, however, as well as their twin predilections for the startling leap, controls were always, for Nixon and Connally, at least on the outer rim of possibility. But at the beginning of his administration, Nixon was not even prepared to accept, though he did not rule out, an "incomes policy"—some governmental effort, far short of mandatory controls, to achieve a moderating effect on private wage-and-price decisions affecting the entire economy.

As his new administration settled down to work, Nixon found, in practice, little room for budget cutting that he thought either a Democratic Congress or the public would support. He certainly did not want to raise taxes. Nevertheless, his economic advisers—at that point, principally McCracken and Stein—insisted on sufficient fiscal and monetary restraint to bring inflation down from 5.5 percent, then considered excessive. They assured the president that this could be done without driving unemployment much above 4 percent.

So the first Nixon budget was balanced—the last balanced budget the nation has had—by *continuing* the Vietnam-forced income tax surcharge Johnson and Congress reluctantly had agreed on in June 1968. The Federal Reserve (where Nixon's supposed nemesis, William McChesney Martin, still reigned) also was urged to restrain the money supply throughout 1969. After that, the administration supposed, inflation would have declined enough so that some expansion of the economy could be permitted.

But "gradualism"—McCracken's term—didn't quite work; the best-laid economic plans often don't. Chairman Martin, at the Fed, kept an even tighter lid on money growth than the administration had wanted; but neither that nor the gradual rise in unemployment from the 3.3 percent of January 1969 had the expected effect of reducing inflation. For the first time, the nation was experiencing "stagflation"—rising unemployment *and* inflation.

Two overall reasons suggest themselves. By 1969, long-term union contracts and corporate power had intervened in the functions of the market; all prices no longer rose and fell according to supply and demand. Many, in John Kenneth Galbraith's description, were "administered"; wages, moreover, went up regularly because of annual contractual increases and cost of living adjustments. These rising wages pulled prices after them.

The other reason probably was an influx of young people and women into an expanding work force. To have the expected effect on inflation, unemployment therefore would have to rise *above* the 4 percent or so that administration economists had calculated as the level that would do the job. But Nixon did not want the jobless rate driven so high; and he feared, anyway, that in 1970 the distrusted Martin's tight-money policy once again, as in 1960, would force a recession. Nineteen-seventy was, of course, an election year in which the president hoped to win stronger Republican representation in Congress.

"Stagflation" predictably increased calls from congressional Democrats, from the general public and even from many businessmen for an "incomes policy"—a moderating government influence on private price and wage decisions. "Jawboning," or speaking out against increases, had been the Johnson administration's concession to incomes policy. Nixon's advisers counseled him against this un-Republican practice—who was the government to lecture to business?—and insisted that jawboning was ineffective anyway.

But close to Nixon's ear, and frequently heard in public, was one prominent voice offering an exception—that of Arthur Burns. In early 1970, Nixon happily sent Burns to replace Martin as chairman of the Fed (also putting, as we have seen, an end to the Moynihan-Burns tug-of-war in the White House). Burns's open advocacy of an incomes policy was bound to have an effect on Nixon, however the president reacted publicly; it had been Arthur Burns, after all, who had offered the pump-priming economic advice in 1959 that, had Eisenhower and George Humphrey listened, might have saved Nixon from defeat in 1960—so Nixon believed, anyway.

Burns was out of step with most of Nixon's advisers because, like Galbraith but for different reasons, he had come to the conclusion that the revered laws of economics were no longer functioning as they were supposed to; wages and prices were no longer simple functions of the market. In a memo to Nixon, Burns elaborated what he thought were the reasons: the assumptions of labor and business, for instance, that the government would always act to stimulate a sluggish economy; the unions' belief that their demands could not be resisted; a weakening of the power of union leaders over their rank and file, which lessened the leaders' ability to negotiate moderate wage settlements.

Burns also cited a general fear of inflation that caused labor to seek higher wages and businessmen higher prices, whether or not the market made them necessary. Consumers, similarly fearful, offered less resistance to price increases, believing worse was sure to come; and borrowing had increased on the expectation that loans could be repaid in cheaper—inflated—dollars.

All this led Burns to suggest to Nixon that "We thus face an entirely new economic problem—one that our nation has never before had to face: namely, an inflation feeding on itself at a time of substantial unemployment.[8]

Paul McCracken had arrived at a similar idea at about the same time. The nation, he told Nixon, was in "a situation where the price-cost level is rising because the price-cost level is rising."[9]

These memos were not written until June 1971; but by 1970, the economy had slowed to a point that everyone except the White House called "recession." Nixon's economists, who had expected an upturn in 1970, had to push back their predictions—not once but several times. Maddeningly, inflation did not decline either. Demands for an incomes policy became louder and more frequent, including those of Arthur Burns.

Acting on his own apprehensions, Burns as Fed chairman eased the money supply in 1970 and 1971, but not enough to generate an expansion. Stagflation persisted; in mid-1970, unemployment topped 5 percent and the inflation rate remained at about the same level. And this situation *seemed* worse than it was—perhaps even to Nixon—because of the administration's confident early predictions of a stable expansion after a small rise in unemployment.

The clamor for an incomes policy, remarkably, reached its height in the business community. With inflation unconquered, businessmen faced strong wage demands from unions; but owing to the recession, they feared passing increased wage costs to consumers, as they had been accustomed to doing. In the time-honored way of American capitalists under pressure, they forgot ideology and turned to the government for help, demanding some policy to hold down wages, though most understood that it would have to include downward pressure on prices, too.

In June 1970, with the fall elections in mind, Nixon appeared to yield. He announced creation of a National Commission on Productivity, a labor-management forum to which no one could object, and a board to review government practices that might be raising prices and costs. His Council of Economic Advisers also was instructed to issue "inflation alerts"—a disguised form of jawboning.

None of this had much effect economically, nor had much been expected; Nixon had tried to throw a political bone to his critics. But because the president had done *something,* he was accused immediately and loudly of not having done enough. As such half-measures often do, these had backfired, consequently unlatching the door to a *real* incomes policy.

Meanwhile, as unemployment rose, so did the federal deficit picture— owing to declining revenues and increased benefits for the jobless. But in a recession, it made no economic sense either to raise taxes or to cut expenditures. A proposed solution came from George Shultz—who had risen high in Nixon's estimate because of the Philadelphia Plan, his leadership in school desegregation and his general common sense, and who therefore had been promoted to director of the Office of Management and Budget in mid-1970.

Shultz persuaded Nixon to present for fiscal year 1972 a "full-employment budget," a Keynesian concept then familiar mostly to economists but never *openly* adopted by a president—though several had tacitly accepted the idea. A full-employment budget would have been in balance had the economy been operating at a peak, with employment and federal revenues at the maximum; its actual deficit of spending over income thus represented the difference between *current* employment and *full* employment, and was calculated to stimulate the economy by precisely that amount—a stimulus seemingly determined "scientifically," or at least by a well-defined rule.

"By [government] spending as if we were *at* full employment," Nixon announced in his State of the Union message in January 1971, "we will help to *bring about* full employment."

Nixon was the first president so frankly to embrace the full-employment concept. Later, in an interview with Howard K. Smith of ABC news, he went so far as to assert that "now I am a Keynesian." He had nevertheless promised too much for his full-employment budget, perhaps because he was proud that in its adoption he finally had thrown something of a "long bomb."

Whatever its origins, liberals and congressional Democrats—conditioned by the expansionist Kennedy-Johnson years—in 1971 saw *Nixon's* full-employment budget rule as a *conservative* exercise, one that placed a ceiling on expansionary policy. But conservatives and businessmen scoffed because *they* saw institutionalized deficit spending, rather than such a ceiling, and because a budget "balanced" with revenues that did not exist appeared to them to deny conventional budget-balancing theology. Besides, a "Keynesian" Republican president was an electric shock to the GOP faithful.

Worse, the full-employment budget did not deliver the goods. As 1971 advanced toward 1972, unemployment continued in the 5 to 6 percent range and the inflation rate fluctuated indecisively. Even a further plunge by Nixon into incomes policy—in the same month as his proclamation of the full-employment budget—seemed to make little difference.

That January, Nixon rolled back a 50 percent steel price increase that probably had been set high enough to take into account presidential resistance the steel companies had anticipated. Nixon then took the far bolder political step of suspending the Davis-Bacon Act, beloved of organized labor; it required the federal government to pay union wages on federal construction projects. Coming on top of the Philadelphia Plan, the suspension of Davis-Bacon made it all the more remarkable that the hard-hat unions most affected nevertheless strongly supported Richard Nixon on the war in Vietnam and in his collisions with the peace movement.

Underneath all this "action," Nixon and his economists still believed, at least hoped, that their original policy of "gradualism"—gradual restraint of demand—ultimately would bring down inflation without ruinous unemployment. Given enough time, they might have been proven right; but by comparison to the Kennedy-Johnson years, the overall Nixon economic record seemed stodgy, unimaginative—not even three yards gained in the cloud of dust—if not a demonstrable failure. The quest for reelection also began to weigh ever more heavily on the president.

In June 1971, in the memoranda previously quoted, both Arthur Burns and Paul McCracken, in effect, sounded a death knell for gradualism (which Burns never had expected to work): "Finally, and I say this with no joy," McCracken wrote, "we must be prepared at a suitable time to use the ultimate weapons of wage and price control."

Burns was more specific:

> Our monetary and fiscal policies have not been working as expected; they have not broken the back of inflation, nor are they stimulating economic activity as expected. . . . I recommend . . . emphatic and pointed jawboning, followed by a wage and price review board . . . and in the event of insufficient success (which is now more probable than it would have been a year or two ago), followed—perhaps no later than next January [1972]—by a six-month wage and price freeze.

That summer of 1971, twelve Republican senators joined to introduce legislation that would establish a wage-price board. Public opinion polls showed strong national support for a more active economic policy. And two important events already had sped Nixon down the slippery slope toward more radical action:

In August 1970, after much oratory denouncing stagflation, Congress had enacted legislation empowering the president to impose comprehensive wage and price controls. The Democrats in control did not urge Nixon to do it and hardly expected that a Republican president would; they only wanted to put the monkey squarely on Nixon's back. They could, and did, say that they had handed him the necessary tools to manage the economy; depending on what he did, they could add either that he had refused to use those tools, or had used them unwisely and ineffectively.

Then, in December 1970, the charismatic Connally had accepted Nixon's offer to make him secretary of the treasury. To that office Connally brought Texas-sized self-confidence, a strong influence on the president, an indifference to economic orthodoxy and—perhaps most important—a liking for the long bomb that matched Richard Nixon's.

"Closing the gold window," as we have seen, was no longer unthinkable—though still a shocking idea—as the Nixon economic officials gathered at Camp David on August 13, 1971. And though few observers expected wage and price controls from a group supposedly so conservative, the case for them could be argued with much persuasiveness.

In the summer of 1971, the economy was not expanding, as the Nixon administration repeatedly had promised it would—which made the actual economic situation look worse than it really was. Inflation continued, with food prices rising rapidly. As a result, Republicans in Congress were worried about running in 1972, and were urging the White House to stronger economic action. So were businessmen who wanted help against union wage demands. The news media echoed these forces, and provided a forum for liberals and congressional Democrats to point out that the president had the power to impose controls if that were the necessary medicine.

Everything seemed to point in that direction. On the other side, few administration economists or Republicans or businessmen had so strongly opposed incomes policy that they had been able to stop Nixon's ventures into it. In effect, the forceful free market position that might have been expected from a Republican administration had been undermined, even by the administration itself. Such a position could no longer be offered as a plausible alternative to the "stronger action" that, as was more apparent every day, soon would have to be taken.

Against that background, and during the week of August 9, 1971, a British official appeared at the Treasury with a fateful demand: $3 billion in gold in redemption of Britain's dollar hoard. The Briton could not have known it at the time, so closely had the secret been held, but his demand triggered a decision already made.

Several months earlier, at about the time of the sudden flow of dollars into West German marks, Connally and Nixon—yearning for the long bomb and seeing no other way out of the balance-of-payments dilemma— had made a secret resolution to suspend gold convertibility, even though

that would signal to the world that "the dollar was . . . too weak to lead."
They had determined to act when some major foreign demand for redemption would appear to force their hands. The proposed British withdrawal
was sufficient pretext.[10]

But the failure to meet obligations that would be announced by that
renunciation "would be mainly a failure of the U.S. Treasury—which
meant John Connally." So Connally had advocated that gold convertibility
be suspended only *in tandem* with a strong anti-inflationary domestic
policy that would make larger headlines in the U.S. than "closing the gold
window," and which would make the gold decision look less inflationary
and less a failure of American obligation.

Nixon readily agreed with his persuasive treasury secretary. Perhaps
also remembering the cold reception for his innovative full-employment
budget, the president had no more halfway measures in mind; if he moved,
he confided to his economists, he would "leapfrog them all . . . get out there
so far that nobody will ever be able to say I didn't do enough."

Thus did the gold decision drive a further resolution Nixon and Connally had made in the spring of 1971—to announce the suspension of gold
convertibility, if that became necessary, at the same time that they imposed
wage and price controls on the American economy."[11]

So the basic decisions had been made before anyone reached Camp
David on August 13; but many details remained to be determined. How
long would a wage-price freeze last? How would it be enforced? What
would follow? Would the dollar be allowed to float or could a new exchange rate be negotiated? Aside from such cosmic matters, when would
Nixon announce all this to the world?

He was opposed to speaking in prime time on Sunday night, August 15,
because that would preempt "Bonanza," then one of the public's—that is,
the *voters'*—favorite programs. But financial experts knew that other kinds
of bonanzas were to be made in Monday's markets by those with inside
information; and political experts realized that the slightest delay would
mean that the momentous Camp David decisions surely would leak.

"Rushing it through just to save a couple of billions in gold on Monday
does not appeal to me," Nixon huffed; but he was persuaded finally that
"Bonanza" would have to give way. He agreed to speak on Sunday before
the markets opened again.[12]

The atmosphere at Camp David was set by the tight secrecy on which
Nixon insisted, and by the high spirit of collegiality among the sixteen men
present, animated in the heady belief that they were making history. "It
was . . . more fun," William Safire observed, "than any of the men there
had ever had in their lifetimes."[13]

In these memorable circumstances, a ninety-day wage and price freeze
was decided upon, to be followed by further restraints still to be deter-

mined. And to back up the closing of the gold window, a temporary 10 percent import tax would be levied—in effect, devaluing the dollar by 10 percent.

That would *raise* about $2 billion in revenues. Since wages and prices were to be frozen, the domestic need was for economic *stimulus;* so the Kennedy administration's investment tax credit, repealed earlier, was to be reinstated with a different name. The 7 percent excise tax on automobiles also would be lifted. In obeisance to conservative demands for spending reduction, revenue sharing was delayed and a 5 percent personnel cut was planned. The New Economic Policy was a hodgepodge of conflicting and compensating devices.

Arthur Burns, though enthusiastically in support of the wage-price freeze, alone among those present opposed the closing of the gold window. Even Paul Volcker, who had spent his career in support of the fixed exchange system based on American gold, was reluctantly in favor of that once-unthinkable step.

"I hate to . . . close the window," he said in reply to Burns. "All my life I have defended exchange rates, but I think it is needed." Coming from Paul Volcker, that was stronger than Dick Nixon proclaiming himself a Keynesian.

Burns argued that all the other actions to be taken would "electrify the world," increase its confidence in American policies, and therefore stop the gold outflow; closing the window would not be necessary. If it became so, he pointed out—for instance, if there should be a run on gold—the window could be closed later. A smaller meeting—Nixon with Volcker and the "Quadriad" (the administration's economic Triad plus the chairman of the Fed)—was required to overcome Burns's dissent. After that, perhaps because he so favored the freeze, he became a "good soldier" for the entire project.[14]

Nixon took an active part in the weekend discussions, though Volcker in later years was disdainful of the president and his understanding:

> Poor old Nixon was not a deep thinker in these matters. He had no intellectual conviction about floating [currency rates]. His position was, "You tell me which rules you want to play under, fixed or floating, and I'll play it that way, but you're to make sure the best interests of the United States are taken care of."[15]

That echoes Connally's version of the LBJ round-or-flat story. It also raises a question: in such arcane matters *should* a president be an authority himself, or rest confident in the ability of his administration's experts and specialists to tell him how to protect the "best interests" of the nation? Volcker's condescension might have vanished had *he* been required also to deal with, say, school desegregation and nuclear arms control, rather than only with that single matter in which he had been engaged all his life.

At one point, Nixon gave Safire a lesson in effective speech writing. On the vexing question of whether to concede a devaluation of the dollar, Volcker wanted to insist that, instead, other currencies would be revalued *upward* in relation to the dollar—technically true but a transparent evasion. In his own hand, Nixon substituted for the relevant passage in Safire's proposed speech text:

> Let me lay to rest the bugaboo of devaluation. Will this action reduce the value of the dollar? The long term purpose and the effect of this action will be to strengthen the $—not weaken it.
> Short term—the $ will buy less.
> But for overwhelming majority who buy American products in America—your $ will be worth same tomorrow as it is today.[16]

That could be called having it both ways, and it was. It also effectively concealed, at least for the crucial first public reaction to the NEP, what could have been a topic of critical "instant analysis" on television and a rallying point for hostile armchair economists.

Arthur Burns, vindicated in his advocacy of intervention in the economy, swallowed his opposition to closing the gold window and observed that Nixon was acting like a president: "He has a noble motive in foreign affairs to reshape the world, or at least his motive is to earn the fame that comes from nobly reshaping the world. Who can say what his motive is?"[17]

This curious pronouncement poses a central question about Richard Nixon. Did he want to do great things, or only to get credit for doing them? Or perhaps the true question is whether that really matters, for Nixon or anyone, assuming the great things get done—or, if they don't, that a genuine effort has been made. Does purity of motive confer some finer quality upon achievement? If the urge to do good is really the desire for credit, or if the urge is stimulated by the desire, is the good that may be done diminished? Can that desire, or at least the *consciousness* that credit is possible, ever be separated entirely from the urge to do good? Not, it seems clear, in the case of Richard Nixon, or perhaps that of any politician; not perhaps in *any* case, the definition of motive, even one's own, being so often imprecise.

Besides, the urge to do good, however pure, does not necessarily result in good being done. At Camp David, Burns suggested that whatever Nixon's motive in formulating his NEP, at least "it's moving him in the right direction." That subjective judgment has not stood the test of time, and even as Burns was making it things were happening, or not happening, that would invalidate it.

Herbert Stein, for example, though he too was caught up in the euphoria of sweeping and historic action, realized in retrospect that there had been too little thought about how to get out of the wage-price freeze, once it was imposed; about the long-term consequences of closing the gold window; and as to how much economic stimulus was enough. No attention at all, he lamented, was paid to domestic monetary policy.

These were substantial omissions; and all would come back to haunt the president and the Camp David conferees.[18]

Nixon feared, as usual, that his bold new policies would get a bad press; but he was wrong, as he often was in that fear. The American press, though not economically sophisticated, usually does well with "big stories" that call out all its resources; and the NEP was a big story indeed. It turned out, moreover, to be one of the more popular actions of Nixon's years in office.

The Dow Jones average soared by 32.9 points the day after Nixon's speech. By every available test, most Americans greeted controls with relief and the closed gold window with indifference—even a certain chauvinistic satisfaction, since the president cannily presented it as a selfless action by reliable Uncle Sam against greedy international speculators.

The popularity of controls did not, of course, last. As the months came along, one interest after another found itself disadvantaged; one apparent inequity after another turned off various segments of the public. But declining enthusiasm for the system focused largely on its *administration;* no widespread public disillusionment with the *principle* of controls surfaced even after prices began to rise again in 1973.

This demonstrated, in Stein's clearly disappointed view, a "shallow" public commitment to "the basic characteristics of a free market economy." The popularity of controls, moreover, had unfortunate and largely unforeseen consequences, one of which was abandonment of the original plan for a short freeze.[19]

"What worries me," the president had remarked even before leaving Camp David, "is putting the economy in a straitjacket under the control of a bunch of damn bureaucrats for any length of time."

That has the ring of a former OPA underling's unforgotten experience; and his advisers felt much the same. Administration political specialists— including Nixon and Connally—were well aware, moreover, that the sudden abandonment of traditional free enterprise would not sit well with hardy conservatives.

"American fascism arrived on August 15, 1971," one Republican remarked; and with elections coming, the president did not need such discontent in his party.[20]

General public enthusiasm meant, however, that neither quick decontrol after the ninety-day freeze nor a sharp retreat to some less drastic program would be possible; if Americans generally—probably including most Republicans—felt themselves rescued by controls from the harsh judgments of the market, to abandon controls and return to the market too abruptly was to risk political disaster.

After the ninety-day freeze, Phase II—in which moderate wage and price increases were allowed by the vast bureaucracy that had been hastily assembled—only continued the public's fear that prices would explode when and if *all* controls were ended. That apprehension was justified, because prices did not decline under controls. Most ultimately *rose* to, or remained at, the ceilings imposed by the government, and were held at that level only by those ceilings—or not held at all in some cases.

That happened primarily because, with controls in place and successful at first in stabilizing prices, both the administration and the Federal Reserve concluded that room had been created for economic expansion to reduce unemployment. The predictable result was overstimulation—an error into which economic controllers usually fall. Stein provides an incongruous picture of a Republican president urging Republican cabinet officers to "get out and spend."

Worldwide crop failures, especially in the Soviet Union, put upward pressures on American food prices; and in late 1973, the Arab oil embargo began to drive up oil prices and spread inflation throughout the economy. Food and oil prices could not be capped without causing severe shortages; and once prices of these essentials rose, wages as well as other prices could not easily be prevented from rising too. Inflation had not been subdued; it was precariously capped, but ready to roar upward once the cap was removed.

Oil price increases were especially ironic; they represented one element of the NEP negating the other. They also justified Herbert Stein's uneasy sense that the consequences of closing the gold window had not been sufficiently analyzed at Camp David or before.

When OPEC raised its prices, in fact, the sheiks were making a logical and justified response to the American suspension of gold convertibility. That suspension had permitted declines in the dollar's value—and oil was traded throughout the world in dollars. As the real value of the dollar declined, therefore, so did the real revenues from the oil producers' product.

Six months after the Nixon administration permanently abandoned the gold guarantee it supposedly had only "suspended" at Camp David, the OPEC nations, in the fall of 1973, quadrupled their prices—regaining what they had lost, plus adding a little something extra to guard against future dollar declines. Chickens from that August weekend in Camp David had come rapidly home to roost, first in long lines waiting for higher-priced gasoline, ultimately throughout the nation's economy.

In 1973, under Phase II regulation, the effectiveness of controls began to waver and decline. Even after his reelection, Nixon was restive at creeping price increases (and at the same time was feeling the increasing heat of the Watergate controversy). In those uncomfortable circumstances, he began to look back nostalgically at the happy times of the early wage-price freeze, and its enthusiastic public support; but he could find no backing among his economists for another freeze—not even from Connally, who by then had departed the administration but who finally had turned Republican and who came back from time to time to discuss economic and political matters with the president.

When Nixon raised the second-freeze question with Herbert Stein, who had become chairman of the Council of Economic Advisers, Stein replied with a proverb: "You cannot step into the same river twice."

But in what Stein considered "the best joke I ever heard him make," Nixon topped him: "You can if it's frozen."[21]

Ultimately, in June 1973, in search of another gain that might help counteract Watergate—certainly not because of any economic advice he received—Nixon did impose a second wage-price freeze. But since it was primarily an effort to cap rising farm and food prices, it had little chance to succeed; and it was hastened to its predictable demise by television pictures of baby chicks and calves being slaughtered by farmers who could no longer afford to feed them.

The second freeze was quickly lifted, and the entire control program came to an end in April 1974—after two and a half years instead of the expected ninety days plus a phaseout. Congressional authority for controls expired and Nixon, by then fighting for his political life against the Watergate charges, did not seek renewal. There was little public outcry at the death of a system widely seen by then as exhausted and ineffective. Just over three months later, Nixon's presidency itself came to an end.

The end of controls—not with a bang but a whimper—had little to do with his resignation; but had the New Economic Policy maintained its early success it conceivably could have saved him by making the nation so prosperous that his impeachment would have been politically impossible. As it was, however, from mid-1971 to the end of 1974, inflation rose at an average annual rate of 6.6 percent, well above the rate of increase in the precontrol years; and after all controls were lifted in 1974, inflation quickly jumped into double digits.

Things might have been worse *without* controls, but that can't be established; and, as Herbert Stein observed years later, though imposing wage and price controls proved to be a mistake, it was a mistake "shared and welcomed" by many people, including some of Nixon's strongest opponents.

Nixon's own judgment in *RN*, long after the fact, was straightforward but not quite satisfying: "I believe that [using controls] was wrong . . . there

was an unquestionably high price for tampering with the orthodox economic mechanisms." Tampering hardly seems an apt description of all that
happened at Camp David.

Nixon thought "the best thing that came out of" that memorable August weekend was the closing of the gold window, though he offered no
evidence for his belief. In fact, "an unquestionably high price" was paid
for that decision, too, and not just by Americans.

Nixon and Connally decided on closing the gold window *and* imposing
wage and price controls. It's not clear, however, that the idea of linking
these steps was their own, or either's.

At about the same time, Paul Volcker was chairing a Treasury Department group in which the same linkage was under discussion. Domestic
controls were viewed in the Volcker group as a way to demonstrate that
the suspension of gold convertibility—if that ever had to happen—would
not mean the U.S. was courting inflation. Connally and Nixon may well
have derived their secret plan from the deliberations of the Volcker
group—without informing Volcker.

At Camp David, and in Nixon's speech to the nation on August 15,
1971, the reference always was to a "suspension" of gold convertibility, to
emphasize that this was a temporary expedient. Paul Volcker certainly
believed—at least hoped—it was.

"We had to have a breathing space," he said later, "but I looked hopefully for a reconstruction of the orderly system." That is, Volcker wanted
to return as soon as possible to a fixed exchange rate based on the dollar.
"I didn't think floating was a good policy. . . . I was concerned as an
economist about it because [floating] conveniently removes the need for
internal economic discipline to protect the external value of the currency."[22]

Immediately after the momentous Camp David weekend, Volcker took
off for the financial capitals of the world, not just to explain the administration's actions and reassure those upset by them, but to begin the process
of restoring the dollar's fixed value as the currency against which all others
would be measured.

Over the next two years he labored in vain for a "reconstruction of the
orderly system." But foreign governments did not want to return to a
dollar standard, because a highly valued dollar had enabled American
investors to buy up many foreign businesses and take heavy advantage of
foreign labor and material; some foreign governments, moreover, already
were saddled with bigger dollar balances than they wanted.

In December 1971, owing to the failure to renegotiate a fixed exchange
rate, the Nixon administration was forced to devalue the dollar again, by
7.9 percent. In early 1973, with worldwide turmoil continuing in trade and
currency, the administration was forced to do it again, this time by 11

percent. In March of that year, the pretense of a "suspension" was abandoned; the gold window was not only closed but nailed down for good; fixed exchange ratios among the major currencies were permanently abandoned. All, in future, would have to find their value in the marketplace.

A few months later, OPEC quadrupled its prices, as we have seen. For developing nations dependent on imported oil, the problem was particularly acute, and a peculiarly circular system developed: banks in the U.S. and Europe accepted enormous "petrodollar" deposits from the OPEC nations, to which vastly increased oil revenues were pouring in; then these banks lent dollars to nations that, without such loans, could not pay OPEC prices for the imported oil on which their economies depended.

Thus, OPEC dollars were lent to countries that immediately returned them to OPEC in the form of payments for OPEC oil, after which the process started again. How were the original loans to be repaid to the banks by the developing nations? Here was a major source of the continuing "Third World debt problem" with which international organizations, banks and nations—including the U.S. and its commercial institutions—still are wrestling today.

To the extent that closing the gold window was part of an effort to correct the American imbalance of payments, it proved self-defeating. Third World economies, particularly in Latin America, have been forced by international institutions into austerity measures as the price of further loans to enable them to pay interest on foreign indebtedness (most are able only marginally to repay principal). These economies have little to spare for imports from the U.S.—a significant cause of the persisting American trade deficit.

The postwar monetary system based on fixed exchange rates, moreover, had underwritten Japanese and West German recovery by undervaluing the yen and the mark against the dollar. These nations' exports thus sold at unrealistically low prices in the United States, while they accumulated dollars in exchange. Not least for that reason, Japan and West Germany recovered and prospered. They also exported more, primarily to the United States, which ultimately began paying out more dollars than it earned abroad.

By 1970, the American balance of payments was in deficit by $3 billion. In 1971, the deficit ballooned to $10 billion, and it became only a matter of time before Nixon and Connally had to act. They responded by closing the gold window, forcing an end to the system of fixed exchange rates.

Devaluation then diminished the amount of a foreign currency the dollar could buy; conversely, the number of dollars for which a unit of that currency could be exchanged *increased*. American prosperity necessarily suffered, as import prices rose, driving up inflation, and the postwar advantages of an overvalued currency were lost.

Overall, the suspension and ultimate renunciation of gold convertibility did shut off the long-threatened outflow of gold; that made possible the lifting of controls on the export of capital. Had the gold window remained open, protectionist measures against imports—Japanese imports in particular—might have been hard to resist.

But closing the window failed to reverse the payments imbalance, not least because of the continuing—into the nineties—heavy fixed costs of defending Europe, Japan and Korea. Extensive global economic dislocations resulted from the lack of discipline that the fixed value of the dollar once had provided. Floating exchange rates meant constantly shifting currency values; that, in turn, meant constantly unstable trade relations; exporters and importers, individuals and corporations, were forced to become veritable speculators, as currency values shifted in unpredictable fashion. Trade was inhibited as floating rates forced nations to develop ingenious new protectionist devices, such as marketing agreements.

As the dollar continued to decline and Nixon's controls petered out in the U.S., domestic inflation kept on climbing. As noted earlier, both the administration and the Federal Reserve overstimulated; to a considerable extent, they were deluded by the idea of controls into overestimating the capacity for noninflationary expansion in the economy. To some unknowable extent, moreover, both were almost certainly influenced by Nixon's fierce desire for reelection in 1972.

That is not surprising in the case of administration fiscal policy; rather, it would have been unusual had Nixon—with his demonstrated sensitivity to unemployment—pursued fiscal restraints as he approached reelection. He certainly didn't; government spending was increased, federal deficits grew larger, and by one economic model, fiscal stimulation in the two years before the election resulted in almost $9 billion added to gross national product.[23]

Nixon was not responsible for—he merely capitalized upon—one major stimulus: a 20 percent rise in Social Security benefits beginning one month before the election, and totaling $8 billion handed out to voters in that October alone. This federal largesse helped account for a 3.3 percent rise in 1972 in real disposable income per capita, one of the best measures of voters' economic well-being.

The powerful chairman of the House Ways and Means Committee, Wilbur Mills, forced these benefit increases through Congress in the unrealistic hope that they might propel him into the presidency. Passage wasn't difficult; few members of Congress, whatever their economic reservations, were willing in an election year to vote *against* greater Social Security benefits.

Mills's campaign, such as it was, did not survive the early Democratic primaries. And when Americans began receiving those additional Social Security benefits in October, they were accompanied by a letter that did

not mention Wilbur Mills but predictably declared that the increase resulted from "a statute signed into law by President Richard Nixon."

Considerably more surprising than Nixon's expansionary *fiscal* approach was the stimulative *monetary* policy of the Federal Reserve under
Chairman Arthur Burns—a consistent public Jeremiah on the subject of
inflation. Though Burns always denied it, sometimes angrily, and Herbert
Stein at the Hofstra conference denigrated the notion, it's hard to explain
away the empirical evidence that Burns and the Fed actively aided Nixon
in 1972.

If Nixon was to be successful in his strategy of stimulus to reduce
unemployment while capping prices with controls, the Fed would have to
provide the necessary money growth; and whatever its reasons were—
political or not—the Fed did just that. The rate of expansion of the money
supply bounded up from an average of 3.2 percent monthly in the last
quarter of 1971 to a monthly average of *11 percent* in the first quarter of
1972. Throughout the election year, money growth was about 25 percent
faster than in 1971.

The most important interest rate, the Fed's discount rate, was *lowered*
to 4.5 percent until after the election. Despite repeated pleas for restraint
from all the Federal Reserve banks and from a minority on the board of
governors, Chairman Burns held his ground throughout 1972. To all warnings of an inflationary surge in 1973, he replied that he saw no signs of
it—even when reminded that in that year the administration planned to
begin relaxing wage-price controls.

The same economic model that measured 1971–1972 fiscal stimulus at
about $9 billion was applied to monetary stimulus. The startling result
suggested that in the eight quarters of those two years the monetary policy
of Burns and his colleagues had added more than $66 billion to GNP. With
that kind of growth underpinning prosperity and his reelection effort,
Nixon scarcely needed dovish George McGovern as his Democratic opponent or the financial shenanigans of CREEP (the Committee to Re-Elect
the President) to win the landslide he did—up to that time, the biggest in
history.[24]

Burns in later years denied he had been acting politically on Nixon's
behalf, and his colleagues on the board of governors generally sustained
him. In fact, Nixon bluntly—and often—told Burns what the White House
expected of him. On December 15, 1970, for example, in an Oval Office
conversation, Nixon informed him that "domestically we should err on the
side of a too-liberal monetary policy, Arthur. We should risk some inflation."

"That's a question of degree," Burns replied.

"Err toward inflation," Nixon insisted in a "peremptory" voice.[25]

Nixon also "released" Charles Colson on Burns—so Burns told me—

with obvious intimidation in mind. Colson leaked to the press that Nixon planned to expand the board of governors to shake Burns's control of it, and to bring the Fed under the Treasury Department. Burns recognized these as empty threats but he was angered by a further Colson leak that Burns, the supposed inflation-fighter, was seeking an increase in his own salary.

This was untrue and Burns was sufficiently outraged that Nixon ultimately, at a news conference, knocked down the story himself. Years later, after Colson became a Christian evangelist, he visited Burns, confessed and claimed that Nixon himself had put him up to the false story; then Colson got down on his knees and asked for the forgiveness of Burns and God.

"He got mine," Burns told me.[26]

Also suggesting Burns's election-year complicity were comments by George Shultz, who had become one of the strongest economic voices in the administration. Sherman Maisel, then a member of the board of governors of the Fed, remembers Shultz saying that monetary policy had to supply the "real juice" for economic expansion by allowing growth far in excess of the 4.2 percent average of 1969–1970.

Shultz's "estimates of how fast money was to grow were not as precise but in various speeches and off-the-record briefings, the range of 6 to 9 percent became clear."[27]

Herbert Stein has defended the expansionary policies of 1972 as a natural response to 6 percent unemployment and denied that the approach of the election affected policy—though in his book he concedes that there was overstimulation in that period. He agreed that the Fed was hardly non-political but argued at Hofstra that the political interests it served were its own, not the president's.

Stein scoffed at the "amusing" idea of Nixon instructing Arthur Burns on monetary policy and remarked that Burns lectured Nixon "ten times as much." No doubt; Burns was incurably professorial. His position was secure enough, moreover, that he could hardly be intimidated, even by a Colson.

Yet the record of Nixon's direct and indirect approaches to the Fed chairman on the subject of monetary policy in 1971 and 1972 is well established. Burns himself told me that during his chairmanship, his experience with Nixon, a "political animal," was "not good." The president so often urged various actions on him, Burns said, that it was possible he had done some things with a "political tinge" that would have been hard to distinguish from his official responsibilities.[28]

What finally matters, of course, is that the Fed's monetary policy in late 1971 and 1972 amply accommodated Nixon's expansionary economic— and political—strategy, hence his reelection. And what matters equally is that in 1973, and later, the piper had to be paid.

With the election over, the administration turned to a more restrictive fiscal policy. The dollar continued to weaken internationally and the attempt to negotiate a fixed exchange rate collapsed. OPEC ran up oil prices, to make things worse, and inflation—averaging 8.8 percent in 1973, double the 1972 rate—finally forced the Fed to increase interest rates.

By the end of 1973, the economy was in the most severe recession since the thirties. Unemployment rose to a peak of 9.1 percent, while inflation—though it declined slowly—remained above the levels that had caused Nixon to invoke the freeze in 1971. Burns and the Fed suffered much angry criticism, particularly from Democrats aware of the economic expansion in 1972. Why, a 1975 Congressional resolution demanded to know, had the money supply risen by nearly 9 percent per year in 1972 and 1973 but by only 2 percent per year in the second half of recession-ridden 1974?

It was a good question to which there was no ready answer. And if the nation paid the piper in the recession of 1973–1975, the Republican party may have done so in 1976. Many reasons for the defeat of Gerald Ford, Nixon's appointed successor, can be adduced; surely one of them, and perhaps not the least, was the long and painful recession inexorably following the New Economic Policy.

One price control mechanism that did not die with the others in 1974 was the "immense Rube Goldberg structure . . . erected simply to deal with the problems created by unwillingness to let the prices of oil rise to a free market level." Oil price controls—one of the least admirable legacies of the Nixon administration—were continued in separate legislation owing to congressional sensitivity to consumers' needs for gasoline and heating oil, and were not to meet their deserved end until Ronald Reagan's free marketeers came to power.[29]

To describe the jerry-built "structure" would require pages, and add little to a study of Richard Nixon. It needs only to be said that because price controls existed in 1973, when OPEC imposed its astronomical increases, there were two prices of oil—one (controlled) for domestically produced oil, and a considerably higher (uncontrolled) price for imported oil. Refiners procured controlled and uncontrolled oil in different proportions and at widely differing costs, but the resulting petroleum products had to be sold to consumers at roughly the same retail price.

The consequent problem of equalizing costs to refiners led the administration into a nightmare of regulation, allocation and bureaucracy—"old oil" from existing domestic wells, for instance, remained controlled while "new oil" from new American wells rose to the import price level. Retail prices were forced lower than they would have been if freed—though a high price would have been the most effective conservation measure. The system also contributed to long and frustrating lines at gas stations, made it easier for OPEC to sell dear, and encouraged imports, thus decreasing American energy independence to a degree that never has been regained.

The oil price fiasco was a low point of the Nixon administration before Watergate, and lingered on for years afterward. Controls also complicated the problem of food prices, but with a far different result. When worldwide crop failures led to exceptionally high food prices everywhere, the increases in the U.S. threatened to undercut efforts to hold down wages. In 1972 and 1973, the administration met the problem by removing all restrictions on the production of food crops, some of which had existed since the New Deal. This venture into deregulation expanded the food supply to relieve price pressures.

The administration's only real excursion into tax reform was forced on it by the Johnson administration's late revelation that a number of millionaires and other rich Americans were paying no income taxes. Even a Republican president had to deal with the outcry that resulted, though Nixon's effort proved less than satisfactory.

He coupled a minimum-tax proposal with the repeal of the Kennedy administration's investment tax credit in such a way that *more* revenue would have been raised; but the Democratic Congress tailored this combination into a stimulative package that *reduced* tax receipts. Two years later, moreover, in his NEP, Nixon reversed himself and restored the investment tax credit.

Another innovation promised more than it delivered. In his 1968 campaign, Nixon, as shown, had made little overt appeal to blacks and other minorities, certainly not in the usual terms of civil rights laws and powerful government jobs. He *had* professed to know that blacks really wanted "a piece of the action"; so he proposed a rather vague program of "black capitalism" to help blacks get businesses started, or to push shaky black firms to success. In pursuit of this good Republican, free market approach, Nixon had set up by March 1969 the Office of Minority Business Enterprise under Secretary Maurice Stans in the Department of Commerce.

Stans claimed later that this "genuine commitment on the part of the Nixon administration" had been "one of the most worthwhile" of its accomplishments. There had been fourteen minority auto dealerships in the country in 1969, but 271 were in business by 1976; major corporation purchases from minority firms had grown from $83 million in 1968 to $8 billion in 1986, while federal government purchases from minority vendors rose from $13 million in 1969 to $9 billion in 1986.

Even Stans conceded, however, that the overall growth of the economy and the general opening of opportunity to minorities by private companies accounted for much of this improvement. The minority enterprise program is generally considered to have withered on the vine, because of a lack of funds resulting from Nixon's greater interest, in 1969, in holding down spending to fight inflation, and because of the president's failure to push the program vigorously—again, no doubt, a reflection of his lack of real personal interest.

Nixon loyalists sometimes make much of the fact that during his administration the Pentagon's proportion of the budget declined, while social spending rose. Nixon's fiscal 1974 budget, for example, proposed nearly 60 percent more for social programs than Lyndon Johnson had sought in 1968. Defense costs were less than a third of Nixon's last budget, but had been nearly half the total in the Kennedy years.[30]

The facts are undeniable and the figures are remarkable. In the Nixon years, "payments to individuals"—Social Security, Medicare and the like—rose steadily from 6.3 percent of gross national product in 1969 to 8.9 percent in 1974; expenditures for "public assistance and food," to take only one social category, increased from $6.6 billion (in 1972 dollars) in 1969 to $9.1 billion in 1974. In the same years, Pentagon spending *declined* from 9.1 percent of GNP to 5.8 percent.

Such comparisons, though true enough, are somewhat misleading. Nixon's years in office, for one thing, coincided with the "winding down" of the war in Vietnam; and however controversial his handling of it may have been, military costs dropped along with the decline of American participation in the war. Nixon consistently asked *more* for the Pentagon, while the Democrats in Congress sought more for nonmilitary programs, with the predictable result that both got less than they wanted.

During the same period, "entitlement" programs previously enacted (by Democratic Congresses during Democratic administrations) grew phenomenally, accounting for much of the rise in social spending—"payments to individuals," for example. One major component, as noted, was the increase in Social Security benefits engineered in 1972 for the political hopes of Wilbur Mills, but adroitly turned to Nixon's advantage.

The tax burden on the American people also climbed while this Republican president was in office, owing to the effect of inflation that tended to push middle- and upper-income taxpayers into higher brackets—but owing even more to a sharp increase in the most onerous of major taxes, the regressive Social Security levy on payrolls. As a percent of GNP, "social insurance contributions" rose by nearly a third, from 4.3 in 1969 to 5.4 in 1974.

For all his fears, fiscal gyrations and monetary manipulations, Nixon's five-year tenure saw a net *increase* in unemployment, from the yearly rate of 3.5 percent in 1969—a figure perhaps never to be seen again—to 5.6 percent in 1974 (before the roof fell in on Gerald Ford in 1975, at 8.5 percent). The inflation rate fluctuated, but despite all efforts averaged 8.7 percent in 1974 against 5.1 percent in 1969.

In cold numerical terms, that is hardly a successful economic record—

though we cannot know what might have happened had a different president, with different advisers and a different approach, been in office. A liberal Democrat, for only one example, might have been too politically inhibited to impose wage and price controls—or might have pursued them more vigorously; a more conservative Republican might have been too ideologically rigid for controls—or less concerned about unemployment, hence willing to brake expansion more sharply. Any of those courses *might* have managed the economy to better effect than the Nixon administration did—or to worse.

But Richard Nixon, not some other president, was in the Oval Office—pursuing his pragmatic course, nursing his personal nightmares, drawing on his lengthy and wounding experience. Whatever else, he did not overturn the most basic products of the New Deal and its successor administrations, and his most fundamental economic choice was not the usual Republican preference for price stability and "sound money" but an effort to keep ordinary Americans at work and on a payroll.

Herbert Stein's judgment, though it is partial to his own labors, is irrefutable: "Nixon did not come into office to make a conservative revolution in economic policy. . . . [S]till the actual developments were surprisingly different from what might have been expected."[31]

And, he might have added, from what many still believe.

14

★

Bomber

★

I had never imagined that at the end of my first year as President I would be contemplating two more years of fighting in Vietnam.

—Richard Nixon in *RN*

Anatoly Dobrynin was a familiar figure around the Nixon White House. The avuncular Soviet ambassador frequently met and lunched with Henry Kissinger and also saw the president more often than most diplomats; and he had no difficulty getting an appointment with Nixon on the afternoon of October 20, 1969.

Even the long-experienced Dobrynin must have had some difficulty, however, in saying to Nixon's face what Moscow had instructed him to say:

> If someone in the United States is tempted to make profit from Soviet-Chinese relations at the Soviet Union's expense, and there are some signs of that, then we would like to frankly warn in advance that such line of conduct, if pursued, can lead to a very grave miscalculation and is in no way consistent with the goal of better relations between the U.S. and the USSR.

Clearly, Moscow was not deceived by the administration's protestations that its approaches to China were not directed at the Soviet Union. The aide-mémoire from which Dobrynin was reading, moreover, made another harsh point—that "the [American] method of solving the Vietnam question through the use of military force is not only without perspective, but also extremely dangerous."

This was a gloves-off message but Nixon—to use an expression he liked—"hung tough." As he recalled the occasion in *RN,* he gave Dobrynin a yellow pad, advised him to take notes, and—as Kissinger listened—delivered a round-the-world critique of Soviet policy. Concerning China, he warned that in ten years it would be a "nuclear power, capable of terrorizing many other countries." He intended to "make moves" toward friendship with China but not with the intent "to embarrass the Soviet Union."

Then Nixon shifted the subject to what he really wanted to say, and had planned in advance. Moscow had promised President Lyndon Johnson that if he stopped the bombing of North Vietnam in 1968, "the Soviet Union would be very active with its help" in ending the war in Indochina.

"The bombing halt then was agreed to," Nixon reminded Dobrynin, "but the Soviet Union has done nothing to help. . . . [a]ll the conciliatory moves for the past year have been made by us."

Perhaps, Nixon suggested, Moscow did not really want the war to end.

> You may think that you can break me. You may believe that the American domestic situation is unmanageable. Or you may think that the war . . . costs the Soviet Union only a small amount of money while it costs us a great many lives.
>
> [But] I want you to understand that the Soviet Union is going to be stuck with me for the next three years and three months, and during all that time I will keep in mind what is being done right now, today. If the Soviet Union will not help us get peace, then we will have to pursue our own methods for bringing the war to an end. . . .
>
> If the Soviet Union found it possible to do something in Vietnam, and the Vietnam war ended, then we might do something dramatic to improve our relations. . . .
>
> But let me repeat that we will not hold still for being diddled to death in Vietnam.

Thus, Nixon shifted the emphasis of the meeting from Dobrynin's warning on China to his own hard stand on Vietnam. And when Dobrynin left, the delighted Kissinger exulted: "No President has ever laid it on the line to them like that."

He must have forgotten a tongue-lashing Harry Truman had given Vyacheslav Molotov in 1945; and in his own memoir, Kissinger barely mentioned the Nixon-Dobrynin meeting in October 1969. Kissinger did cite "about ten occasions in 1969" when he, too, tried through Dobrynin to enlist Soviet aid in ending the war; but the ambassador was "always evasive." Not even Nixon's lecture to Dobrynin produced the desired result of effective Soviet pressures on North Vietnam.[1]

Important and unprecedented though Richard Nixon's persistent approaches to China were, they were never more than parallel, and were at times subordinate, to his desperate four-year search for an "honorable" way out of Vietnam. Before it could be achieved, Nixon proved willing, if necessary, to sacrifice the historic China exercise, as well as the possibility of a SALT treaty, to achieve that "honorable"—which became finally only an "acceptable"—peace in Indochina.

Nixon and Kissinger had had no idea, at the outset of the administration, of the torturous ordeal Vietnam would pose for them—differently, but to no lesser degree, than it had for Lyndon Johnson. Six weeks after his inaugural, Nixon ruefully recalled in *RN,* he "confidently told the Cabinet that I expected the war to be over in a year."

He did not have, however, a "secret plan" to end the war, as had been widely believed; nor had he ever claimed to have such a plan. He had pledged, during his campaign, that "new leadership will end the war and win the peace in the Pacific." That expansive promise, combined with his politically astute refusal to divulge during the campaign any details of what he had in mind, had given rise to the secret-plan myth—so enduring that it sometimes crops up even today.

But Nixon also had told the Associated Press, on March 14, 1968, long before his nomination, that he saw "no magic formula, no gimmick" for winning the war: "If I had a gimmick I would tell [President] Johnson." Thus, he did not take office in January 1969 under the illusion that he could get out of the war by threatening North Vietnam with nuclear bombing, as Eisenhower supposedly had threatened North Korea in 1953, or with any other "savage blow" that would win a quick military victory.

Any lingering hopes he might have had for striking such a blow had been dashed during the interregnum at the Pierre Hotel, when Nixon considered and discarded the ideas of using tactical nuclear weapons and/or bombing North Vietnam's extensive irrigation-dike system to cause floods across the country. Even if either of these would have provided the necessary knockout punch—a dubious proposition—Nixon concluded that public reaction at home and in the world "would have got my Administration off to the worst possible start."

Fundamentally hawkish, Nixon was convinced that Johnson had not used sufficient force to win in Vietnam, particularly in the early stages. He was not himself reluctant to escalate ground and air warfare in order to win a quick victory, which with wild overoptimism he thought could be done in six months; but his honed political instincts told him he could not hold public support even for so short a time, owing to the rise in casualties that would surely occur. It was not so much the casualties that deterred him; it was the *reaction* to the casualties that he shied from.

But to let the war drag on indecisively was not an acceptable option: it was costing $30 billion a year, 200 American deaths a week (about 31,000 altogether by early 1969), and rising turmoil in American society. No end was in sight. Nor, to Richard Nixon, was immediate withdrawal of American troops—a "bug-out," in Lyndon Johnson's phrase—a choice he could let himself make. As early as 1966, he had argued to Elmer Bobst that the U.S. could not too quickly pull out the "cork in a bottle"—Vietnam—without serious dislocations of American power and influence (see chapter 1). So he had concluded at the outset of his administration as he said eleven months later in his "silent majority" speech, that a quick withdrawal

> would result in a collapse of confidence in American leadership, not only in Asia but throughout the world. . . . A nation cannot remain great if it betrays its allies and lets down its friends.

Neither of these actions, moreover—withdrawal or fighting on at the same rate—would redeem his campaign pledge to end the war and win the peace.

Nixon's conclusions are repugnant to those who believe he should have ended the war quickly and at almost any price; and he is often scoffed at as a man of no principle, motivated only by political advantage. On the question of continuing the war, however, critics can't have it both ways—that he refused to withdraw *and* had no principles. Had the latter been true, he almost surely would have abandoned the war in his first months in office. Not everyone shares the principle that did guide him, or accepts the reasoning by which he reached it; but that it may have been misguided does not mean that it was unprincipled.

Essentially by a process of elimination, Nixon decided to seek "honorable" peace through a negotiated settlement. In a *Foreign Affairs* article written just before Kissinger joined the Nixon administration, the man who would be the new national security adviser had provided the basic terms of the "honor" he and Nixon had in mind: "the United States *cannot accept* a military defeat, or a change in the political structure of South Vietnam brought about by external military force."[2] (Emphasis added.)

Kissinger's reasoning ran along the same lines as Nixon's. In the necessary effort both men envisioned for an orderly world in which American power and diplomacy would be the stabilizing factors, a defeat in Vietnam—a defeat that would be made undeniable by a forced change in the Saigon government the U.S. was defending—would critically reduce the nation's credibility and prestige. Defeat would pull the cork from the bottle as disastrously as a "bug-out." American deterrent and retaliatory power, as Nixon and Kissinger saw it, would no longer be a vital force in maintaining an orderly balance of power.

As Nixon later put it rhetorically (in a televised address on April 30, 1970, when he sought to explain the American and South Vietnamese campaign into Cambodia), a defeat or withdrawal would be ruinous to the American position and mission in the world:

> If, when the chips are down, the world's most powerful nation . . . acts like a pitiful, helpless giant, the forces of totalitarianism and anarchy will threaten free nations and free institutions throughout the world. . . .
>
> I would rather be a one-term president and do what I think is right than to be a two-term president at the cost of seeing America become a second-rate power and to see this nation accept the first defeat in its proud 190-year history.

Setting aside the blustery one-term remark, the rest would have done for a text had Nixon set out in early 1969 to explain the policy he settled upon for Vietnam. Whatever the goal of the war had been before, in his administration it became geopolitical—to maintain American credibility by denying the North Vietnamese a military victory that Kissinger had defined as a "change in the political structure of South Vietnam brought about by external force."

Put another way, the war's aim was the survival of the government in Saigon beyond the moment of settlement and the final American troop withdrawal. Kissinger's article was explicit as to what might happen ultimately: "once [North] Vietnamese military forces and pressures are removed, the United States has no obligation to maintain a government in Saigon by force."

An honorable settlement, therefore, involved no guarantees for the people of South Vietnam, or for the Saigon government, once the U.S. had gathered up its credibility and gone home. Nixon had a principle, all right, but it had far more to do with American self-interest than with his frequent claims about "standing by an ally."

Kissinger's article also suggests one of the two damaging illusions that, despite their realpolitik, Kissinger and Nixon *did* bring to the search for a way out of Vietnam.

One was the idea that had fatally afflicted the Johnson administration: that it would be possible to negotiate with Hanoi for a *mutual* withdrawal of American and North Vietnamese forces from South Vietnam. In fact, the North Vietnamese never were willing to consider mutual withdrawal; as long as the U.S. insisted on it, negotiations went nowhere.

The other Nixon-Kissinger illusion was that the Soviet Union, perhaps in return for an arms control agreement and trade favors, would bring effective pressures on the North Vietnamese to end the war on terms "acceptable" to the Nixon administration. At a news conference on March 4, 1969, Nixon voiced this hope:

I believe the Soviet Union would like to use what influence it could appropriately bring to bear to help bring the war to a conclusion. What it can do, however, is something that only the Soviet Union would be able to answer to, and it would probably have to answer privately, not publicly.

That was a clear invitation to Moscow to confer secretly with the U.S. on a peace settlement for Indochina, and it reflected a clear and persisting assumption that the Soviets *could* help if they would. On April 14, 1969, in a frank meeting with Dobrynin, Kissinger first outlined the "linkage" he had in mind: American-Soviet relations could improve "on a broad front," but Vietnam was "a major obstacle"; if Washington could not get Soviet help in ending the war and removing the obstacle, American-Soviet relations could not advance.

Did this mean, Dobrynin asked, that no progress on the Middle East, trade relations or strategic arms was possible if no settlement in Vietnam was reached? Progress on such issues, Kissinger replied, would be more rapid if Vietnam were out of the way. If the war continued, the unpredictable Nixon would be likely to escalate; that would create a "complicated situation" between Washington and Moscow.[3]

Even under that kind of pressure, Moscow protested that it did *not* have the power to bend Hanoi to its will; and when Nixon took a hard line on relaxing restrictions on trade with the Soviet Union, Moscow still did not or could not bring Hanoi around. Kissinger, at least, never really believed Soviet claims that Moscow could not persuade Hanoi; but in the end it was retreat in Washington, not Soviet pressure, that produced an end to American fighting in Vietnam.

If he was to sustain the war even until a settlement, Nixon had to face the problem of rapidly declining support at home. The "peace movement" continued to grow; huge antiwar rallies in Washington in October and November 1969 were to be the proof of that. With the departure of the Democratic administration that had begun and waged the war, the Democratic Congress that had supported it quickly turned its back, as Kissinger angrily noted:

Those who had created our involvement in Vietnam moved first to neutrality and then to opposition, saddling Nixon with responsibility for a war he had inherited and attacking him in the name of solutions they themselves had neither advocated nor executed when they had the opportunity.[4]

If Kissinger felt that way, with much reason, it can only be imagined how Richard Nixon, with his paranoid suspicion of a perpetual liberal conspiracy to destroy him, felt about former Democratic officials (Clark Clifford and Averell Harriman, to name two) and journalists (the author, for example) who had turned against the war—hence, in Nixon's eyes, against (or further against) Richard Nixon.

It's nevertheless fair to point out that the American "involvement" in Vietnam dated at least to the Eisenhower administration's establishment of the Saigon regime and its sabotage of the North-South elections scheduled for 1956 by the Geneva conference of 1954. Not all war critics, moreover (the author again included), shared the Nixon-Kissinger conviction that American withdrawal in 1969 would have been a geopolitical disaster, or that such a possibility had to be the primary consideration.

"Vietnamization" became Nixon's instrument for "buying time" necessary to work out the settlement he was confident the Soviets could wring out of Hanoi. Developed and named by Secretary of Defense Laird, with the help of Paul Warnke, a briefly held-over Democrat in the Pentagon, Vietnamization was a program that sprang from Laird's acute sense of the domestic political costs of the war.

It also complemented Nixon's inner determination. Just before his nomination, he had told a group of journalists of his belief that Soviet pressure on Hanoi would bring about a settlement of the war. If not, he said, there would have to be "a phased withdrawal."[5]

Vietnamization included just such a withdrawal, while the U.S. attempted both to build up and train the Army of the Republic of Vietnam (ARVN) to provide the manpower needs of the war. The announcement of the program—in June 1969, at a meeting between Nixon and South Vietnamese President Thieu on Midway Island—signaled the beginning of the end of American military participation in the war (which nevertheless would continue at declining levels until the last American troops were evacuated on August 12, 1972).

Nixon was disappointed in his hopes that Vietnamization would silence domestic opposition to the war; and ARVN never did develop the capacity to defeat or even hold its own against North Vietnamese and Vietcong forces. Vietnamization, however, did help to rally for a while the support of "the silent majority" to which Nixon appealed so effectively in his speech of November 3, 1969. And the program had good effect, as we shall see, on the Chinese view of Nixon's intentions in Indochina; that may have had some influence on Hanoi.

Vietnamization eventually did "bring the boys home," too, although its pace was so slow that nearly as many Americans were killed during Nixon's administration as in the previous years of the war. It may be, however, that "phased withdrawal" spared American society from even worse contortions and divisions than those it actually suffered, as war and resistance continued for the four long years of Nixon's first term.

Even before he was sworn in as president, Nixon was pursuing, secretly and cautiously, a rapprochement with the People's Republic of China—although to use that name was then taboo in American politics, the theological nature of which required patriots to refer only to "Red China" or more moderately to "Communist China," or—barely acceptably—to "Mainland China."

Not since before the Korean War, antedating even Nixon's service as vice president to Eisenhower, had decent relations—or any formal relationship—prevailed between the U.S. and an apparently arch-hostile China. That nation, many Americans believed, had been "lost" by the "free world," owing to treason and conspiracy in high places; and it was viewed as a place of Communist evil second only to the Soviet Union.

As a man who had built his political career on staunch anticommunism and suspicions of Communist subversion, Richard Nixon seemed hardly the leader to break down a barrier he had done as much as anyone to build. As late as 1960, when he had advised President-elect Kennedy not to recognize China (see chapter 6), Nixon had maintained orthodox Republican animosity to the "Chinese Reds."

At least as early as 1966, however, he had privately agreed with Elmer Bobst, an old China hand, that the most important thing Richard Nixon could do if he became president would be to "bring China into the world" (see chapter 1). The developing ideological, political and territorial conflict between the Soviet Union and China, becoming ever more visible during the early sixties, had led him—as it did others—to wonder if differences between the two great Communist powers might not be exploited.

Besides, Nixon in the White House was less Nixon the anti-Communist than Nixon the pragmatist; and he could make a clear distinction between authoritarian states, depending on how he defined American self-interest. How much he may have developed this view later, to justify his presidential actions, is not clear; but in 1977, in a television interview with David Frost, Nixon observed during a discussion of his actions against the Marxist government of Salvador Allende Gossens in Chile:

> In terms of national security, in terms of our own self-interest, the right-wing dictatorship, if it is not interfering with its neighbors, if it is not taking action against the United States, it is therefore of no security concern to us. . . . A left-wing dictatorship, on the other hand, we find that they do engage in trying to export their subversion to other countries, and that does involve our security interests.[6]

China's dictatorship was, of course, left-wing by definition—although in terms of the authority of the state, "left" and "right" designations tell us little about dictatorships. But Nixon's tolerant attitude toward right-wing dictatorships (by no means unique to him) was easily transferred to Sino-Soviet relations; for if to the pragmatist "the enemy of my enemy is my friend," China as the enemy of the Soviet Union obviously was a potential friend of the U.S. Richard Nixon would have no trouble making peace with such an enforced friend, whether left-wing or right, if he saw it as in American self-interest to do so.

The public may not have realized that this renowned anti-Communist was so flexible; but by mid-1967 Nixon was letting his views be known selectively—to Bobst, for example. On one of his globe-trotting forays that year, as he recalled in *RN,* Nixon also told Nicolae Ceausescu, the Communist leader of Romania (a theoretically "left-wing" dictatorship that, like China, suffered difficult relations with Moscow):

> I doubted that any true détente with the Soviets could be achieved until some kind of rapprochement could be reached with Communist China. If its 800 million people remained isolated, within 20 years China could pose a grave threat to world peace. . . . I thought the United States could do little to establish effective communications with China until the Vietnam war was ended. After that, however, I thought we could take steps to normalize relations with Peking.

As a likely presidential candidate late in 1967, Nixon disclosed his basic attitude toward China, outlining his views to the limited but influential audience that reads *Foreign Affairs,* the publication of the Council on Foreign Relations:

> For the short run . . . this means a policy of firm restraint, of no reward, of a creative counterpressure designed to persuade Peking that its interest can be served only by accepting the basic rules of international civility. For the long run, it means pulling China back into the world community—but as a great and progressing nation, not as the epicenter of world revolution.

As president, he signaled his flexibility through travel. Much to the displeasure of the Soviets, for example, Nixon visited and established closer relations not only with Romania but with Yugoslavia, still another Communist state not subservient to Moscow.

In Nixon's scheme of things, an acceptable dictatorship must not be threatening to the security interests of the U.S. China qualified, because Nixon did *not* believe Dean Rusk's insistence that the war in Vietnam was the product of "Asian communism with its headquarters in Peiping." (Rusk clung loyally but not helpfully to this outdated Kuomintang appellation for the Chinese capital.) Nixon knew the Chinese had not instigated the war, nor done as much as he thought the Soviets had to sustain it, and he did not expect that rapprochement with China would end it.

He *did* calculate that improved American relations with the Chinese might so alarm the Soviets that, to appease Washington, Moscow would put pressure on Hanoi and hasten to enter an arms control agreement. Again a pragmatist, not an ideologue, was at work in the White House; his eventual "opening to China" was, at root, a power play designed to improve the power position of the U.S., most particularly in its relations with the other nuclear superpower.

Candidate Nixon managed to display a decent Republican hostility to "Red China" during his 1968 campaign—although in September he did say in an interview with *U.S. News and World Report* that "we must always seek opportunities to talk with [China], as with the USSR. . . . We must not only watch for changes, we must seek to make changes."

Two weeks after Nixon's narrow election on November 5, the Chinese chargé d'affaires in Warsaw proposed the resumption on February 20, 1969, of a series of talks, long suspended, between Chinese and American representatives in that city. Whether Peking was moved by the exigencies of its dispute with Moscow, or by Nixon's numerous hints, or by both, is unclear; but Lyndon Johnson, the lame-duck president, put the response up to the president-elect and Nixon immediately advised that the invitation be accepted.

That exchange—which took place before Nixon asked Henry Kissinger to join his administration—as well as his other prepresidential statements, establishes that the Nixon administration's ultimate policy toward China originated with Richard Nixon himself. In January, moreover, as he awaited inauguration, Nixon told his old friend, General Vernon Walters, that one of the things he wanted to do as president was to reestablish contact with China. Not long after he was sworn in, while chatting in the White House with Senator Charles Mathias of Maryland, Nixon also observed: "We're going to do a great deal more in our relations with China." Mathias, a liberal Republican, was enthusiastic.[7]

Thus, despite Kissinger's later enthusiasm for the China project, he had little to do with its inception. As Kissinger himself conceded, "China had not figured extensively" in his writings through 1968, nor had it been a major subject of his academic interest. He immediately perceived, however, upon hearing Nixon's plans, that an opening to China meshed well with his own geopolitical purposes—particularly "linkage."

Aside from his personal desire to be the president to "bring China back into the world," Nixon saw clearly, and perhaps earlier than any American political leader, that if the U.S. had active relations with China as well as with the Soviet Union, it would give him greater leverage for dealing with either one—a sort of whipsaw approach. Nixon perceived also that the real possibility of a Sino-Soviet war, possibly nuclear war, as well as the ideological differences within the Communist world—becoming vitriolic after the Czech invasion in 1968—might make a Sino-American rapprochement possible without undue American concessions to the Chinese.

Neither Nixon's developing attitude of conciliation nor his broad-gauged inaugural appeal to "those who are willing to join [us] to strengthen the structure of peace," seemed *publicly* to impress Peking. The day after the new president took the oath from his old antagonist, Chief Justice Earl Warren, a Chinese spokesman branded Nixon as the newest "puppet" of imperialism to pursue the "vicious ambitions" of the U.S. for "aggression and expansion in the world."

With such epithets possibly ringing in his ears, the new president said he saw "no immediate prospect of any change in our policy," though he carefully noted at his first news conference that the U.S. "looks forward" to the first of the Sino-American meetings, then scheduled for Warsaw on February 20, 1969.

Just three days after meeting reporters on January 30 and suggesting how powerful was his fixation on renewing relations with China, Nixon instructed Kissinger to plant a new "signal" in an Eastern European channel—probably Romania—that the U.S. was "exploring possibilities" for a rapprochement with China. Kissinger considered this primarily a move to alarm the Soviet Union and spur it into helping to end the war in Vietnam; undoubtedly, however, the signal reached Peking.

Taking his cue from the president's interest, Kissinger also ordered detailed policy reviews on China. On February 18, however, Peking abruptly canceled the scheduled Warsaw ambassadorial meeting, charging that the U.S. had seduced a Chinese diplomat who had defected in the Netherlands.

Nixon was to tell a later news conference that the cancellation meant "breakthroughs . . . at this time" were not to be expected, though "further down the road . . . a better understanding" with China might be possible. In the meantime he had made his early-administration trip to Europe, during which—apparently undiscouraged—he confided to Charles de Gaulle that he planned a "step-by-step" campaign to open a "dialogue" with the Chinese. De Gaulle concurred, and delivered a Gaullist pronouncement that Nixon recalled in *RN:* "It would be better for you to recognize China before you are obliged to do so by the growth of China."

Shortly afterward, de Gaulle came to Washington for the funeral of Dwight D. Eisenhower. Nixon asked de Gaulle to convey to Peking his administration's intent to improve relations—particularly that he planned to withdraw American troops from Vietnam "come what may." In May, when de Gaulle dispatched a new French ambassador, Etienne M'nach, to China, M'nach carried Nixon's message with him and ultimately delivered it "at the highest level." The message was timely, because Peking's relations with Moscow were worsening, and the Chinese had recent reasons to take such American overtures more seriously.[8]

On March 2, a major armed clash on the Sino-Soviet border had resulted in considerable loss of life—thirty-one Russians are known to have been killed, as well as an unknown number of Chinese. The affair is believed to have been instigated by Peking, no doubt as a warning; but on March 15, the Soviets staged their own attack, apparently as a response to the events of March 2. Larger forces were involved this time, and numerous casualties resulted (exactly how many is unclear). Lesser fighting erupted sporadically well into the summer of 1969.

Moscow, at a meeting in Budapest, even requested the Warsaw Pact powers to send forces to the Far East to help counter the belligerent Chinese; but the Soviets were publicly rebuffed by their supposed puppets. On March 21, the Peking government actually refused a phone call from Premier Kosygin. Nixon, in *RN,* called this an "amusing incident" as described to him by Chou En-lai, in which a Chinese "hot-line" operator, "completely on his own, said [to Kosygin], 'You are a revisionist, and therefore I will not connect you.' " Kosygin was *not* amused.

On March 14, Nixon announced the conversion of McNamara's "thin" Sentinel antimissile system into the more comprehensive and "thick" Safeguard, but described it as still having a role against a possible Chinese attack. He added, somewhat mysteriously in view of his approaches to Peking, that there should be a common interest in the U.S. and the Soviet Union in not being "naked" against a potential Chinese Communist threat.

That was only one day before Moscow launched its responsive attack along the Ussuri River on the Sino-Soviet border. Peking promptly labeled Nixon's statement as evidence of his "collusion with the Soviet revisionists."

In April, the Ninth Congress of the Chinese Communist Party formally turned Peking's international policy line somewhat *away* from hostility to the U.S. and toward "dual confrontation" with Moscow and Washington. The Soviets, at least, thought they saw in this a Chinese bid for rapprochement with the Americans, and they may have been right.

On May 14, addressing on television the overriding problem of the war in Vietnam, Nixon impressed Peking rather more favorably than Hanoi. Among other "peace proposals," he junked the so-called Manila Formula over which he and Johnson had wrangled in 1966 in the incident that, as much as any other, had launched Nixon's successful presidential bid (see chapter 8).

The Manila Formula had called for mutual American and North Vietnamese troop withdrawals from South Vietnam, with a residual American force to remain for six months after all North Vietnamese forces were gone. Nixon's new position—despite his three-year-old criticism of Johnson's harder-line proposal—was for a *simultaneous* withdrawal of all forces. This warmed Hanoi not at all, for the government there had no intention of pulling out; but it caused the Chinese to take more seriously M'nach's message that Nixon intended to withdraw "come what may."

On June 8, Peking was given further reason to believe Nixon meant what he said. Meeting on bleak Midway Island in the Pacific with President Nguyen Van Thieu of South Vietnam, Nixon announced plans to withdraw twenty-five thousand American troops from Indochina as the first step in Vietnamization. Periodic withdrawal announcements thereafter—Nixon found that public pressures permitted no turning back—convinced the Chinese that he was, indeed, pulling out of Vietnam.

This was important to them because it could hasten the end of a war against a neighboring Communist state they had little choice but to support, materially and politically, and which therefore carried some threat of drawing them in—particularly if the supposedly unpredictable Nixon of the "madman theory" escalated the war and spread it further into Indochina and along the Chinese border. If he was "winding down," instead, that tended to validate his several signals that he wanted better relations with Peking.

Chinese leaders also may have taken in their own way another point Nixon sought to make—that if the U.S. were *forced* to withdraw from the war, the resulting victory would strengthen those in the Communist world who sought confrontation, rather than negotiation. Nixon was bidding for Soviet help in ending the war, but the Chinese knew very well that both Hanoi and Moscow would be strengthened against China by a North Vietnamese military victory over the U.S.

On July 25, again on an island in the Pacific, Nixon announced the "Guam Doctrine" or "Nixon Doctrine"; in the future, he said, threatened nations would have to supply their own fighting manpower, even when the U.S. supported them. That must also have appealed to Peking as further confirming American disengagement in Indochina—enough so, perhaps, that the Chinese could overlook Nixon's gratuitous remark that their country posed "the greatest threat to the peace of the world." Or perhaps they took into consideration that all his remarks in Guam were extemporaneous and—in Kissinger's opinion, at least—"not intended [as] a major policy pronouncement."[9]

The late spring and summer of 1969 was an eventful period—and for Nixon productive—in the planned "opening to China." On May 24, William Rogers, traveling in Pakistan, asked President Yahya Khan to inform Peking of the American desire to improve relations. Two days before

Nixon's remarks on Guam, on the occasion of American astronauts' return from the moon, the president lamented that the Soviet and Chinese peoples had not been able to see this great occasion on television, and added: "I want the time to come when the Chinese people and the Russian people and all the peoples of the world can walk together and talk together."

On the way back to Washington, after Guam, Nixon stopped in Pakistan and heard Yahya Khan report that Peking had neither encouraged or discouraged better relations. Yahya promised to keep the channel open. The next day, in Romania, Nixon urged Ceausescu also to impress on China the American desire for dialogue; he managed, in addition, to make a public criticism of a plan Brezhnev had proposed, to build a Communist security system in Asia that would isolate China.

Meanwhile, unknown to the Chinese, Kissinger's Senior Review Group of the NSC had met to review China policy options—decades after the last such meeting. One result was a National Security Decision Memorandum directing relaxation on trade with China, a move duly announced on July 21.

But if Peking's view to the West was somewhat sunnier, its outlook in the other direction was ominous. Formal talks with the Soviets on border disputes began, but armed clashes continued and the atmosphere between the two nations grew more heated. The Soviets started a major military buildup on the border that continued into 1973. In June 1969, they moved bomber units into Siberia and Mongolia and practiced attacks on simulated Chinese nuclear facilities; heavy hints began to emerge from Moscow that a Sino-Soviet war inevitably would become nuclear. The Chinese may or may not have learned at the time that a Soviet diplomat had inquired of a State Department official how the U.S. would react to a Soviet attack on Chinese nuclear facilities.[10]

As the summer neared its end, Secretary Rogers journeyed to Australia; on August 8, in an unauthorized speech that irritated Nixon and Kissinger, he declared that the U.S. had been "seeking to open up channels of communication" with the Chinese, who had been, he said, too long isolated and would someday play a great role in Asia. The U.S. would welcome "renewal of talks" with them. Rogers was expressing his own views, since—remarkably—he had not been allowed to know of the administration signals to China through French and Romanian channels.

What Peking thought of Rogers's open supplication is not known; but, as a result, Nixon called another NSC meeting and disclosed his views, to the surprise of most in the room, who knew no more than Rogers had of Nixon's several approaches to Peking. The Soviets were more aggressive than the Chinese, Nixon explained, and it would be contrary to American interests to allow the latter to be "smashed" in a Sino-Soviet war.

That the Chinese were not fully prepared to risk being so smashed was indicated in September, when they made a grudging gesture of limited reconciliation with Moscow. Following the death of the Communist hero, Ho Chi Minh, Premier Kosygin had traveled to Hanoi—through India, not China—to pay his respects; obviously avoiding a meeting, he departed before Chou En-lai arrived. During Kosygin's return through Central Asia, however, he was suddenly invited to talk with Chou. The Soviet premier detoured to Peking, and the two leaders met at the airport—the first Sino-Soviet encounter at such a level in nearly five years.

The meeting on September 11 does not appear to have been cordial. It was brief, and described later by the Chinese as "frank," diplomatic parlance for argumentative; and the Soviets were to remember, when Nixon later was received in Peking with red-carpet treatment, that the Chinese had not let Kosygin out of the airport lounge. Nor did the encounter halt the rumors of war, so that four days later Elliot Richardson announced for the administration—reflecting Nixon's remarks at the NSC meeting— that the U.S. would be "deeply concerned" if there should be a "massive breach of international peace and security."

As the commander in chief of a huge fighting force in Vietnam, Nixon was preoccupied from the start with the so-called sanctuaries in Cambodia, then a neutral nation friendly, if not allied, with the U.S. North Vietnamese forces found shelter in Cambodia along its long border with South Vietnam; they then struck across the border when they saw the chance, retreating when neccssary into their Cambodian sanctuaries. This violated Cambodian neutrality, of course, but the Cambodians had neither the force nor the will to prevent it, or even to protest.

South Vietnam and the U.S. ostensibly *had* respected Cambodian neutrality, but in 1965 an International Control Commission charged that there had been 375 South Vietnamese incursions across the border during 1964 and 385 during the first five months of 1965, "none . . . provoked by the Royal Government of Cambodia."

After that, reports surfaced frequently of South Vietnamese "hot-pursuit" missions into Cambodia; the U.S. conceded having participated in at least one of these in January 1968. Respect for Cambodian neutrality thus was a fiction maintained by both sides, and by a Cambodian government that did not want to admit its helplessness to defend its own sovereignty and neutrality.[11]

Nixon and Kissinger decided soon after taking office—as Lyndon Johnson never had—to go after the sanctuaries systematically. The president ordered and Kissinger arranged a sustained bombing campaign, kept secret from the American public, and requiring doctored Air Force records to remove all traces of the bombing from the history of the war. When on May 8, 1969, the *New York Times* nevertheless published a story by William

Beecher about the bombing, the public and the rest of the press blissfully ignored this sensational revelation. Nixon and Kissinger, however, were enraged to have their secret scheme apparently endangered, so they set in motion with the FBI the wiretaps that presaged Watergate and the "plumbers" (see chapter 15).

The illegal and criminally concealed bombing of Cambodia continued, and was to become in 1974 a possible count in the impeachment of Richard Nixon. The House Judiciary Committee, in deference to traditional congressional reluctance to interfere with a president in his role as commander in chief, finally rose above the evidence and dropped the charge, while endorsing others that were considerably less serious.

In March 1970, General Lon Nol, a strong anti-Communist, overthrew the neutralist Cambodian government of Prince Norodom Sihanouk. Both Nixon and Kissinger, in their memoirs, strongly deny that the coup was ordered or organized by Washington, and the available evidence tends to support them. Nixon went so far in *RN* as to complain of the CIA, which had not predicted Lon Nol's move: "What the hell do those clowns do out there in Langley?"

The Cambodian coup, nevertheless, may have been inspired *tacitly* from Washington. Lon Nol is known to have been in touch with American officials a number of times before he took action. He could have been in little doubt that he would receive American support if he rid Cambodia of Sihanouk's weak government. When he did, Washington's backing was immediate.

On the other hand, Lon Nol's new government and armed forces immediately came under heavy attack from North Vietnamese troops. The Cambodians resisted with some initial success—enough so that on April 20 Nixon could announce the withdrawal of another 150,000 Americans from Vietnam for the coming year. The Cambodian emergency caused him to arrange, however, that the bulk of these troops were not to leave until after August 1, 1970.

As April neared its end, Lon Nol's position weakened and became desperate. Nixon saw the likely North Vietnamese victory in Cambodia as threatening South Vietnam from the west as well as the north; and that, he argued in *RN*, "would jeopardize our troop withdrawal" and "virtually assure a Communist invasion of South Vietnam [from Cambodia] as soon as the last American had left."

He listened to strong advice from Kissinger, Admiral Thomas Moorer of the Joint Chiefs, and Vice President Agnew—among others. But Nixon needed little urging before he decided to send American as well as ARVN troops across the Cambodian border; his intention to act was so strong that Richard Helms, the director of Central Intelligence, *suppressed* a CIA analysis setting out the military impracticability of an invasion of Cambodia.[12]

Helms did not want to stand in the way of Nixon's stated desire "to protect our men who are in Vietnam and to guarantee the continued success of our withdrawal and Vietnamization programs"; or perhaps he sensed that the president really wanted to demonstrate both his own strength and his army's power—to himself as well as to his critics. Whatever his motives, Nixon's decision put him on a deeply controversial course—to "widen the war" into Cambodia, when his public position was that he was "winding down" the conflict.

The Cambodian campaign, announced on national television on April 30 in Nixon's "pitiful, helpless giant" speech, was one of the decisive events of the war, though not as he had planned. That suppressed CIA analysis had been on target; the operation neither captured the Communist headquarters in Cambodia, as Nixon had predicted incautiously, nor in spite of early success did it clean out the sanctuaries or stop Communist attacks across the border into South Vietnam. It led, arguably, to the engulfment of Cambodia in the war, ultimately to the triumph in that unhappy country of the despicable Khmer Rouge with their murderous "resettlement" and "reeducation" programs.

Nixon professes in *RN* to have anticipated the "uproar at home" that resulted from the Cambodian operation; but he hardly could have foreseen its extent. The macho terms in which he addressed the nation ("I would rather be a one-term president . . .") reinforce the possibility that his decision may have been influenced by his tendency toward a certain reckless defiance (perhaps to bolster his own confidence)—as when he unnecessarily confronted mobs in Burma and South America during his vice presidential tours, and in California during the political campaign of 1970. Kissinger remarked that when Nixon "was pressed to the wall, his romantic streak surfaced and he would see himself as a beleaguered military commander in the tradition of [General George S.] Patton"—the movie about whom he viewed frequently in the spring of 1970.[13]

Nixon not only inflated his rhetoric in the April 30 speech; he falsified it, claiming that "for five years neither the U.S. nor South Vietnam moved against those enemy sanctuaries [in Cambodia] because we did not wish to violate the territory of a neutral nation." That would come back to haunt him with the disclosure of the secret and illegal bombing of the Cambodian sanctuaries that he had started in 1969.

The day after the April 30 speech, while he seems—to judge from his account—still to have been in the exhilaration of what he considered a Churchillian decision, Nixon visited the Pentagon for a progress report and ordered *more* sanctuary areas cleaned out. As he departed, he spoke to a small crowd in the Pentagon lobby and carelessly referred to some protesting students as "bums."

That added to the conflagration the Cambodian operation already had ignited on hundreds of campuses. May 1970 quickly became a national

trauma—on the 4th, protesting students were killed by National Guards-
men at Kent State in Ohio; on the 15th, other students were killed by state
police at Jackson State in Mississippi. Huge protest crowds gathered in
Washington, and even the silent majority barely stayed with Nixon; a
Gallup poll found exactly 50 percent of respondents in support of the
Cambodian campaign (see chapter 15).

The fierce national reaction obviously shook his self-confidence—never
too strong. But unlike earlier protests, the massively hostile response to the
Cambodia operation also may have had direct effect on the war—most
specifically, in the reaction of Congress.

On June 30, 1970, driven by members' and their constituents' anger at
Nixon's widening of the war, the Senate voted by 58 to 37 to approve the
so-called Cooper-Church Amendment *prohibiting* use of government
funds for American military operations in Cambodia after July 1. The
House later rescued the administration from the Senate ban, although not
until all the invading Americans had left Cambodia. But that strong Senate
majority was impressive—particularly since sixteen Republicans had
joined forty-two Democrats in approving Cooper-Church. In *RN,* Nixon
called it "the first restrictive vote ever cast on a president in wartime"; and
he was too experienced a politician to discount or ignore such a setback.

The amendment's bipartisan nature was symbolized by its sponsors—
Frank Church of Idaho, the second-ranking Democrat on the Foreign
Relations Committee, and the respected Republican moderate, John Sherman Cooper of Kentucky. The big vote for it in the Senate clearly meant
that Congress—including influential Republicans—would no longer stand
aside to allow Richard Nixon a free hand in Indochina.

For a year and a half, relatively free of congressional hindrance, he had
had the opportunity to carry out his promise to "end the war and win the
peace." Despite Vietnamization, he had come nowhere near that goal and,
instead, had expanded American participation into another country; still
no notable progress toward ending the war had been achieved. The Cambodian operation even overshadowed the huge troop withdrawal he had
announced on April 20. Nixon finally had overplayed the hand he had held
since January 1969, and Congress had shown its willingness to call him to
account.

His lunge into Cambodia, admittedly a gamble though hardly an impulsive move, marked another turning point of sorts; after that, Nixon in effect
gave up on the sort of negotiated settlement he had set out in 1969 so
confidently to achieve. For one thing, the Soviets were not cooperating; in
the State of the World report Nixon and Kissinger had issued in February,
they had complained:

> To the detriment of the cause of peace [in Vietnam], the Soviet
> leadership has failed to exert a helpful influence on the North

Vietnamese. . . . This cannot but cloud our relationship with the
Soviet Union.

But this sort of threat, consistently failing to move the Soviets, had become
more nearly an excuse for failure to end the war than a useful tactic; it was
an empty threat anyway, as SALT continued.

In the secret talks with North Vietnam that had opened in August 1969,
for another thing, Kissinger had encountered mostly stolid intransigence,
shrewd opportunism and stubborn unwillingness to compromise. A meeting on September 7, 1970, months after the Cambodian incursion, slightly
encouraged Kissinger; but a subsequent meeting on September 27 found
the North Vietnamese not only as uncooperative as before, but "argumentative and repetitive"—Nixon's phrase.

On October 7, 1970, therefore, in a speech to which too little attention
has been paid, Nixon took a fateful step—in retreat. He proposed a cease-
fire and stand-fast for "all armed forces throughout Indochina," to be
followed by *unilateral* and complete withdrawal of the American troops
on a timetable to be negotiated. *Mutual* withdrawal was no longer demanded and no residual American force was to remain behind; when the
Americans were gone, the North Vietnamese would still be in position in
the South. Unless Vietnamization had stiffened ARVN beyond anyone's
real expectations, that meant that the South Vietnamese regime for which
the U.S. since 1965 had sacrificed so lavishly, in lives and money, could
not long survive the American departure.

In *RN* Nixon put the best face he could on this abandonment of the key
point of the war—what might cynically be termed a "delayed bug-out."
The "success" of the Cambodian operation, he wrote, denied "supplies,
ammunition and reinforcements" to the North Vietnamese, and Vietnamization soon would have ARVN ready to stand alone in defense of the
Saigon regime. "I felt that now, for the first time, we could consider
agreeing to a cease-fire in place in South Vietnam without first requiring
that the North Vietnamese agree to withdraw their forces."

Five days later, Nixon announced that 40,000 American troops—part
of the 150,000 designated for withdrawal on April 20—would be out of
Indochina before Christmas.

The troop withdrawal was anticlimactic—except, of course, to the
"grunts" who would be pulled out of Vietnam. More than two years and
many deaths later, what mattered was that Nixon had made the essential
concession that would allow Hanoi to agree to what the president and
Kissinger could still call, in geopolitical terms, an "honorable" settlement—even though it would cut the jugular of the South Vietnamese
government.

Timing and circumstance strongly suggest that Nixon made that move,
not because it had become, in reality, safe to do so—no soldier would say

that it had—and for more reasons than the lack of promise of his negotiating efforts. He could not escalate *and* continue Vietnamization; and since, politically, he could not abandon the troop withdrawals—though they had failed to give him the undivided support of the American public for which he had hoped—he could not escalate significantly, either. The results of the Cambodian invasion—uproar in the streets, revulsion in Congress, continued stalemate in Indochina—made it clear, moreover, that he could not sustain the war long enough to wear down the rocklike North Vietnamese and cause them to agree to the long-demanded *mutual* withdrawal.

Nixon must also have been influenced by the fall congressional elections of 1970, in which he and his party were waging an all-out effort to improve his support in Congress. Only four days after the pivotal speech of October 7, he made the impulsive decision to take over and lead personally a national political campaign that, for more than a month, had been entrusted to Agnew—then at the height of his ephemeral popularity (see chapter 15).

In July 1970, Nixon had told Kissinger that he would accept a separate ABM treaty with the Soviets, though officially he and the SALT delegation had been insisting on a comprehensive agreement including limits on offensive weapons. In the fall of 1970, almost any treaty and a summit with the Soviets would have been good domestic politics for the president and his party. So, too, was a new peace proposal for Vietnam.

Just as the Chinese in their long isolation from the U.S. could not know all that was happening in Washington, Nixon and Kissinger appear to have had no inkling, at first, that a bitter struggle was going on in Peking over the American approaches. Chou and Mao Tse-tung favored a friendly response; Marshal Lin Piao, Mao's designated successor, opposed that idea; and leadership factions formed behind each position.

This internal battle, or Chinese fears of being "smashed" in a real war with the Soviets, or both, may have caused them to ease relations with Moscow in the fall of 1969. After the Chou-Kosygin airport meeting, the Chinese upgraded the border talks, cooled the border fighting and sent representatives to a Soviet embassy reception in Peking. Taking note, Brezhnev—referring to "Comrade Chou" for the first time in three years—expressed hope for "positive" results in the border talks.[14]

Despite this minirapprochement, and though they returned ambassadors to each other's capital in 1970, the two Communist giants remained distant and mistrustful. The Sino-American relationship, in contrast, and largely unrealized by the world, had been set by the end of 1969 on a conciliatory course.

In November, Nixon had withdrawn the navy patrol that, since the Truman administration, ostensibly had protected China and Taiwan from each other. Various American and Chinese representatives were getting in touch around the world; and in Warsaw, American Ambassador Walter Stoessel managed on December 3 to inform the Chinese chargé d'affaires personally that the U.S. was ready to resume the ambassadorial talks the Chinese had proposed, then canceled, a year earlier.

On December 11 the Chinese publicly accepted Stoessel's proposal, and a week later the U.S. announced further relaxation of trade restraints. In January, the State Department referred, for the first time, to "the People's Republic of China," a milestone of sorts. By then, to experienced diplomats, what was going on seemed obvious; and Kissinger had to reassure Dobrynin—with tongue in cheek—that the Sino-American contacts were not directed against the Soviet Union. No doubt Dobrynin knew better.

At the first Warsaw meeting on January 20, 1970, Stoessel wasted no time in making the bid for which Nixon had been seeking opportunity: he proposed that a special, high-level American emissary be sent to China to open a reliable channel of communication—over which, of course, Nixon and Kissinger could maintain complete control, as they might not be able to do if ambassadors were exchanged. Stoessel sweetened the proposal by expressing the "hope" that American forces on Taiwan might be reduced "as tensions in the area diminish."

In February, Nixon and Kissinger issued that first State of the World report, including a first public step in the China initiative:

> The Chinese are a great and vital people who should not remain isolated from the international community. . . . It is certainly in our interest, and in the interest of peace and stability in Asia and the world, that we take what steps we can toward improved practical relations with Peking.

At a second Warsaw meeting later in February, the Chinese accepted the special envoy proposal. The old wall of separation had been breached, although the agreed trip of the high-level visitor was kept a deep secret on both sides, and no date or other details were agreed upon. For its part, the administration empowered Stoessel to state that his "hope" of January 20 had become an American "intention" to reduce its military forces on Taiwan. That was also a well-kept secret, against the political power in the U.S. of the "China lobby" that supported the claims of Taiwan.

The internecine struggle in Peking had not been settled, however. On March 2, Radio Peking blasted Nixon's "hypocrisy" in calling for better relations with China. It's now believed, moreover, that the Warsaw agreements had been engineered by Chou and Mao without informing Lin Piao.[15]

Fierce internal debate in Peking may have been the reason why in June, and again in September, General Vernon Walters was unable to open another channel through the Chinese military attaché in Paris; the attaché may have represented the Lin Piao faction. Or the Chinese may have been put off momentarily by the May "incursion" into Cambodia.

In response to this clear provocation—an exercise of American military power near China's borders—Peking did cancel a Warsaw ambassadorial meeting that had been scheduled for May 20; on that day, instead, Mao sharply attacked "U.S. aggressors and all their running dogs," momentarily infuriating Nixon. Kissinger deftly converted this setback into the closing of the Warsaw channel, though the Chinese carefully had expressed a willingness to hold the scheduled meeting later. But Kissinger wanted greater White House control over Sino-American exchanges and was glad to be rid of any channel shared with the State Department. No further Warsaw meetings were held.[16]

Peking did *not*, as Nixon and Kissinger had shrewdly calculated, break off secret negotiations with the U.S. because of Cambodia. Instead, for two weeks in August and September 1970, in what must have been a titanic clash in the Central Committee, the contending Chinese factions fought out their differences. That Chou carried the day—after what struggles and confrontations still is not clear—was confirmed later when Chinese policy was explicitly shifted from "dual confrontation" to the recognition of the Soviet Union as a more threatening enemy than the U.S.

For the rest of 1970, much signaling back and forth ensued—some of it unrecognized or unacknowledged—with Nixon and Kissinger doggedly pursuing their object of sending a special emissary to China. Primarily they wanted to use a rapprochement with Peking *to influence Moscow* to help with a settlement of the war in Vietnam and to enter an arms control agreement; secondarily they wanted to establish more leverage with both the Soviets and the Chinese. Then, too, as he approached midterm, President Nixon began to think more and more about his reelection prospects in 1972.

On December 8, 1970, the White House received from Chou a personal message to Nixon relayed through the Pakistani channel. Chou welcomed again the sending of a special American envoy but only to "discuss the subject of the vacation [by American troops] of Chinese territories called Taiwan."

In January 1971, the Romanians sent along another message, this time from Chou *and* Lin, confirming the earlier message, and adding an invitation for Nixon himself to visit—carefully linking that suggestion to his earlier visits to the capitals of those other thorns in Moscow's side, Romania and Yugoslavia.

The American journalist Edgar Snow had met with Mao in December—a friendly signal to the U.S. that no one in Washington picked up, since Snow was considered too far left to be in good standing there. Nixon would be welcome to come to China, Mao told Snow, "either as a tourist or as president." If Nixon came, the shrewd Chinese patriarch suggested, it would probably be in the election year 1972; and he wondered to Snow—as well he might have—why the White House did not want the State Department to know about the proposed visit of a special envoy.

Knowing nothing of Mao's talk with Snow, Nixon replied in writing to Chou's message of December 8. The U.S. was willing to discuss Taiwan and the reduction of its forces there, he said, but wanted also to talk about "the broad range of issues which lie between the People's Republic of China and the United States." He made no reference to the later suggestion that he, too, might come to China—although in the previous October he had told *U.S. News and World Report* that "if there is anything I want to do before I die, it is to go to China."

"The first months of 1971," Nixon reflected in *RN,* "were the lowest point of my first term as president." The congressional elections of the previous November had been a disappointment, the economy was lagging, antiwar sentiment was high, the war itself dragged on endlessly and SALT seemed stagnant. The opening to China, though promising, had not been assured; and the president had started to worry, with reason, that he might not be reelected. Edmund Muskie, the "Lincolnesque" Democratic Senator from Maine, led in the early presidential polls.

Worse was to come. Supplies for North Vietnamese and Vietcong forces were pouring down the Ho Chi Minh trail—not really a "trail," at all, but an interlocking maze of pathways running through Laos from the north, generally parallel to the border of South Vietnam. The system of trails and roads was so complex that it had defied all attempts at serious interdiction. On January 16, Nixon authorized a major operation to choke off the tonnage coming down from North Vietnam, much of it transshipped from the Soviet Union and China.

The president had learned, however, from the Cambodian incursion seven months earlier. Gone were the Churchillian pretensions, the macho language. Operation Lam Son across the Ho Chi Minh trail would be carried out by ARVN ground troops only, though they were to be ferried in by American helicopters and gunships, and supported by American B-52s. ("You could never go wrong," Philip Caputo wrote of the war in Vietnam, "if you killed people at long range with sophisticated weapons.")

Lam Son would test the efficacy of Vietnamization's second purpose—to improve ARVN's fighting qualities. Primarily, however, Nixon hoped the absence of American troops would avoid the firestorm of home-front anger that had followed the Cambodian operation in the previous spring.

On February 8, 1971, the five-thousand-man ARVN force was carried into Laos. In *RN* Nixon claimed that "most" of Lam Son's military purposes were achieved and that "the Communists were deprived of the capacity to launch an offensive against our forces in South Vietnam in 1971." In fact, the Laotian operation plainly was a disaster.

As American and South Vietnamese forces had claimed in the Tet offensive three years earlier, ARVN troops may have had a technical military success; more important, they and their American backers suffered a devastating psychological and political defeat. Even Nixon, in *RN,* concedes that the North Vietnamese opposition was stronger than expected, the American air cover was insufficient, the ARVN commanders pulled out early (beginning March 18) and the "strategic retreat" then became a rout. ARVN morale was badly shaken, rather than reinforced as hoped. Television pictures of South Vietnamese troops clinging to helicopter skids as they fled Laos destroyed claims that Vietnamization was turning ARVN into a fighting force that could "hack it"—a phrase much heard at the time.

Contrary to Nixon's hopes, moreover, the Laotian campaign again aroused intense opposition in the U.S. Despite his insistence that the operation had been staged to protect the withdrawal of American troops, much of the public saw it as still another widening of an endless and debilitating war, still another desperate gamble for military victory. In a speech at the time, I described as inexplicable a policy that "required the bombing of three countries and the invasion of two in order to evacuate one."

Lam Son backfired in another way. The war leaders in Hanoi correctly took the withholding of American ground troops from the campaign as a clear signal that Nixon was not prepared to accept more domestic turmoil or casualties in waging major offensive operations on the ground; American troops really were being taken off the board. That only increased Hanoi's confidence in the battlefield outcome and stiffened its resistance to compromise at the conference table. Why help the Americans slip out of a war that North Vietnam obviously was winning?

The North Vietnamese leaders got something of a jolt in March, however, when Chou En-lai visited Hanoi. At a news conference, Nixon had insisted that nothing in the Laotian campaign was directed against China; nevertheless, Peking had sharply criticized the Laos operation—though not so sharply as it had condemned the invasion of Cambodia the year before. Chou, too, had read Lam Son's exclusive reliance on ARVN troops as proof that the U.S. was serious about pulling out of Vietnam. He relayed that view to the North Vietnamese—but *because* of it, he did not offer to increase Chinese aid or to enter combat on Hanoi's behalf. Though, in any case, China was unlikely to have done either, Chou's reinforced view of American intentions was one of the few real gains that Lam Son—on balance, a net loss—brought Nixon.

The hard-eyed men who ran the North Vietnamese government were not noticeably less perceptive after the death of their senior colleague, Ho Chi Minh. They understood the meaning of Chou's performance; he was tacitly advising them to settle the war and not to count on China for more assistance if they chose to fight on. But they had no intention to settle, which meant compromise; they aimed, as they always had, to win.

Laos in February and March 1971 may have been one reason that the Chinese delayed their answer to the Nixon message of December 16, 1970, in which he had proposed an agenda for the projected visit of his special emissary to China. But by then things were beginning to look up a little for Nixon. In April, following an NSC meeting on China during which Rogers, Laird and other high officials were *not* told how far the secret diplomacy with Peking had carried rapprochement, the Nixon administration announced the most important of its numerous steps to ease trade with China—the lifting of major elements of a twenty-one-year-old trade embargo. Perhaps more important in the short run, a further withdrawal of one hundred thousand American troops from Indochina was announced, to be carried out between May and December 1971.

April also was the month of Peking's famous "ping-pong diplomacy." The American table tennis team was invited to participate in world championship matches in China, an important breakthrough in contacts between the two nations. On April 14, Chou personally and ostentatiously received the American team; in his remarks to its members, he said that a "new chapter" had been opened in Sino-American relations. The Cambodian and Laotian operations obviously had not closed that new chapter.

Late in the month, the Pakistani ambassador delivered the long-awaited response from Chou. It confirmed that discussions with the American emissary could follow the lines Nixon had suggested. The next day, as was all but foreordained, the president—after consulting the ubiquitous H. R. Haldeman—chose Henry Kissinger to make the historic trip to China. Who else would have the White House perspective, would guard the White House interest against the grasping bureaucracy and would respond most ardently to Nixon's every wish?

Yahya Khan was asked in a back channel to inform Chou that a formal reply would be forthcoming in May. In the meantime, would Chou be sure to confine any messages to the Pakistani channel? Nixon and Kissinger did not want leaks; even more so, they did not want Peking communicating with or inviting other Americans without White House knowledge. They wanted the triumph for themselves, not unjustly. On May 9, in the promised formal response, Chou was told that Kissinger would arrive sometime after June 15. Perhaps to his puzzlement, the Chinese premier was urged once again to use only the Pakistani channel.

The good news continued, as the Kissinger-Dobrynin talks and Kissinger's end runs around the SALT delegation brought a "breakthrough" with the Soviets on May 12, 1971. A week later, on May 20, Nixon announced in Washington the terms of the breakthrough deal, as they also were being made public in Moscow; the superpowers had agreed to work out in the coming year an ABM treaty and, separately, "certain measures" to limit offensive weapons (see chapter 11).

Tight secrecy, however, had raised the possibility of trouble with the Chinese. A State Department spokesman, knowing nothing of Kissinger's planned trip, remarked that the question of whether Peking or Taiwan was entitled to a seat in the U.N. was "an unsettled question subject to future international resolution"—a position both claimants opposed and which might have nettled Peking at the wrong time.

Secretary Rogers, equally ignorant, responded unfortunately in London to questions about Edgar Snow. At the request of the Chinese, Snow had not written about his interview with Mao at the time; his account of their talk, including Mao's remark about a Nixon visit, finally appeared in an issue of *Life* on the newsstands in late April. Rogers dismissed Mao's invitation to Nixon as "not serious," termed China "expansionist" and confounded Kissinger's assurances to Dobrynin by saying that if improved Sino-American relations stimulated the Sino-Soviet feud, that would be a "dividend" for Washington.

Nixon sought to repair the damage at a news conference on the same day, saying "I hope, and as a matter of fact I expect, to visit Mainland China sometime in some capacity. I don't know in what capacity."

He must have been successful, and no doubt the alert Chinese had long since detected the extraordinary fact that the secretary of state was "out of the loop" during one of the great diplomatic episodes of the postwar era—perhaps of the twentieth century.

The SALT "breakthrough" in May 1971 all but guaranteed a summit meeting with the Soviets—and began to put a redeeming light on Nixon's election prospects. They looked even better after June 2, when another message from Chou confirmed that neither the American-Soviet SALT announcement nor Rogers's remarks had offended the Chinese enough for them to back away from their willingness to receive Nixon's envoy.

On July 9, 1971, Kissinger made his secret trip to Peking, while Nixon's assistant press secretary, Gerald Warren, put out the word in San Clemente that Kissinger—supposedly in Pakistan—was indisposed with a stomachache. On July 6, however, as Kissinger was still on his way to Pakistan to begin his adventure, Nixon himself had come close to giving away the game in an extemporaneous discussion of world affairs with news executives meeting in Kansas City. During one of his spontaneous *tours d'horizon,* he could not resist remarking that it was "essential" for his administration to "take the first steps toward ending the isolation of Mainland China."

No American reporter paid any attention. Jim Deakin of the *St. Louis Post-Dispatch,* a splendid but sometimes choleric correspondent, complained afterward that it was "the worst speech [he] ever heard a president make." British and Asian reporters, however, picked up the hint and had to be put off with White House blandishments. Despite Nixon's near-gaffe, the secret held.[17]

From late July 9 until July 11, Kissinger conferred in Peking with Chou and other Chinese officials in long meetings and meals. One consequence was that Nixon's official visit to China was set for the spring of 1972, *before* he would go to Moscow, if a summit there ever were arranged. A joint statement about Kissinger's trip and Nixon's proposed visit also was agreed upon, to be issued in China and the U.S. at the same hour on July 15, 1971.

Kissinger's Peking experience, described in lavish detail in his memoir, was extraordinary—more so for the Chinese, perhaps, than for his small party, he suggests perceptively, because it so unmistakably marked the Chinese leaders' emergence as a major force on the world scene, after the isolated and traumatic years since the Long March. Kissinger, for his part, obviously was charmed by Chou, Huang Hua and other Chinese officials, and deeply impressed—who would not have been?—to be at the center of such a momentous undertaking.

Perhaps a little carried away by the occasion, he assured Chou that the U.S. would inform him "of any understanding affecting Chinese interests that we might consider with the Soviets"—a pledge, to say the least, that skirts the edge of evenhanded diplomacy. Kissinger never made such a pledge to the Soviets. He also shared with Chou some highly classified American intelligence photos and documents on Soviet military forces along the Chinese border—a dubious gesture not mentioned in his memoir.[18]

It's still not clear what substantive concessions Kissinger might have made on American forces in Taiwan—the ostensible reason China accepted Kissinger's visit. Nor is it known to what extent the Chinese overtly agreed to try to help the U.S. extricate itself from the Vietnam War. These issues, Taiwan for the U.S., Vietnam for the Chinese, could have been devastating in the two nations' internal politics.

Kissinger's mission did not prove so salutary for my great colleague, James Reston. Characteristically taking quick advantage of Chou's invitation to American journalists to visit China, Reston and his wife, Sally, arrived in Canton on July 8, a day before Kissinger's Pakistani jet landed in Peking. Though the Chinese were puzzled and slightly hurt at the inscrutable Americans' insistence on keeping Kissinger's presence secret, they obligingly delayed the Restons briefly in Canton, then put them on a slow train that would not bring them to Peking until Kissinger had left.

Never before in his distinguished career had "Scotty" Reston been so near to, yet so far from, a big exclusive story. Adding injury to insult, he came down with appendicitis on the day he was told—too late!—of Kissinger's coming and going; he had to undergo surgery and acupuncture at the Anti-Imperialist Hospital of Peking.

The secret thus preserved from the *New York Times* was disclosed to the world in a brief statement Nixon read on television from Los Angeles on the evening of July 15. Kissinger's trip was made public and the president's visit was announced for "an appropriate date before May 1972." The American desire for "a new relationship with the People's Republic of China," Nixon ritually observed, "is not directed against any other nation."

It was one of the most stunning news announcements I can recall, and the world reacted generally with shock and amazement—and with anxiety and anger in Moscow, where officials were too shrewd to accept Nixon's obligatory disclaimer. The Japanese were upset, too, at what they called the *Nixon shokku,* about which they had not been consulted despite their proximity to China and their own approaches to Peking.

Hanoi, as was only to be expected, felt betrayed by the Chinese—who, in any case, had been historically an enemy of the Indochinese nations. Most of the rest of the world saw the news as a step toward relief of a major international stress.

Events now began to fall happily into place for the Nixon administration—except for Vietnam. On July 26, Kissinger arranged with Chinese representatives in Paris that he would make a public visit to China in October; the announcement was held up for clearance in both capitals. And it was not only in foreign affairs that Nixon's star—and his reelection prospects—were rising; in August, he announced his New Economic Policy, including wage and price controls that were immediately—if all too briefly—popular among inflation-conscious Americans (see chapter 13).

Mao Tse-tung, meanwhile, resurrected an early article citing the necessity for a united front with a less immediately dangerous adversary, when in the presence of a "principal enemy." This document had been written in 1940 to justify Chinese Communist cooperation with the Kuomintang against the Japanese; with extraordinary economy, Mao adapted it to the circumstances of three decades later, and no one doubted—certainly not Moscow—who formed the united front against whom this time around.

Nevertheless, in September, even as American-Soviet work continued on the ABM treaty and the interim offensive-arms agreement, difficult quadripartite negotiations on Berlin were completed favorably; the agreement removed long-standing East-West tensions involving that divided city, and confirmed that the Soviets were still willing to do business even with the new friend of their old enemy in Peking. A minor but useful American-

Soviet agreement to reduce risks of accidental war also was reached late in September 1971.

Shortly after a second Kissinger visit to China was made public on October 5, Nixon was able to announce another stunning achievement for his diplomacy: an American-Soviet summit, in Moscow in May 1972, at which an ABM treaty was to be signed (see chapter 11). That would be *after* Nixon's planned visit to Peking. Linkage had succeeded to the extent that the opening to China undoubtedly had made Moscow more eager to advance its relations with Washington; and Nixon was in the happy position of being sought by both of his country's principal rivals for power and influence—without having made politically damaging concessions to either.

George Meany, the crusty chief of the AFL-CIO and an ardent anti-Communist, huffed that Nixon also should visit Castro in Cuba and Allende in Chile. "If he's going to visit the louses of the world," Meany wanted to know, "why doesn't he visit them all?" But most Americans, save the "China lobby" (really the Taiwan lobby) and the most devout anti-Communists, were pleased at what they took to be improved prospects for peace, international amity and American prestige.

Unknown to Americans at the time, moreover, Prime Minister Pham Van Dong of North Vietnam traveled to Peking in November and appealed to Mao Tse-tung to reverse the Chinese decision to receive Nixon in 1972. Mao not only refused; he took the occasion to urge Dong to accept a compromise settlement of the war—advice the disgruntled Dong did not immediately accept but an occasion he did not forget.[19]

Thus, 1971, which had begun so badly, became for Nixon a year of mounting success, and closed on an appropriate note. Richard Fecteau, a CIA agent, had been captured in China in 1952—when a younger Nixon was running for vice president and defending himself in the fund crisis. The president personally asked the Peking authorities to release Fecteau; when they did so in December 1971, it seemed a good omen for the future—even though the unfortunate Fecteau had served nearly all of his twenty-year term and was about to go free anyway.

The most remarkable circumstance of the Peking summit—February 21–28, 1972—was that it was held at all, bridging what Chou called "the vastest ocean in the world, twenty-five years of no communication" (see chapter 4).

The most extraordinary aspect of the Moscow summit—May 22–26, 1972—was that it was held despite the Peking summit *and* last-minute developments in Vietnam over which either side might well have withdrawn.

That these meetings came off smoothly, within three months of each other, is a tribute to the sharp calculation by Nixon and Kissinger of the vital interests of all three powers. Summits back-to-back, within three months and with powers hostile to each other, marked the apogee of the Nixon administration's diplomacy—in skill and professionalism, if not necessarily in consequences.

That vast ocean was an immense barrier to Sino-American rapprochement. Aside from the natural suspicions and fears it caused in Washington and Peking, the historical, cultural and political differences of the two societies (barely understood on either side), and the real difficulties of adequate communication, both governments had a great deal to lose domestically if their attempts at an "opening" were prematurely exposed or publicly shut down.

As a conservative president, heavily dependent on the conservative wings of both American parties, and the anti-Communist cultural mainstream of American politics, Nixon could have been heavily damaged by the charge that he was "conniving" with "Red China"—particularly that he was "selling out" Taiwan, on behalf of which a powerful public lobby exerted great influence in Congress. His reputation as a trickster without ethical concerns would have aided this picture.

The president's other strong identification, as an anti-Communist, gave him some political protection, and that undoubtedly encouraged him to proceed as he did; nevertheless, one false step could have roused fatal public and congressional opposition, which would have prevented further dealings with Peking, and would have done Nixon and his administration little political good—perhaps much harm.

The dangers for Nixon were political; in China, heads were quite literally at stake. As we have seen, and as Mao later confirmed to Nixon, a major internal battle had to be waged—between a Mao-Chou faction that favored and a Lin Piao faction that opposed rapprochement. So ferocious was the struggle that it certainly ended in the death of Lin, and possibly involved an attempted coup d'état by his faction against Mao and Chou.

Lin apparently died in a plane crash in Mongolia on September 12, 1971, less than two months after Nixon's forthcoming visit to China had been announced on July 15. Not until July 1972 was Lin's death in the wrecked plane "confirmed"; later charges were made that the crash had occurred while he was in flight to the Soviet Union following a failed coup—in which, perhaps, the murders of Mao and Chou were projected. It's also been alleged that Lin was carrying Chinese secrets—such as the tapes of the Chou-Kissinger conversations of July 1971.

Considering these shadowy circumstances, all taking place in a closed society, it is not strange that speculation continues whether the plane crash was accidental or whether, in fact, Lin died in that manner. The Soviet press, moreover, has had to deny charges that Moscow was in collusion with Lin in the alleged coup attempt.

It's possible that Lin did *not* attempt a murderous coup, or even plan one, but was the victim of a purge by Chou and Mao. In any case, the struggle within the Peking government obviously was not a casual game; it was about power itself, and the loser paid the ultimate price.

If the stakes were high, the results justified the effort. Renewed relations between China and the U.S. (interrupted only slightly by the repressed student revolt in June 1989) made inevitable the economic reforms that since have moved China toward a more capitalistic system. Nixon's opening to China also relieved the threat of Sino-Soviet war; it permitted the Chinese to concern themselves with internal needs rather than doctrinal and border disputes; and certain echoes of the events of 1972 undoubtedly still rang in the ears of some of the students and others who electrified the world with their stand in Tiananmen Square for a more open democracy.

Nixon's approach to China moved Moscow to hasten the Nixon-Brezhnev summit and to try, not too successfully, to be more helpful in Vietnam; the Soviets also quickly reached a number of agreements—notably on Berlin—that might otherwise have taken longer or never have been reached.

Since the agreements at the Moscow summit set the superpowers on an all but irrevocable course—surviving through SALT, intermediate nuclear forces (INF), and strategic arms reduction talks (START)—the Peking summit's pressure on the Soviets also may take substantial credit for some significant advances in strategic arms control.

In an effort to soothe Japanese sensibilities, the U.S. announced in July 1971 that the Ryukyu Islands, including Okinawa, would be returned to Japan's sovereignty the next year; and when Japan and China then agreed to reopen diplomatic relations, an important three-nation link had been joined in the Pacific, sharply limiting the possibilities of Soviet influence there following the ultimate North Vietnamese triumph in Indochina.

Sino-American friendship also assured the two Koreas that no repetition was likely of the alignments of the early fifties, when China had intervened against American troops advancing toward its borders. What effect that recognition might yet have on Korean reconciliation, hence on the maintenance of American forces in South Korea, has yet to be seen.

For all these reasons and because a "sleeping giant" was brought more actively into the world community, the opening to China is Richard Nixon's true monument in international affairs—all the more rare and impressive because he planned it just about as it happened.

In late 1971, North Vietnamese forces had stepped up military activity in South Vietnam, including the shelling of Saigon itself. This was seen in Washington as a clear violation of the old agreement of 1968, as a result of which Lyndon Johnson had stopped the bombing of the North; so Nixon promptly *resumed* bombing, reawakening fierce domestic opposition to the war.

In January 1972, however, he announced the withdrawal of seventy thousand more Americans; and two weeks later he took to television to sweeten his peace proposals. Repeating his offer to withdraw all American forces while the North Vietnamese remained in place after a cease-fire, he also offered internationally supervised elections in the South with President Thieu stepping aside, so that all candidates would be competing on a level playing field.

In a dramatic effort to put the U.S. in a more favorable light, Nixon even detailed Kissinger's fruitless private meetings with the North Vietnamese and outlined numerous previous American peace proposals. He was interested, he insisted "in almost any potential peace agreement [but] the only kind of plan we would not consider was one that required us to accomplish the enemy's goals by overthrowing our South Vietnamese ally."

Thus, his and Kissinger's original basic requirement for a settlement still held; the U.S. would not "accept" a change in the South Vietnamese regime that appeared to have been forced by military action. That, however, was exactly the reverse of what Nixon, in *RN,* called the North Vietnamese "bottom line": "they would not agree to a settlement unless [the U.S.] agreed to overthrow Thieu."

So on that sticking point the diplomatic stalemate continued—until, on March 30, 1972, *after* Nixon's visit to China but *before* his trip to Moscow, the North Vietnamese launched a powerful offensive across the Demilitarized Zone into South Vietnam—not a guerrilla uprising but a conventional, tank-led assault by a force eventually estimated at 120,000 men, and an obvious bid to end the war by the military conquest of the South.

Nixon was convinced, he confided to his diary, that "the U.S. will not have a credible foreign policy if we fail [in Vietnam]." To Kissinger, who took a less apocalyptic view, the president railed that if the North Vietnamese succeeded in driving the U.S. out of Indochina, "sitting in this office wouldn't be worth it. The foreign policy of the United States will have been destroyed."

He was certain, too, as was Kissinger, that the Soviets were behind the invasion, and perhaps had planned it. Intelligence indicated that the North Vietnamese offensive relied heavily on Soviet arms shipments.

Nevertheless, Nixon risked the Moscow summit by responding powerfully to Hanoi's attack, though American ground forces had been mostly withdrawn from Vietnam. Virtually unchallenged American air power, operating from navy carriers and including a big buildup of B-52s, enabled him eventually to thwart the offensive with devastating attacks on both the invading force and on North Vietnam itself. ARVN bore the brunt of the fighting on the ground, performing well at first, but soon showing once again that Vietnamization had not yet made it a first-class combat force.

ARVN never developed sufficient morale and confidence in itself or its officers or, above all, in the Saigon government.

Nixon also responded diplomatically, again fiercely, to Hanoi's drive. To Dobrynin's face, Kissinger accused the Soviets of "complicity" in the offensive and threatened a hardening American position on matters of interest to the Soviets. The Chinese were told that their expressions of support for the invasion were "not helpful"; but to signal that the U.S. held its new friend, China, less responsible than its old adversary, the Soviet Union, Nixon played some ping-pong diplomacy of his own. On April 18, 1972, even as the battle raged in Vietnam, he received a Chinese table tennis team at the White House.

Despite events in Peking, Indochina and Washington, and the stiffening American attitude toward the Soviet Union, or perhaps because of them, Moscow invited Kissinger to Moscow before the summit. During his visit in April 1972, and despite Nixon's instructions to talk only about Vietnam, Kissinger accepted—as will be recalled from chapter 11—Brezhnev's proposal (originally Kissinger's own) for a freeze on SLBMs in the SALT agreements.

Brezhnev seized the occasion also to deny that the Soviet Union was behind the North Vietnamese offensive; he blamed not only Hanoi itself but Peking as well, on grounds that both wanted to scuttle the planned American-Soviet summit. The North Vietnamese, he disclosed, had formally requested their supposed ally, Moscow, to cancel the summit with their active adversary, the U.S.—just as they had asked Peking not to receive Nixon in February. As the Chinese had done, Brezhnev refused. He, like they, had interests to pursue, allies or no allies.

Brezhnev apparently was angered that Hanoi had withheld its hand before the Sino-American summit, then had unleashed its mightiest attack of the war just before Nixon was scheduled to visit Moscow—an act that obviously and perhaps purposely endangered the summit. His protestations convinced Kissinger that Moscow was not, in fact, in collusion with Hanoi in the North Vietnamese offensive.

The Soviet leader would not agree, however, to put pressure on Hanoi for a settlement; he would only promise Kissinger to transmit American negotiating proposals to the North Vietnamese, and he did send a senior Communist party official to Hanoi after Kissinger's departure. The North Vietnamese, who also had interests, continued on their chosen course.

As May opened, with the North Vietnamese offensive not yet turned back, bad news from Vietnam rained down on the White House. On May 1, General Creighton Abrams, the commander of American forces, reported that Quangtri had fallen to the North Vietnamese and the crucial battle for Hue was beginning; worse, the brittle morale of ARVN—no matter how "Vietnamized" by American training—was collapsing.

This makes perhaps more understandable Nixon's remark at an NSC meeting on arms control on the day he received Abrams's news. The president had interrupted Gerard Smith's objections to the SLBM agreement with Brezhnev by exclaiming: "Bullshit!"

In his exasperation Nixon also was preoccupied with the decision whether to cancel the summit because of what he then continued to believe was Moscow's complicity with Hanoi. His mood was not improved by a blunt note from Brezhnev, urging him to refrain from further action in Vietnam that might hurt chances for a successful summit.

On May 2, Kissinger met again in Paris with Le Duc Tho—and found not only the usual unyielding foe across the table but one so confident of victory that he was willing to spurn even the pretense of negotiation. It was not only the shortest but the testiest of their secret meetings, crowned by Le Duc Tho's private, parting boast to Kissinger that Hanoi's war prospects were "good."[20]

Kissinger flew back to Washington that night (one can only stand in awe of his resistance to jet lag) and in their first discussions—aboard the *Sequoia*—he and Nixon agreed that the Moscow summit should be canceled. Not only were North Vietnamese troops in Soviet tanks moving on Hue but Soviet influence, if it ever had been exercised, certainly had not restrained Hanoi from its great offensive.

On further reflection, however, the president and his national security adviser saw that cancellation would not help to end the war; it would only further arouse domestic dissent and hand Moscow a golden chance for a worldwide campaign blaming the U.S. for the summit's cancellation. Besides, the summit had been scheduled in May 1972 to help along Nixon's reelection six months later; to cancel it could have the opposite effect and surely would hand the Democrats an issue against him.

Secretary of the Treasury John B. Connally was influential in this reconsideration. Cancellation would be bad politics for Nixon, he argued; if anyone canceled, it should be the Soviets, and he doubted that they would. These arguments were persuasive, particularly as it was obvious that canceling would mean continuing war *and* loss of the summit, a worse bargain than going through with the summit despite the war.

Nixon was determined, however, as he makes clear in *RN,* to punish North Vietnam severely if no settlement was to be had; Connally strongly supported that idea; and after the May 2 meeting with Le Duc Tho, Kissinger agreed. They decided to make good on this determination, even though that might—in view of Brezhnev's note of May 1—cause the *Soviets* to cancel the summit. To aides including Kissinger and Connally, Nixon observed, however:

The summit isn't worth a damn if the price for it is losing Vietnam. My instinct tells me that the country can take losing the summit, but it can't take losing the war.

Therefore, in a televised speech on May 8, 1972—the Moscow summit was scheduled for May 22—the president took the most drastic military step since the invasion of Cambodia. He announced the mining of North Vietnamese harbors to cut off its war supplies, a "savage blow" that both he and Lyndon Johnson previously had refused to permit. Continued and expanded bombing of North Vietnamese cities also was ordered; and from May 9 to October 23, they were heavily pounded. At least 41,500 attack sorties against the North were carried out by more than two hundred B-52s from Guam and Thailand, and from five attack carriers in the Tonkin Gulf.

This warlike response to the fruitless Kissinger–Le Duc Tho meeting of May 2 was combined, in Nixon's speech, with the most forthcoming of his peace offers: the promised unilateral American withdrawal after a cease-fire, he said, would be completed in four months rather than the six previously proposed.

New outrage at the escalation—in Congress, the press and among opponents of the war—was nevertheless immediate and high-pitched, though later polls put the public firmly on Nixon's side. One reason was the many Americans who had come to oppose or resent the war only because they thought it was not being won; Nixon's stiff new action looked to them like a proper application, at last, of American power.

The *opposition* to escalation, which found greater voice in the press, was focused on the likelihood that the Soviets now would break off the summit—as, at an NSC meeting earlier in the day of Nixon's speech, the CIA had predicted they would. Kissinger also had predicted a "better than even chance" that Moscow would cancel. John Connally dissented again.

The response to the assault on North Vietnam in the Communist world, Kissinger noted acidly in his memoirs, was "much more restrained" than in the U.S. Peking expressed concern about Chinese ships rather than North Vietnamese harbors, and continued preparations for visits in June by the Republican and Democratic leaders in the House, Gerald Ford and Hale Boggs. Moscow protested—but more about the American bombing of Soviet ships in Haiphong harbor than about the mining of the harbor itself. The Soviets did not even hint at cancellation of the summit in a routine denunciation of Nixon's moves by Tass, or in a careful protest note from Brezhnev.

Even Hanoi, the target of the mining, reacted in a way that tended to confirm Kissinger's belief that the North Vietnamese were more tractable when threatened, and most intransigent when they believed themselves in the strongest position. On May 12, at a news conference in Paris, Le Duc

Tho affirmed the willingness of his government to resume the Paris peace talks and remarked that "there is no reason not to arrive at a negotiated solution to the Vietnamese problem."[21]

There's little doubt, therefore, that Nixon's harsh military measures finally sent—with vital assistance from Moscow and Peking—a decisive message to Hanoi. The Nixon speech of May 8, 1972, marked the beginning of the end of the war in Vietnam—not so much because of the mining and bombing he decreed (which, though effective, were well within North Vietnam's vast capacity to absorb punishment) but because of the interpretation Hanoi was forced to place upon this tough announcement and its aftermath.

Nixon had not flinched before the massive North Vietnamese invasion of the South, he had not been cowed by Le Duc Tho's imperious treatment of Kissinger at the May 2 meeting and—most important—*he had not hesitated to risk the Moscow summit and a probable SALT treaty* in order to announce and carry out the most severe American military actions of the war. And his air power, by mid-May, had blunted the great offensive from the North, enabling ARVN to hold strategic points like Hue, Kontum and An Loc.

In sharp contrast, Moscow unmistakably had spurned the pleas and plight of its ally in Hanoi in order to receive and conclude agreements with an American president who—even as he signed—was mining North Vietnamese harbors, bombing its cities and hitting some Soviet ships. Peking, which had reversed nearly twenty years of its history to receive that same president just three months earlier, had offered only token protests of his war measures.

No genius was required of the leaders in Hanoi to reach the conclusions that Richard Nixon was not going to settle the war on their terms (the ouster of the Saigon government) or yield tamely to their military pressures; and—perhaps more important—that neither of their great Communist allies and supposed socialist brothers was going to penalize him. As a matter of hard fact, Hanoi was bound to conclude, both its allies would continue—in their own interests rather than Hanoi's—to *improve* relations with the greatest of the imperialist powers, the last barrier to North Vietnamese control of Indochina.

That conclusion was driven home a month after the Moscow summit, when Soviet President Nikolai V. Podgorny appeared in Hanoi personally to present the latest American peace proposals, to emphasize that they would allow the North Vietnamese army to remain in South Vietnam, and to urge a "negotiated settlement" rather than continued pursuit of military victory. In the summer and fall of 1972, Hanoi's leaders—supreme realists—began reluctantly but surely to move toward such a settlement.

It's still not clear how intense was the pressure, if any, felt by the North

Vietnamese from Moscow and Peking—upon which Hanoi was to a large extent reliant for supplies. Nixon leaves the impression in *RN* that *his* pressures on the Soviets and the Chinese were constant, as he urged them to coerce or persuade the North Vietnamese into settling. The likelihood is that not much more pressure was needed.

Kissinger exulted that because of the summits, the U.S. had achieved "a free hand in Vietnam." That August, *Nhan Dan,* the official North Vietnamese Communist publication, echoed the point. The U.S. had contrived "a balance of the great powers" to gain "complete freedom of action in checking by use of force the national liberation movement, first of all in pushing back the patriotic struggle" of the Indochinese peoples. And some Communist countries had taken "the dark muddy road of compromise," preferring "peaceful coexistence over proletarian internationalism, serving their own immediate interests at the expense of the revolutionary movement."[22]

During the same period of late 1972, the astute North Vietnamese observed the presidential campaign closely enough to understand that Nixon's opponent, George McGovern, stood little chance to win; after Nixon's nearly certain reelection, vastly aided by the Moscow and Peking summits, the president obviously might be harder to deal with—might not even want a settlement at all. On the other hand, Hanoi undoubtedly calculated that Nixon would want to reach an agreement—hence might be more accommodating in negotiations—*before* the election, in order to influence voters opposed to the war. On the last point, they proved to be wrong.

For all these reasons, by October 12, a month before the American election and after crucial negotiations with Le Duc Tho in Paris, Kissinger could report to Nixon that Hanoi was willing at last to meet the unvarying minimum condition for a settlement that the administration had maintained for nearly four years: the Saigon government, with Thieu as president, could remain in place after the war ended. The U.S. would not be judged, at least by *that* standard, to have lost the war; the Nixon-Kissinger geopolitical goal had been achieved.

But just barely. What finally brought Hanoi to accept this key point was American agreement to include representatives of the Saigon government *and* the Vietcong—now reorganized as the Provisional Revolutionary Government (PRG)—in a hybrid body established to supervise elections for a future government of South Vietnam. The other roles, if any, of this strange entity were murky. It was clear, however, that if this "Administration of National Concord" was not quite a coalition government, it to some extent legitimated the PRG; the Saigon regime would not be the *only* governing body in South Vietnam.

Of course the North Vietnamese army also would remain in the South, which was the *real* measure of victory or defeat; but Nixon coolly dismissed that problem in *RN*—years after Hanoi's ultimate takeover in Saigon—with the bald statement that

> the provisions of the agreement regulating the replacement of forces and closing the border sanctuaries in Laos and Cambodia would effectively cut [the North Vietnamese troops] off from their source of supplies and force them either to return to the North or gradually to wither away in the South.

President Nguyen Van Thieu, for one, did not believe such rationalizations for one minute. He saw, too, that if he accepted the Administration of National Concord, he would be granting some degree of recognition to the PRG. Besides, he had no intention of holding elections in South Vietnam.

But despite the reservations Thieu and his advisers had expressed in a string of memos passed through Ambassador Ellsworth Bunker to Kissinger, the negotiations proceeded toward agreement. Then, despite Thieu's anguish and anger, expressed personally and emotionally to Kissinger in Saigon, the security adviser—in his first nationally televised news conference, on October 26, just before the American elections—expressed confidence that "peace is at hand."

By loose definition, that might have been true; but strictly speaking, peace was far off. Thieu's strong objections had prevented the U.S. from carrying out a schedule agreed upon with Hanoi for signing the peace documents. That could be made to look as if Washington were reneging. More serious, Thieu's most powerful objection was to the major concession Nixon had made to Hanoi—*two years earlier,* in October 1970, and surviving into the October 1972 agreement—when he dropped his demand for a North Vietnamese withdrawal from the South.

The North Vietnamese obviously would not accept any change in that provision; so Thieu just as obviously could not be satisfied. Kissinger had greatly overstated the case—not only driving up public expectations but therefore indicating to Hanoi that, one way or another, the U.S. now would *have* to go through with a peace agreement—almost certainly the one arranged in October.

Kissinger's news conference did serve one important purpose. Predictably, Hanoi had responded to the delay in the schedule for signing the peace accords by making public the negotiating record, detailing its own concessions and accusing the Nixon administration of reneging on the deal. Still, Kissinger's "peace is at hand" statement stole the headlines from these North Vietnamese charges.

This was important because the one thing that might have damaged

Nixon's glowing 1972 election prospects was clear evidence that, in fact, he had reneged on the Paris accords—which, he had twice assured Hanoi, he regarded as "complete." Kissinger made it appear that the North Vietnamese had misunderstood; the U.S. had promised, he argued, only a "good faith" effort to have the accords signed on schedule. With characteristic nationalism, the American press and public generally accepted this sophistry and blamed Hanoi for standing in the way of peace.

Nixon had *not* particularly wanted an agreement before the election anyway, because he was confident of winning without it and because he feared that a last-minute accord would be considered phony and politically motivated (as he had considered Johnson's bombing halt in 1968)—particularly if it had to be accomplished by publicly dragooning South Vietnam into signing. Nixon believed that could cost him the support of "hard-hat Democrats"—blue-collar voters who would be upset by the appearance of selling out an anti-Communist ally.

To Kissinger's distress, Nixon refused to twist Thieu's arm before the election; and on that issue, the relationship of president and national security adviser apparently reached its lowest point—Kissinger fearing he would be made a scapegoat for failure to end the war, Nixon worrying that Kissinger was out of his control. And in the background, at least on Nixon's part, in late 1972, was the growing shadow of Watergate.

Once the president had achieved his landslide victory over McGovern—by the biggest margin, up to that time, in presidential history—Nixon's attitude changed. He did not want to begin his second term with the war still going on. But he wanted even less to have it taken out of his hands when Congress returned in January; Nixon believed members then would vote an end to funds for the war or for support of South Vietnam, particularly if Thieu and/or Nixon rather than Hanoi came to be seen as the barrier to peace. With the election over, he had no further fear of strong-arming Thieu.

The public was enthusiastic, moreover, that peace was at hand, and believed from Kissinger's statements that another meeting or two in Paris would end the war. If that prospect slipped away, and the war resumed as before—bloody, costly, endless—Congress surely would act and disaster could strike the political standing of even a president just reelected by a landslide.

Later in November, Kissinger resumed negotiations with Le Duc Tho; but the prospects seemed hopeless. He was demanding on Thieu's behalf a total of sixty-nine changes that the North Vietnamese had no reason to grant; and since that amounted to reopening the October accord, Le Duc Tho retaliated by retracting some of the concessions he had made to reach that agreement. His proposed alternative to this impasse—one that seems reasonable enough—was essentially a return by both sides to the October agreement that Nixon had assured Hanoi was complete. Tho had a strong position and did not hesitate to assert it.

Le Duc Tho's superiors in Hanoi, after four years of long-distance contention with Richard Nixon, had learned something about him. On December 4, they ordered the evacuation of children from the capital city. Two days later, Kissinger cabled Nixon from Paris that the renewed talks were at a "crossroads," owing to the North Vietnamese negotiator's hard stance. The president's options, he suggested, included the resumed bombing of North Vietnamese cities; during the downturn in negotiations since October 12, Nixon had reduced but had not ended the bombing of North Vietnam.

On December 14, Nixon ordered mines sown again in Haiphong harbor, and round-the-clock B-52 strikes against that city, Hanoi, and the crowded urban area between them; more than two hundred planes were marshaled for the assault. Despite Kissinger's urging, Nixon made no public explanation of his reasons for this renewed air war; he claimed in *RN* that he doubted whether he could any longer rally public support, and that he did not want to put the North Vietnamese under the psychological pressure of appearing to be bombed into a settlement.

This labored explanation overlooks polls that had shown heavy public support for the assault he had ordered in May; many Americans wanted *more* power used in Indochina, not less. Moreover, the bombing itself, rather than anything Nixon might say about it, would appear to put the North Vietnamese inescapably under the kind of psychological pressure he said he wanted to avoid.

Probably what Nixon *really* wanted to avoid was any more personal association than necessary with what became known and condemned worldwide as the "Christmas bombing." He correctly anticipated that after the high peace hopes of October and November, many Americans would be disappointed and shocked; and he knew, also, that heavy American casualties would be suffered in the skies above cities expecting attack and strongly defended by Soviet-provided surface-to-air missiles.

He was right on both counts. Probably no single act of the long Vietnam drama has been more heavily or passionately criticized than Nixon's indiscriminate Christmas bombing, in which the North Vietnamese suffered up to sixteen hundred deaths in a largely evacuated city. Its costs, moreover, were as high as Nixon had feared: fifteen B-52s shot down in twelve days, ninety-three American airmen officially listed as missing.

Nixon's ostensible purpose in risking such criticism and taking such losses—not to mention the damage his bombers inflicted, and the continuing war in the South—was outlined by Kissinger in a news briefing on December 16. Accusing Hanoi of raising new issues to prevent a settlement, Kissinger justified the bombing as an effort to convince Hanoi to accept a peace settlement—though Hanoi *had* accepted a settlement two months earlier.

"The obstacle to an agreement at this moment is not Saigon," he insisted at one point; at another, he said that the U.S. could not "accept the proposition that North Vietnam has a right of constant intervention in the South"—though since October 1970 the administration had been willing to leave the North Vietnamese army in the South after American troops had been withdrawn.[23]

Kissinger's version of events was widely accepted, but the necessity for Nixon to resume the Christmas bombing was not. To many observers, the timing and the circumstances of the Christmas bombing conveyed a sense of the president's undoubted frustration, of a need to lash out; James Reston referred in the *Times* to "war by tantrum."

A diary entry quoted in *RN* does hint at old angers unleashed; in it, Nixon suggests that criticism of the bombing was coming from

> those in the media who simply cannot bear the thought of this administration under my leadership bringing off the peace on an honorable basis which they have so long predicted would be impossible.
>
> The election was a terrible blow to them and this is their opportunity to recover.

This may be no more than Nixon's persistent animus against the press; but it seems unusually paranoid. No peace had been brought off, and the "honorable basis" for one achieved by bombing Hanoi was doubtful. Nixon's reelection victory, moreover, had been expected for months.

By trying to exonerate himself from responsibility, Kissinger may have helped along the suspicion that Nixon was indulging in personal vengeance; he let it be known among journalists that he had *opposed* Nixon's resumption of the bombing—which does not square with Nixon's repeated assertions in *RN* that Kissinger urged it more than once. Long after the fact, moreover, Kissinger concedes that he favored the bombing "at first with slight reluctance, later with conviction."[24]

To those who understood or believed that it was *in Saigon,* not Hanoi, that the October agreement had been torpedoed, such retaliation against the North Vietnamese seemed a particularly senseless and unwarranted policy, not worthy of American traditions or the administration's protestations. But even such critics did not know the shocking dimensions of the whole story.

Not for years was it generally understood that Nixon was *not* retaliating against Hanoi for holding up a settlement (though he may have been

venting the frustrations of the war and his rising fear of Watergate). Nixon
was bombing Hanoi *to persuade Saigon to accept the October agreement.*
The North Vietnamese were taking a terrible pounding and high casualties
to impress Nguyen Van Thieu with Richard Nixon's sincerity.

After his reelection, Nixon had given Thieu—in addition to promises of
lavish economic aid and abundant military resupply—a strong secret guarantee: swift, certain and powerful American retaliation "with full force"
if North Vietnam violated terms of a peace settlement. The Christmas
bombing was designed to impress Thieu with Nixon's ruthlessness—ultimately to convince the South Vietnamese president that Nixon would not
hesitate to keep his secret commitment.[25]

In his farewell speech as president of South Vietnam, on April 21, 1975,
Thieu reverted bitterly to those December days of 1972:

> Mr. Nixon told me as follows, "All accords are, in the final analy-
> sis, mere sheets of paper. They will be worthless if they are not
> implemented and if North Vietnam violates them. Therefore, the
> important thing is what you will do after the agreement, and what
> facilities we will make available to you if North Vietnam reneges
> or violates the agreement. . . . So you should not be concerned
> about the signing of the agreement.

Thieu's speech came after Nixon's own forced departure from the White
House but its meaning was clear. I tried to spell it out in a *Times* column:

> It was not Hanoi that reneged on the October agreement but
> Saigon that at first refused to accept the agreements negotiated by
> Mr. Kissinger and Le Duc Tho. That is almost entirely contrary
> to the official version given the American people.

Nevertheless, as 1972 turned to 1973, the Christmas bombing—even
when it was deplored—was generally regarded as Nixon's effort to force
Hanoi to negotiate. Once again Moscow and Peking came to the president's aid; they protested, but neither took any concrete steps to help
Hanoi, as must have been noticed in that beleaguered city. And once again,
the North Vietnamese leaders must have been impressed, if not so much
by the bombing itself, by Nixon's willingness to undertake it in the teeth
of so much public opposition, and by their supposed allies' failure to react.

On December 22, Kissinger cabled Hanoi that if negotiations were
resumed, the bombing of the cities would be stopped on December 31.
Nixon allowed a one-day halt to the bombing on Christmas day; but on
December 26, he specified—personally, he claims in *RN*—116 B-52 sorties
against the Haiphong-Hanoi area. That afternoon in Washington he re-

ceived a message from the North Vietnamese agreeing to another negotiating session in Paris on January 8—a telltale signal, he argues, that his attacks had succeeded in convincing Hanoi to return to the table.

No doubt Hanoi was eager for a halt to the destructive bombing; but the North Vietnamese had long since shown their ability to take punishment. It seems more likely that they agreed because it was not they who had broken off the talks. Kissinger, moreover, probably had conveyed to them that the resumed talks would be for the purpose of *renewing the October agreement.*

In his December 16 news briefing, he had said that the U.S. wanted "to continue in the spirit of the negotiations that were started in October"— *before* Saigon made its objection. He made the point all but explicit in another message to Hanoi on December 27: the January 8 meeting would be a "final effort to conclude the October negotiations."[26]

Again, on December 28, and not surprisingly, Hanoi agreed; the October agreement, after all, was what the North Vietnamese had been demanding since Saigon first blocked it. On December 29, Nixon ordered the bombing restricted to the area below the 20th parallel, excluding Hanoi, Haiphong and most of North Vietnam.

The question arose, when this was made public, whether Hanoi had knuckled under to well-calculated bombing, or had agreed to resume talks *despite* fruitless bombing. This chicken-or-egg question was irrelevant. The bombing not only had been for Saigon's education rather than Hanoi's intimidation; it had covered up the fact that when Kissinger and Le Duc Tho met in Paris on January 8, it would be to reinstate the basic terms of the October agreement, to which everyone but Saigon had agreed three months earlier. Hanoi had *held out* for the substance of that original accord, rather than knuckling under to anything.

Was it Nixon, then, who was settling for less than he wanted? He certainly got little more than he had had in October. Kissinger points out that "we thought the agreement of October adequate or we would not have proceeded with it." In an effort, however, to satisfy Saigon and confirm that the breakdown of the October negotiations was the fault of Hanoi, he details in his memoir some of "about twenty changes" in the October text—all presented as improvements—negotiated in January.

None are much more than cosmetic or technical—so slightly substantive that even Kissinger asks: "Were the changes significant enough to justify the anguish and bitterness of those last months of the war?" (He does *not* ask whether they justified the deaths and havoc in Hanoi, or in the continuing war.) Kissinger's answer is sadly telling: for the U.S., he conceded, the textual changes "probably" were *not* worth what it had taken to win them; for Saigon, they "almost surely" were.[27]

That is weak justification indeed, for the Christmas bombing and for three months more of war and destruction. The speed with which the changes were worked out further suggests how little was gained; after only *two days* of renewed meetings with Le Duc Tho, Nixon wrote in *RN,* Kissinger reported from Paris that "a major breakthrough [had] settled all the outstanding questions."

On January 15, 1973, all bombing and mining of the North was stopped. "The bombing had done its job," Nixon wrote in *RN,* "and now it could be ended."

But the bombing had *not* quite done the job, which was to persuade Nguyen Van Thieu that Nixon would protect the Saigon government. After the talks in Paris had been concluded, Alexander Haig still had to be dispatched to Saigon to make sure Thieu did not balk again; Haig went armed with a letter from Nixon, who wrote that it flatly expressed his intention to sign the agreement "if necessary, alone." Nixon's letter also restated his assurances that the U.S. would "react strongly" against any North Vietnamese violation of the peace settlement.

These assurances never were detailed to Congress or to the public, nor was either likely to have approved them or the return to the war they clearly suggested. Without the necessary congressional assent, Nixon's assurances seem likely to have been unconstitutional and—if not deliberately deceptive—at least overstated.[28]

Thieu had little choice but to rely on these assurances, even though the accord, in fact, constantly referred to "the two South Vietnamese parties" as if the PRG and Thieu's government were of equal standing. But Thieu continued to hold out through two meetings with Haig. On January 18, however, Washington and Hanoi publicly agreed to meet in Paris on January 23 "for the purpose of completing the text of the agreement." Thieu must have known that the game was up, but even then he made what Nixon called "one last stab at resistance." Finally, under intolerable pressures, he tearfully told Ambassador Bunker that he had held out as long as he reasonably could: "I have done all that I can do for my country."

So, in the end, it was Nguyen Van Thieu who knuckled under, as he might have done in October or November, had Nixon been willing then—risking whatever consequences there might have been to his own reelection—to bring on Thieu the relentless pressures he used in January. It is not certain that earlier agreement could have been reached and the Christmas bombing avoided, but it's hard to see—as Kissinger's rare self-questioning suggests—much improvement over the October text in the one Thieu was forced to swallow in January. The difference three months had made was therefore in the strengthening of Nixon's *private* but questionable assurances to Thieu.

On January 23—one day after Lyndon Johnson died in Texas, not quite having seen the end of "the bitch of a war" that had ruined his presidency—the agreement ostensibly concluding that war was initialed in Paris. A cease-fire, Nixon said, would begin in Vietnam on January 27: Peace with Honor.

But amazingly, in the same statement, he declared in effect that *he* did not intend to honor the agreement, in at least one major regard: "The United States will continue to recognize the Government of the Republic of South Vietnam as the sole legitimate government of South Vietnam."

That not only confounded the semirecognition of the PRG in the Council of National Concord; more important, it informed Thieu that Washington did not intend to honor that part of the agreement and that Thieu needn't either; and Thieu already had been assured that, whatever North Vietnam's response, he would have the backing of the Nixon administration.

The president said nothing, however, about what was so painfully plain to Thieu and his advisers, no secret to those who read the fine print in the agreement, and the prime reason why Hanoi, after so many years of struggle, was willing to accept a settlement: *the North Vietnamese army would remain in South Vietnam, in position soon to take over.*

In the long run, neither the toughness nor the agility of the Nixon-Kissinger diplomacy extricated the U.S. from Vietnam. What finally did it, instead, was their willingness to grant Hanoi's primary war aim— *unilateral* American withdrawal. That was a far cry from the campaign pledge of 1968 to "end the war and win the peace."

Neither the Soviets nor the Chinese, by representations to Hanoi, helped achieve a settlement, as Nixon had confidently hoped in the beginning; but they helped negatively when they did *not* thwart his schemes for rapprochement with Peking and arms control with Moscow. When the U.S. pursued China and gained its friendship, despite North Vietnamese protests, Hanoi was effectively isolated from Peking. Sino-American rapprochement caused the Soviet Union, in turn, also to seek and achieve better relations with Washington, again over North Vietnamese objections. Thus, Hanoi was isolated from Moscow, too.

In effect, the two great Communist powers—in order to pursue their own interests with the U.S.—*allowed Nixon a free hand in Indochina.* He used it to extract what he might not have been able to get otherwise—an agreement that he could call "peace" and characterize as "honorable," though it left the North Vietnamese in position to win the real war.

On January 24, 1973, the day after the agreement was initialed in Paris, John Ehrlichman encountered Henry Kissinger "in the doorway of the Roosevelt Room" of the White House and asked him: "How long do you figure that the South Vietnamese can survive under this agreement?"

Ehrlichman "expected Henry to give me some assurances. Instead he told me the truth and it shook me badly.

" 'I think,' Henry said, 'that if they're lucky they can hold out for a year and a half.' "[29]

He was a trifle pessimistic. The last Americans were driven from Saigon by the impending fall of the city to the North Vietnamese on April 30, 1975.

15

★

Hard-hat

★

[The D.C. crime bill] is as full of unconstitutional, unjust, and unwise provisions as a
mangy hound dog is full of fleas . . . a garbage
pail of repressive, nearsighted, intolerant,
unfair and vindictive legislation. . . .

—Senator Sam J. Ervin, Jr.

Law and order—considered imprecisely as a single value, if a redundant
phrase—formed a principal theme of Richard Nixon's 1968 campaign for
the presidency. That was to be expected in a nation growing more fearful
every day of crime in the streets, riots in the cities, disorder on the campus.

Law and order, pronounced as one word—"law'n'order"—also was the
fraudulent promise of the Southern demagogue, George Wallace, who had
learned since 1964 that a presidential candidate needed to keep his racism
implicit, his language symbolic. Nixon had little choice but to present
himself as a better bet than Hubert Humphrey and a more respectable
choice than George Wallace to keep law and order in the land.

Law and order, however, and Nixon's preoccupation with them—a
veritable obsession that included a far-fetched and self-serving view of
"national security"—were to lead him to fatal excesses. If the excesses were
not predictable, the obsession was manifest from the outset.

During the inaugural parade on January 20, 1969, for example, as Nixon
recalled in *RN:*

> Suddenly a barrage of sticks, stones, beer cans and what looked
> like firecrackers began sailing through the air toward [my limou-
> sine]. Some of them hit the side of the car and fell into the street.

I could hear the protesters' shrill chant: "Ho, Ho, Ho Chi Minh, the NLF is going to win."[1]

Among those lining Pennsylvania Avenue for the parade was Dr. Hunter S. Thompson, the self-proclaimed "gonzo journalist" who produced irreverent and often penetrating political articles for *Rolling Stone* magazine. He saw little need for alarm that the occupants of the car might be injured. It seemed, Thompson wrote,

> to be a huge, hollowed-out cannonball on wheels. It was a very nasty looking armored car, and God only knows who was actually inside it. . . . It was just barely possible to detect a hint of human movement through the slits that passed for windows.

Richard Nixon was in there, with Mrs. Nixon, and he did not like what he heard, or saw through those "slits"—even though the trouble soon subsided. Richard Kleindienst, an old Goldwater loyalist who was to become deputy attorney general, ordered standby troops to move toward the demonstrators. That, together with the passing of the new president's car, cooled things off.

But after a *Washington Evening Star* editorial commented the next day that none of those who had shouted obscenities at the president had been arrested, Nixon sent a copy to John Ehrlichman and asked: "Why not? I think an opportunity was missed when people would have suggested strong action."

In a separate note, he *demanded* action: "John E. It is of the highest priority to do something meaningful on DC crime *now*. Talk to Mitchell— give me a timetable for action."

To Gwen Cafritz, a renowned Washington hostess, Nixon sent a handwritten note on the same day, declaring: "We are going to make a major effort to reduce crime in the nation—starting with D.C."[2]

Nixon apparently had violent crime confused with the kind of demonstrations that had marred his inauguration. But all disturbances of the peace were distasteful to the new president and his campaign pledges to do something about "law and order"—mostly made in competition with Wallace—were clear.

Crime of all varieties, moreover, was then as now a major problem in the District of Columbia; and that federal fief is the one jurisdiction in America where a determined president has the actual authority to do something about crime. Richard Nixon had pledged to do it. He meant to keep that pledge.

In his first presidential news conference, on January 27, 1969, Nixon recalled the "major commitment" he had made in his campaign. So he had asked Attorney General Mitchell, he said, to prepare a program of legislative and administrative action "on an urgent basis." Four days later, a White House "Message on Crime in the District of Columbia" was made public.

The message, and later bills, featured a "preventive detention" plan for those who might have been set free on bail after being charged with the commission of a crime, but who were considered likely to commit another. The legislative bills included a "no-knock" provision allowing policemen to enter premises unannounced, ostensibly to seize evidence before it could be destroyed.

Nixon proposed, also, for District officials the same expanded power that state authorities had been granted in the 1968 Safe Streets and Crime Control Act—to use wiretaps and "bugs," a power already under heavy criticism as threatening wholesale violations of the Fourth Amendment guarantee against "unreasonable searches and seizures."

On that same January 31, when Nixon hardly could have had time to furnish the Oval Office as he desired, he let it be known at the highest levels of the administration that no crackdown on J. Edgar Hoover and FBI excesses was in prospect. In a crafty memo to the new president, the old director, Washington's master bureaucrat, had pumped up the potential for the FBI's National Crime Information Center. Nixon sent the document to Ehrlichman and Mitchell with the query: "Should we not ask J.E.H. how much more he could use for his programs?"[3]

That was hardly the way to begin reining in Hoover. After decades of managing to remain above criticism, the director had become a hated figure to the "New Left," the peace movement and minority groups; his autocratic ways had been controlled only partially by three successive Democratic attorneys general, Robert Kennedy, Nicholas deB. Katzenbach and Ramsey Clark. But Lyndon Johnson—as Nixon remembered in *RN*—had assured his successor in a preinauguration meeting:

> Dick, you will come to depend on Edgar. He is a pillar of strength
> in a city of weak men. You will rely on him time and time again
> to maintain security. He's the only one you can put your complete
> trust in.

The new president certainly did not forget or forgive those who had thrown beer cans at his inaugural parade. In a speech at General Beadle State College in South Dakota,* he offered the pointed warning that stu-

---

*Nixon was on this obscure campus for two reasons: to dedicate a library named for Karl Mundt, his old colleague on the House Un-American Activities Committee; and because widespread student unrest made it inadvisable for him to appear at a more prominent college. The next day, he gave the commencement address at the Air Force Academy, another unlikely site for a demonstration.

dents and demonstrators had better begin to exercise some self-restraint. If not, he said ominously, "we have the power to strike back and prevail."

The new lineup of officials at the Justice Department elaborated rather indiscriminately on Nixon's law-and-order theme. Six weeks after being sworn in, Attorney General Mitchell announced that he was ready to prosecute "hard-line militants" who crossed state lines to incite riots. The FBI had collected "a great deal of evidence . . . on this aspect of campus disorders," he said—though it was unclear how even the FBI could know what was on someone's mind when he or she crossed a state line, or what a person's purpose was in doing so.

Kleindienst, a man neither of moderate view nor restrained tone, was even more threatening:

> We're going to enforce the law against draft evaders, against radical students, against deserters, against civil disorders, against organized crime, and against street crime. . . . If we find that any of these radical, revolutionary, anarchistic kids violate the law, we'll prosecute.

It was hard to discern, in this pell-mell statement, any distinction between organized and street crime, on the one hand, and radicalism and dissent on the other—or, for that matter, between federal and traditional state responsibilities for law and order.

Thus, the new Nixon administration appeared as ready to use questionably constitutional means—or, as those who shared its attitudes would have said, "strong action"—against dissenters and demonstrators as against drug dealers and murderers. When questions of law-and-order procedure arose in the Nixon White House and Justice Department, the decision in every case was to "get tough."[4]

"You've got to crack down," Kleindienst told a group of Harvard Law School alumni, and that could have been the motto of Mitchell's Justice Department and Nixon's White House.[5]

These early indications rather accurately forecast, had anyone read them properly, some of the most troubling and dangerous directions—to itself as well as the country—the Nixon administration was to take. But the new president and his hard-line associates soon showed themselves *not* prepared to embark on what many authorities on crime believed was the most effective remedy available.

Owing to the assassinations of Martin Luther King, Jr., and Robert Kennedy within two months in 1968, each by gunshot, a Senate subcommittee was weighing a bill to require gun owners to obtain a five-year federal license, at no cost, for their weapons. Expert after expert testified to the necessity for strict gun control in any effective battle against crime;

felons, for example, would not be able to buy guns legally if the bill became law.

During the presidential campaign, even in the echoes of the shots that had murdered King and Kennedy, Richard Nixon had refused to support even a milder version of such legislation. When hearings were held in early 1969, no one was surprised that Associate Deputy Attorney General Donald Santorelli was sent to Capitol Hill to register the *opposition* of the new, tough, law-and-order administration.

The gun-licensing bill, Santorelli said, would be too expensive to administer and would be "an unwarranted invasion into the province of state and local governments." He did *not* say that it also would be highly unpopular with the millions of gun owners who regularly voted against any form of gun control, as well as against those few politicians bold enough to support it.

Nixon's tough-looking anticrime program for the District of Columbia consisted largely of leftover proposals from the Johnson administration that Congress had not approved. Among them were court reorganization, a thousand more policemen, ten more judges, twenty more prosecutors, an expansion of court and jail facilities, and a larger role in the District for the Bureau of Narcotics and Dangerous Drugs. The request for more policemen was obvious window dressing; Congress already had authorized such an addition to the D.C. force; but a dearth of qualified candidates had left nine hundred slots unfilled.

The core of the message, however, and its headline-grabber, was the proposal for the preventive detention of "dangerous hard-core recidivists." It was widely believed that crime rates were sharply increased by criminals who were arrested for one offense, freed on bail by "soft" judges, then committed more crimes before being tried for the first one.

George Wallace, with his gift for the memorable phrase, had dramatized the issue during his ugly presidential campaign, saying repeatedly that if one of his listeners were injured by a criminal, "he'll be out of jail before you're out of the hospital."

This perceived danger had been made more threatening, it often was argued, by the federal Bail Reform Act of 1966. It had been designed to prevent a judge from setting high bail for any defendant he might think dangerous, while the same judge turned other defendants free on little or no bail. That common practice often left the poor and uneducated and unprepossessing in jail awaiting trial, for want of bail, while wealthier persons and professional criminals "walked," sometimes on their mere pledge to show up in court.

The 1966 reform prohibited *any* bail requirement in noncapital cases in the federal courts—which included *all* D.C. courts—unless a judge had demonstrable reason to believe a defendant would "skip"—fail to appear for trial. As the crime rate rose in Washington, where most offenders (and most victims) were poor blacks, the Bail Reform Act came to be considered a large part of the problem.

Statistics showed, however, that only about six percent of *all* reported crimes—not just serious or violent crimes—were committed by persons free on bail. The bail reform legislation, moreover, had been sponsored by two conservative senators, Roman L. Hruska, Republican of Nebraska, and Sam J. Ervin, Jr., Democrat of North Carolina, neither a partisan of criminals. But the *fear* of crime is seldom lessened by such facts.

Preventive detention, if imposed in the District of Columbia, would most heavily affect blacks; that made the idea appear to some critics as an extension of Nixon's "Southern strategy." I wrote in the *Times* that preventive detention was

> sure to be perceived in the ghetto as one more way of making second-class citizens of black Americans—one more way of reacting punitively to the victims of conditions that breed and even encourage crime and violence, rather than of launching any real or effective attack upon those conditions.

Preventive detention also was denounced as an unconstitutional suspension of due process, since it would punish someone before he or she had been tried and found guilty of anything. It required a judge, moreover, to predict the commission of a new crime and to jail the person he believed might perpetrate it—*before* any law had been violated.

The need for preventive detention, if any, rested on the District's inability to provide what the Constitution supposedly required—speedy trial. In Washington, the average elapsed time between arrest and trial then was more than *three hundred days.* Thus, preventive detention appeared to be an unconstitutional remedy for an unconstitutional situation.

In practical fact, the Nixon bill allowed accused persons to be detained without bail only for a maximum of sixty days—far short of the more than three hundred that typically expired before a trial could be held. So in most cases it would not be a "remedy" at all; and that led to the suspicion that the proposal was addressed to voters' *fear of crime*—including the public outside the District—rather than to *crime itself.*

Preventive detention evoked particular outrage from a man Nixon was to have cause to remember for other reasons—Senator Sam Ervin, a North Carolina conservative on civil rights and most other issues but a zealous defender of civil liberties and the Constitution as he interpreted it. Nixon's plan "smacks of a police state," Ervin said, and added:

I have misgivings about imprisoning a man for crimes he has not yet committed and may never commit. Preventive detention in non-capital cases is repugnant to the traditions of a liberty-loving people. . . . If you lock everybody up, or even if you lock up everybody you think might commit a crime, you'll be pretty safe. But you won't be free.

Ervin no doubt would have denied it, but his early outrage at the D.C. crime bill, vigorously expressed, must surely have influenced his general attitude toward the Nixon administration. When he later became chairman of the Senate committee investigating the so-called Watergate offenses, he may already have been subconsciously convinced that Nixon and his men had little basic respect for the Constitution that Sam Ervin so often extolled.

Nixon's D.C. proposals served their immediate purpose—to tell the nation that he was living up to his tough-talk campaign and quick-action promises. Talk was one thing, however; real action was another, as was quickly realized by Tom Charles Huston, a twenty-eight-year-old Hoosier who was part of the Nixon speech-writing team.

As early as February 5, 1969, less than a week after Nixon's statement on crime in the District, Huston urged in a memorandum to Pat Buchanan that "presidential rhetoric on this issue must be matched by presidential action. . . . Consideration should at least be given to creating the impression of continuing *Presidential* action." (Huston's emphasis.)

Huston thought Nixon ought to issue some directives for minor executive actions and "get at least a limited D.C. Crime message up to the Hill as soon as possible." Buchanan forwarded his memo, and when it reached the Oval Office, Nixon endorsed it in his own hand: "Burns + Moynihan (copy to Haldeman). I completely agree with this memo—have the messages and directives on my desk Monday at 2 P.M."[6]

The administration nonetheless was unable to get proposed D.C. crime legislation before Congress until July 1969; even then, its highly controversial nature assured much further debate and acrimony. None of the legislation cleared Congress in Nixon's first year in office.

That hardly mattered politically; administration rhetoric caused it to be seen as standing up for law and order. Since some of the proposed muscle-flexing, like preventive detention, probably would not work, the president actually could have been better off if Congress had turned it down. He then could claim to have redeemed his law-and-order pledges, only to be thwarted by Congressional Democrats and "libs," who were constantly billed anyway as more concerned for criminals than for victims.

During congressional deliberations, the Justice Department attempted to shore up the case for preventive detention by ordering a study of the

rearrest rate of persons freed on bail. But when the study was released in
April 1970, it hardly suggested a need for such a drastic step. Of all persons
who had been charged with felonies *or* misdemeanors, during four weeks
of 1968 in the District, 11 percent had been rearrested on some charge
while awaiting trial; but of every 20 of those rearrested persons who had
been charged originally with *a violent or dangerous* crime, only *one* had
been rearrested on charges of committing another violent or dangerous
crime.

Ervin pointed out that if these Justice Department findings were typical,
twenty persons could be held without bail under the proposed legislation,
in hope of preventing a violent crime by just one of them. The study further
showed that two of every three persons charged with a *serious* crime,
released on bail, then rearrested, were arrested the second time for a *minor*
offense.

The House, however, had approved preventive detention before the
Justice Department study was published; the public's fear of crime was
pushing Congress finally toward action to mollify that fear. But in June
1970, a crime in the District that at first seemed to validate the need for
preventive detention again disclosed its shaky rationale.

A police officer was critically wounded by a robbery suspect who had
been arrested twice for armed robbery, but who was free on bail. The
wounded officer then shot and killed the suspect. Senator William Saxbe
of Ohio noted in debate that the dead man had been charged with armed
robbery on January 23 and freed on bail, then had been charged with the
same crime on June 1 and released again. He could have been held and the
officer would not have been wounded, Saxbe argued, had preventive detention been in effect.

In response, Ervin pointed out that the robbery suspect would have been
free on June 1 even if he had been detained for the permitted sixty days
after January 23. What might actually have prevented the second arrest
and the shootout with the policeman, Ervin contended, was a speedy trial
after the January offense.[7]

The "no-knock" and wiretapping provisions also encountered strong
opposition. Not only was a no-knock entry arguably a violation of the
Fourth Amendment; it might also provoke a violent reaction. Representative Abner Mikva of Illinois, the leader of the Nixon legislation's opponents in the House and now a member of the District of Columbia Court
of Appeals, pointed out that "the reaction of the average citizen to an
unexpected attempt to break into his home is to fight like hell."

Wiretapping also threatened wholesale violations of citizens' privacy
and constitutional rights—but would have little effect on the most feared
crimes: violence of all kinds, most of which was impulsive, or incidental
to other crimes—street muggings, for example—that could not be coun-

tered by eavesdropping. In fact, the state of the eavesdropping art at that time would mean taking officers off the street to man the taps and bugs; so the new law might even *increase* the incidence of violent street crime.

These arguments ultimately were to no avail. "Law and order," in a time of high and rising crime rates, was a call hard to resist by legislators who had to face a fearful public at the ballot box. Though the Senate at first rejected preventive detention, the House approved it and the provision became part of the compromise version between the two Houses. The final bill, in an effort to meet constitutional speedy-trial requirements, did include an important proviso: the cases of persons detained under the new law would have to be placed on an expedited court calendar, to be tried as soon as possible.

The final D.C. crime bill was approved by the House on July 15, 1970, and by the Senate on July 23—more than a year and a half after Nixon's original proposals. The legislation gave the administration an early but lasting reputation—not just with Sam Ervin—for putting anticrime expediency above the protections of the Constitution. That reputation was to be damaging later; but at the time the debate and the publicity surrounding it solidified the administration's law-and-order claims with those most concerned about crime and disorder. That political fact was more important than the legislation.

This "model anticrime program," as Mitchell called the D.C. bill, never proved itself an actual model that the states would follow, as the administration had said it would. Even preventive detention, with its superficial appeal, never has been much used in the crime-ridden District; the requirement for quick trial of those detained could not be met by crowded D.C. courts. District jails usually have been too overcrowded, anyway, to "accommodate" detainees.

Egil Krogh, a young Ehrlichman aide who had been given large responsibilities for crime programs, told the Hofstra conference in 1987 that the Nixon administration never was able actually to reduce crime in the District. But by such measures as additional policemen, increased narcotics treatment programs, and sodium vapor lights to illuminate crime-ridden streets, the administration did cut down "the rate of increase." Krogh did not mention preventive detention.

The year after he spoke, 372 people were murdered in the federal city, and D.C. police said 60 percent of the killings were drug related. In the first three months of 1989, 120 more murders were recorded, and President George Bush contemplated calling in the National Guard to help cope with what was still the District of Columbia's overwhelming crime problem.[8]

In its earliest weeks, the Nixon administration also moved to exploit new wiretap authority Congress had granted in 1968. With a judge's approval, anyone who had committed, was committing or was believed to be *about to commit* a crime punishable by a year or more in prison could be tapped or bugged. To protect "national security," that vaguest of grab-bag concepts, the president also was authorized to wiretap—*without* the concurrence of a judge—anyone or any group he believed to pose a threat.

In his 1967 State of the Union message, President Johnson had called for the outlawing of *all* wiretapping and bugging; but he had not vetoed the 1968 legislation, thus preserving other provisions that he approved and had sought. His last attorney general, Ramsey Clark, had refused to take advantage of the wiretapping authority.

Clark contended that the legislation probably was unconstitutional, surely permitted wholesale invasions of citizens' privacy, and would not be effective against most crime—since murderers, rapists, thieves and muggers rarely discussed their intentions or confessed their actions over the phone. (Gamblers did use the phone extensively in their business dealings; but could such sweeping legislation be justified by arresting bookies?)

Nixon had campaigned, however, on the premise that the "carefully considered and carefully drawn" 1968 legislation—a judgment not everyone shared—was necessary in his promised battle against crime. During John Mitchell's confirmation hearing, the attorney general–designate also assured a pleased John McClellan, the Democratic senator from Arkansas and principal sponsor of the anticrime legislation, that the new administration planned an active wiretap program.

Within a month, to much acclaim, Mitchell announced that taps had been placed on Mafia leaders—though the announcement must have placed those leaders on notice and lowered the value of the taps to law enforcement, if not to politics. Soon the attorney general disclosed, to less acclaim, that taps also had been placed on eight men indicted for conspiring to incite street rioting during the 1968 Democratic National Convention.

It was not at all clear that the so-called Chicago Eight—even if they had conspired to do *something*—had posed a threat to national security, or even had planned to commit crimes. They were charged under another section of the wide-ranging 1968 crime legislation, providing that anyone who crossed a state line "to aid or abet any person" in inciting a riot could be fined and jailed for five years.

Ramsey Clark also had refused to pursue this section of the 1968 act. Since it was impossible to know anyone's motive in crossing a state line— perhaps at thirty thousand feet in a jet airliner—and since those who planned peaceful protests could not necessarily know that they would turn into riots or result in criminal acts, Clark and many legal authorities regarded the provision as a palpable violation of the First Amendment rights of free speech and assembly.

Thus, indictment and trial of the Eight was dubious from the start. In a brief filed in federal court in Chicago, however, Mitchell asserted that those tapped and indicted were planning to "attack and subvert the government by unlawful means." Therefore, the government had not been required to get a judge's consent to the taps. And anyway, the president's duty to protect national security, in the administration's view, overrode the Fourth Amendment's prohibition against "unlawful search and seizure." As the nation was to learn, Richard Nixon regarded that duty as paramount—at least, he found it convenient to take that extreme position.

Here first appeared another fateful attitude: not only did the Nixon administration seem willing to subordinate constitutional protections to perceived emergencies, as in the D.C. crime bill; it also appeared to believe in the preeminence of presidential power if it came into conflict with constitutional procedure. "National security," in the White House view, was a magic incantation that could justify almost any presidential act.

In a trial so uproarious that one of the defendants, the Black Panther leader Bobby Seale, was bound and gagged in the courtroom, the Chicago riot defendants were acquitted—though Seale served time for contempt of court. In their cases, the national security wiretaps had proved worthless, except perhaps for the purpose of frightening some other dissidents into conformity; but the power to install such taps without a court order was there for a suspicious, security-minded, highly secretive president to use— and Lyndon Johnson had tipped that president to a man who could be trusted to exercise that power for him.

Actually, Nixon needed no recommendation from LBJ in order to rely on J. Edgar Hoover, the director of the FBI for nearly a half century and in 1969 the most feared man in Washington. As far back as the Hiss case in 1948, young Congressman Nixon had received helpful information from FBI agents and officials (see chapter 2). One of these sources was Louis Nichols, then Hoover's liaison with Congress, to whom Nixon in return passed along information from the House Un-American Activities Committee; the two had even colluded to keep information from Harry Truman's attorney general.[9]

The bureau also provided, in that period so crucial to Nixon's career, important documentary assistance—including copies of papers turned over to the FBI by Whittaker Chambers. It's highly unlikely that Nixon did not know that this arrangement had Hoover's approval, though both men denied and concealed their connection.

Just over a year later, by then a famous man for exposing Hiss, Nixon had returned the favor. The National Lawyers' Guild was preparing a damning report on FBI improprieties, but Hoover beat the Guild to the punch by leaking information purporting to show that the Guild was a Communist front. Then, the day before the Guild report was to be released,

Nixon made headlines with a demand for HUAC to investigate the organization. All this effectively blunted the damaging impact the Guild's charges might have had on Hoover and the FBI.

Nixon was not in doubt about Hoover's scruples, either. In 1956, the FBI chief had detailed for a meeting of Eisenhower's NSC the range of the bureau's surveillance tactics, including break-ins, bugs, mail openings, and wiretaps—all of which were to some degree illegal. No objection was heard from President Eisenhower, Vice President Nixon or Attorney General Herbert Brownell, who were among those present.[10]

A few months later, Hoover launched the COINTELPRO—for "counterintelligence program"—against the Communist party. That step, in the fifties, marked a fateful turn for the bureau—from more or less approved surveillance to secret harassment and disruption of persons and groups under some kind of suspicion.

Nixon also had consulted Hoover in 1962 on whether to run for governor of California and had received the bad advice to do it. On all his trips abroad in the sixties, he had been faithfully attended, on Hoover's instructions, by the FBI agents who posed as "legal attachés" at American embassies. And it had been, of course, to Hoover that Nixon had turned in 1963 (see chapter 7) immediately after he heard the news of John Kennedy's assassination—another significant point in Nixon's career.

It is not surprising, therefore, that it was also to the durable and "trustworthy" J. Edgar Hoover that President Nixon turned in early 1969, when he and Kissinger were outraged by a leak to the press concerning the secret bombing of Cambodia that they had ordered, and were desperate to conceal.

On May 8, the day the offending story (by William Beecher) appeared in the *New York Times,* Henry Kissinger and his closest aide, Colonel Al Haig, demanded of Hoover a "major effort" to ferret out the leak. Both the Cambodian bombing and the inquiry into a newspaper's sources were so sensitive that Haig ordered no record to be kept of the White House demand. The wily Hoover was too experienced to follow such an order; he kept a record anyway—though not in the regular FBI files—as a protection to himself and as a possible source of leverage on the White House.

FBI wiretaps—with no other authorization, even from the attorney general, as was legally required—were instituted on Beecher, three other reporters and thirteen administration officials, including such apparently trusted Nixon associates as William Safire and John Sears. Even so, Hoover never identified the leaker—which makes a significant point about the supposed efficacy of wiretaps.

Nor did Beecher's story alert the rest of the press, or even the *Times,* to a major story unfolding in secrecy in the skies over Cambodia—which makes a significant point about the complacency of the press. Hoover did suggest, however, that Kissinger's associate on the NSC staff, Morton Halperin, a member of "the Harvard clique" and one of those tapped, *could* have been the culprit.

Kissinger asked Hoover—who naturally made a secret record of the secret request—to "follow it up as far as we can take it and they [the White House] will destroy whoever did this if we find him, no matter where he is." This savage remark sheds interesting light on Kissinger's later contention that in wiretapping associates and reporters he merely "went along with what I had no reason to doubt was legal and established practice."[11]

Neither Hoover nor "they" ever did find or "destroy" that particular leaker, but the taps continued nevertheless—in the cases of Halperin and Anthony Lake, another NSC staff man, even after they quit the Nixon administration in protest and went to work for Senator Muskie's Democratic presidential campaign. Thus, these taps came to have political value to Nixon beyond their original purpose; they were a listening post on the Muskie campaign, and for that reason were even more sensitive than before. They also increased Hoover's potential leverage on the White House.

Recognizing the heightened sensitivity, if not yet the leverage, the president ordered in May 1970 that the reports from the taps were either to be handed personally to Haldeman or given in a sealed envelope to Haldeman's aide, Larry Higby. Hoover made a secret record of that instruction, too.

What a man so experienced as Nixon in the ways of politics and Washington may have suspected, we do not know; but Nixon officially learned of Hoover's bureaucratic treachery only belatedly. William Sullivan, an assistant to the director, was the custodian of the secret records, but Sullivan and Hoover were not getting along; so in an effort to gain White House support for himself, Sullivan in the summer of 1971 sent word of the secret records' existence, through Assistant Attorney General Robert Mardian (as he had then become).

Nixon then was forced to recognize the records' potential for blackmail and embarrassment, or worse. He ordered Mardian to retrieve them; with Sullivan's help, they were removed to the White House and preserved there.

This repellent story—Nixon and Kissinger betray their associates, Hoover betrays Nixon and Kissinger, Sullivan betrays Hoover—did not end as poetic justice would have had it, with Nixon turning on Hoover to fire him. Hoover obviously knew too much, and no one could be sure how much *more* he knew than was represented by the wiretap records.[12]

To Nixon and his closest aides, however, it must have been obvious that Hoover's knowledge of dubious White House activities was extensive; after all, he had participated in many of them. For example, at Nixon's personal request he had secretly funneled information to Representative Gerald Ford during the latter's White House–inspired effort to impeach Supreme Court Justice William O. Douglas.

Beginning just after Nixon's inauguration, Hoover sent the White House *thousands* of reports on the president's political adversaries, journalists critical of him, actress Jane Fonda, other unfriendly personalities and dissident organizations—including even those planning Earth Day, which was to have so much impact on the administration's environmental policies. In November 1969, the director formalized this service in Operation Inlet, a heightened effort to provide the White House with "high-level intelligence data in the security field" on a more permanent basis.[13]

At Nixon's request, Hoover eagerly assisted Vice President Agnew in his attacks on students, dissidents, intellectuals and the press—though the FBI supposedly was precluded from political activity. A bureau report on these targets, in summary form, went regularly to Agnew, including one on a student protest against a Nixon speech at a Billy Graham revival in Knoxville. Hoover also forwarded to Agnew all available derogatory information on Ralph Abernathy, the president of the Southern Christian Leadership Conference—and threw in for good measure the FBI's eavesdrop reports on the sexual indiscretions of Abernathy's predecessor, the late Martin Luther King, Jr.

As early as January 30, 1969, Henry Kissinger—acting on Nixon's instructions—had asked Hoover if the FBI could substantiate the president's suspicion that student and other demonstrations against the war in Vietnam were directed from abroad. Whether Nixon actually believed this or not—Lyndon Johnson apparently did—a report even tenuously linking dissent to foreign direction would be useful in battling the president's critics. Hoover assented to the White House request, as usual, but his report did not contain the kind of hard evidence of foreign influences that Nixon and Kissinger needed.

The White House therefore redefined what it was looking for, to make it easier to find. In a memorandum to the FBI and the CIA signed by Tom Charles Huston, the agencies were instructed to report practically *any* activities by foreign Communists that might encourage or further protest movements in the U.S. Huston then met with William Sullivan to impress on him the president's desire for such information.

Sullivan ultimately confided to Huston that one reason no hard evidence was being found was Hoover's order, dating to 1965, that put restrictions on FBI wiretapping and bugging, and prohibited mail openings and break-ins. This order reflected no ethical considerations on the director's part; rather, he had been faced with and had retreated before a rare congressional investigation of the bureau. Instead, moreover, of the quick acquiescence to FBI requests for authorization of such activities that he was accustomed to, Hoover had encountered stiff resistance from Nicholas Katzenbach, Ramsey Clark's predecessor as attorney general. Hoover's fear that the bureau's illegal activities would be exposed, its reputation damaged and his own position endangered, had caused him to issue the 1965 restraints on surveillance.

In 1970, after a dispute with the CIA, the irate director broke off relations with the intelligence agency. Thereafter, he made clear, if the CIA wanted the FBI to do sensitive domestic work—wiretaps, break-ins, and so on—the CIA, not J. Edgar Hoover, would have to get an authorization from the attorney general. But Richard Helms, the director of Central Intelligence, had no intention of making an official request for permission to do something the law specifically prohibited the CIA from doing. Neither did officials of the National Security Agency, who sometimes needed FBI help in code-breaking activities.

Thus, these agencies' frustrations with Hoover coincided with that of the White House; and when a storm of campus protest erupted in May 1970—about which more later—Sullivan and Huston concocted a plan to bypass him. On June 5, Nixon agreed to it, and appointed a committee of representatives from the intelligence agencies to consider improvement and coordination of their activities. As befitted his seniority, Hoover was given the chair; but in practice, the committee's activities were guided by his representative—William Sullivan.

The staff coordinator was Tom Charles Huston—"an intense, cadaverous, fiercely conservative former national chairman of Young Americans for Freedom," who seemed to his nominal superior, Ray Price, "overly obsessed with such matters as internal security and insufficiently sensitive to civil liberties." After the interagency committee was formed, Huston "gradually disappeared from [Price's] writing staff, slipping away into a double-locked office down the hall doing nobody seemed to know just what."[14]

What Huston was doing was helping the interagency committee draft the report he and Sullivan had planned from the beginning, advising the president that *he* could authorize an increase in wiretapping and bugging, as well as modify or set aside restrictions on break-ins and mail openings, to permit their use in investigating radical activities and organizations. Not only was Hoover to be reversed; he was to be made more subordinate to the president.

Other intelligence agency heads quickly approved, no doubt gleefully. Sullivan, anticipating Hoover's anger at this undercutting of his authority, tried to persuade the director that the report only followed the president's request and made no actual recommendation to him; it only advised him of his options, Sullivan argued. Hoover, the shrewd old bureaucrat, saw through this at once; he peppered the report with dissenting footnotes to the effect that all the illegal activities discussed carried with them dire risk of public exposure and great damage to the intelligence community.

Hoover conceded, however, that he would not oppose use of these sensitive techniques by other agencies—provided *they* sought the attorney general's approval, then carried out the operations themselves. The FBI would not do it for them—the problem that had caused the committee to be formed and the report drafted. Worse, Hoover's footnotes constituted a written record—the sure sign of the master's touch—that he, at least, had objected to these illegal activities.

Huston was not intimidated. In his own report to the president, he denigrated Hoover's objections and urged Nixon to approve the report. Emphasizing Hoover's supposed loyalty, Huston suggested that the president could call in the old director, explain the decision personally, and flatter him into cooperation.

Like Hoover himself, however, Nixon was wise in the bureaucrat's need to "CYA"—"cover your ass." He had no intention of signing his name to an authorization or even a request for illegal investigative actions. Instead, he instructed Haldeman to let Huston know the report was approved, and that Huston could put it into effect. Huston, more zealot than bureaucrat, immediately *signed* a memorandum reporting to the agencies that the president had made certain decisions—in effect, to proceed with wiretaps, break-ins and the like.

Thus, Nixon had set in motion the investigatory zeal he wanted, but he also had "deniability" because he had not explicitly approved the report; Tom Charles Huston only *said* he had. The monkey was on Huston's back, and the so-called Huston Plan therefore entered into the seamier side of the Nixon administration's history. But still another twist was yet to come in this dubious saga.

Hoover perceived without difficulty that Huston's memo gave him no grounds to claim that the FBI was only following direct *presidential* orders, should an illegal FBI wiretap or break-in be discovered. He went to Attorney General Mitchell—who, remarkably, had not previously been involved—and declared that he was making a written record to show that it was *the president* who had lifted the restraints the director had imposed on FBI investigations. He would also continue to seek, Hoover said, the *attorney general's* written authority every time the FBI undertook the kind of operation outlined in the Huston Plan.

Mitchell hastened to the White House to report Hoover's reaction. Nixon's account of their conversation stated that Mitchell told him "that it was his opinion that the risk of disclosure of the possible illegal actions . . . was greater than the possible benefit to be derived."[15]

Nixon already had Hoover's footnotes making that point, but the added weight of Mitchell's opinion may have been decisive. In *RN,* however, Nixon gave a different account:

> I knew that if Hoover had decided not to cooperate, it would matter little what I had decided or approved. Even if I issued a direct order to him, while he would undoubtedly carry it out, *he would soon see to it that I had cause to reverse myself.* [Emphasis added.]

What "cause" would that be? Undoubtedly, Nixon saw that Hoover's obstinacy could destroy the president's "deniability." If given a direct order, Hoover could lay the burden of authorizing illegal actions directly on Nixon, and to protect himself would not hesitate to do it. Only five days after Huston's memo had gone out, Nixon prudently withdrew the indirect approval he had conveyed through Haldeman.

Price quotes Huston's responding memo, "which verged on the hysterical":

> At some point Hoover has to be told who is President. . . . For eighteen months we have watched people . . . ignore the President's orders, take actions to embarrass him, promote himself at his expense, and generally make his job more difficult. It makes me fighting mad, and what Hoover is doing is putting himself above the President.

Hoover was doing that, indeed, and successfully. The Huston Plan was dead—so dead that the public knew nothing of it until the Watergate investigating committee leaked it to the *New York Times* in 1973, when the Nixon administration was falling rapidly into disrepute. Publication of the abortive plan produced widespread shock and revulsion, some of it genuine. Sam Ervin called it a program "to spy on the American people" as well as evidence of a "Gestapo mentality" in the White House. J. Edgar Hoover's worst fears had come true.

Two years after this furor, however, a clearer perspective was offered. A Senate committee investigating the CIA disclosed—as many old Washington hands had known all along—that the investigative techniques the Huston Plan would have authorized would only have *restored* to the intelligence agencies the ability to carry out operations they had used regularly in every administration back to Franklin Roosevelt's.

The committee chairman, Frank Church, a liberal Democrat from Idaho and not a friend of Richard Nixon, conceded that the Huston Plan "was limited to techniques far more restrictive than the far-reaching methods" the FBI had employed in five administrations before Nixon's. But the difference was immense; the only president ever linked directly to these distasteful activities was Richard Nixon.

In Nixon's first year in office, despite the fears that led to his early request for derogatory information on the antiwar movement, demonstrations were not the crucial problem that he had expected—although there were huge antiwar rallies in Washington in October and November 1969. The president, by then, was so confident that the nation was behind him and the war in Vietnam that he let the press know he was watching a televised football game while the second demonstration spilled through the streets outside the White House.

Public reaction to a speech the president had made on November 3, between the two rallies, had enhanced his confidence. This was the occasion of his television appeal to "the silent majority"; in it he not only pledged to continue the war but promised not to permit "the policy of this nation to be dictated" by a minority staging "demonstrations in the streets." Antiwar forces were disappointed and infuriated, but polls showed the silent majority indeed was with the president.

American colleges, though students remained unhappy with the war, were reasonably quiet in early 1970—until the night of April 30, when Nixon again took to national television, this time to announce the "incursion" into Cambodia. The next day, campuses exploded all across the nation, as enraged students poured out of classrooms into the streets. The National Student Association called for the president's impeachment; student body presidents from ten universities joined in the demand. Representatives of more than a hundred colleges began planning a nationwide student strike.

Nevertheless euphoric from his "tough decision" and his "bold stroke" into Cambodia—the kind of action that always exhilarated him, at least briefly—Nixon chose that day to make his most severe statement about student protesters, and at the Pentagon, of all places. After being briefed on military progress in Cambodia, the president remarked during an informal exchange with persons gathered in the Pentagon lobby:

> You see these bums, you know, blowing up the campuses. Listen, the boys that are on the college campuses today are the luckiest people in the world, going to the greatest universities, and here they are burning up the books, storming around about this issue. You name it. Get rid of the war, there will be another one.

The penurious Duke law student with his "iron butt" in a library chair and his heart set on "getting ahead" could be heard in that statement; so could the Orthogonian resentful of more fortunate young men in their black ties. But Nixon's unvarnished words, not surprisingly, were enough to fan the campus fires—almost literally.

The next night—Saturday, May 2—at Kent State University in Ohio, as raucous student demonstrations continued, the Reserve Officers' Training Corps building was burned down; ROTC was a favorite campus target in 1970. Governor James Rhodes sent in the National Guard—mostly nervous young men not much older or more experienced than the Kent State students.

On Monday, May 4, as the guardsmen sought to assert control of the campus, some of them suddenly opened fire; four demonstrators were killed and eleven wounded. Later investigation established that the guardsmen had had no provocation—other than their own fears—severe enough to justify the shooting.

That was not so clear at the time, and Nixon and Agnew did nothing to cool things off with statements that condemned *student* violence for provoking such a response. The campus eruptions that had followed the April 30 speech on Cambodia then broke out all over again, even more destructively than before; marches, burnings, building takeovers, student strikes, blazed everywhere.

To many Americans, the day of revolution may have seemed at hand, not least because the attention of newspapers and television naturally was on the exploding campuses, not on the rest of the nation going routinely about its business. In fact, Nixon was correct that the war protesters, however much attention they attracted, were not really representative of the whole people, and that he, rather than they, had the sympathy of the silent majority.

But the president, as Kissinger observed years later, was not "emotionally" the right leader to contest the peace movement—which carried on, in Kissinger's view, a "civil war" directed not only at the conflict in Vietnam but at American institutions generally. Nixon was too much a loner to be willing to educate the public about the national interest, Kissinger said in a speech at Hofstra, and the opposition to the war "touched too many insecurities and brought out too many defensive attitudes" in Nixon's psyche for him to counter it effectively. Thus, Nixon and the peace movement angered rather than persuaded each other.

Walter Hickel, the secretary of the interior, a maverick in Nixon's official family, weighed in on May 6 with a letter accusing the administration of lacking "appropriate concern for the attitude of a great mass of America—our young people." Nixon was enraged, but the letter—plus Hickel's temerity—made him a hero to the young people he had championed. Somewhat chastened by the campus uproar, Nixon chose not to fire Hickel (yet), lest that make matters worse.

Instead, the president met with Kent State students, received a delegation of college presidents—and in a news conference on May 8 abandoned his hard line. "I agree with everything that [students] are trying to accomplish," he insisted—*not,* however, agreeing with everything they had done.

If this switch from the careless remarks at the Pentagon a week earlier had any impact on student opinion generally, it was too late to stop the hordes of striking students—more than a hundred thousand—who were then gathering in Washington for another enormous rally. But Nixon now was eager to "communicate," as most protesters claimed *they* were.

Hours after the May 8 news conference ended and long after midnight, with his valet Manolo Sanchez in tow, the president of the United States paid a surprise visit to the Lincoln Memorial. The Secret Service was appalled; and the students who were spending the night at the memorial were astonished.

Nixon has been derided, no doubt properly, for talking to these radicalized students about football, World War II, his travels around the world and surfing—all irrelevancies to those young people of the Vietnam era who were willing to travel to Washington to protest the war. The incongruity of his talk is what most of them remembered, and scorned, about this bizarre episode, one of the strangest in modern presidential history.

For a shy and introverted man, no more in touch with the impassioned youth of the sixties than were most Americans his age (probably less, due to his isolation in the White House)—for a man, moreover, who had just committed thousands of other young Americans to a bloody military operation, and whose self-confidence (never secure) had been shaken by a public reaction confounding to his experience—for such a man as Richard Nixon in the spring of 1970, the visit to the Lincoln Memorial seems in retrospect more nearly sad and moving than comical.

He was at least trying to "get in touch"—a value ordinarily touted by the youths who later derided him; but Nixon did not know how to do it, and he was probably too late anyway. Still, in his own limited way, he reached across formidable barriers; but no one of his startled listeners took his hand. Perhaps, for all their talk of "communication," they did not know how either—not, at least, with the representative of "the system" so many believed uncaring.

Nixon did communicate effectively, if not affectionately, with one student. As the presidential limousine began to pull away from the extraordinary scene at the memorial, a bearded youth braved the Secret Service to dash alongside. Right by the rear window, right in the face of the president, he extended his middle finger from his clenched fist in one of the less delicate gestures of defiance. Right in the same window, right in the bearded young face, Nixon put up his own fist and extended his middle finger, too. *They* understood each other; and Nixon for once was amused rather than angered by confrontation.

"That SOB," he said to Sanchez, "will go through the rest of his life telling everybody that the president of the United States gave him the finger. And nobody will believe him!"[16]

Whatever else Nixon's appearance among the startled students accomplished, it did not quiet the campus convulsion. Just one week later, on May 15, state highway patrolmen opened fire on demonstrating students at Jackson State College, a black institution in Mississippi, with no more reason than the Kent State guardsmen had had. Two students died and eleven were wounded.

Nixon, no longer talking about "bums" or student violence, promptly met with a delegation of black college presidents—fortuitously scheduled before the Jackson State shootings. But as many in the black community angrily perceived, the nation seemed not quite as shocked by the murder of black students in Mississippi as by the shooting of white students in Ohio.

In-house defections were another problem that spring of 1970. Hickel had leaked his letter even before Nixon had a chance to see it; the Cambodian incursion had caused Halperin and Lake to leave Kissinger's national security staff (neither then knowing that he had been and still was being wiretapped); and next came Dr. James Allen, a well-known liberal educator, a Finch appointee who as assistant secretary of HEW was far out of place in the Nixon administration anyway.

Allen said publicly that he did not "understand the rationale to move into Cambodia, or indeed to continue the war in Vietnam." Again Nixon was angered, but again he hesitated to fire a man who had become an overnight hero on the campus. But Allen soon got the Panetta treatment (see chapter 12); his "resignation" was announced before he submitted it.

Campus reaction slowly cooled from the fiery peaks of May, but Nixon made one more conciliatory gesture. In June, he named a commission under former governor William Scranton of Pennsylvania to explore ways of satisfying protesting students. The president even refused to remove the commission's only student member, Joseph Rhodes, a war critic whose comments caused Spiro Agnew to demand his ouster. But the commission episode turned out predictably: its September report called the war in Vietnam the central cause of student unrest—thus blaming Richard Nixon for disrupting the campus by continuing the war.

By the time that report appeared, Nixon was preoccupied with the 1970 state and congressional elections rather than with colleges that had peacefully reopened that same September. Campus dissidence and the elections, however, were not unconnected.

Nixon planned for political purposes to fan silent majority resentments of youthful violence, drug abuse and lack of patriotic support for the war;

on that issue, he calculated, he and his party could make gains in the House and take control of the Senate—if not literal Republican control, then *ideological* control through a combination of Republicans and hawkish Democrats. Agnew was to be Nixon's campaign instrument just as Nixon himself once had been for Eisenhower—Agnew, Eugene McCarthy quipped, was "Nixon's Nixon."

Agnew had made a reputation in the 1968 campaign for blunders and ethnic slurs; by 1970 he was celebrated, instead, for outspoken hostility to dissenters ("who detest everything about this country and want to destroy it"), intellectuals ("an effete corps of impudent snobs") and news commentators ("a small and unelected elite"). Nixon found Agnew a shallow malcontent within the White House, but appreciated the public acclaim he had aroused for views the president shared.

As Agnew began his 1970 campaign with great national hoopla, he stated succinctly the issue the administration wanted to emphasize— "whether policies of the United States are going to be made by its elected officials or in the streets." Adapting a phrase of Pat Buchanan's, the vice president also coined the term "radiclibs" for those who were willing—he said—to abandon Vietnam to communism, and who were "weak" on law and order. As he barnstormed the country on these themes in September and early October, Agnew dominated the campaign and eclipsed Democratic responses.

But Nixon's high hopes were unrealistic: the White House party historically had *lost* rather than gained seats in midterm elections; Agnew's rhetorical blasts, though popular with many in the silent majority, were divisive, too, and often excessive; announcement of the Peking and Moscow summits would not come until the next year; and the Democrats had an issue of their own, one more meaningful to most Americans than the doings of "radiclibs" and one that must have echoed hauntingly in Nixon's long memory—recession.

As we have seen (chapter 13), by mid-1970 "gradualism" had not done the economic job and unemployment had risen 1.7 points from its inauguration level, to 5 percent; inflation hovered at about the same rate. In June 1970, Nixon—his eye already on the elections—had taken his first limited venture into incomes policy. Even so, by August unemployment was up again, to 5.1 percent, its highest level since 1964. In midcampaign, a strike against General Motors left hundreds of thousands of workers idle in Michigan, Illinois and the Republican "heartland" states, Indiana and Ohio.

Consequently, as Americans worried more and more about jobs and prices, Agnew's impact weakened. So during the weekend of October 10–11 at Key Biscayne, Nixon made the risky decision to take over the campaign himself—deciding also, despite earlier warnings from Bryce

Harlow and Bob Finch, to continue emphasizing the law-and-order theme. By then, if the president was going to campaign for his party, he actually needed to blunt Democratic charges that an unfeeling Republican administration, in the footsteps of Herbert Hoover, did not care how much economic suffering ordinary Americans had to endure.

Between October 17 and November 2, instead, Nixon campaigned in twenty-three states, repeatedly assaulting

> A small group that shouts obscenities . . . that throws rocks . . . a group of people that always tear America down; a group of people that hate this country, actually, in terms of what it presently stands for; who see nothing right with America. . . .

Campaigning day after day on this line, John Mitchell later lamented, Nixon looked less like a president than like a man "running for sheriff." He certainly did not sound like one distressed by joblessness and rising prices. Only one rock, moreover, and that one coming nowhere near the president, had been thrown—in Burlington, Vermont, on the first day of Nixon's frantic campaign.

Near its end, on October 29 at San Jose, California, an unusually hostile crowd tried to interrupt his speech, then booed and reviled Nixon as he walked to his car after his sixth appearance of the day: *"One, two, three, four, we don't want your fucking war!"*

Instead of making a rapid exit, Nixon—the same Nixon who had unwisely challenged threatening mobs in South America a decade earlier, had harangued another in Burma on his first vice presidential trip abroad, and had adopted Churchillian airs in announcing the invasion of Cambodia— that same recklessly defiant Nixon jumped on the engine hood of the presidential limousine and stood there for a moment in the television lights, flashing the V-for-Victory sign at the noisy crowd.

Was he again, as on those earlier occasions, in the grip of his own kind of machismo and seeking to demonstrate—perhaps to himself as well as to a mob—a lack of fear, a refusal to be intimidated? Was his judgment impaired, as it often was when he was overtired? Or did he deliberately invite an attack he thought would swing the election by dramatizing his condemnation of rock-throwers, obscenity-shouters and those who supposedly hated America?

As Nixon recalled it in *RN*, "I could not resist showing them how little respect I had for their juvenile and mindless ranting." No doubt all these reasons influenced his impulsive action; and it did evoke what seemed to be political justification for his campaign: a shower of rocks, eggs, vegetables, invective, a shocking scene caught for the nation, its president targeted in the harsh light of television.

When the first rocks sailed out of the darkness, however, Nixon quickly slipped off the hood and into his car; but as the presidential motorcade moved out, the assault continued. A window was cracked in the press bus—not a lick amiss, some might have said in echo of Tom Sawyer's Aunt Polly—and the White House limousine was dented in several places.

Two days later, Nixon sharply attacked his attackers, calling them "violent thugs" in a speech at Phoenix. Then he ordered a tape of the Phoenix speech to be televised nationally on election eve. The result was disaster: the black-and-white tape was badly filmed, the sound was screechy, the angry and arm-waving Nixon was "hot" in a cool medium. Worse, he was followed on the screen by a cool Senator Edmund Muskie, speaking for the Democrats from his quiet home in Maine, and reminding Americans in his calm manner that the recession was hurting them in the pocketbook while the Republicans—in Muskie's telling—did nothing about it.

Typically, Nixon drew from this fiasco no real lesson about himself or his 1970 strategy but only the conclusion that "in this age of television, technical quality is probably more important than the content of what is said." He claimed also an "excellent showing" in the election—and since the Republicans gained a net of two Senate seats, the results *were* better than might have been expected at midterm and in a recession year.

In hard fact, however, the Democrats still controlled the Senate, 55 to 45, and even Nixon's "ideological" gain was marginal. His party lost nine House seats and eleven governorships—retaining control in only twenty-one states. Political overkill on the law-and-order issue by both Agnew and the president had left their candidates vulnerable on the recession issue. Ed Muskie had been propelled (temporarily) into leadership for the Democratic presidential nomination in 1972; but Spiro Agnew had peaked in October. The subsequent Republican defeat in November seriously damaged the vice president's prospects for higher office.

For Nixon, 1970 had not been a good year on the domestic front. But one bright spot, in the general dreariness of the spring, summer and fall, cheered him up. On May 8, in the lurid days after Nixon's announcement of the Cambodian invasion, construction union workers in New York City had come spectacularly to his support. Wearing their hard-hats, they swarmed down from a skyscraper project on Wall Street and violently squelched an antiwar demonstration, beating up a number of the protesters while New York City policemen looked on and did nothing to stop the one-sided "battle."

At the Hofstra conference, Donald Rodgers, then an official of the Department of Labor but in 1970 a union business agent in New York, told the story from the viewpoint of the attackers. Many, he said, were themselves Vietnam veterans and regarded it as a "lousy war." But they had done their part in it patriotically, and had friends and relatives who were still fighting and dying in the jungle. The Cambodian invasion, they thought, would reduce the toll of Americans killed in Vietnam; so how could other Americans be opposed to it?

The hard-hats had watched, Rodgers said, as for more than a week protesters marched through New York streets, carrying Vietcong banners, sometimes desecrating American flags, proclaiming the war immoral and demanding that the U.S. get out of it. On May 8, one of the protesters lit the fuse of the hard-hats' barely contained anger.

He climbed on a statue of George Washington in Wall Street near the Subtreasury Building and "peed on it." That, said Rodgers, was too much; the hard-hats charged the demonstration and silenced it.

A few other battles around the city caused union leaders to fear that someone would be killed—whether workers or protesters, Rodgers did not specify. Mayor John Lindsay sought the leaders' help in cooling things off. Union officials then scheduled a march of their own for May 20. That day, twenty-five thousand hard-hats showed up at City Hall and marched through lower Manhattan in support of Richard Nixon, the invasion of Cambodia and the war in Vietnam.

This showing was all the more remarkable because construction workers had felt themselves aggrieved the year before by the Philadelphia Plan for racial integration of their unions (see chapter 12). They could not know, either, that after their march Nixon's zeal to enforce the Philadelphia Plan was to cool considerably (though, in 1971, in pursuit of incomes policy, he nevertheless suspended the Davis-Bacon Act that prescribed union wages for federal construction projects).

On the night of the hard-hats' march, the president—who in *RN* put the total number of marchers on May 20 at "more than 100,000"—called Peter Brennan, the head of the New York Building Trades Council, to thank him. According to Donald Rodgers, Nixon also read Brennan "an interminable list" of weapons captured in the previous two days in Cambodia, then declared that "not one of those things will be fired against any of our troops over there."

In that turbulent May, Nixon doubtless was happy to have *any* public display of support. But when he later invited the New York union leaders to the White House, met with them personally and had himself photographed in a hard-hat inscribed COMMANDER-IN-CHIEF, many thought him a little too willing to applaud vigilante action against lawful—even if rowdy—demonstrations, and to celebrate what, after all, had been the violent suppression of dissent.

Richard Nixon had thanked the hard-hats, many Americans concluded, for what he wished he could have done himself.

·   ·   ·

The "excellent showing" in the 1970 elections that Nixon claimed many years later left him disgruntled at the time, and seeking a scapegoat. As usual, he sought it first in the press.

Not long after Election Day, Bob Haldeman dutifully relayed to J. Edgar Hoover a request from the president for "a run down on the homosexuals known and suspected in the Washington press corps." Haldeman added that Nixon would like the names of "some of the others rumored generally to be [homosexuals] and also whether [the FBI] had any other stuff; that he, the President, has an interest in what, if anything else, we know."[17]

As usual, Hoover made a record of the White House request, from which the quotations above are extracted. As usual, also, he readily agreed to do the job, promising a report within the week. It was delivered on time, but so far as is known no use ever was made of any facts it may have contained. Most likely, Hoover's report was composed of the same rumors, innuendo, supposition, malicious suggestions and tenuous conclusions featured in many such FBI documents.

As is now known, in 1970 and for several years earlier, the once-formidable Hoover was losing his fabled grip on himself, the bureau, and even on Washington's fearful imagination. Both he and the FBI were under rising public criticism and examination, and Hoover's responses often were intemperate and obviously self-serving. He dabbled more and more openly in politics, he was at public loggerheads with the antiwar movement, and his right-wing and racist personal views frequently were exposed. Hoover's vendetta against Martin Luther King, Jr., as its extent came slowly to light, was perhaps the offense that had brought him the most criticism.

Ehrlichman soon learned that the New York Police Department was a better source than Hoover's FBI for the intelligence information Nixon craved—on domestic violence, bombings, protests and the like. In Ehrlichman's opinion, Hoover was by the fall of 1969 "like an old boxer who had taken too many punches . . . He had lost his judgment and vigor. He had become an embarrassment."[18]

Thus, Hoover posed a problem beyond the restraints he had imposed on bureau investigations, beyond even his increasing garrulity (Nixon met with the director infrequently in order to escape what had become his rambling monologues). The president, however, did not really grasp the Hoover problem until 1971. That summer, William Sullivan's revelation about Hoover's secret wiretap records was coupled with an ineffective FBI performance after the publication of the Pentagon Papers—which was "probably the seminal event," Egil Krogh said at the Hofstra conference, "that caused the downfall of the administration."

Krogh was in Vietnam studying the narcotics problem in the American military when the New York Times printed the first installment of the

Papers on June 13, 1971. That event did not particularly upset President Nixon; the history the Papers recounted predated his administration, after all, and he was soon informed that his name was nowhere mentioned in the forty-three volumes. The publication seemed basically Lyndon Johnson's problem.

Henry Kissinger, however, was beside himself with rage and fear; when Charles Colson arrived at the White House on the Monday after the *Times* publication had begun on Sunday, he found Kissinger "as angry as I had ever seen him." Colson was used to Kissinger's "sharp flashes of temper which, like summer cloudbursts, quickly passed." This time, Kissinger's anger was more like a hurricane.

"There can be no foreign policy in this government," he shouted to Colson and Haldeman. "We might just as well turn it all over to the Soviets and get it over with. These leaks are slowly and systematically destroying us."[19]

Kissinger had reasons to be upset, though the difficulty of conducting a foreign policy was not really among them. He figured frequently in the Pentagon Papers, for one thing, owing to his work as a consultant for the Johnson administration; and he did not wish to be connected with that earlier and none too admirable history.

Even as early as June 14, moreover, the administration believed that the Papers had been leaked by Daniel Ellsberg, a young defense intellectual with whom Kissinger had been close. Ellsberg, in fact, had drafted—at Kissinger's instigation—an important transition paper on Vietnam that at first had guided Nixon's policy in Southeast Asia. But Ellsberg had turned against the war publicly; and their work together was another connection that Kissinger did not wish publicized—certainly not by the Pentagon Papers.

The national security adviser also had a somewhat more serious concern: he feared publication of the Papers would cause other governments to lose confidence in the ability of the Nixon administration to keep secrets. At the moment of this "massive hemorrhage of state secrets," as he later termed the Pentagon Papers, secret negotiations were going forward with North Vietnam and with the Soviets on SALT and Berlin. Nixon and Kissinger also were deeply enmeshed in the secret talks leading to the latter's trip to China later that summer of 1971. Kissinger's "nightmare . . . was that Peking might conclude our government was too unsteady, too harassed, and too insecure to be a useful partner."[20]

If not a later rationalization of his anger, this was a panicky departure from Kissinger's usually hardheaded geopolitical approach. The government in Peking was dealing with the U.S. because its interests recommended rapprochement; it was not likely to set those interests aside because of such apprehensions as Kissinger conjured up. The Chinese, after all, in June 1971, already had absorbed both the American incursion into Cambodia and the American-Soviet agreement to reach a strategic arms treaty, and nevertheless were about to receive Kissinger; the Pentagon Papers surely must have seemed to them, by comparison, a minor matter.

But to support his nervous argument Kissinger showed Colson protest cables soon in from Australia, Great Britain and Canada—but not, notably, from China or the Soviet Union or North Vietnam, partners in the secret negotiations about which Kissinger professed to be concerned. His fears did not prove realistic, but it's fair to say that Kissinger could not have known that in June 1971.*

Kissinger fully aroused Nixon, however, with two more specific lines of argument:

One was that Ellsberg, who had worked for the Rand Corporation and was believed to have obtained the Pentagon Papers from its files, knew a great many national security secrets. What might he leak next, and to whom? Kissinger cleverly salted this argument with anecdotes about Ellsberg's sexual activities and supposed use of drugs—items sure to arouse the interest and ire of the rather prurient Nixon.

This aspect of the president's personality was well known in the White House. The FBI, always eager to please, once informed Nixon that one of his aides, a married man, was carrying on an affair with an airline stewardess. Affronted, Nixon ordered the accused fired.

Ehrlichman stalled for nearly two months, while the culprit sought another job; but Nixon kept pressing to know what had been done. Finally the man found a place in a law firm, and Ehrlichman duly fired him, to Nixon's satisfaction.

Kissinger played on another Nixonian nerve-end by insisting that the necessary respect for classified documents had been scorned. That the Papers were "top secret," but had been leaked and published anyway, indeed offended Nixon's sense of propriety, his belief in the sanctity of secrets, his regard for the government's prerogatives. In the case of classified documents, the authority for which rested on presidential directives rather than legislation, those prerogatives were largely his own. Kissinger sincerely shared these views, and he knew they would have powerful effect on Richard Nixon.

"Had some process removed the Top Secret stamps from those pages,"

---

*To my knowledge, no substantive damage to national security ever has been shown to have resulted from publication of the Pentagon Papers—a matter of considerable interest to me, since as an associate editor I was one of the twenty-one *New York Times* reporters and editors named in the federal court injunction that temporarily halted publication, and since I was the first *Times* editor with whom the possibility of publishing the Papers was raised by anyone who could make them available. I encouraged publication, and would again.

John Ehrlichman came to believe, "Nixon would have had no objection to their publication." Ehrlichman thought it was primarily this reason and Kissinger's protestations that caused Nixon to act to restrain publication.[21]

Ronald Ziegler—the White House press secretary in 1971—contended later that Nixon had little idea of what was in the Pentagon Papers, but was sympathetic to repeated arguments from Kissinger that their publication might cause codes to be broken, intelligence sources to be disclosed, untold harm to that sacred value—national security. Ziegler claimed at Hofstra that Nixon consented to an injunction against further publication only to give the administration time to evaluate the Pentagon Papers for such damage, even to consider possible declassification.

Herbert Klein observed that in the days immediately after publication, "in meetings around the White House, Kissinger seemed to be everywhere." But Klein said the decision to seek an injunction to halt publication—a move he thought mistaken—came basically from Attorney General Mitchell (who believed, according to Colson, that Daniel Ellsberg was part of a Communist spy ring).

"Most of us who worked on the problem," Klein wrote, "were not aware of the decision [to ask for an injunction] until after Mitchell had ordered the U.S. attorney in New York to seek restraint of publication."

With unprecedented speed, however, first a federal district court, then the Supreme Court following expedited procedures ruled that insufficient justification for prior restraint on publication had been furnished by the administration. Publication resumed, and as Klein pointed out, "the losing battle led to the attempt to further discredit Ellsberg and to the break-in of the office of his psychiatrist."[22]

Immediately after the Supreme Court ruling came down, Nixon decided—perhaps in one of his "Alice in Wonderland" rages—to ask the House Internal Security Committee (formerly HUAC, which he had known so well) to conduct hearings designed to show that publication of the Pentagon Papers was part of a conspiracy damaging to national security. For this purpose, J. Edgar Hoover and the FBI would have to furnish derogatory information, particularly on Ellsberg and on Neil Sheehan, the *Times* reporter to whom Ellsberg was believed to have given the Papers.

Hoover agreed, but the aging director never provided anything more damning than a report on an alleged affinity for Communist causes displayed by Ellsberg's attorney, the well-known Leonard Boudin—a report both Colson and the FBI duly leaked. The Internal Security Committee, as a result of Hoover's failure to provide real raw meat, never was asked to conduct the "conspiracy" hearings.

Ehrlichman had access to an internal FBI audit of the effort against Ellsberg, and concluded from it and from the lack of results that Hoover had assigned the investigation "a very low priority," and that the bureau had been less than effective in pursuing the matter. One reason no doubt was Hoover's restraining hand on sensitive investigations which, if discovered, could bring criticism and rebuke to his cherished bureau.[23]

In any case, Hoover's latest failure, together with William Sullivan's report on the secret wiretap records, marked the downturn of the director's standing in Nixon's eyes. But far more important consequences flowed from the president's intense frustration—by the FBI as well as by the Supreme Court—at being unable to make an example of the Pentagon Papers leaker, and to head off more such disclosures. Colson furnishes a vivid picture of Nixon at this time, "pounding his fist on his desk and leaning forward in his chair, his face flushed. 'I don't care how it's done. I want these leaks stopped. Don't give me any excuses. Use any means.' "[24]

Nixon and Kissinger had succeeded in creating around them in the White House a high sense of the "national security crisis" Kissinger insisted had been caused by publication of the Pentagon Papers. His argument that other nations would mistrust the administration's ability to keep secrets, for example, had convinced Ehrlichman that publication of the papers should be stopped; after the Supreme Court ruling, he was even more concerned about administration credibility in security matters.

Colson was persuaded by Kissinger's and Nixon's "genuine alarm" that "serious security violations" had occurred, and might occur again. Even the normally levelheaded Ray Price found the tension in the White House "deadly serious" and believed that "it was vital to know more about Daniel Ellsberg."[25]

This angry, even vindictive atmosphere, rather than anything actually contained in the Pentagon Papers, made their publication and its aftermath what Egil Krogh called a "seminal event" in the Nixon administration. At that point, Colson too came to believe, "the Nixon Presidency passed a crossroads of sorts." Within the White House "the ground rules began to change."[26]

Krogh walked innocently into this highly charged environment in July 1971, upon his return from his drug investigation in Vietnam. On a sunny afternoon at San Clemente, he sat with Nixon on a terrace and gave the president the bad news that the "drug problem" among American troops fighting in Vietnam had become a "drug condition." The difference was that Nixon might plan to *solve* a problem. He could only hope somehow to "deal with" a condition.

But the Pentagon Papers, not drugs, were on Nixon's mind. Ehrlichman was called in and handed Krogh a file on the security violations the White House believed had, or might have, resulted from publication. Krogh was young, eager, patriotic, fervently admiring of Richard Nixon, deeply impressed by the term "national security," and in no doubt whatever that the president of the United States was empowered to protect it by any means necessary. He took the file to his motel room, studied it intensively, and became convinced that publication of the Pentagon Papers threatened consequences of the "highest national security importance." Krogh took that "very seriously," he said at Hofstra.

There at San Clemente, Nixon authorized Krogh to put together a team of investigators, keeping it secret from the FBI and the CIA and even from the families of those involved, to do what J. Edgar Hoover had failed to do. If the president couldn't get intelligence and security action from the agencies charged with them, he aimed to get it from his own staff. This determination was redoubled on July 24, when the *New York Times* enraged him again with another story by William Beecher, who in 1969 had made the fateful disclosure of the secret bombing of Cambodia. This one described the American "fallback" position in SALT.

Thus were "the plumbers," so referred to because of the group's supposed mission to stop leaks, approved from the top. Operating out of room 16 in the Executive Office Building next door to the White House, with scrambler phones and a shredder at hand, Krogh recruited David Young, Gordon Liddy, and Howard Hunt. Liddy's zeal already had caused him to be discharged from the FBI and the Treasury. Hunt as a CIA specialist in covert operations had been deeply involved in Eisenhower's overthrow of the Arbenz government in Guatemala (see chapter 4).

Hunt and Liddy proposed to break into the office of Dr. Lewis Fielding—Ellsberg's psychiatrist—in Los Angeles to obtain whatever information Fielding's files might disclose. Krogh claimed at Hofstra that he had not been able to check out this idea with experienced persons at the FBI or elsewhere, owing to Nixon's orders for strict secrecy; but he agreed to the plan because he thought the doctor's files might show whether Ellsberg was acting under Soviet influence.

"Others," Krogh added without naming names, merely wanted facts with which to discredit Ellsberg—Colson later pleaded guilty to conspiring to defame Ellsberg—or to learn the names of his allies, if any. But all, Krogh insisted, believed that "national security was at stake."

Few in the White House knew what the plumbers were doing, or even that the group existed. Colson directed some of their activities, Ehrlichman authorized or knew about others; what Nixon and Haldeman knew is not clear—probably more than has been disclosed. But the plumbers acted fundamentally on Nixon's overall instructions, confirmed to Krogh by Ehrlichman, "to find out what Ellsberg was up to."

Whatever other orders or authorizations the president may have given or implied, directly or otherwise, remains a mystery. Ehrlichman insists that, despite the general belief, *he* did not authorize the Fielding break-in. He believes Richard Nixon did. But whether Nixon *literally* ordered it or not, he had said enough to set that foolish scheme in motion.

The Fielding break-in—on Labor Day weekend of 1971—produced nothing of use to the plumbers, much less to national security. Liddy and Hunt, unabashed, then wanted to burgle Dr. Fielding's apartment. Krogh phoned Ehrlichman for permission; but Ehrlichman, by his account, was horrified to learn of the first break-in and absolutely forbade the second. Later, Krogh said at Hofstra, he and Young were stricken with remorse and fear; they resolved not again to allow such a violation of the law.

After Krogh's phone call following the break-in, Ehrlichman "barely considered," but fatefully rejected, reporting the plumbers to the police. "Someone was betraying national secrets," he reasoned. "Hunt and Liddy did what the FBI had been doing in such cases for years with the blessing of the Attorney General and the President. . . . I conceived my job as being to protect the President, not to expose him."[27]

Though Ehrlichman did not believe at the time that Nixon had ordered the break-in, and though he could not have known the consequences of his decision to "protect the President," the Watergate cover-up may be said to have started at that moment.

The break-in, moreover, actually helped its target, Ellsberg, and backfired on its perpetrators. When it became known among other Watergate disclosures, the government's illegal invasion of Ellsberg's and Fielding's rights and privacy was largely responsible for the mistrial that then was declared in the administration's effort to prosecute Ellsberg and his alleged associate, Anthony Russo, for "stealing" and leaking the Pentagon Papers.

Egil Krogh, however, became the first Watergate defendant to go to prison.

In October 1971, with Watergate far in the future, the problem of J. Edgar Hoover came to a head in the White House. Though Nixon, in *RN*, maintained that he did not believe Hoover would use the secret wiretap records against a president, he conceded that if the records fell into the hands of someone like Daniel Ellsberg, they could do great harm. That they even existed was a black mark against Hoover. Besides, the director had become all but useless; he had been an obstinate barrier to the Huston Plan; and by forcing William Sullivan out of the FBI in September 1971, he had removed a valuable White House "mole" from the bureau.

What Nixon called in his memoirs "Hoover's increasingly erratic conduct" was impairing the bureau's morale and contributing to a rising chorus of criticism of both. The president worried that if he were not reelected in 1972, a Democratic president would replace Hoover with a new director who would investigate Republicans (with the aid of records Hoover had kept on the clandestine activities of the Nixon White House.)

So in October 1971, even Richard Nixon concluded that it was time for Hoover to go; as with another old friend, Joe Martin, more than twenty years before, the fact had to be faced (see chapter 2). Hoover's age—seventy-six—and his tenure—back to 1924 and the Coolidge administration—clearly warranted his retirement.

Attorney General Mitchell concurred but warned that Hoover was still something of a hero to many Americans—the leader whose G-men had shot John Dillinger, captured Nazi spies in World War II and exposed the Communist threat. The silent majority would not want Hoover fired outright, Mitchell argued; nor would the old man go gentle into that good night. Besides, Nixon told Ehrlichman, he couldn't have Hoover out in the country criticizing a president who had fired him.*

But "Mr. President," Mitchell warned, if voluntary retirement was to be suggested, "both you and I know that Edgar Hoover isn't about to listen to anyone other than the President of the United States." Nixon would have to do the job himself, much as he hated such confrontations.

The president reluctantly arranged to have the director come to the White House for breakfast. Ehrlichman was enlisted to prepare a "talking paper" outlining what the president should say to Hoover to persuade him to go quietly.

Whether Nixon followed the Ehrlichman script we do not know. In *RN* he said only that he had tried "as gently and subtly as I could" to point out that in the current and foreseeable national atmosphere attacks on the FBI and its director would increase; and that it would be a shame for Hoover's long career to come to an end under such fire.

But Hoover was not quite as punch-drunk as Ehrlichman had supposed; he had anticipated the subject of the breakfast and was ready. The attacks would not bother him, he assured Nixon, but

> more than anything else, I want to see *you* re-elected in 1972. If you feel that my staying on as head of the Bureau hurts your chances for re-election, just let me know.

It's hard not to admire the indomitable old man, with all his faults, at that crucial moment. He had correctly gauged Richard Nixon and made precisely the right move to thwart him. He knew the president hated to say "you're fired"—everyone in the administration knew that; he knew, too, that after the apparent magnanimity of the quoted remark, Nixon would never go through with whatever ultimatum or proposition he had planned. And Nixon didn't—not least because Hoover's maneuver echoed what Nixon himself had said to Eisenhower at the time of the fund crisis in 1952: "He would submit his resignation only if I specifically requested it." And, like Eisenhower, Nixon "decided not to do it."

---

*LBJ, facing the same problem, found a vivid if vulgar way to put it: he told aides he'd rather have Hoover "inside the tent pissing out than outside pissing in."

Nixon does not add, in *RN,* that he *could* not do it. Hoover knew too much. His vindictiveness was legendary. All Nixon's long association with him, every favor the director had done for him over the years, particularly in the White House, had come back to haunt the president. He had to let Hoover stay on the job because the director had the power to ruin him, and might be goaded into doing it.

Retaining high position and great power would have been triumph enough for most men. But J. Edgar Hoover had not become Washington's most accomplished bureaucrat for nothing. He knew something about timing; while he had Nixon on the ropes, the old fighter moved in for the kill.

When Hoover left the Oval Office that October morning, he not only was still director; he had the president's approval for what the attorney general and the secretary of state had *refused* for two years to allow: a 20 percent increase in the FBI's overseas force, with the bureau's "legal attachés" to be newly stationed in the Philippines, Argentina, the Dominican Republic, Australia, Malaysia and India.

He had outwitted or outlasted everyone else, but even J. Edgar Hoover could not overcome death. On May 2, 1972, he died in his sleep. At his funeral, President Richard M. Nixon announced that the massive new FBI building on Pennsylvania Avenue would be named for the one and only director.

That same day, Nixon ordered all Hoover's secret personal files brought to the White House. But the director scored one last great victory for the bureau that had been his life—his secretary seized the files first.[28]

16

★

Loner

★

He had a room up over the garage that was
his room where he could be alone to study
. . . He liked to be alone to study.

—Merle West, recalling
Richard Nixon's youth

After years of almost unimaginable dedication to a single goal had made him president of the United States, Richard Nixon still liked to be alone to study. He would shut himself away from the world, in the jealously guarded isolation he established in the Oval Office, or in his hideaway in the Executive Office Building, as he worked out in solitude his ideas for a speech or a policy statement or a letter, in longhand on his yellow legal pad.

The White House was "liberating" to Nixon in at least one respect; he no longer felt he had to do things he didn't want to do—for example, the typical posturing and glad-handing of American politics that he had for a lifetime steeled himself to endure. As inflation continued to be a problem in his presidential years, his domestic advisers, John Ehrlichman and Pat Moynihan, tried to get him to visit a Washington supermarket to be photographed checking the prices housewives had to pay. Nixon refused; "too hokey," he insisted.

Only by insisting could the two aides even persuade him to stop in the telephone room in the Executive Office Building and speak to the hard-working White House operators, who could and did connect him virtually anywhere in the world in a minute or two. Nixon is a man who uses the phone like a third arm; but he had thought that if he visited the operators, that would appear hokey, too.

For him, the White House was a haven where he could indulge his penchant for privacy, his lack of interest in many of the people who wished to see him—including some of his associates in the administration—and his relatively limited range of interests. In Bob Haldeman, he had the perfect doorkeeper—a man totally devoted, keenly aware of Nixon's preferences and prejudices, who had organized the White House to take advantage of the former and shield him from the latter.

If Haldeman had no after-hours relationship with the president, it was because Mrs. Nixon disliked him. *No one* seemed to have such a relationship with the president, except Bebe Rebozo, the Florida banker, a lightweight whose prime talent was a seemingly endless capacity for listening to Nixon's monologues. So at one point Haldeman became concerned about the president's reclusiveness. He seemed *too* much alone with himself for his own good.

Nixon needed a real confidant, Haldeman decided, one who could give as well as receive. With typical thoroughness, the staff chief set out to find his boss a friend, beginning by researching the acquaintances of Nixon's prepresidential past. That was not an extensive task, and Haldeman soon settled upon a man the Nixons were reported to have liked during their residence in Los Angeles, between Nixon's electoral defeats in 1960 and 1962.

The man, an oil company executive, was tracked down and offered a place in the administration—not a demanding position but a make-work job that would leave him plenty of time to spend with his old friend, now the president. Haldeman brought the executive and his wife to Washington and settled him in the Executive Office Building; then he told the president what he had done.

"You *what?*" Nixon said, clearly astonished.

Haldeman's bright idea was a predictable flop. The Nixons saw the recruited couple once or twice, no doubt out of courtesy, but the president showed little interest in renewing what was supposed to have been a friendship. After a while, the oil man was eased out of his office; he went quietly and nothing more was done about finding a designated friend for Richard Nixon.

He makes much, in *RN,* of the loving support his family gave him during the Watergate ordeal; and it is not for any outsider to question that testimony, or to discount what that support meant to him. But in Nixon's account of his family's return to the White House from San Clemente, at one particularly low point in his fortunes, he quotes a telling passage from Tricia Nixon's diary:

> In the hall of the second floor of the White House we said goodby to Daddy and Mama before Ed [Tricia's husband] and I departed

for New York. *Daddy came as close to outward emotion as he ever does* when he said how much it had meant to him for us to be in California with him. [Emphasis added.]

Even in the bleakest hours, though he obviously tried, Nixon could not be a man of warmth and easy affection, a fact apparently accepted even by his daughters. Nixon himself has made a point of his inability to relax with other people, to accept the comforting intimacies of normal human relations. When he told Stewart Alsop in 1959 that "it doesn't come natural to me to be a buddy-buddy boy," he sounded almost as if he were contemptuous of those who were.

In the same conversation, Nixon said he couldn't "really let my hair down with anyone . . . not even with my family." This does not necessarily mean, however, that there was no consolation for him among his wife and daughters; they displayed constant devotion during the long Watergate crisis. Tricia's diary entry suggests, moreover, a tacit understanding among the Nixon women that their aloof husband and father was not unloving or uncaring—nor were they with him.

Perhaps they understood, too, that his childhood background continued to influence his manner—as with most of us. In a television interview in 1990, he recalled that Hannah Nixon

> never said "I love you" because she considered that to be very private and very sacred. And I feel the same way. . . . I don't say "God bless you," "I love you," and the rest. . . . That's just the way I was raised.

Under further questioning, Nixon acknowledged that he did not even say "I love you" to his grandchildren, though Mrs. Nixon did—"she's more outgoing in that respect than I am."

> In [my early] family, we considered religion to be very private, we considered affection and love to be very private. . . . [W]e loved each other. But we didn't think we had to prove it by saying publicly all the time, "I love you."[1]

In later life, as he told Alsop (in one of the more personally informative interviews he ever gave):

> A major public figure is a lonely man. . . . [Y]ou can't enjoy *the luxury* of intimate personal friendships. You can't confide absolutely in anyone. You can't talk too much about your personal plans, your personal feelings.[2] [Emphasis added.]

Richard Nixon as president, as in all his years as "a major public figure," remained a man alone—just as he once had been a boy alone, rising dutifully in the darkness to make those predawn trips into Los Angeles, hoping not to be seen by classmates when he brought back produce for the Nixon grocery. If, in the end, Nixon was a loner by rationalized preference, surely in the beginning nature and circumstance were at work.

In his early years, he had a cantankerous father to avoid and a mother whose unrelenting goodness certainly inspired but does not appear, in Nixon's or any account, to have radiated warmth and physical affection. The only evidence of demonstrable love readily discernible in Nixon's childhood and youth is a deeply emotional essay he wrote about his younger brother, Arthur—and that was after Arthur's death, a loss that profoundly disturbed the seventeen-year-old Richard.[3]

At school and in what free time the Nixon store left him, he was introverted, cerebral, hardworking, inwardly bent on great deeds that probably would have seemed far-fetched to his contemporaries, and determined to the point of fanaticism to overcome his disadvantages (witness his virtually suicidal determination to make the Whittier College football squad and the long study habits at Duke law school). Nixon never appears to have had much interest in or time for the distracting "luxury" of close relationships.

In his later public life, by his own account, he believed he could not afford that particular luxury. Perhaps, in time, he did not even consciously want it, having become used to aloneness and to loneliness—if not comfortable in them, at least able to get along on his own. In describing the traumas and triumphs of his public life—the Hiss case, the fund crisis, the "dump Nixon" episode, his losing campaigns, his victory in 1968, the major events of his presidency, even his resignation—in all these he describes important periods of seclusion, of silent contemplation, of deliberate retreat from the consolations or plaudits of family, staff, advisers. Solitude was Richard Nixon's chosen reward in victory, his solace in defeat.

Bryce Harlow ventured an explanation: "As a young person, he was hurt very deeply by somebody he trusted . . . a sweetheart, a parent, a dear friend, someone he deeply trusted. He never got over it and never trusted anybody again. But in life we get back what we plow into it."[4]

That, of course, was only Harlow's speculation, and he did not pretend to know who might have scarred Nixon so deeply, or how. Nixon's own comments to Ken Clawson (see chapter 1) suggest that he was the victim of a more generalized bitterness, not just at one event or one person. But in personal relations he probably did get back from life about what he had plowed into it.

"Do you think," Arthur Burns asked me, in the course of a long conversation about Nixon, "that he ever had a really good, close, personal friend?" He did not know of Haldeman's ill-fated find-a-friend experiment and he dismissed Bebe Rebozo as a "drinking buddy." Burns meant a *friend,* he said, in whom Nixon not only could have confided his deepest thoughts, but from whom he could have expected sympathetic understanding—from whom even a president might have been willing to hear and heed "straight talk."

When neither of us could think of any such person in what we knew of Nixon's life, Dr. Burns shook his head sadly. "A friend like that could have saved him," he said.[5]

Not long before Nixon's resignation, Hugh Sidey of *Time* talked with Henry Kissinger. "Can you imagine," Kissinger said, "what this man [Nixon] would have been had somebody loved him?"

"What do you mean?" Sidey asked.

"Had somebody in his life cared for him," Kissinger said. "I don't think anybody ever did, not his parents, not his peers. There may have been a teacher but nobody knows, it's not recorded. He would have been a great, great man had somebody loved him."[6]

Kissinger's conception of a totally unloved Nixon is somewhat grayer than the picture that derives from oral histories by relatives and acquaintances in Nixon's youth; but those, of course, are hindsight, recorded in most cases long after Nixon became a senator, vice president, president, and were almost surely colored by knowledge of his later prominence. Kissinger was asking a question, in any case, that probably no college classmate or first cousin—or perhaps even Nixon himself—could answer.

But that Kissinger and Burns, each of whom could claim to know Nixon better than most, asked such questions suggests much the same (I believe essential) insight as Harlow's: that Richard Nixon was a man alone, a man who was not much loved because he could not love—at least not openly and fully.

If so, it may well have been that this brooding and introverted man, even when at last in the White House of his dreams, lacked the sense of self-worth, of his own human value, that might have enabled him to give and inspire love, receive love and feel deserving of it. Without such a sense of worthiness, neither the applause of an audience nor the devotion of an intimate is likely to be accepted unreservedly.

Nixon had ample "self-confidence in his own judgment," William Rogers told me, but believed that people simply did not like Richard Nixon. His "body language indicated uncertainty," Rogers said; and the sweating upper lip during Nixon's television speeches, the clasped and twisting hands, the wooden gestures and awkward movements, are readily recalled by old Nixon watchers.

Perhaps the lack of an innate sense of self-worth was *why* the introvert made the apparently contradictory choice to enter the exhibitionary world of politics, with its recurring opportunities for public and reassuring victory. Perhaps that's why "battle" and challenge, often imagined, yielded his preferred environment: the struggle to prove himself *to himself* would have been constant, necessary, life's blood. But it could not finally be won by the greatest achievement, the biggest share of the vote, the most daring decision, because it was not the outer world or the cheering crowd that demanded proof or could give assurance. The insatiable doubt within gnawed at every external triumph, demanding another to clinch the case, and then another, and still another.

The quip once current in Washington may have had a sharper point than I then realized—that Richard Nixon ordered the invasion of Cambodia because he could never make the first string.

His public life remarkably paralleled the course of the U.S., as it assumed and played its superpower role in the years following World War II. In that unfamiliar world both the man and the nation, it seems to me, came to believe more in power than in ideas. That may have been unavoidable, given the nature of the times; but it may also have been a fundamental flaw that limited their greatness.

In retirement in 1963, while preparing his memoirs for publication, Dwight Eisenhower recalled at length his decision not to intervene at Dienbienphu in 1954, against the Vietminh.

> The strongest reason of all for the United States refusal to respond by itself to French pleas is the fact that among all the powerful nations of the world the United States is the only one with a tradition of anti-colonialism. . . .
>
> The standing of the United States as the most powerful of the anti-colonial powers is an asset of incalculable value to the Free World. It means that our counsel is trusted where that of others may not be. It is essential to our position of leadership in a world wherein the majority of the nations have at some time or another felt the yoke of colonialism.
>
> *Thus it is that the moral position of the United States was more to be guarded than the Tonkin Delta, indeed than all of Indochina.* [Emphasis added.]

This striking passage unfortunately was cut from the published version of *Mandate for Change,* apparently for reasons of length. It was preserved by William Ewald, one of the writers who helped Eisenhower with the memoir, and who published it in a book of his own in 1981.[7]

The passage probably was not written or dictated by Eisenhower, but was based on his views. He had not always himself refrained from risking the nation's "moral position"—notably in Iran and Guatemala. But the overthrow of governments in those nations was accomplished in "covert operations" that mostly *were* secret, at the time; for the most part, as in Indochina and later during the assault on Egypt by Britain, France and Israel, Eisenhower acted in the anticolonialist tradition and to preserve the nation's "moral position."

That the U.S. had no colonialist past was an overstatement, of course, as Filipinos and Panamanians could testify; and the interventionist record of the Colossus of the North had earned it no reverence in Latin America. But Eisenhower's fundamental point was that, in most of the world, the U.S. *did* have a moral position of "incalculable value" to sustain, one that was "more to be guarded" than anything likely to be gained in wars that smacked of imperialism.

He was pointing to the *idea* of an America based on the Declaration of Independence and the Constitution, the writings of Jefferson, Tom Paine and Abraham Lincoln, Roosevelt's promotion of the "Four Freedoms"— an idea that largely prevailed after the defeat of Hitler and the surrender of Hirohito. America was seen not just as the home of the brave but as the land of the free—the world's foremost exponent of democratic values and individual rights, its preeminent spokesman for the right of peoples everywhere to independence, self-determination, justice under law . . . not just words but powerful ideas. Lincoln had called the American experiment in liberty "the last best hope of earth," and in mid-twentieth century, the world largely agreed.

It was significant, for instance, that Ho Chi Minh was a student of the Declaration and the Constitution. Had not President Truman been so intent on keeping postwar France from "going Communist" in Europe, thus having to support the French in Indochina, Ho might well have been brought, as he originally hoped, into some sort of tacit good relations with the U.S. Much future grief might have been avoided.

But Truman *did* focus on Europe, adding the weight of the U.S. to a French colonialist war—and sacrificing some significant part of the prevailing idea of America to the *power* he and most Americans thought more important. Truman faced a difficult choice, of course; but from his administration straight through that of Richard Nixon, American presidents— often including Eisenhower—virtually always opted for *power* over whatever remained of the "moral position" of America.

The decisive turn had come on that day in 1947 when Dean Acheson seized the floor from George Marshall to argue passionately to Republican congressional leaders that the U.S. had to take on the defense of the "free world" against the Communist intent to dominate the globe. Washington and Moscow were Rome and Carthage all over again, and not since their era—in Acheson's apocalyptic formulation—had there been "such a polarization of power on this earth."

Put that way—and Stalinist Russia and Communist China provided ample evidence for the thesis—not only the congressional leaders of the time but the American people for the next forty years saw the world divided between the almost unquestioned good of democracy and the secular evil of communism (however it might have been confused with the imperialist goals of the Soviet Union). In such a war to the death, even if it was a war *for* ideas, it would not be ideas but power that counted.

Power had to meet power; that was the political theology of the era, seldom questioned by "right-thinking" Americans. Only power could thwart or even "contain" power; only fire could fight fire. *The Communists only respect force.*

"How can you persuade a paranoid adversary to disarm 'by example'?" Acheson scoffed at the scientists who resisted American development of the hydrogen bomb. His question might have been asked by any American confronted with the heretical notion that the power of an *idea* might be greater than that of arms.

By the broadest standard, moreover, power worked. The line was held in Europe. Soviet expansionism was largely contained. The Communist lunge into South Korea was halted and turned back. A Soviet military toehold in Cuba was stamped out. The "free world" stayed mostly free, and the iron curtain failed to sustain the Communist empire.

But the cost was immense—and not just in mammoth "defense" expenditures in the U.S. for NATO, Japan, South Korea. As the two great giants waged their Cold War across the world, many other peoples, particularly in the Third World, saw fewer and fewer differences in superpower *uses* of power. The idea of a freedom-loving nation living by its ideals of justice and democracy—the idea that had so exalted the standing of the U.S. at the end of World War II—seemed more and more tarnished, by the CIA, the Pentagon, the arms race, the iron fist of power in Washington as in Moscow.

In either capital, nations and leaders were viewed as being for one side and against the other; in both, "neutralism" was suspect if not denounced. In West as well as East, all conflicts were treated as cold war battlegrounds, all political movements were targets for penetration, all nations were subject to military, economic and diplomatic discipline from the superpowers.

As in any war, pressures for conformity against the enemy rose and flourished, and the fear of disloyalty deeply influenced American politics. Zeal for the anti-Communist cause threatened reason and restraint. Few questioned, as long as the war went well, the absurd idea that the U.S. in Vietnam was fighting against Communist expansion that could turn the Pacific into a "Red Lake" lapping at the shores of California.

Anticommunism, the cold war, the superpower struggle for influence, advantage anywhere and everywhere on the globe—"Is this the real world?" Stanley Hoffman asked.

Or does it not substitute for the real world an artificially simple and tidy one, in which friends and foes, radicals and moderates are neatly lined up, and in which nationalism—surely as important a force as communism—gets thoroughly discounted?[8]

Real world or not, it was the world of Richard Nixon's political life, and he accepted it without apparent qualm. From the day he set out to unseat Jerry Voorhis in 1946 (not long before Acheson defined the American idea of the cold war), Nixon took the hard line of power for himself, his party, his country. Though his speeches and positions sometimes rang with a moralism that bordered on piety, their content was militant. He was relentless in pursuit of enemies abroad and subversives at home, and not even his greatest admirers doubted that he was a "gut-fighter" for the cause, his own as well as the nation's. Reinforced by his view of life as battle, Richard Nixon would have derided the notion that his or the country's political success depended upon an abstract "moral position."

He accepted cold war values as completely as he absorbed that other conventional ethic of his time and background—hard work brings success; anyone willing to work can get ahead. But Nixon was not only a political beneficiary of Cold War attitudes; he was among their foremost instigators. His early campaigns in California, the Hiss case, his selection for Eisenhower's ticket, his national campaigns from 1952 to 1958—all capitalized upon and reemphasized the anti-Communist orthodoxy that then dominated American politics. As vice president during the first Indochina crisis, he clearly was prepared to go further—perhaps even to atomic weapons—than Eisenhower's remotest intention. From 1960 on, Nixon's anti-Communist focus became somewhat diffused only because he was responding politically to changing circumstances—the Sino-Soviet split, the new importance of domestic issues like crime and race, the broader gauge required of a presidential contender.

Even when, as president, he sought rapprochement with China and détente with the Soviet Union, he was not trying to *end* the Cold War or retreat from the world competition with communism. He sought to *strengthen* the U.S. for the race—as Elliot Richardson observed—by bringing about its adaptation

to the end of the era in which our margin of military and economic superiority was so great that we could afford to neglect the careful delineation of U.S. interests, the farsighted shaping of contingency plans, and the husbanding of U.S. resources.[9]

No matter how he and the country he led adapted, however, Nixon remained a creature of the Cold War he had helped to make a reality; as crises, of whatever magnitude or authenticity, arose during his presidency, he all but invariably considered them geopolitically, as confrontations at first or second hand between Moscow and Washington. Like his predecessors, more ruthlessly and pragmatically than most but often more skillfully too, he met power with power. For him, the "moral position" of America, like his own, was still an abstraction; the *consequence* of an act or a policy was his concern, and if the consequence was favorable or even acceptable, the apparent morality or immorality of the act itself meant little. Nixon's was "situational morality," not a fixed and accepted code of conduct; and the same might have been said, in much of the postwar era, of American foreign policy.

By so often taking the course of power, the nation had lost much of that "moral position" Eisenhower cited: Whether by doing so it had survived, when it could not have otherwise, or whether in defending its values it had sacrificed them—these are historical questions too demanding to be answered briefly. Richard Nixon, in choosing the same course personally and politically, also had taken a decisive turn—not just from a moral position but from the cool, "saintly" Quaker who had dominated his early life, and from the peaceful ideals she had exemplified. He had followed, instead, the combative way of Frank Nixon; and for Richard Nixon as well as for the nation, the choice of power over an idea, and an ideal, had been costly, even if outwardly successful.

For both man and nation, the political necessity to profess belief in the ideal, even when their actions undermined it, was a reminder of a lost Arcadian age. Nations may not collectively suffer guilt, even for such self-betrayals, but individuals do; and whatever the reason Richard Nixon may have thought himself unworthy, his failure or inability to follow Hannah Nixon's gentle ways cannot have eased his pain.

It was quintessentially as a *public* man that Nixon chose to lead his life, and therefore as a public man that he most demands and deserves to be summarized. It's a cliché of current comment that he was more successful as president in his foreign policy than in his domestic activities; and those who lament his forced departure from the White House usually suggest that had he remained in office he would have accomplished further great deeds in world, not necessarily national, affairs.

Nixon himself, in *RN* and subsequent books, has assiduously fostered an essentially correct idea of himself as especially knowledgeable about world affairs. That view is widely shared, by those who served in his administration as well as by disinterested observers.

Elliot Richardson, Nixon's undersecretary of state (later secretary of defense, still later attorney general), termed Nixon "the conceptualist, the architect, the chief strategist of his own foreign policy." Stephen Ambrose, an admiring biographer of Eisenhower and a less admiring biographer of Nixon, argued at Hofstra that of the two presidents in world affairs, Nixon "thought on a larger scale." Dr. Kenneth Thompson of the Miller Center of Public Affairs at the University of Virginia put it roundly: "No president before or since has had the same strategic sense, the grasp of foreign policy, that Nixon achieved."*

Nixon took office at the end of the sixties, when keen eyes could see that American power and resources no longer were adequate for a hegemonic position in the world; the U.S. could not be everywhere at once, the policeman in every dispute, the guardian of every legitimate interest. It was Nixon's almost unprecedented task to set priorities and define essential interests for a nation not accustomed to such limits, not happy with the necessity to choose.

Americans, moreover, in their brief post–World War II period of singular world leadership, had tended to form political judgments and make international choices, when they had to—as Kissinger has observed—in "moral and legal terms," without much regard for realistically conceived national interest. Communists were bad, elections were good, nations who paid their debts were honorable, people who didn't speak English or French were suspect and—perhaps worse—not modern.

Nixon wanted to instill an approach that would impose orderly and rational choices on American foreign policy but also move it away from abstract moralism and legalism. This may have been partially a reaction against the policies of John Foster Dulles that Nixon had watched at close range in the Eisenhower administration, when American economic and military power was preeminent and the fixed notion of Communist world versus free world was largely unchallenged—and when Vice President Nixon had resented his status as a lightweight best fitted for ceremonial junkets and domestic political drudgework.

On a more important level, the world had changed since the fifties. Nixon, watching the change, had changed too; he took office convinced, for example, that a serious American foreign policy could not "exclude one-fourth of the human race"—China. He understood, too, that the arena was no longer bipolar, divided between Washington and Moscow, but multipolar, with Peking, Tokyo, and Western Europe able to play major roles. The U.S. would not be able again to dominate such a world, even if it wanted to; its interests would have to govern its commitments, rather than the other way around.*

"Five great economic superpowers" watching and challenging each

*All these remarks were delivered at the Hofstra conference.
*This overall view of Nixon's basic approach was detailed at the Hofstra conference in several panels and speeches, one of the most important of which was by Henry Kissinger.

other, Nixon predicted on July 6, 1971 (in the same Kansas City speech in which he almost gave away Kissinger's mission to China), would not be "a bad thing." In fact, he suggested, general economic progress probably would be promoted by the competition. No doubt he also saw, too, that this was a world in which his and Kissinger's balance-of-power approach might work best.[10]

Two other Nixonian perceptions influenced his policies toward China and the Soviet Union. Sino-American relations might be improved and that would give the U.S. new leverage against Moscow. Once communications were opened, moreover, the Chinese proved to be delighted with Nixon's multipolar-world concept; the Kansas City speech, which Kissinger had not seen when he arrived in China, was one of the first subjects they wanted to discuss with him. For their own reasons, they opposed superpower hegemony in the world as well as Soviet dominance of the Communist nations.[11]

Technological advances, moreover, meant that the U.S. had to adapt to something like military parity in the world—particularly with the Soviets. Nixon foresaw and acted on the resulting "era of negotiation," concluding SALT I, a vitally needed demonstration (however flawed the actual agreements) that nations need not go on lemminglike to nuclear catastrophe. In a world of nuclear deterrence, moreover, military parity was in the U.S. as well as the Soviet interest—hard though that was to explain to some American hawks.

Nixon was prepared, however, to negotiate arms control agreements only if linked to political issues. That is, he believed arms agreements with Moscow could not last unless the Soviets restrained their external behavior—a point generally borne out by congressional revulsion against SALT II after the Soviet invasion of Afghanistan in 1959. "The primary purpose of arms control is to reduce the danger of war," Nixon later wrote,

> But arms control by itself cannot do this. Political differences, not arms, are the root causes of war, and until these are resolved, there will be enough arms for the most devastating war no matter how many arms control agreements are reached.[12]

Nixon also realized that if the U.S. had interests, so did Moscow. Those Soviet interests needed to be respected as the best means of bringing Moscow to understand and respect American interests in return. As was seen in chapter 12, this attitude—respect for both sides' genuine concerns—also served Nixon well in a domestic crisis, his necessary effort to bring about unitary schools in the South in 1970.*

Nixon was not, certainly, the only American to realize that when rela-

---

*I am indebted to Ray Price for pointing out this parallel.

tions between the Soviet Union and China were troubled, the time was ripe
to improve American relations with both. But he perhaps knew better than
any other leader of his time how to exploit the opportunity—with his
anti-Communist credentials, he certainly was better situated politically—
without alienating either of the Communist powers (or his own following).
As a result, in Raymond Garthoff's words, "the U.S. had the greatest
leverage in the triangular relationship."[13]

But another, less prepossessing perception guided Nixon's approach: his
long and hard experience in American politics. From the start, partially
propelled by Murray Chotiner's advice, but surely urged on by the legacy
of his father's bullying intensity, Nixon seemed to regard the law of politics
as something like the law of the jungle, in which—as Ken Thompson put
it at Hofstra—"the Marquis of Queensberry rules did not apply." This
attitude carried over into Nixon's conduct of foreign policy.

The world was a place, if not of abstract good and evil, of the weak and
the strong, where the big fish ate the little fish anytime they could, and it
was justifiable practice to bomb one country in order to send a message to
another. Nixon was a big fish who had scant concern for little fish—for the
Third World generally, for "third-rate" powers like North Korea, for black
Africa in its liberation struggles, for human rights as a guiding concept of
foreign policy. Aided and abetted by Henry Kissinger, he proceeded usually by secrecy, often by threat and manipulation, sometimes by duplicity,
and rarely believed enough in his own principal associates or the American
people to take them into his confidence, share with them his goals and
ideas.

For that, Nixon paid a high price—not just ultimately in Watergate, but
in the widespread lack of support and goodwill of a public that could
seldom see his world vision for the "crafty atmospherics" in which he
beclouded it. Surely he was "the leading strategist we've had in the White
House since World War II," but just as surely he was "a realist whose
realism [was] infused with cynicism"; and for these flaws of character he
came to grief personally, and left incomplete the soaring structure of peace
he envisioned.[14]

The SALT I agreements, the American-Soviet détente of the seventies,
the opening to China—all are achievements often adduced as empirical
evidence of Nixon's superior strategy and foreign policy. His extrication
of the nation from Vietnam—long, bloody and deceptive though it was—is
sometimes cited. But the SALT negotiations themselves, the whole four-
year drama of Vietnam, and a number of other episodes, reflect also the
less admirable side of Richard Nixon's White House and call into question
the strategic vision and the sophisticated diplomacy claimed for his administration.

Nixon's moves, for one example, were usually restricted by his persistent
view of all the world as a Cold War battleground, where every clash and

competition was in some sense an extension of the Moscow-Washington rivalry. His fetish for secrecy, for another example, may have aided his diplomacy in the short run; but it kept him too often out of the "bully pulpit." He could not build up lasting public support among a people accustomed to considering foreign policy in moral and legal terms—a people, consequently, who did not naturally share Nixon's capacity for ruthless pragmatism.

His abandonment of the outspoken anticommunism of his early career, which so many Americans shared, his about-face on China after twenty years of hostility, his dealings with the Soviets who, in his telling, supposedly had menaced the U.S. for so long—such realpolitik needed more convincing explanations, more open discussion, if they were to be translated into permanent American attitudes. Nixon, operating so much in secrecy, was unable to function as a good teacher, with confidence in his students' capacity to understand.

Kissinger and others have suggested that the North Vietnamese would not have dared to challenge Nixon by taking over South Vietnam had he been able to remain in the White House. But Kissinger himself, *before* Nixon's resignation was dreamed of, had predicted the Saigon regime could hold out for no more than "a year and a half" (see chapter 14).

The more interesting question, therefore—and perhaps the *most* important that can be asked about Nixon's foreign policy—is "what if" he had been willing to end American participation in the Indochinese war soon after he took office? He might well have been able to do it on roughly the same terms he ultimately accepted—unilateral American withdrawal from the South.

"There were never any other [North Vietnamese] terms," Kissinger said at Hofstra—although he insisted that to say that the war could have been settled in 1969 was "playing games with the honor of the American people."

Had Nixon, however, moved as quickly to end the war as Eisenhower had done in order to cut American losses in Korea, some of the events most damaging to the Nixon administration (in some cases to the nation) could have been avoided—the secret bombing and invasion of Cambodia, the campus explosions of 1970, the incursion into Laos, the Christmas bombing, the huge peace demonstrations in the U.S., the gradual alienation of Congress.

Perhaps even the long chain of events collectively known as "Watergate" would not have been set off, leading as it did to Nixon's resignation. Without the war and the challenges of the peace movement and the Pentagon Papers, there would have been no plumbers and no break-in at Dr. Lewis Fielding's office in Los Angeles. It was to a large extent for fear of exposure of that crime and other plumbers' activities that Nixon made his fatal decision to "stonewall" and cover up the relatively unimportant Watergate break-in itself.

The American position in the world *might* have been drastically weakened by such an early termination of the war, if the Nixon-Kissinger geopolitical rationalization is accepted. Nixon's determination to meet every challenge with a tough response would have had to be curtailed. But it's hard to see, in retrospect, even the geopolitical advantages of four years of war and destruction, four years of violent controversy at home and abroad, when the war finally was ended on such terms that its supposed goal—to defend South Vietnamese independence—could not be achieved.

Beyond these conceptual objections, some literal results of Nixon's foreign policy do not square with the idea of his mastery. He went straight from the first Moscow summit, for example, to Teheran to conclude an agreement under which Riza Pahlevi, the shah of Iran, could buy any U.S. weapons (save nuclear warheads) and have any assistance he wanted. Nor were there to be any of the customary Pentagon, State Department or White House staff reviews. These were unprecedented favors, even to a trusted ally, and ultimately neither in his interest nor that of the U.S. More immediately, this Nixonian contribution to a "position of strength" on the border of the Soviet Union must have caused Moscow to wonder about the sincerity of his desire to relax American-Soviet tensions—SALT I or no.

The Senate Foreign Relations Committee pointed out in 1976 that Nixon's extraordinary decision had resulted in arms sales to Iran totaling $10 billion, including four destroyers more sophisticated than any then in the U.S. Navy, plus eighty advanced F-14 fighter planes. At that time, twenty-four thousand American technicians were in the shah's service, owing to these arms sales and the need to service the weapons.

Yet, despite this enormous investment in Pahlevi's regime, Nixon—having designated the shah the West's "protector" in the Persian Gulf region, as well as the guarantor of the American oil supply—ignored the growing repressiveness of the shah's government and the rising disquiet and anger among the Iranian people. As we have seen (chapter 4), on his first vice presidential trip abroad in 1953 Nixon had been greatly impressed by the shah, then newly restored to the Peacock Throne by an American-British covert operation. Over the next twenty years, Nixon, the supposed master of foreign affairs, never changed or even seems to have reexamined his early judgment.

The limitless arms sales he authorized were aimed substantially at recycling Iranian "petrodollars" into the American economy. But as Pahlevi's indebtedness increased, he raised oil prices to pay for his continuing arms purchases, to the detriment of American consumers and in derision of the shah's "guarantor" role. Nixon's open-hand, blind-eye policy also contributed heavily to Pahlevi's ultimate downfall—although that was the last thing Nixon would have wanted, had he still been in the White House—by tacitly encouraging the shah's megalomania and his ambition to make Iran a Western-style superpower. That also fed the resentments, popular and religious, that led to the Islamic revolution and the accession to power of the Ayatollah Ruhollah Khomeini.

Thus, the resulting damage to American interests in the Middle East— not to mention the short-term hostage crisis of 1979–1980—are more nearly chargeable to Nixon's policy and his unexamined support for the shah than to anything done or not done by President Carter, who was in office when the revolution erupted.

Pahlevi also served as a conduit for secret American arms aid to Kurdish rebels in Iraq. Iran and Iraq were traditional adversaries; and when the Iraqi government signed a treaty of friendship with the Soviet Union in 1972, Nixon and Kissinger characteristically turned hostile to Baghdad, too. The shah then proposed American aid to the Kurds, who had been fighting Baghdad for autonomy off and on since 1961; and Nixon and Kissinger assented, over the objections of the State Department and the CIA. The president's purpose was not to win Kurdish autonomy, about which he cared nothing, or to overthrow the Iraqi government, but to weaken and harass the latter—more nearly an example of aggressive meddling than of shrewd foreign policy management.

A House committee, later examining the matter, reported that Nixon and Kissinger

> hoped [the Kurds] would not prevail. They preferred instead that the insurgents simply continue a level of hostilities sufficient to sap the resources of our ally's [Iran] neighboring country [Iraq]. This policy was not imparted to our clients [the Kurds] who were encouraged to keep fighting. . . . [O]urs was a cynical enterprise.

Iranian and Iraqi animosities subsided somewhat, after they settled a long-standing boundary dispute in an agreement the shah considered favorable to his country. He then took counsel of his fears of the Kurdish revolt spreading from Iraq into Iran.

In 1975, therefore, Pahlevi brutally cut the aid pipeline, sealing the Iranian border against further arms deliveries to the Kurds. The result was no doubt in his own interest; but this action by an ally left the Nixon administration with no alternative—owing to its blind determination to maintain good relations with the shah—to a dishonorable abandonment of the two hundred thousand Kurds it had encouraged to fight. They were left, with bloody results, to the untender mercies of the Iraqis.

It was President Gerald Ford, Nixon's successor, with the encouragement of his secretary of state, Henry Kissinger, who acquiesced in this sell-out of the Kurds; but it had been Richard Nixon, in 1972, who authorized the arms aid that caused the Kurds to continue their doomed rebellion.

"We never trusted the Shah," said Mulla Mustafa Barzani, the Kurdish leader, who later lived and died in exile in the U.S. "Without American promises, we wouldn't have acted the way we did."

Thus, two American presidents accepted and acted upon the shah's leadership in a policy that caused the shedding of other people's blood for limited American and Iranian geopolitical purposes, and in the end brought the U.S. much opprobrium throughout the Third World—a deserved stain on its good repute. The Kurds, having served their purpose, suffered near genocide.

In 1976, nevertheless, Secretary of State Kissinger announced that arms sales to the shah would be *increased* by the Ford administration, with the latest American aircraft and airborne warning systems included.[15]

Iran is one of the worst examples of the grim side of Nixon's foreign policy but not the only one. His "tilt" to Pakistan during the Indo-Pakistan War, for example, jeopardized long-term American interests in the region. Was he influenced, again, by memories of that vice presidential trip abroad in 1953, when he had disliked Jawarharlal Nehru and considered Muhammad Ayub Khan of Pakistan "more anti-Communist than anti-Indian"?

In any case, the Nixon-Kissinger team, as usual operating virtually alone in the interpretation of intelligence and the making of decisions, several times came to the wrong conclusions and took the wrong course. They viewed India as the aggressor—Ambassador George Bush so labeled her at the U.N.—when the evidence plainly establishes, as it should have at the time, that Pakistan struck first, on December 3, 1971, in air attacks on Indian bases and an armored drive into Indian-administered areas of Kashmir. Indian troops only then moved into East Pakistan.

Even before that, and even before India and the Soviet Union, influenced by Kissinger's visit to China, signed a friendship treaty in the summer of 1971, Nixon had demanded an American "tilt" toward Pakistan in the event of war. When it began, he and Kissinger thought the Indians had acted at the instigation of the Soviets, who supposedly hoped the world would see the U.S. and China stand idly by while their friend, Pakistan, was attacked.

Nixon and Kissinger persisted in and acted upon the far-fetched geopolitical assessment—not supported by the State Department or the CIA—that the Indo-Pakistan conflict was a confrontation by proxy between the Soviet Union and the U.S., and that the Soviet client, India, intended to invade and dismember the American client, West Pakistan.

"A number of us quite frankly felt that the intelligence reports that were coming in this regard were exaggerated," the experienced State Department official, Joseph Sisco, later remarked. "The dangers of Pakistan being snuffed out seemed exaggerated. [But] they were used to justify the tilt in that direction."[16]

The war actually was about the brutal repression by a government dominated by West Pakistan of ninety-five million Bengalis in East Pakistan (the two Pakistans were separated by India). It soon became clear, and all parties accepted—the U.S. only reluctantly—that East Pakistan would have to be given independence (it became Bangladesh). Not only the Soviets but Prime Minister Indira Gandhi assured Washington that India had no intention of invading or dismembering West Pakistan; but Nixon and Kissinger could not be convinced. They also believed China would intervene on behalf of Pakistan, until Peking managed to disabuse them of the idea.

Laboring under such misconceptions, Nixon and Kissinger flailed about—delivering ultimata to Moscow, broadly hinting that they would break off summit negotiations, threatening to come to the military assistance of Pakistan, dispatching a naval force to the Bay of Bengal (without consulting the NSC, the secretary of defense, the secretary of state, the Joint Chiefs or the navy), though giving that force no defined mission. They even discouraged Pakistan from offering a cease-fire in the East, believing that would free India to make the attack in the West that they feared.

That fear was not really for the integrity of Pakistan or in sympathy for a friendly nation (one that had just facilitated Kissinger's visit to China); it arose from the convoluted notion that if India attacked West Pakistan, the U.S. would have to come to Pakistan's defense or be judged, by friends and enemies alike, a paper tiger.

Ultimately, the war was settled more or less as it had to be. East Pakistan won its independence. Cease-fires were arranged in both East and West. There was no Indian attack on West Pakistan, and the status quo was accepted there. Historical records disclose that this was about what Moscow, New Delhi and Peking had worked for all along, and what the Pakistanis came to see as the best they could expect. The Nixon-Kissinger maneuvers, threats and manipulations had had little effect on the outcome of the war.

There were numerous other effects, none favorable to Washington: India was turned more toward the Soviet Union—though it was far from being a proxy, much less a puppet. The U.S. was seen to be ignoring the millions of Bengali refugees from Pakistani oppression. The Soviets demonstrated their ability to match an American naval presence in Asian waters. It can even be speculated that deployment of a nuclear-armed American task force in the Bay of Bengal influenced India's decision to develop nuclear weapons; its giant Chinese neighbor was doing so, the Indians could not count on American support, and they did not want to become dependent on Moscow.

Despite Kissinger's plodding efforts in a seventy-six-page chapter of his memoirs to justify his and Nixon's actions, and Nixon's claim in *RN* that "we had once again avoided a major confrontation with the Soviet Union," this is hardly an account of sophisticated mastery of foreign policy. Certainly, as Kissinger understates the matter at one point in his account, it was "not an ideal way to manage crises."[17]

Another example of fumbled foreign policy was the "destabilization" of Chile, leading ultimately to the overthrow and death of an elected president, Salvador Allende Gossens in 1973, and to the long run of the repressive, *un*elected government of General Augusto Pinochet, who still was in power sixteen years later. That "accomplishment" could be celebrated only by those willing to accept any regime and any method of achieving it in preference to Communists or "Marxists" or "Soviet puppets"—three terms often, if erroneously, used interchangeably.

Allende was an avowed Marxist, and Nixon apparently considered him an out-and-out Communist, therefore necessarily a puppet or a potential puppet of Moscow. He had no intention of watching Allende convert Chile into "another Cuba" in the Western Hemisphere—not on Richard Nixon's watch.

First, in 1970, he sought to prevent Allende's predicted election, through CIA covert operations in support of more palatable opponents. The president ignored or overruled the objections of Charles Meyer, the assistant secretary of state for Latin America, that such operations would tarnish the American "image" south of the border; and when covert action failed to stop Allende's election (by a minority in a multicandidate race) in September, Nixon further ordered the CIA to stop the president-elect's inauguration.

On September 15, Richard Helms, the director of Central Intelligence, made a note of Nixon's instructions: "$10,000,000 available, more if necessary—full time job—best men we have—game plan—make the economy scream." The CIA subsequently spent $8 million to shore up old and create new preinaugural opposition to Allende, but its efforts again failed.[18]

The president's demands and agency bungling did result, unfortunately, in the death of General Rene Schneider, the commander of the Chilean armed forces and an anti-Allende *friend* of the U.S. The CIA had set up a kidnapping of General Schneider, in the hope that the Chilean military would seize power in response. The general evaded two attempts to seize him, but was fatally shot in a third—and Allende was inaugurated anyway.

In subsequent years, however, Nixon certainly helped to make Allende's economy "scream." Chile depended on massive imports of food and machinery, 40 percent of them from the U.S. Combined with a decline in the international price of copper, Chile's main export, this dependence made Chile in the Allende years exceptionally vulnerable to American economic pressure. Richard Nixon had learned that game at the feet of Dwight Eisenhower, as the old general squeezed Britain in the aftermath of the Suez crisis of 1956.

The U.S. Export-Import Bank, which had extended $600 million in credits to Chile in the quarter century before Allende took office, not only cut off new loans, it stopped disbursement on old loans—under orders from the White House, through Nixon's treasury secretary, John B. Connally. That had its impact; Chile's imports from the U.S. dropped from 40 percent of the total to 15 percent. Without machine-part replacements, Chilean industry suffered; worse, politically, the important Chilean middle class was hard hit by the unavailability of accustomed imports, and blamed Allende.

Similarly, Nixon used American influence on the Inter-American Development Bank and the World Bank to make the Chilean economy scream more loudly. In the eleven years before Allende, the IADB had granted fifty-nine loans to Chile totaling more than $310 million; after his inauguration, IADB assistance dropped to nothing. Not even emergency relief for the terrible 1971 earthquake was granted. Similarly, the World Bank—which had lent Chile $235 million B.A. (Before Allende)—refused all Allende's loan requests; and the bank's president, Robert S. McNamara, repeatedly criticized Chile in such a way as to damage its credit rating.

The International Monetary Fund, over which the U.S. exerts somewhat less control, apparently saw little wrong with the Chilean economy; the IMF extended $148 million to Chile in 1971 and 1972. Nixon himself told David Frost in 1977 that on the issue of international aid he had "indicated that wherever we had a vote, where Chile was involved, that unless there were strong considerations on the other side, that we would vote against them."

The reason he gave was that Allende had expropriated foreign, including American, businesses and property. When Frost pointed out that no expropriation had occurred when Nixon first moved to stop Allende's election in 1970, Nixon replied: "I know, I know, but I knew that it was coming. . . . There wasn't any question but that he was cooperating with Castro."

Frost did not point out, as he might have, that Allende's expropriation of American copper companies was specifically ordered by a constitutional amendment approved by the anti-Allende Chilean congress.

Thus, Nixon's policy toward Chile was less that of a shrewd and sophisticated master of world affairs than that of a single-minded anti-Communist who had made up his mind not to tolerate another Communist government in the Western Hemisphere. Had he done nothing, he told Frost, Cuba and Chile would have made of Latin America "a red sandwich, and eventually it will be all red."[19]

Allende had needed little help in creating an economic mess in Chile. He did not have the support of the armed forces, or congress, or the judiciary, and had been elected by a minority. He tried to do too much too rapidly, alienating many Chileans who believed in democracy but deplored his failures. Some actually supported the military coup in which Allende was killed, foolishly expecting General Pinochet to honor Chilean tradition and return power to an elected regime.* Instead, he maintained his repressive military government until 1989.

Many years after the coup, a former member of the Allende government conceded to me that "Sweden was not the model" for its policies, and that Chile under Allende was "not all peaches and cream." But he pointed out that there had been no human rights violations—commonplace under General Pinochet—and argued that Allende himself was an "incompetent" who had neither power nor will to become a Communist dictator. He added sadly: "I wouldn't vote for him again. But the coup was not necessary."

No evidence has come to light that the CIA instigated that coup, which was carried out on September 11, 1973; and the agency has roundly denied involvement ever since. Nevertheless, the years of destabilization, of making the economy scream, speeded Allende's loss of popularity and support. A private trucking strike, for example, set off the Chilean political crisis which ended in the military coup; the truck owners cited as a reason for the strike their inability to obtain replacement parts through imports— imports that had been cut off by the Nixon administration.

Nixon's opposition also reinforced the Chilean military's decision to get rid of Allende. In every way possible, the administration had signaled that it would welcome Allende's overthrow; and when that was accomplished, the CIA immediately embarked on a public-relations program to make the right-wing Pinochet government appear more acceptable and legitimate to the American public.

That, too, proved largely beyond the agency's means. But Nixon's main purpose had been achieved—"the single darkest side," Roger Morris said at Hofstra, "to the Nixon-Kissinger record." Nor had there been anything innovative about the "destabilization" of Chile, save the word itself. U.S. intervention, armed or otherwise, in the affairs of Latin nations was one of the oldest American traditions, to be repeated again in Nicaragua when Ronald Reagan came to power.

*One of these was Patricio Aylwin, a Christian Democrat, who in 1989 was elected Chile's first post-Pinochet president.

In the same summer of 1970 that saw Allende elected—the summer that followed the Cambodian invasion in the spring—Nixon had to deal with a situation in the Middle East that he later told Congress "presented the gravest threat to world peace" since he had been in office. But did it?

Nixon's and Kissinger's focus on the Soviet Union as the instigator of virtually any international problem once again convinced them that they were facing, however camouflaged, a Soviet challenge. On that assumption, they took actions risking war primarily in order to send the message to Moscow that its supposed geopolitical move in the Middle East was being stiffly resisted.

Twenty years later, not least because of Nixon's and Kissinger's claims at the time and in their later memoirs, the notion persists that Nixon faced down the Soviets in the Middle East crisis of 1970. But what in fact precipitated that crisis was a decision by King Hussein of Jordan to confront the Palestine Liberation Organization and break its power within his kingdom. The PLO had become something like a state within the state of Jordan, particularly after Hussein lost the West Bank to Israel in the 1967 war.

Then as now, Hussein was seen as a moderate Arab leader; but the PLO of that time craved immoderate action against Israel. In June 1970, PLO terrorists tried unsuccessfully to assassinate Hussein and take over in Jordan. In September, Hussein responded by forming a military government and launching an anti-PLO civil war with the intention of restoring and consolidating his own kingly authority.

The Soviets had made what Washington considered client states of Egypt and Syria; but the historical record does not suggest that Moscow had much, if anything, to do with what was happening in Jordan. Nixon and Kissinger, in keeping with their worldview and anti-Soviet fixation, nevertheless concluded that Moscow must have urged Syria, which had a strongly anti-Hussein government, to incite the PLO revolt against the king.

"We could not," Nixon wrote in *RN,* "allow Hussein to be overthrown by a Soviet-inspired insurrection." Though he knew Hussein himself had launched the civil war, Nixon—urged on by Kissinger—was convinced that the earlier PLO attack on Hussein had been inspired by Moscow and Damascus and had forced the king to act.

As the president saw this intricate situation, if King Hussein fell, Israel would intervene against the resulting radical, Syrian-dominated government in Jordan; Gamal Abdel Nasser, Syria's Egyptian ally, then would have to react against Israel, opening a two-front war against the Jewish state; and the Soviets would have to aid both the Egyptians and the Syrians, who were their clients. The U.S. could not afford to do nothing while the

Soviet-Syrian-Egyptian combination drove Israel into the sea; Washington would have to intervene to protect *its* client and ally. Thus, Nixon concluded, as he was to do in the Indo-Pakistan War, that the Soviets had concocted through secondhand means a direct challenge to the U.S.

Nixon seems to have been almost eager to confront it. He quickly moved strong naval forces into the eastern Mediterranean, readied a Marine landing force, and put various air force and army units in Europe and the U.S. on alert. These military actions, though unannounced, were telegraphed to the Soviets in the kind of geopolitical "signals" on which Nixon and Kissinger so heavily relied.

Nixon's reasoning required one illogical leap. The Soviets surely knew, too, that Israel would see no alternative but to react militarily against a Syrian-PLO takeover in Jordan. That would set off, as Nixon saw it, a Middle East war into which both superpowers might easily be drawn. So if Moscow really was encouraging Syria to encourage a PLO takeover in Jordan, the Soviets were not just playing a game of chicken with the U.S. They were assuring a Middle East war that might well draw down nuclear bombs on themselves.

Even in 1970, an unbiased analyst would have been hard put to explain why Moscow would want to risk setting off a Middle East war with such fatal consequences, and there is no evidence that the Soviets did—quite the opposite. Moscow quite obviously, for example, kept its own Mediterranean naval forces out of the way of the American task force.

The crunch came on September 20. Washington learned that a heavy Syrian tank column had crossed the border into Jordan, headed for Amman, undoubtedly to help the PLO against Hussein. Nixon's version in *RN* includes two separate Syrian tank attacks, the first turning back after he sent a warning note to the Soviets, the second and heavier column of three hundred tanks moving three days later. Various movements of American military forces, in his account, alerted Moscow to his readiness to intervene, whereupon the Soviets again forced Damascus to withdraw the attacking tanks.

Even today, little is known about those Syrian tank forces and their brief expedition into Jordan. There were no solid sources of American intelligence in the area at the time—no reliable agents in place and no satellite coverage. Washington was getting its information from the Israelis and the Jordanians, both of whom had reason to exaggerate the dangers in order to draw the U.S. further to their support, and—in the Israelis' case— possibly to take advantage of the crisis by capturing and holding, with American backing, strategic ground in the north of Jordan.

Neither Nixon nor Kissinger mentions in his memoir another development, purely regional and having no Cold War linkage, that was a major factor in turning back the tanks. The Syrian defense minister and air force commander, Hafiz al-Assad, was engaged in a political struggle for power within the radical Ba'athist regime of Salah Jadid in Damascus. When Jadid sent the tanks into Jordan on behalf of the PLO, Assad denied air cover to the invading forces, allowing the Jordanian air force to batter them at will and force their withdrawal.

It might be argued that Assad acted as Nixon thought Moscow did—in response to U.S. troop movements that raised the possibility of American intervention on the side of Hussein and Israel. But because of their internal differences, Assad opposed the Syrian intervention *before* Jadid ordered it. The subsequent weakening of Jadid's domestic political position after the defeat his tanks suffered at the hands of Jordan was a major factor in Assad's seizure of power in Syria a few months later. He promptly arrested Jadid and Yussef Zaylin, who had commanded the tank column, and Assad has been in power ever since.[20]

Nixon's military movements cannot be discounted. But Assad's decision to withhold air cover, a matter of Syrian domestic politics, was of at least equal significance. Together with another regional factor—Israel's demonstrated military prowess, willingness to use it, and designs on strategic territory—Assad's action suggests that Nixon's Soviet-challenge scenario was more imagined than real.

The Jordanian-PLO death toll—perhaps as many as twenty thousand—was real enough, and remains today a factor in the West Bank Palestinians' refusal to accept Jordan as their "Palestinian state." Real, too, was the ultimate consolidation of Hussein's authority in Jordan, and Assad's in Syria—and a new direction in American-Israeli relations. The Nixon administration's early interest in an "evenhanded" Middle East policy disappeared, and so did the primacy in Middle East affairs of Secretary of State Rogers, who had espoused that policy.

Thereafter, Henry Kissinger—the hard-line advocate of tough responses to supposed Soviet maneuvers—was Nixon's primary adviser on Middle East matters, as he was on the rest of world affairs. In their view, they had turned back another Soviet challenge, with the indispensable help of Israel. Nixon's Middle East policy consequently "tilted" toward Israel, and Israel became the main instrument of his determination to offset the influence of the Soviet Union in that region.

Not everyone would agree that the Soviets were the real problem, then or later.

Even a partial list of developments during Richard Nixon's presidency returns repeatedly to the "dark side" of the foreign policy over which he presided, and forces difficult questions about his supposedly effective conduct of the nation's foreign relations.

He consistently supported, for example, the cruel colonels' junta he found in power in Greece when he himself took office. He even managed, by conniving with the colonels to make their regime look better, to lift the arms embargo that had been imposed on Greece by the Johnson administration. Strong evidence suggests that, in following this line, Nixon was influenced more by Greek-American political contributions than by diplomatic or ideological concerns.

Nor was he always, in crises, the cool-headed analyst self-pictured in his books. In April 1969, he wanted to bomb North Korea after one of its fighters inadvertently shot down an American EC-121 reconnaissance plane ninety miles off the Korean coast. Kissinger egged him on, even talking of nuclear weapons—while simultaneously presenting himself to the press as a force for restraint. In that early stage of the administration, cooler heads prevailed, as they might not have been able to do after Kissinger's power escalated.

Similarly, in 1970, when Palestinian extremists hijacked several airliners and held more than five hundred passengers as hostages, Nixon ordered a punitive air strike on guerrilla bases. It may be imagined what would have happened to the five hundred hostages, many of them Americans, had not Secretary of Defense Melvin Laird deflected the bombing order—which, in any case, was calculated mostly as another "signal" of Nixon's toughness.

Nixon's zealous pursuit of a flawed SALT agreement, as we have seen, ignored some important security considerations; and his overpraise of the result made future arms control agreements less credible in Congress. His manipulation of intelligence estimates to serve his purposes undermined the CIA and the role of reliable and measured intelligence. For only one example, he and Kissinger insisted that the Soviets were developing MIRVs faster than they actually were, in order to bolster their arguments for a ballistic missile defense.[21]

Nixon's lack of real interest allowed thousands of black Africans to starve in the crucial months just after the tragic Biafran war. His fetish for secrecy resulted in the damaging *shokku* to Japan caused by the opening to China, about which he had refused to consult the Tokyo authorities, and his later explanation relied on the unflattering implication that the Japanese might have "leaked" and "jeopardized the whole China initiative."[22]

Nixon did not manage substantial improvement in prospects for an Arab-Israeli peace in the Middle East, although his and Kissinger's diplomacy partially prepared the ground for the Camp David agreements reached between Israel and Egypt during the Carter administration. The fall of Cambodia into the hands of the murderous Khmer Rouge was at least an indirect consequence of the illegal secret bombing and the later invasion of that country.

Nixon's high-handedness, sometimes exceeded by that of his national security adviser, led to unprecedented congressional restraints on presidential power. One example: the Case-Zablocki Act of 1972 providing for congressional review of executive agreements (and sponsored in the Senate by the liberal Republican, Clifford Case of New Jersey, for whom in 1954 Vice President Nixon had insisted on campaigning, despite the antagonism of conservatives).

The War Powers Act of 1973, ostensibly preventing a president from waging undeclared war for more than sixty days, was another response to Nixon's uses of power, particularly in Indochina. Brent Scowcroft, national security adviser to President Ford and later to President Bush, called this legislation "almost certainly unconstitutional." But he conceded that it was an expression of frustration at presidents' unwillingness to consult Congress on foreign affairs—an unwillingness exemplified by Richard Nixon and Henry Kissinger.

Congressional restraints and Nixon's resignation—though his departure was specifically forced by domestic rather than foreign policy acts—left the office of the presidency substantially weaker than Nixon found it. Inevitably, that meant that the chief executive's ability to lead in foreign affairs was weakened too.

Diminishing the office he inherits is the one sin against which every president swears eternal hostility. Even after losing his bid for the office in 1960, Nixon had had too much respect for it to challenge the legitimacy of John Kennedy's election. But when he finally attained the office himself, Richard Nixon committed that cardinal sin; his actions weakened the presidency. And that fact alone deeply flaws the conventional belief that his was an unsurpassed mastery of foreign affairs.

Owing to the general belief that President Nixon made his greatest contributions in foreign policy—a belief he has been at pains to encourage—his achievements in domestic affairs have been underrecognized and underrated. It was not merely in self-defense that Daniel Patrick Moynihan termed the Nixon administration in which he had served "the most progressive" of the postwar era. The proposition can be plausibly argued (see chapter 12).

Nixon, however, is not a likable man save to a few close associates. His is not a riveting television presence. Throughout his career, the shadow of duplicity, like the shadow of his beard, has clung to him—all three factors alienating opponents, even restricting the affection of his political supporters. His early encounters with Hiss, Helen Douglas, Truman, Acheson, Stevenson, made his career but dimmed it too; and he never escaped the exaggerated impression that he was closely linked to the disreputable Joe McCarthy. As John Kennedy's opponent in 1960, he became the man Kennedy idolaters—and there are many—love to hate. His determined waging of the war in Vietnam and his ambiguous withdrawal from it remain more prominently in memory than many less dramatic events. All this has helped deny him his due for domestic achievement.

Above all, however, and without question, Richard Nixon is associated in the public mind not with domestic or foreign accomplishments but with Watergate. The complex of offenses lumped under that rubric, the number of his aides involved in it, his own fatal participation, the "Saturday-night massacre" arising from his futile efforts to coverup, the televised hearings that brought the country nearly to a standstill, the unprecedented drama of a president's resignation to avoid impeachment—no one who lived through the period is likely to forget it, and few can or want to remember, as a consequence, the more positive aspects of the Nixon administration.

Watergate is the indelible mark Richard Nixon left on the consciousness of his time. It caused many Americans to believe him an evil man who had schemed deliberately to subvert the Constitution and undermine liberty; it convinced others that he was the victim of nefarious schemes by the press, the liberals, the Democrats, those who "hate America," even the CIA and/or the Pentagon.

Either way, and even considering the "elder statesman" position he since has labored, characteristically, to attain, it is Watergate and his resignation in disgrace for which Richard Nixon is best known today.

Yet Watergate was a live possibility in any postwar administration, for a reason long antedating the Nixon presidency, and going back at least to World War II—perhaps even to Abraham Lincoln's strong assertion of presidential war powers unknown before the Confederate attack on Fort Sumter. Because power corrupts, and because the real and effective power of an American president had been so greatly expanded, by the time Richard Nixon reached the White House Watergate or something equally disreputable was a disaster waiting to happen.

Power corrupts whether the corruption occurs in dollar terms—graft and bribery—or in political action, such as the "arrogance of power" that led the Johnson administration into the jungles of Indochina. Every postwar president before Nixon, as power steadily accumulated in the White House, suffered its corrupting touches—whether it was the "influence-peddling" of the Truman years, the Eisenhower administration's illegal overthrow of governments in Iran and Guatemala, the attempts to assassinate Fidel Castro during Kennedy's thousand days, or FBI investigation and harassment of dissidents in Lyndon Johnson's time.

From Franklin Roosevelt to Richard Nixon, moreover, and no doubt beyond, the federal government engaged in eavesdropping, illegal entry, mail covers and openings, payoffs and other surreptitious, often illegal, means of investigating enemies and opponents, real or imagined. In some administrations, income tax investigations were used for harassing individuals, and in others crass favoritism enriched the few. In all, the heavy hand of power exposed itself malignly—in certain administrative rulings, executive orders, bureaucratic indifference, harassing investigations, passport and visa decisions, improper influence, political rewards, contract awards—in any number of ways that ranged from injustice and inequity to persecution and preference.

This is not to say that all postwar administrations were corrupt; but all had rising opportunity for the misuse of their rising power, and none had a leader with the impossible capacity to control or monitor all the deeds done under his expanding aegis. Thus, all postwar administrations succumbed to the corruptions of power, in one degree or another, and with varying levels of connivance, acquiescence or ignorance in the White House.

That is hardly to be wondered at in a world of fallible men and women, and is a process replicated in any number of corporations, municipalities, private institutions—even sometimes in churches. As power accumulates, so do the opportunities to misuse it, and the temptations. And nowhere, in the years beginning with World War II, did power accumulate more rapidly than in the White House.

Franklin Roosevelt, for example, not only presided over the biggest military and industrial buildup in American history, projecting the White House into every corner of American economic life; he was the first president in the modern era to function as commander in chief of the armed forces in wartime *and* to achieve recognized status as a world leader— perhaps *the* world leader, as photos from Casablanca and Yalta suggest. The sight of Roosevelt in his black cape, as he reshaped with Churchill and Stalin the future of the world—a sight carried to millions of Americans by newsreels in the movie palaces of the time, and reinforced by radio broadcasts reaching even more millions—Roosevelt as world statesman gave the presidency itself a new aura of power and importance.

Harry Truman launched the Marshall Plan, stood up to the Communists in Korea and fired General MacArthur, all of which made the president, as commander in chief and world leader, an even more impressive figure. Truman, as one joke about the plain man from Missouri would have it, proved that anyone could be president, and the remark was not without point; the office was believed in his time to confer something of its majesty mysteriously upon the man. Above all, however, Harry Truman dropped the Bomb—and the president became forever the man with his finger on the button, the one American who could destroy an enemy, perhaps the world, with a single order.

Dwight Eisenhower, with Churchill and Stalin removed from the world scene, became clearly its most imposing figure—a distinction only Roosevelt and Woodrow Wilson (briefly in 1919) had achieved. Eisenhower also was the first television president, visible virtually every night on the home screen. After Eisenhower, *any* president was to be the single most familiar figure to every American, far more so than anyone's mayor or senator or governor.

John Kennedy, in his youth and good looks, brought a new generation to replace the dour faces of the Eisenhower administration, and added social glamor and greater public-relations skills to the presidency's power. He was the first president for whom television—particularly his witty and informative news conferences, broadcast live—became a calculated political instrument. In his term, too, the president's responsibility for managing the national economy was acknowledged and accepted. Kennedy's brief tenure, coinciding with the apogee of American power in the world, made him a sort of young emperor; and his murder was doubly shocking because Americans, by 1963, considered their president somehow preeminent over mere mortals, as superior as the nation itself, thus lacking ordinary human vulnerability.

Lyndon Johnson had fallen into popular disfavor by the time Nixon succeeded him in the White House; but in succeeding Kennedy, winning a landslide over Goldwater, and pushing through Congress not only Kennedy's remaining initiatives but his own Great Society program, Johnson had been by late 1965 perhaps literally more powerful than any of his predecessors. The Tonkin Gulf resolution he maneuvered through Congress left him and for a while Nixon virtually a free hand in Indochina; and in waging one of the biggest wars in American history without congressional declaration, Johnson notably expanded the already extensive "war powers" of the presidency.

All these presidents, moreover, served in a time when American military supremacy was unchallenged, when the American economy led the world in productivity and profits, when the country had never suffered defeat in war—a time when American certainties were firmly in place and American self-doubt was largely nonexistent or suppressed, when the nation believed itself by right and without question Number One in the world, and when the president was the conceded champion of the "free world" against the Communists.

In this buildup to power that had transformed the presidency in the postwar years, some disastrous abuse of power was sure to happen. In 1969, Richard Nixon brought to the White House a combination of personality, experience and attitudes likely to make it happen sooner rather than later.

He had participated in most of the significant events of the previous twenty-three years, had spent eight years in close study of President Eisenhower, and had a keen sense of presidential powers and prerogatives. He had watched them, after all, as they were magnified to imperial status, and he meant, as a matter of right and poetic justice, to have and to exercise them all. Little in his experience—directly with Eisenhower, or vicariously in his scrutiny of Kennedy and Johnson—could have led him to see any real limits on those powers and prerogatives. If a president was sufficiently clever and determined—Nixon was both—he could have his way. He could get it done, whatever "it" was.

Nixon's closest advisers—Bob Haldeman, John Mitchell, later Charles Colson on the domestic side, Henry Kissinger in foreign affairs—reinforced this expansive attitude, because they agreed with him, because the greater the president's powers, the greater their own, and often, notably in Kissinger's case, to gain and keep Nixon's favor. Those in his closest circle rarely contradicted him—though, as noted, some quickly learned to ignore the impulsive, often quixotic instructions he seldom really intended for them to carry out. The isolation he sought and they enforced walled him away from those who might have played devil's advocate.

Nixon's personal insecurities and self-doubt, his paranoid sense of enemies hovering everywhere to do him in, the fear of treachery he had harbored at least since the fund crisis of 1952, served to underpin his insistence on presidential powers. *He* had the power, he was going to use it, and *they* were not going to take it away, though they certainly would try. Power was Nixon's security blanket.

He was realistic about his political interests (except that in the presidency he confused them with the nation's, sometimes deliberately), unblinking in his willingness to gull the press and the public in the pursuit of those interests, and relentless in his insistence on the secrecy in which he believed he could operate with best effect. The public's "right to know" was a concept to which he might occasionally pay lip service, but which he profoundly believed inimical to the public interest—and certainly to Richard Nixon's.

Thus, he was all but tailor-made for Watergate: a man who brooked few limits on what he believed to be his legitimate powers, whose inner circle acquiesced or even encouraged him in that attitude, whose insecurities demanded isolation from dissent and whose preferred operating atmosphere was secrecy and seclusion.

For such an experienced and studious man, he could be strangely ignorant, too, or simply rationalize his preferences into truth. Though a lawyer and a student of politics for more than a quarter century, Nixon insisted that he had a constitutional right to appoint Supreme Court justices. With similar certainty, he managed to find in his conception of the Constitution a presidential right to convert illegal acts into lawful functions, if the president was acting "because of the national security, or . . . a threat to internal peace and order of a significant magnitude."*

*This and following Nixon comments are from a broadcast interview with David Frost, May 19, 1977.

Even if products of rationalized hindsight, these are extraordinary assertions of power that probably originated in Nixon's Orthogonian sense that
others had been given greater leeway, allowed more advantages, than he;
that in becoming president, he was entitled to his turn; and that no fruit
of his triumph was to be snatched from him.

Nixon appeared to dumbfound his interviewer, David Frost, with this
explanation:

> Well, what I, at root I had in mind . . . was perhaps much better
> stated by Lincoln during the War between the States. Lincoln said,
> and I think I can remember the quote almost exactly, he said,
> "Actions which otherwise would be unconstitutional could
> become lawful if undertaken for the purpose of preserving the
> Constitution and the nation."

When Frost protested that Nixon's and Lincoln's situations were different—obviously having in mind that Lincoln was trying to cope with an
armed insurrection by the Southern Confederacy—Nixon persisted: "This
nation was torn apart in an ideological way by the war in Vietnam, as much
as the Civil War tore apart the nation when Lincoln was president."

Lincoln and few historians would agree that Nixon faced in public
dissent a problem as formidable as that presented in 1861 by the secession
of eleven states and the formation of the Confederacy and its army. Even
if so wild a claim were conceded, Lincoln hardly would have contended
that therefore he had the power to make *burglary* of private premises legal;
he had been referring to the seizure and holding, without *habeas corpus,*
of suspected secessionist agents and activists. Lincoln acted, moreover,
under his asserted war powers in a time of armed insurrection—not merely
because largely peaceful dissenters were marching in the streets.

Nixon was uncompromising, nevertheless, in his insistence that he had
had good reason for taking extraordinary action:

> The people on the other side were hypocritical, they were sanc-
> timonious and they were not serving the best interests of the
> country. That is why . . . Henry and I felt so strongly about it. And
> call it paranoia but paranoia for peace isn't that bad. I don't mean
> . . . that everybody who was out talking against the war deliber-
> ately, with intent, was prolonging [it], but the effect of what they
> did was to prolong the war. Had it not been for the division in
> America, the war would have been ended one to two years earlier.

Paranoia seems about the right word; Hanoi maintained the war, not the
peace movement. Sanctimony and hypocrisy are not crimes, and "the best
interests of the country" are not ipso facto what the president may say they

are. But owing both to his own experience and to conventional American attitudes that he shared, Nixon's view of presidential power and the national interest were entangled; if a president's approval could make lawful an otherwise illegal act, then obviously a president's definition of "the best interests of the country," and what might damage them, was unchallengeable.

These attitudes led straight to the Huston Plan, to the activities of the plumbers and to what John Mitchell called the "White House horrors," including illegal wiretaps and the burglary of Daniel Ellsberg's psychiatrist's office—all under the supposed color of "national security." Nixon told Frost that he could not recall whether John Ehrlichman had alerted him to the planned break-in at Dr. Fielding's office. But he conceded that Ehrlichman *might* have, and added: "And if he had I would have said, *'Go right ahead.'*" (Emphasis added.)

(Ehrlichman denies [see chapter 15] that he authorized the Fielding break-in or even knew about it in advance; therefore, he argues, he *could not* have told Nixon about it before it happened.)

Nixon also denied that he authorized Charles Colson to firebomb the Brookings Institution, a plan aborted by protests from other White House aides—if Colson ever really meant to do it. Almost incredibly, in that context, Nixon insisted that had he been convinced that Brookings was about to release sensitive national security documents, he would have used "very strong methods" to stop it.

The Huston-Colson-plumbers excesses are primarily responsible for the widespread belief that Nixon schemed to subvert the Constitution. In the Frost interview, Nixon set out the following defense: first, he was trying to protect national security; second, he sought to shorten the war; and third, he had both the constitutional authority and the necessity to do everything he did.

No doubt Nixon convinced himself that all of that was true; but even conceding the pressures he was under, he clearly exaggerated, in a mind ever alert for enemies, the security crisis he thought resulted from the peace movement and the publication of the Pentagon Papers. The *necessity* to approve burglary was largely imaginary, and the constitutional *authority* to make it legal in any kind of crisis has been discerned by few disinterested scholars or historians.

Even J. Edgar Hoover, whose agents perpetrated many a black-bag job and planted many an illicit listening device with the tacit approval of every president from FDR to RN, never claimed that this approval could make such activities *lawful*. On the contrary, they might be done under a presidential claim of necessity, but only at risk of public disclosure and legal and political consequence—against which Hoover always tried to protect himself and the FBI.

When President Nixon, moreover, was asked to approve in his own name the "clearly illegal" security measures outlined in the Huston Plan—including break-ins—he carefully withheld his signature; and five days later he scrapped the whole scheme, not without regrets for the "strong methods" he longed to use but dared not. Apparently, he did not then believe that his approval could convert otherwise unlawful acts to legality. That idea came later, in hindsight, when public disclosure called him to account.

Nixon put the plumbers in business because of the Pentagon Papers, and because of his dissatisfaction with FBI efforts to find information linking the antiwar movement to foreign influences. So whether or not the president *specifically* authorized the plumbers to make the Fielding break-in—Ehrlichman makes a strong case that he probably did—that illegal entry was a direct result of Nixon's often-expressed zeal to obtain derogatory information about Daniel Ellsberg.[23]

Nixon personally had nothing to do with the subsequent authorization of the Watergate break-in—except that, again, his attitudes and the atmosphere of his White House must have encouraged John Mitchell, the chairman, and Jeb Magruder, the staff director of Nixon's reelection committee, to believe that he would *want* such a thing done. *They* authorized but he implicitly inspired the scheme by Gordon Liddy and Howard Hunt to obtain political "intelligence" through a listening device in the office of the Democratic national chairman, Larry O'Brien, in the Watergate office building.

When the original entry into O'Brien's office to plant the tap produced no such intelligence, Mitchell called Liddy and "chewed him out." Liddy then, on his own authority, ordered the second entry, during which the burglars were caught—with the whole sordid Watergate story spinning itself out from that point on, not with the inevitability of tragedy but in a macabre parade of errors, misjudgments, lies and ineptitude.

Elliot Richardson, who as attorney general resigned rather than follow Nixon's panicky order to fire the Watergate special prosecutor, Archibald Cox, was not particularly surprised to learn that the supposedly shrewd and sensible Mitchell had authorized such a dangerous scheme, then let himself be connected to it. (Mitchell ultimately served a prison term and was disbarred.)

Richardson believed Mitchell was *not* so shrewd. In his view, Nixon drafted Mitchell, his law partner but a political neophyte, as his 1968 campaign chairman because

> there would be no question of Mitchell's asserting his own independent judgment on any important aspects of the campaign; it

would be clear between Mitchell and himself and indeed any other key people that Nixon was the real campaign manager.[24]

Nixon won that election, though narrowly, as shown, and it was the general impression that Mitchell had been the architect of the victory; he was given much credit in the press. Richardson thought, however, that Nixon had won the election for himself but

> Mitchell then took office as attorney general of the United States with a reputation as a political mastermind. My own view is that he was a political ignoramus whose only recourse in the circumstances was either to confess that he was no mastermind or to do what he did do, which was to keep his mouth shut, puff on his pipe, listen to the argument until the last possible moment, and then deliver himself of some sententious and pithy observation and get out of the room. I saw him do this many times.

Richardson suggested that when Liddy and Hunt informed Charles Colson of their "intelligence-gathering" scheme, it appealed to Colson's aggressive spirit, and he called Mitchell, the campaign manager, to say something like:

> "John, I've got these great guys here, Hunt, Liddy. . . . You'd better talk to them because they could be very useful to you." So they go over and see Mitchell and present a $700,000 plan. . . . Mitchell doesn't know whether or not national campaigns normally spend that kind of money on intelligence gathering, and his only immediate recourse is to say, "Well, um, that sounds a little rich, $700,000, I mean, couldn't you maybe go back and see if you could scale that down some?"

They scale it down, in Richardson's theory, Colson probably puts on more pressure, and Hunt and Liddy lobby Mitchell again:

> The plan now costs $250,000 or something like that, and Mitchell can't think of any good reason to stall any more. He says, "Well, why don't you go ahead and just stay in touch with Jeb Magruder here. Anything that comes up, just talk to Jeb."

That is only one hypothesis of how the Watergate break-in was authorized, but Richardson added:

> Nixon . . . contributed to creating an inflated political reputation for Mitchell which, in turn, led to the creation of the monster that brought [Nixon] down.

There's no doubt, in any case, that Mitchell and Magruder authorized the Hunt-Liddy scheme for entering Larry O'Brien's office and tapping his phone. But why, then, did not a shrewd politician like Richard Nixon immediately *expose,* rather than try to cover up, an illicit plan he had not authorized? Had he done so, his presidency might have been saved.

One reason undoubtedly was the ever-present trauma of the fund crisis, when a young senator had felt betrayed by those he had trusted and served. "That's what Eisenhower—that's all he cared about," Nixon recalled in the depths of the Watergate crisis, as his hidden tapes rolled. "He only cared about—Christ, 'be sure he was clean.' Both in the Fund thing and the Adams thing. But I don't look at it that way . . . We're going to protect our people, if we can."

But if loyalty to "our people" was a relatively defensible reason for Nixon's participation in the cover-up, it seems clear that fear, too, was a motive. If Nixon really had authorized the Fielding break-in, or knew about it in advance—or even if he only learned of it later and did nothing— he would have wished to keep that secret buried deep within the White House. The involvement of Hunt and Liddy in both the Fielding and the Watergate break-ins would have been enough to suggest that exposure of the latter could lead to trouble about the former.

Nixon also may have remembered, as Leonard Garment has suggested, Eisenhower's sweeping invocation of executive privilege to keep administration documents and "reproductions" out of the hands of Joe McCarthy (see chapter 5). Eisenhower had made that order stand, and it had become a precedent. How then, Nixon might well have thought, could investigators get at the evidence they would need to involve him in Watergate—particularly the tapes turning silently within the White House walls, tapes the investigators did not even know about?

Executive privilege, besides, was only one facet of the power of a president, power that must also have been an element in Nixon's decision—if "decision" it was, rather than an instinctive reaction—to stonewall. The president had immense authority over the Justice Department, the FBI, the CIA; he could issue executive orders and pardons, raise money, silence subordinates, fire the insubordinate, influence the press, appeal to the public from his unmatched eminence. He could invoke national security. How could anyone counter a president's powers, if he were fully to mobilize them? How could "a third-rate burglary"—as Ron Ziegler termed Watergate—bring down a president?

Nixon would not have been alone if he asked himself such questions. The *New York Times,* for example, did not in the crucial early stages pursue the Watergate case as relentlessly as did the *Washington Post* because the *Times* relied on essentially *political* reporters and editors, few of whom could believe that an imperial president could be deeply involved in, much less destroyed by, such an otherwise trivial event. They thought the 1972 election campaign more important and devoted more manpower and attention to it. The *Post*, in contrast, was using police reporters not concerned with the election, reporters who were tracking a criminal case wherever it led.

John Ehrlichman was another who could not believe at first that Watergate was a serious threat, and he doubts that Nixon did, either. But in Ehrlichman's view, Nixon loved intrigue too much to stay safely out of even the minor challenge Watergate must have seemed at first to present. Thus, in retrospect, Ehrlichman believes Nixon could *not* let Watergate alone. In his thirst for battle, his eagerness to respond to challenge and prove his mettle, he couldn't pass up a chance to outmaneuver the investigators, the Nixon haters, the press—the world.

Within days of the Watergate break-in, John Mitchell and John Dean had devised a cover-up scheme worthy of the most extreme ideas about Tricky Dick Nixon. It relied, moreover, on Nixon's cherished powers; not only was it a clever move, it was a *power* move—the kind Nixon preferred. The Number Two man at the CIA, Vernon Walters (a Nixon loyalist), would call the Number One man at the FBI, Pat Gray (another loyalist appointed by Nixon to replace the late Edgar Hoover), and deliver the message that the FBI should stay out of the Watergate investigation because it involved "national security," a judgment Gray would know could only have been made by the president. If the FBI were kept out of it, the plan assumed, the investigation would collapse.

On June 23, 1972, Bob Haldeman put the scenario before Nixon ("We're really set up beautifully to do it," Haldeman said). The president, either forgetting the tapes recording his every word, or believing no one had the power to take them from him, no doubt excited by so ingenious a scheme, taking time for only a few clarifying questions, can be plainly heard to reply: "All right, fine. . . ."

A bridge had been burned behind him. Ehrlichman, knowing his man—though he did not hear the fatal tape until years later, when preparing for his own trial—believes that Nixon must have realized quickly what he had done: not just a foolish thing, but a criminal act, an obstruction of justice. The June 23 tape was a true smoking gun, so incriminating that when one of Nixon's lawyers, James St. Clair, finally heard it he said that he himself would become a party to the obstruction of justice if the tape were not handed over to investigators.

Ordering the cover-up scheme was irrevocable; the evidence, if discovered, was irrefutable. This knowledge "suffused" Nixon with guilt, in Ehrlichman's retrospective judgment; he knew thereafter that he could never "make a clean breast" of it, as he was so often urged to do; he could never truly "put it all behind him."

Beyond that he is a person who having been in politics for thirty years, is simply emotionally and constitutionally unable to deliver himself to his enemies to any degree. He will fight, bleed and die before he will admit to [columnist] Jack Anderson that he's wrong or that he's made a mistake.

So he would have to lie to the world, to his closest associates, even to his family. It's possible that under this burden, as the lie was repeated and embellished, Nixon even convinced himself for a while that he was telling the truth. Before Ehrlichman resigned in April 1973, he

> began to feel that [Nixon] didn't know what the truth was. He didn't know what he had said, he didn't know what he had done, and the fact was whatever he was saying was truth at that particular moment.[25]

On election night, November 7, 1972, when the worst of Watergate was unforeseen, Richard Milhous Nixon received over forty-seven million votes, nearly twenty million more than his Democratic opponent, George McGovern, and 60.7 percent of the total. Only Lyndon Johnson, winning 61.1 percent in his unique campaign against Barry Goldwater less than a year after John Kennedy's murder, had been supported by a larger proportion of the electorate.

No Republican ever had won the White House by so large a margin; no president ever had won more popular votes or carried so many states. Nixon had every reason to believe, that night and in the days and weeks following, that he had an irresistible mandate for his second term (which may have influenced the Christmas bombing six weeks later), that he could move on to even greater purposes than those vindicated by the Moscow and Peking summits, to that "structure of peace" that might make him worthy of Hannah Nixon's grace—perhaps even to feel, at long last, that he had nothing left to prove to anyone, including himself.

Instead, he recorded in his diary, an inexplicable "melancholy . . . settled over me on that victorious night."

Nixon had no inkling at the time—nor would he until early 1973—that the Watergate cancer would metastasize into disaster. Nevertheless, the "foreboding" he felt, even in his triumph, seems hardly surprising; he need not have foretold the end to have started already to feel an inchoate knowledge of what later, nearly in tears, he told David Frost—that he had "let down my friends . . . let down the country . . . let down the American people."[26]

Like Conrad's Lord Jim, he had "jumped—it seems," and the rest of the Watergate calamity would follow inexorably. "I wished I could die," Jim cried out to Marlowe; and Richard Nixon was to tell John Ehrlichman, on the day he forced Ehrlichman and Haldeman to resign, that he had hoped the night before not to wake up the next morning. By then, Nixon knew as clearly as had Jim that "there was no going back. It was as if I had jumped into a well."

That was April 1973. Sixteen months were yet to be spent in the White House, amid splendors and powers that must have become more and more unreal, less and less compensating, as the tides of Watergate eroded the political and personal ground under Nixon's feet. Another summit in Moscow, one in Washington, the October war in the Middle East, numerous bear-pit news conferences, the return of prisoners of war from Indochina, the shabby revelations about and departure of Spiro T. Agnew, the appointment of Gerald Ford to replace him, the elevation of Kissinger to be secretary of state—none of it, nor all of the legal turning and twisting, provided any real escape from the agonizing retreat to resignation on August 9, 1974.

Richard Nixon believed in hard work, worked hard and got ahead; but he was fatally subject to the allure of power. He preached the virtues of home and family, yet was unable to yield much of his private self to others; beneath a public mask of good fellowship, he was a man lonely and alone.

Nixon exalted American values and traditions but seldom hesitated to ignore or distort them for his own advantage. He sought peace but made war, proclaiming the American faith that an American war must be a war *for* peace.

He spoke well of his fellow man, but mistrusted him—"You've got to be a little evil to understand those people out there," he once said of the American voters he both extolled and courted all his adult life. "You have to have known the dark side of life to understand those people."[27]

Perhaps that was true in reverse, too; if John Kennedy embodied, as Norman Mailer once wrote, something like the nation's "romantic dream of itself," perhaps Richard Nixon represented a harder and clearer national self-assessment. In the dark of their souls, which Nixon seems to have perceived, Americans could have seen in him themselves as they knew they were, not as they frequently dreamed of being. They could have recognized in Nixon their own sentimental patriotism and confidence in national virtue, their professed love of God and family, their theological belief that hard work would pay off, their desire to get ahead and live well, their preference for action over reflection—hardhead over egghead—and their vocal if not always practiced devotion to freedom and democracy.

They also might have seen reflected in the ambiguous figure of Richard Nixon—even in his reputation for sharp practice and his transparent presentations of himself—their own melancholy knowledge, hard earned in a demanding world, that ideals sometimes had to yield to necessity, right to might, compassion to interest, principle to circumstance. They might even have understood that Nixon, or anyone, could believe himself forced on occasion to cheat a little, lie a little, find an edge, get out front of more favored competitors any way he could—as they themselves had done, or would do—in the unrelenting battles of life.

Romantic dreams play their necessary part in lives too often drab and unchanging; but they cannot replace for long the ever-present reality, the daily recognition of things as they are. Rarely if ever, in my judgment, has the extent to which dreams and reality live side by side within a people been so dramatized as it was in the great Kennedy-Nixon confrontation of 1960; and that Richard Nixon came so close to victory in that election, with all his strengths and weaknesses, his virtues and deceits, his lack of grace in his self-willed ascent to the summit, suggests how many Americans sensed, if they did not fully understand, that he was "one of us" and the more to be embraced for that.

He was, in fact, Richard Nixon, American—working and scheming without let to achieve his dreams, soured by the inequities of life, perhaps by his own fallibilities, surely by the cynical lesson that "in politics, most people are your friends only as long as you can do something for them, or to them." If, as president, he swore to uphold the Constitution but skirted it when he could, that was American still; which of us in the national rush to get ahead has never cut a corner or winked at the law?

But surely Nixon was one of us, too, at our occasional best, when in the blackest hours of his life he managed to rise above his bitterness and his cynicism, refusing to challenge the legitimacy of Kennedy's election and peacefully surrendering the tapes that ruined him, when the Supreme Court commanded.

Notes

★

1 CARDBOARD MAN

The account of the Nixon-Bobst friendship, the 1963 phone call and its aftermath is from Elmer Bobst, *The Autobiography of a Pharmaceutical Pioneer* (New York: David McKay, 1973), chapter 23 and later pages. Hereafter cited as *Bobst*.

The account of Nixon's arrival at his new law firm in New York, of his participation in the *Hill* case, and of the Nixon-Garment trip to Florida and visit with Bobst, is from the interview with Leonard Garment cited below.

Specific notes follow:

1. Jules Witcover, *The Resurrection of Richard Nixon* (New York: G. P. Putnam's Sons, 1970), pp. 42–43. Hereafter cited as *Resurrection*.

2. Nixon was admitted to the New York bar on January 1, 1964, after becoming "of counsel" to Nixon, Mudge on June 1, 1963.

3. Interview with William P. Rogers, New York, September 13, 1986. Hereafter cited as *Rogers*.

4. Interview with Leonard Garment, Washington, November 5, 1985. Hereafter cited as *Garment*.

5. Lucille Parsons Oral History, Richard Nixon Project, California State College, Fullerton. Unless otherwise noted, all other recollections by Nixon's contemporaries during his youth in California are from oral histories in that collection. When necessary, it is cited as *RNP, CSC.*

6. Stewart Alsop, *Nixon and Rockefeller, A Double Portrait* (New York: Doubleday, 1960), p. 194. Hereafter cited as *Alsop.*

7. Ken Clawson, "A Loyalist's Memoir," the *Washington Post,* Outlook Section, August 9, 1979. Hereafter cited as *Clawson.*

8. This account of Nixon's participation in the *Hill* case and the following account of the Nixon-Garment trip to Florida are from *Garment.* Mr. Garment later recounted the Nixon-Garment trip to Florida and gave a detailed account of the *Hill* case in an article in the *New Yorker* for April 17, 1989.

9. *Clawson.*

10. *Public Papers of the President of the United States, 1971,* p. 782; Richard Nixon, *RN: The Memoirs of Richard Nixon* (New York, Grosset & Dunlap, 1978), p. 288. Hannah Nixon died in 1967, before her son was elected president.

11. Fawn Brodie, *Richard Nixon: The Shaping of His Character* (New York: W. W. Norton, 1981), p. 36. Hereafter cited as *Brodie.*

12. Bela Kornitzer, *The Real Nixon: An Intimate Biography* (Rand McNally, 1960), pp. 75, 78, 79. Hereafter cited as *Kornitzer.*

13. Ibid., pp. 70, 74.

14. Ibid., p. 41.

15. *Resurrection,* pp. 147–148.

16. Earl Mazo, *Richard Nixon: A Political and Personal Portrait* (New York: Harper and Bros., 1959), p. 2. Hereafter cited as *Mazo.*

17. Richard Rovere, *Affairs of State: The Eisenhower Years* (New York: Harcourt, Brace and Co., 1950), pp. 306–307.

18. Interview with Bryce Harlow, October 23, 1985, at his house near Harper's Ferry, West Virginia. Hereafter referred to as *Harlow.*

19. William Costello, *The Facts About Nixon* (New York: Viking Press, 1974), p. 161. Hereafter cited as *Costello.*

20. *Alsop,* p. 200.

21. Interview with James R. Schlesinger, Washington, D.C., 1985.

22. A series of discussions with former officials of the Nixon administration was conducted in the eighties by the White Burkett Miller Center for the Study of Public Affairs at the University of Virginia. The texts have been published by the Center in *The Nixon Presidency: Twenty-two Intimate Perspectives of Richard M. Nixon,* vol. 6 in the series *Portraits of American Presidents* (New York: University Press of America). Material culled from these discussions is cited to the person quoted, in this case Arthur Burns, and to the book, as *TNP,* p. 150.

23. *Maurice Stans in TNP,* p. 30.

24. Elliot Richardson spoke at a conference on the Nixon administration at Hofstra University, November 19–21, 1987. Other citations to speakers at this event will be cited by name, as *Richardson at Hofstra.* (See general notes for chapter 10.)

25. Interview with Raymond K. Price, December 16, 1988. Hereafter cited as *Price.*

26. *RNP, CSC; Kornitzer,* p. 74.

27. *Kornitzer,* p. 65.

28. Ibid., pp. 60, 57.

29. *Harlow.*

2   TRICKY DICK

A major source for this chapter was an independent study of the Nixon-Voorhis campaign, compiled as course work in History 190 at Fresno State College in 1971 by John T. Balch: *Richard M. Nixon vs. H. Jerry Voorhis for Congress, 1946.* Where necessary it is cited as *Balch,* but I have relied upon Mr. Balch's research and insights for far more than the details and quotations noted.

The most authoritative account of the Alger Hiss affair, upon which I have drawn heavily, is by Allen Weinstein: *Perjury—The Hiss-Chambers Case* (New York: Alfred

A. Knopf, 1978). It is cited where necessary as *Weinstein*. Mr. Weinstein also was the author of the enlightening article "Nixon vs. Hiss," in *Esquire* magazine (November 1975). It is cited several times as *Esquire*. Robert Stripling, who was in 1948 the chief investigator for the House Un-American Activities Committee, also provided me with much useful material, by mail and in a telephone conversation nearly two hours long on April 30, 1990.

Specific notes follow:

1. *Brodie,* p. 244.
2. *Kornitzer,* p. 160.
3. Robert Donovan, *Conflict and Crisis* (New York: W. W. Norton, 1977), p. 211. Hereafter cited as *Conflict.*
4. William H. Chafe, *The Unfinished Journey: America Since World War II* (New York: Oxford University Press, 1986), p. 97. Hereafter cited as *Chafe.*
5. *Brodie,* p. 175; *RN,* p. 42.
6. *Balch,* pp. 56–57 and Appendix H.
7. Jerry Voorhis, *Confessions of a Congressman* (Garden City, N.Y.: Doubleday and Co., 1947), p. 339. Hereafter cited as *Voorhis.*
8. *Balch,* p. 14.
9. *Balch,* p. 16; *Costello,* p. 40; *RN,* p. 35.
10. *Balch,* pp. 17, 19.
11. *Balch,* pp. 42–43; *Voorhis,* pp. 284–285.
12. *Kornitzer,* pp. 160–161.
13. *Costello,* p. 50.
14. *Balch,* p. 20.
15. *Costello,* p. 57.
16. *Balch,* pp. 56, 47.
17. *Brodie,* p. 182.
18. *Balch,* p. 17.
19. *Costello,* p. 179.
20. *Brodie,* pp. 158, 172.
21. Philip M. Stern, *The Oppenheimer Case* (New York: Harper and Row, 1969), pp. 118–122. Hereafter cited as *Stern.*
22. Interview with Robert Finch, now an attorney in California, in his office in Pasadena, March 27, 1987. Finch was on the staff of Representative Norris Poulson of California in 1947 and became a close friend of Nixon; later he served on Nixon's staff and as his presidential campaign director in 1960. Hereafter cited as *Finch.*
23. *Kornitzer,* p. 163.
24. *Finch;* interview with Herbert Klein, now editor in chief of the Copley Newspapers, at San Diego, March 30, 1987. Hereafter cited as *Klein.*
25. Gary Wills, *Nixon Agonistes: The Crisis of the Self-Made Man* (New York: New American Library, 1971), pp. 35–37. Hereafter cited as *Wills; Weinstein,* pp. 7–8.
26. This account of how suspicion gathered around Alger Hiss is taken from *Weinstein,* pp. 356–372, and *Brodie,* pp. 203–204.
27. *Weinstein,* pp. 21–22.
28. *Wills,* p. 37.
29. Whittaker Chambers, *Witness* (New York: Random House, 1952), p. 793n.; Robert Stripling to the author, April 30, 1990.
30. Hannah Nixon, as told to F. R. Schreiber, "Richard Nixon, a Mother's Story," *Good Housekeeping,* June 1960, p. 54ff.
31. *The Red Plot Against America,* Robert Considine, ed. (Drexel Hill, Pa.: Bell, 1979), p. 143.
32. *Mazo,* p. 59; *Esquire,* p. 152.
33. This and the following account of Nixon's involvement in the espionage case

against Hiss is taken from *Esquire,* pp. 144–151. They are based on the similar recollections of Vazzana and Stripling. Allen Weinstein went to San Clemente in 1975 to seek Nixon's comments on the Vazzana-Stripling account, and repeated it to Nixon's research aide, Frank Gannon. Nixon himself has never confirmed, denied or otherwise commented on the *Esquire* story. Weinstein repeated it in *Perjury* (cited herein as *Weinstein*). And Robert Stripling later repeated it to me in great detail.

34. The *Esquire* account of the Andrews-Nixon conversation is confirmed in a book by Bert Andrews and Peter Andrews, *A Tragedy of History* (Washington: Robert B. Luce, 1962), pp. 175–176. Hereafter cited as *Tragedy.*

35. Bert Andrews, who claimed to have been present, contradicts at almost every point the *Esquire* account of Nixon's reaction to the film mix-up. *Tragedy,* pp. 188–189.

36. *New York Times,* op-ed page, January 8, 1986. See chapter 3 for details on how Nixon actually was chosen to run with Eisenhower.

37. *Costello,* p. 68; *Mazo,* p. 76.

38. *Stern,* pp. 160–162.

39. *Brodie,* pp. 240, 535n; *Mazo,* p. 141; *Costello,* p. 70.

40. William Safire, *Safire's Political Dictionary* (New York: Random House, 1968), p. 82.

41. *Mazo,* p. 81.

42. *Mazo,* pp. 79–80; *Costello,* pp. 64, 67, 68, 70; *Brodie,* p. 242; *RN,* p. 77.

43. *Costello,* p. 73.

3 HONOR, IF POSSIBLE

The main source for the attitudes and actions ascribed to Richard Nixon and others during the fund crisis of 1952 is *Six Crises* (Garden City, N.Y.: Doubleday, 1962), written only a decade later. To a lesser extent, *RN* also is a valuable source for this period.

Except where otherwise noted, quotations, thoughts and actions described in this chapter are from those two books.

Specific notes follow:

1. Sherman Adams, *Firsthand Report: The Story of the Eisenhower Administration* (New York: Harper and Bros., 1961), p. 37. Hereafter cited as *Adams.*

2. *Kornitzer,* pp. 192–193.

3. *Alsop,* p. 192.

4. Except for the "pot" remark, *Six Crises, RN, Mazo, Alsop* and Stephen E. Ambrose, *Eisenhower,* vol. 1, *Soldier, General of the Army, President-Elect, 1890–1952* (New York: Simon and Schuster, 1985), essentially agree on what was said in this Eisenhower-Nixon exchange. The Ambrose book is hereafter cited as *Ambrose 1.*

5. *Mazo,* p. 5.

6. Floyd Wildermuth in *RNP, CSC.*

7. *Alsop,* p. 192.

8. *Rogers.*

9. *Mazo,* p. 124–125.

10. *Costello,* p. 111.

11. *Mazo,* p. 129.

12. *Wills,* p. 110.

13. *Ambrose 1,* pp. 559–560.

14. *Alsop,* p. 65.

15. Ibid., p. 193.

16. House Judiciary Committee transcripts, conversation of March 23, 1973, p. 48.

17. *Ambrose 1,* p. 555.

18. The thesis of a continuing relationship of suspicion and mistrust between Eisenhower and Nixon is asserted in *Ambrose 1,* pp. 558–561, but has been most persuasively stated in *Wills,* pp. 94–144.

19. *Mazo,* p. 119.

20. *Alsop,* p. 197.

21. Ronald Steele, *Walter Lippmann and the American Century* (Boston: Little, Brown and Co., 1980), p. 483. Hereafter cited as *Lippmann.*

22. *Rogers.*

23. *Costello,* p. 115.

4 MASTER AND STUDENT

Sources for this chapter were the public record of events and numerous publications by participants, historians and journalists; those points that seem to require it are specifically cited. The opinions and conclusions are entirely the author's.

Particular reliance was placed upon the two volumes of Harry Truman's biography, *Conflict and Crisis* and *Tumultuous Years* (New York: Doubleday and Co., 1979, 1982) by my admired colleague, Robert J. Donovan, formerly of the *New York Herald Tribune* and the *Los Angeles Times;* on *Korea: The War before Vietnam* (New York: The Free Press, 1986) by Callum A. McDonald, cited as *McDonald;* on *The Unfinished Journey* by William H. Chafe, cited as *Chafe;* and of course on *RN.*

Many details of the covert operations that drove Mohammed Mossadegh from power in Iran in 1953 and overthrew the Arbenz government in Guatemala in 1954 still are classified; the full story of these events probably never has been told. The brief accounts in this chapter rely heavily on *The Declassified Eisenhower: A Divided Legacy* (New York: Doubleday and Co., 1981) by Blanche Wiesen Cooke; and on *Presidents' Secret Wars* (New York: William Morrow and Co., 1986), by John Prados. They are cited as *Cooke* and *Prados.*

Specific notes follow:

1. Churchill to Eisenhower, April 16, 1956, Eisenhower Diary, Box 8, in the Eisenhower Library, Abilene, Kansas.

2. An experienced foreign correspondent and assistant to James Reston in the Washington Bureau of the *New York Times,* Carroll later was publisher of the *Winston-Salem Journal* and *Sentinel.* He quoted Acheson in a speech in 1967, later reprinted in the *Journal,* and hereafter cited as *Carroll.*

3. *Carroll.*

4. George McT. Kahin, *Intervention: How America Became Involved in Vietnam* (Garden City, N.Y.: Doubleday Anchor Books, 1987), p. 22. Hereafter cited as *Intervention.*

5. McGeorge Bundy, *Danger and Survival: Choices About the Bomb in the First Fifty Years* (New York: Random House, 1988), p. 231, quoting David Rosenberg, *The Origins of Overkill,* p. 23.

6. *Mazo,* pp. 206, 250.

7. H. R. Haldeman, *The Ends of Power* (New York: Dell Publishing, 1978), pp. 82–83. Hereafter cited as *Haldeman.*

8. *McDonald,* p. 183.

9. *Costello,* p. 250.

10. *Cooke,* p. 186.

11. Ibid., p. 233, quoting State Department memorandum of conversation.

12. Ibid., p. 269.

13. Robert H. Ferrell, ed., *The Diary of James C. Hagerty: Eisenhower in Mid-Course, 1954–1955* (Bloomington: University of Indiana Press, 1983), pp. 48–49.

14. Dwight D. Eisenhower, *Mandate for Change* (Garden City, N.Y.: Doubleday and Co., 1963), p. 427.

15. Stephen Ambrose, *Eisenhower,* vol. 2, *The President* (New York: Simon and Schuster, 1985), p. 196. Hereafter cited as *Ambrose 2.*

16. *Cooke,* p. 281.

17. *Ambrose 2,* p. 173.

18. *Prados,* pp. 115–116.

19. Richard Nixon, *Leaders* (New York: Warner Books, 1982), p. 10. Hereafter cited as *Leaders.*

20. *Ambrose 2,* p. 184.

21. *Lippmann,* p. 567.

22. The *Washington Post,* article by William Brannigan, May 17, 1984.

23. *Intervention,* p. 46.

24. Diane Kunz, a scholar of the exercise of economic power in the Eisenhower administration, in a lecture at the White Burkett Miller Center at the University of Virginia, February 11, 1988. Hereafter cited as *Kunz.*

25. Ibid.

26. Peter Lyon, *Eisenhower: Portrait of a Hero* (Boston: Little, Brown, 1974), p. 851.

27. *Kunz.*

28. *Klein.*

5   PRAT BOY

The story of Sherman Adams's downfall and departure from the White House is taken mostly from *RN, Ambrose 2, Costello, Ewald* and *Finch.* Adams in his memoir, *First-hand Report,* devotes a chapter to the episode but it is blandly unrevealing.

Kevin McCann's memory of Eisenhower's meeting in Peoria with Joe McCarthy is from William B. Ewald, Jr., *Eisenhower the President: Crucial Days, 1951–1960* (Englewood Cliffs, N.J.: Prentice-Hall, 1981) [hereafter cited as *Ewald*], p. 60, but for reasons given in the text I am somewhat skeptical of it—particularly the verbatim quote.

Most of Nixon's activities as vice president, of course, are described on the public record. For some of his second term, I was an active reporter in Washington, first for the *Winston-Salem Journal,* in 1960 for the *New York Times.* I have cited specific sources only where it seemed necessary.

These notes follow:

1. *Mazo,* p. 198.

2. *Adams,* p. 446.

3. *Ewald,* pp. 60–61.

4. Ibid.

5. William H. Lawrence, *Six Presidents, Too Many Wars* (New York: Saturday Review Press, 1972), pp. 194–197. Hereafter cited as *Lawrence.*

6. *Ambrose 2,* p. 81.

7. *Mazo,* p. 144; Richard Rovere, *Senator Joe McCarthy* (New York: Harcourt, Brace and Co., 1959), pp. 248–254. Hereafter cited as *Senator Joe.*

8. Rhodri Jeffreys-Jones, *The CIA and American Democracy* (New Haven: Yale University Press, 1989), pp. 115, 75. Hereafter cited as *Jeffreys-Jones.*

9. Charles E. Bohlen, *Witness to History, 1929–1969* (New York: W. W. Norton, 1973), p. 335.

10. For further details of these adventures with McCarthy, see *Costello,* pp. 275–276, and *RN,* pp. 140–141.

11. *Stern,* p. 204; *Ambrose 2,* p. 166.

12. *Lawrence,* p. 199.

13. Leonard Garment, "The Guns of Watergate," *Commentary,* April 1987, p. 17.

14. *Stern,* pp. 267, 272–73, 296–297.

15. *Ewald,* pp. 171–172.

16. *Senator Joe,* p. 246.

17. *Burns in TNP;* author's interview with Burns, Washington, D.C., June 25, 1986 (hereafter cited as *Burns Interview*).

18. *Burns Interview.*

19. *Burns in TNP,* p. 16.

20. *Mazo,* p. 254.

21. *Burns in TNP,* p. 4.

22. For Eisenhower's heart attack and its aftermath, *Ambrose 2,* pp. 273, 275, 277; *RN,* p. 166; Herbert Parmet, *Eisenhower and the American Crusades* (New York: Macmillan and Co., 1972), pp. 417–418. For the Dulles-Nixon conversation following Eisenhower's stroke, *Ambrose 2,* pp. 438–439.

23. This account of the "dump Nixon" episode is based on *RN,* pp. 169–170; *Ambrose 2,* pp. 292–294; *Finch; Ewald,* pp. 187, 178.

24. *Finch.*

25. *Ambrose 2,* pp. 331–332.

26. *Harlow.*

27. Emmett Hughes, *The Ordeal of Power: A Political Memoir of the Eisenhower Years* (New York: Atheneum, 1963), p. 173.

28. *Ewald,* p. 199.

29. For all these remarks, see *Ambrose 2,* pp. 370, 281; *Ewald,* pp. 26, 28, 32; *RN,* p. 379.

30. Arthur M. Schlesinger, Jr., *A Thousand Days: John F. Kennedy in the White House* (New York: Houghton Mifflin, 1965), p. 18. Hereafter cited as *Thousand Days.*

31. *Ambrose 2,* p. 298.

32. *Ewald,* pp. 178–179.

33. *Alsop,* pp. 154–155.

6   "IF ONLY . . ."

In 1982, Abby Wasserman, a researcher, compiled for me a summary report entitled *South America 1958.* The account of Nixon's Latin American tour that year, and information in this chapter about economic and political conditions in the region at that time, are from Ms. Wasserman's report, except where otherwise cited in text or footnotes. Her report includes her translation of the Luis Alberto Sanchez *cuaderno,* or loose-leaf publication. *Six Crises,* of course, was another indispensable source for this episode.

My principal reliance for the election campaign of 1958 was on the published record and the account in *Costello,* written soon after the campaign. Exceptions are noted.

For Nixon's visit to the Soviet Union in 1959, I drew heavily on *RN, Ambrose 2, Costello,* and the published record; again, exceptions are noted.

I covered the 1960 presidential campaign as a reporter for the *New York Times,* though most often I was assigned to travel with one of the two vice presidential candidates. I was present at the Eisenhower news conference of August 29, a significant episode in this chapter. The Nixon-Kennedy campaign has been written about more extensively than any of modern times, and my account of it is primarily from this public record and from my own recollections, notes and files, and from another summary by Abby Wasserman. Again, exceptions are cited in text or footnotes.

Specific notes follow:

1. Milton Eisenhower, *The Wine Is Bitter* (New York: Doubleday and Co., 1963), pp. 209–212.

2. *Costello,* p. 258.

3. Ibid., p. 172.

4. William Safire, *Before the Fall: An Inside View of the Pre-Watergate White House* (Garden City, N.Y.: Doubleday and Co., 1975), p. 33. Hereafter cited as *Before the Fall.*

5. *Klein; Before the Fall,* pp. 3–5.

6. Interview with Jacob D. Beam, June 30, 1987, Washington, D.C. Senator Thurmond wrote President Nixon, citing an alleged lack of security in the Warsaw embassy during Beam's tenure and suggesting that his appointment to Moscow might therefore result in "serious embarrassment." Nixon referred the letter to Secretary of State Rogers but took no other action. President's Handwriting File, Box 1, February 3, 1969, Nixon Records Center, 825 South Pickett Street, Alexandria, Virginia. This file is hereafter referred to as *PHF* and the center as *NRC.*

7. *Brodie,* pp. 385–386.

8. *Burns Interview.*

9. *Ewald,* pp. 236–238.

10. *Burns in TNP,* pp. 4–5.

11. David Halberstam, *The Powers That Be* (New York: Dell Publishing, 1979), p. 477. Hereafter cited as *Powers.*

12. *Alsop,* pp. 148–149.

13. *Thousand Days,* pp. 73, 225, 232.

14. *Powers,* p. 479.

15. *Brodie,* pp. 429, 415.

16. *Thousand Days,* p. 68.

17. All statistics of the 1960 election are from Nelson W. Polsby and Aaron B. Wildavsky, *Presidential Elections,* 3d ed. (New York: Charles Scribner's Sons, 1971), pp. 23–27. These authors are not responsible for my interpretations of their statistics.

18. *Thousand Days,* p. 72.

19. William Safire, "A View from the Grandstand," *New York Times,* April 13, 1987, p. 19.

20. *Thousand Days,* pp. 73–74. The Kennedy-King story is detailed in, and the pledge by Daddy King is quoted from, Taylor Branch, *Parting the Waters* (New York: Simon and Schuster, 1988).

21. *Ewald,* p. 310.

22. Ibid., pp. 312–313.

23. *Powers,* p. 472.

24. *Harlow.*

25. *Ewald,* pp. 307, 313–314.

26. *Burns in TNP; Finch; Ewald,* p. 293.

27. *Thousand Days,* p. 74.

28. *Harlow.*

29. *Harlow; Thousand Days,* p. 75.

30. Neal Peirce, *The People's President* (New York: Simon and Schuster, 1968), p. 20. Hereafter cited as *Peirce.*

31. Turner Catledge, *My Life and The Times* (New York: Harper and Row, 1971), p. 212.

32. Benjamin Bradlee, *Conversations with Kennedy* (New York: W. W. Norton and Co., 1975), p. 32.

33. *PHF,* Box 1, March 21, 1969, *NRC.*

34. Thomas A. Flinn (of Oberlin College), "How Mr. Nixon Took Ohio: A Short Reply to Senator Kennedy's Question," *Western Political Quarterly,* June 1962, pp. 274–279. I am indebted to my friend James Baughman, who teaches "History of

Journalism" at the University of Wisconsin, for providing this and other information about voting in his native state in 1960.

35. *Jeffreys-Jones,* p. 115.

36. *Ewald,* p. 313.

37. *Bobst,* chapter 23.

38. *Thousand Days,* pp. 64–65.

39. *Brodie,* p. 546. She quoted the remark from "Press and Prejudice" by David Halberstam in *Esquire,* April 1974, p. 109.

40. *Thousand Days,* pp. 75, 116.

7 TIDES

The best overall account of Richard Nixon's years out of office after 1960, his return to the political wars, and his election to the presidency in 1968 is *The Resurrection of Richard Nixon,* by Jules Witcover (New York: G. P. Putnam's Sons, 1970), cited herein as *Resurrection.* Mr. Witcover, now a political columnist for the *Baltimore Sun,* is a colleague whose work I have long admired, and I rely heavily on his book.

In this period, too, I was first an active correspondent for the Washington Bureau of the *New York Times,* then its chief; in both capacities, I wrote much about Nixon's public activities. I covered the 1964 primary campaign and the Republican convention in San Francisco that year, and heard Nixon's convention speech urging support for Barry Goldwater. Later, I traveled with Nixon during part of his campaign on behalf of congressional candidates in 1966. I was present at the White House news conference on November 4, 1966, when President Johnson denounced Nixon as a "chronic campaigner."

Thus, much of this chapter is based on my own experience and reporting. I also reviewed *Six Crises,* when it appeared in 1963, for the *New York Times Book Review*— not entirely to its author's liking. From 1964 to 1968, as Washington Bureau chief for the *Times,* I had numerous occasions to report on or talk not only with Nixon but with President Johnson, Nelson Rockefeller, George Romney, Eugene McCarthy and others involved in this chapter.

Specific notes follow:

1. *Resurrection,* pp. 59–60.

2. *New Republic,* November 7, 1960.

3. *Resurrection,* p. 130.

4. Doris Kearns, *Lyndon Johnson and the American Dream* (New York: New American Library, 1977); hereafter cited as *Kearns.*

8 SHOCKS

The main resources for this chapter were Witcover's *Resurrection,* the files of the *New York Times* and my own reporting. I covered the entire primary campaign in 1968, beginning with New Hampshire in the winter and ending in California in June. During the McCarthy-Kennedy battle in California, I reported from that state until the Sunday before the voting on Tuesday, and Robert Kennedy's murder on primary night.

Throughout the year, therefore, I had opportunity to follow and interview all the active presidential candidates.

Specific notes follow:

1. *Resurrection,* p. 223.

2. *Chafe,* p. 370.

3. Ibid.

4. Clark M. Clifford, "A Vietnam Reappraisal," *Foreign Affairs,* vol. 47, no. 4 (July 1969), p. 607. Hereafter cited as *Clifford.*

5. *Clifford,* pp. 611–612.

6. *Kearns,* quoted in *Chafe,* p. 360.

7. Interview with Morton Halperin, a White House special assistant in both the Johnson and Nixon administrations, November 5, 1985. Hereafter cited as *Halperin.*

8. Conversation with Lawrence F. O'Brien, July 21, 1988 (notes are in my possession). Hereafter cited as *O'Brien.*

9. James R. Jones, "Behind LBJ's Decision Not to Run in '68," *New York Times,* April 16, 1988, p. 31. Hereafter cited as *Jones.*

10. *O'Brien.*

11. From a personal conversation between the author and Ramsey Clark in 1969.

12. Tom Wicker, "The Terrible Toll of Violence," *New York Times,* June 9, 1968.

13. Bruce Oudes, "The Reagan-Nixon Letters," *Washington Post,* January 25, 1981, p. C1.

14. *Resurrection,* p. 307.

9   REDEMPTION

My own reporting and the files of the *New York Times* were the primary resources for this chapter, as will be evident. I wrote that newspaper's lead stories from both the Miami Beach convention that nominated Nixon in 1968 and the violence-ridden Chicago convention that wanted to draft Edward Kennedy but nominated Hubert Humphrey instead. I was present at the riotous Boston Democratic rally described here and I listened in by radio as Humphrey made his crucial speech from Salt Lake City. I traveled briefly with both presidential candidates, and on election night wrote the election lead for the *Times.*

Important printed sources were Witcover's *Resurrection* and *An American Melodrama,* the excellent work of a team of British correspondents, Lewis Chester, Godfrey Hodgson and Bruce Page. I am indebted to Clark Clifford for extensive conversations, some years after the events, about President Johnson's decision to seek a negotiated peace in Vietnam and about the "peace negotiations" of 1968.

Specific notes follow:

1. *Clifford,* p. 616.

2. Norman Mailer, *Miami and the Siege of Chicago* (New York: Donald I. Fine, 1986), p. 44.

3. William Manchester, "Recapturing Bobby," *New York Times Book Review,* August 7, 1988, p. 23.

4. Lewis Chester, Godfrey Hodgson, Bruce Page, *An American Melodrama* (New York: Viking Press, 1969), p. 351. Hereafter cited as *Melodrama.*

5. *O'Brien.*

6. Richard Tuck, "Teddy, We Hardly Know Ye," *Washington Post,* November 11, 1979.

7. *Jones.*

8. Tom Wicker, "In the Nation," *New York Times,* September 22 and 26, 1968. These two columns were the basis for the preceding paragraphs.

9. Thomas J. Schoenbaum, *Waging Peace and War: Dean Rusk in the Truman, Kennedy and Johnson Years* (New York: Simon and Shuster, 1988), p. 487. Hereafter cited as *Rusk.*

10. *Resurrection,* p. 388; *Melodrama,* p. 615.

11. *Price.*

12. *Harlow.*
13. *Melodrama,* p. 725.
14. *Rusk,* pp. 485–486.
15. *Rusk,* p. 459; Lyndon B. Johnson, *The Vantage Point* (New York: Holt, Rinehart and Winston, 1971), p. 421.
16. *Melodrama,* pp. 732–733.
17. *O'Brien.*
18. *Melodrama,* pp. 624–625, 763.
19. *Rusk,* pp. 489–490. Of course, it cannot be known whether the course of the war would have been substantially different had Humphrey been elected.

10 PRAGMATIST

In this and following chapters, *The Nixon Presidency*—cited, where necessary, as *TNP*—was a major resource (see note 22, chapter 1). Unless cited to other sources, or obviously taken from the public record, direct quotations in this chapter are to be found in *TNP.* Those quoted are identified in the text and their remarks are from their oral history interviews in the book.

Since I separately interviewed many of those whose recollections also are gathered in *TNP,* I have tried to distinguish between the book and my interviews. The latter are specifically footnoted. In many cases, of course, material told to me is also to be found in *TNP.*

Another primary resource about the Nixon presidency was the sixth annual "Presidential Conference" at Hofstra University, November 19–21, 1987. Hofstra sponsors these conferences on the administrations of presidents who have served since the university's founding in 1935. The chronological turn of the Nixon administration came up in 1987; former officials of that administration, interested academics and journalists active in Washington during the Nixon era participated in three days of seminars, round tables and plenary sessions, well attended by Hofstra students and the general public.

Audio tapes of the discussions are available from Minute Tapes International, 1066 Sunnyvale-Saratoga Road, Suite 14, Sunnyvale, California, 94087. Quotations and references are taken from those tapes, or from the author's notes. If not identified in the text, they will be cited by speaker and the occasion—as *Ehrlichman at Hofstra,* or *Kissinger at Hofstra,* for example.

Also of considerable value, of course, was my own coverage of the first Nixon term. During most of it, I was a *New York Times* columnist resident in Washington and familiar with many of those quoted and discussed in this chapter, as well as with the memorable events of the period.

Specific notes follow:

1. *Ehrlichman in TNP.*
2. Interview with John Ehrlichman, Santa Fe, New Mexico, February 1, 1989. Hereafter cited as *JE.*
3. *Price.*
4. *Harlow.*
5. *JE.*
6. Theodore White, *The Making of the President, 1968* (New York: Atheneum Press, 1969), p. 147. Hereafter cited as *Making '68.*
7. *Harlow.*
8. *Burns Interview.*
9. *Harlow.*
10. *JE.*

11. John Ehrlichman, *Witness to Power* (New York: Simon and Shuster, 1982), p. 78. Hereafter cited as *Witness.*

12. *Safire,* pp. 280–281.

13. *JE.*

14. *Schlesinger.*

15. *Harlow.* The story of Nixon telephoning the congressional leaders is in *TNP.*

16. Interview with Senator Daniel P. Moynihan of New York in Washington, D.C., October 22, 1985. Hereafter cited as *Moynihan.*

17. Henry Kissinger, *White House Years* (Boston: Little, Brown, 1979), pp. 7–10. Hereafter cited as *WHY.*

18. *Harlow.*

19. Letter from Moynihan to the author, dated August 17, 1988.

20. *Burns Interview.*

21. Ibid.

22. Ehrlichman, or someone, excised this passage from *TNP,* but it appears in the original transcript of his remarks, at p. 13.

23. Herbert G. Klein, *Making It Perfectly Clear* (New York: Doubleday and Co., 1980), p. 45. Hereafter cited as *Perfectly Clear.*

24. *Ehrlichman at Hofstra.*

25. Robert V. Remini, *Andrew Jackson and the Course of American Democracy,* vol. 3: *1835–1845* (New York: Harper and Row, 1984), p. 140.

26. *PHF,* Box 9, *NRC.*

27. *Moynihan.*

28. *JE.*

29. Richard Harris, *Justice* (New York: E. P. Dutton, 1969), pp. 107–108. Hereafter cited as *Justice.*

30. *PHF,* Box 9, *NRC.*

31. *RNP, CSC.*

32. Raymond Price, *With Nixon* (New York: Viking Press, 1977), p. 203. Hereafter cited as *With Nixon.*

33. *Price.*

34. Interview with Gerard Smith, October 25, 1985. Smith said Henry Kissinger disagreed with this view of Nixon's attitude in 1969. Hereafter cited as *Smith.*

35. *Making '68,* p. 147.

36. Alfred Steinberg, *The Man from Missouri: The Life and Times of Harry S. Truman* (New York: G. P. Putnam's Sons, 1962), p. 417.

37. *Price.*

38. *Price in TNP,* p. 388.

39. *WHY,* pp. 7–10. For detailed allegations about Kissinger's dealings with the Nixon campaign in 1968, see Seymour M. Hersh, *The Price of Power* (New York: Summit Books, 1983), chapter 1. Hersh flatly charges Kissinger with spying for Nixon.

40. *WHY,* pp. 11–14.

41. *Price; Burns Interview.*

42. *WHY,* p. 31.

43. *Perfectly Clear,* pp. 66–69.

44. Box 229, White House Special Files, Staff Member and Office Files, H. R. Haldeman, January 9, 1970, *NRC.* Hereafter cited as *WHSF, SMOF,* and by the name of the official who kept the file.

45. Ibid., January 6, 1970.

46. *PHF,* Box 1, April 16, 1969, *NRC.*

47. *Kornitzer,* pp. 79–80.

48. *Perfectly Clear,* p. 47.

49. See *Lawrence* for an account of this controversy.

50. *Perfectly Clear,* pp. 85–93.

51. *Price.*

52. Ibid.

53. Box 228, *WHSF, SMOF,* H. R. Haldeman, March 16, 1970, *NRC.*

54. For a more detailed discussion of the press in the Kennedy years, see the author's *On Press* (New York: Viking Press, 1978).

55. A. Scott Berg, *Goldwyn: A Biography* (New York: Alfred A. Knopf, 1989).

56. *Perfectly Clear,* p. 69.

57. Richard Nixon, *The Real War* (New York: Warner Books, 1980), p. 250. Hereafter cited as *Real War.*

11   CHANNELS

The indispensable sources for any account of the Nixon administration's foreign policy, of course, are Richard Nixon's memoirs, *RN,* and the first volume of Henry Kissinger's memoirs, *White House Years.* Both have been previously cited; in this chapter, I continue to identify *RN* as a source directly in the text, without footnotes. The Kissinger book, as before, is cited in the notes as *WHY.*

Equally indispensable in recalling—and setting straight—the history of the first strategic arms negotiations with the Soviet Union is the first-person account by Gerard Smith, the chairman of the American negotiating team: *Doubletalk: The Story of SALT I*—a title with a double meaning—(Garden City: Doubleday, 1980). I cite this too-little-known book as *Smith,* and a helpful interview with Smith himself as *Smith Interview.* Gerard Smith served also in the Truman, Eisenhower, Kennedy, Johnson and Carter administrations and is one of the most knowledgeable Americans on arms control matters.

One of Chairman Smith's key associates in the SALT I negotiations was Raymond L. Garthoff, a distinguished Foreign Service officer with much experience and expertise in Soviet affairs; later, he was American ambassador to Bulgaria, before joining the Foreign Policy Studies program of the Brookings Institution in 1960. Garthoff's magisterial study, *Détente and Confrontation: American-Soviet Relations from Nixon to Reagan* (Washington, D.C.: Brookings Institution, 1985), is deeply detailed on the SALT negotiations and on the development of "triangular diplomacy" with China and the Soviet Union during the Nixon administration.

It is also, like *Doubletalk,* a necessary antidote to the Nixon and Kissinger memoirs. *Détente and Confrontation* provided me with many details and insights, far more than specific citations to *Garthoff* might suggest. A stinging and detailed criticism of the Nixon-Kissinger foreign policy is available in *The Price of Power: Kissinger in the Nixon White House* (New York: Summit Books, 1983) by the redoubtable investigative reporter, Seymour M. Hersh.

For the years of the Nixon administration, of course, I could also call on my own recollections and records as a columnist active for the *New York Times.* Overnight journalism, let alone commentary, is not necessarily accurate source material; but it does provide a useful framework in which to fit later studies and documentation.

Detailed notes follow:

1. Interview with Morton Halperin, deputy assistant secretary of defense for international affairs in the Johnson administration, later a member of Kissinger's national security staff in the early stages of Nixon's term. When I talked to Halperin, he had developed a deep distrust of Kissinger and was no longer sure that the security adviser actually had made this suggestion to Nixon. Interview hereafter referred to as *Halperin.*

2. *Halperin.* The following account of the evolution of arms negotiations in the

Johnson administration is based, except as noted, on this interview and on Halperin's article, "The Decision to Deploy the ABM: Bureaucratic and Domestic Politics in the Johnson Administration," *World Politics,* vol. 25, no. 1 (October 1972), p. 62.

3. Glenn T. Seaborg with Benjamin S. Loeb, *Stemming the Tide: Arms Control in the Johnson Years* (Lexington, Mass.: Lexington Books, 1987), p. 430. Seaborg was chairman of the Atomic Energy Commission during the Johnson administration. Hereafter cited as *Seaborg.*

4. Roger Labrie, ed., *SALT Hand Book: Key Documents and Issues, 1972–1979* (Washington, D.C., American Enterprise Institute for Public Policy Research), p. 6; *Seaborg,* p. 427.

5. *Hand Book,* p. 8; *Seaborg,* p. 430.

6. *Hand Book,* p. 8.

7. *Halperin; Seaborg,* pp. 436–437.

8. *Seaborg,* pp. 438–439.

9. *Garthoff,* pp. 71–72.

10. *Hand Book,* p. 9.

11. *WHY,* p. 145.

12. Gerard Smith, *Doubletalk: The Story of SALT I* (Garden City, N.Y.: Doubleday & Co., Inc., 1980) pp. 88–89. Hereafter cited as *Smith.*

13. Quoted in *Seaborg,* p. 442.

14. *Hand Book,* p. 11, quoting a study by Raymond L. Garthoff.

15. *Smith,* p. 177.

16. Ibid., pp. 155, 164.

17. *Garthoff,* p. 138; *Smith,* p. 119.

18. *Smith,* p. 169; interview with Sidney Drell, April 17, 1989; *Halperin.*

19. *Halperin.*

20. *Smith,* p. 155.

21. *WHY,* pp. 542–543.

22. *Garthoff,* p. 139n.

23. *WHY,* p. 209; *Garthoff,* p. 144, quoting NSDM-33 of November 12, 1969.

24. *Smith,* p. 226; *WHY,* p. 556.

25. *Smith,* pp. 222–228.

26. Ibid., pp. 225–226.

27. Ibid., pp. 223, 225.

28. Ibid., pp. 373–376.

29. *Garthoff,* p. 146.

30. The following account of the back-channel conversations culminating in the announcement of May 20, 1971, is derived, except where noted, from *WHY,* pp. 814–822.

31. *WHY,* pp. 525, 544–545.

32. *Garthoff,* pp. 60–61.

33. *Smith,* pp. 364–369.

34. *Garthoff,* pp. 150–152.

35. This account of the Nixon administration's dealings with the maritime unions, and the grain sales to the Soviet Union, is based on the reporting of Seymour M. Hersh in *The Price of Power: Kissinger in the Nixon White House* (New York: Summit Books, 1983), pp. 343–348.

36. Garthoff, pp. 305–307.

12   REFORMER

Great reliance has been placed in this chapter on the recollections of John W. Ehrlichman, the director of the Domestic Affairs Council in the Nixon White House until April

1973. Ehrlichman's views were available to me first in his memoir, *Witness to Power* (New York: Simon and Schuster, 1972), which I cite as *Witness;* in the long and informative oral history taken from him by scholars at the White Burkett Miller Center for the Study of Public Affairs at the University of Virginia, published in *The Nixon Presidency* by the University Press of America, and cited by me as *TNP* (except where identified in the text); in his remarks at the Hofstra conference in 1987; and finally in a five-hour interview with me in Santa Fe, New Mexico, on February 1, 1989, supplemented by later telephone calls, and cited as *JE.*

Even where not specifically cited, these Ehrlichman sources have guided many of the ideas and conclusions in this chapter. So have other oral histories of former Nixon associates included in *TNP.*

I am indebted also to Dr. Barry D. Riccio of the history department at the University of Illinois. Dr. Riccio's paper, *Richard Nixon Reconsidered: The Conservative as Liberal?,* is a brief but well-considered survey of the Nixon administration's domestic activities, particularly those not always credited by the general public. Dr. Riccio, however, did not deal with school desegregation. His paper is cited as *Riccio.*

I have been enlightened, too, by the work of Joan Hoff-Wilson, professor of history at the University of Indiana, with whom I appeared on a panel at a meeting of the American Historical Association in Chicago on December 30, 1986. The paper Professor Hoff-Wilson presented on that occasion is not available for quotation but its content had considerable effect on my own views. She presented some of the same material in a panel discussion of the Nixon social welfare policies at the Hofstra conference on November 19, 1987.

As will be seen from citations, Senator Moynihan of New York also was helpful on the domestic policies of the first Nixon term. Throughout the period, of course, I was a *New York Times* columnist active in Washington and commenting on the policies, deeds and, frequently, the perceived inadequacies of the Nixon administration and its enigmatic leader.

Specific notes follow:

1. This account of the June 24, 1970 meeting is based on *With Nixon,* pp. 208–210; and on Harry S. Dent, *The Prodigal South Returns to Power* (New York: John Wiley and Sons, 1978), pp. 146–150 (hereafter cited as *Dent*).
2. *PHF,* Box 9, *NRC.*
3. *Witness,* p. 235.
4. *JE.*
5. *Dent,* p. 136.
6. *Witness,* pp. 229, 223.
7. *PHF,* Box 12, *NRC.*
8. *Dent,* p. 128.
9. *New York Times,* July 5, 1969, p. 1; July 6, p. 1.
10. *PHF,* Box 1, *NRC.*
11. *Dent,* p. 134.
12. Ibid.
13. *Witness,* p. 122.
14. *Dent,* p. 210.
15. *Witness,* p. 126.
16. *JE.*
17. *With Nixon,* p. 200.
18. *Before the Fall,* p. 267.
19. *Dent,* p. 212.
20. *Witness,* p. 226.
21. *Garment; Before the Fall,* pp. 233–242. The "historic issue" quotation is not from Garment's memo but from his interview with the author.

22. *With Nixon,* p. 206.

23. *Dent,* p. 155.

24. Herbert Stein, *Presidential Economics: The Making of Economic Policy from Roosevelt to Reagan and Beyond,* 2d ed. (Washington, D.C.: American Enterprise Institute for Public Policy Research, 1988), p. 195. Hereafter cited as *Stein.*

25. *JE.*

26. *Witness,* p. 326.

27. *Stein,* pp. 429– n. 16.

28. Interview with William Ruckelshaus, then the director of the FBI, November 13, 1973. Within minutes after the interview, I dictated to a tape recorder my recollection of Ruckelshaus's remark. The tape is still in my possession.

29. *JE; Before the Fall,* p. 592.

30. *JE.*

31. *Witness,* p. 207.

32. *JE;* Warren and Sive spoke at the Hofstra conference.

33. Both the Blue Lake and Alaska native claims issues were discussed in the interview cited as *JE.*

34. *Riccio.*

35. *JE.*

36. *PHF,* Box 10, *NRC.*

37. *Witness,* p. 239n.

38. *Before the Fall,* p. 317.

39. Ibid., p. 230.

40. *PHF,* Box 10, *NRC.*

41. *Rogers.*

42. *Riccio,* p. 13.

43. *Stein,* pp. 137, 144.

44. *PHF,* Box 1, *NRC.*

45. Quoted in *Riccio,* p. 20.

46. *Moynihan.*

47. *New York Times,* June 2, 1989, p. A13.

48. *Riccio,* p. 10; *JE.* Herbert Stein considered establishment of the volunteer army "a market solution" (*Stein,* p. 144).

49. Garment was speaking at a dinner honoring Nixon and Maurice Stans at the New York Hilton.

50. William Greider in the *Washington Post,* June 22, 1980, pp. D1 and D3.

51. "Beyond the Shuttle," ABC News "Closeup," September 18, 1988. Transcript available from Journal Graphics, Inc., New York, N.Y.

13 KEYNESIAN

A detailed and generally dispassionate account of economic policy in the Nixon administration is available in *Presidential Economics: The Making of Economic Policy from Roosevelt to Reagan and Beyond,* previously cited as *Stein,* by Herbert Stein, a member and the second chairman of the President's Council of Economic Advisers. As its title indicates, Stein's book—from which the epigraph for this chapter is taken—is not limited to the Nixon years, but it benefits from his personal experience during that period. His interview with the scholars of the Miller Center at the University of Virginia (cited as *TNP*) is highly informative too.

My *Times* colleague, William Safire, was present as a Nixon speech writer during the historic weekend at Camp David in August 1971 when the "New Economic Policy" was developed. He includes an engaging chapter on that episode in *Before the Fall,* his account of the Nixon White House before Watergate.

At the Hofstra conference, a panel discussion on the economics of the Nixon period was extremely helpful, particularly since Herbert Stein and Maurice Stans, Nixon's secretary of commerce, were participants.

Specific notes follow:

1. *Before the Fall,* pp. 509–510.
2. *Stein,* p. 176.
3. Quoted in *Stein,* p. 162. LBJ was fond of telling how he had applied for a school-teacher's job early in his career and had been asked by the school board if he taught that the earth was round or flat. "I can teach it round or flat," he claimed to have replied, and got the job. The story is no doubt apocryphal, but, if anyone could have done it, Johnson—and perhaps Connally—could have.
4. Both Nixon remarks about Connally are quoted in *Before the Fall,* p. 498.
5. *Stein in TNP.*
6. *Stein,* p. 165.
7. William Greider, *Secrets of the Temple: How the Federal Reserve Runs the Country* (New York: Simon and Schuster, 1987), p. 334; hereafter cited as *Secrets.*
8. *PHF,* Box 12, *NRC.*
9. Ibid.
10. *Secrets,* p. 329.
11. *Stein,* p. 166. The "leapfrog" remark is quoted in *TNP,* at p. 181.
12. *Before the Fall,* p. 518; *Stein,* p. 177.
13. *Before the Fall,* p. 522.
14. Ibid., pp. 513–514, 518.
15. *Secrets,* p. 339.
16. *Before the Fall,* p. 523.
17. Ibid., p. 524.
18. *Stein,* pp. 177–179.
19. Ibid., pp. 180–181.
20. *Before the Fall,* p. 516. The "fascism" remark is quoted in Leonard Silk, *Nixonomics* (New York: Praeger Publishers, 1972), p. 200.
21. *Stein in TNP.*
22. *Secrets,* pp. 335, 338.
23. The model results were reported in a paper presented at the Hofstra conference by Ann Mari May, an assistant professor of economics at the University of Nebraska, and Robert R. Keller, professor of economics at Colorado State University. Hereafter cited as *May-Keller.*
24. *May-Keller.*
25. *Witness,* p. 254.
26. *Burns Interview.* See also *Before the Fall,* pp. 491–496.
27. Maisel is quoted in *May-Keller.*
28. *Burns Interview.*
29. *Stein,* p. 191.
30. *Riccio,* p. 8.
31. *Stein,* p. 206.

14 BOMBER

As in chapter 12, Richard Nixon's memoirs, *RN;* Kissinger's account of his *White House Years* (*WHY*); and *Détente and Confrontation* (*Garthoff*) were the prime for this account of the end of the war in Vietnam and the culmination of triangular diplomacy with China and the Soviet Union.

The war in Vietnam and the negotiations to end it were matters that I followed closely at the time, owing to my work as a journalist, and on which my own observations and reporting were highly relevant. I made several reporting trips to Vietnam in the years 1966–1972, though I was never a resident correspondent in Saigon.

Detailed notes follow:

1. *WHY,* p. 144.
2. Henry A. Kissinger, "The Viet Nam Negotiations," *Foreign Affairs*, vol. 47 (January 1969), pp. 211–34.
3. *WHY,* pp. 267–268.
4. Ibid., p. 227.
5. A. James Reichley, *Conservatives in an Age of Change* (Washington, D.C.: Brookings Institution, 1981), pp. 110, 107. Hereafter cited as *Reichley.*
6. Transcript from the *New York Times,* May 26, 1977.
7. Vernon Walters, *Silent Missions* (New York: Doubleday and Co., 1978), p. 525; interview with Charles Mathias, October 23, 1985.
8. Ross Terrill, *800,000,000: The Real China* (Boston: Little, Brown, 1972), pp. 144–145. Quoted in *Garthoff,* pp. 218, 255.
9. *WHY,* p. 224.
10. Ibid., p. 183. It is not true, as H. R. Haldeman erroneously suggested in 1978, that the Soviets approached the U.S. about the possibility of a joint attack on China. H. R. Haldeman, *The Ends of Power* (New York: Times Books, 1978), pp. 89–93.
11. Williams, McCormick, Gardner and LaFeber, eds., *America in Vietnam: A Documentary History* (New York: Anchor Press, 1985), p. 285, hereafter cited as *Documentary.*
12. *Jeffreys-Jones,* p. 182.
13. *WHY,* p. 407.
14. In fact, they went on desultorily for years, without large consequence.
15. *Garthoff,* p. 225.
16. *WHY,* p. 693.
17. Gerald Warren at the Hofstra conference.
18. *WHY,* p. 765; *Garthoff,* p. 233.
19. Nguyen Co Thach, a North Vietnamese foreign ministry official who was present during the exchange between Mao and Pham Van Dong, later told about it in an interview with Seymour Hersh, cited in *Garthoff,* p. 255.
20. *WHY,* pp. 1169–1174, 1176.
21. Ibid., pp. 1191–1196.
22. Nhan Dan, quoted in *Garthoff,* p. 259. The Kissinger remark is in *WHY,* p. 1197.
23. In his memoir, Kissinger omits the statements quoted but concedes that "the aim of my briefing . . . was to place the blame where it belonged—on Hanoi—and again to leave no doubt in Saigon of our determination to conclude the agreement." *WHY,* p. 1451.
24. Ibid., pp. 1445–1448.
25. *Documentary,* pp. 308–309.
26. *WHY,* pp. 1451, 1458.
27. Ibid., pp. 1466–1467.
28. For a detailed discussion of this point, see McGeorge Bundy, "Vietnam, Watergate and Presidential Powers," in *Foreign Affairs,* winter 1981, pp. 377–407. In Bundy's

view, Henry Kissinger's extravagant claims, in *WHY*, for the assurances to Thieu are "a discredit to its author."

29. *Witness*, p. 316.

15 HARD-HAT

This chapter was guided primarily by my own reporting at the time, though John Ehrlichman's *Witness to Power* and my interview with him were particularly helpful. So was a biography of J. Edgar Hoover by Athan G. Theoharis and John Stuart Cox, cited as *The Boss*, which provided many insights I have not acknowledged.

Specific notes follow:

1. "NLF," which stands for the National Liberation Front of South Vietnam, was a familiar set of initials in 1969.

2. All these notes of January 22, 1969, are in *PHF*, Box 1, *NRC*. Ehrlichman came to believe that Nixon habitually addressed him as "E" because the president never learned to spell his name (*Witness*, p. 77).

3. *PHF*, Box 1, *NRC*.

4. *JE*.

5. Both Kleindienst statements are quoted in *Justice*, p. 162.

6. *PHF*, Box 1, *NRC*.

7. Both the Justice Department study and the Ervin-Saxbe exchange are detailed in *Congressional Quarterly*, 1970 Chronology, vol. 3, Congress and the Nation, pp. 270, 272.

8. *New York Times*, March 26, 1989, p. 20.

9. This account of the Hoover-Nixon relationship is from Athan G. Theoharis and John Stuart Cox, *The Boss: J. Edgar Hoover and the Great American Inquisition* (Philadelphia: Temple University Press, 1988), pp. 251–252, 259–265, 312. Hereafter cited as *The Boss*.

10. In September 1969, President Nixon went to dinner at Hoover's house and heard from the director the same kind of details about FBI buggings and black-bag jobs. Neither Nixon nor Attorney General Mitchell, who was present, offered objection. Not surprisingly, Hoover took this for their approval (*Witness*, pp. 161–162).

11. *The Boss*, p. 415; *WHY*, p. 253.

12. Hoover forced Sullivan into retirement in September 1971, but this was not directly a result of Sullivan's warning to the White House.

13. *The Boss*, p. 408.

14. *With Nixon*, p. 227.

15. Quoted in *The Boss*, p. 423.

16. *Michael Raoul-Duval in TNP*, p. 292.

17. *The Boss*, p. 409.

18. *Witness*, pp. 159, 166.

19. Charles Colson, *Born Again* (Old Tappan, N.J.: Chosen Books, 1976), p. 57. Hereafter cited as *Born Again*.

20. *WHY*, p. 730.

21. *Witness*, pp. 300–302.

22. *Perfectly Clear*, pp. 345, 347, 350; *Born Again*, p. 59.

23. *Witness*, p. 165.

24. *Born Again*, p. 60.

25. *Witness*, p. 300; *With Nixon*, p. 366.

26. The "crossroads" statement is in *Born Again*, p. 60. Colson made the other remark at the Hofstra conference.

27. *Witness,* pp. 165, 400–407.

28. Ibid., pp. 167–168.

16 LONER

This summary chapter relies heavily on oral histories by Richard Nixon's youthful contemporaries (from one of which the epigram is taken), by colleagues in his administration and my own interviews with some of them—all specifically cited. This chapter was particularly informed by my notes and tapes from the conference on the Nixon presidency at Hofstra University in 1987, at which many persons who had worked with Nixon spoke of the experience, and a number of scholars shared the fruits of their studies of his years in office.

As in other chapters, *RN* by Richard Nixon and *White House Years* by Henry Kissinger were invaluable. A counterwork to both volumes is *The Price of Power* by Seymour M. Hersh, a highly critical but informed account of Nixon-Kissinger foreign policy. My brief paragraphs on the Indo-Pakistan War follow closely a detailed study by Raymond Garthoff in *Détente and Confrontation.* Many accounts of the Watergate drama, of course, are in print.

As previously noted, I was active as a Washington reporter or columnist covering national affairs for the *New York Times,* starting early in 1960, and therefore followed Richard Nixon's career, at journalist's range, from his campaign against John Kennedy to the sad end of his second administration in 1974. Without that personal background, I would not have attempted to write this book.

Specific notes follow:

1. From "Today" on NBC, May 2, 1990, interview with Bryant Gumbel.

2. *Alsop,* p. 195.

3. *Kornitzer,* pp. 61–66.

4. *Harlow.*

5. *Burns Interview.*

6. *TNP,* p. 301. The quoted remarks are from Siney's recollection, not directly from Kissinger.

7. *Ewald,* pp. 118–20.

8. *New York Review of Books,* December 6, 1979.

9. *TNP,* p. 53.

10. *Reichley,* p. 1223.

11. *WHY,* pp. 748–749.

12. *Real War,* p. 269.

13. *Garthoff,* p. 247.

14. Kenneth Thompson used the phrase "crafty atmospherics" and the other two quoted remarks are by Elliot Richardson. Both men spoke at the Hofstra conference.

15. James A. Bill, *The Eagle and the Lion: The Tragedy of American-Iranian Relations* (New Haven: Yale University Press, 1988), pp. 204–208. The House committee report is quoted in this account; and Mustafa Barzani was personally interviewed by Mr. Bill.

16. *TNP,* p. 410.

17. *WHY,* p. 910.

18. *Jeffreys-Jones,* p. 183, quoting a report of a Senate select committee on intelligence (the Church committee), 1975, vol. 7, p. 96.

19. Nixon-Frost interview broadcast May 25, 1977.

20. Moshe Ma'oz, *Asad, the Sphinx of Damascus* (New York: Weidenfeld and Nicholson, 1988), pp. 34–40.

21. *Jeffreys-Jones,* pp. 179, 188.
22. *Real War,* p. 258.
23. *Witness,* pp. 400–403.
24. Richardson made this and the following statements in *TNP,* pp. 56–57.
25. *Witness,* p. 346; *JE; TNP,* pp. 137–138.
26. Nixon-Frost interview broadcast May 4, 1977.
27. Quoted by Hugh Sidey in *TNP,* p. 312.

Index

★

ABOUT THE AUTHOR

TOM WICKER joined the Washington Bureau of the *New York Times* in 1960 after working for four Southern newspapers, including the *Winston-Salem Journal* and the *Nashville Tennesseean.* He succeeded James Reston as chief of the Washington Bureau in 1964, serving until 1969; he followed Arthur Krock as author of the *Times* column "In the Nation," from 1966 to the present. He lives in New York and Vermont with his wife, Pamela Hill, a vice president of the Cable News Network.